CAMBRIDGE GREEK AND

GENERAL ED

P. E. EASTERLING
Regius Professor Emeritus of Greek, University of Cambridge

PHILIP HARDIE
*Fellow, Trinity College, and Honorary Professor of Latin Emeritus,
University of Cambridge*

†NEIL HOPKINSON

RICHARD HUNTER
Regius Professor of Greek Emeritus, University of Cambridge

S. P. OAKLEY
Kennedy Professor of Latin, University of Cambridge

OLIVER THOMAS
Assistant Professor in Classics, University of Nottingham

CHRISTOPHER WHITTON
Professor of Latin Literature, University of Cambridge

FOUNDING EDITORS

P. E. EASTERLING

†E. J. KENNEY

HORACE
ODES
BOOK III

EDITED BY
A. J. WOODMAN

CAMBRIDGE
UNIVERSITY PRESS

University Printing House, Cambridge CB2 8BS, United Kingdom

One Liberty Plaza, 20th Floor, New York, NY 10006, USA

477 Williamstown Road, Port Melbourne, VIC 3207, Australia

314–321, 3rd Floor, Plot 3, Splendor Forum, Jasola District Centre, New Delhi – 110025, India

103 Penang Road, #05–06/07, Visioncrest Commercial, Singapore 238467

Cambridge University Press is part of the University of Cambridge.

It furthers the University's mission by disseminating knowledge in the pursuit of education, learning, and research at the highest international levels of excellence.

www.cambridge.org
Information on this title: www.cambridge.org/9781108481243
DOI: 10.1017/9781108666558

© Cambridge University Press 2022

This publication is in copyright. Subject to statutory exception and to the provisions of relevant collective licensing agreements, no reproduction of any part may take place without the written permission of Cambridge University Press.

First published 2022

Printed in the United Kingdom by TJ Books Limited, Padstow Cornwall

A catalogue record for this publication is available from the British Library.

Library of Congress Cataloging-in-Publication Data
NAMES: Horace, author. | Woodman, A. J. (Anthony John), 1945–editor.
TITLE: Odes : book iii / Horace ; edited by A.J. Woodman.
DESCRIPTION: Cambridge ; New York, NY : Cambridge University Press, 2022. | Series: Cambridge Greek and Latin classics | Includes bibliographical references.
IDENTIFIERS: LCCN 2021030911 (print) | LCCN 2021030912 (ebook) | ISBN 9781108481243 (hardback) | ISBN 9781108740548 (paperback) | ISBN 9781108666558 (ebook)
SUBJECTS: LCSH: Horace. Carmina. Liber 3. | Laudatory poetry, Latin. | Rome – Poetry. | BISAC: HISTORY / Ancient / General | LCGFT: Laudatory poetry. | Literary CRITICISM.
CLASSIFICATION: LCC PA6393 .C53 2022 (print) | LCC PA6393 (ebook) | DDC 874/.01–dc23
LC record available at https://lccn.loc.gov/2021030911
LC ebook record available at https://lccn.loc.gov/2021030912

ISBN 978-1-108-48124-3 Hardback
ISBN 978-1-108-74054-8 Paperback

Cambridge University Press has no responsibility for the persistence or accuracy of URLs for external or third-party internet websites referred to in this publication and does not guarantee that any content on such websites is, or will remain, accurate or appropriate.

*To the memory of my beloved Dorothy
and to David and John.
My family.*

> We must just read and be ready for anything
> David West, *Reading Horace*

CONTENTS

Preface	*page* ix
References and Abbreviations	xi
Introduction	1
1 Politics and Poetry	1
Chronological Table	8
2 Book 3	11
(a) The First Six Odes	12
(b) The Book as a Whole	16
3 Vocabulary	23
(a) Word Choice	23
(b) Word Order	25
4 Models and Metres	27
(a) Intertextuality	27
(b) Metres	29
5 'Artiste de sons'	34
6 Scholarship	36
7 The Text	39
Q. HORATI FLACCI CARMINVM LIBER TERTIVS	43
Commentary	77
Select Bibliography	382
Indexes	389
General Index	389
Latin Words	398

PREFACE

Horace has been my favourite author for close on sixty years, ever since I first read Book 2 of the *Odes* for A-Level in the Latin class of Ronald Fox, for whose wonderful teaching I remain grateful to this day. Until very recently it never entered my head that I might have the privilege of writing a commentary on a work of Horace, but, once the opportunity of *Odes* 3 arose, I found myself more tempted by the prospect than deterred by the responsibility. The odes of Book 3 are particularly challenging even by Horace's own high standards, and, although it is inevitable that a commentary will reflect the interests and idiosyncrasies of the commentator, my principal endeavour throughout has been to try to understand the Latin and logic of each ode and to convey to readers such understanding as I have acquired. The commentary makes no claim to definitiveness (as if such a thing were ever possible in the case of the *Odes*), but, given that the series Cambridge Greek and Latin Classics describes itself as being 'aimed primarily at undergraduate and graduate students', I hope at least to have provided these readers with 'all the guidance needed' for their enjoyment of this exceptional and much loved author.

In the course of writing the commentary I have been even more importunate than usual in seeking advice and information from others, and for various kinds of help (sometimes on repeated occasions) I am most grateful to J. N. Adams, A. Bonnell Freidin, W. W. Briggs, F. Cairns, H. Clements, K. M. Coleman, D. C. Feeney, C. H. George, S. J. Harrison, D. Kovacs, J. E. Lendon, D. S. Levene, R. Maltby, R. G. Mayer, E. A. Meyer, J. D. Morgan, T. Morton, F. Muecke, K. S. Myers, D. P. Nelis, J. Nelis-Clément, J. J. Paterson, A. Petrovic, J. G. F. Powell, J. W. Rich, Z. Stamatopoulou, R. J. Tarrant, T. P. Wiseman, A. T. Zanker, G. Zanker and J. E. G. Zetzel. Much gratitude is owed to the Editors, P. R. Hardie and S. P. Oakley, for their customary comments and advice and especially for endorsing a somewhat flexible word limit (even so, the amount of quoted Greek has had to be reduced to a regrettable minimum). It is a cause of much sadness that I was unable to consult E. Courtney, who would have relished the opportunity of engaging once more with the *Odes* of Horace, the subject of his last ever scholarly paper.

By far my greatest debt is to I. M. Le M. Du Quesnay, who devoted an enormous amount of time and labour to commenting extensively on the whole book, correcting mistakes, questioning assumptions, responding to countless emails, and making suggestions (whose adoption almost always goes shamelessly unacknowledged). There is scarcely a page which has not benefitted from his critical attention, and, on the occasions where

I declined to follow his advice, I have done so with great misgivings; he is certainly not to be held responsible for any remaining errors. Every author should be so fortunate.

It is never an ideal time to consign one's book to one's publisher. There is always more to be said, always other books on the horizon which may prove relevant, disputing one's conclusions or solving problems which one could not solve oneself. But there comes a moment when one has to let go. This is the eighth volume of commentary which I have had the pleasure of being published by Cambridge University Press, where Michael Sharp and Muriel Hall have given me, as always, the great benefit of their helpfulness and expertise. I am extremely grateful to them.

On the one occasion in my teaching career when I had the opportunity of offering Horace's *Odes* as an option for special study, only one undergraduate took up the offer, and I am happy to say that (such being the poet's *callida iunctura*) subsequently she became my wife. We were married for forty-three years.

23 October 2020   A. J. W.

REFERENCES AND ABBREVIATIONS

Horace's works are abbreviated as follows: *Satires* (*S.*), *Epodes* (*Epo.*), *Odes* (*C.*), *Carmen Saeculare* (*CS*), *Epistles* (*Epi.*), *Ars Poetica* (*AP*). Commentators on these works are usually referred to by name only (thus e.g. 'Brink on *AP* 99'). References to the *Odes* usually omit the title (thus '1.12.2').

Greek Lyric, Elegy and Iambic. Wherever possible I have referred to the Greek lyric poets as edited and translated by D. A. Campbell in the Loeb edition *Greek Lyric* (5 vols., 1982–93). For Pindar I have used the Loeb *Pindar* (2 vols., 1997) by W. H. Race. There are helpful commentaries on selections of Greek lyric poetry by D. A. Campbell (1967), G. O. Hutchinson (2001) and F. Budelmann (2018). There are Loeb editions of Greek elegy and iambic poetry by D. E. Gerber (1999), from which my references are taken; there is a recent commentary on selections from each genre by W. Allan (2019).

Cross-references. In the Commentary I use 'Intro.' to refer to the Introduction to the volume, and 'intro.' to refer to the introductory notes to each ode.

OTHER ABBREVIATIONS

BA	Talbert, R. J. A. (ed.) (2000). *Barrington Atlas of the Greek and Roman World*. Vols. 1–2 and Maps. Princeton
BCH	Günther, H.-C. (ed.) (2013). *Brill's Companion to Horace*. Leiden/Boston
BNP	*Brill's New Pauly*. Vols. 1–15. Leiden/Boston
CAH	Bowman, A. K. et al. (edd.) (1996). *Cambridge Ancient History*. Vol. 10. 2nd edn. Cambridge
CCC	Du Quesnay, I. M. Le M. and Woodman, A. J. (edd.) (2021). *The Cambridge Companion to Catullus*. Cambridge
CCGL	Budelmann, F. (ed.) (2009). *The Cambridge Companion to Greek Lyric*. Cambridge
CCH	Harrison, S. (ed.) (2007). *The Cambridge Companion to Horace*. Cambridge
CH	Davis, G. (ed.) (2010). *A Companion to Horace*. Chichester
CLE	Buecheler, F. and Lommatsch, E. (1895–1926). *Carmina Latina Epigraphica*. Vols. 1–3. Leipzig

DBC	Todd, R. B. (ed.) (2004). *The Dictionary of British Classicists*. Vols. 1–3. Bristol
EJ	Ehrenberg, V. and Jones, A. H. M. (1955). *Documents Illustrating the Reigns of Augustus and Tiberius*. 2nd edn. Oxford
EO	Mariotti, S. (ed.) (1996–98). *Enciclopedia oraziana*. Vols. 1–3. Rome
FLP	Courtney, E. (2003). *The Fragmentary Latin Poets*. Rev. edn. Oxford
FRH	Cornell, T. J. (ed.) (2013). *The Fragments of the Roman Historians*. Vols. 1–3. Oxford
GL	Keil, H. (1855–80). *Grammatici Latini*. Vols. 1–8. Leipzig
G&L	Gildersleeve, B. L. and Lodge, G. (1992). *Latin Grammar*. Repr. Walton-on-Thames
HH	Harrison, S. J. (ed.) (1995). *Homage to Horace*. Oxford
ILS	*Inscriptiones Latinae Selectae*
Inscr. Ital.	Degrassi, A. (ed.) (1947). *Inscriptiones Italiae*. Vol. 13. Rome
LH	Woodman, A. J. (2015). *Lost Histories: Selected Fragments of Roman Historical Writers. Histos* Suppl. 2. Newcastle upon Tyne
LIMC	*Lexicon Iconographicum Mythologiae Classicae*
MRR	Broughton, T. R. S. (1951–86). *The Magistrates of the Roman Republic*. Vols. 1–3. New York/Atlanta
NA	Navarro Antolín, F. (1996). *Lygdamus. Corpus Tibullianum III.1–6*. Leiden/New York/Cologne
N–H	Nisbet, R. G. M. and Hubbard, M. (1970, 1978). *A Commentary on Horace: Odes Book I* and *Odes Book II*. Oxford
NLS	Woodcock, E. C. (1959). *A New Latin Syntax*. London
N–R	Nisbet, R. G. M. and Rudd, N. (2004). *A Commentary on Horace: Odes Book III*. Oxford ['Nisbet' refers to comments attributable to him alone.]
OCD	*Oxford Classical Dictionary*. 4th edn. Oxford
OLD	*Oxford Latin Dictionary*
OLS	Pinkster, H. (2015). *The Oxford Latin Syntax*. Vol. 1. Oxford
OR	Lowrie, M. (ed.) (2009). *Oxford Readings in Classical Studies. Horace: Odes and Epodes*. Oxford
ORF	Malcovati, H. (1953). *Oratorum Romanorum Fragmenta*. Vol. 1. Turin

PH	Woodman, A. J. (2012). *From Poetry to History: Selected Papers*. Oxford
RG	*Res Gestae Diui Augusti*
RIC	Mattingly, H. et al. (1923–67). *Roman Imperial Coinage.* London [Vol. 1 rev. by C. H. V. Sutherland and R. A. G. Carson (1984)]
SB	Shackleton Bailey, D. R.
TC	Woodman, A. J. and Feeney, D. (edd.) (2002). *Traditions and Contexts in the Poetry of Horace.* Cambridge
TLL	*Thesaurus Linguae Latinae*
W.	Woodman, A. J.
W–M	Woodman, A. J. and Martin, R. H. (1996). *The Annals of Tacitus: Book 3*. Cambridge

INTRODUCTION

1 POLITICS AND POETRY

Aktion today is the site of an airport on the Adriatic coast of Greece, offering seasonal access from various European cities to the nearby holiday island of Lefkada. On 2 September 31 BC, just offshore, there took place a naval battle to which the ancient village of Actium gave its name. On the one side were Mark Antony and Cleopatra, the Egyptian queen; on the other was Octavian, the heir and adopted son of Julius Caesar. Octavian emerged the winner from a conflict which contemporaries saw in terms of global domination (Nep. *Att.* 20.5). Such an outcome demanded commemoration, and on the promontory opposite that of Actium Octavian founded a colony, to which he gave the name Nicopolis ('Victory City'), and set up an elaborate memorial on the site where he had had his camp. The remains are still visible today.[1]

Although the matter is the subject of scholarly controversy, it is remarkable to think that the poet Horace was almost certainly a member of Octavian's entourage on that early September day more than two thousand years ago.[2] He owed his presence at the battle to his friendship with Gaius Maecenas, who was a member of Octavian's inner circle and may aptly be described as a 'minister' of the newly victorious leader.[3] In his first collection of poems, Book 1 of the *Sermones* or 'Satires', published in 36/35 BC, the poet describes his first meeting with Maecenas two or three years earlier.[4] His name had been mentioned to the great man by his friends and fellow poets Virgil and Varius,[5] but, when he came into Maecenas' presence, overcome by the occasion, he was tongue-tied. Nevertheless, after nine months he was summoned back and 'ordered' to be counted among Maecenas' *amici* (*S.* 1.6.54–62). It was a dramatic change of fortune for a poet who, elsewhere in the same satire, says that people criticise him for being 'the son of a freedman'

---

[1] See W. M. Murray and P. Petsas, *Octavian's Campsite Memorial for the Actian War* (1989), K. L. Zachos, *An Archaeological Guide to Nicopolis: Rambling through the Historical, Sacred, and Civic Landscape* (2015).
[2] Du Quesnay, *TC* 19 and n. 17; so too Nisbet, *CCH* 11–12, in his discussion of Horace's life and chronology.
[3] A recent study is C. Chillet, *De l'Étrurie à Rome: Mécène et la fondation de l'Empire* (2016); note also Lyne, *Hor.* 132–8.
[4] The precise date is uncertain (see Muecke on *S.* 2.6.40–2).
[5] For L. Varius Rufus see A. S. Hollis, *Fragments of Roman Poetry c. 60 BC–AD 20* (2007) 253–81.

(*S.* 1.6.6, 45–6). Class and status were of vital importance in the elitist society of ancient Rome.

It may be objected that it is naïve to read Horace's satires in a straightforwardly autobiographical manner, and it is undoubtedly true that in certain respects his self-presentation is modelled on such predecessors as Lucilius, the second-century inventor of the satirical genre and himself said by Horace to be an autobiographical poet (*S.* 2.1.30–4), and Bion, the Cynic sage, who flourished around 300 BC.[6] But the fact remains that Horace's verse – and this goes for the *Odes* as well as the *Satires* – is an amalgam of literature and life and gives every impression of supplying readers with precious details which are not to be found in the *Vita Horati* which has come down to us under the name of Suetonius, the second-century AD biographer.[7]

Suetonius in his *Vita* tells us that Horace was born on 8 December 65 BC, when L. Aurelius Cotta and L. Manlius Torquatus were consuls:[8] he was thus two years older than Octavian, the future emperor Augustus. In *Odes* 3 he himself mentions the year of his birth (3.21.1), and perhaps also alludes to the month and the day (3.28.1–2n.); his birthplace was Venusia (modern Venosa) on the border of Apulia in the south of Italy (cf. *S.* 2.1.34), an area he twice recalls with pride and affection in Book 3 (3.4.9–20, 30.10–12). He describes his beloved father as both a smallholder and a *coactor*, rendered in Gowers' commentary as 'an embryonic bank-manager' (*S.* 1.6.71, 86). From the jibe 'son of a freedman' scholars used to infer that the father was a former slave, but Gordon Williams argued that this was misleading.[9] In the so-called Social War of 91–89 BC, which Horace in *Odes* 3 calls the 'Marsian War' (3.14.18), various allies (*socii*) of Rome rebelled, Venusia prominent amongst them. Williams suggested that, when Venusia at last succumbed to siege towards the end of the war, Horace's father was one of the three thousand taken prisoner and sold into slavery, regaining his freedom and citizenship only a few years afterwards. The jibe reported by Horace was true, but it was not the whole truth.

Shortly after Horace's fifth birthday there was formed the so-called 'First Triumvirate', an unofficial alliance of power between Pompey the Great, Julius Caesar and M. Licinius Crassus. Each of the three entered the alliance for what he could get out of it, and the belief that the alliance

---

[6] For Bion see Moles, *CCH* 165–8. Even Horace's self-description as 'libertino patre natum' has a literary parentage (*PH* 112–15).
[7] Suetonius' *Vita* is discussed by Fraenkel 1–23. On the general question see Tsitsiou-Chelidoni; also below, pp. 20–1.
[8] See Bradshaw, *TC* 2–10. [9] Williams, *HH* 296–313.

made civil war ultimately inevitable 'was the standard view in antiquity and still is today'.[10] We do not know the point in Horace's childhood when his father took him to Rome to be educated (*S.* 1.6.76–8, *Epi.* 2.2.41–2), but, since a boy might enter into the care of a *grammaticus* at the age of 11 or 12, Horace's relocation to Rome was perhaps in 53 BC, the year when Crassus, who had led a campaign against the Parthians, was killed at Carrhae in one of the worst disasters in Roman military history. Revenge against the Parthians and recovery of the legionary standards which they had seized would reverberate in political life during the last days of the Roman Republic and well into the principate of Augustus, as various references in Book 3 of the *Odes* attest (see esp. 3.2). Meanwhile Julius Caesar, Crassus' partner in the Triumvirate, was extending his reach from Gaul to the southern shores of Britain, an achievement mentioned by Catullus (11.10–12, 29.4, 20) shortly before the poet's presumed death in 54; Lucretius died at about the same time, but Cicero would continue speaking and writing for another decade until his murder in December 43.

Crassus' death left Caesar and Pompey as rivals, neither of them able to tolerate the power of the other, and civil war broke out when Caesar, in pursuit of Pompey, transferred his army from Cisalpine Gaul to Italy across the River Rubicon in 49 BC. Pompey fled to Greece but was defeated at Pharsalus in Thessaly on 9 August the following year. After an interval during which he eliminated Pompeian resistance in Africa and Spain but was unable to prevent the escape of Sex. Pompeius, Pompey's youngest son, Caesar returned to Rome but seemed to be nurturing monarchical ambitions: in 44 BC, now *dictator perpetuus* as well as consul, he was killed on 15 March in a plot led by M. Junius Brutus and C. Cassius Longinus. Caesar's will revealed that he had adopted Octavian, his nineteen-year-old grand-nephew, as his son and named him as his heir.

Whether Horace was still in Rome at the time of Caesar's murder is unknown, but a late-republican or Augustan inscription has been found at Montemilone, about 11 miles from Venusia, marking the burial place of one Cinura, slave of a Lucius Salvius.[11] Her name is a transliteration of the Greek κινύρα, which in turn renders the Phoenician word for 'lyre'. Now Horace in his later works looks back repeatedly on an early girlfriend who evidently died young and whose name is printed by modern editors as 'Cinara' (κινάρα means 'artichoke').[12] But the manuscripts of Horace

---

[10] A. W. Lintott, *CQ* 21 (1971) 498. The First Triumvirate was formed in 60 BC or (see *PH* 133–7) early 59.
[11] *L'Année Épigraphique* 1994, No. 472: 'Cinura | L. Salui h(ic) | sita est. | Silo L. Sal(ui) | posuit'.
[12] *C.* 4.1.3–4, 4.13.21–2, *Epi.* 1.7.28, 1.14.33.

transmit the middle vowel of her name in numerous different ways, including -y- ('Cinyra'), prompting the tantalising suggestion – made by J. D. Morgan – that the slave recorded on the inscription and the girl remembered by Horace are one and the same.[13] If that is so, then Horace was back in Venusia at some point in the mid-40s.

Popular hostility to Caesar's death made natural allies of Octavian and Mark Antony, Caesar's colleague in the consulship. Brutus and Cassius were compelled to leave Rome, and in the autumn of 44 Brutus is found in Athens, recruiting young Roman students for his army (Plut. *Brut.* 24.2); Suetonius tells us that amongst the recruits was Horace, who had gone to Athens to study philosophy at the famous Academy (*Epi.* 2.2.43–5): since this was a normal stage in a young Roman's higher education,[14] it should not be inferred that the experience necessarily denotes any special propensity for philosophy, although some scholars believe that Horace's poetry is seriously philosophical.[15] Two years later the future poet was serving as one of the officers (*tribuni militum*, of whom there were six in a legion) in Brutus' and Cassius' army when it was confronted by the forces of Antony and Octavian at the battle of Philippi in Thrace (cf. *S.* 1.6.48, *Epi.* 2.2.49): no other engagement was bloodier for its slaughter of distinguished men, says the historian Velleius (71.2). Brutus and Cassius were defeated; Horace, as he famously puts it in the *Odes*, left his shield behind on the battlefield (2.7.9–12; cf. 3.4.26). Subsequently, as a member of the losing side, he, like Alcaeus centuries earlier (130B.5–9), was deprived of the farm which he had inherited from his father, and he was compelled by *paupertas* to write poetry (*Epi.* 2.2.50–2; cf. *S.* 1.6.71); Horace's eviction was only one of many, as the victors sought to settle their veterans on the land, and the misery of the age is eloquently voiced in the *Eclogues* of Virgil (1, 9), whose poetic career had started a little earlier than that of his friend.

The relationship between Antony and Octavian had been formalised in 43, when, along with M. Aemilius Lepidus, they had been appointed to the so-called 'Second Triumvirate'. Their combined efforts eventually saw the defeat of the troublesome Sex. Pompeius in 36 BC, but Lepidus was always the least important member of the alliance and in the latter years

---

[13] 'The name of Horace's first mistress', Archaeological Institute of America, 113th Annual Meeting Abstracts (Philadelphia, January 2012), pp. 145–6. I am most grateful to Professor Morgan for allowing me to refer to his suggestion in advance of its formal publication.
[14] Ll. W. Daly, 'Roman study abroad', *AJP* 71 (1950) 40–58.
[15] The matter is highly controversial; good bibliographical summary in Moles, *CCH* 180.

1 POLITICS AND POETRY

of the decade the struggle for power essentially rested between Octavian and Antony, culminating in the battle of Actium in 31. It was during the 30s that, as Suetonius reports, Horace successfully sought pardon for his past association with Brutus and procured the position of *scriba quaestorius* (administrative assistant to the quaestors who were in charge of the public finances: cf. *S.* 2.6.36–7).[16] It is unclear whether his new position provided him with sufficient income to write poetry or whether his early poetry elicited subsidies from wealthy patrons which enabled him to buy his position as *scriba*;[17] either way, as we have already seen, early in the decade he came to the attention of Maecenas, whose patronage guaranteed him financial security for the rest of his life. To Maecenas was dedicated the first book of the *Sermones*, whose socio-political concerns exactly reflect those of the Octavianic coterie to which Horace now belonged.[18] A second book of *Sermones*, comprising eight poems, was published in perhaps 30, and, though not dedicated to Maecenas, features the patron prominently.

Also published around 30 were the *Epodes*, a heterogeneous collection of seventeen poems which in many ways foreshadow the *Odes*. Two of them express anguish and despair at the ongoing civil war (7, 16); two of them are centred on the battle of Actium, one being set before the battle (1), the other a celebration of the victory (9). Both Actium poems are addressed to Maecenas and serve to dedicate the book to him: since in the first of them Horace expresses gratitude for his patron's generosity (1.31–2), many readers have believed that the poet is referring to the Sabine farm, to which he alludes, or seems to allude, frequently in his verse (e.g. 3.1.47–8):[19] in fact Horace never says explicitly that he ever received the farm as a gift, nor is there any independent evidence to this effect, but the probability is deemed to be very high.[20]

Victorious from his defeat of Antony and Cleopatra and the subsequent military operations, Octavian returned to Rome in mid-August 29 BC and celebrated a series of triumphs. Eighteen months later, on 16 January 27 BC, he was given the name 'Augustus' – used twice in Book 3 (3.3.11, 5.3) – on the occasion of the first so-called 'constitutional settlement', whereby 'rem publicam ex mea potestate in senatus populique

---

[16] For 'Horace in the Thirties' see J. Griffin in Rudd (1993) 1–22.
[17] See *PH* 112–13. [18] Du Quesnay (1984).
[19] The 'farm' or 'villa' is traditionally sited in the valley of the Digentia (mod. Licenza), about 30 miles ENE of Rome (*BA* Map 44: C1): see Frischer, *CH* 75–90 (map on p. 77).
[20] Cairns, *RL* 241–3, in response to A. Bradshaw, 'Horace *in Sabinis*', in C. Deroux (ed.), *Studies in Latin Literature and Roman History* (1989) 5.160–86, who points to other possibilities, such as personal purchase by Horace.

Romani arbitrium transtuli' (*RG* 34.1).[21] He then left Rome for Gaul and Spain, where in 26–25 BC he campaigned against the Cantabrians and Astures in the NW of the country; there are repeated allusions to this campaign in Book 3. In 24 he returned to the capital, a moment marked by Horace in 3.14.

It is generally, but not universally, accepted that Books 1–3 of the *Odes* were published in the second half of 23 BC, that being the date of the suffect consulship of L. Sestius, whose address amidst a series of luminaries at the start of Book 1 (1.1 Maecenas, 1.2 Octavian, 1.3 Virgil, 1.4 Sestius, 1.6 Agrippa, 1.7 Plancus) is regarded as otherwise inexplicable.[22] If the date is correct, publication coincided with the second and last of the constitutional settlements by which Augustus formalised and consolidated his position of power.[23] Three or so years later Horace dedicated to Maecenas his first collection of verse letters, in which the poet reveals his disappointment with the contemporary reaction to his lyric poetry (*Epi.* 1.19.35–6). An exception, however, was the *princeps* himself, to whom Horace had sent a special copy (cf. *Epi.* 1.13): according to Suetonius in his Life of Horace, Augustus so approved of the *Odes* and believed in their immortality that he enjoined on the poet the composition of the *Carmen Saeculare*. This was the hymn which was sung by a choir of boys and girls on the last day of the Ludi Saeculares or Secular Games, which, as we know from the long inscription of the events which has survived (*CIL* 6.32323 = *ILS* 5050), were celebrated on three successive days and nights (31 May–2 June) in 17 BC to mark the start of a new era.[24] Line 149 of the inscription exhibits one of the most evocative of all Latin epigraphic sentences to have survived from the ancient world: 'CARMEN COMPOSVIT Q. HORATIVS FLACCVS'. Apart from Augustus and other direct participants, Horace is the only person whose name appears on the inscription, and its position directly above those of Augustus and Agrippa in the following

---

[21] On this see Cooley ad loc., and, for Octavian in the years 30–27, R. Kearsley, *CQ* 59 (2009) 147–66. Augustus and his principate have been the subject of much recent scholarship, e.g. P. J. Goodman, 'Twelve Augusti', *JRS* 108 (2018) 156–70, A. E. Cooley, 'From the Augustan Principate to the invention of the Age of Augustus', *JRS* 109 (2019) 71–87, T. P. Wiseman, *The House of Augustus* (2019).

[22] See Lyne, *Hor.* 73–5. O. Murray (in Rudd (1993) 103) favoured 24 BC, though he never published his reasons. Hutchinson (2008) disputes the relevance of Sestius and argues that each book was first published separately, suggesting e.g. 26 for Book 1, early 24 for Book 2, and early 23 for Book 3 (138–9, 147).

[23] For a summary see e.g. Rich on Dio 53.32.5.

[24] For the relevant lines of the inscription see Thomas' commentary on the *Carmen Saeculare*, pp. 274–6 (translation in M. G. L. Cooley (ed.), *The Age of Augustus* (LACTOR 17, 2003) 275).

line[25] would have been appreciated by a poet who took such evident pride in his name.[26] But there is a further refinement if the poet's name is spelled out in full, something precluded by the naming conventions of the inscription:

Cārmēn cōmpŏsŭīt ́ Quīntŭs Hŏrātĭūs | Flaccus.

The inscribed sentence incorporates an Asclepiad line, the 'signature' metre of *Odes* 1–3, which are framed by Horace's only two poems in stichic Asclepiads.[27] In identifying the author of the *Carmen Saeculare*, the sentence also acknowledges the collection of poems which won him the commission.[28] This refinement too would have been appreciated by a poet who himself enjoyed transferring metres from one context to another.[29]

Four years later, and a decade after the publication of Books 1–3, Horace published his fourth and final book of odes, in which at least a third of the poems deal with the poet and the power of poetry (4.2, 3, 6, 8, 9): now Horace is pointed out by passers-by as a virtuoso of the Roman lyre (4.3.22–3 'monstror digito praetereuntium | Romanae fidicen lyrae'). The fifteen odes of Book 4 were followed by the Letter to Augustus (*Epi.* 2.1), the Letter to Florus (*Epi.* 2.2) and the Letter to the Pisones (the *Ars Poetica*), which together constitute a second collection of verse letters and seem to have been published at some point later than 12 BC.[30] Whether or not Maecenas in his later years had lost favour with Augustus,[31] the fact that neither of these collections is dedicated to Horace's patron has led to speculation that there was a cooling in relations with the poet. Yet 'Maecenas meus' is the description he is given in *Odes* 4 (4.11.19) and, when he died

---

[25] For this see J. Nelis-Clément and D. Nelis, '*Furor epigraphicus*: Augustus, the poets, and the inscriptions', in P. Liddel and P. Low (edd.), *Inscriptions and their Uses in Greek and Latin Literature* (2013), 317–47, at 322–3.

[26] He mentions his *praenomen* once in his work (*S.* 2.6.37), his *nomen* and *cognomen* twice each (4.6.44, *Epi.* 1.14.5; *S.* 2.1.18, *Epo.* 15.12), but this is not the limit of it. When at *S.* 1.9.20 he says 'I lowered my little ears like a bad-tempered donkey' ('demitto auriculas ut iniquae mentis asellus'), we are certainly intended to remember that *flaccus* means 'floppy-eared'; and scholars have detected numerous puns involving the noun *hora* – appropriately for a poet so preoccupied with the concept of time (see K. J. Reckford, 'Horatius: the man and the hour', *AJP* 114 (1997) 583–612).

[27] The metre recurs in the troublesome 4.8.

[28] See A. J. Woodman, '*Numerosus Horatius*?', *CQ* 69 (2019) 911–12. Compare Sall. *C.* 19.5 'Cn. Pompeii ueteres fidosque clientis', which becomes a hexameter line when *Gnaei* is spelled out in full.

[29] See Fraenkel 349 on the incorporations of Terence at *S.* 2.3.264 and *Epi.* 1.19.41; see also 3.3.70–2n.

[30] For the dating (controversial) see S.J. Harrison, *PLLS* 13 (2008) 173-86.

[31] See Tac. *A.* 3.30.4 and W–M ad loc.

in 8 BC, Maecenas' last words to Augustus, perhaps in his will, were 'Horati Flacci ut mei memor esto': this instruction was adduced by Suetonius as evidence of Maecenas' strong affection, adding that Horace held an important place in the friendship of both him and Augustus. This is certainly the impression we derive from the poetry, and modern attempts to suggest otherwise – that Horace is somehow subversive and that his praise of such great men is not to be taken at face value – are based on a mistaken view of Roman social conventions and the reciprocity expected between friends.[32] To him it was a virtue that he had pleased the leaders of Rome in war and peace (*Epi.* 1.20.23 'me primis urbis belli placuisse domique').

According to Suetonius, the poet himself died on 27 November 8 BC, thus fulfilling the prediction in Book 2 of the *Odes* that he and Maecenas would die together (2.17);[33] they were buried side by side on the Esquiline Hill. Few poets have had as great an influence on the literature of Western Europe.[34]

Chronological Table

BC	HISTORICAL EVENTS	AUTHORS AND WORKS	
91–89	Social War between Rome and her Italian allies (*socii*)		
		Catullus born (?)	84
81	Sulla dictator	Cicero's first speech	81
		Philodemus in Rome (?)	75
		Parthenius in Rome	72
		Virgil born (15 October)	70
		Horace born (8 December)	65
63	Cicero consul; Octavian born (23 September)		

---

[32] An enormous amount has been written on patronage at Rome: a standard account is P. White, *Promised Verse: Poets in the Society of Augustan Rome* (1993); for Horace and Maecenas in particular see e.g. Du Quesnay (1984) and *TC* 17–37.

[33] For the date of Horace's death see Bradshaw, *TC* 11–16.

[34] The influence of Horace is much too large a subject for even a cursory summary here; for a brief survey see S. Harrison, *Horace* (2014) 84–94; also *EO* Vol. 3. See too below, p. 26 n. 87.

1 POLITICS AND POETRY

BC	HISTORICAL EVENTS	AUTHORS AND WORKS	
60	'First Triumvirate'		
59	Julius Caesar consul	Livy born (?)	59
58–50	Caesar in Gaul		
55	Caesar invades Britain		
54	Caesar invades Britain again	Catullus and Lucretius die (?)	54
53	Battle of Carrhae (May): Parthians kill Crassus, capture standards		
49	Julius Caesar crosses Rubicon (January): civil war		
48	Battle of Pharsalus (9 August): Caesar defeats Pompey, who is subsequently killed		
44	Caesar killed (15 March): Octavian adopted as his heir		
43	Second Triumvirate; Octavian cos. I	Ovid born (20 March); Cicero murdered (7 December)	43
42	Battle of Philippi (23 October): Brutus and Cassius defeated; Horace escapes	Sallust starts writing (?)	42
		Virgil's *Eclogues* published (?)	39
		Horace is now Maecenas' *amicus* (?)	37

BC	HISTORICAL EVENTS	AUTHORS AND WORKS	
36	Battle of Naulochus (3 Sept.): Sex. Pompeius defeated	Horace, *Satires* 1 published (?)	36
34	Octavian cos. II	Livy starts writing (?)	34
31	Octavian cos. III; Battle of Actium (2 Sept.): Antony and Cleopatra defeated		
30–23	Octavian/Augustus cos. IV–XI	Horace, *Satires* 2 and *Epodes* published (?)	30
29	Octavian's triple triumph (13–15 August): civil war formally ended; Temple of deified Julius Caesar dedicated (18 August)	Virgil's *Georgics* published (?)	29
28	Temple of Palatine Apollo dedicated (9 October)	Propertius' Book 1 published (?)	28
27	Octavian named 'Augustus' (16 January); 'first constitutional settlement'; Augustus departs for Gaul and then Spain	Tibullus' Book 1 published (?)	27
26	Augustus campaigning in Spain; Aelius Gallus invades Arabia	Cornelius Gallus kills himself	26
25	Augustus taken ill, receives Indian embassy; Temple of Janus closed		
24	Augustus returns to Rome	Book 2 of Propertius published	24
23	'Second constitutional settlement': Aug. resigns consulship, receives *imperium maius*; Marcellus, his nephew, dies (September)	HORACE PUBLISHES ODES 1–3	23

BC	HISTORICAL EVENTS	AUTHORS AND WORKS	
22	Augustus in the East		
		Propertius' Book 3 published (?)	21
20	Augustus receives captured standards from Parthians	Horace, *Epistles* 1 (?)	20
19	Augustus returns to Rome	Virgil dies (21 Sept.), the *Aeneid* unfinished; Tibullus dies, Book 2 perhaps unpublished	19
18	Moral legislation		
17	Secular Games	Horace, *Carmen Saeculare*	17
16–13	Augustus campaigns in Gaul	Propertius' Book 4 published (?)	16
		Ovid, *Heroides* published; *Amores* already out (?)	15
		Propertius dies	14
13	Augustus returns to Rome (4 July); Ara Pacis vowed	Horace, *Odes* 4	13
12	Augustus become Pontifex Maximus	Horace, *Epistles* 2 and *Ars Poetica* (?)	12
9	Ara Pacis dedicated		9
8	Month Sextilis renamed 'Augustus'	Maecenas dies; Horace dies (27 November)	8

2 BOOK 3

A Horatian ode is a Latin poem written in a metre borrowed from Greek lyric poetry. It varies in length from eight lines to eighty, although the usual range is between sixteen and forty. Each ode is expressed in relatively unexceptional language, although the words will usually be arranged in striking and often memorable ways, with illustrations regularly drawn from mythology. Almost every ode has an addressee, who, if male, may be of high status, and, if female, seems usually to be one of numerous apparent girlfriends. The odes are used to convey a wide variety of messages: to dispense advice, issue convivial invitations, offer consolation, comment on the politics of the day, communicate moral or philosophical reflections. Readers derive the attractive impression of a congenial and worldly-wise friend. No other Latin poetry remotely resembles Horace's *Odes*.[35]

(a) The First Six Odes

Book 3 begins with six poems in the Alcaic metre, a sequence unparalleled elsewhere in the *Odes*; they are almost always referred to as the 'Roman Odes', a title which Fraenkel traced back at least as far as T. Plüss in 1882.[36] The title is absurd: it implies that the other eighty-two odes in Books 1–3, even though written in the language of the Romans by a Roman poet who lived and worked in Rome and its immediate vicinity, are somehow *not* Roman. Yet this is what many scholars appear to think. 'That Horace is a Greek lyric poet', writes Rossi, 'is almost obvious.'[37] If this is thought to be a mere oxymoron, designed to catch the reader's attention, consider the following statements by Nisbet and Rudd in their commentary on Book 3:

> 'The underlying situation is Roman' (114, on 3.9);
> 'Horace gives his serenade a Roman setting' (142, on 3.10);
> 'he sets the scene in the Campus Martius, so the characters are felt to be Roman' (166, on 3.12);
> 'The ilex or holm-oak...is an Italian touch' (179, on 3.14);
> 'Horace's ode is very Roman' (366, on 3.30).

These statements presuppose an expectation that Horace's odes will somehow *not* be Roman, that he is writing *Greek* poetry, into which the occasional introduction of Roman or Italian elements is worthy of bringing to the reader's attention.[38]

Such statements are an unfortunate throw-back to the nineteenth century, a time when, under the influence of Romanticism, literary and aesthetic judgement assigned priority to the glory that was Greece,

---

[35] The classic definition of a Horatian ode is that of Heinze, *OR* 11–32.
[36] Fraenkel 260 n. 1. The bibliography on 3.1–6 both collectively and individually is extensive even by Horatian standards. Much of the earlier scholarship is given in the monograph by C. Witke, *Horace's Roman Odes* (1983). Syndikus, *CH* 193–209, offers a brief summary; the most recent survey is Günther, *BCH* 373–406.
[37] Rossi, *OR* 356.
[38] Such statements are naturally to be distinguished from cases where a Greek character uses Roman terminology: thus *penates* in Europa's mouth at 3.27.49 is rightly described as a 'Roman touch' (N–R). This is an example of the so-called *interpretatio Romana*, which is omnipresent in the Latin historians.

downgrading the claims of the Eternal City;[39] Victorian scholars, assuming instinctively that Roman poets agreed with their views, believed that what the poets were trying to do was to write Greek poetry in Latin. It was in 1883, the very next year after Plüss, that one Horatian commentator could write: 'It is a remarkable defect in Roman poetry that it is to so great an extent an imitation of Greek models and not the result of native inspiration.'[40] Since the first six odes of Book 3 explore socio-political themes which seemed not to fit into this preconceived framework, they earned the title 'Roman'.

We need to rid ourselves of this misnomer, and, since the six odes are linked together by the Alcaic metre, my suggested alternative is the 'Alcaic Hexad'. It would be gratifying to think that this apparently neutral title, unlike 'Roman Odes', has no unfortunate implications, but, alas, this is not so. In the fourth century AD the grammarian Diomedes described *Odi profanum* as the first ode in Book 3 and *Quid fles, Asterie* (3.7) as the second:[41] it is therefore clear that he regarded 3.1–6 as a single long poem, a view in which he may well have been anticipated by the Horatian commentator Porphyrio.[42] Although some modern scholars too believe in a single long poem,[43] the notion is highly unlikely.[44] The most objective evidence in its favour is the Alcaic metre itself, whose continuity across a quite unparalleled sequence of 336 lines is likely to impress those whose principle is that 'a new poem begins only where the metre changes'.[45] But the metrical principle has an in-built problem: there are some cases in the *Odes* where the metre changes but appears not to. There is no example of this

---

[39] See e.g. R. Jenkyns, *The Victorians and Ancient Greece* (1980), F. M. Turner, *The Greek Heritage in Victorian Britain* (1981).

[40] Page on 1.12.39 (first edition 1883). Page, who also wrote a standard school commentary on Virgil, was a schoolmaster at Charterhouse until his retirement in 1910, whereupon he was appointed the first Editor of the Loeb Classical Library series (*DBC* 3.737–9). For other examples along the same lines see S. Harrison, *Victorian Horace: Classics and Class* (2017) 26, 31–2.

[41] *GL* 1.525.1–4 (Keil). Unfortunately he then proceeded to describe 3.9 as the *tertia ode* and 3.10 as the *quinta ode*, thus seeming to imply that 3.7 and 3.8 are also a single poem, which is impossible (they are in different metres): scholars assume there is something wrong with Diomedes' text.

[42] Since Porphyrio's comment ('haec autem ᾠδὴ multiplex per uarios deducta est sensus') comes *after* his note on *Odi...arceo*, it is theoretically possible to interpret the words 'haec...ᾠδή' as referring only to 3.1 itself and not to 3.1–6 as a whole. It is true that he does not use the '(In) this ode...' formula again until 3.7–9; on the other hand, the formula is not invariable (thus omitted for 3.10 and 3.11).

[43] See Heyworth (1995) 140–5, and 'Segmentation and interpretation in *Odes* 2', *Dictynna* 14 (2017) 1–21; A. Griffiths, *TC* 73–9.

[44] See further Woodman (2020) 278–9.   [45] Heyworth (1995) 144.

phenomenon in Books 2 or 3, but there are three instances in Book 1. The famous Pyrrha ode (1.5) is written in the metre known as the Third Asclepiad, which begins with two Asclepiad lines; the following ode is in the Second Asclepiad metre, which begins with three Asclepiad lines: it is therefore not until readers reach the third line of 1.6 that they realise that the metre has changed. The same sequence of metres is evident in 1.14 ~ 1.15 and 1.23 ~ 1.24, in the former case with an additional complication: 1.14, the so-called Ship of State ode, is addressed to a ship ('O nauis...') and refers to ships (plural) in line 14 (*puppibus*); 1.15 begins with a reference to ships ('Pastor cum traheret per freta nauibus...'). In each of these three cases, but especially in 1.14 ~ 1.15, readers guided by metre alone will be misled into thinking that they are reading a continuation of the preceding poem, and, when they come to realise that the metre has in fact changed, they will think that the author has performed on them a cruel and pointless trick. This evidence suggests that readers needed more than metre to tell them that one poem had finished and another one was about to begin. In the Gallus papyrus, which perhaps dates from exactly the time when Books 1–3 of the *Odes* were published, the separate poems are divided from each other by a special sign somewhat resembling a lower-case *h*;[46] perhaps the original text of Horace's *carmina* was similarly equipped.[47]

If we continue to regard the Alcaic Hexad as consisting of six individual poems, their varying lengths may be set out as follows:

1	**48**	
2	32	
		} = **104**
3	72	
4	80	
5	56	
		} = **104**
6	**48**	

Scholars have different reactions to what is sometimes called 'numerology',[48] but the numerical coincidences in the above scheme seem more

---

[46] See R. D. Anderson, P. J. Parsons and R. G. M. Nisbet, 'Elegiacs by Gallus from Qaṣr Ibrîm', *JRS* 69 (1979) 129–30, 138; Hutchinson 24–5.

[47] The titles with which all the odes are prefixed in the MSS are deemed to derive from later in antiquity (Tarrant (2016b) 226–30).

[48] For the case of the *Eclogues* see e.g. O. Skutsch, 'Numbers in Virgil's Bucolics', *BICS* 27 (1980) 95–6, who parallels *Odes* 3.1–6, pointing out additionally (n. 8) that 80 is the total not only of 3.4 but also of 3.2 + 3.6 (and indeed also of 3.1

than simply accidental. It is surely intentional that the opening and closing poems are each of the same length in a form of ring composition; and, since the hexad is divided into two groups of three (see 3.4 intro.), it seems plausible to think that each group is closed by a pair of poems whose line-totals correspond.[49]

The correspondence between 3.1 and 3.6 extends beyond line-totals: each deals with a social problem in which building plays a significant part: in the case of 3.1 the virtues of *quod satis est* are contrasted with the greed of the man who builds on the sea, while in 3.6 neglect of the gods needs to be remedied by the restoration of temples and statues. The second poem, which advocates dying in battle (3.2.13) and emphasises *uirtus* halfway through (3.2.17–24), has been described as a recruiting call for the invasion of Parthia, which is likewise the theme of 3.5, where *uera uirtus* is mentioned halfway through (3.5.29) and dying in battle features throughout (3.5.13–40). Of the two central poems of the hexad, 3.3 features a long speech by Juno which is epic in nature and draws from the poet an apologia addressed to the Muse at the very end; the next poem is cast in a Hesiodic mould, also features a speech, and begins with an address to the Muse. Although all of these odes are naturally far more complicated and varied than these brief summaries suggest, it nevertheless seems possible to regard the hexad as arranged on a series of concentric rings.[50] This pattern is perhaps reflected in the arrangement of the

---

+ 3.2) and that 128 is the total not only of 3.1 + 3.2 + 3.6 but also of 3.3 + 3.5. Skutsch, whose paper was a response to an attack by D. West (*CR* 28 (1978) 76–8), was also involved with numbers in Propertius (*CP* 58 (1963) 238–9, supported by E. Courtney, *Phoenix* 22 (1968) 250–8). Contemporary interest in numbers as evidenced by e.g. Varro's *De principiis numerorum* (see E. Rawson, *Intellectual Life in the Late Roman Republic* (1985) 160–2) has to be balanced against the fact that in antiquity 'smaller units of Latin texts are seldom if ever numbered' (A. M. Riggsby, *Mosaics of Knowledge* (2019) 17), although Asconius' commentary on Cicero's speeches exhibits references such as 'around line 80' (p. 4.21 'circa uers. LXXX'), 'around line 320 from the beginning' (p. 6.18 'cir. uer. a primo CCCXX'), 'around line 900 from the end' (p. 12.22 'cir. uer. a nou. DCCCC'), if they are not later insertions. The whole question of line-numbers has been discussed by Ll. Morgan, *Patterns of Redemption in Virgil's Georgics* (1999) 223–9, whose point is that Virg. *G.* 4.400 alludes to Hom. *Od.* 4.400 (for similar discussions apropos of other texts see Wills 159 n. 82, J. Farrell, *Phoenix* 59 (2005) 105 n. 20). Other examples are Virg. *Ecl.* 9.43 ~ Theocr. 11.43 (T. Keeline, *CP* 112 (2017) 457 n. 6) and *Aen.* 1.37 ~ *Aen.* 7.37 (D. Nelis, *REA* 109 (2007) 269–71).

[49] I am not claiming that any particular meaning is to be attached to Horace's numerical correspondences. Poets just seem to like such things as e.g. acrostics, lipograms, *technopaegnia* ('shape poems') and abecedarian poems, and I cannot see that numerical composition is very different.

[50] See Santirocco 113–15 for this and the other arrangements which have been suggested.

odes' addressees: the two central odes of the six are each addressed to a Muse (3.3.70 *Musa*, 3.4.2 *Calliope*), while the implicit address *uirginibus puerisque* of the first ode (3.1.4) is matched by the explicit address *Romane* of the last (3.6.2). The two remaining odes have no addressee (3.2 ~ 3.5). It has also been pointed out that each ode leads neatly into the next.[51] The first ode, addressed 'uirginibus puerisque' (3.1.4), ends with the memorable image of the horseman and a recommendation of the simple life (3.1.40–8), while the second ode begins by advising a *puer* to take kindly to 'narrow poverty' and to fight bravely as a horseman (3.2.1–4). The loyalty which enjoins silence at 3.2.25–32 prepares for the man whose sense of justice and tenacity of purpose introduce 3.3. The third ode ends with an address to the Muse (3.3.69–72); the fourth ode begins by addressing a Muse (3.4.1–4). The connection between the fourth and fifth odes is in one sense less immediate; but the relationship established between Augustus and Jupiter in the course of 3.4 (37–68) is encapsulated by the correspondences between the same two in the first stanza of 3.5. Likewise Regulus in 3.5 was so anxious to prevent a bad precedent being set for the future that he declined the embrace of his chaste wife (13–16, 41–3), whereas earlier generations in 3.6 were so unthinking of the future that, thanks to divine vengeance, young wives were now acting as prostitutes (7–8, 17–32).[52]

(b) The Book as a Whole

Book 1 comprises thirty-eight odes (876 lines): the longest is 60 lines (1.12), the two shortest are 8 lines (1.11, 30); between these limits there is considerable variation in the length of each ode, although Horace likes juxtaposing odes of identical length (thus a run of 16 lines each in 1.32–34). The character of Book 2, comprising twenty odes (572 lines), is quite different. As if complementing the book's lack of metrical variation (below, p. 29), three-quarters of the odes are between twenty-four and thirty-two lines in length; of the remaining five odes, one is twenty lines in length (2.15) and four are forty lines (2.1, 13, 16, 18). Comprising thirty odes, Book 3 is the longest book (1008 lines) and different again, strikingly so.[53] Not only does it contain the longest ode of all (3.4: 80 lines), incorporating 22½ lines of speech, but it also contains four other odes which are longer than the longest ode of Book 1; only one of these,

---

[51] For such links see again the very helpful summary of Santirocco 115–18.
[52] This section has included a revised and abbreviated version of Woodman (2020).
[53] See also Hutchinson 156–61.

featuring 50½ lines of speech, occurs within the Alcaic Hexad (3.3: 72 lines): the remaining three (3.24, 27, 29) occur towards the end of the book (respectively 64, 76 and 64 lines), with 3.27 again including a substantial amount of speech (32 lines). Hence the odes of Book 3 are even more varied in length than those in Book 1 (3.22 is 8 lines).

The first book of the *Odes* begins with an introductory poem which Horace opens by addressing his patron in royal terms (1.1.1 'Maecenas, atauis edite regibus') and continues by discussing his role as a lyric poet (1.1.35–6). Since there are thirty-eight poems in Book 1, the poem which begins the second half of the book is 1.20, where he again addresses Maecenas, this time referring to him as a distinguished *eques* (1.20.5 'clare Maecenas eques'). These various features are mirrored in Book 3. In the poem which begins the second half of the book, Maecenas is again addressed as a distinguished *eques* (3.16.20 'Maecenas, equitum decus'). His address in royal terms comes in the penultimate ode of the book (3.29.1–3 'Tyrrhena regum progenies, ... Maecenas'), the final ode being reserved for Horace's lyric achievement (3.30). Thus the collection as a whole is unified and rounded off by ring composition. It is possible that Horace was influenced in such symmetries by those of his friend Virgil in the *Georgics*, where Maecenas is addressed in the second line of Books 1 and 4 and in the forty-first line of Books 2 and 3, while the programmatic passage which starts Book 3 (1–48) is balanced by the *sphragis* at the end of Book 4 (559–66). The third address to Maecenas in *Odes* 3 occurs in the central ode (8) of the first half of the book, although the three addresses to his patron in Book 2 betray no such symmetry (2.12, 2.17, 2.20).

The circular arrangement and thematic sequences of the Alcaic Hexad (above) prompt the question of whether similar patterns are detectable in remaining odes of Book 3. The dialogic courting of 3.9 is followed by the wooing of Lyce in the paraclausithyron of 3.10; the reference to Formiae at 3.17.6 may be anticipated by a reference to the Laestrygonians at 3.16.34. The prayer to Diana at 3.22 is set in the countryside and features a sacrifice, while Phidyle, the addressee of 3.23, is described as praying and sacrificing in the countryside; her rustic simplicity contrasts markedly with the luxury and extravagance attacked in 3.24, from which the people are to be rescued by Augustus (3.24.25–30), in whose honour Horace promises a poem in 3.25. Yet, while these sequences seem reasonable enough, they differ from those discerned by Santirocco, who proposes in addition that the Alcaic Hexad is followed by two sets of ring composition (7 ~ 15, 16 ~ 29).[54] The fact is that, while many scholars believe that

---

[54] Santirocco 125–49.

Horace arranged his *Odes* in a particular way, they often disagree on what that arrangement actually is.

Horace's liking for symmetry extends to the structure of individual odes. The stanzaic form of many odes means that often they will fall into logical blocks of stanzas: thus 3.8, for example, consists neatly of three blocks (3+1+3), and the vocative 'Maecenas' is placed significantly in the central stanza: as has been shown particularly by Moritz, middles can be at least as important as openings and endings.[55] On other occasions the divisions of an ode can occur in mid-line: this is the case with every division in 3.25, which also constitutes a perfect example of ring composition (A¹ B¹ C B² A²); and, whereas A¹ and A² have an equivalent number of lines, there is no numerical correspondence between B¹ and B² (see ad loc.). Ring composition, which is frequent in Horace, is one of the poet's many regular ways of signalling closure,[56] but, as with many such structures, one reader's analysis of a poem will often differ from another's. Horace has a well-deserved reputation for the deceptive nature of his transitions.[57]

It is one of the defining characteristics of the *Odes* that almost all of them have an addressee (the exceptions in Book 3 are 2, 5 and 24).[58] Young women constitute the largest group in Book 3 (7 Asterie, 9 Lydia, 10 Lyce, 12 Neobule, 15 Chloris, 23 Phidyle, 27 Galatea, 28 Lyde),[59] followed by divinities (11 Mercury, 18 Faunus, 22 Diana, 25 Bacchus, 26 Venus), although in 3.11, whose implied addressee is in fact Lyde, Mercury seems merely a foil for the lyre; inanimate objects are likewise

---

[55] Cf. also S. Kyriakides and F. De Martino (edd.), *Middles in Latin Poetry* (2004).
[56] See Schrijvers, *OR* 56–71.
[57] An enormous amount has been written on the structure of Horace's odes (e.g. Syndikus and Tarrant, *HH* 17–49, and Mayer's Introduction to Book 1, pp. 12–16). The first seventeen odes of Book 3 have been studied by J. Y. Nadeau, *Latomus* 42 (1983) 303–31, 45 (1986) 522–40, and *QUCC* 31 (1989) 85–104.
[58] On this see also Citroni, *OR* 72–105, and Barber, Chap. 4.
[59] 'Every time Horace has addressed a woman in these odes, the relationship between the woman and the man, usually Horace himself, is or has been sexual, or one of them has wished it to be' (West, *DP* 226, noting that Phidyle in 3.23 is the only exception). In Books 1–3 as a whole Horace addresses or expresses a personal interest in about twenty women (the exact number will vary depending on how one calculates), the great majority being in Books 1 and 3 (women hardly feature at all in Book 2); sometimes a name is repeated from poem to poem (thus 1.8, 1.13, 1.25, 3.9 Lydia; 1.23, 3.7, 3.9, 3.26 Chloe; 2.5, 3.15 Chloris; 2.11, 3.11, 3.28 Lyde; 1.19, 1.30, 1.33, 3.19 Glycera). Scholars have been divided on the question whether these Greek-named women are entirely fictitious or whether the names are pseudonyms for real women, as in the famous examples mentioned at Apul. *Apol.* 10.3 (but note the case of Cinyra above, pp. 3–4 and n. 11). The status of the women in erotic (especially Augustan) Latin poetry has been endlessly debated. Williams has an interesting discussion of women in elegy (*TORP* 525–42), but his half-page on Horace (565) is inconclusive. Also of interest is Griffin 1–29, esp. 27–8.

addressees in 3.13 (a spring) and 3.21 (a wine-jar). Addresses to a Muse bring closure to 3.3 and 3.30; in 3.4 Calliope is addressed at the start and the Camenae later on. Two odes are addressed to otherwise unidentified young men (3.19, 3.20), and it is striking that only one ode is addressed to a high-status figure of the type so common in Books 1–2 (3.17 Aelius Lamia), although M. Valerius Messalla Corvinus, the consul of 31 BC, is the honorand of 3.21. The vocative 'Romane' in 3.6 is in my opinion an address to Augustus (see ad loc.), although it is generally thought that Horace is referring to the Roman people, who are also addressed implicitly in 3.1 and explicitly in 3.14 (see below). There are 'asides' to slaves at 3.14.17, 3.19.10 and (by implication) 3.26.6.

Given that most of the odes have an addressee, there are some odes 'which read, to all intents and purposes, as verse epistles'.[60] This is especially true of odes such as 3.29 (in which Horace invites Maecenas to visit him in the country), since invitations would often be issued by means of real letters. Another invitation to Maecenas, however, is very different: in 3.8 the great man is envisaged as arriving at Horace's house and being taken aback by the celebrations which are in progress and which require an explanation from the poet. The difference between the two poems is that in the latter case the reader is expected to imagine a dramatic situation, and a similar expectation is required in a significant number of odes. One ode (3.9) constitutes a dialogue between Lydia and an unnamed interlocutor (often but not always identified as Horace), each character speaking in turn. At the start of 3.4, after Horace has asked Calliope to present herself and sing (1–4), a short interval is to be imagined during which the Muse is given a chance to start her performance; otherwise Horace's question to his unidentified audience (5 'auditis?') makes no sense. The passing of time is expressed rather differently in another ode where poetic inspiration is again the topic: in 3.25 Horace begins by imagining himself in the process of being swept away by Bacchus (1–8a); only halfway through the poem (8b–14a) does it become clear that his destination has now been reached. In 3.19 Horace and Telephus have been drinking and are now making their way through the streets of Rome at night: Telephus is maundering on, while Horace is more concerned about where their next drink is coming from. There is another night-time

---

[60] Quinn, *LE* 87, a comment with precedents in antiquity, where 'even some among the *epinicia* of Pindar and Bacchylides are commonly treated as verse epistles' (R. Ferri, *CCH* 121, also mentioning Sappho and Solon). Herodotus regards Alcaeus 428A as a kind of letter (5.95.2). On the problems associated with epistolography and its identification see R. Morello and A. D. Morrison (edd.), *Ancient Letters* (2007) 1–16, 215–25.

walk in 3.26: the speaker is on his way to Chloe's house as a komast, when he has second thoughts and tells the slaves accompanying him to hang up his komastic equipment in the temple of Venus which they have just reached (6 'Hic, hic ponite...'); but he then changes his mind yet again and decides on one last attempt on Chloe.[61] Komastic situations are dramatic of their very nature, as is clear in 3.10, where Lyce is asked by the *exclusus amator* whether she can hear the wind howling; at the other end of the scale, 3.7 might be a verse letter in all but name, were it not for its first three words ('Quid fles, Asterie...?'), which envisage Horace in the presence of the woman. Quinn, who rightly points out that some odes are 'neither clearly epistolary nor clearly dramatic', uses the term 'dramatic monologues' to describe all such poems, with the exception of the dialogic 3.9;[62] but, since 'monologue' may carry the misleading implication that the speaker is alone, it is perhaps best avoided. Whatever nomenclature is adopted,[63] it is worth noting that these dramatised poems account for a full third of the total in Book 3.

Some dramatised poems raise a question which applies to the *Odes* more generally. On encountering the komast of 3.10, lying in the snow outside Lyce's door in a howling gale, contemporary readers would be unlikely to identify him with a poet who elsewhere describes himself as in his early forties (3.21.1) and an intimate of Maecenas: unless they assumed that Horace had inserted into Book 3 a poem relating to a youthful incident two decades earlier (cf. 3.14.25-8), which seems equally unlikely, such readers would understand that the 'I' of the ode (3.10.2 *me*) is no more to be identified with the author of the *Odes* than is the lover in 3.26, who equips himself with crowbars when en route to serenade Chloe (3.26.7-8).[64] In these odes Horace is adopting the *persona* of a komast, and it is natural to ask whether, or to what extent, the speaker of other odes is likewise fictitious or is the 'real' Horace.[65] In some cases

---

[61] For this interpretation see ad loc.; there is an imagined pause between lines 8 and 9.
[62] Quinn, *LE* 84-109.
[63] Another term is 'mimetic': see W. Albert, *Das mimetische Gedicht in der Antike* (1988).
[64] 'If any of Horace's compositions are purely fanciful, this may be pronounced to be so' (Macleane ad loc.).
[65] For a sceptical discussion see N. Horsfall, 'The first person singular in Horace's *Carmina*', in P. Knox and C. Foss (edd.), *Style and Tradition: Studies in Honor of Wendell Clausen* (1998) 40-54. On the other hand R. Mayer has argued that the ancients' concept of *persona* differed from ours and that ancient readers read poetry biographically ('Persona<l> problems', *MD* 50 (2003) 55-80). Cf. the nineteenth-century division between K. Lehrs ('The real Horace is never found in his *Odes*') and O. F. Gruppe ('Horace is Horace only in his *Odes*').

(such as the odes addressed to Maecenas) the question does not even arise; but in 3.9, for example, Nisbet and Rudd argue strongly that Lydia's wooer is Horace himself,[66] whereas for D. A. Russell such a reading is 'naïve'.[67] Of particular interest are cases where the role and nature of the speaker changes within the same ode. The clearest example is 3.14, where in the last four stanzas the speaker (13–14 *mihi, ego*), who seems to identify himself almost explicitly as Horace (27–8 *ego*), orders a young slave to arrange a party (17 'i, pete…, puer'); but in the first three stanzas the speaker addresses the people at large (1 'o plebs') and boys and girls in particular (10 'o pueri et puellae'). It is evident that the speaker of lines 1–12 is different from the speaker of lines 13–28: he is imagined not to be Horace himself but some kind of public orator, whose role the poet has temporarily adopted. Boys and girls are again the intended audience of the first ode of the Alcaic Hexad: on this occasion Horace adopts the role of priest while speaking to them (cf. 3.1.1–4), before reverting to himself in the last two stanzas (41–8). This pattern is mirrored in the last ode of the Alcaic Hexad, except that there the role adopted at the start is that of prophet or the like (3.6.1–8: see ad loc.). Although it is natural and convenient to assume that in most of the odes, for most of the time, the speaker is Horace himself, the demonstrable exceptions show that the assumption of roles is an aspect of his lyric *uarietas* (ποικιλία),[68] and there will certainly be readers who prefer to imagine that in an ode such as 3.27 Horace has not been abandoned by Galatea but is playing the role of an abandoned lover;[69] but it would be tedious if not impossible to qualify almost every reference to 'H.' in my Commentary.[70]

Two of the dramatised poems begin with a day's date (3.8.1, 3.28.1–2); the latter includes also a consular date to denote the year in which wine was sealed into its amphora (3.28.8 'Bibuli consulis', 59 BC). The same motif is used to open 3.21, which Horace also identifies as the year of

---

[66] N–R 133; so too Tsitsiou-Chelidoni 176, 189 n. 63. In their commentary on Book 1 of the *Odes* N–H were heavily influenced by the so-called 'biographical fallacy' and were predisposed to downplay elements of 'real life', but such scepticism is not a feature of their work on Book 2 and Rudd had always expressed misgivings about the 'fictionalised' approach to Latin poetry (*Phoenix* 18 (1964) 216–31, *Lines of Enquiry* (1976) 145–81): see further Griffin 1–31 and 48–64.
[67] D. A. Russell, 'Self-disclosure in Plutarch and in Horace', in G. W. Most et al. (edd.), *Philanthropia kai Eusebeia: Festschrift für A. Dihle* (1993) 426–37, at 432.
[68] For the application of this concept to the *Odes* see e.g. Santirocco 5–9.
[69] So e.g. Courtney (2016) 44–5.
[70] The strategy of Y. Nadeau in *Erotica for Caesar Augustus* (2008) is to distinguish between the historical person Horace (whom he calls 'Horatius'), the character within the poems ('Quintus') and the author ('Flaccus'). There are good and sensible remarks in D. West, *Reading Horace* (1967) 126–41.

his own birth ('consule Manlio', 65 BC). A third consular date concludes 3.14 to connote Horace's youth (28 'consule Planco', 42 BC), but readers are intended to remember also that that was the momentous year of the battle of Philippi (above, p. 4); the date sustains the theme of memory which suffuses the second half of an ode which earlier had looked to the future (3.14.13–15 'hic dies...eximet... nec...metuam'): the celebratory wine-jar requested by Horace remembers the Social War of 91–89 BC and witnessed Spartacus' slave revolt of 73–71 BC (3.14.18–20). The complex interweaving of past, present and future is on brilliant display in 3.3, which is dated by the mention of Augustus' name to 27 BC or later (3.3.11) but consists largely of a speech by Juno which, if we follow the clues, is placed seven centuries earlier during the later period of Romulus' reign (see intro.); the speech itself looks back to the relatively recent Trojan War but embraces a vision of Rome's destiny – which is in the distant future for the gods listening to Juno but in the present for the readership of Horace's ode (3.3.42–8).

Although it is difficult to determine the dramatic season of some odes, such as 3.18 (April or December?) and 3.28 (July or December?), others are firmly fixed at a definite point of the year: spring (3.8), summer (3.29), autumn (3.13 (?), 17) and winter (3.7, (?) 19). Almost every ode expresses more or less awareness of the passage of time. The Myth of Ages is in the background of 3.6, a poem which not only incorporates references to earlier versions of the Myth but suggests that Augustus can halt the downward spiral of decline. Lyce is reminded of old age in 3.10, Chloris is not acting her age in 3.15, and the komast is too old for love (or is he?) in 3.26. In the invitation to Maecenas which occupies the penultimate position in the book, the central portion of the ode is entirely taken up with the theme of time (3.29.29–48).[71]

This final invitation to Maecenas is dated to the month of July (3.29.17–20), when the great man should exchange his city dwelling for Horace's villa in the country. The countryside evokes a simpler and more upright way of life (3.6.37–44), where the changing seasons are marked by rustic rituals and the sacrifices of the devout (3.13, 18, 22, 23). Since Horace, like other authors, associated living off the land with olden times (*Epo.* 2.1–2, *Epi.* 2.1.139), his evident sympathy for the countryside harmonised with Augustus' explicit desire to resurrect old-fashioned customs and morality (*RG* 8.5): 'By means of new laws carried on my initiative I brought back many examples of ancestral practices which were already disappearing from our age, and I personally handed down to posterity

---

[71] On time in the *Odes* see Evans; also *EO* 2.883–90 (F. Citti).

3 VOCABULARY

examples of many things for them to imitate.' No one doubts that among these 'new laws' were the Lex Iulia de Maritandis Ordinibus and Lex Iulia de Adulteriis Coercendis of 18–17 BC:[72] although these postdate the publication of the *Odes*, they were the practical result of socio-ethical thinking which had been common in the imperial circle for many years.[73] The deplorable practices of an unfaithful young wife and her conniving husband (3.6.17–32) contrast with the virtuous behaviour of the Scythians on the remote steppes (3.24.19–30), while the approval of a husband's loyalty (3.7) is matched by a celebration of wifely fidelity (3.10), the latter followed by a recommendation of marriage in the form of an elaborate myth (3.11). Yet none of this prevents Horace from proclaiming his own bachelor status (3.8.1) or commemorating his career as a lover (3.28): we have to assume that in such cases the women are *meretrices* or otherwise not of the social status that would incur official disapproval.[74]

3 VOCABULARY

The components which contribute to an author's 'style', as it is called, are almost beyond counting. The third volume of D. Bo's edition of Horace has roughly three hundred pages of statistics, listing everything from the poet's use of prepositions to his Grecisms. It is obviously impossible in this Introduction to do justice to such evidence, which is discussed in an invaluable survey by F. Muecke (*EO* 2.755–87). In what follows I shall focus on word choice and word order.

(a) Word Choice

The Romans had at their disposal a remarkably large number of adjectives with which to describe and categorise individual words,[75] and this number reflects the importance which they, like the Greeks, attached to choosing the right word in the right context.[76] In the Epistle to Florus, for example, Horace himself discusses the use of ordinary words, archaisms and neologisms (2.2.111–19; cf. *AP* 46/45–72), which is a convenient division for

---

[72] See 3.6.25–6n.
[73] See Du Quesnay (1984). Whether there had been an earlier attempt at marriage legislation is disputed (see 3.6.25–6n.). West prefaces his commentary on Book 3 with an 'Augustan Inventory', in which he lists ten socio-political themes prominent in the book (*DP* 3–11).
[74] For Horace's love poetry see e.g. Lyne, *LLP* 192–238.
[75] See e.g. those listed by Lausberg 795–6, Index 1 s.v. 'verbum'.
[76] See L. P. Wilkinson, 'The language of Virgil and Horace', *CQ* 9 (1959) 181–92.

illustrating his own vocabulary. Axelson famously identified in the *Odes* a large number of words which he considered to be more characteristic of prose than of poetry. Those in Book 3 include: *amabilis* (3.4.5), *atqui* (3.5.49, 3.7.9), *attinet* (3.23.13), *cena* (3.29.15), *condicio* (3.5.14), *luctuosus* (3.6.8, 3.8.19), *merces* (3.2.26, 3.3.22), *negotium* (3.5.53, 3.29.49), *nequam* (3.6.47), *ordino* (3.1.9), *pecunia* (3.16.17, 3.24.61), *plerumque* (3.21.14, 3.29.13), *praesidium* (3.29.62), *prauus* (3.3.2). Although Axelson's analysis has encountered occasional criticism (see N–R on 3.5.53–4), his findings were largely endorsed in a detailed study by P. A. Watson (1985). The overall effect of Horace's vocabulary in the *Odes* is that it 'is marked more by the artistic deployment of words drawn from the neutral register of everyday Latin rather than the consistent use of elevated diction'.[77] Axelson provided only incidental remarks on adjectives ending in *–osus*, which have often been described as colloquial or even vulgar: Horace uses many of them in the *Odes* and there are almost two dozen in Book 3, perhaps a greater proportion than in any of the other books, ranging from the rare (*caliginosus*, 3.29.30) to the common (e.g. *iocosus*, 3.3.69, 3.21.15). It has been emphasised by J. N. Adams, however, that most of the 'sweeping characterisations' about the stylistic level of these formations result from misapprehension: the suffix almost always has a specific meaning ('abounding in') and each example needs to be treated on its merits.[78] Since an ode is usually framed as an address by the poet to an individual within his own society, as Mayer has observed, 'much of the language normally used by the élite in familiar conversation ought to be entirely at home in lyric'.[79]

Since archaisms are often found in verse, they can be difficult to distinguish from language which is itself poetic, as Cicero pointed out (*De Or.* 3.153).[80] Two of the nouns exemplified by Cicero occur in *Odes* 3 (*proles*, 3.6.38, and *suboles*, 3.13.8); other words which fall into a similar category are *aeuum* (3.5.16, 3.11.36), *catus* (3.12.15), *duellum* (3.5.38), *hosticus* (3.2.6), *nauita* (3.4.30, 3.24.41) and *pubes* (3.5.18). Horace is responsible for a fair number of neologisms, some of them *unique.[81] Those

---

[77] P. E. Knox, *BCH* 540.
[78] J. N. Adams, *Social Variation and the Latin Language* (2013) 571–8.
[79] Mayer, Intro. p. 10.
[80] Deciding whether a word is or is not 'poetic' can also be tricky and is easiest in cases where one can apply the so-called 'synonym test' (for which see esp. H. M. Hine, 'Poetic influence on prose: the case of the Younger Seneca', in T. Reinhardt et al. (edd.), *Aspects of the Language of Latin Prose* (2005) 211–37). A standard example is the poetic *ensis*, since it has the non-poetic synonym *gladius* (see 3.1.17–18n.).
[81] It should always be borne in mind how much Latin literature is no longer extant.

in Book 3 embrace verbs (3.3.33 *redono* (also 2.7.3), 3.7.28 **denato*, 3.29.47 *diffingo* (also 1.35.39, perhaps *S.* 1.10.37)), nouns (3.4.71 **temptator*, 3.24.30 **postgenitus*), adjectives (3.4.69 *centimanus* (also 2.17.14), 3.14.11 **ominatus* (if the text is right), 3.23.8 *pomifer* (also 4.7.11)), and an adverb (3.11.10 **exsultim*). He is particularly fond of negative adjectives compounded with *in-*, such as the sequence *imbellis…intaminatis…immeritis…incesto* at 3.2.15–30;[82] of these, **intaminatus* is unique, as are **immiserabilis* (3.5.17), **impermissus* (3.6.27), **inaudax* (3.20.3), **immetatus* (3.24.12). Sometimes these novelties imitate Greek forms (thus *irrepertus* (3.3.49; elsewhere only at Sen. *Med.* 468) = ἀνεύρετος and *centimanus* = ἑκατόγχειρ): such formations are the linguistic equivalent of literary allusion.

Horace also likes using words in new ways, a favourite resort being to construct adjectives with an infinitive (as 3.2.21 *immeritus*, 3.3.50 *fortis* (also 1.37.27, *S.* 2.7.85), 3.11.4 *callidus* (also 1.10.8), 3.12.15 *catus*, 3.12.13 *celer* (also 1.15.18, 4.6.40, *Epi.* 1.20.25), 3.19.2 *timidus* (also 4.9.52), 3.21.22 *segnis*, 3.29.50 *pertinax*). Whether this habit is also influenced by Greek, which likes such constructions, or is to be regarded as an extension of an existing Latin practice,[83] is unclear. On two occasions Horace seems to endow verbs with a new meaning (3.1.23 *fastidire* = 'to look down on from a height', 3.16.27 *occultare* = 'to store') on the analogy of near-synonyms which have this semantic dimension (respectively *despicere* and *condere*).

(b) Word Order

Coleridge, a poet and critic like Horace himself, famously defined poetry as 'the best words in the best order'. In 1922 H. Darnley Naylor listed a very wide variety of Horace's favoured word patterns, focussing especially (but not exclusively) on the arrangement of nouns and adjectives.[84] Amongst many other patterns he noted a great fondness for 'golden lines' (adj.¹ adj.² verb noun¹ noun²), e.g. 3.18.5 'si tener pleno cadit haedus anno', 'silver lines' (adj.¹ adj.² verb noun² noun¹), e.g. 3.1.16 'omne capax mouet urna nomen', interlacing (abab), e.g. 3.6.37–8 'rusticorum mascula militum | proles', and chiasmus (abba), e.g. 3.14.5 'unico

---

[82] Such adjectives are regularly paired in asyndeton (see J. N. Adams, *Asyndeton and its Interpretation in Latin Literature: History, Patterns, Textual Criticism* (2021), Chap. VI), although there are no examples in the *Odes*.

[83] See Coleman 83 (in the course of a long and very helpful discussion of 'poetic diction, poetic discourse and the poetic register').

[84] See Naylor xiii–xxx; the bulk of his book (pp. 1–274) consists of selected comments on each individual ode and epode.

gaudens mulier marito'. Sometimes interlacing and chiasmus will alternate, as at 3.3.5-6:

> dux[a] inquieti[b] turbidus[a] Hadriae[b]
> nec fulminantis[c] magna[d] manus[d] Iouis[c]

Wilkinson in his *Golden Latin Artistry* was interested in the effects of Horace's word patterns (see further below, p. 34), while West (1973) investigated various examples of what he called 'polar tension', where Horace plays off one word against another, as at 3.12.13-16:

> **celer** idem per apertum
> fugientes agitato
> grege ceruos iaculari et **catus** arto latitantem
> fruticeto excipere aprum;

here there is both the *uariatio* of the ablative *arto...fruticeto* corresponding not with *agitato grege* (which has no correspondent) but with *per apertum* and also the extra refinement of *latitantem* 'lurking' mimetically within the dense thicket. Nisbet in his own detailed study of Horatian word order alleged that mimetic word order affects only 'a very small proportion' of the *Odes*,[85] but in fact it is very common, e.g. 3.1.33 'contracta pisces aequora sentiunt', 5.31-2 'extricata densis cerua plagis', 10.5-6 'nemus inter pulchra satum tecta', 15.5 'inter ludere uirgines', 16.34-5 'Laestrygonia Bacchus in amphora', 18.13 'inter audaces lupus errat agnos', 27.51-2 'utinam inter errem nuda leones', 29.2 'non ante uerso lene merum cado'. Particularly Horatian is the creative juxtaposition of opposites, often producing paradox or oxymoron: e.g. 3.4.5-6 'amabilis insania', 44 'sustulerit caduco', 3.5.48 'egregius...exsul', 3.6.44 'agens abeunte', 3.7.13 'perfida credulum', 3.11.35 'splendide mendax', 3.20.3-4 'inaudax...raptor', 3.24.59 'periura...fides', 3.27.28 'palluit audax', 41-2 'fugiens...ducit', 3.29.17 'clarus occultum', 3.29.49 'saeuo laeta negotio', 50 'insolentem...pertinax'.[86] It is this facility with words which has made Horace such a memorable epigrammatist: many of his *sententiae* remain in common parlance today, such as *Dulce et decorum est pro patria mori* (3.2.13) or *Vis consili expers mole ruit sua* (3.4.65).[87]

---

[85] *OR* 384. The useful term 'mimetic syntax' was coined by D. Lateiner, *AJP* 111 (1990) 204-37.
[86] It is this type of linguistic phenomenon which is held to illustrate Horace's famous words at *AP* 47-8: 'notum si callida uerbum | reddiderit iunctura nouum'.
[87] In both the *Oxford Dictionary of Quotations* and *The Penguin Dictionary of Quotations* Horace is cited more times than Ovid and Virgil combined.

When the poet Eumolpus in Petronius' *Satyrica* commends Horace for his 'curiosa felicitas' or 'painstaking felicity' (118.5), he seems to have been referring to Horace's success at integrating his *sententiae* into their context; but the praise would be equally appropriate for his way with words.[88]

4 MODELS AND METRES

(a) Intertextuality

Greek and Latin are imitative literatures. From the earliest times, when the lyric poets of archaic Greece were routinely using the language and phraseology of Homer, classical authors were as aware of writers in the past as they were of their readers in the future. Such consciousness of a literary tradition, which in one form or another lasted until relatively modern times, was heightened in a society where – before the invention of paper and printing, and when texts were expensive to produce and therefore rare – memory played a decisive role. Ancient writers carried round in their heads the works of their predecessors, which could be reproduced either intentionally or involuntarily. The reproduction might be coextensive with an original, as in Catullus' translation of Callimachus (66), or circumscribed, as when Callimachus himself (*Hymn* 1.90) reused the single noun ἄνη ('fulfilment') from Aeschylus. Sometimes the reproduction will act as a generic indicator, as when Virgil at the start of the *Aeneid* recalls the start of both *Iliad* and *Odyssey*; sometimes there will be a dramatic point, as when Nero's 'marriage' to Pythagoras is described by Tacitus (*A.* 15.37.4) in terms reminiscent of Dido's rather different 'marriage' to Aeneas (Virg. *Aen.* 4.351–2); at other times a verbal similarity will result from nothing more than a reverberation in an author's mind.[89] Modern scholars have developed a whole range of vocabulary – imitation, echo, reference, allusion, intertextuality – to describe and theorise about this phenomenon.[90]

Like Virgil (p. 15 n. 48), Horace was extraordinarily well read. In their editions of his odes, Keller–Holder and Shorey (below, pp. 37–8) quote a vast range of parallel expressions to illustrate his thought and language, to which more recent scholars, such as Nisbet and his co-editors, have added

---

[88] For the reaction to Horace in antiquity see Tarrant, *CCH* 277–90.
[89] See e.g. *PH* 385.
[90] For an extensive bibliography see Y. Baraz and C. S. van den Berg, *AJP* 134 (2013) 133–48; they omit D. West and A. J. Woodman (edd.), *Creative Imitation and Latin Literature* (1979).

further material. If we take references to Homer as a given, Horace's allusions in Book 3 extend from Hesiod's *Theogony* (3.4 intro.) to Virgil's *Georgics* (3.3 intro., 3.25 intro.), a period of roughly seven centuries; capitalising on his friendship with Virgil, he may even have alluded to the as yet unpublished *Aeneid* (3.3 intro.). The opening ode seems to allude to Callimachus (3.1.1n.), the last to Pindar (3.30.2n., 3–4n.). These and innumerable other works acted as sources of inspiration. Catullus is a particularly challenging case: Horace's allusions to his verse (e.g. 3.2.9n., 3.25.8–9n.) have to be reconciled with his dismissive reference to the poet in his satires (*S.* 1.10.19).[91] On the other hand, it is likely that Catullus had a significant influence on Horace's choice of Sappho and Alcaeus as metrical models (see below).

From the frequency with which Horace mentions Alcaeus and Sappho and implies that his odes are modelled on their poetry (1.1.34, 1.26.11, 1.32.3–12, 2.13.24–32, 3.30.13–14, 4.3.12, 4.9.7–12) we might have expected a disproportionate number of allusions to them; is this what happens? We have already noted that Virgil at the start of the *Aeneid* alludes to the *Iliad* and *Odyssey*, indicating that these two Homeric poems will be his principal epic models. This technique is quite common. At the start of the *Eclogues* Virgil alludes to Theocritus' first *Idyll*; at the start of the *Annals* Tacitus alludes to Sallust's *Bellum Catilinae*. It is well known that the technique is adopted by Horace in his *Odes*, where opening allusions are called 'mottoes' or 'epigraphs'.[92] A famous example is the Cleopatra ode (1.37), whose three opening words, *Nunc est bibendum*, constitute a verbal and partly aural imitation of Alcaeus 332.1 Νῦν χρῆ μεθύσθην ('Now we must drink'). Yet Mayer, the latest commentator on Book 1 of the *Odes*, finds only two other Alcaic mottoes (1.18, 1.22), of which the second is uncertain; there are no cases in Book 2; and the one alleged example in Book 3 (12) can be discounted (see ad loc.). There are no Sapphic mottoes in any of the three books.[93] In short, there seems to be a mismatch between Horace's references to Alcaeus and Sappho and his verbal

---

[91] For a full study see M. C. J. Putnam, *Poetic Interplay: Catullus and Horace* (2006).

[92] Fraenkel 159 n. 2 for 'motto'; for 'epigraph' see G. B. Conte, *The Rhetoric of Imitation* (1986) 25–6.

[93] We must always bear in mind (a) that only a fraction of archaic Greek lyric poetry has survived, (b) that scholars will differ in what they think constitutes a 'motto'. J. A. Richmond ('Horace's "mottoes" and Catullus 51', *RhM* 113 (1970) 197–204) finds six Alcaic mottoes in *Odes* 1–3; he omits 1.22, included by Mayer, because the text of Alcaeus 130B was yet to be satisfactorily emended. There is a monograph by A. Cavarzere, *Sul limitare: Il 'Motto' e la poesia di Orazio* (1996), which is very inclusive.

allusions to their poetry.[94] The reason, as may be inferred from those of his statements that are programmatic in nature, is that Horace conceived of his debt to Alcaeus and Sappho principally in metrical terms.[95]

(b) Metres

In Books 1–3 of the *Odes* Horace uses eleven different lyric metres, all of them modelled (sometimes with modifications) on those of the Greek lyric poets.[96] All but two of these metres are paraded in the first nine odes of Book 1, which as a result are often called the 'Parade Odes'.[97]

By far the commonest metre in *Odes* 1–3 is the Alcaic stanza, named after Alcaeus, the sixth-century poet from the Aegean island of Lesbos: in all three books it outnumbers every other metre (**1**: 10; **2**: 12; **3**: 11) and generates the greatest number of lines (**1**: 27.3%; **2**: 60%; **3**: 46.8%). The Sapphic stanza, named after Alcaeus' contemporary, Sappho of Lesbos, is the second most common (**1**: 9; **2**: 6; **3**: 7) and accounts for the second highest total of lines (**1**: 25.1%; **2**: 28%; **3**: 22.2%). These two 'Lesbian' metres together account for half the poems in Book 1 (19 = 52.4% of lines), all but two of the poems in Book 2 (18 = 88% of lines), and the majority of poems in Book 3 (18 = 69% of lines).[98]

Most of the remaining odes are written in one or other of the five Asclepiad-based systems, as they are called, and each book has at least one metre which does not feature in the other books: thus the Third Archilochian and Greater Sapphic in Book 1 (1.4, 1.8), the Hipponactean in Book 2 (2.18), and Ionics *a minore* in Book 3 (3.12).[99] It is hardly surprising that Horace was described by Ovid as 'numerosus Horatius', 'metrical Horace' (*Tr.* 4.10.49): his metrical versatility was the most immediately conspicuous quality of his lyric poetry.

---

[94] There is a brilliant discussion of Horace and the Greek lyric poets by Feeney in Rudd (1993) 41–63 (= *OR* 202–31); see also Hutchinson 162–76 (= *CCH* 36–49) and Barchiesi, *CCGL* 319–35, *OR* 418–40. For a discussion of Alcaeus and Book 1 of the *Odes* see Lyne, *CP* 293–313.

[95] 'His pride at having introduced Aeolian lyric to Italy is very likely due, not to the phrases or ideas, nor even to the small amount of spirit, which he derived from Alcaeus and Sappho, but to his success in mastering and adapting their metres' (Wilkinson, *HLP* 11).

[96] For Greek see M. L. West, *Introduction to Greek Metre* (1987); for Greek lyric metres see Battezzato 130–46. There is an excellent account of Horatian metre in N–H 1.xxxviii–xlvi; see also Wilkinson, *GLA* 102–18.

[97] See Lyne, *CP* 296 and n. 20.

[98] Like Lyne (*Hor.* 98–9), I am assuming that the Alcaic stanza was so named in Horace's own day and hence that the Sapphic stanza was so named too.

[99] This practice is continued in Book 4 with the unique Second Archilochian (4.7).

Of these eleven metres, seven are used in Book 3:

Alcaic stanza (1–6, 17, 21, 23, 26, 29)
– – U – – ´ – U U – U ×
– – U – – ´ – U U – U ×
– – U – – – U – ×
– U U – U U – U – ×

In the first three lines the first syllable is usually long but, following Alcaeus' practice, is sometimes short, including eight times in Book 3 (1.2, 1.26, 3.34, 3.71, 4.78, 5.22, 6.10, 29.11).[100]

Sapphic stanza (8, 11, 14, 18, 20, 22, 27)
– U – – – U U – U – ×
– U – – – U U – U – ×
– U – – – U U – U – ×
– U U – ×

Four of the remaining five metres are called **Asclepiads**, since either they consist entirely of Asclepiad lines or they combine an Asclepiad line with a Glyconic and/or a Pherecratean.[101]

First Asclepiad[102] (30)
– – – U U – ´ – U U – U × (Asclepiad)
A continuous series of Asclepiad lines.

Second Asclepiad (10, 16)
– – – U U – ´ – U U – U × (Asclepiad)
– – – U U – ´ – U U – U × (Asclepiad)
– – – U U – ´ – U U – U × (Asclepiad)
– – – U U – U × (Glyconic)

---

[100] I have not mentioned here the other technical modifications which Horace made to this and the other metres, but individual points will be made in the Commentary; for full details see N–H 1.xxxviii–xlvi. Though these modifications may seem unimportant to us, their significance to the ancients is well illustrated by the elder Pliny's remarks about his own modification of Catullus (*NH* 1 *praef.* 1).

[101] The term 'Asclepiad' derives from the poet Asclepiades of Samos, an older contemporary of Theocritus, but the reason for the derivation is unknown. 'Glyconic' derives from a putative Glycon, who probably did not exist, and 'Pherecratean' from a fifth-century Greek comic poet named Pherecrates, its supposed inventor. Catullus has various combinations of Glyconics and Pherecrateans in Poems 17, 34 and 61; he uses the Fifth Asclepiad in Poem 30.

[102] I am using the names as given in N–H 1.xxxviii–xl.

Third Asclepiad (7, 13)

– – – U U – ´ – U U – U × (Asclepiad)
– – – U U – ´ – U U – U × (Asclepiad)
– – – U U – × (Pherecratean)
– – – U U – U × (Glyconic)

Fourth Asclepiad (9, 15, 19, 24, 25, 28)

– – – U U – U × (Glyconic)
– – – U U – ´ – U U – U × (Asclepiad)

The alternating sequence is repeated throughout.

One poem (12) is written in **Ionics** *a minore*, a metre which is unique in Latin and consists of a series of ten quadrisyllabic metra (U U – –). Most editors arrange these ten into four 3-line stanzas, but the arrangement looks highly anomalous in the context of the book as a whole: in most cases, as will be seen, the other poems are either divided into clear stanzas of four lines each or, in the cases of the First and Fourth Asclepiad, the line-totals of the poems are divisible by four. This phenomenon obtains for every other ode in Books 1–4,[103] with the exception of 4.8, where there are textual problems. It therefore seems virtually certain that Goold (1977) and Quinn (1980) were right to divide 3.12 into four *four*-line stanzas: if we follow them, the six odes of the Alcaic Hexad will comprise exactly half as many lines (336) as the remaining twenty-four odes in Book 3 (672). This ratio seems too neat to be accidental:[104] if it is significant, as I believe, it means that we should not try to solve textual problems by resorting to the deletion or insertion of lines or stanzas.

Tennyson famously described Virgil as 'Wielder of the stateliest measure | ever moulded by the lips of man', and no one can fail to marvel at the variety of effects which the poet can conjure from his succession of hexameter lines. But he had many poets – including Ennius, Cicero, Lucretius and Catullus – as his precedents, and it was perhaps the only metre which Virgil ever used.[105] Horace not only matched Virgil in hexameters (and to outrageous effect in the *Satires*) but ventured upon the iambic and other metres of the *Epodes* before presenting himself with the lyric challenges of the *Odes*.[106] No one, as far as we know, had ever made

---

[103] This is known as Meineke's Law, after the 19th-century scholar who discovered it; see further Wilkinson, *GLA* 204–7.
[104] It was pointed out by Moritz 118.
[105] The authorship of some of the poems in the Appendix Vergiliana is disputed.
[106] For the metres of the *Epodes* see Mankin's commentary, pp. 14–22.

a concerted attempt on these metres before,[107] and few would make the attempt afterwards. Horace's metrical achievement in the *Odes*, sustained over three (and subsequently four) books, was unparalleled. In the words of L. P. Wilkinson he was quite simply 'the greatest of Roman metrists'.[108]

In the first ode of the first book Horace expresses a hope that his 'Lesbian lyre' will not fail (1.1.34 *Lesboum...barbiton*) and he lets it be known that his ambition is to be included in the canon of nine Greek lyric poets (1.1.35).[109] These juxtaposed statements mean that he aspires to being canonised on the basis of having composed in the metres used by the Lesbian poets, Alcaeus and Sappho: that is, not merely the two metres to which they gave their names but also some or all of the other metres which they used and to which modern scholars have given the name 'Aeolic',[110] including, for example, the First Asclepiad in which that first ode is written. When Horace later in Book 1 says that it is fitting to immortalise his friend Lamia 'with a new lyre and Lesbian plectrum' (1.26.10–11 'fidibus nouis | ...Lesbio...plectro'), he is claiming to be the first Latin poet to use the metres used by Alcaeus and Sappho. A few odes later he demands a 'Latin song' from the 'lyre first played by the Lesbian citizen' (1.32.3–5 'dic Latinum, | barbite, carmen, | Lesbio primum modulate ciui'): *primum* here looks back to *nouis* in the earlier ode: a key element which Horace has in common with Alcaeus, the 'Lesbian citizen', is that they are both metrical pioneers. It is true that there is no reference to Sappho in 1.32; but, since this very ode is written in the Sapphic metre, we cannot infer that his other references to 'Lesbian' poetry necessarily exclude Sappho. Scholars are agreed that, when he repeats his claim to metrical originality in the last ode of Book 3 (3.30.13–14), he is referring to both poets.[111]

It may seem strange for Horace to make a series of claims which include the work of a female poet, and it is certainly true that Nisbet in his

---

[107] Catullus used the Sapphic metre in Poems 11 and 51, in addition to the metres mentioned above (n. 101).

[108] *GLA* 102. The case for Catullus is made by D. Butterfield, 'Catullus and metre', *CCC* Chap. 7.

[109] The nine comprised six practitioners of choral lyric (Alcman, Stesichorus, Ibycus, Simonides, Pindar and Bacchylides) and three of so-called monodic lyric (Alcaeus, Sappho and Anacreon): see T. A. Hadjimichael, *The Emergence of the Lyric Canon* (2019). For the geographical distribution of the poets see D. Driscoll, I. McMullin, S. Sansom, A.-E. Peponi, *Mapping Greek Lyric: Places, Travel, Geographical Imaginary* [accessed 6 June 2019] (http://lyricmappingproject.stanford.edu).

[110] Lesbos had been settled by colonists from Aeolia on the west coast of Asia Minor. For Aeolic metres see Battezzato 134–6.

[111] See *PH* 41. Text and interpretation of 3.30.13–14 are controversial (see ad loc.).

commentaries, for example, consistently gives priority to Alcaeus, often to the exclusion of Sappho.[112] I have suggested elsewhere, however, that Horace was responding to Catullus,[113] one of the striking features of whose poetry is its gender dualism:[114] Catullus frequently depicts men, including himself, in female terms, the most famous example being Poem 51, his translation of Sappho 31, in which he applies Sappho's self-description to himself. Horace had no wish to portray himself or others similarly, but he was an admirer both of Catullus and of Greek lyric and he realised that, by imitating the metrical achievements of both Alcaeus and Sappho, he could reproduce, albeit in a radically different form, the gender dualism which he found in Catullus. It may be significant that Aristides Quintilianus, a musicologist of perhaps the late third century AD, says that much of the world is to be seen in terms of masculine and feminine, a combination which, when applied to the soul, means that the masculine part of the soul is the seat of 'anger and boldness', while the feminine part is that of 'pain and pleasure' (*On Music* 2.8). He contends that 'all sensible objects' – including poems, and even the letters, words, figures and tropes of which poems consist – have powers corresponding to these elements of the soul: those 'which entice us to pleasure and gently relax the mind are to be reckoned as feminine, while anything that excites anxiety or activity belongs to the realm of the male. Those that are neither or both should be assigned to an intermediate category.'[115] If we apply such a framework to the *Odes*, we should conclude that Horace's appeals to both Sappho and Alcaeus assign the collection as a whole to just such an 'intermediate category'. It is noteworthy that Quintilian attributes to Horatian lyric the complementary qualities of 'charm' and 'boldness' (10.1.96 'plenus est iucunditatis et gratiae et…uerbis felicissime audax'): boldness is clearly a masculine quality, whereas *gratia* is the Latin for χάρις, the very quality for which Sappho was famous.[116] Of particular interest is the fact that, without any reference to Sappho, Cairns has suggested χάρις as a helpful critical term in the explication of Horace's odes.[117]

To sum up. The interval which separated Horace from Alcaeus and Sappho is equivalent to that which separates us from Chaucer. As he

[112] See e.g. N–H 1.xii. [113] *PH* 41–58.
[114] See e.g. K. S. Myers, 'Gender and sexuality', *CCC* Chap. 4.
[115] The translations of Aristides are taken from D. A. Russell and M. Winterbottom, *Ancient Literary Criticism* (1972) 552–8. See also T. J. Matthiesen, *Aristides Quintilianus: On Music* (1983).
[116] For rather different and much more extended discussion of this topic see Morgan (2010) 410 (Index s.v. 'metrical form, gendered quality of').
[117] Cairns, *RL* 390, 418. At *AP* 42 ('ordinis haec uirtus erit et uenus') H. refers to word order in gendered terms (see Rudd's n.).

surveyed the history of literature across this vast tract of time, Horace recognised in the Lesbian poets a joint achievement which he believed he could replicate in the world of early imperial Rome. Each had produced a body of poetry in a wide variety of metres, each had pioneered a metre which bore their own name, each of them used the other's eponymous metre as well as their own.[118] This achievement is exactly mirrored by that of Horace, who in his odes gives pride of place to the Alcaic and Sapphic metres but sets them in a dazzling context of metrical variety.

5 'ARTISTE DE SONS'

It is important to recognise that metres are not simply inert patterns of long and short syllables;[119] metre can make a vital contribution to the expressiveness of Latin verse. An excellent guide in this area is the Horatian scholar L. P. Wilkinson, whose book *Golden Latin Artistry* (1963), though now unaccountably unfashionable, is full of the most suggestive examples and sensitive readings.[120] Wilkinson also draws attention to the work of the French scholar J. Marouzeau, who in 1936 had published an article entitled 'Horace artiste de sons' which deserves to be more widely known.[121] Most of Marouzeau's examples are chosen from Horace's hexameter poetry, but we should not follow some distinguished scholars in alleging that expressiveness is alien to the *Odes*. Consider a couple of lines in the very first ode of Book 3 (18–19):

non Si<u>c</u>ulae <u>d</u>apes

<u>d</u>ul<u>c</u>em elab*or*abunt s<u>a</u>p*or*em

or Regulus' eyewitness testimony (3.5.21–4):

de<u>r</u>epta **uidi; uidi** ego ci<u>ui</u>um

ret*orta* te<u>r</u>go bracchia lib<u>er</u>o

p*orta*sque non <u>c</u>lausas et <u>a</u>r<u>u</u>a

M<u>ar</u>te <u>c</u>oli **po**pulata nostro;

---

[118] That Sappho used the Alcaic metre is not definite but possible (Lyne, *CP* 297 n. 26): see 137, 138 and 168c.
[119] Some scholars refer to 'heavy' and 'light' syllables respectively, reserving the terms 'long' and 'short' for vowels.
[120] See now also Morgan (2010).
[121] *Mnem.* 4 (1936) 85–94 (= *Quelques aspects de la formation du latin littéraire* (1949) 193–201); see also C. Facchini Tosi, *EO* 2.841–50, 930–2.

5 'ARTISTE DE SONS' 35

or the final stanza of the Bandusia ode (3.13.13-16):

> fies nobi_l_ium tu quoque fontium
> me d_ice_nte cauis _im_positam il_ice_m
> saxis, un_de_ loquaces
> l_ymph_ae d_e_s_ili_unt tuae.[122]

or the first four stanzas of 3.16:

> Incl_us_am D_anaen_ _tur_ris aēnea
> _r_ob_us_taeque f_or_es et _ui_gilum ca_num_
> tristes excubiae _mun_ierant satis
> noc_tur_nis ab adulteris,   4
>
> si non Ac_ris_ium, _ui_rginis abditae
> custodem pa_ui_dum, Iupp_iter et_ V_enu_s
> _r_isiss_ent_: fore _eni_m **tu-tum** _iter et_ **pat**_ens_
> conu_er_so in p_r_etium deo.   8
>
> Au_rum per_ medios ire **sat**ellites
> et p_errumper_e amat **sax**a potentius
> ictu f_ul_mineo; concidit auguris
> Argi_ui_ domus ob _lu_crum   12
>
> demersa exitio; diffid_it ur_bi_um_
> portas uir Macedo et s_ub_r_uit_ ae_mu_los
> reges _muner_ibus; _muner_a nauium
> saeuos illaqueant duces.   16

Such examples could easily be multiplied; in fact, if you take almost any Horatian ode, you will find it alive with assonance, alliteration, anagrams and wordplay.[123] Horace is in no sense unique in this respect: almost every Latin author, prose as well as verse, aimed at similar effects; but Horace's are more extensive than anyone else's and more subtle.

Since almost all these effects involve sound, they invite the questions of whether or not the *Odes* were intended for performance, and, if so,

---

[122] Wilkinson said that the repeated *l* sounds 'suggest running water' (*HLP* 141), but there is clearly more to it than that.

[123] The standard commentators on the *Odes* allege that Horace by and large 'avoids alliteration, onomatopoeia, and haunting vowel sounds' (N–H 1.xxii). A similar response from Norden is quoted by Wilkinson (*GLA* 84 and n.).

what kind of performance. It is well known that 'The vocabulary of song, instruments, Muses and other singing gods, verbs of utterance or singing, and the like abound in Horace.'[124] Over the years there has been intermittent speculation about whether the *Odes* were sung to musical accompaniment; my own view is that Horace's references to song and the like are metaphorical and no more to be taken literally than Milton's reference to his 'adventurous song'.[125] A mimetic ode such as 3.19 would lend itself to dramatic performance in a kind of mime; and we may assume that Horace recited odes to friends, as he did in the case of his satires (*S.* 1.4.73), since recitation was an established stage on the road to eventual publication in the ancient world. Nevertheless, despite powerful voices urging that the oral communication of Latin literature in a public forum was regular and frequent in Roman times,[126] Horace himself stated that 'it is a pleasure for the bearer of things hitherto untold to be read and held by frank eyes and hands' (*Epi.* 1.19.33–4 'iuuat immemorata ferentem | ingenuis oculisque legi manibusque teneri'). The 'things hitherto untold' are the *Odes*, and their bearer is of course Horace himself: evidently he expected his poems to be read by individuals in silence, exactly as happens today.[127]

6 SCHOLARSHIP

L. P. Wilkinson began his book on Horace and his lyric poetry by noting that Horace shared with Homer the distinction of having his own special volume in the catalogue of Cambridge University Library.[128] In

---

[124] M. Lowrie, *Writing, Performance, and Authority in Augustan Rome* (2009) 73–4, with a valuable collection of the evidence and lengthy discussion.

[125] For discussion see Rossi, *OR* 356–77.

[126] T. P. Wiseman, *The Roman Audience* (2015); *contra* H. N. Parker, 'Books and reading Latin poetry', in W. A. Johnson and H. N. Parker (edd.), *Ancient Literacies: The Culture of Reading in Greece and Rome* (2009) 186–229 (pp. 220–1 for Horace).

[127] Cf. also *OLD manus* 12. It is a myth that the ancients read aloud to themselves (A. K. Gavrilov, 'Techniques of reading in classical antiquity', *CQ* 47 (1997) 56–73 (with a postscript by M. F. Burnyeat, pp. 74–6), R. W. McCutcheon, 'Silent reading in antiquity and the future history of the book', *Book History* 18 (2015) 1–32).

[128] Wilkinson, *HLP* iv. As an undergraduate at Cambridge in the late 1920s Wilkinson had attended A. E. Housman's lectures on the text of *Odes* 1–3. 'Textual criticism was not a preoccupation of mine', he wrote in old age, 'but to be shown how to go about it by the greatest living expert was a fascinating privilege. For examination purposes the best thing to do was to learn all the eighty-eight odes by heart, so that you would know the content of the *cruces* set. This I proceeded to do.' When Wilkinson himself began lecturing on Horace's *Odes* at Cambridge in the early 1930s, a member of the audience was Professor F. Solmsen, a refugee from Nazi Germany and already publishing on Horace (*FL* 56, 66). Later in the decade, Wilkinson took on the responsibility of delivering Housman's course of lectures on

6 SCHOLARSHIP

the seventy-five years since those words were written, the quantity of published scholarship in Classics has expanded beyond recognition, and publications on favourite authors such as Catullus, Horace and Virgil have increased disproportionately. Some current trends in Horatian scholarship will be found illustrated in the three handbooks which appeared in the early years of the third millennium.[129]

The most important development in scholarship on the *Odes* during the past half-century has been the three volumes of commentary by R. G. M. Nisbet in collaboration with M. Hubbard on Books 1 (1970) and 2 (1978) and with N. Rudd on Book 3 (2004).[130] The first volume drew from Wilkinson the following verses:[131]

> This is a book of Hubbard and Nisbet:
> Some of it's her bit and some of it's his bit.
> I leave it to you to decide who did what,
> But all of it's sense and none of it's not.

The division of labour and opinion remained anonymous in the second volume, but in the third the different views of Nisbet and Rudd are identified by their initials.[132] The work has replaced that of Kiessling and Heinze as the standard commentary on the *Odes*, and its authoritativeness is such that I thought it prudent not to consult the third volume until I had written my first draft of commentary on each ode, instead relying primarily on two late-nineteenth-century student commentaries, by J. Gow (1896) and the remarkable P. Shorey (1898),[133] and the revised version of the

---

Horace after the great man's death in 1936 (see L. P. Wilkinson, 'A. E. Housman, scholar and poet', *Housman Society Journal* 1 (1974) 32–46).

[129] *CCH* (2007), *CH* (2010), *BCH* (2013): see list of Abbreviations.

[130] See S. J. Harrison, 'Two-author commentaries on Horace: three case studies', in C. S. Kraus and C. A. Stray (edd.), *Classical Commentaries* (2015) 71–83.

[131] See S. J. Harrison, *PBA* 13 (2014) 365–82.

[132] Rudd was the ideal replacement for Hubbard, his Horatian expertise being complemented by an extensive knowledge of English literature, on which he also published. His two autobiographical memoirs (*Pale Green, Light Orange: A Portrait of Bourgeois Ireland, 1930–1950* (1994) and *It Seems Like Yesterday* (2003)) are as amusing as they are informative.

[133] Gow was successively Headmaster of Nottingham High School (1885–1901) and of Westminster School (1901–19); he died in 1923. A. S. F. Gow, the commentator on Theocritus, Machon and the Greek Anthology, was his son (see *DBC* 2.388–90 for both men). Shorey moved from Bryn Mawr College (1885–92) to become Professor of Greek at the University of Chicago; on his death in 1938 an obituarist declared 'Shorey was a genius'. It was said that he knew the *Iliad* by heart, and his commentary on the *Odes* is remarkable for its 'copious illustration… by passages from all literatures' (*CP* 29 (1938) 186): see https://dbcs.rutgers.edu/all-scholars/9117-shorey-paul.

edition by O. Keller and A. Holder (1899), where an invaluable repertory of Greek and Latin parallels may be found. In producing my first draft I nevertheless did allow myself to consult the first two volumes of Nisbet and Hubbard, and it goes without saying that, whenever readers of my Commentary on Book 3 encounter even plain cross-references to poems in Books 1 or 2, it is very likely indeed that Nisbet and Hubbard will have something helpful and interesting to say on the quoted passage.

In 1969 Gordon Williams produced a commentary on Book 3 of the *Odes* which he described as 'experimental'. The text of each ode was accompanied by an English translation and a commentary which, rather than being lemmatised in the traditional manner, offered a continuous interpretation of the text. Williams hoped that the presence of a translation would help those readers 'whose knowledge of Latin is uncertain', while the innovative commentary was designed to explain 'the poet's process of thought'. Shortly afterwards, in 1972–73, a two-volume study of Horatian lyric was published by the German scholar H. P. Syndikus: while lacking a text, the volumes consisted of 'paraphrastic commentary on the *Odes*' and rapidly established themselves as a standard work, a third edition being issued in 2001.[134] In 1980 Kenneth Quinn, who for more than twenty years had been pioneering a literary-critical approach to Latin texts, followed his traditionally formatted commentary on Catullus (1970) with one on Horace's *Odes*, replacing that by T. E. Page, which had held the field in British schools for more than a century. Finally, between the years 1995 and 2002, David West devoted to *Odes* 1–3 three stimulating volumes which in format, if not in tone, resemble that of Williams on Book 3.

For many generations the study of Horace was dominated by Fraenkel's *Horace* (1957).[135] Innumerable other scholars have written books or articles on Horace in the decades since the Second World War, and their quantity is such that it is almost impossible even to keep track of them, let alone read and study them;[136] certainly it is quite beyond the capacity of a 'green-and-yellow' commentary to do justice to the many, varied, and often competing interpretations of an individual ode. The pres-

---

[134] The description is that of Günther, *BCH* ix, xii.

[135] One evening in 1943, Wilkinson and Fraenkel found themselves on the same train from Oxford to Bletchley and in the course of conversation each discovered that the other was writing a book on Horace. Fraenkel asked to read Wilkinson's typescript, which the latter sent to him; when reminded of this some considerable time later, Fraenkel returned it without acknowledgement or comment and, when prompted again, replied 'I advise you to put it away for nine years' (*FL* 167).

[136] In the decade 1991–2001, for example, books on Horace averaged almost one a year, and that covers only those written in English. Conspicuous for their excellence are the Horatian papers by Francis Cairns in his *Roman Lyric* (2012).

ent volume represents a personal view, informed (I hope) by selected interpretations by others. It is taken for granted that, if readers of *Odes* 3 desire further information, they will consult Nisbet–Rudd and (if they have German) Syndikus. Happily there are online bibliographies by W. Stroh (http://stroh.userweb.mwn.de/bibl/horaz.html) and – even more up to date – N. Holzberg (http://www.niklasholzberg.com/Homepage/ Bibliographien.html). An invaluable and comprehensive resource for all aspects of Horace is the *Enciclopedia oraziana* (3 vols., 1996–98). These reference works allow scholars to follow up in more detail those matters of particular interest to them. An extremely helpful and readable guide to recent scholarship on Horace was produced by S. J. Harrison in 2014, No. 42 in the series *Greece & Rome* New Surveys in the Classics, replacing the earlier Horatian volume by Gordon Williams (1972) in the same series.

7 THE TEXT

Our modern texts of Horace depend principally upon manuscripts which in some cases date back to the ninth century,[137] although editors also report readings found in the ancient commentaries on Horace which are attributed to Porphyrio and (pseudo-)Acro.[138] Some of these manuscripts are available digitally:

A (Paris lat. 7900A:
https://gallica.bnf.fr/ark:/12148/btv1b10546779x.r=7900A?rk=21459;2);

δ (London, B.L., Harley 2725:
(http://www.bl.uk/manuscripts/Viewer.aspx?ref=harley_ms_2725_fs001r);

ψ (Paris lat. 7971 (digitised microfilm):
https://gallica.bnf.fr/ark:/12148/btv1b10035299t.r=7971?rk=21459;2);

λ (Paris lat. 7972 (digitised microfilm):
https://gallica.bnf.fr/ark:/12148/btv1b90664859.r=7972?rk=21459;2);

π (Paris lat. 10310 (digitised microfilm):
https://gallica.bnf.fr/ark:/12148/btv1b10035300f.r=10310?rk=64378;0);

---

[137] For discussion see R. J. Tarrant in L. D. Reynolds (ed.), *Texts and Transmission* (1983) 182–6, E. Courtney, *BCH* 547–60.

[138] These 'are works of the fifth century at the earliest, and although they represent an older tradition, they do not reflect it completely or accurately' (J. E. G. Zetzel, *Critics, Compilers, and Commentators* (2018) 149–50, who on pp. 149–57 and 267–8 discusses them and their complicated genesis). The likely archetype of MSS of Porphyrio is available digitally: https://digi.vatlib.it/view/MSS_Vat.lat.3314.

C/E (Munich BSB clm 14685 (digitised microfilm): http://daten.digitale-sammlungen.de/0010/bsb00109437/images/ index.html?id=00109437&groesser=&fip=eayaewqeayaeayaeayaeayaeayaqrssdasyztsyzts&no=&seite=2)[139]

In 1969 and 1971 C. O. Brink argued that some manuscript readings were unjustly neglected in modern editions of the *Odes*, an argument which had the commendable result of showing that the text of Horace's lyrics was not as settled as it was thought to be.[140] In 1977 G. P. Goold produced an 'editionem vix a vulgata discrepantem': it was privately printed, had neither critical apparatus nor notes, and was never reissued as a mainline publication. In the 1980s Germany was still divided into East and West, and Horace was one of the Latin authors whose text, newly edited, was published by both arms of the Teubner publishing house. In 1984 there appeared from the Leipzig branch an edition by S. Borzsák, and in the following year, from Stuttgart, came the edition by D. R. Shackleton Bailey. The latter is as radical as the former is conservative; both were subjected to magisterial reviews by R. G. M. Nisbet.[141] Nisbet himself was always interested in textual criticism and increasingly bold in his proposed emendations of Horace, especially in Book 3 of the *Odes*. It will be interesting to see how his conjectures fare in the new Oxford Classical Text of Horace which is being prepared by R. J. Tarrant.[142]

In my presentation of the apparatus criticus for *Odes* 3 I have not been concerned to identify the individual manuscripts, or classes of manuscript, which exhibit this or that reading; in the interests of simplicity and (I hope) clarity, I have merely attempted to distinguish manuscript readings from modern conjectures.[143] The source of each conjecture may be traced via *Repertory of Conjectures on Horace* (http://tekstlab.uio.no/horace/), the wonderful website hosted by the University of Oslo. Where manuscripts

[139] Many later MSS may be found by going to https://digi.vatlib.it/?ling=en (Vatican) and typing in 'Horatius' or to http://mss.bmlonline.it/?search=Horatius (Florence, Laurenziana).
[140] C. O. Brink, *PCPS* 15 (1969) 1–6, 17 (1971) 17–29; Brink (1982), the third article in the sequence, dealt mainly with the *Epodes* but included the case of *C*. 3.16.5–7.
[141] Nisbet, *Gnomon* 58 (1986) 611–15, *CR* 36 (1986) 227–34 (= *Collected Papers on Latin Literature* (1995) 192–201).
[142] See Tarrant (2016a); also (2016b).
[143] This practice resembles, but is even more basic than, that of S. J. Harrison and R. F. Thomas in their editions of *Odes* 2 and 4 respectively. R. G. Mayer's edition of Book 1 has no apparatus criticus.

7 THE TEXT

themselves differ in the readings they offer, I have separated the preferred reading from the rejected by means of a square bracket, thus:

> 3.4.15 Forenti] Ferenti   3.4.38 addidit] abdidit *uel* redditis

In presenting the text of the *Odes* I have tried to use punctuation to clarify the sense (e.g. 3.6.13, 10.13–16, 14.1–2, 17.2–9), but there are some phenomena which are beyond clarifying by modern typography. For example, at 3.4.73–4 Horace writes:

> INIECTA MONSTRIS TERRA DOLET SVIS
> MAERETQVE…

When we read the first three words of this sentence, it is natural to assume that Horace is referring to the burial practice of casting earth on the dead (compare Sen. *Ben.* 5.20.5 'si terram…mortuo inieci'), but, when we reach the two verbs, we realise that Earth is being personified and requires an initial capital letter. Now Horace will often juxtapose personification with non-personification in the same sentence or even, as here, superimpose (as it were) one upon the other; there is no way in which this ambivalence can be represented in a modern text which uses both upper-case and lower-case letters, and the decision whether to use initial capitals to indicate personification will inevitably vary from place to place, resulting in inconsistency.

The difficulties posed by direct speech are even more complicated, especially since every ode which has an addressee is a form of direct speech. Editors conventionally place quotation marks around speeches which are delivered by characters in the text and are introduced by a verb of speaking, such as those of Juno (3.3.17 *elocuta*), Regulus (3.5.20 *dixit*), Hypermnestra (3.11.37 *dixit*) and Europa (3.27.35 *dixit*), whose own long speech is followed by a much shorter speech from Venus (3.27.70 *dixit*). The presence or absence of quotation marks is particularly helpful in cases where editors disagree on what constitutes direct speech. In the great ode to Maecenas (3.29) direct speech is introduced by *dixisse* (43), but does it extend only to the following word (most editors) or to the end of the following stanza (Shackleton Bailey) or to the very end of the poem (Vollmer)? At 3.2.9 most editors do not infer direct speech from *suspiret*; but, if there is speech, as I believe, does it extend only to the following word (this edition) or to the rest of the stanza (Vollmer)? Since no earlier editor, as far as I know, infers from *scimus* at 3.4.42 that a speech by the Camenae begins at this point and extends to line 64, the insertion of quotation marks makes the interpretation clear.

This last ode raises a further difficulty. The Camenae start to be addressed by the poet at line 21, but the ode begins with an address to the Muse Calliope (1–4); what is the relationship between these two addressees? Moreover the address to the Muse is followed immediately by a question directed at an anonymous plural 'you' (3.4.5 *auditis?*). No editor attempts to distinguish these variations, presumably because the speaker remains unchanged throughout and a lyric ode is incompatible with the insertion of stage-directions. Similar considerations no doubt apply in 3.19 and 3.26: most of the former is addressed to Telephus, but the third stanza is addressed to a slave who has evidently been accompanying them (3.19.10 *puer*); in 3.26, after introductory lines apparently addressed to no one (1–6), there are suddenly addresses, in quick succession, to attendant slaves (6–8 *ponite*) and Venus (9–12).

We have already noted that 3.9 takes the form of a dialogue. Many editors, such as Kiessling–Heinze and Williams, use quotation marks to indicate that in the even-numbered stanzas Lydia rather than Horace is speaking. Since Kiessling–Heinze and Williams also believe that Neobule, not Horace, is the speaker in 3.12, logically they ought to place the whole of that ode within quotation marks, yet they do not. Some editors, such as Shackleton Bailey, additionally place quotation marks around the odd-numbered stanzas of 3.9, presumably to indicate that Lydia's interlocutor is not Horace but her ex-lover, the role which Horace is adopting. Yet no editor places quotation marks around the first three stanzas of 3.14, where, in his address to the *plebs* and to boys and girls (1, 10–12), Horace is universally agreed to be adopting the *persona* of a public speaker, in contrast to his 'personal' address to his slave later in the poem (17 *puer*). In another address to boys and girls at the start of 3.1 Horace explicitly tells us that his role is that of a priest (3.1.3), while he is likewise assumed not to be speaking in his own voice at the start of 3.6: should an editor insert quotation marks into these two odes to signify as much? Consistency is difficult to achieve, and it is easy to sympathise with Denis Feeney's argument that Latin texts should dispense with quotation marks altogether.[144]

---

[144] Feeney (2011) 60–3.

Q. HORATI FLACCI
CARMINVM LIBER TERTIVS

Q. HORATI FLACCI
CARMINVM LIBER TERTIVS

1

Odi profanum uulgus et arceo.
  fauete linguis: carmina non prius
    audita Musarum sacerdos
      uirginibus puerisque canto.   4
regum timendorum in proprios greges,
  reges in ipsos imperium est Iouis,
    clari Giganteo triumpho,
      cuncta supercilio mouentis.   8
est ut uiro uir latius ordinet
  arbusta sulcis, hic generosior
    descendat in Campum petitor,
      moribus hic meliorque fama   12
contendat, illi turba clientium
  sit maior: aequa lege Necessitas
    sortitur insignes et imos;
      omne capax mouet urna nomen.   16

destrictus ensis cui super impia
  ceruice pendet, non Siculae dapes
    dulcem elaborabunt saporem,
      non auium citharaeque cantus   20
somnum reducent; somnus agrestium
  lenis uirorum non humiles domos
    fastidit umbrosamque ripam,
      non Zephyris agitata tempe.   24
desiderantem quod satis est neque
  tumultuosum sollicitat mare
    nec saeuus Arcturi cadentis
      impetus aut orientis Haedi,   28

> non uerberatae grandine uineae
> fundusque mendax, arbore nunc aquas
>   culpante, nunc torrentia agros
>   sidera, nunc hiemes iniquas.   32
>
> contracta pisces aequora sentiunt
> iactis in altum molibus: huc frequens
>   caementa demittit redemptor
>   cum famulis dominusque terrae   36
>
> fastidiosus; sed Timor et Minae
> scandunt eodem quo dominus, neque
>   decedit aerata triremi et
>   post equitem sedet atra Cura.   40
>
> quod si dolentem nec Phrygius lapis
> nec purpurarum sidere clarior
>   delenit usus nec Falerna
>   uitis Achaemeniumque costum,   44
>
> cur inuidendis postibus et nouo
> sublime ritu moliar atrium?
>   cur ualle permutem Sabina
>   diuitias operosiores?   48

2

> Angustam amice pauperiem pati
> robustus acri militia puer
>   condiscat et Parthos feroces
>   uexet eques metuendus hasta   4
>
> uitamque sub diuo et trepidis agat
> in rebus. illum ex moenibus hosticis
>   matrona bellantis tyranni
>   prospiciens et adulta uirgo   8
>
> suspiret 'Eheu!', ne rudis agminum
> sponsus lacessat regius asperum
>   tactu leonem, quem cruenta
>   per medias rapit ira caedes.   12

[1] 36–7 dominoque...fastidioso *Nisbet*: alii alia
42 sidere *codd.*: Sidone *Nisbet*
[2] 1 Anguste amictam *Stroh*: Angusto amictu *A. Allen*   amici (*uoc.*) *Bentley*

CARMINVM LIBER TERTIVS 47

dulce et decorum est pro patria mori;
Mors et fugacem persequitur uirum
  nec parcit imbellis iuuentae
    poplitibus timidoque tergo. 16

Virtus, repulsae nescia sordidae,
intaminatis fulget honoribus
  nec sumit aut ponit secures
    arbitrio popularis aurae. 20

Virtus, recludens immeritis mori
caelum, negata temptat iter uia
  coetusque uulgares et udam
    spernit humum fugiente penna. 24

est et fideli tuta silentio
merces: uetabo qui Cereris sacrum
  uulgarit arcanae sub isdem
    sit trabibus fragilemque mecum 28

soluat phaselon: saepe Diespiter
neglectus incesto addidit integrum;
  raro antecedentem scelestum
    deseruit pede Poena claudo. 32

3

Iustum et tenacem propositi uirum
non ciuium ardor praua iubentium,
  non uultus instantis tyranni
    mente quatit solida neque Auster, 4

dux inquieti turbidus Hadriae,
nec fulminantis magna manus Iouis:
  si fractus illabatur orbis,
    impauidum ferient ruinae. 8

hac arte Pollux et uagus Hercules
enisus arces attigit igneas,
  quos inter Augustus recumbens
    purpureo bibet ore nectar; 12

[2] 13 dulci decorum *Nisbet olim*   16 timidoque] -oue
[3] 12 bibet] bibit

hac te merentem, Bacche pater, tuae
uexere tigres indocili iugum
   collo trahentes; hac Quirinus
      Martis equis Acheronta fugit,   16

gratum elocuta consiliantibus
Iunone diuis: 'Ilion, Ilion
   fatalis incestusque iudex
      et mulier peregrina uertit   20

in puluerem, ex quo destituit deos
mercede pacta Laomedon, mihi
   castaeque damnatam Mineruae
      cum populo et duce fraudulento.   24

iam nec Lacaenae splendet adulterae
famosus hospes nec Priami domus
   periura pugnaces Achiuos
      Hectoreis opibus refringit   28

nostrisque ductum seditionibus
bellum resedit. protinus et graues
   iras et inuisum nepotem,
      Troica quem peperit sacerdos,   32

Marti redonabo; illum ego lucidas
inire sedes, ducere nectaris
   sucos et adscribi quietis
      ordinibus patiar deorum.   36

dum longus inter saeuiat Ilion
Romamque pontus, qualibet exules
   in parte regnanto beati;
      dum Priami Paridisque busto   40

insultet armentum et catulos ferae
celent inultae, stet Capitolium
   fulgens triumphatisque possit
      Roma ferox dare iura Medis.   44

---

23 damnatam *Glareanus*: -tum *codd.*   34 ducere] discere

horrenda late nomen in ultimas
extendat oras, qua medius liquor
    secernit Europen ab Afro,
        qua tumidus rigat arua Nilus,   48

aurum irrepertum et sic melius situm,
cum terra celat, spernere fortior
    quam cogere humanos in usus
        omne sacrum rapiente dextra.   52

quicumque mundo terminus obstitit,
hunc tangat armis, uisere gestiens
    qua parte debacchentur ignes,
        qua nebulae pluuiique rores.   56

sed bellicosis fata Quiritibus
hac lege dico, ne nimium pii
    rebusque fidentes auitae
        tecta uelint reparare Troiae.   60

Troiae renascens alite lugubri
fortuna tristi clade iterabitur,
    ducente uictrices cateruas
        coniuge me Iouis et sorore.   64

ter si resurgat murus aëneus
auctore Phoebo, ter pereat meis
    excisus Argiuis, ter uxor
        capta uirum puerosque ploret.'   68

non hoc iocosae conueniet lyrae;
quo, Musa, tendis? desine peruicax
    referre sermones deorum et
        magna modis tenuare paruis.   72

4

Descende caelo et dic – age! – tibia
regina longum Calliope melos,
    seu uoce nunc mauis acuta,
        seu fidibus citharaque Phoebi.   4

[3] 54 tangat] tanget   [4] 4 citharaque] -aue

auditis? an me ludit amabilis
insania? audire et uideor pios
  errare per lucos, amoenae
    quos et aquae subeunt et aurae.   8

me fabulosae Vulture in Apulo
nutricis extra limina sedulae
  ludo fatigatumque somno
    fronde noua puerum palumbes   12

texere, mirum quod foret omnibus
quicumque celsae nidum Aceruntiae
  saltusque Bantinos et aruum
    pingue tenent humilis Forenti,   16

ut tuto ab atris corpore uiperis
dormirem et ursis, ut premerer sacra
  lauroque conlataque myrto,
    non sine dis animosus infans.   20

uester, Camenae, uester in arduos
tollor Sabinos, seu mihi frigidum
  Praeneste seu Tibur supinum
    seu liquidae placuere Baiae;   24

uestris amicum fontibus et choris
non me Philippis uersa acies retro,
  deuota non exstinxit arbor
    nec Sicula Palinurus unda.   28

utcumque mecum uos eritis, libens
insanientem nauita Bosphorum
  temptabo et urentes harenas
    litoris Assyrii uiator,   32

uisam Britannos hospitibus feros
et laetum equino sanguine Concanum,
  uisam pharetratos Gelonos
    et Scythicum inuiolatus amnem.   36

10 limina sedulae *Bentley*: limina Pulliae *uel* limen Apuliae *codd.*: limina dum uagor *Courtney*: *alii alia*   16 Forenti] Ferenti   32 limitis *Nisbet*

uos Caesarem altum, militia simul
fessas cohortes addidit oppidis,
    finire quaerentem labores
        Pierio recreatis antro;   40

uos lene consilium et datis et dato
gaudetis, almae. 'Scimus ut impios
    Titanas immanemque turmam
        fulmine sustulerit caduco   44

qui terram inertem, qui mare temperat
uentosum et urbes regnaque tristia
    diuosque mortalesque turbas
        imperio regit unus aequo.   48

magnum illa terrorem intulerat Ioui
fidens iuuentus horrida bracchiis
    fratresque tendentes opaco
        Pelion imposuisse Olympo.   52

sed quid Typhōeus et ualidus Mimas
aut quid minaci Porphyrion statu,
    quid Rhoetus euulsisque truncis
        Enceladus iaculator audax   56

contra sonantem Palladis aegida
possent ruentes? hinc auidus stetit
    Vulcanus, hinc matrona Iuno et,
        numquam umeris positurus arcum,   60

qui rore puro Castaliae lauit
crines solutos, qui Lyciae tenet
    dumeta natalemque siluam,
        Delius et Patareus Apollo.'   64

uis consili expers mole ruit sua;
uim temperatam di quoque prouehunt
    in maius; idem odere uires
        omne nefas animo mouentes.   68

38 addidit] abdidit *uel* redditis   43 turmam] turbam   46 urbes *codd.*: umbras *Bentley*   47 turbas] turmas

testis mearum centimanus Gyges
sententiarum, notus et integrae
   temptator Orion Dianae,
      uirginea domitus sagitta.   72

iniecta monstris Terra dolet suis
maeretque partus fulmine luridum
   missos ad Orcum; nec peredit
      impositam celer ignis Aetnen,   76

incontinentis nec Tityi iecur
reliquit ales, nequitiae additus
   custos; amatorem trecentae
      Pirithoum cohibent catenae.   80

5

Caelo tonantem credidimus Iouem
regnare; praesens diuus habebitur
   Augustus adiectis Britannis
      imperio grauibusque Persis.   4

milesne Crassi coniuge barbara
turpis maritus uixit et hostium
   (pro curia inuersique mores!)
      consenuit socerorum in armis   8

sub rege Medo Marsus et Apulus
anciliorum et nominis et togae
   oblitus aeternaeque Vestae,
      incolumi Ioue et urbe Roma?   12

hoc cauerat mens prouida Reguli
dissentientis condicionibus
   foedis et exemplo trahenti
      perniciem ueniens in aeuum,   16

---

[4] 69 Gyges *Bentley*: gigas *codd.*
[5] 7 curia *uix sanum*   8 aruis *Faber*   10 et nominis] nominis
15 trahenti *Comm. Cruq.*: -entis *codd.*

CARMINVM LIBER TERTIVS 53

si non periret immiserabilis
captiua pubes: 'Signa ego Punicis
   adfixa delubris et arma
   militibus sine caede', dixit,   20

'derepta uidi; uidi ego ciuium
retorta tergo bracchia libero
   portasque non clausas et arua
   Marte coli populata nostro.   24

auro repensus scilicet acrior
miles redibit. flagitio additis
   damnum. neque amissos colores
   lana refert medicata fuco,   28

nec uera uirtus, cum semel excidit,
curat reponi deterioribus.
   si pugnat extricata densis
   cerua plagis, erit ille fortis   32

qui perfidis se credidit hostibus,
et Marte Poenos proteret altero
   qui lora restrictis lacertis
   sensit iners timuitque mortem.   36

hic, unde uitam sumeret inscius,
pacem duello miscuit. o pudor!
   o magna Carthago probrosis
   altior Italiae ruinis!'   40

fertur pudicae coniugis osculum
paruosque natos ut capitis minor
   ab se remouisse, et uirilem
   toruus humi posuisse uultum   44

donec labantes consilio patres
firmaret auctor numquam alias dato
   interque maerentes amicos
   egregius properaret exul.   48

17–18 si non periret *et* captiua pubes *transposuit Edwards*
17 perirent *Glareanus*   iam miserabilis *Düntzer*

atqui sciebat quae sibi barbarus
tortor pararet; non aliter tamen
   dimouit obstantes propinquos
      et populum reditus morantem   52

quam si clientum longa negotia
diiudicata lite relinqueret,
   tendens Venafranos in agros
      aut Lacedaemonium Tarentum.   56

6

Delicta maiorum immeritus lues,
Romane, donec templa refeceris
   aedesque labentes deorum et
      foeda nigro simulacra fumo.   4

dis te minorem quod geris, imperas:
hinc omne principium, huc refer exitum.
   di multa neglecti dederunt
      Hesperiae mala luctuosae.   8

iam bis Monaeses et Pacori manus
inauspicatos contudit impetus,
   nostrorum et adiecisse praedam
      torquibus exiguis renidet;   12

paene, occupatam seditionibus,
deleuit Vrbem Dacus et Aethiops,
   hic classe formidatus, ille
      missilibus melior sagittis.   16

fecunda culpae saecula nuptias
primum inquinauere et genus et domos:
   hoc fonte deriuata clades
      in patriam populumque fluxit.   20

motus doceri gaudet Ionicos
matura uirgo et fingitur artibus
   iam nunc et incestos amores
      de tenero meditatur ungui.   24

[6] 1 meritus *Peerlkamp*: heu meritus *Lehrs*   10 *post* impetus *interpunxit Shackleton Bailey*   11 nostrorum *Bentley*: nostros *codd.*   19 labes *Peerlkamp*   22 nuptura *Delz*: innupta *Shackleton Bailey*: *alii alia*

mox iuniores quaerit adulteros
inter mariti uina, neque eligit
   cui donet impermissa raptim
     gaudia luminibus remotis,   28

sed iussa coram non sine conscio
surgit marito, seu uocat institor
   seu nauis Hispanae magister,
     dedecorum pretiosus emptor.   32

non his iuuentus orta parentibus
infecit aequor sanguine Punico
   Pyrrhumque et ingentem cecidit
     Antiochum Hannibalemque dirum,   36

sed rusticorum mascula militum
proles, Sabellis docta ligonibus
   uersare glaebas et seuerae
     matris ad arbitrium recisos   40

portare fustes, sol ubi montium
mutaret umbras et iuga demeret
   bobus fatigatis, amicum
     tempus agens abeunte curru.   44

damnosa quid non imminuit dies?
aetas parentum, peior auis, tulit
   nos nequiores, mox daturos
     progeniem uitiosiorem?   48

7

Quid fles, Asterie, quem tibi candidi
primo restituent uere Fauonii
   Thyna merce beatum,
     constantis iuuenem fide   4

Gygen? ille Notis actus ad Oricum
post insana Caprae sidera frigidas
   noctes non sine multis
     insomnis lacrimis agit.   8

[6] 46–8 *pro interrogatione interpretatus est Trenkel*

atqui sollicitae nuntius hospitae,
suspirare Chloen et miseram tuis
　　dicens ignibus uri,
　　　　temptat mille uafer modis.　　　　　　12

ut Proetum mulier perfida credulum
falsis impulerit criminibus nimis
　　casto Bellerophontae
　　　　maturare necem refert;　　　　　　16

narrat paene datum Pelea Tartaro,
Magnessam Hippolyten dum fugit abstinens,
　　et peccare docentes
　　　　fallax historias mouet.　　　　　　20

frustra: nam scopulis surdior Icari
uoces audit adhuc integer. at tibi
　　ne uicinus Enipeus
　　　　plus iusto placeat caue,　　　　　　24

quamuis non alius flectere equum sciens
aeque conspicitur gramine Martio,
　　nec quisquam citus aeque
　　　　Tusco denatat alueo.　　　　　　28

prima nocte domum claude neque in uias
sub cantum querulae despice tibiae
　　et te saepe uocanti
　　　　duram difficilis mane.　　　　　　32

8

Martiis caelebs quid agam Kalendis,
quid uelint flores et acerra turis
plena miraris positusque carbo in
　　caespite uiuo,　　　　　　　　　　　4

docte sermones utriusque linguae?
uoueram dulces epulas et album
Libero caprum prope funeratus
　　arboris ictu.　　　　　　　　　　　8

[7] 20 mouet] monet　　30 cantum] cantu

CARMINVM LIBER TERTIVS 57

hic dies anno redeunte festus
corticem adstrictum pice dimouebit
amphorae fumum bibere institutae
   consule Tullo.   12

sume, Maecenas, cyathos amici
sospitis centum et uigiles lucernas
perfer in lucem; procul omnis esto
   clamor et ira.   16

mitte ciuiles super Vrbe curas:
occidit Daci Cotisonis agmen,
Medus infestus sibi luctuosis
   dissidet armis,   20

seruit Hispanae uetus hostis orae
Cantaber sera domitus catena,
iam Scythae laxo meditantur arcu
   cedere campis.   24

neglegens ne qua populus laboret,
parce priuatus nimium cauere et
dona praesentis cape laetus horae.
   linque seuera.   28

9

Donec gratus eram tibi
   nec quisquam potior bracchia candidae
ceruici iuuenis dabat,
   Persarum uigui rege beatior.   4

'donec non alia magis
   arsisti neque erat Lydia post Chloen,
multi Lydia nominis,
   Romana uigui clarior Ilia.'   8

me nunc Thressa Chloe regit,
   dulces docta modos et citharae sciens,
pro qua non metuam mori,
   si parcent animae fata superstiti.   12

[8] 25–8 *secl. Guyet*   25 ne cliens *Edwards*   26 parte *Bonfinius*   priuatis
Shackleton Bailey

'me torret face mutua
    Thurini Calais filius Ornyti,
pro quo bis patiar mori,
    si parcent puero fata superstiti.'   16

quid si prisca redit Venus
    diductosque iugo cogit aëneo,
si flaua excutitur Chloe
    reiectaeque patet ianua Lydiae?   20

'quamquam sidere pulchrior
    ille est, tu leuior cortice et improbo
iracundior Hadria,
    tecum uiuere amem, tecum obeam libens.'   24

10

Extremum Tanain si biberes, Lyce,
    saeuo nupta uiro, me tamen asperas
porrectum ante fores obicere incolis
    plorares Aquilonibus.   4

audis quo strepitu ianua, quo nemus
    inter pulchra satum tecta remugiat
uentis, et positas ut glaciet niues
    puro numine Iuppiter?   8

ingratam Veneri pone superbiam,
    ne currente retro funis eat rota:
non te Penelopen difficilem procis
    Tyrrhenus genuit parens.   12

o – quamuis neque te munera nec preces
    nec tinctus uiola pallor amantium
nec uir Pieria paelice saucius
    curuat – supplicibus tuis   16

parcas, nec rigida mollior aesculo
    nec Mauris animum mitior anguibus:
non hoc semper erit liminis aut aquae
    caelestis patiens latus.   20

[9] 20 reiectoque *Peerlkamp*

11

Mercuri (nam te docilis magistro
mouit Amphion lapides canendo)
tuque, testudo, resonare septem
    callida neruis,   4

nec loquax olim neque grata, nunc et
diuitum mensis et amica templis,
dic modos Lyde quibus obstinatas
    applicet aures,   8

quae, uelut latis equa trima campis,
ludit exsultim metuitque tangi,
nuptiarum expers et adhuc proteruo
    cruda marito.   12

tu potes tigres comitesque siluas
ducere et riuos celeres morari;
cessit immanis tibi blandienti
    ianitor aulae   16

Cerberus, quamuis furiale centum
muniant angues caput atque agatur
spiritus taeter saniesque manet
    ore trilingui.   20

quin et Ixion Tityusque uultu
risit inuito, stetit urna paulum
sicca, dum grato Danai puellas
    carmine mulces.   24

audiat Lyde scelus atque notas
uirginum poenas et inane lymphae
dolium fundo pereuntis imo
    seraque fata   28

quae manent culpas etiam sub Orco.
impiae (nam quid potuere maius?),
impiae sponsos potuere duro
    perdere ferro.   32

[11] 17–20 *secl. edd. nonnulli*   18 atque agatur *Woodman*: eius atque *codd.*: exeatque *Bentley*: aestuatque *Cunningham*

       una de multis face nuptiali
       digna periurum fuit in parentem
       splendide mendax et in omne uirgo
           nobilis aeuum,   36

       'Surge', quae dixit iuueni marito,
       'surge, ne longus tibi somnus, unde
       non times, detur; socerum et scelestas
           falle sorores,   40

       quae, uelut nactae uitulos leaenae,
       singulos – eheu! – lacerant; ego illis
       mollior nec te feriam neque intra
           claustra tenebo.   44

       me pater saeuis oneret catenis
       quod uiro clemens misero peperci;
       me uel extremos Numidarum in agros
           classe releget.   48

       i pedes quo te rapiunt et aurae,
       dum fauet nox et Venus, i secundo
       omine et nostri memorem sepulcro
           sculpe querelam.'   52

                              12

            Miserarum est neque Amori
            dare ludum neque dulci
       mala uino lauere aut exanimari metuentes
           patruae uerbera linguae.   4

            tibi qualum Cythereae
            puer ales, tibi telas,
       operosaeque Mineruae studium aufert, Neobule,
           Liparaei nitor Hebri,   8

            simul unctos Tiberinis
            umeros lauit in undis,
       eques ipso melior Bellerophonte, neque pugno
           neque segni pede uictus;   12

[11] 52 sculpe] scalpe
[12] 3 lauere *codd*.: eluere *Withof*

celer idem per apertum
fugientes agitato
grege ceruos iaculari et catus arto latitantem
    fruticeto excipere aprum.   16

13

O fons Bandusiae, splendidior uitro,
dulci digne mero non sine floribus,
cras donaberis haedo
    cui frons turgida cornibus   4

primis et uenerem et proelia destinat.
frustra: nam gelidos inficiet tibi
rubro sanguine riuos
    lasciui suboles gregis.   8

te flagrantis atrox hora Caniculae
nescit tangere, tu frigus amabile
fessis uomere tauris
    praebes et pecori uago;   12

fies nobilium tu quoque fontium
me dicente cauis impositam ilicem
saxis, unde loquaces
    lymphae desiliunt tuae.   16

14

Herculis ritu – modo dictus, o plebs,
morte uenalem petiisse laurum –
Caesar Hispana repetit penates
    uictor ab ora.   4

unico gaudens mulier marito
prodeat iustis operata sacris
et soror clari ducis et decorae
    supplice uitta   8

---

[12] 13–15 celer...catus *Bentley*: catus...celer *codd.*
[14] 5 unice *Cunningham*   6 sacris] diuis (uotis *Palmer*)   7 clari] cari

uirginum matres iuuenumque nuper
    sospitum. uos, o pueri et puellae,
    iam uirum expectate. male ominatis
        parcite uerbis!   12
hic dies uere mihi festus atras
    eximet curas; ego nec tumultum
    nec mori per uim metuam tenente
        Caesare terras.   16
i, pete unguentum, puer, et coronas
    et cadum Marsi memorem duelli,
    Spartacum si qua potuit uagantem
        fallere testis;   20
dic et argutae properet Neaerae
    murreum nodo cohibere crinem.
    si per inuisum mora ianitorem
        fiet, abito: 24
lenit albescens animos capillus
    litium et rixae cupidos proteruae;
    non ego hoc ferrem calidus iuuenta
        consule Planco.   28

15

Vxor pauperis Ibyci,
    tandem nequitiae fige modum tuae
    famosisque laboribus;
        maturo propior desine funeri   4
inter ludere uirgines
    et stellis nebulam spargere candidis.
    non, si quid Pholoen satis,
        et te, Chlori, decet: filia rectius   8

[**14**]   11 iam...expectate *J. Gow*: iam...expertae *codd.*: non...expertae *Bentley*: iam...expertes *Cunningham*   male ominatis] male nominatis (male inominatis *Bentley*)   14 eximet] exiget   19 uagacem *Charisius*   20 testis *Woodman*: testa *codd.*: cista *Nisbet*   22 cohibente *Muretus*

expugnat iuuenum domos,
pulso Thyias uti concita tympano:
illam cogit amor Nothi
lasciuae similem ludere capreae; 12

te lanae prope nobilem
tonsae Luceriam, non citharae decent
nec flos purpureus rosae
nec poti uetulam faece tenus cadi. 16

16

Inclusam Danaen turris aënea
robustaeque fores et uigilum canum
tristes excubiae munierant satis
nocturnis ab adulteris, 4

si non Acrisium, uirginis abditae
custodem pauidum, Iuppiter et Venus
risissent: fore enim tutum iter et patens
conuerso in pretium deo. 8

aurum per medios ire satellites
et perrumpere amat saxa potentius
ictu fulmineo; concidit auguris
Argiui domus ob lucrum 12

demersa exitio. diffidit urbium
portas uir Macedo et subruit aemulos
reges muneribus; munera nauium
saeuos illaqueant duces. 16

crescentem sequitur cura pecuniam
maiorumque fames. iure perhorrui
late conspicuum tollere uerticem,
Maecenas, equitum decus. 20

quanto quisque sibi plura negauerit,
ab dis plura feret: nil cupientium
nudus castra peto et transfuga diuitum
partes linquere gestio, 24

[15] 9 expugnet *Nisbet*   11 cogat *L. Müller*

contemptae dominus splendidior rei
quam si quidquid arat impiger Apulus
occultare meis dicerer horreis,
magnas inter opes inops.   28

purae riuus aquae siluaque iugerum
paucorum et segetis certa fides meae
fulgentem imperio fertilis Africae
fallit sorte beatior.   32

quamquam nec Calabrae mella ferunt apes
nec Laestrygonia Bacchus in amphora
languescit mihi nec pinguia Gallicis
crescunt uellera pascuis,   36

importuna tamen pauperies abest,
nec, si plura uelim, tu dare deneges.
contracto melius parua cupidine
uectigalia porrigam   40

quam si Mygdoniis regnum Alyattëi
campis continuem. multa petentibus
desunt multa; bene est cui deus obtulit
parca quod satis est manu.   44

17

Aeli uetusto nobilis ab Lamo
(quando et priores hinc Lamias ferunt
    denominatos et nepotum
        per memores genus omne fastos,   4

auctore ab illo ducis originem
qui Formiarum moenia dicitur
    princeps et innantem Maricae
        litoribus tenuisse Lirim,   8

late tyrannus), cras foliis nemus
multis et alga litus inutili
    demissa tempestas ab Euro
        sternet, aquae nisi fallit augur   12

[**16**] 30 curta *Nisbet*
[**17**] 2–9 *de interpunctione edd. dissentiunt*   4 fastos] fastus   5 ducit *Heinsius*
(ducet *Shackleton Bailey*): ducere *Lenchantin*

CARMINVM LIBER TERTIVS 65

annosa cornix. dum potes, aridum
compone lignum: cras Genium mero
curabis et porco bimenstri
cum famulis operum solutis. 16

18

Faune, Nympharum fugientum amator,
per meos fines et aprica rura
lenis incedas abeasque paruis
aequus alumnis, 4

si tener pleno cadit haedus anno
larga nec desunt Veneris sodali
uina creterrae, uetus ara multo
fumat odore. 8

ludit herboso pecus omne campo,
cum tibi Nonae redeunt Apriles;
festus in pratis uacat otioso
cum boue pagus; 12

inter audaces lupus errat agnos,
spargit agrestis tibi silua frondes,
gaudet inuisam pepulisse fossor
ter pede terram. 16

19

Quantum distet ab Inacho
Codrus pro patria non timidus mori
narras et genus Aeaci
et pugnata sacro bella sub Ilio; 4
quo Chium pretio cadum
mercemur, quis aquam temperet ignibus,
quo praebente domum et quota
Paelignis caream frigoribus, taces. 8
da lunae propere nouae,
da noctis mediae, da, puer, auguris

[17] 13 potes] potis
[18] 7 creterrae] craterae   9–10 *transposuit Peerlkamp*   9–16 *secl. Cucchiarelli*
(13–16 *iam Peerlkamp*)   10 Apriles *Woodman*: Decembres *codd.*
12 pagus] pardus   14 arentis (*iam Cornelissen*) ubi *L. Müller*
[19] 4 sacra *Haupt*

Murenae: tribus aut nouem
    miscentur cyathis pocula commodis? 12
qui Musas amat impares,
    ternos ter cyathos attonitus petet
uates; tres prohibet supra
    rixarum metuens tangere Gratia 16
nudis iuncta sororibus.
    insanire iuuat. cur Berecyntiae
cessant flamina tibiae?
    cur pendet tacita fistula cum lyra? 20
parcentes ego dexteras
    odi: sparge rosas! audiat inuidus
dementem strepitum Lycus,
    et uicina seni non habilis Lyco. 24
spissa te nitidum coma,
    puro te similem, Telephe, Vespero
tempestiua petit Rhode;
    me lentus Glycerae torret amor meae. 28

20

Non uides quanto moueas periclo,
Pyrrhe, Gaetulae catulos leaenae?
dura post paulo fugies inaudax
    proelia raptor 4

cum per obstantes iuuenum cateruas
ibit insignem repetens Nearchum –
grande certamen, tibi praeda cedat
    an magis illi. 8

interim, dum tu celeres sagittas
promis, haec dentes acuit timendos,
arbiter pugnae posuisse nudo
    sub pede palmam 12

fertur, et leni recreare uento
sparsum odoratis umerum capillis,
qualis aut Nireus fuit aut aquosa
    raptus ab Ida. 16

[19] 12 miscentor *Rutgers*
[20] 8 an magis *Woodman*: maior an *codd.* (maior an illa *Peerlkamp*)
13 feruet *Unger*: gaudet *Rosenberg*   15 fuit *codd.*: puer *Peerlkamp*

21

O nata mecum consule Manlio,
seu tu querellas siue geris iocos
  seu rixam et insanos amores
    seu facilem, pia testa, somnum,   4

quocumque lectum nomine Massicum
seruas, moueri digna bono die,
  descende, Coruino iubente
    promere languidiora uina.   8

non ille, quamquam Socraticis madet
sermonibus, te neglegit horridus:
  narratur et prisci Catonis
    saepe mero caluisse uirtus.   12

tu lene tormentum ingenio admoues
plerumque duro; tu sapientium
  curas et arcanum iocoso
    consilium retegis Lyaeo.   16

tu spem reducis mentibus anxiis
uiresque et addis cornua pauperi,
  post te neque iratos trementi
    regum apices neque militum arma.   20

te Liber et (si laeta aderit) Venus
segnesque nodum soluere Gratiae
  uiuaeque producent lucernae,
    dum rediens fugat astra Phoebus.   24

22

Montium custos nemorumque uirgo,
quae laborantes utero puellas
ter uocata audis adimisque Leto,
  diua triformis,   4

imminens uillae tua pinus esto,
quam per exactos ego laetus annos
uerris obliquum meditantis ictum
  sanguine donem.   8

[21] 10 neglegit] -et

23

Caelo supinas si tuleris manus
nascente luna, rustica Phidyle,
  si ture placaris et horna
    fruge Lares auidaque porca,   4

nec pestilentem sentiet Africum
fecunda uitis nec sterilem seges
  robiginem aut dulces alumni
    pomifero graue tempus anno.   8

nam quae niuali pascitur Algido
deuota quercus inter et ilices
  aut crescit Albanis in herbis,
    uictima pontificum secures   12

ceruice tinguet; te nihil attinet
temptare multa caede bidentium
  paruos coronantem marino
    rore deos fragilique myrto.   16

immunis aram si tetigit manus,
non sumptuosa blandior hostia,
  molliuit auersos Penates
    farre pio et saliente mica.   20

24

Intactis opulentior
  thesauris Arabum et diuitis Indiae,
  caementis licet occupes
    terrenum omne tuis et mare publicum,   4
si figit adamantinos
  summis uerticibus dira Necessitas
  clauos, non animum metu,
    non Mortis laqueis expedies caput.   8
campestres melius Scythae,
  quorum plaustra uagas rite trahunt domos,
  uiuunt et rigidi Getae,
    immetata quibus iugera liberas   12

---

[23] 17 manus *codd.*: malis *Unger*
[24] 4 terrenum *scholia quaedam, Lachmann*: Tyrrhenum *codd.*   publicum] apulicum *uel* ponticum   5 sic *Bentley*   5-6 figit *et* summis *transpos. Axt*

fruges et Cererem ferunt;
  nec cultura placet longior annuā
defunctumque laboribus
  aequali recreat sorte uicarius.   16
illic matre carentibus
  priuignis mulier temperat innocens
nec dotata regit uirum,
  coniunx nec nitido fidit adultero;   20
dos est magna parentium
  uirtus et metuens alterius uiri
certo foedere castitas;
  et peccare nefas, aut pretium est mori.   24
o quisquis uolet impias
  caedes et rabiem tollere ciuicam,
si quaeret 'PATER' urbium
  subscribi statuis, indomitam audeat   28
refrenare licentiam,
  clarus postgenitis, quatenus – heu nefas! –
uirtutem incolumem odimus,
  sublatam ex oculis quaerimus inuidi.   32
quid tristes querimoniae,
  si non supplicio culpa reciditur,
quid leges sine moribus
  uanae proficiunt, si neque feruidis   36
pars inculta caloribus
  mundi nec Boreae finitimum latus
durataeque solo niues
  mercatorem abigunt, horrida callidi   40
uincunt aequora nauitae?
  magnum pauperies opprobrium iubet
quiduis et facere et pati
  uirtutisque uiam deserit arduae: 44
uel nos in Capitolium,
  quo clamor uocat et turba fauentium,
uel nos in mare proximum
  gemmas et lapides aurum et inutile,   48
summi materiem mali,
  mittamus, scelerum si bene paenitet.
eradenda cupidinis
  praui sunt elementa et tenerae nimis   52

20 laedit *Shackleton Bailey*: fallit *olim Nisbet*   30 clarus] carus   32 inuidis *Crusius*   37 inculta *Woodman*: inclusa *codd*.: exclusa *Nisbet*
44 deserere *Bentley*   arduam *Lambinus*

  mentes asperioribus
   formandae studiis. nescit equo rudis
  haerere ingenuus puer
   uenarique timet, ludere doctior   56
  seu Graeco iubeas trocho
   seu malis uetita legibus alea,
  cum periura patris fides
   consortem <et> socium fallat et hospites,   60
  indignoque pecuniam
   heredi properet. scilicet improbae
  crescunt diuitiae, tamen
   curtae nescioquid semper abest rei.   64

25

Quo me, Bacche, rapis tui
 plenum? quae nemora aut quos agor in specus
uelox mente noua? quibus
 antris egregii Caesaris audiar   4
aeternum meditans decus
 stellis inserere et concilio Iouis?
dicam insigne, recens, adhuc
 indictum ore alio. non secus in iugis   8
exsomnis stupet Euhias,
 Hebrum prospiciens et niue candidam
Thracen ac pede barbaro
 lustratam Rhodopen, quam mihi deuio   12
rupes et uacuum nemus
 mirari libet. o Naïadum potens
Baccharumque ualentium
 proceras manibus uertere fraxinos,   16
nil paruum aut humili modo,
 nil mortale loquar. dulce periculum est,
o Lenaee, sequi deum
 cingentem uiridi tempora pampino.   20

[**24**] 60 consortem <et> *Bentley*
[**25**] 6 concilio] consilio   12 quam *Porphyrio*: ut *uel* ac *codd.*
13 rupes *Muretus*: ripas *codd.*

26

Vixi puellis nuper idoneus
et militaui non sine gloria;
nunc arma defunctumque bello
   barbiton hic paries habebit,   4

laeuum Marinae qui Veneris latus
custodit. hic, hic ponite lucida
funalia et uectes acutos,
   oppositis foribus minaces!   8

o, quae beatam, diua, tenes Cyprum et
Memphin carentem Sithonia niue,
regina, sublimi flagello
   tange Chloen semel arrogantem.   12

27

Impios parrae recinentis omen
ducat et praegnans canis aut ab agro
raua decurrens lupa Lanuuino
   fetaque uolpes;   4

rumpat et serpens iter institutum,
si per obliquum similis sagittae
terruit mannos. ego, cui timebo
   prouidus auspex,   8

antequam stantes repetat paludes
imbrium diuina auis imminentum,
oscinem coruum prece suscitabo
   solis ab ortu.   12

si licet, felix, ubicumque mauis,
et memor nostri, Galatea, uiuas,
teque nec laeuus uetet ire picus
   nec uaga cornix.   16

[**26**] 1 duellis *Franke*   7 acutos *Woodman*: et arcus *codd.*: securesque *Bentley*: *alii alia*
[**27**] 10 imminentum] -ium   13 si licet *Woodman*: sis licet *codd.*: ilicet *Nisbet*:
scilicet *Courtney*

> sed uides quanto trepidet tumultu
> pronus Orion? ego quid sit ater
> Hadriae noui sinus et quid albus
>   peccet Iapyx.   20
>
> hostium uxores puerique caecos
> sentiant motus orientis Austri et
> aequoris nigri fremitum et trementes
>   uerbere ripas.   24
>
> sic et Europe niueum doloso
> credidit tauro latus et scatentem
> beluis pontum mediasque fraudes
>   palluit audax.   28
>
> nuper in pratis studiosa florum et
> debitae Nymphis opifex coronae
> nocte sublustri nihil astra praeter
>   uidit et undas.   32
>
> quae simul centum tetigit potentem
> oppidis Creten, 'Pater – o relictum
> filiae nomen pietasque', dixit,
>   'uicta furore! –   36
>
> unde, quo ueni? leuis una mors est
> uirginum culpae. uigilansne ploro
> turpe commissum an uitiis carentem
>   ludit imago   40
>
> uana, quam porta fugiens eburna
> somnium ducit? meliusne fluctus
> ire per longos fuit an recentes
>   carpere flores?   44
>
> si quis infamem mihi nunc iuuencum
> dedat iratae, lacerare ferro et
> frangere enitar modo multum amati
>   cornua monstri.   48

27 mediasque *suspectum*   41 quam *Sanadon*: quae *codd.*   43 ac *E. Baehrens*

impudens liqui patrios Penates,
impudens Orcum moror. o deorum
si quis haec audis, utinam inter errem
   nuda leones! 52
antequam turpis macies decentes
occupet malas teneraeque sucus
defluat praedae, speciosa quaero
   pascere tigres. 56

"Vilis Europe", pater urget absens,
"quid mori cessas? potes hac ab orno
pendulum zona bene te secuta
   laedere collum. 60

siue te rupes et acuta leto
saxa delectant, age! te procellae
crede ueloci – nisi erile mauis
   carpere pensum 64

regius sanguis dominaeque tradi
barbarae paelex."' aderat querenti
perfidum ridens Venus et remisso
   filius arcu. 68

mox, ubi lusit satis, 'Abstineto',
dixit, 'irarum calidaeque rixae,
cum tibi inuisus laceranda reddet
   cornua taurus. 72

uxor inuicti Iouis esse nescis?
mitte singultus; bene ferre magnam
disce fortunam; tua sectus orbis
   nomina ducet.' 76

28

Festo quid potius die
   Neptuni faciam? prome reconditum,
Lyde, strenua Caecubum
   munitaeque adhibe uim sapientiae. 4

    inclinare meridiem
  sentis et, ueluti stet uolucris dies,
    parcis deripere horreo
      cessantem Bibuli consulis amphoram!   8
nos cantabimus inuicem
  Neptunum et uirides Nereidum comas;
tu curua recines lyra
    Latonam et celeris spicula Cynthiae,   12
summo carmine, quae Cnidon
  fulgentesque tenet Cycladas et Paphon
iunctis uisit oloribus.
  dicetur merita Nox quoque nenia.   16

29

Tyrrhena regum progenies, tibi
non ante uerso lene merum cado
  cum flore, Maecenas, rosarum et
    pressa tuis balanus capillis   4

iamdudum apud me est. eripe te morae!
ne semper udum Tibur et Aefulae
  decliue contempleris aruum et
    Telegoni iuga parricidae.   8

fastidiosam desere copiam et
molem propinquam nubibus arduis;
  omitte mirari beatae
    fumum et opes strepitumque Romae.   12

plerumque gratae diuitibus uices,
mundaeque paruo sub Lare pauperum
  cenae sine aulaeis et ostro
    sollicitam explicuere frontem.   16

iam clarus occultum Andromedae pater
ostendit ignem, iam Procyon furit
  et stella uesani Leonis
    sole dies referente siccos;   20

[29] 6 ne] nec

iam pastor umbras cum grege languido
riuumque fessus quaerit et horridi
   dumeta Siluani caretque
      ripa uagis taciturna uentis. 24

tu ciuitatem quis deceat status
curas et Vrbi sollicitus times
   quid Seres et regnata Cyro
      Bactra parent Tanaisque discors. 28

prudens futuri temporis exitum
caliginosa nocte premit deus,
   ridetque si mortalis ultra
      fas trepidat. quod adest memento 32

componere aequus; cetera fluminis
ritu ferentur, nunc medio alueo
   cum pace delabentis Etruscum
      in mare, nunc lapides adesos 36

stirpesque raptas et pecus et domos
uoluentis una, non sine montium
   clamore uicinaeque siluae,
      cum fera diluuies quietos 40

irritat amnes. ille potens sui
laetusque deget cui licet in diem
   dixisse 'Vixi'. cras uel atra
      nube polum Pater occupato 44

uel sole puro; non tamen irritum
quodcumque retro est efficiet, neque
   diffinget infectumque reddet
      quod fugiens semel hora uexit. 48

Fortuna saeuo laeta negotio et
ludum insolentem ludere pertinax
   transmutat incertos honores,
      nunc mihi, nunc alii benigna. 52

34 ferentur] -untur   alueo] aequore

laudo manentem; si celeris quatit
pennas, resigno quae dedit et mea
uirtute me inuoluo probamque
Pauperiem sine dote quaero. 56
non est meum, si mugiat Africis
malus procellis, ad miseras preces
decurrere et uotis pacisci
 ne Cypriae Tyriaeque merces 60
addant auaro diuitias mari;
tum me biremis praesidio scaphae
tutum per Aegaeos tumultus
aura feret geminusque Pollux. 64

30

Exegi monumentum aere perennius
regalique situ pyramidum aptius,
quod non imber edax, non Aquilo impotens
possit diruere aut innumerabilis 4
annorum series et fuga temporum.
non omnis moriar multaque pars mei
uitabit Libitinam; usque ego postera
crescam laude recens, dum Capitolium 8
scandet cum tacita Virgine pontifex;
dicar, qua uiolens obstrepit Aufidus
et qua pauper aquae Daunus agrestium
regnauit populorum, ex humili potens 12
princeps Aeolios carmen ad Italum
deduxisse modos. sume superbiam
quaesitam meritis et mihi Delphica
lauro cinge uolens, Melpomene, comam. 16

---

[29] 62 tum] tunc
[30] 2 aptius *Woodman*: altius *codd.*   13 Aeolios...Italum *Fuss, Kovacs*: Aeolium
...Italos *codd.*

COMMENTARY

1

The first ode of the book adopts a dramatic form (Intro. 19–20). In the opening stanza H. identifies himself as a priest of the Muses and declares that his role is to utter *carmina* to maidens and boys (2–4). Such an utterance then follows in lines 5–40 (see 2–3n.). It begins with a generalised statement of enigmatic expression and unclear relevance (5–8) and then proceeds by a series of asyndetic sentences in which the imagined listeners are obliged to articulate for themselves the successive stages of the argument. The priestly utterance comes to its unannounced end in line 40, after which H. abandons the role of priest and, as we know from the reference to his Sabine farm (47), concludes by expressing his own personal endorsement of the argument put forward in the body of the ode. The switch from public address to personal statement is very similar to that found in 3.14 and *Epode* 7.

The opening thesis of the priestly utterance is that socio-political hierarchies, of which four examples are given (vignerons, two types of politician, patrons), are a fact of life (9–16). But, since grandees are thought to be more fortunate than their inferiors and are therefore (so it is implied) envied, H. next alludes to the story of Dionysius and Damocles in order to make the new point that even an individual considered to enjoy supreme felicity, such as a tyrant, in fact is plagued by terror and anxiety, unlike humble rustics (17–24). These two stanzas are transitional: the tyrant is a further seemingly enviable grandee (cf. *Epi.* 1.2.58–9 'inuidia Siculi non inuenere tyranni | maius tormentum'), but the anxiety which distinguishes him from the rustics looks forward to the next four stanzas (25–40), where the contented man (evidently replacing the rustics) is contrasted with three neurotics (merchant, vigneron, builder). If riches therefore do not bring happiness, says H. in conclusion (41–8), I have no reason to prefer them to my present contentment.

The argument proceeds via a series of foils: the priestly utterance begins with kings and Jupiter (5–8), who turn out to be a foil for the four sets of grandees (9–16), who themselves are a foil for the tyrant and rustics (17–24). Only when we are exactly halfway through the poem are we given the theme *desiderantem quod satis est* (25), which, along with its opposite, will occupy the entire second half, where the three *exempla* of 25–40 balance the four of the first half. There is some similarity with the movement of H.'s first satire, where the theme of discontent (μεμψιμοιρία) gives rise naturally to an attack on *auaritia*; and, just as the satire chimed in with the political climate of the early 30s (Du Quesnay (1984) 34–5), so it cannot be doubted that the ode's theme of contentment, one of H.'s favourite topics (e.g. 2.16, *Epi.* 1.2.46 'quod satis est') and repeated at the start of the second half of the book (3.16.44 'quod satis est'), would have met with the approval of Augustus. In the old days, said Sallust, everyone was content with what he had (*BC* 2.1 'sua cuique satis placebant'), and one of the *princeps*' principal concerns was to restore old-fashioned morality (*RG* 8.5). Even the seemingly preparatory foils play their part in the Augustan programme. The reference to kings and Jupiter (5–8) reminds us of the ruler's relationship with the gods (cf. 3.5.2–3, 3.6.5), while continuity with the republic is suggested by the grandees' activities in 9–16.

The stanzaic arrangement of the ode seems to be 4 + 2 + 4 + 2, with the qualification that the first four stanzas are really 1 + 3 (see above). For a wide-ranging discussion of the whole and selected individual problems see Cairns, *RL* 292–349.

METRE Alcaic

1 Odi profanum uulgus et arceo: both the book and the poem open strikingly with a line framed by two forceful verbs; their common object is inserted after the first of them, which is co-ordinated with the second by *et*: this form of arrangement – whereby two elements are joined by the interposition of a third – is known as *coniunctio* (*Rhet. Herenn.* 4.38) or, in modern terminology, 'conjunct hyperbaton' (e.g. Cic. *Caec.* 59 'congregat homines et conuocat'): see A. M. Devine and L. D. Stephens, *Latin Word Order* (2006) 586–91. Fraenkel (263) argued that *Odi* here does not mean 'hate' but 'have nothing to do with'; *arceo* ('repulse, keep away') etymologises *pro-fanum* as meaning 'away from the temple, *fanum*' (Maltby 499): similar is Virg. *Aen.* 6.258 'procul este profani' (see also 2n. below). We are to imagine a crowd of people who are not only uninitiated (*OLD profanus* 2) but excluded from a sacred precinct: the first Orphic Fragment, which, exactly like the ode (line 4), begins with the speaker's stated intention of singing to a privileged group,[1] continues with θύρας δ' ἐπίθεσθε, βέβηλοι ('close the doors, you profane ones'); and in the ancient *Carmen Aruale* the priests are enclosed within the sacred precinct ('ibi sacerdotes clusi') as they recite their ritual utterance ('carmen descindentes'): see Courtney, *ML* No. 1 (pp. 34–5, 199–204). Such religious exclusion zones

---

[1] The beginning of the fragment is transmitted in alternative versions: see J. N. Bremmer, 'The place of performance in Orphic poetry (*OF* 1)', in M. Herrero de Jáuregui et al. (edd.), *Tracing Orpheus* (2011) 1–6.

COMMENTARY 1.2–3

are cynically parodied by Tacitus to highlight the 'divine' status of Sejanus, henchman of the emperor Tiberius (*A.* 4.74.4 'foedum illud in propatulo seruitium' and W.). Gellius alludes to Horace when stating whom he does not want as readers of his *Attic Nights* (*praef.* 20 'ut ea ne attingat neue adeat profestum et profanum uolgus a ludo musico diuersum'). H.'s line bears a strong resemblance to line 4 of Callim. *Ep.* 28 (= *Anth. Pal.* 12.43), a poem which also begins with a synonym of *Odi*:

Ἐχθαίρω τὸ ποίημα τὸ κυκλικόν, οὐδὲ κελεύθῳ
χαίρω, τίς πολλοὺς ὧδε καὶ ὧδε φέρει·
μισέω καὶ περίφοιτον ἐρώμενον, οὐδ' ἀπὸ κρήνης
πίνω· σικχαίνω πάντα τὰ δημόσια.
Λυσανίη, σὺ δὲ ναίχι καλὸς καλός – ἀλλὰ πρὶν εἰπεῖν   5
τοῦτο σαφῶς Ἠχώ φησί τις 'ἄλλος ἔχει'.

I hate the roundabout poem and I take no pleasure in the path which carries many people this way and that. I loathe too the wandering beloved, and I do not drink from that well. I abhor everything that is common. Lysanias, you are indeed lovely, lovely – but, before Echo says this clearly, someone says 'He belongs to another'.[2]

On the epigram see further below.

2 fauete linguis: lit. 'Be favourably inclined with your speech' (*linguis* is abl.), which in a ritual context is equivalent to saying 'Keep silent' (*OLD faueo* 5a: see Sen. *Vit. beat.* 26.7 'hoc uerbum...imperat silentium, ut rite peragi possit sacrum, nulla uoce mala obstrepente'): compare Pind. *Pyth.* 6.1 Ἀκούσατ' ('Listen!'). The plural imperative is explained by H.'s revelation that he is speaking as a priest (3): as in 3.14 and *Epodes* 7 and 16 (see Watson's nn.), he is to be imagined as addressing an audience. Assonance links the call for silence (*fauete*, repeated in the semi-acrostic of *f- a- u-* in 2–4) with *profanum*, and, since the ancients derived *fanum* from *fari* 'to speak' (Maltby 223), perhaps an alternative derivation of *profanum* from *profari* 'to speak out' is activated retrospectively (see 1n.). For further discussion of multiple etymologising here see Cairns, *RL* 296–8. For *fauete* see Intro. 30.

2–3 carmina non prius | audita: this phrase raises two related questions: What are the *carmina*? What is the meaning of *non prius audita*?

---

[2] Scholars disagree on the punctuation and interpretation of the two final lines, which are sometimes deleted.

(a) Is H. referring to the originality of the *Odes* in general? He was intensely proud of his lyric achievement (3.30.13–14 'princeps', *Epi.* 1.19.32 'non alio dictum prius ore'), and 'songs not previously heard' would receive support from the allusion to Callimachus' epigram (above); Propertius, addressing the shades of Callimachus and echoing H.'s priestly role, likewise claims originality at the start of his third book (3.1.3 'primus...sacerdos'). Yet a statement of originality would be directed at all readers, whereas the *carmina* are being sung to a limited audience of 'maidens and boys' (4). (b) Following Meineke, many (perhaps most) scholars believe that the first stanza of the ode is (as it were) separable from the body of the poem and functions as a prelude to the entire Alcaic Hexad: on this view *carmina* refers specifically to the first six poems of the book. It follows from this view that the 'maidens and boys' of line 4 are being addressed throughout the Hexad; yet, even if we except the addresses to the Muse(s) as a special case (3.3.70, 3.4.2, 3.4.21–42), 3.6 has a different addressee altogether (2 'Romane'). Scholars of this persuasion have therefore argued that 3.6 is an earlier composition, tacked on to 3.1–5 to form a cycle of six 'Roman' odes (so Syndikus 2.4–6). This is quite implausible in a series of odes on whose singular importance everyone is agreed. (c) My suggestion (*PH* 71–4) is that *carmina* refers to ritual utterances which H. issues in his role as the Muses' priest and of which a specimen is given in lines 5–40 of the ode: for the various senses of *carmen* ('ritual utterance', 'poem', 'poetry') see *OLD*. The priestly framework is intended to enhance the seriousness of the message. That message is summed up in the exact centre of the ode with the words *desiderantem quod satis est* (25), a commonplace of popular philosophy and very familiar elsewhere in H. (see ad loc.): since *carmina* on that theme, as on every virtue advocated by H. in the *Odes*, can in no sense be described as 'not previously heard', *non prius audita* must mean 'not previously listened to', i.e. ignored, not obeyed (*OLD audio* 11). This meaning, rightly advocated by Silk 132–8, coheres perfectly both with the demand for attention on the present occasion (2 'fauete linguis') and with the focus on maidens and boys, who he hopes will be more receptive to the message than were older generations (for whom see 3.6.46–7 at the end of the Alcaic Hexad).

3 Musarum sacerdos: if the poet is a priest (Virg. *G.* 2.475–6, Prop. 3.1.3, Ov. *Am.* 3.8.23 'Musarum...sacerdos'), he is likely to be associated with a temple: an Aedes Herculis Musarum in Rome had been founded by M. Fulvius Nobilior in 179 BC in the Circus Flaminius and recently restored by L. Marcius Philippus, Augustus' stepbrother (Suet. *Aug.* 29.5 with Wardle): see e.g. A. Hardie, 'Juno, Hercules, and the Muses at Rome', *AJP* 128 (2007) 551–92, at 560–4.

4 uirginibus puerisque canto: H.'s *profanum uulgus* (1) is a foil for the young audience at whom he is directing his words (cf. 3.14.10, 3.24.51–4), in the same way as lines 1–4 of Callimachus' epigram (above) act as 'foils' for the final couplet (if it is genuine). Cicero envisaged a young readership for his philosophical works (*Div.* 2.4 'quod enim munus rei publicae adferre maius meliusue possumus quam si docemus atque erudimus iuuentutem, his praesertim moribus atque temporibus quibus ita prolapsa est ut omnium opibus refrenanda ac coercenda sit?'); it has been argued that the intended readership for Augustus' *Res Gestae* was the Roman *iuuentus* (Z. Yavetz, 'The *Res Gestae* and Augustus' public image', in F. Millar and E. Segal (edd.), *Caesar Augustus: seven aspects* (rev. edn 1990) 14–20, 36); and Tiberius' *laudatio* for the dead Germanicus was evidently expected to be useful to the same readership (*Tab. Siar.* IIb.17 'esse utile iuuentuti liberorum posterorumque nostrorum iudicaret' = Crawford 1.518 [top]). See also West, *DP* 8. For *canto* see Intro. 36.

5–6 regum timendorum in proprios greges | ...imperium est 'Fearful kings have power over their own flocks': when *est/sunt* is used with a possessive genitive rather than a possessive dative, the emphasis is on the possessor rather than the possession (G&L 224 §349 R. 2); the notion is complemented by *proprios* (*OLD* 2c), which 'implies absolute ownership' (Page). In this stanza kings and Jupiter, as variously superior beings, act as foils for the hierarchies listed in 9–14 below. *imperium in* + accus. is regular (exs. in *OLD*). *greges* indicates that the kings are seen as shepherds of the people, an image as old as Homer and very common (R. Brock, *Greek Political Imagery from Homer to Aristotle* (2013) 43–52).

6 reges in ipsos imperium est Iouis is chiastic with 5; the anaphoric polyptoton (*Regum ~ reges*) and paronomasia (*grĕges ~ rēges*) are suggestive of a ritual utterance. *ipsos* has a reciprocal function (almost 'over kings in their turn') and combines with the polyptoton to evoke the notion that kings enjoy a special relationship with Jupiter and are appointed by him (N–H on 1.12.50). This relationship, already applied to Augustus at 1.12.51–2, will be hinted at again at 3.5.2–3 below (see n.; also 3.6.5); in general see Weinstock 300–5. West notes that Augustus' adoptive father, Julius Caesar, as a young man had delivered a funeral speech for his aunt which included the words 'deorum, quorum *ipsi* in potestate *sunt reges*' (Suet. *DJ* 6.1). For anaphora starting the first and second lines of a stanza see also 3.4.65–6, 11.37–8, 19.9–10, 25.17–18, 27.49–50 (see Thomas on 4.1.21).

7 clari Giganteo triumpho 'famous for his triumph over the Giants' (as Ov. *Ex P.* 4.3.45 'Iugurthino clarus Cimbroque triumpho', Stat. *Theb.* 12.617).

In post-Homeric myth the Giants (sons of Earth) rebelled against Zeus and the other gods but were defeated; the story, illustrated on the frieze of the great Altar at Pergamum, is told at 3.4.49–60 below. Symbolising the victory of order over disorder, good over evil, the Gigantomachy was important in the Augustan era as an allegory for Augustus' suppression of his opponents (see esp. P. Hardie 85–90). For the various ways of expressing the victims of a triumph see *OLD triumphus* 2b.

8 cuncta supercilio mouentis: Zeus in Homer nods assent with his dark eyebrows; the locks on his head move; and he makes great Olympus shake (*Il.* 1.528–30); H. condenses the three separate actions into the bizarre picture of Jupiter 'literally' moving the world by means of his eyebrow. The absence of *cunctus* from Terence perhaps suggests that the word was without real currency in ordinary speech in earlier times; and, although it is quite common in Cicero and Caesar, the context often implies an association with officialese: its earliest extant appearance is in fact in the *Carmen Aruale*: 'aduocapit conctos' (see above, 1n.). Cf. J. N. Adams, *BICS* 20 (1973) 129–31.

9–14 Lists of occupations had appeared in the first ode of Book 1 (1.1.3–28) and likewise in the first of the *Satires* (1.1.4–19). N–R agree with those who think that the members of the present list are being criticised, but criticism is hard to reconcile with *est ut, generosior* and *moribus... melior.*

9–10 est ut uiro uir latius ordinet | arbusta sulcis 'It is the case that one man lays out his plantations with furrows over a wider area than another man' (*OLD sum* 7a); polyptoton of the type *uiro uir*, which is as old as Homer, can be used instead of reciprocal forms of *alius* or *alter* (Wills 195, 223). *ordinare*, a largely prosaic verb, is used 'esp. with abl.' of laying out in rows (*OLD* 1a); *sulci* are the furrows into which the vines will be planted (Cato, *RR* 32.1, 33.3; *OLD* 1a). An *arbustum* is 'a plantation of trees on which vines were trained' (*OLD* 2): since there was a limit on the maximum distance between individual host trees (cf. Virg. *G.* 2.284–7), H. must be referring to the overall area occupied by the plantations (*latius* suggests *latifundia*): the wealthier the vigneron, the more land he owns (and the more wealth he proceeds to acquire). On planting vines etc. see Thurmond Chap. 3, esp. 100–3; also Thomas or Mynors on Virg. *G.* 2.259–89.

10–11 hic generosior | descendat in Campum petitor: H. moves from the countryside to Rome: this and the next example (~ *hic*, 12) are taken from politics. Since the Campus Martius was the place where the electoral assemblies (*comitia*) met, *Campus* alone can stand for *comitia* by the figure metonymy (cf. Cic. *De or.* 3.167). *descendere* is often used of going to the Campus Martius for one reason or another; this man is a candidate for office (*petitor*), so he is presumably canvassing for votes. His advantage over his rivals is that he is of nobler birth (*OLD generosus* 1); see also next n.

12–13 moribus hic meliorque fama | contendat: the regular order would be *moribus hic famaque melior*: such dislocation of *-que* (again at 3.4.11, 3.4.18–19; probably *et* at 3.21.18) is common in the *Odes* (N–H on 1.30.6, 2.19.27). In the later republic there was an often voiced contrast between the traditional *nobilitas* of the *nobiles*, which was dependent on *genus*, and the *nobilitas* of the *noui homines*, which was attainable through *uirtus* (see esp. T. P. Wiseman, *New Men in the Roman Senate 139 BC–AD 14* (1971) 107ff. on 'the ideology of *novitas*'). H., having dealt with the genuine *nobilis* in 10–11 above, now turns to the new man, who relies on character; there is a similar contrast at Lucr. 2.11 'certare ingenio, contendere nobilitate', where there is the same absolute use of *contendere* (again at Sall. *BC* 11.2) and *ingenio* is used instead of *moribus* (see also 41n. below). H.'s new man relies on his reputation as well as his character (cf. Liv. 23.23.4 'de fama ac moribus senatoris'), although the co-ordinated terms are perhaps to be regarded as a hendiadys: 'this man competes on the basis of his superior moral reputation'.

13–14 illi turba clientium | sit maior: whereas the repeated *hic* (10, 12) linked the two types of politician, the change here to *illi* indicates a move to society more generally. '*Clientela* on a grand scale was associated with the nobility and was routinely listed among the noble's advantages over his rivals, often as an object of envy on the part of his competitors' (W. J. Tatum on *Comm. petit.*, Intro. p. 28): cf. Plaut. *Men.* 573–4 'optumi maxume morem habent hunc: | clientes sibi omnes uolunt esse multos'. Readers of H.'s *Satires* would know not to associate Maecenas with 'morem hunc' (*S.* 1.6.51–2 'cautum dignos assumere, praua | ambitione procul', 1.9.44 'paucorum hominum'). For the change of pronoun see *OLD ille* 16b; Courtney on Juv. 3.69. Apart from *Laus Pis.* 134–5, *turba clientium* is otherwise found only in the Senecas, e.g. *Ep.* 68.11 'ille me gratia forensi longe antecedet,...ille clientium turba'.

14–15 aequa lege Necessitas | sortitur insignes et imos 'Necessity draws by lot the distinguished and the lowly on equal terms' (*OLD sortior* 2a). Orelli rightly saw that Necessitas here is equivalent to Fate, as at 1.35.17

and 3.24.6; the term looks back to *est ut* (9), and lines 14b–16 as a whole explain lines 9–14a: H. is summing up, in the generalised and sententious manner appropriate to a closural passage, the point that inequalities are an inexorable fact of life. The system operated by Necessitas is fair ('aequa lege') because every man's name is in the lottery (16) and each person has an equal chance of emerging as either high or lowly. (Most scholars believe that Necessitas is Death, but on this view the lot can only symbolise the random timing with which Death comes for each individual (so N–R), which seems quite irrelevant to the ode: see further Silk 139–45, esp. 144.) The metaphor of drawing lots is especially relevant in Roman public life: though sortition was not used for the installation of regular magistrates, it was used for the selection of juries or to decide areas of magisterial jurisdiction such as provincial commands (*BNP* 7.818; A. Lintott, *The Constitution of the Roman Republic* (1999) 101). For *aequa lege* cf. Plaut. *Cist.* 532–3 'quando aequa lege pauperi cum diuite | non licet', Cic. *Verr.* 3.118; for *lege...sortitur* cf. Quint. 3.10.1.

16 omne capax mouet urna nomen: the line concludes the first section of the ode (intro.). Closure is often effected by universalising vocabulary (*omne*) and wordplay (*omne ~ nomen*): see e.g. Smith 161–6 and 182–6. Here the effect is heightened by the so-called 'silver line', whereby adjectives and nouns are arranged chiastically around a central verb (Wilkinson, *GLA* 216, 219). *mouet* refers to the shaking of the urn which contains the lots (cf. e.g. Virg. *Aen.* 6.432 'Minos urnam mouet' with Horsfall); since this action strictly precedes the process of sortition, lines 14–16 illustrate the figure *hysteron proteron*.

17–21a These lines allude to the famous story of Dionysius I, tyrant of Syracuse in Sicily (405–367 BC), and his courtier, Damocles, which is told by Cicero (*TD* 5.61–2). When Damocles listed to the tyrant the latter's many advantages and declared that no one had ever been happier, Dionysius asked him whether he would like a taste of the tyrant's life ('eam degustare'). Damocles agreed and was immediately surrounded by all the trappings of luxury, including tables laden with feasts ('mensae conquisitissimis epulis exstruebantur'). But then Dionysius arranged for a gleaming sword to hang from the ceiling by a single horse-hair, directly over Damocles' neck ('ut impenderet illius beati ceruicibus'). The courtier was unable to partake of any of the food or other luxuries and asked to be released from the experiment, realising that no one could be happy if he was threatened by a continuous terror. In 17–21a H. transfers the suspended sword from the courtier to the tyrant, as is indicated by *impia ceruice* (17–18), and the tyrant is no longer Dionysius specifically but any tyrant: the lines, which mention no names, are a generalisation (see nn. below).

17–18 destrictus ensis cui super impia | ceruice pendet '<For him> over whose impious neck a drawn sword hangs...': the omitted antecedent is the unexpressed dat. *ei*, which is to be understood with *elaborabunt* (19) and *reducent* (21). When the antecedent of a relative clause is a form of *is*, as here, it is often omitted, especially when its case would be the same as that of the relative pronoun (G&L 398 §619), also as here (again at 3.16.43–4, 3.27.7–8). *cui* is an example of the so-called 'sympathetic' dative, distinguished from a possessive construction by 'denoting a warmer interest of the person concerned' (*NLS* 46), as would certainly be the case if a drawn sword were suspended over one's neck. *impia* refers to Dionysius' notorious cruelty ('maleficum natura et iniustum', in Cicero's words); the suspended sword symbolises the constant threat of assassination under which a tyrant lives. H.'s use of the tyrant is transitional. Being a classic case of a hierarchical figure, the tyrant seems to continue the examples listed in 5–16; but his description in terms of his disadvantageous life (18–21a) leads into the themes of the following stanzas. *ensis* is preferred by Latin poets to *gladius*, which H., like Propertius and Tibullus, does not use at all (P. A. Watson (1985) 441).

18–19 non Siculae dapes | dulcem elaborabunt saporem 'Sicilian feasts will not produce their sweet taste': *elaborabunt*, like *reducent* below (21), is a 'gnomic' future, 'often used in statements of a general character, such as general truths' (*OLS* 1.425–6; cf. G&L 162 §242 R. 3, N. 1). H. has here transferred to the food the taste of the lifestyle which Damocles thought he wanted to enjoy (n. on 17–21a). Sicilian banquets were proverbial for their luxury (Otto 321) and Dionysius was tyrant of Syracuse. *elaborare*, when transitive, is more normally found in the passive (as *Epo.* 14.12): for a similar use to ours cf. Sen. *Ep.* 16.8 'quicquid ars ulla luxuriae elaborauit'.

20 non auium citharaeque cantus: a slight syllepsis:[3] *cantus* means 'song' with *auium* but 'tune' or 'music' with *citharae* (*OLD* 4a, 5a). Birdsong in a *locus amoenus* was associated with sleep (Heyworth on Ov. *F.* 3.17–18), but here *auium*, positioned between *dapes* and cithara, denotes caged birds, beloved by the Romans and indicative of luxury (F. M. A. Jones, 'The caged bird in Roman life and poetry', *Syllecta Classica* 24 (2013) 105–23).

---

[3] Syllepsis is the use of a word in more than one correct sense, e.g. 'I surveyed the scene with interest and binoculars', where 'with' is used sylleptically.

cithara (again at 3.4.4, 3.9.10, 3.15.14) is one of various words for 'lyre', others being *lyra* (3.3.69, 3.19.20, 3.28.11), *barbitos* (3.26.4), *fides* (3.4.4), and *testudo* (3.11.3); the first three are borrowed from Greek. The cithara was a box lyre, of which there were several types (M. L. West (1992) 50–6, Battezzato 144; *BNP* 9.355–6 for illustrations), although Greek and Latin poets often use the various terms interchangeably.

21–3 somnus agrestium | lenis uirorum non humiles domos | fastidit: H. customarily deploys verbal repetition in various forms and for various purposes (Bo 3.397–405); here the asyndetic polyptoton of *somnus* is adversative: '<But> gentle sleep does not look down on the humble homes of country men'. The contrast between the sleep of the poor and the insomnia of the rich is conventional (N–H on 2.16.15). *lenis* is a standard epithet for sleep from Enn. *Ann.* 5 and Lucr. 4.1009 onwards. *humiles* perhaps suggests that H. is using *fastidire* ('disdain') as an equivalent to *despicere*, which means 'to look down on' literally as well as metaphorically (a similar view seems possible at Vell. 2.15.2 'in id ipsum peruenisset *fasti*gium ex quo homines...*fasti*dire posset'): either way, *fastidit* (like *reducent* above) perhaps hints at the personification of *somnus*. For another place where H. seems to extend the meaning of a verb see 3.16.27n.

22–4 non...umbrosamque ripam, | non Zephyris agitata tempe: two typical haunts of *agrestes uiri* (21–2); *–que* = 'or' (*OLD* 7); the repetition of *non* echoes 18 ~ 20 above. *ripam* implies water, 'a constant element in the *amoenus locus*' (N–H on 2.3.12); the shade implies trees or an idyllic grove (N–H on 2.3.9). Tempe (neut. plur. in Greek) was a famously beautiful valley (in places a gorge) in Thessaly; the word came to be applied to any such valley (*OLD*) and is here used metonymically for the trees or air within the valley. The scene (like Virg. *Ecl.* 5.5 'incertas Zephyris motantibus umbras') is self-evidently calmer than many other cases where *agito* is used of the wind (e.g. 1.9.12, 2.10.9–10; *TLL* 1.1334.11–39). Since 'the Zephyr is conventionally associated with spring' (N–H on 1.4.1), it is as if in the valley it is always springtime – the *uer aeternum* of the Golden Age (Virg. *G.* 2.149, Ov. *Met.* 1.107–8). For sleep in the *locus amoenus* cf. e.g. Virg. *Ecl.* 1.55, *G.* 2.469–71.

25 desiderantem quod satis est 'The man who desires only what is sufficient'; words for 'only' are often omitted in Latin (W. on Vell. 68.5). It is characteristic of H. to place a moral message at the halfway point of an ode (Moritz 117, quoting this example). *satis est* is one of his most frequent expressions (over 20×), and contentment with what one has – a common theme of popular philosophy – is one of his most frequently expressed ideas (Oltramare 143, 274). *desiderantem* here does not have the verb's usual implication of desiring something which is lost or missing; the man already has that with which he is content (cf. Publil. Syr. Q 74 'Quod uult habet qui uelle quod satis est potest'). For the proverbial 'nothing to excess', *ne quid nimis*, cf. Tosi 785-7 §1761.

25-6 neque | tŭmultuosum sollicitat mare: the negative characterisation of the contented man conjures up a picture of his opposite – the individual who *would* be made anxious by rough seas, namely, the merchant (for so-called 'description by negation', again at 3.16.33-6, see M. Davies, *Prometheus* 13 (1987) 265-84, although the exs. are quite different). *tumultuosum*, a word not commonly used of natural forces, suggests the time of year when seafaring was impracticable (27-8n.); but the merchant's anxiety shows that he has put to sea nevertheless, and the only reason can be his unworthy desire for further profit (a topos: see N-H on 1.3, intro.). Cf. *Epo.* 2.6 'neque horret iratum mare' and Watson. For *tŭmultuosum* see Intro. 30.

27-8 nec saeuus Arcturi cadentis | impetus aut orientis Haedi: sc. *sollicitat* from 26. Arcturus, the brightest star in the constellation Bootes, sets at the start of November (Plin. *NH* 18.313) and was a sign of bad weather (Plaut. *Rud.* 71 'occido uehementior'). The Kids (the name is usually plural) are two stars in the constellation Auriga: their rising is ascribed to late September or early October (Colum. 11.2.66 and 73) and is also associated with bad weather (Gow on Theocr. 7.53). These stars, which had earlier been conjoined by Virgil (*G.* 1.204-5 'sunt Arcturi sidera nobis | Haedorumque dies seruandi'), broadly indicate the start of the period when seafaring was regarded as perilous if not impossible;[4] but they are also relevant to the vigneron too (29n.). *cado* (*OLD* 6a) and *orior* (*OLD* 1a) are technical of heavenly bodies' setting and rising respectively; *impetus* is regularly used of forces of nature (*OLD* 1a).

29 non uerberatae grandine uineae: sc. *sollicitant* from 26. A further negative statement conjures up a picture of the vigneron to match that of the merchant; *uineae* and *arbore* (30) look back to *arbusta sulcis* (10). Agriculture and seafaring are often juxtaposed in ancient texts (Watson on *Epo.* 2.6, Thomas on Virg. *G.* 1.50), and the above references to autumnal weather are as applicable to the vine-grower as to the merchant: the

---

[4] The sailing season is said by Vegetius (*Mil.* 4.39) to have lasted from 27 May to 14 September, although in exceptional circumstances it could be extended to 10 March-10 November: see Casson 270-3.

agricultural writer Columella mentions the vintage directly after his two references to the Kids (27–8n.). In Italy grapes were normally harvested in October (Varro, *RR* 1.34.2), a month when freak hailstorms are sometimes recorded: Pliny complains of hail at harvest time (*Ep.* 4.6.1 'Tusci grandine excussi'). *uerberare* is used of natural forces (3.27.23–4n.; *OLD* 3b), perhaps esp. hail (e.g. *Priap.* 61.5 'grandine uerberata dura'); Virgil may be alluding directly to H. at *Aen.* 9.668–9 ('quantus ab occasu ueniens pluuialibus *haedis* | *uerberat* imber humum, quam multa *grandine nimbi*...'), although a lost common source is also possible.

30 fundusque mendax: sc. *sollicitat* from 26. The estate-owner accuses his farm of 'lying' because it fails to fulfil its promise (cf. *Epi.* 1.7.87 'spem mentita seges', Petron. 117.9).

30–1 arbore nunc aquas | culpante: the estate, here designated by its trees (singular for plural: see *OLD arbor* 2, an uncommon usage), replies to the owner's accusation by blaming the weather (*mendax* ~ *iniquas*); for vocal trees see Ogilvie on Liv. 2.6–7.4 (p. 248), Hunt 197. *aquas* = 'rain' (*OLD* 2a). H.'s habit of appending an abl. abs. to the main sentence (again at 34 below) is esp. evident in Book 3 (Nisbet, *OR* 397): see 3.3.17–18, 3.52 (not a certain case), 5.3–4, 5.12, 6.28, 13.14, 14.15–16, 16.8 (also not certain), 21.7–8, 29.20; in other books at e.g. 2.7.9–10, 4.5.27.

31–2 torrentia agros | sidera: the reference is to the Dog-star in July (3.13.9–10n.): cf. Tib. 1.4.42 'Canis arenti torreat arua siti', Colum. 2.20 'seges antequam torreatur uaporibus aestiui sideris, qui sunt uastissimi per exortum Caniculae'.

33 contracta pisces aequora sentiunt: the fish are hemmed in by the contracting waters (mimetic syntax).

34 iactis in altum molibus has two different meanings. As the fish (the subject of the sentence) watch each barrowful of rubble cascading past them and adding to the height of the underwater pile, they think that 'foundations are being piled up into the sky' (*OLD iacio* 6a, *altum* 2a); but from the viewpoint of the builders, 'foundations are being laid in the deep' (*OLD iacio* 6b, *altum* 1a). Rich men famously built out over the sea (see D'Arms, esp. Chap. 5 and Plates 14–15B; M. Zarmakoupi, *Designing for luxury on the Bay of Naples* (2014)): such defiance of the laws of nature was a commonplace of moralistic literature, e.g. Sall. *BC* 13.1, 20.11: see N–H on 2.18.21, J. E. G. Whitehorne, 'The ambitious builder', *AUMLA* 31 (1969) 28–39.

34–6 frequens | caementa demittit redemptor | cum famulis: *frequens* is probably adverbial ('the contractor frequently sends down...': see 3.3.70–2n.) but may perhaps mean 'many a contractor', i.e. in relays. *cum famulis* = 'at the head of his slaves' (*OLD cum*[1] 4a): the implication is that the slaves are doing the actual work (see also next n.). *famulus*, again at 3.17.16, is more stylistically elevated than *seruus*, which H. does not use in the *Odes* (see P. A. Watson (1985) 434–5). *caementa* = 'rubble' (3.24.3).

36–7 dominusque terrae | fastidiosus: if the text is right, *dominus* is a second subject of *caementa demittit*, the owner's defiance of nature (33n.) being underlined by the enjambed *terrae | fastidiosus* (the genit. is rare but regular: *OLD* 2). But the owner would scarcely cart rubble himself: one would have to assume that with *dominus*, if not also with *redemptor* (34–6n.), the verb has a causative dimension (akin to a Greek middle): the owner 'causes rubble to be sent down'. Numerous scholars, however, have expressed serious doubts about the transmitted text (see N–R). Rudd was attracted by Nisbet's *cum famulis dominoque terrae | fastidioso*, but the equalising of slaves and owner under the direction of the contractor seems both pointless and perverse. SB, more radically, placed a full stop after *redemptor* (35) and started a new sentence with *tum famuli dominusque*, with *scandunt* as the verb (understood from 38): 'When the building is ready, the servants and then the master move in, but so do Fear and Threats. The verb *scandunt*...pictures them as climbing on board ship' (*Profile* 93). This is quite implausible and takes no account of line 40. If the text is unsatisfactory, a less radical change would be *dominoque terrae | fastidio sunt*, 'the owner regards dry land/solid ground with disdain' (*-que* is epexegetic). *fastidio est/sunt* is a common predicative dat. (*TLL* 6.1.315.17–30), though not elsewhere found in verse; for the plural *terrae* see *OLD* 1a, 3a.

37 Timor et Minae: the personification of fear is as old as Hom. *Il.* 4.440 (West on Hes. *Theog.* 934); the only parallel quoted for Threats is Stat. *Theb.* 7.51 'innumeris strepit aula Minis' (in a list of personifications: see Smolenaars on 7.47–54, also Horsfall on Virg. *Aen.* 6.274–89).

38 scandunt eodem quo dominus: 'it was normal...for the houses of great men to be high and dominating' (T. P. Wiseman, '*Conspicui postes tectaque digna deo*: the public image of aristocratic and imperial houses in the late republic and early empire', in *Historiography and Imagination* (1994) 101; see also W–M on Tac. A. 3.9.3); they might also boast a *turris* (3.29.9–10n.). The height of the *dominus*' house, implied by the depth of its foundations (34), is confirmed by *scandunt*; but, no matter how high, its owner will be assailed by Fear and Threats. The image is perhaps that of scaling a city wall during a military assault (cf. N–H on 2.19.22), leaving the *dominus* no option but to try to escape: he has the two possibilities of sea or land (38–40), because maritime villas (33n.) had access to both. Augustus acted to regulate the height of buildings and houses (Strabo 5.3.7, Suet. *Aug.* 89.2; D. Favro, *JSHA* 51 (1992) 73–5), but whether, or to what extent, the regulations included the private houses of the rich is not clear.

38–40 neque | decedit aerata triremi et | post equitem sedet atra Cura: the third personified abstraction of the stanza is Care, as Virg. *Aen.* 6.274 (see Horsfall) and elsewhere: in particular H. repeats the language and some of the imagery of 2.16.21–2 'scandit aeratas uitiosa naues | Cura nec turmas equitum relinquit' (see N–H ad loc. and on 2.16.11). *triremis* and *aerata nauis* would normally denote a warship, but the former is used of a rich man's craft at *Epi.* 1.1.93, while *aerata* (contrasting with and partly anagrammatising *atra*) emphasises the wealth of the ship's owner (*dominus*): no matter how well-equipped his ship or how fast his horse, he cannot escape Black Care (cf. *S.* 2.7.115 'comes atra [sc. *Cura*] premit sequiturque fugacem' and Muecke's n.; note too 3.14.13–14n., 3.16.17–18n.): *neque decedit* suggests not abandoning one's post. Black Care riding pillion is one of H.'s most memorable images, turned into a drawing by Keith Douglas, the WWII poet who was killed near Bayeux three days after D-Day (it features on the cover of his *Complete Poems*, ed. D. Graham, 1979); three months later a despondent Churchill quoted H.'s line to his War Cabinet to illustrate his perception – quite misconceived – of Stalin's relationship with his henchmen (*The Second World War* (1954) Vol. 6, p. 208).

41–8 In the last two stanzas H. returns to first-person verbs (*moliar, permutem*), completing a ring with the first stanza (*Odi, arceo, canto*); but, whereas at the start he had clearly adopted a public role (see nn.), here the reference to his Sabine farm (47), of which readers of the collected *Carmina* were reminded as recently as 2.18.14, indicates that he is now speaking as the private individual Q. Horatius Flaccus, giving his personal reaction to the arguments in 5–40. It follows that his address as the Muses' priest has now finished: there is no explicit sign of its closing, but this is often the case with speeches (see Feeney (2011)), although the appearance of *quod si* is perhaps a hint (41n.).

41 quod si...: this is the first time in the ode that a sentence has begun with a connecting word, assisting the notion that the *Musarum sacerdos* has now finished his speech (see above). *quod si* also concludes the opening of Lucr. 2 (47), a passage which H. may have had in mind throughout the ode (above, 12-13n.; N-R 3-4).

41-3 dolentem...| delenit 'soothes...the man suffering' (from Care): the language is medical (cf. Phaedr. 3 *praef.* 44 'nec his dolorem delenirem remediis'; Pease on Virg. *Aen.* 4.393). Ironically the four subjects of *delenit*, while primarily symbolising luxury, also hint secondarily at genuine medical treatments (see below), thereby underlining the inappropriateness of each luxury item.

Phrygius lapis: a luxury kind of marble (*OLD Phrygius* 1b; NA on Lygd. 3.13), such as would be used by the builder of 33-7; but marble, ground down, was also used in medical treatments (Cels. 5.22.6).

42-3 purpurarum sidere clarior | ...usus: *purpura* is 'purple-dyed cloth (esp. as a sign of wealth or power)' and in the plural is used rather like Eng. 'whites' (for cricket); but *purpura* is also the name of a shellfish recommended by the medical writer Celsus for dietary purposes (2.24.3): see *OLD* 3a-b, 1. *usus* refers to the wearing of clothes (e.g. Suet. *Galba* 11.1 'usum togae'; *OLD* 1a); *clarior* is an example of enallage, viz. the transference to a governing noun (*usus*) of an adj. which more properly should be taken with an expressed dependent genitive, in this case *purpurarum*. Nisbet (*LCM* 5 (1980) 151-2) suggested replacing *sidere* by *Sidone* (*OLD Sidon*), largely on the grounds that the three other subjects of the verb are characterised by an adjectival form of a proper name. The emendation is adopted by N-R, but the sense is poor ('the wearing of purple garments brighter than Sidonian purple'), the prosody irregular (the *-o-* is usually long), and the Homeric comparison of a fine robe to a star (*Il.* 6.295 ἀστὴρ δ' ὣς ἀπέλαμπεν, *Od.* 15.108) eliminated.

43-4 Falerna | uitis: Falernian wine, reckoned the second most noble by the elder Pliny (*NH* 14.62), looks back to the estate-owner of 29-32, although wine was also an extremely common ingredient in medicines.

44 Achaemeniumque costum: *costum* (a Greek loan-word, seemingly first here in extant Latin) was an aromatic plant associated with the East (Isid. *Orig.* 17.9.4; J. I. Miller, *The Spice Trade of the Roman Empire* (1969) 84-6) and hence evokes the merchant of 26; it appears regularly in medicinal recipes (e.g. Cels. 6.6.24). Achaemenes was the legendary founder of the Achaemenid dynasty in Persia (N-H on 2.12.21), Persia being a byword for luxury (N-H on 1.38.1).

45–6 cur inuidendis postibus et nouo | sublime ritu moliar atrium 'why should I pile up a lofty atrium with enviable doors and in the new style?' (the rhetorical question is equivalent to a negative statement). *inuidendis postibus* is an abl. of description (*NLS* 64–5 §83); the same is probably true of *nouo…ritu*, though abl. of manner (to be taken with *moliar*) is another possibility (*NLS* 33–4 §48). The atrium, being the place where clients were received (cf. *Epi.* 1.5.31), resonates with *turba clientium* (13); *sublime* contrasts with the lowly dwellings of the countryfolk (22 *humiles*); *moliar* looks back to *molibus* (34). *postibus* refers to the leaves of a door (P. Howell, *Philol.* 112 (1968) 134; *OLD* 2b): they are described as 'enviable' not simply because 'the ancients took it for granted that grand houses aroused envy' (N–H on 2.10.7) but also because the word makes explicit the logical connection between the grandees of 9–16 and the tyrant of 17–21a (see intro.). H.'s rejection of the new style indicates his contentment with his present arrangements, like the individual in 25.

47 ualle…Sabina refers to H.'s Sabine farm (Intro. 5). *ualle* looks back to *tempe* (24) and the contented life of the countrymen; the Sabine region was proverbial for its frugality and generally old-fashioned virtue: see e.g. *Epo.* 2.41–2 and Watson, *Epi.* 2.1.25 'rigidis…Sabinis', Cato, *ORF* 128, Cic. *Vat.* 36, *Lig.* 32 'agrum Sabinum, florem Italiae ac robur rei publicae', Liv. 1.18.4, Virg. *G.* 2.532, Mart. 10.33.1 'priscis…Sabinis'. For H. the area is associated with the Muses (3.4.21–2) and conviviality (3.29.1–16, 1.9.7–8; cf. 1.20.1–2). See further Harrison, *CCH* 245–7.

48 diuitias operosiores 'more vexatious riches'. The comparative form is explained by the fact that his present 'riches' are his life of rural contentment (cf. 25); why should he exchange them for literal riches, which would only bring him trouble?

2

H. ended the first ode of the Alcaic Hexad by drawing a contrast between riches and his own modest circumstances; the second ode begins with the toleration of *pauperies* (1), as if the poet were about to continue or develop similar themes. But this turns out not to be the case. H. is more interested in the military life which would train a *puer* to tolerate straitened circumstances (2–6a). The central experience of a military life is combat, which H. proceeds to describe in vivid and epic terms and appears to see sympathetically from the viewpoint of the enemy women, as they observe from the walls of their citadel their menfolk fighting the young Roman (6b–12).

The prospect of an unequal contest between an enemy prince and the young Roman warrior evokes from H. one of his most famous aphorisms (13 'It is sweet and fitting to die for one's fatherland'), which is followed by the statement that Death will catch up with the warrior even if he flees (14–16). Since the natural corollary to this grim truth is that the warrior should have the courage to stand his ground and fight to the death (a theme to which H. will return in 3.5), *uirtus* is the subject of the next two stanzas (17–24).[5] Although *uirtus* can be rewarded by the acquisition of political honours, such honours are at the mercy of a volatile electorate; it is better to see *uirtus* as its own reward (17–20), capable of bestowing immortality on those who die undeservedly in its cause (21–4).

Hitherto we have had two complementary sets of three stanzas on the subject of warfare, but at lines 25–6 there suddenly appears another aphorism: 'There is also a reward for loyal silence.' Although the notion of reward provides a link with the preceding, there seems to be no explanation at all for the reference to silence, which, via mention of the contrasting fate that awaits the blabber, takes up the remaining two stanzas of the ode (26–32). On the present analysis, therefore, the stanzaic structure of the ode is 3 + 3 + 2, but the transition at lines 25–6 is extremely puzzling: it is as if H. expects his readers to be aware of some unspoken background or context which will help to articulate his sequence of thought. Since lines 14 and 25–6 exhibit two very clear allusions to some fragments of Simonides, the Greek lyric poet of the 6th/5th centuries BC, and since the second of these allusions coincides precisely with the seemingly unexplained transition, W. J. Oates suggested that the ode derives from a single, now lost, poem of Simonides (*The Influence of Simonides of Ceos upon Horace* (1932) 1–55; cf. Harrison (2001) 261–2): if we knew the Simonidean original (so the hypothesis goes), we would understand the ode much better. But it is questioned whether there ever was such a Simonidean poem (R. Rawles, *Simonides the Poet* (2018) 64–6) and, even if there was, whether H. would have made the articulation of his ode so dependent on it. Perhaps, as in 3.16 (intro.), H. was aiming to imitate the general manner of Pindar, in whose odes transitions are as notable a feature as his aphorisms (γνῶμαι).[6]

---

[5] Some scholars, such as N–R (22), think that in 17–24 H. is not talking about the '*uirtus* of the soldier' but about some broader quality.
[6] Some have seen 25–6 as a 'Pindaric' motif whereby the poet calls upon himself to fall silent (R. Stoneman in *Aischylos und Pindar* (ed. E. G. Schmidt, 1981) 257–67, G. Davis, *CA* 2 (1983) 9–26), but this would require an adversative (like Pind. *Isth*. 5.51 ἀλλ' ὅμως, quoted by both scholars) rather than *et*, as Stoneman seems aware (262).

It is significant that in our ode the *puer* is urged to fight the Parthians (3): they are mentioned here explicitly for the first time in Book 3 and will recur in three of the following odes of the Alcaic Hexad (3.3.44, 5.4–9, 6.9). This is such a 'notable concentration' of references that it has led Powell, in a most helpful discussion,[7] to suggest that one might with only slight exaggeration think of renaming the first six odes of the book the 'Parthian Odes' (189; cf. 159–60). The context is Augustus' relations with Parthia (Intro. 3): already at 1.35.30–1 H. had referred to the newly recruited force of young men who will strike terror into the eastern parts of the world; and we are told by Trogus (Just. 42.5.10) and Dio (54.8.1) that Phraates IV, the king of Parthia, was afraid that Augustus would invade his kingdom. Virgil (*Aen.* 7.604–6) and Propertius (2.10.13–14) as well as H. give the unambiguous impression that Augustus was planning an invasion of Parthia (Powell 168–73). The present poem is 'Horace's great recruiting ode', says Powell; 'Augustan youth is to go and show its mettle on the battlefield against the Parthians' (181). See further 3.5 intro.

METRE Alcaic

1–12 The four main verbs (*condiscat, uexet, agat, suspiret*) are all jussive subjunctive.

1–3 Angustam amice pauperiem pati | robustus acri militia puer | condiscat: the emphasis of the first sentence is not on the toleration of poverty for its own sake, the desirability of which is taken for granted (cf. 4.9.49), but on its being learned through the hard life of a soldier (2–3a), which is elaborated in 3b–6 (a similar point is made in Marius' speech at Sall. *BJ* 85.33 'illa multo optuma rei publicae doctus sum: hostem ferire...humi requiescere...inopiam et laborem tolerare', and probably in the elder Cato's speech *De suis uirtutibus*: cf. *ORF* 129 'quid mihi fieret, si non ego stipendia...omnia ordinarius meruissem semper?'); the alliterative first line simply provides an arresting beginning to the poem and a link with the previous ode.

According to Suetonius (*Aug.* 38.2), Augustus wished both to reduce the age at which the sons of senators participated in public life and to encourage their experience of campaigning ('ne qui expers castrorum esset'). Suetonius does not mention a date, but Augustus' aspirations would provide a context for the ode. For the importance of addressing the young see 3.1.4n. (also next n.); for H.'s use of *puer* cf. esp. *Epi.*

---

[7] It should be added to the extensive bibliography on the Parthian question in Nabel 322–5.

COMMENTARY 2.3-4   95

1.18.54-5 'saeuam | militiam puer et Cantabrica bella tulisti', Stat. *Silv.*
5.2.8-10 'quid si militiae iam te, puer inclite, primae | clara rudimenta
et castrorum dulce uocaret | auspicium?' The minimum age for a military tribune seems to have been about 18, although Statius' addressee
is 16. The *princeps*' own nephew, Marcellus, furnished a recent example.
Born in 42 BC, in his mid-teens he had accompanied Augustus to the
Cantabrian war in Spain, from which he returned in 25 (cf. Dio 53.27.5),
an event commemorated in an epigram of Crinagoras (*Anth. Pal.* 6.161 =
1819-22 G-P): 'On his return from the western war laden with spoils...
Marcellus shaved his blonde beard: such was his country's wish, to send
him out a boy and welcome him back a man', βούλετο πατρὶς | οὕτως, καὶ
πέμψαι παῖδα καὶ ἄνδρα λαβεῖν (see Ypsilanti's commentary (2018) ad loc.).
After his death in September 23 BC at the age of 19, Marcellus will be
described as *puer* by Virgil (*Aen.* 6.882).
   amice has caused a great deal of trouble and has generated emendations
elsewhere in the line; but *angustam...pauperiem* seems secure, since it is
imitated by Paulinus of Nola (*Carm.* 18.220-1), and no emendation of
amice itself seems at all convincing. Some scholars state that *amice...pati* is
equivalent to ἀγαπητῶς φέρειν ('to bear contentedly'), as if the latter were
a common expr., but in fact it is almost never found. Nevertheless, if *amice*
can mean 'with good will' (so *OLD*), that seems a reasonable interpretation. *pauperies* (again with *pati* at 1.1.18) is much more recherché than
paupertas and is significantly more common (15×) in H. than in any other
author apart from Apuleius (*TLL* 10.1.850.64-6, 852.63-73): he uses it
7× in the *Odes* (4× in Book 3) as opposed to only once for *paupertas*. H.
is not talking about actual indigence but modest circumstances. *acri militia* (again at 1.29.2), reminiscent of the Homeric ὀξὺν Ἄρηα (*Il.* 2.440),
here perhaps = 'fierce campaigning'; *robustus* is quasi-causal, 'by becoming strong'.

3-4 et Parthos feroces | uexet eques metuendus hasta 'and let him harass the defiant Parthians as a horseman to be feared with his spear': *metuendus* + causal abl. is first in H. (again at 1.12.23-4, 2.19.8, then in a
few subsequent poets: cf. *TLL* 8.906.67-9), though here *hasta* is also felt
as an instrumental abl. with *uexet* (an ex. of ἀπὸ κοινοῦ [*apo koinou* = in
common]). The Parthians are described as 'feroces' because the defeat
of Crassus at Carrhae in 53 BC remained unavenged and, following the
failure of Antony's campaign in the 30s, the Parthians still held on to
the lost legionary standards and prisoners of war (a theme of 3.5); the
young Roman recruit is described as an 'eques' because the Parthians
were horsemen and it was their famous technique of the 'Parthian shot'
(1.19.11) which had to be countered. Training in horsemanship recurs

in the *Odes* (1.8.6, 3.7.25–6, 3.12.8, 3.24.54–5), but it is unclear whether readers are intended to ask themselves how the term *eques* relates to the Roman army of Augustus' day. Possibly H. is imagining a young member of the small units of non-auxiliary cavalry which came to be attached to each legion (for which see K. R. Dixon and P. Southern, *The Roman Cavalry* (1992) 27–30), but he may not be thinking in technical terms at all: 'the principal way in which upper-class Romans displayed *uirtus* was in mounted combat' (McDonnell 152): when in 27/26 BC Cornelius Gallus, the poet and first prefect of Egypt, set up a trilingual inscription (EJ 21) recording his military exploits, it was headed by a relief showing a victorious mounted warrior with a spear. Virgil used the term *eques* in his praise of the famous M. Claudius Marcellus (N–H on 1.12.46), the young Marcellus' ancestor (1–3n.; Plut. *Marc.* 30.6), who as consul in 222 conquered the Gallic Insubres at Clastidium and won the *spolia opima* for killing the enemy leader in single combat (see *Aen.* 6.857–8 'hic rem Romanam magno turbante tumultu | sistet *eques* sternet Poenos Gallumque rebellem'); the man was also commemorated by Naevius in a now lost drama (McDonnell 232–3). A cavalryman's *hasta* in Augustan times is likely to have been a light spear suitable for throwing or thrusting: heavy spears for Roman cavalry, used for charging, seem unknown before the time of Trajan (J. E. H. Spaul, *Ala*² (1994) 97–100). In the end, of course, an expedition against Parthia never took place (see 3.5 intro.).

5 uitamque sub diuo et trepidis agat | in rebus: *sub diuo* (again at 2.3.23) means 'in the open air' (*OLD sub* 9): this is the life to which the Roman soldier will need to adapt if he is to conquer the Parthians, who could not tolerate harsh conditions or camping out in the winter (Plut. *Ant.* 40.2). See Powell 182, who suggests (n. 96) that a source of information about Parthian strengths and weaknesses may have been Q. Dellius, the addressee of 2.3 and historian of Antony's ill-fated Parthian campaign (*FRH* 1.424–5, 2.844–7, 3.518). *in trepidis rebus* is 4× in Book 4 of Livy and again at 34.11.5; he has the sing. form 9×.

6–8 ex moenibus...prospiciens: these words virtually translate *teichoskopia* ('viewing from the walls'), the technical term used in antiquity to describe such episodes as the famous Homeric scene where Helen identifies the Greek leaders from the walls of Troy (*Il.* 3.146–242): see esp. the story of Peisidice in Parthen. *Erot. Path.* 21 with Lightfoot's nn., and for further exs. cf. P.-J. Miniconi, *Les thèmes 'guerriers' de la poésie épique gréco-romaine* (1951) 168; for an early fresco from Thera depicting such a scene see C. G. Doumas, *Thera: Pompeii of the Ancient Aegean* (1983) 40, plate xiv; see also 10–11n. and 13n. below. *hosticus* is archaic, according

COMMENTARY 2.7-11   97

to Porphyrio on 2.1.1 (see the survey of usage by Gaertner on Ov. *Ex P.* 1.3.65); for *moenibus hosticis* cf. Sil. 15.114-15.

7 matrona bellantis tyranni: we have to supply a verb such as *trepidet* from *suspiret* (9) by zeugma. *tyranni* keeps the scene in Parthia (cf. Luc. 7.442-3 'Medique Eoaque tellus, | quam sub perpetuis tenuerunt fata tyrannis'). *matrona* = 'wife' (*OLD* 2).

8 adulta uirgo: she is usually identified as the daughter of the warrior tyrant and his wife (7), but seems more likely to be the anonymous betrothed of their son (9-10n.). *uirgo* is the regular word for a young unmarried woman and is often coupled with *matrona* (P. A. Watson (1983) 125, (1985) 433-4); here there is perhaps also an allusion to the sexual life with her betrothed that she will not enjoy.

9 suspiret 'Eheu!': the words apply to the *uirgo* alone (for sighs as a symbol of love see 3.7.10n.). *Eheu* combines with *prospiciens* (8) in alluding to Cat. 64.61-2 'prospicit, eheu, | prospicit', a familiar passage (cf. 3.25.8-9n.), where *eheu* is authorial but there is the same emotional intensity and Hellenistic 'romance'. Ours seems to be the only occasion when *suspirare* is followed by direct speech, although *suspiratio* is so used at Plin. *NH praef.* 9 and the verb is occasionally followed by indir. speech (*OLD* 1d); see also Intro. 41.

9-10 ne rudis agminum | sponsus lacessat regius: the clause represents the maiden's thoughts and is equivalent to one of fearing (see *NLS* 146 §189). It is usually said that the *sponsus* is an ally of the *tyrannus* (like Coroebus at Virg. *Aen.* 2.344-5); but this leaves *regius* without point: more likely he is the tyrant's son (8n.). *rudis agminum* = 'unversed in fighting': *rudis* regularly takes the genit. (*OLD* 6a); for this meaning of *agmen* see *OLD* 7a. *lacessat* = 'challenge', i.e. to a fight (*OLD* 1a).

10-11 asperum | tactu leonem: (1) Turnus is described as a 'fierce lion' (*OLD asper* 9b) at Virg. *Aen.* 9.792-6 'ceu saeuum turba <u>leonem</u> | cum telis premit infensis; at territus ille, | <u>asper</u>, acerba tuens, retro redit et neque <u>terga</u> | ira dare aut <u>uirtus</u> patitur, nec tendere contra | ille quidem hoc cupiens potis est <u>per</u> tela uirosque'.[8] (2) *asperum tactu* is found also in Lucretius (6.778, 1150; later at Plin. *NH* 27.90). (3) Virgil's *asper, acerba tuens* is also an allusion to Lucretius (5.33 'asper, acerba tuens, immani corpore serpens'). (4) Virgil's simile shares a smattering of other

---

[8] See P. Hardie ad loc. for the Homeric background.

vocabulary (dotted underlining) with lines 10–17 of the ode. These four points perhaps suggest that behind all three authors there lies a lost passage of Ennius' *Annales*; whether such a passage (if it existed) occurred in the vicinity of Ennius' *teichoskopia* (*Ann.* 418 'matronae moeros complent spectare fauentes') naturally cannot be known.

As lions had featured in the Roman arena since the second century BC (see 3.20 intro.), the shaggy mane of the male would be a familiar sight; but such a reference would be without point here: as in the Virgilian passage quoted above, *asperum* means 'fierce' (cf. 1.23.9 'tigris ut aspera') and is explained by *quem...caedes* (11–12). *tactu* is deliberate understatement (like *S*. 2.1.45 'melius non tangere'): the joint evidence of this passage and Ov. *F.* 5.395–6 ('nec se, quin horrens auderent tangere saetis | uellus, Achilleae continuere manus') perhaps suggests a proverb along the lines of *Noli leonem tangere*.

11–12 quem cruenta | per medias rapit ira caedes: *cruenta* combines the notions of 'murderous' and 'bloodthirsty' (*OLD* 2–3), while *caedes* suggests not just the surrounding slaughter but the young Roman's participation in it. *rapit* = 'sweeps along', as Liv. 10.41.1 'Romanos ira...in proelium rapit', Sil. 14.299; Roman soldiers are regularly motivated by *ira* (as Liv. 9.13.5 'Romanos ira...per mediam aciem hostium tulerat'; more exs. listed by Oakley on 9.13.3), which is also a characteristic of lions (e.g. Lucr. 3.298, Virg. *Aen.* 7.15).

13 dulce et decorum est pro patria mori: it has been said that H.'s 'plain prosaic phrase...derives its impact from the vivid images of bravery and violence that surround it' (Coleman 56), but the aphorism also exhibits his characteristic assonance and varied forms of alliteration. The sentiment, of which this is the most familiar formulation, is the theme of 3.5, recurs at 3.19.2 (n.) and 4.9.51–2, and goes back to Homer (*Il.* 15.496–7; cf. also e.g. Tyrtaeus 10, Eur. *Tro.* 386–7, Thuc. 2.42.3, *Rhet. Herenn.* 4.57, Cic. *Phil.* 14.31, *Off.* 1.57 with Dyck's n., Liv. 9.4.10 with Oakley's n.). For the importance of serving one's *patria* cf. Cic. *Rep.* 6.13 'omnibus qui patriam conseruauerint, adiuuerint, auxerint certum esse in caelo definitum locum, ubi beati aeuo sempiterno fruantur', 29 'sunt autem optimae curae de salute patriae; quibus agitatus et exercitatus animus uelocius in hanc sedem et domum suam peruolabit'. *dulce* alludes to the sweetness conventionally evoked by thoughts of one's country: cf. Virg. *Aen.* 10.782 'dulcis moriens reminiscitur Argos' with Harrison (and in *RhM* 136 (1993) 91–3). H.'s words were famously used as the title of a poem by Wilfred Owen, who bitterly applies to his own side the line which in H. is poignantly motivated by the death of the royal fiancé at the hands of the young Roman. See also T. Fuhrer, 'Teichoskopia', in J. Fabre-Serris and A. Keith (edd.), *War and Women in Antiquity* (2015) 56–7.

14 Mors et fugacem persequitur uirum: *Mors*, personified by the verb, picks up the last word of the preceding line (13 *mori*), a modification of the figure illustrated at 3.3.61n.: see Wills 397 for numerous other exs. H.'s words are an almost exact translation (note *et* ~ καί) of Simonides 524/22P ὁ δ' αὖ θάνατος κίχε καὶ τὸν φυγόμαχον ('But Death overtakes even the battle-fleer'), itself an allusion to a formulaic line of Homer (*Il.* 17.478, 672, 22.436); for *persequor* = 'catch up with' see *OLD* 1b. The notion is proverbial (recurring in e.g. Sall. *BJ* 87.2, Liv. 8.24.4 (with Oakley), 22.5.2, Tac. *Agr.* 30.1; Tosi 560 §1246); H. himself had been a 'fugax uir' but had lived to tell the tale (2.7.9–10 'Philippos et celerem fugam | sensi'). For another translation of Simonides see 25–6n. and note too 21–2n.

15–16 nec parcit imbellis iuuentae | poplitibus timidoque tergo: the lines repeat, expand and explain the sentiment of 14 ('theme and variation'), which otherwise could have referred to death catching up with the runaway after his return home (as Callin. 1.13–15). *timido* is to be taken with *poplitibus* as well as *tergo* (Naylor xxii §33). Wounds in the back (as opposed to the frontal *honesta uulnera* of Tac. *A.* 1.49.3) are conventionally shameful (cf. e.g. Hom. *Il.* 8.94–5, Tyrt. 11.19–20, Pind. *Nem.* 9.26–7, Cat. 64.339); inflicting wounds in the back of the knees was 'a speciality of the Roman legionary' (P. Hardie on Virg. *Aen.* 9.762–3: cf. Liv. 22.48.4 'tergaque ferientes ac poplites caedentes stragem ingentem…fecerunt') and young recruits were taught how to do it (Veg. *Mil.* 1.11.7 'poplites et crura succidere'): the perspective is no longer Parthian (as in 6b–13) but Roman. *iuuenta* is concrete and collective here, 'young men', as *CS* 45 (*TLL* 7.2.742.1–14; *OLD* 2b is misleading).

17–24 *uirtus* had been the topic of a now lost book by Brutus, H.'s commander at the battle of Philippi (see Moles on Plut. *Brut.* 2.3); Cicero himself had written a *De uirtutibus*, of which only one fragment survives; and Varro too had written a work with the probable title *Marcellus de uirtute*, evidently with reference to one of the contemporary Marcelli (see further Weinstock 230–3). *uirtus* in this and the following stanza of the ode is the manly courage which the young Roman of 1–16 is expected to display on the battlefield by performing outstanding deeds. Now 'demonstrations of prowess in battle – *uirtus* – were rewarded by election to public office and the prestige the office conferred, both of which were denoted by *honos*' (McDonnell 213); but H.'s points in 17–24 are that *uirtus* is not to be seen in terms of such rewards; rather it can lead to immortality. A comparison between soldiering and politics was natural, since these were the two principal spheres of Roman public life.

17 Virtus, repulsae nescia sordidae 'Courage, unfamiliar with sordid/ignominious electoral rejection' (the word order is interlaced): the point is that true *uirtus* is entirely independent of the political process (*OLD nescius* 2), as the stanza proceeds to explain ('theme and variation' again). *nescia* and *sumit aut ponit* (19) contribute to the personification of *Virtus*. There is a typically Horatian contrast between *sordidae* (cf. *Epi*. 1.1.43 'turpemque repulsam') and *intaminatis* (Intro. 26). N–R maintain that H. is here referring to 'the man of *uirtus*' and that 'Augustus is obviously the example in the poet's mind'; but the references to the electoral and political process would then seem crude and undiplomatic, diminishing the all-powerful position of the *princeps*. It is true that in 27 or 26 BC Augustus was presented with a shield testifying to his *uirtus, clementia, iustitia* and *pietas* (*RG* 34.2), which was placed alongside the statue of Victory in the curia (Dio 51.22.1–2); but, although both date and placement are suggestive, it would be odd to prioritise *uirtus* at the expense of the three other qualities and to claim that the presentation had a significant influence on the ode. *uirtus* is repeated at the start of the next stanza (cf. Thomas on 4.1.21), the anaphora resembling Lucilius' famous fragment on *uirtus* (1196–1208W = 1326–38M), to which H. alludes elsewhere (e.g. *S*. 1.1.92, 106, *Epi*. 1.1.41, 1.2.3, 1.18.9).

18–20 intaminatis fulget honoribus | nec sumit aut ponit secures | arbitrio popularis aurae '(Virtus) gleams with untarnishable honours and does not take up or lay down the axes at the whim of popular favour' (*fulgeo* is regularly constructed with the abl.). The axes (*OLD securis* 2b) are synecdochic for the *fasces*, which in turn are metonymical for magisterial office; such office was conventionally the reward for *uirtus* (17–24n.), of which a classic example was M. Claudius Marcellus (3–4n.), 'the prototype of a man of *uirtus*', whose '*uirtus* was matched by his *honores*: he had been consul five times' (Weinstock 232, 230; cf. McDonnell 206–36).[9] Lists of such *honores* would gleam out from the ancestral portraits which, fashioned in precious metal and shaped like a shield (*imagines clipeatae*), great men displayed as a record in their houses (Plin. *NH* 35.4–14, with R. Winkes, *AJA* 83 (1979) 481–4). But H. points out that political *honores* are dependent

---

[9] Marcellus had vowed the first temple to Honos and Virtus at the battle of Clastidium in 222 (Liv. 27.25.7); the most recent had been built by Marius after defeating the Cimbri and Teutoni in 101 (cf. Cic. *Sest*. 116 'cum in templo Virtutis honos habitus esset uirtuti').

on popular favour, which is proverbially fickle (Horsfall on Virg. *Aen.* 6.816; Tosi 477 §1025), and that, even when *honores* have been won, the record of them can tarnish; the real reward for *uirtus* is simply one's own consciousness of the deeds of which it is constituted (cf. Cic. *Rep.* 6 fr. 12 (p. 134 Powell) 'sapientibus conscientia ipsa factorum egregiorum amplissimum uirtutis est praemium'), and this reward of its very nature can neither be taken away from one nor tarnish. The unique *intaminatus* is one of H.'s characteristic adjs. in *in-* (see Intro. 25); for *uirtus...fulget* cf. Plin. *NH* 7.100, Sen. *Ep.* 92.18, [Quint.] *Decl. mai.* 3.18. For the meaning of *aura* see *OLD* 3a; for *arbitrio* cf. [Quint.] *Decl. mai.* 9.12 'arbitrio uentorum'.

21-2 Virtus, recludens immeritis mori | caelum, negata temptat iter uia: despite the different syntax, these difficult lines combine two allusions to Virgil's *Georgics* (3.8-9 'temptanda uia est qua me quoque possim | tollere humo' + 4.52 'caelumque...reclusit'). The main idea is conveyed not by the main verb but by *recludens* (as 3.6.33-4, 3.10.1-2), which explains too that *temptat* represents a successful journey (cf. Ov. *Met.* 14.113 'inuia uirtuti nulla est uia'): 'Virtus, attempting a journey along a route denied [sc. to others], opens up heaven to those who do not deserve to die'. *uirtus* is often associated with journeying (3.24.44n.), and here the journey leads to heaven and immortality (cf. Cic. *Rep.* 6.16 'ea uita uia est in caelum', 26 'bene meritis de patria quasi limes ad caeli aditum patet', an allusion to Enn. fr. 44.3-4 Courtney). Virtue is the *dux itineris*, testing the path and opening up the destination for the deserving: cf. the epigram ascribed to Simonides at *Anth. Pal.* 7.251.3-4 σφ' Ἀρετὴ καθύπερθε | κυδαίνουσ' ἀνάγει δώματος ἐξ Ἀΐδεω ('glorifying Valour brings them [the dead heroes] up from the house of Hades'), where *Arete* 'is plainly personified; it is neither abstract *virtus* nor their personal heroism which performs the act of "*leading them up*" from Hades to the living' (D. L. Page, *Further Greek Epigrams* (1981) 200). H.'s words anticipate the opening theme of the following ode (3.3.1-16), in which Augustus features prominently.

recludere is technical of opening up territory etc. (*OLD* 2b); for *caelum* cf. also Manil. 1.704. For *immeritus* + inf. cf. Stat. *Theb.* 9.657. *temptare iter* is a regular expr. (e.g. Caes. *BG* 1.14.3, Ov. *AA* 1.456, Manil. 2.943, Val. Fl. 3.734); *negata...uia* is an abl. of route (*NLS* 31 §43 (4)): for *negata* cf. Ov. *Her.* 7.170, Sen. *Phaedr.* 224, Plin. *Ep.* 3.16.12.

23-4 coetusque uulgares et udam | spernit humum fugiente penna: *coetus* contrasts with the deserving few (21 *immeritis mori*), while *uulgares* looks back to *popularis aurae* (20). *humus* was thought to be etymologically connected with *humidus/humor* (Maltby 285), designating the earth as characterised by wetness. Virtus was often associated with elevation (3.24.44 (n.)),

Sen. *Ira* 1.21.1 'sublimis et excelsa uirtus', *Vit. beat.* 7.3 'altum quiddam est uirtus, excelsum'), but its description as winged (again at [Quint.] *Decl.* 6.22) seems unusual: is H. thinking of Pegasus, who used his wings (Ov. *Met.* 4.785–6 'pennisque fugacem | Pegason') to reach the heavens (Hes. *Theog.* 285)?

25–6 est et fideli tuta silentio | merces: 'The Romans valued the ability to keep a secret' (N–H on 1.18.16); this expr. of what they valued ('There is also a secure reward for loyal silence') is again (see 14 above) a translation of Simonides, this time 582/291P ἔστι καὶ σιγῆς ἀκίνδυνον γέρας ('There is also a safe reward for silence'), a saying which Augustus used of himself (Plut. *Mor.* 207C) and close to Pind. fr. 180.2 ἔσθ' ὅτε πιστόταται σιγᾶς ὁδοί, 'there is a time when the ways of silence are surest' (cf. *Nem.* 5.18 καὶ τὸ σιγᾶν πολλάκις ἐστὶ σοφώτατον ἀνθρώπῳ νοῆσαι, 'and silence is often the wisest thing for a man to observe'). The virtue of silence – for *silentii uirtus* cf. [Quint.] *Decl.* 19.7 and Breij's n. – is one which H. mentions elsewhere (*S.* 1.3.94–5, 1.4.84–5, *AP* 200) and illustrates by his own relationship with Maecenas (*S.* 2.6.57–8). Ennius described 'the good companion' as one 'qui dicta loquiue tacereue posset' (*Ann.* 285), and the idea was inevitably proverbial (*Dist. Catonis* 1.3.3 'uirtutem primam esse puta compescere linguam'; Tosi 11 §19). For *fideli* (*OLD* 2a) cf. Virg. *Aen.* 3.112 'fida silentia' (of ritual silence, as 3.1.2n.); *merces* (again at 3.3.22) is largely prosaic.

26–8 uetabo qui Cereris sacrum | uulgarit arcanae sub isdem | sit trabibus 'I shall forbid <the man> who has publicised the secret rites of Ceres to be under the same beams [sc. as me]'; for *ueto* + subjunc. cf. Tib. 2.6.36, Pers. 1.112 (*OLD* 2b). The reference is to the so-called Eleusinian Mysteries, celebrated annually at Athens in honour of Demeter, for whom H. substitutes the equivalent Roman name, Ceres (*arcanae* has been transferred from *sacrum* to *Cereris*): see Bremmer 1–20. Augustus had been initiated into the Mysteries after Actium (Dio 51.4.1), and later at Rome he prevented their secrets from being divulged (Suet. *Aug.* 93 with Wardle). Since *isdem...trabibus*, though here referring to a roof (cf. Ov. *Tr.* 3.12.10 'sub trabibus'), translates the Greek compound adj. ὁμότοιχος, H. in the present context may have in mind a passage of Callimachus' *Hymn to Demeter* (6.116–17 Δάματερ, μὴ τῆνος ἐμὶν φίλος, ὅς τοι ἀπεχθής, | εἴη μηδ' ὁμότοιχος, 'Demeter, may the man who is hateful to you never be my friend or share a wall with me').

28–9 fragilemque mecum | soluat phaselon '...or to cast off a flimsy boat with me [sc. as companion]'; Broukhusius anticipated Bentley in conjecturing *fragilemue*, but *-que* often has a disjunctive sense (as 3.1.23–4,

3.29.47–8; *OLD* 7). It was an 'old Greek commonplace that it was dangerous even for an innocent man to risk the perils of the sea in the company of a perjurer' (Knox on Ov. *Her.* 7.57 'nec uiolasse fidem temptantibus aequora prodest', with parallels); H. has evidently transposed the commonplace from a perjurer to a discloser.

29–30 saepe Diespiter | neglectus incesto addidit integrum 'often has Jupiter, when neglected, linked an innocent man with a sinful/unholy one': this sentence, like the next (*saepe ~ raro*), explains the prohibition of 26–29a; it closely resembles Eur. *Suppl.* 226–8 'Considering their lots to be cast together, the gods destroy the healthy and innocent with the troubles of the diseased' (trans. Kovacs).[10] Diespiter is an archaising alternative for Jupiter (Maltby 187–8): H. uses it again at 1.34.5–8 in connection with thunder storms, a likely source of destruction for the flimsy vessel of 28–9. The exact meaning of *incestus* is uncertain (cf. *OLD* 1–2; *TLL* 7.1.893.71–84); for *integer* = 'morally unblemished, upright' see *OLD* 13a; for *addo* see *OLD* 9 (cf. too 4).

31–2 raro antecedentem scelestum | deseruit pede Poena claudo 'rarely has Punishment with/despite her lame foot abandoned a criminal preceding her': retribution was proverbially slow in coming (Otto 111), while Plutarch in his *De sera numinis uindicta* (549A) quotes Euripides to the effect that Justice 'walks with slow foot' (fr. 979). H. has rationalised the latter by making Poena lame. The pursuit of a malefactor by a personified abstraction mirrors 14–16, where Death pursues the runaway.

3

The third ode is opened by two pairs of stanzas. In lines 1–8 H. describes a man who will not be deterred from his purpose; the man is not identified and it is not clear whether he simply represents an idealised Stoic type. In lines 9–16 H. explains that it was 'this quality', also unidentified (9), which led to the apotheosis of Pollux, Hercules, Bacchus and Romulus, in whose company Augustus will find himself in due course (11–12). Since the obvious conclusion seems to be that Augustus is the unnamed man whose determination is outlined in 1–8, the reader might have expected the ode now to illustrate further the achievements which justify the *princeps*' inclusion in divine company. But this is not what happens. Appended to the mention of Romulus is the information that the apotheosis of Rome's

---

[10] The lines were deleted by Lueders.

first ruler had been supported by Juno in a speech to the gods (17–18a), and it is this speech which, apart from the very last stanza (69–72), takes up the remainder of the ode (18b–68).

Juno's speech is delivered before a divine assembly, of which there are five in the *Iliad* and two in the *Odyssey*, with imitations by Ennius in his *Annales* (51–5, with Skutsch) and by Virgil in the *Aeneid* (10.1–117). Indeed the *concilium deorum* is so defining a feature of epic that it was parodied by Lucilius in his satire (5W = 4M): see further M. Hammond, '*Concilia Deorum* from Homer through Milton', *Stud. Philol.* 30 (1933) 1–16, Ll. Morgan, *CQ* 69 (2019) 636–53. The assembly in Ennius dealt with the question of Romulus' apotheosis, on which Juno delivered a speech (*Ann.* 53 'respondit Iuno Saturnia, sancta dearum'), and it seems highly likely that this passage of the *Annales* provided a model for H. in the ode (see Feeney (1984) 185–7).[11]

The ode is thus a bravura introduction of epic into lyric, as H. himself says in the last stanza by means of a characteristic 'break-off' (69–72),[12] and the epic intrusion seems all the greater when Juno's conditional surrendering of her hatred for Troy (57–68) is placed alongside her speech to Jupiter in Book 12 of the *Aeneid* (12.821–8), where some very similar points are made. A question at once arises. Propertius at the end of his second book refers to the forthcoming *Aeneid* in such a way as to indicate that he was familiar with at least the opening of Books 1 and 7 (2.34.63–6):[13]

> qui nunc Aeneae Troiani suscitat *arma*
> iactaque *Lauinis moenia litoribus.*
> cedite, Romani scriptores! cedite, Grai!
> nescio quid *maius nascitur* Iliade.

Propertius is thought to have been writing his book between the years 28 and 25 BC, the very years during which H. was composing his first three books of odes. If Propertius had knowledge of the *Aeneid*, how much more likely is it that H., who described his friend Virgil as the 'half of his soul' (1.3.8), had even more knowledge? Perhaps H. in the ode was intending to produce a 'trailer', as it were, for his friend's epic, resorting to the same

---

[11] Such an assembly would in due course be parodied by Seneca in his *Apocolocyntosis*, where the gods consider whether the emperor Claudius should be admitted to heaven.

[12] Generic interaction has been much studied over the years, esp. with reference to the *Odes*: see e.g. N–R xxvi–xxvii, Harrison (2007) 168–206. The analogous phenomenon of 'inclusion' was discussed by Cairns, *GC* 158–76.

[13] See Horsfall on *Aen.* 7.44–5 for further possibilities.

Ennian source for his *concilium deorum* as that to which Virgil would turn for Juno's last speech in his epic.[14] It is certainly interesting to note the frequency with which parallels for H.'s diction may be found in the *Aeneid* (1n., 29–30n., 43–4n., 45n.).

Juno uses her speech in the ode to express her opposition to the revival of Troy. In many ways this is a surprising theme. The family of Julius Caesar claimed descent from Ascanius, whose other name, Iulus, was associated with ancient Ilion (Virg. *Aen.* 1.267–8), and they were patrons of the contemporary city of the same name (Weinstock 17). Julius Caesar himself granted Ilium various privileges, which it is thought likely that Augustus will have confirmed 'well before 20 BC', the year he is known to have visited the city (Erskine 250). Augustus' extensive building programme at Ilium was 'probably motivated by the same Julian tie' (M. Sage, 'Roman visitors to Ilium in the Roman imperial and late antique period', *Studia Troica* 10 (2000) 213), and he in his turn 'is honoured as god, saviour, benefactor, patron, and kin' by the city (Erskine 251). Although much of this Augustan activity no doubt belongs to the period after publication of the *Odes*, it was presumably part of an ongoing process.

It may have been Julius Caesar's patronage of Ilium which gave rise to the rumours that he proposed to move the capital of the empire there (Nic. Dam. *Caes.* 20, Suet. *DJ* 79.3). It seems unlikely that the rumours had any foundation in fact, yet they were part of a wider phenomenon (P. Ceauşescu, 'Altera Roma', *Historia* 25 (1976) 79–109). Mark Antony was said to have wanted to move the capital from Rome to Alexandria (Dio 50.4.1); Livy, a contemporary of Antony, attributes to early Roman history a proposal to move the capital to Veii (5.51–4, with Ogilvie); and H. himself, in an earlier poem which is echoed here (40–1n.), dealt with the question of whether the Romans should abandon Italy and move to the Isles of the Blest (*Epode* 16 with Watson). Although these various texts are either rumour or fantasy, it is difficult to deny that collectively they betray some sort of socio-political unease. The speech which H. puts into Juno's mouth is perhaps intended not as a contradiction of such proposals but as a declaration of confidence in the future of Rome.

The imaginativeness of the ode is not only generic but chronological. The naming of the *princeps* as 'Augustus' provides the poem with a precise date in the present (11–12n.), but Juno's speech is set in the very distant past. The Trojan War is finished (18–24) but of relatively recent memory (25–8, especially the words *Iam nec*, 'No longer...'); and, since Juno

---

[14] For a survey of the question whether H. was influenced by Virgil or the latter by H. see M. Wigodsky, *Vergil and Early Latin Poetry* (1972) 147.

describes herself as the grandmother of Romulus and Ilia as his mother (31–2), she must be following the tradition that Ilia was the daughter of Aeneas (32n.). Thus only two generations separate the war from Juno's present, which can be defined still more exactly: since the question of her grandson's apotheosis has arisen amongst the gods, they will have required time to familiarise themselves with the full range of his services to mankind, amongst which the principal was the founding of Rome. Juno is therefore speaking at some indeterminate point during Romulus' later years but before his last moments on earth (17–18n.). Yet the majority of her speech (30–68) is cast in the future, as she presents the listening divinities with a vision of Rome's imperial destiny (42b–56). An essential element is the subjugation of Parthia (43–4 'triumphatisque possit | Roma ferox *dare iura* Medis'), which Virgil, using the very same phrase, had combined with Augustus' apotheosis at the conclusion of the *Georgics* (4.560–2):

> Caesar dum magnus ad altum
> fulminat Euphraten bello uictorque uolentes
> per populos *dat iura* uiamque adfectat Olympo.

Since the *princeps*' apotheosis is the theme with which H. had started (11–12), it seems possible that by means of a 'divided allusion' to this passage H. in the ode is paying tribute to his friend's previous work, even as he looks forward also to the next.[15]

METRE Alcaic

1 Iustum et tenacem propositi uirum: the unnamed man is an analogue for Virgil's Aeneas, 'quo iustior alter | nec pietate fuit' (*Aen.* 1.544–5); *iustitia* and *pietas* were two of the four virtues on the shield which was presented to Augustus in 27 or 26 BC (*RG* 34.2). Verbal adjs. in *–ax* are regularly constructed with the genitive (G&L 240 §375): for *tenax* cf. Virg. *Aen.* 4.188 'prauique tenax' (is it simply coincidence that *praua* occurs in H.'s next line?). For *t. propositi* ('tenacious of purpose', 'holding fast to his objective') cf. Ov. *Met.* 10.405, Val. Max. 6.3.5, Quint. 11.1.90.

2 non ciuium ardor praua iubentium: two subjects linked by anaphora of *non* (2–4a) are followed by two linked by anaphora of *neque/nec* (4b–6); the verb common to all of them is *quatit* (4). *ciuium ardor* (for *ardentes ciues*) is an elevated periphrasis. *iubentium* echoes the technical *populus*

---

[15] For 'divided allusion' see Wills 26–7.

COMMENTARY 3.3-8   107

iussit and similar expressions (*OLD iubeo* 5a); *praua* ('crooked') suggests deviation from the straight path implied by *propositi*.

3-4 non uultus instantis tyranni | mente quatit solida 'the face of a threatening tyrant does not shake (him), given his mental firmness': the abl. (perhaps absolute, as translated) seems unduly divorced from *uirum* (1), to whom it refers; perhaps H. intended it to separate, and to be felt equally with, the two pairs of subjects by which it is surrounded (2n.). *tyranni* (cf. 3.2.7) suggests an eastern potentate (contrasting with *ciuium*); for *instantis* cf. Sen. *Contr.* 2.5.4 'instat...tyrannus...uidet intentum tyranni uultum', 2.5.6 'instabat tyrannus': writers conventionally focus on a tyrant's grim face (e.g. Cic. *Off.* 1.112, [Sen.] *Oct.* 110; W. on Tac. *Agr.* 45.2). For *mens solida* cf. Sen. *Ben.* 7.26.4, [Quint.] *Decl.* 272.10; for *quatit* cf. Vell. 110.6 'ut stabilem illum...Caesaris Augusti animum quateret'.

4-5 neque Auster, | dux inquieti turbidus Hadriae: given the epic background to the ode (intro.), it is perhaps relevant that storms are part of 'the furniture of Epic' (M. P. O. Morford, *The Poet Lucan* (1967) 20). Octavian experienced two violent storms on his way back from Actium (Suet. *Aug.* 17.3, Dio 51.4.3): 'The storms of the Adriatic were and are notoriously' (N-H on 1.3.15 'arbiter Hadriae'; cf. 3.9.22-3, 3.27.18-19). In 5 the word order is interlaced.

6 nec fulminantis magna manus Iouis: since we might have expected H. to say 'the thundering hand of mighty Jupiter', there seems to be a double transference of epithets, generating in the process an Homeric allusion (*Il.* 15.694-5 Ζεύς...| χειρὶ μάλα μεγάλῃ, 'Zeus...with his very great hand', but the context is quite different). Augustus famously escaped being struck by lightning while on campaign in Spain in 26/25 BC, as a result of which he vowed the temple of Jupiter Tonans: the temple, on the Capitoline Hill, was dedicated on 1 September 22 BC (EJ p. 51) and was in the process of construction when H. published *Odes* 1-3 (*RG* 19.2 with Cooley, Suet. *Aug.* 29.3 with Wardle). It would feature on the coinage (*RIC* 1².46 no. 59). Nouns and their adjs. are here chiastic (contrast 5 above).

7-8 si fractus illabatur orbis, | impauidum ferient ruinae: 'The present subjunctive in the protasis indicates a hypothesis, the future indicative in the apodosis implies certainty' (N-R): the combination of moods and tenses is common in Cicero and appears to be regular (Pease on Cic. *ND* 3.47). *orbis* here = 'the vault of heaven' (*OLD* 7c): the image is that of a ceiling breaking up and crashing down (*OLD illabor* 2), the cascading masonry (*OLD ruina* 4) striking anyone beneath; the image relates to the proverbial *caelum ruit* (Otto 61), used by Housman in his famous *Epitaph on an Army of Mercenaries* commemorating the First Battle of Ypres in the autumn of 1914 ('These, in the day when heaven was falling...'). H.'s generalisation forms a hyperbolical climax to lines 1–6. For *ferient ruinae* cf. Sil. 14.678.

9–16 There was a canon of heroes who had achieved divine status by their services to humanity (*Epi.* 2.1.6 'post ingentia facta deorum in templa recepti'). The list varies from text to text (see e.g. 1.12.25–33, 4.8.29–34, *Epi.* 2.1.5) but Castor, Pollux, Hercules, Bacchus and Romulus appear regularly (see e.g. N–H on 1.12.25, Brink on *Epi.* 2.1.5–6, Pease on Cic. *ND* 2.62, Dyck on Cic. *Leg.* 2.19).

9 hac arte Pollux... 'It was because of this quality that Pollux...': *hac* (sc. *arte*) is repeated in anaphora at 13 and 15 below and the whole passage (9–16) presents four individuals (matching the four subjects of 1–6) who have achieved divine status through 'this quality'. The quality itself has not been named: *ars* was sometimes identified with *uirtus* by way of Greek *arete* (Prob. *GL* 4.47.17K 'ἀπὸ τῆς ἀρετῆς, a uirtute'; cf. Maltby 54–5), but the reference is to line 1 and many scholars sum it up by *constantia*. Pollux (along with his brother Castor) protected seafarers, among other benefits (3.29.64; N–H on 1.12.27); see also B. Poulsen, 'The Dioscuri and ruler ideology', *SO* 66 (1991) 119–46; G. S. Sumi, 'Monuments and memory: the Aedes Castoris in the formation of Augustan ideology', *CQ* 59 (2009) 167–86, esp. 181–3.

9–10 uagus Hercules | enisus: 'When a noun has two epithets, Horace frequently places them on either side of the noun' (Naylor xxii §34). Hercules, in addition to his beneficial Labours (to which *enisus* refers), was also seen as a road-builder and the like; he too was prominent in Augustan ideology (3.14.4n.; N–H on 2.12.6) and was indeed a prototype for the deification of Romulus (Feeney (1984) 187–9). For *uagus* cf. Stat. *Silv.* 4.3.155.

10 arces attigit igneas: *attigit* ('reached': *OLD* 6a) applies to both Pollux and Hercules and illustrates H.'s 'tendency to prefer a verb in the singular to one in the plural, in spite of two or more subjects preceding or following it' (Brink (1982) 31); again at *uertit* (20) below. *arces...igneas* are the stars, standing for heaven by metonymy.

11–12 quos inter Augustus recumbens | purpureo bibet ore nectar: the placing of *inter* after the word it governs (anastrophe) is often found in both verse and prose, although this is the only such example in the *Odes*

(3.23.10 is slightly different). H.'s insertion of Augustus' name in the list of deities resembles its official insertion, likewise in a divine list, in the hymn of the Salii (*RG* 10.1 with Cooley). Octavian received the name Augustus on 16 January 27 BC (EJ p. 45): H. repeats it at 3.5.3 but generally prefers the name Caesar, which in Book 3 he uses at 4.37, 14.3, 14.16 and 25.4. Twice he combines both names (2.9.19, *Epi.* 2.2.48). Since nectar was described by Homer as red (*Il.* 19.38, *Od.* 5.93), it seems likely that *purpureo...ore* refers to Augustus' 'purple-stained mouth' (so S. Pulleyn, *Mnem.* 50 (1997) 482–4). Elsewhere similar expressions are used of a girl's mouth (Cat. 45.12 (kissing), Simon. 585/293P (speaking)). Some think the meaning here is 'with shining face' (as Stat. *Theb.* 3.441, of Aurora), as befits a newly deified hero (cf. Virg. *Aen.* 1.589–91 'os umerosque deo similis...|...lumenque iuuentae | purpureum'); whether H. intended us to see Augustus as a *triumphator* (J. S. C. Eidinow, *CQ* 50 (2000) 463–71) will depend on whether triumphing generals painted their faces red, which has been doubted (Beard 231–2). H.'s picture of the *princeps* dining with other divinities (*OLD recumbo* 3a), reminiscent of Ptolemy I Soter feasting with the other Olympians at Theocr. 17.22, supports the argument (of e.g. O. Hekster and J. Rich, *CQ* 56 (2006) 161) that the so-called 'banquet of the gods', at which Octavian and others were accused by Mark Antony of having dressed up as gods for a dinner party (cf. Suet. *Aug.* 70.1), was a fiction.

13–14 hac te merentem, Bacche pater, tuae | uexere tigres 'your tigers, Father Bacchus, conveyed you [*sc.* to heaven], deserving as you were because of this <quality>': *pater*, commonly used of various gods (*OLD* 6a), was esp. applied to Bacchus (N–H on 1.18.6, NA on Lygd. 6.38). For tigers rather than the more normal panthers as Bacchus' draught animals see e.g. Virg. *Aen.* 6.805 (with Horsfall), Ov. *Am.* 1.2.47–8 (with McKeown): scholars believe that the substitution goes back to (now lost) Hellenistic texts, since no tiger was seen in Rome until after *Odes* 1–3 were published (Plin. *NH* 8.65, Suet. *Aug.* 43.4 with Wardle, Dio 54.9.8).

14–15 indocili iugum | collo trahentes 'drawing the chariot with untrainable neck': *trahentes* (rather than, say, *ferentes*) suggests that *iugum* (lit. 'yoke') is here standing for the chariot itself (*OLD* 3b); its combination with *indocili* is an oxymoron.

15–16 hac Quirinus | Martis equis Acheronta fūgit 'it was because of this <quality> that Quirinus escaped Acheron on the horses of Mars' (for *fugere* = 'to succeed in avoiding' see *OLD* 12a). The demonstrative *hac* both concludes the anaphoric sequence (cf. 9, 13) and effects the transition to the case of Romulus (cf. 3.5.13 '*hoc* cauerat mens prouida Reguli',

3.27.25 'sic et Europe...'). Romulus is referred to as Quirinus, an ancient Sabine god, in various Augustan poets (e.g. 1.2.46, *S.* 1.10.32, *Epo.* 16.13, Virg. *G.* 3.27, *Aen.* 1.292, 6.859, Ov. *F.* 2.475–6), reflecting an identity which had come into being at an unknown point in the republic. The name often refers to Romulus in his divinised aspect, as on the statue set up in Augustus' Forum: 'receptusque in deorum numerum Quirinus appellatus est' (*ILS* 64; for the phraseology see 9–16n. above). There were various stories about the end of Romulus' life: according to one of them, perhaps first found in Ennius (*Ann.* 54–5: see Skutsch ad loc. and pp. 260–1), he was carried up to heaven by Mars, his father, in a chariot: this is the version favoured by Ovid in the *Fasti* (2.496 'rex patriis astra petebat equis') and *Metamorphoses* (14.805–28) and alluded to by H. here. Romulus, who was the first Roman to be added to the canon of benefactors (9–16n.), qualified for divine status because he had been the founder of Rome: there had been a proposal that Octavian, as the 'second founder' of the city, should adopt the name Romulus, and the man himself was initially enthusiastic (Dio 53.16.7–8); but it was realised that this might imply monarchic ambitions, so 'Augustus' was chosen instead (11–12n.; see Suet. *Aug.* 7.2 and Wardle). On all this see esp. Myers on Ov. *Met.* 14.805–28 (pp. 200–2) and 818–24 (p. 205). For escaping Acheron see Pind. fr. 143 πορθμὸν πεφευγότες Ἀχέροντος ('having escaped the crossing of Acheron', of the gods); for *Martis equi(s)* cf. Virg. *G.* 3.91, Ov. *RA* 6, Val. Fl. 3.90.

17–18 gratum elocuta consiliantibus | Iunone diuis 'Juno having spoken something welcome to the deliberating gods': *gratum* is the direct object of *elocuta* (the neut. adverbial accus. does not occur until the late writer Dracontius: *TLL* 6.2.2264.84–2265.1); *elocuta* is a genuine past tense rather than a timeless (or 'aoristic') participle: 'It seems to be taken for granted that Horace sets the council after Romulus has been snatched away by Mars...But this snatching away is part of what the council is there to decide' (Feeney (1984) 186 n. 43). It is striking that H. should introduce the principal part of the ode by means of his favourite appended abl. abs. (3.1.30–1n.). *consiliantibus diuis* is H.'s version of the very common expr. *concilium deorum* (for which see also 3.25 intro.); Juno's speech belongs to the *genus deliberatiuum*, which consists 'in consultatione, quod habet in se suasionem et dissuasionem' (*Rhet. Herenn.* 1.2): for this and the two other *genera* (judicial and epideictic) see Lausberg 30–4 §§59–62. The word order of the whole is interlaced.

18b–68 Juno's speech is framed by two passages on Troy, both of which are exactly 12 lines long (18a–30a the Trojan War is over ~ 57–68 Troy must not be reborn); within this frame are three very unequal passages: 30b–33a Juno's surrender [3], 33b–36 Romulus' apotheosis [3½], 37–56 the Roman empire [20]. It will be seen that the apotheosis of Romulus occupies the central portion of the speech (and is placed at almost exactly the mathematical centre of the poem as a whole); yet, though the deification is the principal subject of the speech, it is dealt with in less than a stanza.

18 Ilion, Ilion: this could be the accus. either of feminine *Ilios* or of neut. *Ilion*. Since *Ilios*, the form used by Homer, is used by H. elsewhere in the nom. and accus. (cf. 4.9.18, *Epo.* 14.14 'obsessam Ilion'), feminine seems marginally more likely. Repetition for effect is variously classified and variously named (see Lausberg 274–9 §§607–22); this particular example occurs twice in Euripides (*Or.* 1381, *Tro.* 806), in both cases the context being the destruction of the city; and the same noun occurs at the beginning of four successive lines in the later poet Dionysius Periegetes (815–18). The city's alternative name, 'Troia', is repeated at 60–1 below (n.) and Wills has suggested (145) that H. is alluding to, and varying, the other occasion on which *Troia* is repeated in two passages within the same poem (Cat. 68B.88–90 and 99–100). Repetitions are a striking feature of Juno's speech to Jupiter at *Aen.* 12.819–28 (820 *pro... pro...*, 821–2 *cum...cum...*, 823–4 *ne..neu...*, 826–7 *sit...sint...sit...*, 828 *occidit occideritque*).

19–21 fatalis incestusque iudex | et mulier peregrina uertit | in puluerem: the *iudex* is Paris, the reference being to his famous Judgement, when Aphrodite, bribing him with the promise of Helen, the most beautiful woman in the world, persuaded him to pronounce her the winner over Hera and Athena in a divine beauty contest. He is *fatalis* because his choice was both fateful, in that it led to Hera's unremitting hostility and hence to the Trojan War, and fatal, in that the war brought untold slaughter (*OLD fatalis* 1, 4); the adj. alludes to his names as found in e.g. Alcman 77 Δύσπαρις Αἰνόπαρις κακὸν Ἑλλάδι ('Paris the Evil, Paris the Grim, a disaster for Greece' (Loeb trans.)). Paris is *incestus* (3.2.29–30n.) both because he was corrupted by Aphrodite's bribe and because Helen was already married (to Menelaus). The *mulier peregrina*, like the γυναῖκα βάρβαρον at Eur. *Andr.* 649, is Helen, whom Juno disdains to name; she is 'foreign' because she came from Sparta (H. has perhaps borrowed the expression from the description of Tanaquil at Liv. 1.47.6, although it could equally derive from a now lost passage of Ennius or other author). *uertit in puluerem* seems to be a unique variant on *uertere in cinerem* (at e.g. Ov. *Her.* 1.24 'uersa est in cinerem sospite Troia uiro'); *uertit* (see *OLD* 22a for the constr. with *in* + accus.) is perfect tense: for the singular form with two subjects see above, 10n.

21–3 ex quo destituit deos | mercede pacta Laomedon, mihi | castaeque damnatam Mineruae: the transmitted *damnatum* was changed by Glareanus to *damnatam* on account of the gender of *Ilion* in 18 (n.); a slight ambiguity nevertheless still remains, since *puluis* (21), though usually masc., is very occasionally fem. (see *OLD*). *ex quo* (sc. *tempore* or *die*) = 'from the time that' (*OLD qui*¹ 15c) and is to be taken with *damnatam*. The meaning of *damnatam*, however, is unclear. The background, provided in the *ex quo* clause, is that Laomedon, father of Priam and grandfather of Paris, had promised Apollo and Poseidon a reward for helping to build the walls of Troy but he went back on his word and refused to pay them. Since this story has nothing to do with the hostility of Juno/Hera and Minerva/Athena to Troy (19–21n.), it seems odd to translate 'condemned by me and chaste Minerva from the time that...', as if the two goddesses *were* involved in the story after all. The alternative, supported by numerous scholars, is to render 'consigned to me and to chaste Minerva from the time that...', as if the hostility caused by the Judgement of Paris was preordained from the time of Laomedon's fraud. For the use of *damno* scholars compare Prop. 4.6.21 'altera classis erat Teucro damnata Quirino' (*OLD damno* 4a; Pease on Virg. *Aen.* 4.699). Another question is whether *mercede pacta* is an abl. of separation (as if *destituit* = *fraudauit*) or an abl. abs.; the former (so *OLD destituo* 7) is probably right but it is difficult to be sure. Thus the lines mean: 'consigned to me and to chaste Minerva [sc. for destruction] from the time that Laomedon deprived the gods of the agreed reward'. *castae*, contrasting with *incestus* (19), is an allusion to the virginity of Minerva/Athena (1.7.5).

24 cum populo et duce fraudulento is distantly reminiscent of the Homeric formula which at *S.* 2.3.195 is rendered as 'populus Priami Priamusque'. The *dux* is Laomedon (21–3n.).

25–6 iam nec Lacaenae splendet adulterae | famosus hospes 'No longer does the notorious guest shine for the Spartan adulteress' (*splendeo* + dat. recurs at *Epi.* 1.5.7). Paris had entered Menelaus' house as his guest, and his breach of hospitality – he was called ξεναπάτης, 'host-deceiver', in Greek – was 'a serious aggravation of his offence' (N–H on 1.15.2): see e.g. Aesch. *Ag.* 399–402, Ov. *Her.* 17.3–4 'ausus es hospitii temeratis aduena sacris | legitimam nuptae sollicitare fidem'. *splendet* suggests strongly that H. has in mind the episode in *Iliad* 3 where Aphrodite rescues Paris from his duel with Menelaus and then urges Helen to join him in bed: he is

COMMENTARY 3.26-33   113

'shining in his beauty', says the goddess (3.392 κάλλεϊ τε στίλβων). *famosus* (a word not used by Cat. Lucr. Caes. Virg. Prop. Tib.) is perhaps intended to alert readers to the allusion (that is, a form of 'Alexandrian footnote': see 3.5.41n.).

26-8 nec Priami domus | periura pugnaces Achiuos | Hectoreis opibus refringit 'and the perjurious house/family of Priam does not (any longer) break the Greek fighters with the help of Hector'. The language is elevated. *Priami domus* is an Ennian phrase (*Trag.* 87J) which Cicero quoted three times (*De or.* 3.102, 3.217, *TD* 3.44); *opibus...Hector* occurs earlier in the same Ennian passage (*Trag.* 80J); *pugnaces Achiuos* recalls such Homeric formulae as μεγάθυμοι Ἀχαιοί ('great-souled Achaeans': *Il.* 1.123 etc.); the use of the adj. *Hectoreus* (frequent in the *Aeneid*, e.g. 2.543, 3.304, where Horsfall says that Virgil is the first to use it) instead of the genitive *Hectoris* is a feature of the high style (N-H on 1.4.17, Horsfall on *Aen.* 7.1) and reminiscent of the Homeric Ἑκτόρεος. *refringere* is used by Ennius in a famous line of the *Annales* (226). For *periura* cf. Sen. *Ag.* 863 'mendax Dardanidae domus'.

29-30 nostrisque ductum seditionibus | bellum resedit 'and the war drawn out by our dissensions has subsided': *nostris = de(or)um* or *diuinis*: Juno, Minerva and Neptune opposed the Trojans, while Mars, Apollo and Venus supported them. *ducere bellum* is common in verse and prose (cf. *OLD duco* 24), but *bellum residere* recurs only at Virg. *Aen.* 9.643; the repetition '*sedit*ionibus... re*sedit* ' seems deliberate (cf. [Quint.] *Decl. mai.* 13.9 'si diuersis regibus coorta *seditio* ad bellum inflammauit iras, exiguo puluere uel unius poena ducis re*sidit* omnis tumor') but the point unclear.

30-3 protinus et graues | iras et inuisum nepotem | ...Marti redonabo: the easiest way of understanding this difficult sentence is to assume that the verb, which is almost exclusive to H. (again at 2.7.3 and Apul. *Apol.* 89 but in a different sense), is here being used both instead of *condonabo* and synleptically in the two senses 'to give up or set aside in favour of' and 'to grant the pardon of a person to an intercessor' (*OLD condono* 5, 4): 'forthwith I shall both give up my fierce anger for Mars' sake and shall grant to him the pardon of my hated grandson'. In the *Aeneid* Juno is associated with anger from the fourth line (1.4 'saeuae memorem Iunonis ob iram'; cf. 5.781 'Iunonis grauis ira'); the 'hated grandson' is Romulus (32n.), whose admittance to heaven is the subject of the *concilium deorum* (17-18n.): his father was Mars (32n.), who was therefore also the father of the Roman race (Liv. *praef.* 7).

32 Troica quem peperit sacerdos: Romulus' mother had two identities: she was Ilia, daughter of Aeneas, and she was Rhea Silvia, a Vestal Virgin (the juxtaposition of *sacerdos* with *peperit* is contemptuous): *Troica...sacerdos* combines the two traditions without mentioning either name. Since her son was fathered by Mars, who was himself son of Juno, Romulus was Juno's grandson (*nepotem*, 31). See Feeney (1984) 190 and n. 72.

33–4 lucidas | ĭnire sedes: Olympus was conventionally 'gleaming' (Hom. *Il.* 13.243, Soph. *Ant.* 610); for *sedes* of the gods' heavenly abode, as Virg. *Aen.* 10.3 'sideream in sedem', see *OLD* 5b. For *ĭnire* see Intro. 30.

34–5 ducere nectaris | sucos: it is difficult to choose between *discere* ('to get to know': *OLD* 2a) and *ducere* ('to drink': *OLD* 25b), but the latter both seems more natural and provides a closer parallel between Romulus and Augustus (12 'bibet...nectar'). *nectaris sucos* is imitated by Auson. *Epist.* 12 (p. 207G).

35–6 adscribi quietis | ordinibus patiar deorum: *quietus*, a conventional epithet for the gods (Pease on Virg. *Aen.* 4.379), has been described as 'quite inappropriate here' (Gow). But perhaps Juno is referring to her present audience, sitting in rows in front of her (*OLD ordo* 1b) and listening attentively to her speech (cf. *gratum*, 17) – unlike the gods in Lucian's satirical *Concilium deorum*, who dislike the main character's speech and start hissing (13). Or perhaps she is contrasting the gods' current harmony with the time when they were at loggerheads (29–30n.). *adscribo* = 'to reckon a person as belonging to a category', 'to assign' (*OLD* 3a, quoting this passage).

37–8 dum longus inter saeuiat Ilion | Romamque pontus 'Provided that there is an extensive sea raging between Troy and Rome' (for this sense of *dum* + subjunc. see *NLS* 178–9 §220). *pontus* (Greek πόντος) is an elevated term for 'sea', first found in Ennius (*Ann.* 217) and very common in the *Aeneid*; *longus* seems an unusual adj. to describe the sea (again with *pontus* at Val. Fl. 1.127, Stat. *Ach.* 2.22, with *mare* at e.g. Sen. *NQ* 5.18.10, and with *fluctus* at 3.27.42–3 below (n.)) but is perhaps used 'with reference to the length of time needed to traverse it' (*OLD longus* 4a): Greek and Latin writers regularly describe distance in such terms (Oakley on Liv. 9.9.13 'tridui iter expeditis erat'). The separation of *longus* and *pontus* (hyperbaton) is mimetic. *saeuire* is a regular word for the raging of the sea (*OLD* 3a); its transposition with *inter* here produces 'the illusion of a compound' (Shorey) on the analogy of e.g. *interfluo*.

38–9 qualibet exules | in parte regnanto beati 'let the exiles rule happily in whatever clime they like': *qualibet* is dismissive and *exules* contemptuous. *pars* is a 'geographical' term (3.24.36–8n.) and alludes to the extent of the Roman empire which Juno outlines in the following stanzas. *regnanto* is a third-person plur. fut. imperative.

40–2 dum Priami Paridisque busto | insultet armentum et catulos ferae | celent inultae: evidently the tomb of Paris was pointed out to travellers on the Plain of Troy (Strabo 13.1.33); there were various versions of Priam's death (see Austin on Virg. *Aen.* 2.506–58) but *Anth. Pal.* 7.136 is the only ref. to a tomb; whether the singular *busto*, which is dat. with *insultet* but abl. with *celent* (Grimm 20), is intended to imply that father and son shared a tomb is unclear. *insultet* has reminded scholars of Greek passages where individuals leap on a tomb (Hom. *Il.* 4.177, Eur. *El.* 327), but *armentum* normally applies to plough-animals (Varr. *LL* 5.96), which can scarcely be imagined as leaping anywhere. The verb must either have the less dramatic meaning of 'trample upon' (cf. *OLD* 1a) or the metaphorical meaning of 'behave insultingly towards' (*OLD* 3a): whether the latter constitutes a euphemism for fouling, a frequent fate of tombs (*S.* 1.8.37–8 with Gowers' n., *AP* 471 with Brink's n.),[16] will depend upon whether the imagined edifice can also accommodate the young of wild animals: 'provided that a herd outrages the tomb of Priam and Paris and wild beasts hide their young in it with impunity'. For wild beasts inhabiting graveyards cf. *S.* 1.8.17–18; *inultae* simply means that the animals can use the site undisturbed, because all humans have left. H.'s picture is similar to that which, in despair at the renewal of civil war, he foretold of Rome at *Epo.* 16.9–14; but, whereas those lines were a prelude to the suggestion that Rome should be abandoned immediately and its citizens sail off to the Isles of the Blest, the present passage prefaces a prediction of the opposite – the assured future of Rome and its empire.

42–3 stet Capitolium | fulgens: the temple of Jupiter Optimus Maximus on the Capitoline Hill at Rome symbolised the eternity of the city (1.37.6–8, 3.30.8–9, Virg. *Aen.* 9.448–9, Luc. 10.63; *TLL* Suppl. 2.164.53ff.). According to the elder Pliny (*NH* 33.57) the temple was gilded twice, first in 146 BC and then by Q. Lutatius Catulus after a fire in 83 BC (Cic. *Verr.* 4.69).[17] Hence Virgil's *Capitolia...aurea* (*Aen.* 8.347–8); for *fulgens* cf. Sen. *Contr.* 1.6.4. *stare* here = 'continue to stand/remain stable/endure' (*OLD*

---

[16] A similar question arises at Prop. 2.8.20 'insultetque rogis'.
[17] The temple was restored by Augustus, probably at a much later date (*RG* 20.1 with Cooley).

15–17); the jussive subjunctive ('let the gleaming Capitol...') parallels *regnanto* above (39).

43–4 triumphatisque possit | Roma ferox dare iura Medis: *Medis* is a 'more poetically grandiose' term than *Parthis* (Powell 160) and recurs once in the Alcaic Hexad (3.5.9) and once elsewhere in Book 3 (8.19–20); when taken in the context of H.'s other references to Parthia, it can be seen as an allusion to Augustus' current strategy for dealing with that country (3.2, intro.). In 3.2 it is the Parthians who are 'defiant' (3.2.3 '*Parthos feroces*'), but in our ode Juno is speaking and expressing a wish for the fulfilment of the Augustan policy. Though *dare iura* is a set expression (see *TLL* 7.2.682.70–3), here it seems to allude to Virg. *G.* 4.560–2 (see intro.). For trans. *triumphare* see Horsfall on Virg. *Aen.* 6.836, McKeown on Ov. *Am.* 1.14.46; *OLD* 3b.

45–6 horrenda late nomen in ultimas | extendat oras: the subject of *extendat* (another jussive subjunc.) is *Roma*, continuing on from 44. *horrenda late* = 'widely to be feared' (lit. 'to be shuddered at'); the only other author to combine *horreo* and *late* is Virgil (*Aen.* 11.601–2): in his case the verb is intrans. (cf. 7.525–6 'late | horrescit'), although *horrendus* is in general one of his favourite words. Some edd. take *nomen* (3.5.10–11n.) almost as = 'empire' here; but the actual *name* of Rome was not only talismanic (the Greek ῥώμη = 'strength', a frequent pun) but closely associated with Romulus (Enn. *Ann.* 77) and the obliteration of the name of Troy (Virg. *Aen.* 12.828 '*occideritque sinas cum nomine Troia*'). See Feeney (1984) 191.

46–7 qua medius liquor | secernit Europen ab Afro: the 'intervening water' (for this use of *medius* cf. e.g. Liv. 32.10.8 '*dirempti medio amni*'; *OLD medius*[1] 3) is the Straits of Gibraltar, marking the western extremity of the known world. The clause is said to allude to Enn. *Ann.* 302 '*Europam Libyamque rapax ubi diuidit unda*', but, whereas Ennius has used two place names, *Afro* and almost certainly *Europen* too are personal nouns and stand for their respective continents by metonymy; whether *Afro* intends us to think of Hannibal ('*dirus*...*Afer*' at 4.4.42) is unclear. For other descriptions of the Straits see Pease on Cic. *ND* 3.24.

48 qua tumidus rigat arua Nilus: various aspects of the River Nile attracted the wonder of the ancients, one of them being the flood which irrigated the surrounding countryside each summer (see e.g. Pease on Cic. *ND* 2.130; R. French, *Ancient Natural History* (1994) 110–13): if *tumidus*, regular of swollen rivers (*OLD* 3), suggests also an allusion to the

Nile's deposits of silt (cf. Cic. loc. cit., Cat. 11.7, Virg. *G.* 4.290), there is a contrast with *liquor* (46), which suggests clear water. Since it was a standard theme of encomium that the ruler's empire stretches 'from east to west' (see e.g. W. on Vell. 126.3), the river is presumably intended to represent the east (see last n.).

49–52 aurum irrepertum et sic melius situm, | cum terra celat, spernere fortior | quam cogere humanos in usus | omne sacrum rapiente dextra: this stanza, deleted by some 19th-century edd., is extremely difficult. Many edd. start a new sentence at *aurum irrepertum* (and place a comma after *dextra*, 52), but the reference to buried gold combines well with references to the Straits of Gibraltar (46–7) and the Nile (48): Spain was famous for its gold mines (3.6.31n.), while Diodorus Siculus, an older contemporary of H., describes in detail the gold mines in the territories adjacent to the upper reaches of the Nile (3.11.4–14.5). It therefore seems preferable to place a comma after *Nilus* (48) and to continue the sentence to *dextra* (52); *fortior* (50), like *horrenda* (45), agrees with *Roma* (44): for such continuative adjs. see Nisbet, *OR* 396.

The stanza admits of various interpretations, of which the likeliest seems to be this: '(Rome) more resolved upon spurning undiscovered gold...than upon collecting it for human use with hands which seize everything sacred'. That is: Juno's wish is that Rome will not exploit the mineral resources of distant countries by mining them. (It is obviously pointed that the distant countries in question are those where there were gold mines: see above.) On this interpretation, line 52 has nothing to do with pillaging shrines and temples, as is usually thought, but refers to the gold in the earth: H. is adopting the view that mineral deposits are divine products (cf. Tac. *G.* 5.2), whether the divinity be Nature (Cic. *Div.* 1.116 'aurum...natura diuina genuisset') or sacred mother Earth (Plin. *NH* 33.1 'sacrae parentis') or a nameless god (Sen. *Ben.* 4.6.1 'tot metalla <deus> defodit'):[18] in other words, *aurum irrepertum* is an example of *omne sacrum*. The abl. *rapiente dextra* is perhaps more likely to be instrumental than another ex. of an appended abl. abs. (3.1.30–1n.). A good comment on *rapiente* is the lambasting of the Romans by the British chieftain, Calgacus, at Tac. *Agr.* 30.4–5 'raptores orbis...auferre, trucidare, rapere falsis nominibus imperium...appellant'; for the notion that Roman imperialism is not motivated by mercenary considerations see further 54–6n. below. *irrepertus*, which recurs only at Sen. *Med.* 648, negatives Lucretius'

---

[18] *deus* is an editorial supplement (the sentence otherwise lacks a subject), but Seneca elsewhere (e.g. *Ep.* 94.56–7) regards gold and other precious minerals as products of Nature, which is simply god by another name (*Ben.* 4.8.3, *NQ* 2.45.2).

aurum...repertum (5.1113, 1241) and is only one of several of H.'s favoured negative compounds in the ode (5, 8, 14, 19): see Intro. 25. For *fortis* = 'resolute' etc. see *OLD* 7a; its use + infin., which recurs at 1.37.26 (see N–H) and *S.* 2.7.85–6, illustrates another favoured construction (Intro. 25). For *sacer* = 'sacrosanct' see *OLD* 5.

49–50 et sic melius situm, | cum terra celat: *sic* looks forward to the *cum*-clause: 'undiscovered and better situated thus, when the earth hides it'.[19] For 'hidden' gold see Pease on Cic. *ND* 2.98; for the moral dangers of mining it see e.g. Ov. *Met.* 1.138–40, Sen. *NQ* 5.15.1–2, *Ep.* 90.45, 94.57, Ben. 7.1.6, 7.10.2, Plin. *NH* 33.1–3.

53 quicumque mundo terminus obstitit 'Whatever boundary has acted as a block on the world' (*OLD terminus* 2a): the sense seems equivalent to 'wherever the furthest limit of the world is'. *mundo terminus* perhaps alludes to the Homeric πείρατα γαίης, 'boundaries of the earth' (*Il.* 14.200 etc.): H. is dealing with the notion that the earth is a mass surrounded by boundaries (cf. J. S. Romm, *The Edges of the Earth in Ancient Thought* (1992) 10–13), and, after referring to the western and eastern extremities in 46–8 above, he is about to refer to the remaining two points of the compass in 55–6 below. This is an alternative geographical perspective to that adumbrated at 3.24.36–41 (n.).

54 hunc tangat armis 'this let her reach with her armies' (the subject continues to be *Roma* from 44). For *tangat* see *OLD* 7.

54–6 uisere gestiens | qua parte debacchentur ignes, | qua nebulae pluuiique rores: the subjunc. *debacchentur* indicates that *uisere* is constructed with an indir. question (*OLD uiso* 1b): 'yearning to go and see in what clime...'. Fraenkel (270–2) is eloquent on the theme of Graeco-Roman exploration (see further R. Seager, '*Neu sinas Medos equitare inultos*: Horace, the Parthians and Augustan foreign policy', *Athenaeum* 58 (1980) 108–10, and esp. Powell 179–81). The association of the world's boundaries with a strong desire to see them is above all characteristic of Alexander the Great (see e.g. Curt. 4.8.3 'cupido...incesserat...etiam Aethiopiam inuisere'; Goodyear on Tac. *A.* 1.61.1). *ignes* refers to the sun (*OLD* 4a) and stands for the South: P. Petronius, prefect of Egypt, had advanced into Ethiopia in 25/24 BC and captured the town of Nabata but 'was unable to advance further because of the sand and the heat' (Dio 54.5.5). Mists and drizzle (which is what *nebulae pluuiique rores* seems to

---

[19] SB places commas after *aurum* and *celat*.

mean) are not uncommonly combined (e.g. Luc. 6.375–6 'nec umentis nebulas nec rore madentem | aera') and here stand for the North (cf. Tac. *Agr.* 12.3 'caelum crebris imbribus ac nebulis foedum'): H. elsewhere talks as if an invasion of Britain were imminent (1.21.14–16, 1.35.29–30, 3.5.3–4). South and North here ('qua...qua...') balance the West and East of 46–8 ('qua...qua...'); cf. 1.22.17–22. *pars*, as at 38–9, is a 'geographical' term (3.24.36–8n.). *debacchari* ('to rave, rage'), which otherwise occurs only at Ter. *Ad.* 184–5, is perhaps suitable only for *ignes*; if so, we have to understand some other verb (e.g. *incedant*, 'come on': *OLD* 6a) by zeugma.

57–8 sed bellicosis fata Quiritibus | hac lege dico, ne...: *fata* refers to the Romans' destiny as outlined from 42 (perhaps even from 33) onwards; its combination with *dico* suggests that Juno sees herself as a *fatidica* or prophet. *hac lege...ne...* = 'on this condition, that...not...' (*OLD lex* 12c). Is it simply coincidence that Juno's speech in the *Aeneid* displays the sequence *fati...lege...ne...neu...* (12.819–24)? Although *Quirites* sometimes refers to 'civilians' as opposed to soldiers (*OLD* 1c), *bellicosis* suggests that Juno is associating the name with *Quiritis*, which is one of her own names and said to be derived from the word κύρις, allegedly an ancient word for 'spear' (Plut. *Romul.* 29.1, *Quaest. Rom.* 285c; Maltby 517). Statues of Juno often depict her as leaning on a spear.

58–60 ne nimium pii | rebusque fidentes auitae | tecta uelint reparare Troiae: the Romans' excessive devotion to their ancestors (*nimium pii* is an oxymoron) is identified by Juno as one possible motivation for the rebuilding of Troy (for which see intro.). It is difficult to know exactly what is meant by *rebus*: similar phraseology elsewhere (Plaut. *Capt.* 536, *Merc.* 363, Cic. *Att.* 10.8.2, Sil. 10.379) draws from translators 'situation', 'fortunes', 'success' as seems appropriate; another possibility here is 'wealth'. *nimium* extends also to *fidentes* and constitutes a reluctant tribute to the Rome of the future. For the *fumantia tecta* of Troy (Ov. *Met.* 13.421) see Horsfall on Virg. *Aen.* 3.3. *uelint* is perhaps 'seek, aim' (*OLD* 16).

61 Troiae: the repetition of a word from the end of one sentence at the start of the next (again at 3.16.15, 4.8.11; Bo 3.402) is said by Quint. 9.3.44 to be common in poetry: here the effect is heightened because the repetition occurs not only across lines (often called epanalepsis) but stanzas. For discussion and exs. see Wills 394–7, who notes that *iterabitur* below (62) is a self-referential allusion to the repetition (a modified form of which is at 3.2.13–14 (n.)). See also 18n. above, where an alternative name for Troy is repeated.

61 alite lugubri 'with a sinister omen' (*OLD ales*² 2, *lugubris* 2b). For *renascens...fortuna* cf. Stat. *Silv.* 1.5.65.

62 tristi clade iterabitur '(the fortune of Troy) will be repeated with its grim disaster' (abl. of attendant circumstances: *NLS* 33 §47). For the notion of the Trojan War repeating itself cf. Virg. *Ecl.* 4.35–6 'erunt etiam altera bella | atque iterum ad Troiam magnus mittetur Achilles', *Aen.* 6.86–97.

63 uictrices cateruas is reused at 4.4.23.

64 coniuge me Iouis et sorore: the formulation is conventional (cf. Hom. *Il.* 16.432, 18.356, *Hom. Hymn* 12.3 (to Hera), Cic. *ND* 2.66 'quae est soror et coniunx Iouis' (and Pease's n.), Virg. *Aen.* 1.46–7); perhaps it appeared also in Ennius. For *coniunx* see below, 67–8n.

65 ter si resurgat murus aëneus: perhaps not simply as strong as bronze (*OLD aeneus* 1b) but actually made of bronze, like the walls of Alcinous' palace or of Aeolus' island (Hom. *Od.* 7.86, 10.4): so D. E. W. Wormell, 'Walls of brass in literature', *Hermathena* 58 (1941) 116–20. See also 3.16.1n. For *resurgo* see *OLD* 3c.

66 auctore Phoebo: Apollo had been involved in building the first set of walls (above, 21–3n., 29–30n.): cf. Virg. *G.* 3.36 'Troiae Cynthius auctor'.

66–7 ter pereat meis | excisus Argiuis: both *excido* and *pereo* are regular of the destruction of cities and the like (*OLD excido²* 5a, *OLD pereo* 6a). *meis...Argiuis* is either dat. of agent or, as most edd. prefer, instrumental abl.: the Argives are mere instruments in the hands of Juno (*NLS* 32 §44). Juno's three favourite cities were Argos, Sparta and Mycenae (N–H on 1.7.8).

67–8 ter uxor | capta uirum puerosque ploret: the words seem intended to be taken generally ('three times a captured wife would mourn her husband and children') and to evoke all the horror of a captured city (G. M. Paul, *Phoenix* 36 (1982) 144–55). *uxor*, almost completely absent from epic, is used (7×) as often as *coniunx* (8×) in the *Odes* (see P. A. Watson (1985) 431–2). *ploret* (3.10.2–4n.) leads neatly into the contrasting *iocosae* below (69).

69 non hoc iocosae conueniet lyrae: *hoc* refers to lines 17–68, the *concilium deorum* (intro.). The break-off is characteristically Horatian (see esp. 2.1.37–40 and N–H; Schrijvers, *OR* 63); *lyrae*, a metonymy for lyric poetry

(*OLD* 1b), explicitly indicates that the ode has been 'generically deviant' (Harrison (2007) 188) and that H. is now returning to his lyric mode: *iocosae* is representative rather than definitive (see 70–2n.). The various uses of the future tense can be hard to categorise (*OLS* 1.423–9): here 'the future is used because the Muse is inclined to say yet more, as the next words, *quo...tendis*, show' (Gow). The sentence both functions as a rebuke (like Eng. 'this won't do') and re-asserts generic identity.

70 quo, Musa, tendis?: as if the Muse were getting ahead of herself and proceeding along a path where H. does not wish to go.

70–2 desine peruicax | ...magna modis tenuare paruis 'Stop relentlessly diminishing great themes...': *magna* refers to epic subject matter (as e.g. *S.* 1.4.43–4 'os | magna sonaturum'); *modis...paruis* refers principally to the Alcaic metre ('in short verses'), contrasting with the *uersus longi* of epic (Enn. *Op. incert.* fr. 20 Skutsch), but also connotes the generic limitations of lyric (almost 'in a slight medium': cf. Ov. *Tr.* 2.332 'in paruos... modos'). *referre sermones* suggests the recording of an actual speech (cf. Cic. *De or.* 3.1, 9). H.'s injunction acquires an added edge if he was writing with foreknowledge of the *Aeneid* (see intro.). Similar language is regularly used of the contrast between epic and the lighter genres (see N. B. Crowther, 'Catullus, Horace, and Alexandrianism', *Mnem.* 31 (1978) 40–1; also Brink on *Epi.* 2.1.224–5 and 257–8), but it should be noted that, although *tenuare* (like *tenuis*) can be used of Callimachean refinement (e.g. Prop. 3.1.5), here its meaning is different (as Stat. *Silv.* 5.3.98; *OLD* 5a). Ironically *peruicax* seems to have been capable of meaning 'verbose' (*TLL* 10.1.1869.29–33), suggesting the length of epic, while the fourth line of the Alcaic stanza resembles a hexameter (cf. esp. Lucr. 1.726 'magna modis'): perhaps this illustrates the playfulness to which H. has just referred (69). For the adverbial use of the adj. see G&L 206 §325 R. 6; *desine* is a so-called 'closural allusion' at the end of the poem (Smith 172–82). It is appropriate to have a 'programmatic' passage at the midway point of a sequence, yet the second half of the Alcaic Hexad scarcely accords with H.'s 'playful lyre'.

4

Readers have now reached the halfway point in the Alcaic Hexad, and, just as Virgil had begun the second half of his *Eclogues* and *Georgics* with lines of a programmatic nature (*Ecl.* 6.1–12, *G.* 3.1–48), so H. begins the present ode with two similar stanzas. He first summons Calliope, the Muse, and asks her to utter a 'longum melos' (2): *melos* (only here in H.)

marks a reaffirmation of the lyric genre after the 'epicising' of the previous ode (3.3.69n., 70–2n.), while *longum* means what it says: this is the longest of all H.'s odes.

Gow remarked that 'The thoughts in this ode are unusually abrupt even for Horace', an abruptness well illustrated by the juxtaposition of the first and second stanzas. Having summoned the Muse to come to him, in the second stanza it seems as though the opposite has happened: H. has been transported to the home of the Muses in a similar kind of reverie to that featured in 3.25 (see intro. there). There next follow three stanzas (9–20) in which H. tells a fable-like story of his childhood in Apulia: how he wandered away from his nurse's guardianship and was protected by doves from harm. Only at the very end (20 'non sine dis') is it made clear that this story is evidence that since childhood he has enjoyed a special relationship with the Muses, who from now on are referred to as the Camenae (21). This relationship, as he proceeds to say, remains constant regardless of where he lives (21–4); it has kept him from harm in later life (25–8); and it will protect him in the future, even if he should visit far-off countries on which Rome has military designs (29–36). 'For whomsoever the Muses did not look at askance as a child', Callimachus had said, 'they will not reject as a friend when he is old' (*Aet.* 1.37–8 with Harder). This relationship in its turn authenticates, as it were, the 'reality' of his poetic vision (5–8).

The seven stanzas on H.'s relationship with the Muses/Camenae (9–36) are balanced by the following seven on Augustus' relationship with the same divinities (37–64). The transition is effected both formally and conceptually: the address to the Camenae, with which the new section begins (37–42 *uos...uos...*), continues that in the previous section (21–9 *uester, Camenae, uester...uestris...uos...*), while it was Augustus' perceived intentions which lay behind the militarism of 33–6. In the new address, at the exact centre of the ode, we are told that the Camenae refresh the *princeps* after his labours (40 *recreatis*) and provide him with *consilium*, counsel (41–2). The importance of counsel versus brute force is then illustrated by the story of the Giants' battle with the gods: the battle is told by the Muses in a speech which begins (42) with the actions of Jupiter, who is described obliquely in a double relative clause (45 *qui...qui...*), and ends (64) with those of Apollo, whose description is similarly expressed (61–2 *qui...qui...*). The ring composition suggests closure, that of the speech coinciding with that of the section.

Closure is confirmed by the pivotal nature of the following stanza (65–8n.), where H. first expresses his agreement with the Muses' view of force and *consilium* as illustrated by the Gigantomachy (65–7a), and then adds his own belief that ill-intentioned *consilium* will elicit punishment from the gods (67b–8), of which four examples bring the ode to a conclusion (69–80).

On this reading of the poem, its structure is as follows:

1–8   Introduction (8 lines)
9–36   H. and the Muses (28)
37–64 Augustus and the Muses (28)
65–80 Conclusion (16)

Within this structure the two central sections display various sequences in addition to those mentioned above: three Apulian towns in descending order of height (14–16), four residential areas in the same order (21–4), three near-fatal experiences (26–8), two natural dangers (29–32), four military dangers (33–6); six powers of Jupiter (45–8), five Giants (53–6), four victorious gods (57–60). The poem is rounded off by three aspects of *uis* (65–8) and four criminals (69–80).

These sequences contribute generally to the unity of the ode and underline the similarity forged between poet and *princeps*; both are in receipt of the Muses' favour, which both of them receive in metaphorical landscapes which are strikingly similar (6-7 *pios...per lucos* ~ 40 *Pierio...antro*). It would be facile to conclude that H. is somehow equating himself with Augustus or seeing himself in Augustus' place; the *princeps* occupies a different and exalted level (37 *altum*) and is obliged to deal with problems whose scale in social and logistical terms far outstrips anything which a poet is likely to encounter in his life (37–8). Nevertheless it cannot fail to be significant that H.'s treatment of himself as poet takes up almost half the poem and is so similar to that of the *princeps*. The explanation emerges in the stanza which concludes the first half of the poem. As the recipient of poetry, Augustus is 'refreshed' by the Muses (40); but his response to poetry depends upon there being poetry to which he can respond, and it is poets such as H., inspired by the Muses (5–8), who produce it. The reciprocal relationship of poet and reader is exactly mirrored in the structure of H.'s ode. Moreover, if poets are able to exercise a benign influence on the *princeps*, who is an example to his citizens (W. on Vell. 126.5), it ought to follow that they can do the same for others. The Muse Calliope is not simply an attender on kings (1–2n.) but, according to Lucretius, a relaxation for man in general (6.94 'Calliope, requies hominum'). The poet, in other words, plays a key role in the society of Augustan Rome, and it is no accident that, five years before the publication of Books 1–3 of the *Odes*, Augustus had dedicated the Temple of Palatine Apollo (1.31 with N–H), the empty shelves of its Greek and Latin libraries waiting to receive the works of those authors who passed muster (*Epi.* 2.1.216–18 'si munus

Apolline dignum | uis complere libris et uatibus addere calcar | ut studio maiore petant Helicona uirentem'; see N. Horsfall, *Fifty Years at the Sibyl's Heels* (2020) 318–26).

It is an accepted dogma of modern scholarship that this ode has been heavily influenced by Pindar, *Pythian* 1, which begins with an address to the lyre and proceeds to mention the power of the Muses (1–14). But this dogma has been created largely by Fraenkel, whose extended discussion (276–85) amounts to little more than enthusiastic generalisations and can point to almost no similarity of detail apart from the coincidence of Apollo's names in lines 61–4 (cf. *Pyth.* 1.39); most of Pindar's long ode (it is one hundred lines in length) has nothing at all in common with H.'s poem. By far the most important influence is Hesiod's *Theogony*, as signalled by the address to the Muse Calliope at the very start (1–2n.): this was the poem in which there appeared the notion of the Muses' dual role – both for poets, such as H. himself, and for rulers, such as Augustus. There is nevertheless a significant difference from Hesiod's poem. Hesiod had featured the gods' battle with the Titans (*Theog.* 617–720), whereas what the Muses describe in the ode is the gods' battle with the *Giants* (49–60), which does not feature in the *Theogony* at all. Now numerous ancient authors describe the Titanomachy and Gigantomachy as if they were one and the same conflict, but, at least in H.'s case, this is the result not of some understandable confusion but of deliberate conflation (51–2n.). H. has (as it were) 'updated' Hesiod in the light of the importance of the Gigantomachy in Augustan ideology (3.1.7n.).

This difficult and controversial ode has generated an enormous amount of scholarly discussion. One of the most recent contributions is by A. Hardie (2008) and (2009), a lengthy and exceptionally learned treatment where references to earlier bibliography will be found. Hardie sees the ode as a hymn uttered by the choir of girls and boys to which reference was made at 3.1.4 above.

METRE Alcaic

1 Descende caelo: it was a Homeric formula and repeated by Hesiod (*Theog.* 75, 114; cf. 52) that 'the Muses have their home on Olympus', to which *caelo* is here equivalent. Summoning the Muses is characteristic of Greek lyric rather than early epic, but Hesiod delivers such a summons at *WD* 2 (where see West's n.); for a descent 'from heaven' see Aphrodite's in Sappho 1.11–12.

1–2 dic – age! – tibiā | regina longum Calliope melos: since *regina* and *Calliope* are both vocative (the word order of 2 is interlaced), convention would normally dictate that they be marked off by commas from the rest of the sentence, which would mean commas after each of the last five words. This punctuation is adopted by A. Hardie (2008: 61) as reflecting the 'chopped, halting, word pattern' of H.'s audacious summons; but many editors tend not to punctuate at all. *age* (*OLD* 24a) imitates ἄγε in Greek prayers, e.g. Alcm. 27 Μῶσ' ἄγε Καλλιόπα, Stes. 240 δεῦρ' ἄγε Καλλιόπεια λίγεια ('Come here, clear-voiced Calliopeia'). Calliope, whose name means 'beautiful-voiced' (κάλλος + ὄψ), became associated with epic poetry (N–H on 1.24.3) but had various other associations too (see e.g. Harder on Callim. *Aet.* fr. 7c.4, 75.77); here she is associated with *melos*, a transliteration of the Greek neuter noun μέλος, which tends to be restricted to lyric,[20] while the two-piped *tibia* (3.7.29–30n.) was the instrument accompanying or representing choral lyric (*AP* 202–4). The likelihood is that Calliope appealed to H. because 'she is the greatest of all the Muses, for she attends too upon venerated kings' (Hes. *Theog.* 79–80, where ὀπηδεῖ, 'attends', is perhaps a play on her name): the Muses' relationship with Augustus will become a principal theme of the ode (37–42). So too A. H. F. Thornton, 'Horace's Ode to Calliope', *AUMLA* 23 (1965) 96–102, esp. 97–8. On the other hand, like Fraenkel (281 n. 1), A. Hardie (2008: 59) believes that 'The appeal to Calliope is an appeal to all nine Muses'.

3–4 seu uoce nunc mauis acuta, | seu fidibus citharaque Phoebi: *seu* here = *uel si* (*OLD siue* 2), as often in H.; in full the clauses would read: 'uel, si nunc mauis, uoce acuta uel, si mauis, fidibus citharaque Phoebi' ('or, if you now prefer, with your clear voice or, if you prefer, with the [?] lyre and cithara of Apollo'). Conditional clauses are regular in hymns or prayers, but this passage differs from the commoner types (see 3.18.5n.). *uoce…acuta,* following so soon after *Calliope,* suggests an allusion to the Muse's name (1–2n.); the converse happens in Hesiod's *Theogony,* where ὀπὶ καλῇ (68) appears several lines *before* her name (79). N–R give *fidibus* the very rare meaning of 'strings' and describe its co-ordination with *cithara* (3.1.20n.) as a hendiadys (presumably 'lyre-strings'): they compare Virg. *Aen.* 6.120 'cithara fidibusque canoris',[21] where, however, *fidibus* is given its usual meaning both by *TLL* (6.1.692.34–5) and by Horsfall, who says that the two nouns are synonymous and illustrate 'theme and variation'. Some edd. compare *Hom. Hymn Hermes* 423 λύρῃ…κιθαρίζων, which is not much help with the meaning; and in other lists of three (e.g. Pind.

---

[20] See Pfeiffer 182–3, although his remark about H. is misleading.
[21] The only other occurrence of *fidibus canoris* is in H. (1.12.11).

126 COMMENTARY 4.5–8

Ol. 3.8, Ov. *Met.* 12.157–8 'non illos citharae, non illos carmina uocum | longaue multifori delectat tibia buxi') the media are clearly distinguished from one another. *Phoebi* presumably means 'associated with Phoebus' or 'Apolline' rather than that Calliope is expected to borrow the god's own instruments; yet the genitive is not merely decorative: the association of the two proper names (as at Prop. 1.2.27–8, 2.1.3, and esp. 3.3.13ff., 37ff.) is significant. Virgil in the Fourth Eclogue had expressed the hope that his poetry would vie with that of Orpheus and Linus, whom he describes as offspring respectively of Calliope and Apollo (4.55–7), and in the Sixth Eclogue he had outlined a poetic tradition, headed by Apollo, in which the Muses are said by Linus to pass on to Cornelius Gallus the pipes (*calamos*) which earlier they had given to Hesiod (6.64–73). Since we have already seen that Hesiod lies behind H.'s appeal to Calliope, it seems clear that the mention of Apollo serves to reaffirm H.'s allegiance to that same tradition (see Ross 143–4). See further below, 6–8n.

5 auditis?: we are to envisage a short interval, to allow time for H.'s imagined audience to hear Calliope begin, at which point he asks them whether they hear her (there is no question of seeing her, since the Muses are invisible, as Hesiod tells us, *Theog.* 9): there are similar intervals at 1.27.18, 3.26.9 (n.) and *Epo.* 7.15 (see Fraenkel 180–2), and for a somewhat similar audience address cf. 3.1.2 'fauete linguis!', 3.26.6 'hic ponite', *Epo.* 7.1 'Quo...ruitis?', 7.14 'date', 16.16 'quaeritis'. Although there are no plural forms in 1–4, the Muses/Camenae were thought to be the subject of *auditis* (sc. *me*) by pseudo-Acro, who quoted in support Virg. *Aen.* 9.525 'Vos, o Calliope, precor, aspirate canenti'; but, 'if the passage is to cohere, *auditis* must govern the same object as *audire* in the next line' (N–R).

5–6 an me ludit amabilis | insania?: either H. actually hears the Muse or he is deluded because of the madness conventionally attributed to poets (for *ludo* = 'deceive', again at 3.27.40, see *OLD* 9b); the madness is 'amabilis' (a typically Horatian oxymoron, but cf. also *Anacreontea* 2.6, 53.14, 60(b).2) because it is not craziness of the kind described at *AP* 453–76. H.'s questions, which are alluded to by Ovid (*F.* 5.549–51 'fallor an arma sonant?...caelo descendit'), have some similarity to the end of Keats' *Ode to a Nightingale*: 'Was it a vision, or a waking dream? | Fled is that music:— Do I wake or sleep?'

6–8 audire et uideor pios | errare per lucos, amoenae | quos et aquae subeunt et aurae: 'I seem to hear <her> and to be wandering through the sacred groves...'. *uideor* indicates that H. is hearing the Muse in a dream or vision,[22] an experience which cannot fail to remind readers of Callimachus' encounter with the Muses in a dream (*Aet.* fr. 2d, p. 128 Harder), where Callimachus refers to, and sees his own encounter in terms of, Hesiod's encounter with the Muses at the start of the *Theogony* (*Aet.* fr. 2: see Harder's excellent intro. n., Vol. 2, p. 94). H.'s allusion to Callimachus implies his allegiance to Callimachean poetics, which in turn find their inspiration in Hesiod. Groves too, for which Latin has numerous nouns, are, like dreams, a poetic symbol: see e.g. 1.1.30, *Epi.* 2.2.77 and Brink's n. Apollo is associated with a grove at *Ecl.* 6.72–3, Propertius wishes to enter a Callimachean grove at 3.1.1; for the Muses' grove see Plato, *Ion* 534B Μουσῶν…ναπῶν, while Calliope is described as 'queen of the resounding grove' at Stat. *Theb.* 4.34–5 'o nemoris regina sonori, | Calliope', although there she is the Muse of epic. See further Cairns, *SP* 131–6. Scholars have compared H.'s *errare* with that of Gallus at Virg. *Ecl.* 6.64 'errantem Permessi ad flumina Gallum', while Gallus' words at *Ecl.* 10.58–9 ('iam mihi *per* rupes *uideor lucos*que sonantes | ire') may lie behind those of H. here.

7–8 amoenae | quos et aquae subeunt et aurae: the groves are seen in terms of a *locus amoenus* (cf. Brink on *AP* 16–17): poetic inspiration is suggested both by the idyllic streams (3.13.15–16n.) and by the breezes (N–H on 2.16.38); see also below on *animosus* (20). *subeunt* first refers to water flowing along, or emerging from, the floor of the grove; but with *aurae* it must have the different meaning of 'make their way into' (syllepsis): see *OLD* 10b.

9–13 me fabulosae…fronde noua puerum palumbes | texere 'When I was a child, fabled doves covered me with fresh leaves.' The transition from dream to story, though abrupt, is helped by the early placing of *fabulosae* ('legendary, fabulous': *OLD* 1b, 2), extraordinarily separated from its noun (hyperbaton); Nisbet (*OR* 384–5) thinks that H. is imitating 'the grand style of Pindar'. After 1–8, we are to assume that everything that follows from now on is the result of inspiration from the Muses. As indicated by *fabulosae* and below by *mirum* (13), H.'s story has all the features of the fantastic: similar stories are told of numerous ancient poets (see M. R. Lefkowitz, *The Lives of the Greek Poets* ([2]2012), M. Kivilo, *Early Greek Poets' Lives: The Shaping of the Tradition* (2010); also below, 11n.),

---

[22] Cf. the *Somnium Scipionis* at Cic. *Rep.* 6.18 'quis est qui complet aures meas tantus et tam dulcis sonus?' Whether there is any relationship between H. and *Anacreontea* 62B δοκέει κλύειν γὰρ ἤδε, | λαλέειν τις εἰ θελήσηι ('for she seems to hear, if one wishes to speak') is impossible to say.

although it is hard to parallel the precise combination of every detail: doves, for example, are not usually associated with the Muses, while the mountain location and non-human rescue are elements drawn from stories of exposure. In modern times 'the idea of the future poet marked out from childhood by some sort of supernatural favour had strong appeal in the pre-Romantic and Romantic periods, and proved amenable to much individual adaptation' (Parker 175, with numerous exs.).

9 Vulture in Apulo: the modern Monte Volture (4,350 ft), also referred to at Luc. 9.185 (*BNP* 15.511): see *BA* Map 45: C3. Since the name suggests the bird of prey, there is a contrast with the gentle doves; a vulture returns at the very end of the ode (78). H.'s feeling for his native mountains is clear at *S.* 1.5.77–8 'incipit ex illo montes Apulia notos | ostentare mihi' (Fraenkel 4, 109).

10 nutricis extra limina sedulae 'beyond the house of my attentive nurse' (*limina* is synecdochic). The MSS are divided between *limina Pulliae* and *limen Apuliae*. If *in Apulo* is retained in 9 (it has often been emended), then obviously the latter is impossibly repetitive. Many edd. print *Pulliae*, a name well attested on inscriptions, but the domestic detail seems quite out of place (contrast the reference to Orbilius at *Epi.* 2.1.71, a different genre). E. Courtney (*Phoenix* 40 (1986) 319–20) suggested that a scribe's eye slipped from *limina* to *in Apulo* in 9, causing him to complete line 10 as *liminapulo*, thus ousting the original wording entirely; subsequent readings are attempts to correct the clear mistake. Pointing to the similarity between our passage and 1.22.9–12, Courtney proposed that H. wrote *extra limina dum uagor* (supported by J. Delz, *MH* 50 (1993) 214–15). Somewhat similarly Parker 173–8 has proposed that *Apuliae*, which she obelises, is a marginal gloss which has driven from the text the name of the tiny (and now unknown) Apulian hamlet which it was intended to explain: 'beyond the threshold of X, my nurse' (for *nutrix* used of a place see 1.22.15–16, Cic. *II Verr.* 2.5). Naturally we cannot know what H. originally wrote, but *sedulae*, absolving his old nurse from any blame, is supported by the same phrase at *AP* 116 and Ov. *Her.* 21.95, *Met.* 10.438.

11 ludo fatigatumque somno recalls the Homeric 'sated with toil and sleep' (*Il.* 10.98, *Od.* 12.281; cf. *Od.* 6.2), but H. has transformed Homer's syllepsis into zeugma (with *somno* a participle such as *oppressum* has to be understood from *fatigatum*) and transposed *-que* from *somno* (3.1.12–13n.): 'tired with play and <overcome> by sleep'. It is striking that similar details are told of Pindar, who, as a boy, 'went hunting near Mt Helicon and fell asleep from exhaustion. As he slept, a bee landed on his mouth and built a honeycomb there...he then decided to write poetry' (*Vita Ambrosiana*, transl. Lefkowitz). For other such tales see Pease on Cic. *Div.* 1.78.

12 palumbes: doves are birds of Venus (see e.g. McKeown on Ov. *Am.* 1.2.23–4), and H.'s birthplace was Venusia (*S.* 2.1.35), the 'town of Venus' (cf. Serv. *Aen.* 11.246 'Venusiam, quam in satisfactionem Veneris condidit [sc. Diomedes], quae Aphrodisias dicta est'). See also 18–19n.

13 mirum quod foret omnibus 'which was destined to be a marvel for all...'; the impf. subj. is used in rel. clauses expressing futurity regarded from a past point of view (S. A. Handford, *The Latin Subjunctive* (1947) 84); *foret* (only here in *C.* 1–3) is an archaising equivalent of *esset*: as it is formed from the fut. infin. *fore*, it can have a future aspect which is useful in passages such as this (cf. W. D. Lowrance, 'The use of *forem* and *essem*', *TAPA* 62 (1931) 169–91, esp. 176 for H.). This is also one of those clauses where the neuter rel. pronoun not only refers back to the preceding sentence, as is to be expected, but is itself explained later by some further construction, in this case a repeated indirect question: 'ut..., ut...' (17–18, where see nn.). *mirum...omnibus* renders Bacchyl. *Ode* 17.123 θαῦμα πάντεσσι.[23]

14–16 quicumque celsae nidum Aceruntiae | saltusque Bantinos et aruum | pingue tenent humilis Forenti: the three places, arranged in descending order of height, are within reasonable proximity to Venusia: Ac(h)eruntia is SSE (*BA* Map 45: C3), Bantia is SE (D3),[24] and Forentum due N (C2). *OLD* (1b) gives no parallel for the use of *nidus* in a transferred sense = 'eyrie', although the diminutive seems sometimes so used (e.g. Plin. *Ep.* 6.10.1); *celsae...Aceruntiae* is a definitive genitive. We are left to infer from *celsae* and *humilis* that the *saltus* of Bantia were at an intermediate height. *saltus*, always a difficult word to render in English, here presumably means a region of woodland interspersed with glades, usually in hilly or mountainous country, and used for pasturing (*OLD saltus*² 2a–b); there is thus a further contrast with the ploughland of Forentum (see also West (1973) 34–5). For *tenere* = 'to inhabit, frequent' see *OLD* 8.

17–18 ut tuto ab atris corpore uiperis | dormirem et ursis: the indir. question explains *quod* in 13: 'which was destined to be a marvel...,

---

[23] I owe this parallel to Dr Zoe Stamatopoulou.
[24] The Tabula Bantina, a fragmentary legal document in Latin and Oscan, takes its name from Bantia (mod. Banzi), where it was found (see Crawford 1.193–208 and 271–92).

130   COMMENTARY 4.18–22

namely, how I slept...'. *tutus ab* + abl. is regular (*OLD* 1a). Snakes are often 'black' in Latin poetry: for *ater*, which is taken as = 'deadly' here (*OLD* 8), see Ov. *Met.* 3.63 and Bömer's n. Vipers remain common in Italy, and there are bears in the mountain regions.

18–19 ut premerer sacra | lauroque conlataque myrto 'how I was covered with a pile of sacred laurel and myrtle'. The two nouns are co-ordinated by -*que*...-*que*; one might have expected -*que* to be attached to *sacra* rather than *lauro*, but the suffix gets dislocated elsewhere too (see 11n. above). *sacra* and *conlata* are to be taken with both nouns; and *conlata* ('gathered', 'collected together') is an example of the so-called '*ab urbe condita* idiom' (see *NLS* 75–6 §95), whereby a phrase consisting of a noun + participle (or sometimes an adj.) is rendered by two nouns (one dependent on the other) in English: thus 'from the *founding of the city*'. The construction is commonest with a perfect participle and is frequent in the *Odes* (e.g. 3.4.26, 5.7, 6.7, 10.15, 15.10, 16.29–32, 21.24, 27.75). For *premerer* see *OLD* 14b. For Hesiod the Muses 'plucked a staff, a branch of luxuriant laurel, a marvel' (*Theog.* 30–1: see next n.); as a child Pindar was said to have been laid on branches of laurel and sprays of myrtle (Philostr. *Imag.* 2.12.2).

20 non sine dis animosus infans: the divinities are the Muses, who are often so called (e.g. Prop. 3.3.37 'una dearum', of Calliope); for the form *dis* see Varro, *RR* 3.16.7. Some have seen in *non sine dis* a reference to the Greek adj. ἔνθεος, 'inspired' ('full of the god'), used of poets by Plato (*Ion* 533E, 534B): see D. West in *'Non omnis moriar': La lezione di Orazio a duemila anni dalla scomparsa* (1993) 106. See also 3.25.1–2n. *animosus*, 'spirited' (*OLD* 1a), again recalls Hesiod (*Th.* 31–2 'they breathed a divine voice into me', of the Muses). Lines 9–11 suggest that *infans* must here = 'little child' (*OLD infans*[2]), though its literal meaning ('unable to talk') contrasts ironically with the future poet. *non sine* is a favourite litotes (Thomas on 4.13.27), occurring more often in the *Odes* than in H.'s other works (10:6), and more often in Book 3 (6×) than elsewhere.

21–2 uester, Camenae, uester in arduos | tollor Sabinos: the repeated *uester* is predicative: 'I am yours, Muses, yours, when I am climbing up amongst the high/steep Sabines' *or* 'It is as yours that I climb...' (lit. 'I climb as yours...'); for the passive of *tollo* in a middle sense = 'climb, ascend' see *OLD* 4a. The traditional site of H.'s Sabine farm (Intro. 5) is in hilly country, although here the area is designated by its people, as often (for *arduus* of people cf. Ov. *Met.* 5.289, Sil. 12.486); for the farm's associations see 3.1.47n. The poet switches to the Latin name for the Muses,

COMMENTARY 4.22-6   131

as is appropriate after the autobiographical tale he has just told; for them
see A. Hardie (2016).

**22-4 seu mihi frigidum | Praeneste seu Tibur supinum | seu liquidae plac-
uere Baiae:** the general meaning is clear (I belong to the Muses whatever
my destination of choice) but the syntax much less so: the most straightforward (but by no means the only) way of understanding the words is
to assume that in the previous clause H. had written 'uester sum cum
tollor' in full (so N-R): '(I am yours when I climb...) or if cool Praeneste
or the slopes of Tibur or the clear waters of Baiae take my fancy'; a perfect indic. is regular in a present general condition(*NLS* 150 §194). The
places are again arranged in descending order of height. Praeneste (mod.
Palestrina), roughly 22 miles ESE of Rome (*BA* Map 44: C2), is about
2,000 ft high (a little higher than H.'s presumed Sabine farm) and the
place where H. says he re-read Homer (*Epi.* 1.2.2). Tibur (mod. Tivoli),
15 miles ENE of Rome (*BA* Map 44: C2), is 750 ft above sea level; a fashionable location for villas (see esp. Cat. 44.1-7), it is frequently mentioned by H., who idealised it (2.6.5-8) and evidently had a place there
himself (below, p. 358 n. 142). Baiae is on the Bay of Naples (*BA* Map
44: F4) and was a notoriously luxurious resort (N-H on 2.18.20); it was
where Augustus' young nephew Marcellus would die in September of 23
BC. Juvenal seems pointedly to allude to H. at 3.190-2 'gelida Praeneste...
proni Tiburis arce' (cf. 14.87-8). *supinus* can refer to low-lying ground
but the alternative 'sloping downwards' is required here (*OLD* 3); *liquidae*
not only indicates the coastal location of Baiae but also implies the quality
of its waters (*OLD* 5a).

25 uestris amicum fontibus et choris: the adj. *amicus* + dat. can mean
either 'friendly to ~' or 'welcome/dear to ~' (see *OLD* 1a, 5); scholars are
divided on which meaning is intended here, but the latter seems required
by the context, as at 1.26.1 'Musis amicus' (= μουσοφίλητος, Corinna 674).
At the very beginning of the *Theogony* Hesiod describes the Muses as dancing around a spring, washing in the springs of Permessus or Hippocrene
or Olmeius, and then performing choral dances on Mt Helicon (*Theog.*
3-8); *fontibus et choris* presents the Camenae in identical terms.

26 non me Philippis uersa acies retro... 'the retreat of the line at
Philippi did not...' (another example of the '*ab urbe condita* idiom': above,
18-19n.); *uertere aciem* has various potential meanings: the unexampled
addition of *retro* indicates that H. means reversal. *Philippis* is presumably
locative, though some take it as 'from'. For H.'s participation in the battle
of Philippi in 42 BC on the losing side, famously recalled in 2.7, see Intro. 4.

27 deuota non exstinxit arbor 'an/the accursed tree did not kill (me)'; this rare sense of *deuotus* is earlier at *Epo.* 16.9 and Cat. 64.135. For the falling tree which almost killed the poet see 3.8.7–8n.

28 nec Sicula Palinurus unda: Palinurus (mod. Capo Palinuro) is a cape on the SW coast of Italy (*BA* Map 45: B4): the name is derived from the helmsman either of Aeneas (cf. Virg. *Aen.* 6.381) or (so ps.-Acro) of Hannibal (Maltby 444). The name hints at a storm caused by the wind changing direction, since 'Palinurus' is a combination of the Greek πάλιν ('backwards') + οὖρος ('wind'). We have no other evidence of the shipwreck to which H. refers here, but most scholars assume it will have happened during the war against Sex. Pompeius, which ended in Sept. 36 BC with the Battle of Naulochus off Sicily, Sextus' island stronghold (cf. *Sicula...unda*, local abl.).

29 utcumque 'Whenever' (*OLD* 1c).

29–31 libens | insanientem nauita Bosphorum | temptabo 'as a sailor I will gladly risk the raging Bosphorus': *nauita*, like its quasi-anagrammatised opposite *uiator* below (32), is predicative. The Bosphorus was notoriously dangerous (N–H on 2.13.14); the application of *insanio*, one of H.'s favourite words, to a natural force is most unusual (the only parallel is Sen. *NQ* 6.17.1, of air), although *insanus* is regularly so used (*TLL* 7.2.1835.33ff., esp. 34–52). Cf. *tumultuosum* at 3.1.26 (n.). *nauita* (again at 3.24.41) is an archaising poeticism (Horsfall on Virg. *Aen.* 6.315); the use of *tempto* is like that at 3.2.21–2 (n.).

31–2 urentes harenas | litoris Assyrii: Assyria is roughly equivalent to Mesopotamia (*BA* Map 91) and, being nowhere near any sea, has no shore; and *litus*, unlike *ora* or Eng. 'strand', seems not to be used in a loose sense to mean 'foreign parts'. Scholars have attempted emendation either of *litoris* or of *Assyrii*, but it may be that H. is using *Assyrius* loosely for 'Indian' (as Ov. *Am.* 2.5.40); the shore of India is mentioned at Cat. 11.3, Mela 1.11. For *urentes* cf. Sen. *NQ* 2.30.1 'Aetna...ingentem uim harenae urentis effudit'.

33–6 uisam Britannos...uisam...: on both occasions the verb (for which see 3.3.54–6n.) is to be taken with *inuiolatus* (36): 'unharmed, I shall visit...'. In his account of 26 BC, Dio says that Augustus was prevented from an intended expedition to Britain by a revolt of the Salassi and a war in NW Spain (53.25.2: see 3.5.3–4n.); H. too combines references to Britain and NW Spain (see below), while the subjugation of the Salassi may lie behind his reference to the settlement of veterans (37–8n.). His proposed visit to Britain echoes Cat. 11.10–11 'uisens...ulti- | mos...Britannos' (for which see further 3.5.3–4n.).

33 Britannos hospitibus feros: although the Britons were bestial in their killing of prisoners of war (Dio 62.7.2 θηριωδέστατον, 62.11.4) and the Druids in particular were notorious for the practice of human sacrifice (Tac. A. 14.30.3; cf. Caes. BG 6.16.1), no other text mentions the Britons' cruelty to *hospites*; on the contrary, when some of Germanicus' troops were swept onto the shores of Britain by a storm at sea in AD 16 (thereby falling into the category of *hospites*), they were repatriated by the local princes (A. 2.24.3). It was the Tauri on the shores of the Black Sea who were notorious for sacrificing 'all ship-wrecked men...to the Virgin goddess' (Hdt. 4.103.1; cf. Ov. *Ex P.* 3.2.57–8, Tac. A. 12.17.3). H. has evidently transferred to the Britons a well-known custom of the Tauri. Transferable motifs such as this (*Wandermotive*) are found very commonly in ancient ethno-geographical writing, since they were a convenient way both of describing the unknown and of distinguishing 'the other' from Romans (see e.g. W. on Tac. *Agr.*, Intro. pp. 12–13); for another ex. see next n. For *ferus* + dat. cf. Sen. *Cons. Marc.* 22.5, Stat. *Theb.* 6.313, 11.712; H.'s combination suggests one of the numerous compound Greek adjs. meaning 'guest-killing', such as ξενοκτόνος in Euripides' play about the Tauri (*IT* 53).

34 laetum equino sanguine Concanum 'the Concanians delighting in horses' blood' (*Concanum* is collective singular). Concanum or perhaps Concana (Ptol. *Geog.* 2.6.50) is an 'unlocated toponym' in NW Spain (*BA* 1.383); H. probably knew of its name because Augustus had been campaigning in the area in 26–25 BC (see 3.14, intro.). The Concanians' drinking habit is again mentioned at Sil. 3.360–1, where this evidence of their *feritas* is ascribed to their descent from the Massagetae, a Scythian tribe (see Powell 146), whose drinking of horses' blood is mentioned at Luc. 3.283, Sen. *Oed.* 470, Stat. *Ach.* 1.307. The habit is attributed to the Geloni by Virgil (*G.* 3.463) and to the Sarmatians by the elder Pliny (*NH* 18.100). Evidently an alleged custom of various north-eastern peoples, who were difficult to distinguish from one another, at some point was transferred (presumably not by H.) to the barbarians of NW Spain: in this case the transference was evidently 'rationalised' by the assumption that the Spaniards were descended from one of these north-eastern tribes. See further 33n. above. *laetus* + abl. is regular (*OLD* 4); its combination with *sanguine* formed a convenient hexametrical clausula for Lucr. (2.631), Virgil (*Aen.* 10.787) and Ovid (*F.* 3.63).

35 uisam pharetratos Gelonos: for the Geloni, a Scythian people, see 2.9.23, 2.20.19, Virg. *G.* 2.115, 3.463 (see 34n.), *Aen.* 8.725 'sagittiferosque Gelonos', Mela 2.14; Powell 144–5. *pharetratus*, a favourite of Ovid, occurs first at Virg. *G.* 4.290 and recurs at *Aen.* 11.649. For anaphora starting the first and third lines of a stanza (discussed by Thomas on 4.1.21) see also 3.5.33, 35; 6.5, 7; 11.45, 47; 19.5, 7; 24.33, 35; 24.45, 47.

36 Scythicum...amnem: the Tanais (3.10.1, 29.28, 4.15.24), commonly regarded as dividing Europe from Asia (see Hollis on Gallus 144H/1C). Now called the Don, it flows for over 1,000 miles through Russia and debouches into the Sea of Azov.

37 Caesarem altum: *altus*, more normally applied to divinities, is used of Caesar at Ov. *Ex P.* 2.3.63, *Epic. Drusi* 453 (*TLL* 1.1777.39–49); see further 39n., below. For the name Caesar see 3.3.11–12n.

37–8 militiā simul | fessas cohortes addidit oppidis: in 30 BC, after Augustus' victory at Actium, a large number of veteran soldiers started to be settled on the land (*RG* 16.1, Suet. *Aug.* 17.3, Dio 51.4.2–8; Keppie 73–82). It seems usually to be thought that here (as at *S.* 2.6.55–6) H. is referring to this first wave of post-Actian settlements and that the ode is therefore datable to *c.* 29; but, since a further 3,000 veterans were settled in Augusta Praetoria (mod. Aosta) in 25 or 24 BC after the defeat of the Salassi (Strabo 4.6.7 (an esp. interesting account), Dio 53.25.2–5; Keppie 205–7), whose revolt is perhaps alluded to at 3.14.14–15 (n.), a date later than 29 cannot be excluded and would accord with the above references to Britain and NW Spain (33–6n.).

The MSS are divided between *abdidit* and *addidit*. The former implies an element of concealment which is quite inappropriate (Rudd's 'unobtrusively settled' surely stretches the Latin too much); *addidit*, on the other hand, puts a suitably favourable gloss on the extensive evictions and massive upheaval which many of the settlements involved. *simul* = *simul ac* and introduces a 'generalising clause in the present', for which 'the perfect indicative is the usual tense' (*NLS* 175 [top] §217 (2) (c), quoting as example *Rhet. Herenn.* 4.24 'simul ac fortuna dilapsa est, deuolant omnes', 'As soon as one's fortune has slipped away, all friends fly off').[25] Hence the meaning here is: 'as soon as he attaches [lit. has attached] campaign-weary troops to the towns, you refresh him...'. The statement

---

[25] Two further exs. are Cic. *Mur.* 22 'Simulatque increpuit suspicio tumultus, artes illico nostrae conticescunt', *Rep.* 2.48 'Simulatque se inflexit rex in dominatum iniustiorem, fit continuo tyrannus.'

may refer to one or to more than one occasion, but, like *uos...datis et... gaudetis* below (41–2), to which it is parallel, it is expressed as a general truth. *fessas* is to be taken with *militia* ('tired from campaigning'), as again at 2.7.18. H.'s preference for the more elevated *fessus* over *lassus* in the *Odes* (5:1) resembles that of most other poets (P. A. Watson (1985) 441), although he uses the latter freely in his hexameter verse.

39 finire quaerentem labores: it became a commonplace of imperial texts that the responsibility of administering the empire was a great burden: see e.g. *Epi.* 2.1.1 'Cum tot sustineas et tanta negotia solus', with Brink. In addition to *labor*, other key terms are *onus* and *moles*. Many years later the younger Seneca writes that the most powerful men, elevated to the highest positions, long for *otium* and a respite from their labours (*Brev. vit.* 4.1 'potentissimis et in *altum* sublatis hominibus [cf. *Caesarem altum* at 37 above] excidere uoces uidebis, quibus otium optent, laudent'), and he uses Augustus to illustrate his point (4.2 'hoc *labores suos...*dulci tamen oblectabat solacio'), quoting in support a letter of the emperor's (4.3). Unfortunately there is no way of knowing the date of the letter, but it would not be surprising if Augustus, who was often ill (see Wardle on Suet. *Aug.* 81), had sometimes voiced a desire for an end to his labours. H.'s statement was perhaps designed both to reassure those who thought his powers were now too great and to alarm those – perhaps the majority? – who thought that, without him, the civil wars might flare up again. It was in 23, the year of the *Odes*' publication, that he relinquished the annual consulships which he had held since 31 (Dio 53.32.3–4; W. on Vell. 89.5), and, when in 22 he was offered the consulship in perpetuity, he refused it (*RG* 5.3). *quaero* + infin. (*OLD* 6b) is a favourite construction of H. and reappears in this book at 24.27 and 27.55.

40 Pierio recreatis antro: Pieria is the region immediately to the north of Olympus (*BA* Map 50: B3–4) and was the birthplace of the Muses (Hes. *Theog.* 53 with West's n.); an *antrum* is either a grove or a cave (see Cairns, *SP* 131–6), but of course H. is speaking as metaphorically here as when he saw himself wandering 'pios...per lucos' at the start of the ode (6–7). The restorative power of poetry is often mentioned (e.g. Hes. *Theog.* 98–103; see N–H on 1.32.15); if it seems odd that Augustus should be depicted as seeking relaxation in verse after settling the veteran soldiers, we should remember that the ancients saw great importance in the correct division of one's life into activity and leisure, an ideal represented on the Palatine by the depiction of Apollo with both quiver and cithara (Miller 1–3, with illustration): cf. Xen. *Symp.* 1.1, Cic. *Mur.* 74, *Planc.* 66, Vell. 1.13.3 'Neque enim quisquam hoc Scipione elegantius interualla negotiorum otio dispunxit semperque aut belli aut pacis seruiit artibus: semper inter arma ac studia uersatus, aut corpus periculis aut animum disciplinis exercuit', Colum. 2.21.1, Tac. *Agr.* 9.3. Twenty years earlier, during the war at Mutina, and despite the pressure he was under, Augustus 'is said to have read and written and declaimed daily' (Suet. *Aug.* 84.1); yet Augustus' authorship of poetry was too cursory to feature in an ode such as this (Suet. *Aug.* 85.2 'poeticam summatim attigit'), and *recreatis* suggests rather the relaxation to be afforded by reading or listening. On a famous occasion, en route back to Rome after the Battle of Actium, the *princeps* listened to Virgil reading the *Georgics* on four successive days (Suet. *Vita Verg.* 27), and H. elsewhere, while concerned not to inconvenience the busy ruler, depicts his reception of poetry as attentive and willing (*S.* 2.1.18–19, *Epi.* 1.13.17–18). The validity of the words *uos Caesarem altum...Pierio recreatis antro* is attested by the poets whom the Augustan age produced. See further intro.

41–2 uos lene consilium et datis et dato | gaudetis, almae: for the present indic. verbs see 37–8n. The resumption of a verb by a participle, as here and e.g. Plaut. *Amph.* 278 'optumam operam *das, datam* pulchre locas', constitutes a regular pattern in Latin and is esp. common in Livy and Ovid; although this is the only example quoted for the *Odes*, there are a few exs. in the *Satires* (Wills 311–15). The regularity of the pattern tells against Gow's notion that *dato* means 'when counsel is given to you' and that Augustus is in conversation with the Muses; H.'s words mean 'nurturing ones, you both give soft counsel and rejoice in your gift'. It was in his role as 'counsellor' that Zeus slept with Mnemosyne, the mother of the Muses (Hes. *Theog.* 56); it was in the haunts of the Pierians (see *Pierio...antro* at 40 above) that wisdom resided (Pind. *Pyth.* 6.49 σοφίαν δ' ἐν μυχοῖσι Πιερίδων); and it is the Muses who make a ruler wise and give him 'soft words' as his counsel (Hes. *Theog.* 88–90 μαλακοῖσι...ἐπέεσσιν). Although *almus* is a conventional adj. for female deities (*OLD* b), it is esp. appropriate here because the Muses look kindly upon a ruler from birth (Hes. *Theog.* 81–4); the relationship between the Muses and Augustus is, as it were, confirmed by the link between *almae* (derived from *alo*) and *Caesarem altum* (*altus* being the past part. of *alo*): he is the finished product of their nurturing. Note how cōnsīli(um) ēt is to be scanned: the second -*i*- is regarded as consonantal.

42 Scimus is usually understood as introducing something which 'we' (i.e. H. and his contemporaries) all know, but, of the three alleged parallels for this 'special expression' (Fraenkel 282 n. 1), none is parallel at all ('I know' at Soph. *El.* 837 and *Phil.* 681, and 'Let him know' at Aesch. *Cho.*

602). Rather, this precise verb, coming immediately after an address to the divine Muses/Camenae in which they have been praised for their *consilium* (41–2), suggests a reference to the 'knowledge' which is a defining feature of the Muses (Hom. *Il.* 2.485 'for you are goddesses and...know everything', Pind. *Pae.* 6.54–5 'for you, Muses, know everything', Ov. *Met.* 15.623 'scitis enim', *Anth. Pal.* 2.133 'the much-knowing Muse'). If this is so, then the subject of *Scimus* is the Muses/Camenae themselves and it marks the start of their speech (similarly A. Hardie (2008) 86–90, though for different reasons): in this Hesiodic poem (intro.), see esp. the Muses' words at Hes. *Theog.* 27–8 ἴδμεν..., ἴδμεν... ('We know..., we know...'). This is thus one of those places in Latin poetry where direct speech has no formal introduction but has to be inferred from the context (see Feeney (2011)), here aided by the one first-person plural verb in the whole poem. The speech is parallel to those of Juno in the preceding ode (3.3.18–68) and Regulus in the next (3.5.18–40), while similar speeches will be found later at 3.11.37–52 and 3.27.34–66; they are a feature of Book 3. For the ending of the Muses' speech see 65–8n.

42–4 ut impios | Titanas immanemque turmam | fulmine sustulerit caduco: *ut* = 'how', as 17 and 18 above; the subject of *sustulerit* is the unexpressed antecedent of the *qui*-clauses in 45–8 (3.1.17–18n.), i.e. Jupiter. *impios Titanas* is a reference to the Titanomachy, the ten-year battle between the Titans (offspring of Heaven and Earth) and Zeus which is told by Hesiod in the *Theogony* (617–720; note 707–8 for the lightning-bolt). *immanem* ('monstrous') indicates that *turmam* refers to the Giants, who were often described as having snakes for feet: they too were the offspring of Earth and Heaven and waged a losing battle against Zeus (cf. 3.1.7). In this Hesiodic ode we might have expected to be told the story of the Titanomachy, as in the *Theogony*, but instead H. substitutes the Gigantomachy (49ff.), thereby conflating the two battles in the manner of numerous other authors (N–R on line 53, adding G. D'Alessio, '*Theogony* and *Titanomachy*', in M. Fantuzzi and C. Tsagalis (edd.), *The Greek Epic Cycle and its Ancient Reception: A Companion* (2015) 208, D. Olson, *Broken Laughter* (2017) 54, on Epicharm. fr. 135). *fulmine...caduco* imitates the Greek καταιβάτης κεραυνός, used by Aeschylus (*PV* 359) of Zeus's smiting of Typhoeus (below, 53n.); since *sustulerit* means 'lifted up' as well as 'destroyed', there is a typically Horatian oxymoron with *caduco* (West (1973) 41, 54).

At 43 the MSS are divided between *turmam* and *turbam*, just as they are divided between *turmas* and *turbas* at 47 below. Clearly the same word cannot be used on each occasion, but which is to be read where? The problem with *turma* is that it seems to be used technically of units mounted on horseback; the one possible exception (see *OLD* f) is Ov. *Am.* 2.13.18, where the MSS record the same two variants. In favour of *mortales...turbas* at 47 is the fact that the same expr. recurs (only) in Seneca (*Phaedr.* 475–6), who often echoes H.[26] Since that would oblige us to read *turmam* in the present passage, it may be relevant that at least two of the Giants' names mentioned below, Mimas and Rhoetus (53, 55), are also the names of centaurs, who were half-man and half-horse; it is characteristic of Hellenistic and post-Hellenistic poets to make allusive reference to variant versions of the myth which they are telling (e.g. 3.3.32n., 3.11.17–18n.). *immanem* would be as appropriate for centaurs as for Giants (cf. Germ. *Arat.* 414–15 'immania membra | Centauri'). It therefore seems likely that *turmam* should be read in 43. Indeed H., as again at 51–2 below (n.), is perhaps imitating Hesiod precisely in order to draw attention to his conflation of the two battles: Hesiod had applied to the *Titans* a word which later was used technically of hoplites (*Theog.* 676 φάλαγγας, 'ranks'). Compare *cohors* used of the Giants at 2.19.22.

45–8   These lines (with which compare 1.12.14–16 and N–H) have two finite verbs (*temperat* and *regit*) and three paired objects (*terram ~ mare, urbes ~ regna, diuos ~ turbas*). How are these elements to be distributed? Most scholars see the sentence as divided into two parts by *et* (46), in which case *temperat* governs the two inanimate objects (linked by the anaphora of *qui*) and *regit* governs the four animate objects (linked by the polysyndeton of *-que*): for the resulting *figura etymologica* of *regna...regit* cf. Ov. *Met.* 11.270, Sen. *Ben.* 7.3.2. Yet it could be argued that *imperio regit unus aequo* is best taken only with line 47, from which it would follow that *urbes regnaque tristia* is governed by *temperat* (cf. Sen. *Ep.* 74.28 'regna, urbes, prouincias temperat', of *uirtus*). The pros and cons seem evenly divided.

45–6 qui terram inertem, qui mare temperat | uentosum...:   for Jupiter's regulation of land and sea, here expressed not only assonantally but almost anagrammatically, cf. e.g. Plaut. *Rud.* 1, Cic. *Rosc. Am.* 131. If *inertem* means 'intractable' (*OLD* 4a), H. is perhaps referring to Zeus' ability to soften the dry-hard earth by means of rain (3.10.19–20n.).

46–7 et urbes regnaque tristia | diuosque mortalesque turbas: scholars have seen here two varied examples of the so-called *schema Horatianum* (cf. 3.13.6–7n.): 'gloomy kingdoms' suggests as an opposite *beatas urbes*, the Latin equivalent of πόλις εὐδαίμων, which is a commonplace of Greek

---

[26] See Stöckinger et al., esp. 371–400, though mentioning neither this nor several other parallels.

geographical literature (3.29.11–12n.); and, since the *regna tristia* are those of the dead, there is also the implication that the cities are very much alive. Likewise the noise and bustle implied by *turbas* (above, 42–4n.) invites us to see the divinities as quiet and orderly (cf. 3.3.35–6n.). Some edd. have objected that *mortales...turbas* (below) is pleonastic with *urbes*, which they therefore wish to emend, but cf. Enn. fr. incert. 360J 'mortalis atque urbes beluasque omnis iuuat' (of Jupiter). *regna...tristia* recurs at Luc. 9.869 (of the kingdom of Juba).

48 imperio regit unus aequo: *imperio regere* is a common combination, the most famous ex. of which is Virg. *Aen.* 6.851 (see Horsfall). *aequo* means 'impartial' both as between mortal ~ immortal and in the sense of 'fair'.

49 intulerat: the tense is relative to *sustulerit* (44): the Camenae are describing the aggression which led to the conflict with Jupiter.

50 fidens iuuentus horrida bracchiis: the reference is to three further offspring of Earth and Heaven, namely, the Hundred-Handers or Hecatoncheires (Hes. *Theog.* 147–53; see West on 139–53): they fight against Jupiter also at Virg. *Aen.* 10.565–70 ('Iouis...fulmina contra' with Harrison's n.), although in Hesiod they fight for Zeus against the Titans (*Theog.* 669ff.). *bracchiis* is to be taken primarily with *horrida* ('bristling with ~ '); *fidens iuuentus* suggests the Hesiodic ὑπερήφανα τέκνα, 'presumptuous children', from whose 'shoulders a hundred arms sprang forth' (*Theog.* 149–50), but the participle may also be felt with *bracchiis*, producing the Homeric χείρεσσι πεποιθότες, 'trusting in their arms/hands' (*Il.* 12.135, of Lapiths).

51–2 fratresque tendentes opaco | Pelion imposuisse Olympo: *magnum...terrorem intulerant Ioui* has to be understood from 49. The brothers are the Giants Otus and Ephialtes, whose attempt to pile up mountains in order to reach heaven and attack the gods is described *inter alios* by Virgil in the *Georgics* (1.281–2): 'ter sunt conati imponere Pelio Ossam | scilicet atque Ossae frondosum inuoluere Olympum', Homeric lines (cf. *Od.* 11.315–16) which, as commentators note, Virgil has placed in the middle of a Hesiodic section; perhaps we could say that H. has imitated Virgilian practice but has replaced Homer with Virgil himself (adding the wordplay of *impŏsuisse Olympŏ* and reversing, or perhaps capping, the ordering of the mountains). *opacus*, often used of places shaded by branches and leaves etc., presumably renders the Virgilian/Homeric *frondosum*. *tendentes* means 'straining' (for its use + infin. see *OLD* 13b): since it seems to render the Hesiodic τιταίνοντας (*Theog.* 209), where the participle etymologises the name of the Titans, H. appears to draw attention to his conflation of Titans and Giants (cf. 42–4n.). Here the perf. infin. is used instead of the present, as often in verse (again at 3.18.15–16, perhaps 3.29.43): see G. Calboli, 'Latin syntax and Greek', in P. Baldi and P. Cuzzolin (edd.), *New Perspectives on Historical Latin Syntax*, Vol. 1 *Syntax of the Sentence* (2009) 134–6.

53–8 sed quid...quid...quid...possent...? 'But what would they have been capable of...?': *possent*, here constructed with an accus. (*OLD* 7a), is potential subjunctive (*NLS* 91–2 §121).

53 Typhōeus et ualidus Mimas: Typhoeus (also known as Typhon) was a monstrous Earth-born, like the Giants: after the overthrow of the Titans he took on Zeus single-handed and was defeated by Zeus's lightning-bolt (*Theog.* 820–80, with West's intro. n.). Mimas, another Giant, is *ualidus* because he hurled the island of Lemnos against the gods; according to one version of the myth he too was killed by one of Zeus's lightning-bolts (Eur. *Ion* 215, Sen. *HO* 1384), according to another it was by Hephaestus' missiles (Apollod. 1.6.2). Mimas is a centaur at [Hes.] *Scut.* 186.

54 minaci Porphyrion statu: Porphyrion was king of the Giants (Pind. *Pyth.* 8.17); *minaci...statu* presumably means 'with his threatening posture' (different sense at Sen. *Ag.* 308–9). See also 59n.

55 Rhoetus: a centaur at Virg. *G.* 2.456 and elsewhere but a Giant at 2.19.23 (see N–H).

55–6 euulsisque truncis | Enceladus iaculator audax: *euulsis...truncis* is either an abl. abs. or to be taken as instrumental with the verbal noun *iaculator*. Fighting with trees or branches as weapons is characteristic of centaurs ([Hes.] *Scut.* 184–90, Pind. *Thren.* 6.7, Eur. *HF* 372, Ap. Rhod. 1.63–4, Ov. *Met.* 12.327–9, 356–7, 511–13), who are thus represented in Greek art, as on the François Vase (*LIMC* 8.1.671–727, 8.2.416–93); see also *OLD truncus*[2] 2. *audax* is not just 'bold' but 'subversive': the adj. describes someone who revolts against the status quo (C. Wirszubski, *JRS* 51 (1961) 12–22).

57–8 contra sonantem Palladis aegida |...ruentes: in Homer the aegis – a kind of shield, breastplate or cloak – is associated with both Zeus and Athena; it 'resounds' (*sonantem*) because it was linked with the production of thunder (see Eden on Virg. *Aen.* 8.354). It is somewhat surprising that here (as at 1.15.11) the aegis is described as Athena's, since H.'s story had seemed to concern Zeus/Jupiter (49), but Athena had participated in the Gigantomachy (Z. Stamatopoulou, *CQ* 62 (2012) 72–80). As Minerva she is the only divinity, apart from Apollo, who features both in H.'s ode and in Virgil's Battle of Actium (*Aen.* 8.699): 'It is tempting, in both places, to see in [her] a representative of reason or wisdom, fighting on the side of the legitimate champion of Rome' (P. Hardie 99). *contra ruere* is esp. favoured by Valerius Flaccus, but cf. also Stat. *Theb.* 8.504–5, Tac. *Agr.* 34.2.

58–9 hinc auidus stetit | Vulcanus, hinc…: *hinc* = 'on the side of the gods' (*TLL* 6.3.2806.9–10). In one version of the Gigantomachy, Hephaestus/Vulcan killed Mimas (above, 53n.). *auidus* evidently describes the god's appetite for the fight (*OLD* 4a; Goodyear on Tac. *A.* 1.51.1); it recalls the formulaic ἄατος / ἄτος πολέμοιο ('insatiable for war'), used of Ares by Homer (e.g. *Il.* 5.388) and of Gyges (69 below) by Hesiod (*Theog.* 714). Fire is described as 'eating through' at 75 below.

59 matrona Iuno: it was natural that Juno be called *matrona*, since she was goddess of women, *matronae* (*BNP* 6.1107–8). In the Gigantomachy she was attacked by Porphyrion (54n.), who was struck by a lightning-bolt from Jupiter and then finished off by Hercules (Apollod. 1.6.2).

60 numquam umeris positurus arcum describes the manner in which Apollo, who is identified in the two relative clauses which follow (61–4), participated in the Gigantomachy. The words mean *either* 'never to put the bow <back> on his shoulders' (sc. because he is constantly fighting with it) *or* 'never to put <down> the bow from his shoulders' (i.e. for the duration of the fighting he will not replace it with the lyre). The latter is supported by the facts (i) that *ponere*, when used of weapons, almost always refers to the laying down of arms (e.g. 1.3.40 'Iouem ponere fulmina'; *OLD ponere* 6a), (ii) that H. may be echoing Eur. *Alc.* 40 σύνηθες αἰεὶ ταῦτα βαστάζειν ἐμοί ('It is my custom always to carry them [sc. my bow and arrows]'). For Apollo as archer see also 1.21.11 and 2.10.19–20 with N–H ad locc.; R. F. Thomas, 'Homeric masquerade: politics and poetics in Horace's Apollo', in *Apolline Politics and Poetics* (ed. L. Athanassaki et al., 2009) 329–52; also above, 40n.

61–2 qui rore puro Castaliae lăuit | crines solutos 'who washes his loosened hair in the pure water of Castalia' (*lăuit* is present tense of the third-conjugation form *lauere*). Castalia, the spring at Delphi, was sacred to Apollo as well as the Muses (*BNP* 2.1176): it is mentioned alongside

Lycia and Delos (next n.) also at Pind. *Pyth.* 1.39, where it is described as the spring of Parnassus (the mountain range behind Delphi: see *BA* Map 55: C–D3–4). Apollo's flowing locks symbolised his eternal youth (1.21.2, *Epo.* 15.9); for his washing them cf. 4.6.26. For *ros* of water rather than dew see *OLD* 2a; for *crines* see 3.14.25n.

62–3 qui Lyciae tenet | dumeta natalemque siluam 'who inhabits/holds sway over the thickets of Lycia and his natal wood' (for *tenere* see *OLD* 8, 9b). The clause explains how the god divided up each year (see Serv. *Aen.* 4.143): for the six winter months he was based at Patara in Lycia, on the SW coast of Asia Minor (*BA* Map 65: B5), and for the remaining six months on the island of Delos, where he had been born next to a palm or olive tree (hence *siluam*). These two cult centres are then referred to chiastically in the cult titles provided in line 64.

65–8 In this ascending tricolon of *sententiae*, the first two *sententiae* are introduced by anaphora (*uis...uim...*), whereas the third is not. This pattern corresponds to, and marks out, the topics to which each *sententia* refers: the first two *sententiae* look back to the description of the Gigantomachy in 42–64 (the brute force of the Giants and the 'intelligent' force of the gods, especially Jupiter and Apollo); but the third looks forward to the criminals listed in the last three stanzas of the ode (69–80). Lines 65–8 therefore have a transitional function, which suggests that the speech of the Muses/Camenae has ended with the description of Apollo in 60–4 and that the poet is once again speaking in his own voice (cf. 3.1.41–8n.). His successive references to 'force without *consilium*' (65) and 'force regulated by *consilium*' (66–7a) are designed to reaffirm what he had said about the *consilium* of the Muses/Camenae at 41–2, while his *sententia* about 'misapplied *consilium*' (67b–8) will be proved by what follows. The notion that the poet is speaking in 65–8 is supported by the phrase '*mearum*...sententiarum' at 69–70.

65 uis consili expers mole ruit sua: the combination of mental and physical prowess (compare Eur. fr. 732 ῥώμη δέ τ' ἀμαθὴς πολλάκις τίκτει βλάβην, 'ignorant strength often produces harm', and esp. Gorg. *Epitaph.* fr. 6 δισσὰ ἀσκήσαντες μάλιστα ὧν δεῖ, γνώμην <καὶ ῥώμην>, 'they [sc. the Athenians] cultivated the two most necessary qualities, counsel and strength') is to be expected in an ideal leader (W. on Vell. 79.1). For the notion of collapsing under one's own weight or size (*sua* is emphatic) see E. Dutoit, 'Le thème de "la force qui détruit elle-même"', *REL* 14 (1936) 365–73: it is applied to the Giants by Ovid (*Met.* 1.156 'obruta mole sua'), but its most frequent application is to the civil wars of the late republic to which Augustus put an end at the battle of Actium (see e.g. *Epo.* 16.1–2; Woodman, *RICH* 131–2). *consili expers* is a relatively frequent expr. (Sall. *H.* 1.77.11M/1.67.11R, Cic. *Sest.* 47, *ND* 2.87, Sen. *NQ* 1 *praef.* 15).

66–7 uim temperatam di quoque prouehunt | in maius: *consilio* is to be supplied with *temperatam* (cf. Tac. *A.* 1.67.1 'ea consilio temperanda') and the phrase produces a typically Horatian paradox: force is *enhanced* by being *controlled*. See also 67–8n. below. *quoque* is nicely ambiguous between 'even' and 'also': 'even the gods...' constitutes an example to follow; 'the gods also...' takes it for granted that Augustus is already adopting the policy. For *in maius* ('all the more') cf. *OLD maior* 4c. For the anaphora *uis...uim* see 3.1.6n.

67–8 idem odere uires | omne nefas animo mouentes 'but at the same time they have nothing to do with forces pondering every wickedness in their minds': *idem* (lit. 'the same <gods>') here emphasises a potential inconsistency between two propositions (as 2.10.16, 3.12.13; *OLD idem* 10a): the gods enhance force when it is tempered by counsel, but they reject force when that counsel is wicked: *animo* corresponds to the understood *consilio* in 66, and *uires* is equivalent to 'forceful/violent persons'. This third *sententia* continues the alliteration on *ui-*, to which is now added the double play of *-nĕ nē-* and *-mō mŏ-* ; despite Quintilian's stricture (9.4.41), such effects (again at 'temptātŏr Ōrion' below and e.g. *S.* 2.2.106 'u*ni n*īmirum recte tibi sem*per e*runt res') are extremely common in Latin verse and prose (see e.g. Brink on *AP* 36; *EO* 2.849–50; W. on Tac. *A.* 4.13.2), and indeed the phrase *omne nefas* features commonly in imperial epic. For *odere* see 3.1.1n.; for *mouere* = 'to ponder' see *OLD* 19: its combination with *animo* recurs at Virg. *Aen.* 3.34 and 10.890 'multa mouens animo', which recall the Homeric 'pondering many things in the mind' (*Il.* 10.4, *Od.* 1.427); cf. also Sil. 2.352 'animo patria arma mouebat' (ambiguous).

69–70 testis mearum centimanus Gyges | sententiarum: sc. *est*. The set expr. *testis est* is very common in Cicero (cf. also *OLD testis* 4b); the interlaced word order exhibits chiastic grammar (genit. nom. ~ nom. genit.), which is repeated in the second example below. Gyges, one of the three Hundred-Handers (5n.), and Orion (70–2) illustrate the third of H.'s *sententiae*, namely, 'forces pondering every wickedness' (67–8). A. Hardie (2016) 71–2 sees in the words *centimanus* and *sententiarum* a reference to App. Claudius Caecus (cos. 307, 296 BC), who composed a verse work known as *Sententiae* and was jocularly called 'Centemmanus' on account of his juridical expertise (Pomp. *Dig.* 1.2.2.36).

70–2 notus et integrae | temptator Orion Dianae, | uirginea domitus sagitta 'notorious too is the assailant [*or* and so is the notorious assailant] of the maiden Diana, Orion, tamed by the virgin's arrow.' Orion was a Giant and a hunter, whose attempt on Diana's chastity failed when she shot him (Callim. *Hymn to Diana* 3.264–5, Serv. *Aen.* 1.535), an irony underlined by the description of the hunter as *domitus* (seemingly an imitation of the Greek δαμάζω, from which *domare* was derived by Varro, *LL* 6.96: cf. e.g. Ap. Rhod. 1.483 ἐδάμησαν ὀιστοῖς). *temptator* does not recur in classical Latin (Intro. 25); for *temptare* in this sense see Tib. 1.3.73 and Maltby on 1.2.17.

73 iniecta monstris Terra dolet suis: *dolet* shows that Earth is personified: H. is referring to the goddess who gave birth to both Titans (42–4n.) and Giants (Hes. *Theog.* 184–5 and West's n.): hence *suis*. The sentence refers to those monsters whose fate was to have mountains or islands placed on top of them (75–6n.) or to be condemned to the Underworld (77–8n.); it means *either* 'Earth, superimposed on her own monsters, grieves <because of her own monsters>' *or* 'Earth grieves that she is superimposed on her own monsters' (i.e. a nom. + infin., as in Greek): she bore them and now she buries them. At the same time *iniecta* suggests *terra* as the common noun 'earth', producing an allusive reference to regular burial (e.g. Sen. *Ben.* 5.20.5 'si terram...mortuo inieci'). See further next n.

74–5 maeretque partus fulmine luridum | missos ad Orcum: scholars are agreed that this means 'and mourns that her offspring have been sent by a lightning-bolt to lurid Orcus', although the juxtaposition *fulmine luridum* suggests alternatively that these words might be taken together (for the causal abl. see e.g. Ov. *Tr.* 5.7.16): either way, the word order is interlaced. '*luridus* is applied to anything relating to death or Hell' (NA on Lygd. 3.38 'luridus Orcus').

75–6 nec peredit | impositam celer ignis Aetnen 'and the swift fire has not eaten through superimposed Aetna'. According to certain versions of their story, the fate of Typhoeus (53n.) and Enceladus (55–6n.) was to be imprisoned under Mt Aetna, where they belched forth fire: for Typhoeus see Pind. *Pyth.* 1.13–28, for Enceladus see Virg. *Aen.* 3.578–80 'fama est Enceladi semustum fulmine corpus | urgeri mole hac, ingentemque insuper Aetnam | impositam ruptis flammam exspirare caminis' (with Horsfall). H.'s point is that despite the speed of the fire (*celer* is perhaps concessive) it has not managed to burn away the mountain, which therefore still presses down upon the Giants. Aetna, whose most recent

COMMENTARY 5

recorded eruption was in 32 BC (Dio 50.8.3), was a popular subject for poets, perhaps including H.'s friend Valgius Rufus (cf. 7C/171H with Courtney and Hollis; N–H on 2.9 intro., p. 135). For the proverbial speed of fire see Fowler on Lucr. 2.192.

77–8 incontinentis nec Tityi iecur | rěliquit ales 'and the bird has not left the liver of unrestrained Tityus': a son of Zeus and Earth of gigantic size, Tityus intended to assault Leto but was shot dead by Artemis/Diana and Apollo. In Hades he is stretched out on the ground and his liver is perpetually pecked at by one or more vultures (*BNP* 14.748). The liver was associated with sexual desire (4.1.12 and Thomas's n.), and it is no doubt significant, in view of Augustus' preoccupation with sexual morality, that three of the four criminals named here were punished for crimes of lust. For *rěliquit* see Intro. 30.

78–9 nequitiae additus | custos: the regular expr. for assigning a guard is unexpectedly combined with the abstract *nequitiae* (almost 'lust'), suggesting that Tityus is an incarnation of it.

79–80 amatorem trecentae | Pirithoum cohibent catenae: *trecentae* denotes any large number (*OLD* b). Pirithous (again at 4.7.27) was king of the 'savage Lapiths' (2.12.5, with N–H) and along with Theseus made an attempt on Persephone in the Underworld (cf. Virg. *Aen.* 6.397, Apollod. 2.5.12, with Frazer's long n.). His very name suggests 'one who makes a quick attempt' (πειράω + θοός), while *amatorem* defines the nature of his attempt. It is perhaps significant that the story of his and Theseus' descent into Hades was told by Hesiod (fr. 280 M–W = 216 Most; cf. Pausan. 9.31.4–5). Alliteration, assonance and anagrammatism bring modest closure to a series of examples which otherwise has no formal ending.

5

The ode falls into two distinct and very unequal parts (1–12, 13–56). In the first part H. urges subjugation of the Parthians (1–4), whose customs and way of life have been adopted enthusiastically by the Roman soldiers whom they had taken prisoner after the disastrous battle of Carrhae in 53 BC (5–12). The now ageing prisoners (cf. 8 *consenuit*) are portrayed from two complementary perspectives: the second stanza features the shame and disgrace of the prisoners' Parthian acculturation; the third stanza lists all the familiar symbols which represent Rome and Italy but which the prisoners have shockingly forgotten. The picture is designed both to illustrate the formidable nature of the Parthian empire (4 *grauibus*) and, by raising the reader's indignation, to support the notion of a revenge campaign.

In the second part of the ode H. relates a famous (but probably unhistorical) episode in the life of M. Atilius Regulus (consul 267 and 256 BC), who during the First Punic War (264–241 BC) was captured along with some of his men by the Carthaginians in 255 BC.[27] Five years later, according to the legend (of which there are various versions), Regulus was allowed by Carthage to travel to Rome for negotiations, on the condition that, if his mission was unsuccessful, he himself would return to Carthage; most versions of the story involve a proposal to exchange prisoners, although H. uniquely refers to a ransom (25 *auro*). Unlike their modern-day Parthian counterparts, these prisoners are still young and of military age (18 *pubes*, 26 *miles*), and, so far from being assimilated into Carthaginian society, they are being held captive and treated as slaves (21–2 'ciuium | retorta tergo bracchia libero', 35–6 'lora restrictis lacertis | sensit'); yet Regulus famously advised the senate against their release, even though he knew that he himself would thereby be obliged to return to Carthage and certain death. The central stanzas of the ode (13–48) are devoted to his appearance and speech in the senate, where he argues that the prisoners, if ransomed, will make useless soldiers in the continuing war against Carthage: not only will they themselves be reluctant to return to fighting (25–40), but future generations of soldiers will also be reluctant to fight with true bravery, since they will assume, from the precedent set (cf. 15 *exemplo*), that they too will be ransomed within a relatively short period of time.[28] Regulus, characterised by his far-sightedness (13 'mens prouida'), evidently feared that the process would be cumulative and that the proportion of battle-shy men would grow with the passing years, 'bringing destruction to a future age' (15–16) and resulting eventually in Italy's domination by Carthage (39–40).

Since Carthage and Parthia were successively Rome's principal rivals (3–4n.), it is not surprising that the two great powers should be juxtaposed in the same ode; but the role played by the two sets of Roman prisoners, upon whom the focus rests in each case, could scarcely be more different. Yet that there is a link between them is made explicit by line 13

---

[27] The episode is generally assumed to be unhistorical because it is absent from Polybius (see Walbank on 1.35). For discussion of Regulus see E. R. Mix, *Marcus Atilius Regulus: exemplum historicum* (1970), R. Langlands, *Exemplary Ethics in Ancient Rome* (2018) 267–90; Dyck on Cic. *Off.* 3.97–115, Levene on Liv. *per.* 18.

[28] 'If there were the hope of ransom, Roman soldiers would come to prefer captivity to a brave death' (Wickham).

('hoc cauerat mens prouida Reguli'), upon which depends the interpretation of the ode as a whole. What is that link? Regulus bases his argument on the fact that his soldiers had not fought fiercely enough (20 'sine caede') but had surrendered to the enemy (33 'perfidis se credidit hostibus') and, through their fear of death (36 'timuit...mortem'), had confused war with peace (38 'pacem duello miscuit'). Roman soldiers were expected to fight to the death, and Roman history is full of stories of such bravery.[29] Regulus is above all concerned about true courage: his phrase *uera uirtus* comes at the exact centre of the ode (29a). Because his soldiers had not shown true courage in their first engagement with the enemy, they were even less likely to be courageous if they were ransomed to fight a second time. When H. links the Carthaginian episode with the Parthian by saying '*This* is what the provident Regulus had taken precautions against to prevent' (13: see n.), he means that Regulus had tried to deter future generations from believing that surrender was preferable to a fight to the death. But in the case of the soldiers at Carrhae his efforts proved futile.

In the second ode of the Alcaic Hexad H. had talked of young Romans learning to fight Parthia (3.2.1–4) and he had given memorable expression to the ideal of dying in battle (13 'dulce et decorum est pro patria mori'). Now, in the penultimate ode of the Hexad, he returns ring-fashion to these themes: this ode too opens with the prospect of fighting Parthia (1–4), and the story of Regulus is used to dwell at length on the importance of fighting with true courage. If there is to be a war of vengeance against Parthia, as promised in the second ode of Book 1 (1.2.51 'Medos... inultos'), it has to be fought to the death. The uncompromising nature of this message perhaps helps to explain why the ode concludes obliquely with a characteristically Horatian 'diminuendo' (50–6), where military virtues are replaced by rustic withdrawal.

Although there was much talk of a campaign against Parthia in the 20s BC (see 3.2 intro.), no fighting ever took place. In 20 Augustus reached an accommodation whereby Phraates IV, the king of Parthia, returned the prisoners and military standards captured at Carrhae (cf. Dio 54.8.1–3 with Rich's n.). The event was widely celebrated (see 4.15.6–8, *RG* 29.2 and Cooley, Suet. *Aug.* 21.3 and Wardle), and the standards were eventually displayed in the temple of Mars the Avenger in 2 BC (J. W. Rich, *PBSR* 66 (1998) 71–128).

---

[29] See Oakley on Liv. 9.4.7–16 (p. 78), who refers to N. Rosenstein, *Imperatores Victi* (1990) 135–40.

METRE Alcaic

1–4 The opening stanza consists of a series of characteristically Horatian correspondences (*caelo ~ praesens, tonantem ~ adiectis…Persis, credidimus ~ habebitur, Iouem ~ Augustus, regnare ~ diuus*), the very number of which is intended to heighten the persuasiveness of the analogy. In an amusing reversal Seneca in his satire on Claudius' apotheosis says that, if the emperor is allowed into heaven, no one will believe that the real gods are gods (*Apoc.* 11.4 'dum tales deos facitis, nemo uos deos esse credet').

1–2 Caelo tonantem credidimus Iouem | regnare: *credidimus* is a so-called 'gnomic' perfect (G&L 160 §236 Note), 'a Grecism of which H. is specially fond' (Mayer on *Epi.* 1.2.48) and which may be translated as a present (cf. J. Wackernagel, *Lectures on Syntax* (2009) 231 and n. 14). *tonantem* ('when he thunders') combines with *Iouem* to suggest the title Iuppiter Tonans (Jupiter the Thunderer), whose temple was under construction on the Capitoline Hill (3.3.6n.). Epicureans sought rational explanations for thunder (Lucr. 6.96–155), but H.'s Epicureanism was eclectic.

2–3 praesens diuus habebitur | Augustus: Augustus' divine status on earth was treated at the start of Book 1 (1.2.41–9), where he was identified with Mercury, and his apotheosis was predicted as recently as 3.3.11–12 (n.). H. now returns to the former theme, this time involving Jupiter, with whom (as Zeus) Augustus was readily identified in the Greek east (Weinstock 304–5). A special relationship between the two had been adumbrated at 1.12.49–60 and was suggested at the start of the present book (3.1.6n.). *praesens* is the technical term for a present and efficacious deity (*OLD* 3) and, unlike its Greek equivalent (ἐπιφανής, 'manifest'), need not necessarily imply visibility (see Brink on *Epi.* 2.1.15–17). For more on the name Augustus, 'socium summo cum Ioue nomen' (Ov. *F.* 1.608), see 3.3.11–12n.

3–4 adiectis Britannis | imperio grauibusque Persis 'when the Britons and formidable Parthians have been added to the empire': the abl. abs., appended to the main sentence in H.'s manner (3.1.30–1n.), resembles those used as coin legends to commemorate military or diplomatic victories (e.g. *Armenia deuicta* or *Asia recepta*). Since *imperio* obviously means the 'Roman' or 'our' empire (cf. *RG* 27.1 'Aegyptum imperio populi Romani adieci'), no further identification is required;[30] but there is perhaps some

---

[30] In keeping with his general argument J. Richardson seems to deny that *imperium* here has any kind of geographical connotation (*The Language of Empire: Rome and the Idea of Empire from the Third Century BC to the Second Century AD* (2008) 132–5); this is hard to believe.

COMMENTARY 5.5-6

edge to H.'s use of the word, since the Romans acknowledged that the Parthians had an empire too (Strabo 11.9.2 'in the size of their empire [τῆς ἀρχῆς] they have become, in a way, rivals of the Romans', Just. 41.1.1 'Parthi, penes quos, uelut diuisione orbis cum Romanis facta, nunc Orientis imperium sit'; see further W. on Tac. A. 6.31-9, intro. n.). *grauibus* both hints at the geopolitical reality and prepares for the focus on Parthia in 5-12 below.

The Parthians are here called Persians, 'evoking their role as heirs to the Achaemenid empire and at least potentially tapping into the classical Greek view of the Persians and the imagery of the Persian Wars' (Powell 160): the same equivalence recurs at 1.2.22 'graues Persae' (where they are again coupled with the Britons), 1.21.15 and 4.15.23. Under their own name the Parthians are coupled with the Britons at *Epo.* 7.7-10 (as at Prop. 2.27.5); and, since Scythians may also be identified with Parthians (Powell 147), the two peoples are further coupled at 3.4.35-6 (cf. Virg. *G.* 1.65-6, Ov. *Am.* 2.16.39). Just as there were plans for attacking Parthia (see above, 3.2 intro.), so too plans for the invasion of Britain are mentioned by Dio under the years 34 BC (49.38.2 with Reinhold's n.) and, much more recently, 27 and 26 (53.22.5 and Rich's n., 53.25.2): see esp. 1.35.29-30 'serues iturum Caesarem in *ultimos | orbis Britannos*' (a further allusion to Cat. 11.10-11: see 3.4.33-6n.); A. Momigliano, *JRS* 40 (1950) 39-41. Moreover, since the Britons were conventionally far distant, they lent themselves to polarised expressions such as in lines 3-4, indicating the whole world (see e.g. Pease on Cic. *ND* 2.88); and worldwide empire became a theme of the Augustan age (see e.g. C. Nicolet, *Space, Geography and Politics in the Early Roman Empire* (1991) 29-56). Given the importance of Jupiter in H.'s stanza, it is significant that it is the same god who utters the words 'imperium sine fine dedi' at *Aen.* 1.279; and, while in 1-2a it is implied that Jupiter rules where he thunders (the 'fronted' *caelo* is to be taken *apo koinou* (3.2.3-4n.) with both *tonantem* and *regnare*), in 2b-4 there is the surreal suggestion (typical of H.) that Augustus' 'presence' in Rome depends upon activity in the remotest regions of the world.

5 miles…Crassi: in 53 BC at Carrhae, about 70 miles almost due east from the Zeugma crossing of the Euphrates (*BA* Map 67: H3), in mod. southern Turkey, M. Licinius Crassus (cos. 70, 55 BC) was defeated by the Parthians (*MRR* 2.230); it was one of the worst defeats in the history of Rome, and its avenging recurs as a theme during the age of Augustus. *miles* is collective singular, common in historical writing (Malloch on Tac. A. 11.9.1).

5-6 coniuge barbara | turpis maritus uixit 'has he stayed alive as a husband disgraced by a barbarian wife?' (chiastic): see *OLD turpis* 4 for the abl., although it is possible also to interpret *coniuge barbara* as an abl. abs. Since Roman soldiers were forbidden to marry (Treggiari 46–7), *coniuge* and *maritus* are as loaded as *barbara*. For the criticism implied in *uixit* (*OLD* 5a) see intro.

6–8 hostium | ...consenuit socerorum in armis: the shamefulness of the situation (5–6n.) is continued by the hyperbaton of *hostium...socerorum*, words which ought to be opposites (cf. Val. Max. 5.1.10 'oblitus hostis, soceri uultum induit'). *in armis* seems to refer to service in the Parthian army (cf. Just. 41.2.5); compare Liv. 32.3.5 'consenuisse sub armis'. *consenescere* is 'connected with the wasting away of one's powers and capabilities, with the failure of one's life, with the remoteness of military service overseas or in far off lands, with the tragedy of exile and imprisonment' (P. Treves, *AJP* 63 (1942) 129–53, at 131, whose principal argument is that the verb regularly means 'to die in exile'). The battle of Carrhae had taken place exactly thirty years before the publication of *Odes* 1–3.

7 pro curia inuersique mores: *pro* is an interjection which, regularly found in exclamatory expressions such as 'pro Iuppiter!' or 'pro fidem!', is also used, as here, in exclamations of shame or disapproval (e.g. Liv. 22.14.6 'tantum – pro! – degeneramus a patribus nostris!'): see *OLD pro*² 1 and 2 respectively. *curia* is probably corrupt, since the senate had nothing to do with Carrhae or its aftermath; yet none of the suggested emendations (*gloria, saecula, tempora, patria, munia*) seems at all plausible. The paradosis has been retained *faute de mieux*, in which case the participle is to be taken with both nouns ('Alas, the overturning of *curia* and custom!'); for the *ab urbe condita* idiom see 3.4.18–19n.

9 sub rege Medo Marsus et Apulus: the nominatives are in apposition to *miles* (5), which, being a collective noun, allows more than one appositive. The Marsi, a tribe in central Italy whose name suggested a derivation from Mars, were famously warlike (N–H on 1.2.39); Apulia, further to the SE, was H.'s own district: he refers to the 'Apula gens...uiolenta' at *S*. 2.1.38–9 (and cf. N–H on 1.22.13). For *Medo*, emphatically juxtaposed, see 3.3.43–4n. *rege* adds to the disgrace, given the traditional Roman hatred of kingship. For this metaphorical use of *sub* see Brink on *Epi*. 2.1.99 and Appendix 7; *sub rege* is first at Cic. *Rep*. 2.43.

10–11 anciliorum et nominis et togae | oblitus: the *ancilia* were twelve 8-shaped shields, sacred in origin, which were kept in the Regia and carried ceremonially by the Salii, priests of Mars; the association with the god means that they should have been esp. memorable to the Marsi. See Liv.

1.20.4, 5.52.7. The irregular genit. form (*ancile* is a 3rd-declension noun) is unique to this passage (although the expected *ancilium* is itself found only at Tac. *H.* 1.89.3). *nomen* is capable of a wide range of meanings (3.3.45–6n.): here perhaps 'nationality' is foremost, as in the expressions *nomen Romanum* or *nomen Etruscum* (*OLD* 19a), although other nuances, such as 'reputation' (*OLD* 12), are hard to exclude. The toga symbolised the Roman people, 'rerum dominos gentemque togatam' (Virg. *Aen.* 1.282 with Austin; also Panayotakis on Laber. 28 and 29.2; U. Rothe, *The Toga and Roman Identity* (2019) 45): the point is that the captives will have 'gone native', wearing trousers like their captors (cf. Prop. 3.4.17 'bracati militis', Pers. 3.53 'bracatis...Medis'). The survivor of Carrhae mentioned by Florus is dressed 'Parthico habitu' (2.20.4 = 4.10.4), although Velleius says that he had not lost his loyalty to Rome (82.2). Since the toga was also a symbol of peace (*OLD* 4a), there is a contrast with *anciliorum*.

11 aeternaeque Vestae: the goddess is here metonymical for her sacred fire, which was tended by the Vestal Virgins and never allowed to be extinguished (Cic. *Leg.* 2.20, *Cat.* 4.18 'ignem Vestae sempiternum'), symbolising the eternity of Rome: for the latter cf. K. J. Pratt, 'Rome as eternal', *JHI* 26 (1965) 25–44, who, like others, says that the first occurrence of the famous expression is Tib. 2.5.23, but Liv. 5.7.10 is at least a decade earlier. The name is also metonymical at Virg. *G.* 4.384.

12 incolumi Ioue: another appended abl. abs. (above, 3–4n.). In a common form of metonymy (see e.g. 3.26.5; Smith on Tib. 2.5.22, Courtney on Juv. 13.113ff., Bulloch on Callim. *Hymn* 5.35), the god (Jupiter Optimus Maximus) stands for his temple on the Capitoline Hill (to be distinguished from the temple of Jupiter Tonans in the same area). For the symbolism of the Capitol see 3.3.42–3n.

13 hoc cauerat mens prouida Reguli: poetic for *hoc cauerat mente prouida Reguli*: 'This rather bold personification of *mens*...derives from the high style of epic and tragedy' (Eden on Virg. *Aen.* 8.205 'Caci mens'). For the transitional use of *hoc* see 3.3.15–16n. *cauere* is capable of a wide range of subtly different meanings (see *OLD*); the only one which suits this context is 'to take precautions against so as to prevent' (*OLD* 2c). The way in which Regulus had sought to prevent future Roman prisoners of war from being assimilated into a barbarian culture (*hoc*) was by arguing that soldiers should not allow themselves to be taken prisoner in the first place: that is, they should fight to the death (see further intro.). Despite his arguments, however, some of Crassus' soldiers had preferred survival as prisoners.

According to Livy's version of the Regulus legend, Regulus after returning to Rome was supposed to negotiate about both an exchange of prisoners and a peace treaty (*per.* 18.5);[31] there is no mention of a treaty in the historian Sempronius Tuditanus (fr. 8C = 5P), the earliest surviving purveyor of the story, or in Cicero (*Off.* 1.39, 3.99–100). H. too fails to mention a treaty and is unique in reporting a proposed ransom of the Roman prisoners rather than an exchange (25–6). It is possible that H. has here transferred to the story of Regulus elements of the speech which T. Manlius Torquatus is said to have delivered in 216 BC after the battle of Cannae, condemning the proposed ransom of the Roman prisoners of war (cf. H. Kornhardt, *Hermes* 82 (1954) 106–23). A speech to this effect is put into Torquatus' mouth by Livy (22.60.5–26), and, if Livy began to write his history in (say) the mid-30s BC, it is theoretically possible that Book 22 was published by the early or mid-20s and that H. had Livy in mind; but, since there are no clear verbal similarities between Torquatus' speech in Livy and Regulus' speech in H.,[32] it is more probable that H.'s stanzas are to be explained differently. He may have transferred Torquatus' speech from an author other than Livy; he may have based his version of the Regulus story on a source which is now unknown to us; or he may simply have made it up.[33]

For *mens prouida* cf. Cic. *Div.* 2.117, Ov. *Met.* 7.712, Sen. *Ag.* 872.

14–18 dissentientis condicionibus | foedis et exemplo trahenti | perniciem ueniens in aeuum, | si non periret immiserabilis | captiua pubes: this passage, much discussed and much emended (see N–R), raises far more difficulties than can be discussed here. The imperf. subjunctive in the *si*-clause expresses a regular future condition after a secondary-tense verb of saying or thinking (*NLS* 235–6 §280) and indicates that by the end of the passage we are in virtual indirect speech, representing Regulus' thoughts: this will be most clearly expressed in the text if, like many edd., we accept the variant *trahenti* (agreeing with *exemplo*)

---

[31] One assumes that Livy's epitomator has digested more or less accurately the story of Regulus as told in the missing Book 18, but one can never be sure.
[32] Shorey on 25 had quoted Liv. 22.60.16 'pretio redituri estis eo unde ignauia ac nequitia abistis?', and on 42 he compared Liv. 22.60.15 'sero nunc desideratis, deminuti capite', but these seem to me motific rather than verbal. Yet see 45–6n. below.
[33] H.'s version of the Regulus story shares some features with that of Pyrrhus and Fabricius (280 BC), which also involves an amount of gold and a promise to send back released prisoners in the event of a failed negotiation (Plut. *Pyrrh.* 20.1–2, 5); the latter story as told by Ennius (*Ann.* 183–90) is juxtaposed with the Regulus story by Cicero (*Off.* 1.38–9).

rather than *trahentis*.[34] Thus: 'dissenting from the foul conditions and from a precedent which would bring destruction in its wake for an age to come, unless the young captives perished without pity'. *dissentio* is normally constructed with *ab* + abl., but is occasionally found with the dat. (e.g. Colum. 3.3.8, Quint. 1.5.37; see *TLL* 5.1.1457.28–38, 1458.10–14). We should have expected *tracturo* rather than *trahenti*, but the present tense is used for the sake of vividness. It may seem odd to couple *trahenti* ('to draw behind one, trail, drag') with an expr. denoting the future ('ueniens in aeuum'), but Regulus' point is that, should a similar crisis arise again in the future, its resolution will depend upon the precedent they leave behind now: for this sense of *traho* ('to bring in its wake') see e.g. Virg. *G.* 4.393 'quae mox uentura trahantur'; *OLD* 14c. *condicio* is a largely prosaic word, as are several others in the ode (see below). *aeuum*, by contrast, is choice (Mayer on 1.12.45); *in aeuum* (again at 4.14.3) is a regular expr. meaning roughly 'into the future' (*OLD aeuum* 1c), the meaning of which is filled out by *ueniens* (qualifying *aeuum* again at Sen. *NQ* 7.30.4, Luc. 7.390). For the archaising poeticism *pubes*, 'a collective term for the youth of military age', see Mayer on 1.25.17; *captiua pubes* recurs only at Petr. 89, line 25, but scholars have noted Sil. 6.348–9 'poscentes uinctam inter proelia pubem | captiuamque manum ductore rependere nostro' (of the Regulus story).

Elsewhere H. always has a long syllable at the line-break of the Alcaic hendecasyllabic line: either the final syllable of *periret* is to be regarded as long, an archaism (N–H on 2.13.16, Austin on Virg. *Aen.* 1.308), or it is short in imitation of Alcaeus, who allows a short syllable at this point. The question would not arise if one followed e.g. Vollmer in reading *iam miserabilis* for the otherwise unattested *immiserabilis*; but Regulus' argument requires having no sympathy for the Roman captives in Carthage, and *immiserabilis* belongs to H.'s favourite category of negative compound adjs. (Intro. 25).

18–19 Signa ego Punicis | adfixa delubris: the virtual indirect discourse of the preceding sentence (15–18n.) gives way to direct speech, a technique similar to that in the Roman historians, where *oratio obliqua* sometimes modulates into *oratio recta* (see W. on Tac. *A.* 4.40.4). Regulus' statement, which would immediately remind H.'s readers of the Roman standards currently held by the Parthians, is doubly outrageous. (i) Since

---

[34] The variant was evidently found in a now lost MS whose readings were reported by J. Cruquius in the sixteenth century. Many scholars prefer to retain *trahentis* in the sense of 'inferring/concluding from the precedent' (*OLD* 12b), 'but then *ex* or *ab* might have been expected' with *exemplo* (N–R).

the legionary standards would normally be kept in the *sacellum* or shrine of a Roman fort (see e.g. E. L. Wheeler in C. Wolff (ed.), *L'armée romaine et la religion* (2009) 260), it was a particular disgrace that they should be transferred to a religious repository in a foreign land. (ii) It was evidently a Roman practice to fix enemy trophies to temple walls (Gallus fr. 2.4–5C/143.4–5H 'templa deorum | fixa…spolieis'); the Carthaginians are adding insult to injury.

19–21 arma | militibus sine caede… | derepta: *sine caede* is Regulus' first reference to the *Leitmotif* of his speech, namely, that a Roman soldier should fight to the death: he should not give up his weapons without a fight but should either kill his would-be despoiler or himself be killed in the process.

20 dixit: Regulus' speech is an example of the *genus deliberatiuum* (see further 45–6n.), like Juno's earlier (3.3.17–18n.).

21 uidi ego: the chiastic repetition from *ego…uidi* (18–21) emphasises Regulus' autopsy and hence helps to authenticate the story (for the repetition of a last word by a first see 3.3.61n.). *uidere* is used esp. of witnessing awful scenes (e.g. 1.2.13) or things which test credulity (2.19.2 'uidi…credite, posteri'); both nuances are in play here. See also W. on Tac. *Agr.* 45.1.

21–2 ciuium | rĕtorta tergo bracchia libero 'the arms of free citizens twisted behind [lit. on] their backs' (cf. Ov. *Am.* 1.2.31 'manibus post terga retortis' and McKeown); *libero* has been transferred from *ciuium* to *tergo* (enallage: 3.1.42–3n.), parodying the almost technical expr. *caput liberum*, a 'free person' (*OLD caput* 7a). Cf. [Tib.] 3.7.117 (*Pan. Mess.*) 'libera…colla' (Prop. 2.30.8). For *rĕtorta* see Intro. 30.

23–4 portasque non clausas et arua | Marte coli populata nostro: the syntax of *uidi* changes from direct object, of which *portasque non clausas* is the fourth and final example, to accus. + infin. The gates are those of Carthage, a source of wonder to Aeneas when he first arrived in Africa (Virg. *Aen.* 1.422 'miratur portas'). Open gates and agriculture are both signs of peace: cf. Sall. *H.* 1.14M/inc. 10R 'apertae portae, repleta arua cultoribus', Liv. 6.25.7 'non cultus agrorum intermissus, patentibus portis urbis' and Oakley's additional note (4.525–6; also Brink on *AP* 199). *Marte* + possessive adj. would normally mean 'by one's own prowess' (*OLD Mars* 4), as Cic. *Off.* 3.34 'ut dicitur, Marte nostro', but here the meaning is 'by our armed forces' (*OLD Mars* 7), taking the abl. with both *coli* and *populata*, effectively juxtaposed. As Regulus was the first Roman – and the

COMMENTARY 5.25-32   155

only Roman in the First Punic War – to have led an invasion force to Africa and to have ravaged Carthaginian fields, these two lines are esp. poignant. *populari* is usu. deponent; *populatus* in a passive sense is common (*TLL* 10.1.2709.30–5).

25–6 auro repensus scilicet acrior | miles redibit 'Ransomed by gold, a soldier will naturally return more enthusiastic/fierce': *scilicet* is ironical, indicating that Regulus means the opposite of what he says. For this sense of *repndo* see *OLD* 5b.

26–7 flagitio additis | damnum 'you are adding loss to outrage': i.e. since the ransomed soldier (as Regulus has just said) will not be keen to fight again, his contribution to any future war will be lost, a loss which should be added to the outrage of his being taken captive in the first place (for *flagitium* = 'cowardice' and the like in military contexts cf. *TLL* 6.1.842.23–47). Others take *damnum* as referring to the loss of the ransom money. Either way, *additis damnum* is typically Horatian: one would expect a loss to be subtracted, not added. *damnum* is absent from Cat. Lucr. Virg. and Tib., while *flagitium* is primarily prosaic: they are frequently coupled in Plautus (e.g. *Pseud.* 440).

27–8 neque amissos colores | lana refert medicata fuco: the lines are an analogy for *uirtus* (29–30): once wool has been dyed, it cannot recover its original colour, which is lost for ever. *medico* here = 'to dye' (*OLD* 2c); for *refert* see *OLD* 16.

29–30 nec uera uirtus, cum semel excidit, | curat reponi deterioribus: what is the image? Given that *excidere* and *reponere* appear alongside each other almost exclusively in medical writers (e.g. Cels. 8.11.4 'ut *excidere* omnes articuli possunt, sic non omnes *reponuntur*...ac quibus in pueritia *exciderunt* neque *repositi* sunt...'), H. seems to mean that '*uirtus*, like a dislocated limb, cannot be fitted back into position once "put out"' (S. J. Harrison, *CQ* 36 (1986) 503): 'and true courage, whenever it is once dislocated, does not care to be put back in men <who are now> weaker [sc. because of its dislocation]'; *cum* + perf. indic. = 'whenever' (*NLS* 151 §194 *Note*). The image is undoubtedly strange, esp. since courage seems at the same time to be personified (*curat*), but H. may have a similar notion in mind in his allusion to Philippi, 'cum fracta uirtus' (2.7.11). *deterioribus* (dat.) combines the notions of morality ('more cowardly') and health ('worse').

31–2 si pugnat extricata densis | cerua plagis 'if a doe fights when released from close-meshed nets': H.'s word order is both interlaced and mimetic. Since deer were proverbially timid and flighty (e.g. Lucr. 5.863, Virg. *G.* 3.539), the clause is equivalent to an adynaton or impossibility, setting up the irony of the apodosis (next n.).

32–6 erit ille fortis | qui..., qui...timuitque mortem: the two main clauses are ironical and mean the opposite of what they say: the man who has allowed himself to be taken captive will *not* be brave (*fortis*) and will *not* crush the enemy (*proteret*). *ille...qui...* suggests a generalisation, but, as indicated by the tense of the verbs in the rel. clauses and by *Poenos* in line 34, Regulus is referring to the soldiers whose release he has been sent to negotiate. Since the captivity described in 33 and 35–6a *results from* the fear of death, the two relative clauses perhaps represent a form of *hysteron proteron*.

33 qui perfidis se credidit hostibus: the bad faith of the Carthaginians ('Punica fides') was notorious (cf. Liv. 21.4.9 'perfidia plus quam Punica'; Otto 291, Tosi 113 §245) and contrasts with the *fides* of Regulus himself (Sen. *Prov.* 3.9 'documentum fidei').

34 et Marte Poenos proteret altero 'and he will crush the Carthaginians in another war': *Marte* has a different meaning (*OLD* 2) from that at 24 above. By *altero* Regulus means the campaigning after his death (and the First Punic War continued for almost another decade until 241 BC), but to H.'s readers, for whom Hannibal was a 'bogey-man' (N. M. Horsfall, *Philol.* 117 (1973) 138), *altero* would suggest also the Second Punic War of 218–201 BC (cf. Flor. 1.22.1 = 2.6.1 'post primum Punicum bellum... ecce alterum bellum').

35–6 qui lora restrictis lacertis | sensit iners 'who has spiritlessly experienced the thongs on his tethered arms' (a slightly odd way of referring to the thongs tethering his arms). *inertia* is the opposite of *uirtus* (4.9.29–30: cf. Don. on Ter. *Andr.* 608 'iners sine arte, id est sine ἀρετή'; Maltby 302). *sensit iners* is another of H.'s pointed juxtapositions (cf. Sen. *NQ* 2.1.4 'iners...et sine sensu'). For the adverbial adj. see 3.3.70–2n.

37–8 hic, unde uitam sumeret inscius, | pacem duello miscuit: scholars have been troubled by *hic* referring to the same person as *ille* above (32–6), but 'it is the speaker who decides from which perspective he wants to present an entity or entities within a certain situation. The result may be that the same entity is referred to...with different demonstrative pronouns' (*OLS* 1.1138). Here *hic* = 'a person or thing of the kind just mentioned' (*OLD* 10c), as *Epi.* 1.6.40, 1.15.42. The emphasis of the sentence falls on *unde...inscius* (cf. 3.2.21–2, 3.6.33–4): '<but> this man, confusing war with peace, did not know how he should choose life' (adversative asyndeton); for this particular nuance of *unde* cf. *Epo.* 5.85 'dubius unde rumperet silentium', and for *uitam sumeret* (the imperf. subjunc. represents a present-tense deliberative question in direct speech) cf. Cic. *Fin.* 4.30. The argument is extremely condensed. Confronted with the prospect of death on the battlefield, and asking himself 'how am I to survive?', the true soldier should answer 'by means of the sword' (*ferro*). But the kind of soldier about whom Regulus has been talking chose to survive by surrendering his sword without a fight (~ 19–21) and by becoming a captive in bonds (~ 22).

Housman in his first published paper (1.1–2) objected to the transmitted *duello* on the related grounds that (i) elsewhere H. uses it of a specific war and never of war in the abstract, (ii) H. always uses *bellum* when elsewhere he juxtaposes war and peace. But Housman's emendation (*pacemque bello*) depended upon further emendations in the preceding lines, and, since *duellum* can elsewhere be used of war in the abstract (e.g. Plaut. *As.* 559 'domi duellique'), there seems no reason why H. should not use it thus here, the archaism appropriate in the mouth of a speaker two and a quarter centuries in the past. See further Brink on *Epi.* 2.1.254 and Appendix 14, adding W. Clausen, *HSCP* 75 (1971) 69–72. For *miscere* = 'to confuse one thing with another', as at *Epi.* 1.16.54 'miscebis sacra profanis', see *OLD* 11d.

38 o pudor!: as in 39–40, *o* introduces an exclamation expressing horror (*OLD o²* 2a); for its combination with *pudor* cf. Ov. *Her.* 9.111, Val. Fl. 8.269, Mart. 8.78.4, Flor. 1.22.30 = 2.6.30.

39–40 o magna Carthago probrosis | altior Italiae ruinis! 'To think of great Carthage raised higher by the disgraceful ruin of Italy!' For *o* see 38n.; *ruinis* is a causal abl., since it is no feat to be higher than a ruin (and *altior* is, as it were, 'constructed' out of *Italiae*): Carthage has appropriated the adj. which more properly belongs to Rome (*S.* 1.5.1 'magna... Roma'). After the Third Punic War (149–146 BC) it was in fact Carthage that was razed to the ground and became a famous ruin (*Epo.* 9.25–6), especially associated with the story of Marius (Vell. 2.19.4 'uitam in tugurio ruinarum Carthaginiensium tolerauit', Plut. *Mar.* 40.4 'Marius a fugitive, seated among the ruins of Carthage').

41–3 fertur pudicae coniugis osculum | paruosque natos ut capitis minor | ab se remouisse: the implication of the last four stanzas of the ode is that Regulus, set upon his mission, had sailed the trade route directly from Carthage to Rome, where his family (who had perhaps travelled up from their country estate) were waiting to greet him. Since a returning husband and father would naturally be expected to welcome gestures of affection from his wife and children (Lucr. 3.894–5; Cairns, *GC* 22–3), it was absolutely extraordinary that Regulus pushed his family away and even (43–4) declined to look at them: H. therefore has to guarantee the account by *fertur*, a so-called 'Alexandrian footnote',[35] often used when a poet indicates that he is appealing to a tradition: for discussion and analysis of the exs. in Virgil see N. Horsfall, *The Epic Distilled* (2016) chap. 8 'So the story goes'. The principle involved is Callimachus' ἀμάρτυρον οὐδὲν ἀείδω, 'I sing nothing unattested' (fr. incert. 612).

41 pudicae coniugis: she is the ideal wife (Treggiari 236), contrasting with the barbarian *coniunx* of 5; she and their children feature in the version of the story at Cic. *Off.* 3.99.

42 ut capitis minor 'as being diminished in status': the genitive of reference after *minor* seems unparalleled but is facilitated by the allusion to the legal expr. *capitis deminutio*, 'deprivation of civil rights' (*OLD caput* 6a). Being a prisoner of war, Regulus no longer felt entitled to call himself husband or father. For *ut* see *OLD* 21a.

43–4 uirilem | toruus humi posuisse uultum: casting one's gaze on the ground, a common gesture, is found in a variety of different contexts (see e.g. Virg. *Aen.* 6.862 (Marcellus), 12.220 (Turnus); F. Muecke, *BICS* 31 (1984) 108–9). Here it symbolises Regulus' determination not to be deflected from his purpose. *toruus*, very often used of features (*OLD* 2a), is here used of the man himself; *uirilem* is suggestive of *uirtus* (Maltby 649): the two adjs. reinforce each other (cf. Sen. *Phaedr.* 798 'quam grata est facies torua uiriliter').

45–6 donec labantes consilio patres | firmaret auctor numquam alias dato 'until he as proposer bolstered the wavering senators with advice never given at any other time': H.'s words convey the surreal impression that Regulus kept his gaze averted from his family and fixed on the ground until such time as he could persuade the senate of the correct policy. *auctor* is technical of the mover of a proposal in the senate (cf. Liv. *per.* 18 'auctor senatui fuit' (of Regulus); *OLD* 11), and 'ex tota hac laude Reguli unum illud est admiratione dignum quod captiuos retinendos censuit' (Cic. *Off.* 3.111): a deliberative speech (above, 20n.) is defined

---

[35] The term seems to have been invented by Ross 78.

by the giving and receiving of advice (Quint. 3.4.6). Since similar advice to Regulus' would be given later by Manlius Torquatus in 216 BC (see 13n.), *numquam alias* must mean 'never given before'; interestingly, one of Livy's uses of *numquam alias antea* occurs in his build-up to Torquatus' speech (22.58.2). For the contrast between *labantes* and *firmaret* cf. Sen. *Ep.* 117.21, Plin. *NH* 24.119; the subjunctive is usually explained as occurring in a subordinate clause in indirect speech after *fertur*, but it seems just as likely to indicate intention or purpose (*NLS* 182–3 §224).

47–8 interque maerentes amicos | egregius properaret exul 'and amidst his grieving friends he could hurry away, an exceptional exile' or perhaps, in order to give full weight to *exul*, 'and amidst his grieving friends the exceptional man could hurry away – into exile'; again (see 45–6n.) the subjunctive expresses intention, underlining Regulus' determination to keep to his oath as soon as the senate had accepted his advice. *inter...amicos* anticipates the scene which becomes reality at 51–2 below; *egregius... exul* is another Horatian oxymoron (cf. Cic. *Dom.* 83 'ciuem...egregium... nemo umquam sanus exulem appellauit').

49–50 atqui sciebat quae sibi barbarus | tortor pararet: given Regulus' earlier stress on his eye-witnessing (21), his torture was horribly talionic, according to the version transmitted by pseudo-Acro: 'hunc Poeni...sectis palpebris uigiliis necauerunt' (on 1.12.37). The remarkable sequence of repeated syllables (*bar-bar-*, *tor-tor*, *-ar-ar-*) is perhaps intended to underline the barbarity involved (cf. Tac. *A.* 1.61.3 '*barbarae arae*, apud quas tribunos ac primorum ordinum centuriones mactauerant'). *atqui* (again at 3.7.9) is largely prosaic and common in H.'s hexameters.

50–6 The concluding diminuendo is typical of H. (N–H on 2.1.37, Thomas on 4.2.53–60).

51 dimouit obstantes propinquos: the verb, echoing *remouisse* (43), means 'to cause a group of people to part' (*OLD* 1b); Regulus' relatives and friends (47, above) feature in the version of the story at Cic. *Off.* 1.39.

52 populum reditus morantem 'the people delaying his return'; plur. for sing., as *Epo.* 16.35.

53–4 quam si clientum longa negotia | diiudicata lite relinqueret '(no differently) than if he were leaving behind the lengthy business of his clients after adjudicating their disputes'; in unreal comparative clauses the sequence of tenses is usually observed (*NLS* 210–11 §255): hence the imperf. subjunc. after *dimouit*. One of the responsibilities of a patron (3.1.13–14n.) was to dispense legal advice to his clients (*Epi.* 2.1.104 'clienti promere iura'): see in general R. P. Saller, *Personal Patronage under the Early Empire* (1982). *negotium* (again at 3.29.49 and common in H.'s hexameters) is the last of the largely prosaic words in this ode. Leave-taking is a recognised motif of closure.

55–6 Venafranos in agros | aut Lacedaemonium Tarentum: for Venafrum, a town near the Via Latina in the foothills of the Apennines in the valley of the R. Volturno (*BA* Map 44: F3), see N–H on 2.6.16; Tarentum, a town in southern Italy on the Ionian Gulf (*BA* Map 45: F4), was said to have been founded by the Spartan Phalanthus in the late eighth century BC (2.6.10–11 and N–H). Since the place could be represented as having declined from its Spartan origins (Liv. 38.17.12), *Lacedaemonium* allusively mirrors the decline of Rome which is implied by the behaviour of the Parthians' prisoners (Coleman 67).

When Macaulay in *The History of England* (Vol. 2 (1896 edn), p. 477) described the speech delivered by William III to the States of Holland as he bade them farewell before leaving for England, he portrayed William in terms of the departing Regulus as envisaged by H. (see C. G. Crump, *History and Historical Research* (1928) 151–2).

6

This is an extraordinary ode, both in its own right and as a conclusion to the Alcaic Hexad. In three of its four central stanzas (21–32) H. focusses with extreme vividness on a girl whose youth is spent in learning the techniques of lascivious dancing; then, when later she is married, she attends bibulous parties for the purpose of prostituting herself to the highest bidder with the full connivance of her husband, who therefore becomes a kind of *leno*. The similarity of this cameo to an erotic Greek epigram on a dancing-girl from Asia (*Anth. Pal.* 5.129 = 1509–16 G–P) simply adds to the horror. What kind of a poem can generate a centrepiece such as this?

The situation, by no means clear, seems to be as follows. For three generations now (46–7), the Romans have been neglecting the gods, evidence of which is the dilapidated state of the temples in the city (1–4). As a result, the gods have visited many afflictions on Italy (7–8). There have been defeats and near-defeats in foreign wars (9–16), conflicts made all the more perilous by the defilement of marriage, family and homes (17–20). The causal relationship between domestic defilement and foreign endangerment is by no means obvious and its explanation has to wait until after H. has illustrated the defilement by describing the immoral

COMMENTARY 6   161

girl (21-32). At lines 33-6 H. says that the young Romans who defeated Pyrrhus, Antiochus and Hannibal were not born of parents such as the immoral girl and her husband ('non his...parentibus'), and it is only at this point that the logic of 17-20 becomes clear. The ancients believed that children should resemble their parents, and in an ideal world this meant that virtuous behaviour would be passed on from generation to generation, a notion which had an especial appeal for the Romans, with their devotion to the *maiores*; but, when there was a collapse in the moral order, as described in 21-32, the opposite would happen and parents such as the immoral girl and her husband would have offspring quite unequal to fighting foreign enemies. Things were very different in earlier centuries, when young Romans were brought up to work hard in the countryside under the stern gaze of their virtuous mother (37-44). But everything has become worse with the passage of time (45): the age of our parents was worse than that of our grandparents (46), our own age is worse still (47), and, on the usual view, the generation of our offspring will be even worse (47-8).

Readers have not unnaturally been surprised at the seemingly unrelieved pessimism of an ode which concludes the opening sequence of Book 3, but at least as surprising is the fact that 'there is an extraordinary contradiction between the beginning and end of the poem' (Williams (1962) 32). According to the usual interpretation, 'Romane' (2) is a collective vocative and shows that the ode is addressed to Roman citizens at large: they will be paying for their neglect of the gods until they have restored the dilapidated temples (1-2 'lues...donec templa refeceris'). The contradiction arises because we are explicitly told that the citizens are innocent and do not deserve the punishment which the gods are inflicting upon them (1 'immeritus'), whereas at the end of the ode we are told that the present generation is more wicked than those preceding it (47 'nos nequiores').[36] Some scholars have attempted to remedy the contradiction by emendation, but none is persuasive; others have tried to explain it away, but without success; still others seem prepared to live with it: thus N-R say, with some understatement, that H. 'has not achieved total consistency' (100).

It is inconceivable that in so important an ode H. will have contradicted himself. It is argued below that *Romane* does not refer to the Roman people but is an oracular address to Augustus himself, and that *lues* (1) refers not to punishment but to atonement (not 'you will pay for', as Rudd and

---

[36] The contradiction is not removed by interpreting *immeritus* concessively ('though guiltless'), as do some scholars.

West translate, but 'you will expiate'). On these assumptions Augustus has taken upon himself the responsibility of atoning for society's neglect of the gods (1–2); and his atonement consists in restoring the temples and statues (2–4). Yet this interpretation, while removing the contradiction between *immeritus* and *nequiores* (1, 47), does not eliminate a further problem in the relationship between the first and final stanzas. Regardless of who restores the temple and statues of the gods, the restoration, if completed, makes no sense of an ending which declares that the future generation will be even worse than the current one (48 'progeniem uitiosiorem'). If the degeneration is to continue inexorably into the future, there is no point in even attempting to placate the gods by restoring their temples and statues. This problem is avoided if lines 46–8 are read as a question (see ad loc.).

If Augustus is the restorer referred to in 2–4, as suggested here, we may be confident that he will complete the restoration successfully. It follows that, if the gods are no longer neglected but receive the attention which is their due, they will cease inflicting *multa mala* on Italy as a punishment (cf. 7–8): in other words, Rome's traditional ability to deal with foreign threats, which is as much the subject of the ode as is neglect of the gods, will return, unimpeded by any moral decline. And this successful outcome will be to the credit of the *princeps*.

Structurally the ode is typically Horatian. While it seems broadly divisible into three sections of four stanzas each, it is possible also to discern a frame of generational delinquency (1–8 ~ 45–8) enclosing a central core in which warfare (9–16 ~ 33–6) alternates with upbringing, respectively reprehensible and admirable (17–32 ~ 37–44): see esp. 21–2n.

METRE Alcaic

1–2 Delicta maiorum immeritus lues, | Romane: *delicta* are 'acts which fall short of an approved standard of conduct' (*OLD*), in this case the neglect of the gods' shrines and temples (2–4; cf. 7); for many other exs. of inherited guilt and the like see Pease on Cic. *ND* 3.90 (where note *deliquisset* and *luendis*); for the involvement of the gods (7–8) cf. esp. Cic. *Marc.* 18 'di immortales…poenas a populo *Romano* ob aliquod *delictum* expetiuerunt, qui ciuile bellum tantum et tam luctuosum excitauerunt'. Since many temples in republican times had been set up by victorious generals 'ex manubiis', the responsibility for their maintenance devolved upon later generations of the same family; by *maiorum* here H. seems to be looking two generations back (46n.). *immeritus* is the first of several negative adjs. in the ode (10, 23, 27): see Intro. 25.

COMMENTARY 6.2-4   163

As we have seen (intro.), it is generally assumed (a) that the ethnic address *Romane* is a collective noun and refers to the Roman people, (b) that *lues* means 'you will be punished for' (*OLD luo*² 1), the punishment in question being the *multa...mala* of lines 7-8. The first of these assumptions, however, leads to a significant problem with *immeritus*: how can the present generation of Romans be described as 'undeserving' when at the end of the poem they are described as even more wicked than their parents (47 'nos nequiores')? The clear solution of the problem is to assume that in *Romane* we are intended to see Augustus.[37] Indeed, given the exceptionally close parallel between the *Res Gestae* and lines 2-4 below (see n.), it is almost impossible *not* to see a reference to Augustus. It will be objected that elsewhere *Romane* is 'rarely used to an individual' and that, when it is so used, 'it is spoken exclusively by non-Romans' (Dickey 210). Yet this objection, if it is an objection,[38] will not arise if we assume that, as at the start of 3.1 (see intro. there), H. is not speaking in his own voice. 'The poet speaks, not as Quintus Horatius Flaccus', says Williams, 'but as a prophet' (*TORP* 611); the vocative, according to N-R, 'suits an oracle or a quasi-oracular pronouncement'.[39] Either way, the notion that Augustus is being addressed is strongly supported by what is said immediately below in line 5 (n.). If, then, Augustus is the addressee, he alone clearly cannot be in the process of being punished for 'delicta maiorum'. The meaning of *Delicta...lues* must be 'Without deserving it, you will be expiating ancestral failures' (*OLD luo*² 2, quoting our passage): Augustus is seen as having taken upon himself the responsibility of atoning for the previous derelictions for which society is currently being punished, and the atonement consists of the repair of the temples and shrines of the gods (2-4). Such responsibility is part of the *onus imperii* mentioned earlier at 3.4.39 (n.).

2-4 donec templa refeceris | aedesque labentes deorum et | foeda nigro simulacra fumo: *labentes* is to be taken also with *templa*, and *deorum* is to

---

[37] I am not the first with this suggestion ('Male ad Augustum solum referunt quidam', complains Jani in his edn of 1782), which had also occurred independently to G. Zanker, 'A note on Anchises' *Romane* at Virgil, *Aeneid* 6.851' (*Mnem.* 74 (2021) 329-37).
[38] At *S.* 1.4.85 ('hunc tu, Romane, caueto'), where the vocative occurs amidst a whole series of second-person singular forms denoting the poet's Roman interlocutor (e.g. 90 *tibi*, 95 *te*), it is arguable that *tu, Romane* also denotes the interlocutor. Cf. also Ov. *Met.* 15.654 and Bömer's n.
[39] That H.'s impersonation continues to line 8 is suggested by the triple *deorum...dis...di...*; that H. then starts to speak in his own voice is suggested by the first-person reference in 11, which is echoed in ring composition by *nos* at the end of the ode (47).

be understood with *simulacra*; the word order of 4 is interlaced. *donec* + fut. perf. is regular to indicate 'the limit that will be set to the action of the main verb' (*NLS* 182 §223 (*b*)): Augustus' expiation will continue until he has repaired the temples and shrines. The dilapidation of such buildings seems to have become topical in the 30s (cf. *S.* 2.2.103–4 'quare | templa ruunt antiqua deum?', Nep. *Att.* 20.3, Liv. 4.20.7), and Augustus in the *Res Gestae* claims personal responsibility for their restoration (20.1, 4 'Capitolium...*refeci*...; duo et octoginta *templa deum* in urbe consul sextum [28 BC] ex auctoritate senatus *refeci*, nullo praetermisso quod eo tempore *refici* debebat'): the passage presumably reflects a building programme that was announced in 28 (*ex auctoritate senatus* implies a form of senatorial decree: *OLD auctoritas* 4a), almost certainly on 1 February, the day on which Augustus – recently titled *princeps senatus* (Dio 53.1.3 and Rich's n.) – is commemorated as 'templorum positor, templorum sancte repostor' by Ovid (*F.* 2.63). Livy in a later insertion in his Book 4 refers to 'Augustum Caesarem, templorum omnium conditorem ac restitutorem' (4.20.7); cf. also Suet. *Aug.* 29.4, 30.2 'aedes sacras uetustate conlapsas aut incendio absumptas refecit', Dio 53.2.4. Note too 2.15.19–20 'deorum | templa nouo decorare saxo', and, for smoke, 3.29.11–12n.

5 dis te minorem quod geris, imperas: the subject of the two verbs must obviously be the addressee of line 2: if that addressee is the Romans collectively, as commentators assert, the present complimentary statement produces a further contradiction with the end of the poem, where the current generation is described as more wicked than its parents (47 'nos nequiores'): see 1–2n. above. If the addressee is Augustus, however, no problem arises; and confirmation that Augustus is being referred to is provided by 1.12.57 'te minor laetum reget aequus orbem', where H. makes the similar point that Augustus rules because he recognises that he is subordinate to Jupiter (*OLD minor*² 6a). In both passages the *princeps* enjoys a proper relationship with the divine, unlike those, such as the Giants (3.4.49–64), who set themselves up to rival the gods (Otto 108, Tosi 672–3 §1496). Cf. 3.1.6n. and Plin. *Pan.* 52.2 'sic fit ut di <tibi> summum inter homines fastigium seruent, cum deorum ipse non appetas'. *imperas* will refer to Augustus' full nomenclature 'Imperator Caesar Diui f. Augustus' (on which see Syme, *RP* 1.361–77, esp. 372–3). For the construction of *se gerere* + adj. before H. cf. Sall. *H.* 3.7M/3.4R 'grauiores...se gerere', Liv. 2.27.3 'medium se gerendo'.

6 hinc omne principium, huc refer exitum: *hinc* = *a dis* (*OLD hinc* 7): we have to understand *pete* or some similar verb by zeugma. *huc* = *ad deos* (*OLD huc* 1d). *hinc...principium* is a variation on the proverbial Ἐκ Διὸς ἀρχώμεσθα ('Let us begin from Zeus') or in its Latin form *ab Ioue principium* (e.g. Pind. *Nem.* 2.1–3, Arat. *Phaen.* 1, Virg. *Ecl.* 3.60; cf. Tosi 376–7 §805); it was also a commonplace that 'the end lies with the gods' (West on Hes. *WD* 669): for both together, as here, cf. Scythin. 1, Plato, *Laws* 715E, [Arist.] *Mund.* 401a29–30, Arat. *Phaen.* 14 μιν ἀεὶ πρῶτόν τε καὶ ὕστατον ἱλάσκονται ('men always appease him first and last'), Liv. 45.39.10 'maiores uestri omnium magnarum rerum et principia exorsi a dis sunt et finem statuerunt'. H.'s point, as may be inferred from the adjacent sentences (5, 7–8), is that Augustus is doing what his compatriots have failed to do. The second syllable of *principium* is to be scanned long (the final *-i-* is regarded as consonantal, as 3.4.41).

7–8 di multa neglecti dederunt | Hesperiae mala luctuosae 'Neglect of the gods has inflicted many ills on grief-stricken Hesperia': *di…neglecti* is an example of the *ab urbe condita* idiom (3.4.18–19n.); for this sense of *dare* see *OLD* 24a. There are similar statements of neglect in texts just earlier than H. (cf. Varro *ap.* August. *Civ. Dei* 6.2 'se timere ne pereant, non incursu hostili sed ciuium neglegentia', Sall. *BC* 10.4 'deos neglegere', Liv. 3.20.4 'nondum haec quae nunc tenet saeculum neglegentia deum uenerat'); the ode gives no indication of when the neglect is supposed to have started, but line 46 suggests that the crucial period was two generations earlier. For the anaphora of *dis…di* at the start of the first and third lines of the stanza see 3.4.35n. Hesperia ('the land in the West') is 'a Greek poetic name of Italy' (Skutsch on Enn. *Ann.* 20, its first occurrence in Latin) and appropriate in the mouth of a prophet (e.g. Virg. *Aen.* 3.163) or (cf. 2.1.31–2) focalised by the Parthians (see next n.). *luctuosae,* here in its less common meaning (*OLD* 2; contrast 3.8.19), is proleptic: the grief from which Italy is suffering is caused by the ills sent by the gods. The *mala* are illustrated in the following lines.

9–10 iam bis Monaeses et Pacori manus | inauspicatos contudit impetus: *iam* suggests that there is worse to come. *bis* is distributive and explained by the two named defeats. In 40 BC the Parthians under their leader Pacorus defeated Decidius Saxa, legate of Mark Antony, in a major reversal (Dio 48.25.2–26.4; *MRR* 2.381, *CAH* 10.12–13); four years later Antony himself invaded Parthia but suffered an infamous defeat, an event in which the nobleman Monaeses was evidently involved (Plut. *Ant.* 37.1 and Pelling's n., Dio 49.23.5 and Reinhold's n.; *MRR* 2.400, *CAH* 10.31–2). Whether *inauspicatos* means that the Roman attacks were literally 'not sanctioned by auspices' (*OLD* 1), as was the case with Crassus' notorious expedition (e.g. Vell. 46.3, Plut. *Crass.* 18.5), or were more generally 'ill-fated, unlucky' (*OLD* 2), is unclear. *contundo* ('to pound, crush') is regular in verse from Enn. *Ann.* 386 onwards; *manus* perhaps implies a force which the Romans could have withstood if they had had divine approval. For *ĭnauspicatos* see Intro. 30.

11 nostrorum et adiecisse praedam | torquibus exiguis renidet: in the National Museum in Tehran there is a statue of a Parthian in native dress, with a narrow torque round the neck: *exiguus* is 'the perfect adjective for this item of decoration', says Powell (152), who suggests that H. may have seen such torques for himself in 42 BC, when the army of Brutus and Cassius, in which he served, was augmented by a troop of Parthian cavalry (App. *BC* 4.59, 63, 88). The MSS read *nostros* (to be taken with *inauspicatos...impetus*), which is impossibly flat. SB (*HSCP* 89 (1985) 156) proposed to adopt Bentley's *nostrorum* but to take it with *praedam* rather than with *impetus* (*et* being deferred, as often).[40] This produces excellent sense, but SB did not say whether he regarded the genit. as possessive or definitive: wearing 'loot from our men' alongside one's own finery is a natural enough idea, but there is a typically Horatian surrealism in regarding the enemy himself as the prize to be added to one's own finery (for the defining genit. cf. e.g. Liv. 2.64.3 'praedas hominum pecorumque'; *TLL* 10.2.524.18–30). Hence perhaps: 'and they beam at having added the prize of our men to their meagre torques'. *renidet* applies to each of the chieftains (3.3.10n.) and transfers to them the gleam normally associated with torques (Tac. *H.* 2.89.2 'torques...splendebant'); the construction + infin. seems unparalleled.

13–14 paene, occupatam seditionibus, | deleuit Vrbem Dacus et Aethiops: *paene* is to be taken with *deleuit*, not *occupatam*: hence my commas. In the mid- or late 30s the Dacians, a people who lived north of the Danube, had allied themselves with Antony because they were disillusioned with the unsatisfactory results of an embassy to Octavian. In 29 they made incursions into Macedonia and were opposed by M. Licinius Crassus, the consul of 30 (Dio 51.22.8, 23.2–27.3 with Reinhold's nn. and his Map 5). Other contemporary references to these events are at 3.8.18 (n.), *S.* 2.6.53 '"numquid de Dacis audisti?"', Virg. *G.* 2.497 'coniurato descendens Dacus ab Histro'. The reference to the Ethiopians is taken as an allusion to the forces of Cleopatra (cf. 1.37.6–8), although no other text calls them by this name; on the other hand, Virgil (*Aen.* 8.687–8) describes some of Cleopatra's forces as coming from Bactra, in mod. Afghanistan (3.29.27–8n.), whose people were linked with the

---

[40] In his edition SB printed *nostros*; although he mentioned *nostrorum* in the app. crit., he did not mention his own modification of Bentley's proposal.

Ethiopians by Manilius (4.804 'Bactraque et Aethiopes'). Perhaps H. simply wanted an exotic name which suggested a different compass point from Parthia in the east (9–12) and Dacia in the north (cf. J. Y. Nadeau, *CQ* 20 (1970) 338–48). Whatever the case, his description of Actium as 'almost a destruction of the city' is extraordinary (contrast 1.37.6–8). The dating of the above aggression to 31–29 BC indicates that *occupatam seditionibus*, on which N–R do not comment, is a reference to the young M. Lepidus, son of the triumvir, who in 31 or 30 BC conspired to kill Octavian but was thwarted by Maecenas and executed (Vell. 88.1, Suet. *Aug.* 19.1, Liv. *per.* 133; Woodman (2022)). *occupatam* perhaps = 'in the grip of', as Flor. 2.7.2 = 3.19.2 'occupata tribuniciis seditionibus ciuitate' (slightly different at *HA Car.* 8.1).

15 classe formidatus: for the fleet of Antony and Cleopatra cf. *Epo.* 1.1–2 and Watson's n.

16 missilibus...sagittis: the adj. seems redundant, but N–R explain that it is equivalent to *mittendis*, 'better at the shooting of arrows'. Cf. *pendulum* at 3.27.59.

17–20 This difficult stanza is critical for the interpretation of the poem as a whole. (a) Lines 17–18 deal with domestic defilement (*nuptias, genus, domos*), lines 19–20 deal with endangerment to society at large (*patriam populumque*); the influence of the former on the latter (*hoc fonte deriuata*) will become clear at 33–44 (see intro.). (b) It seems impossible to separate the defilement of marriage and home (17–18) from the immoral behaviour of the married woman and her husband in 21–32: the couple illustrate the defilement. (c) It seems almost equally impossible to separate the *clades* of 19–20 from the events of 9–16. Thus the stanza links 9–16 with 21–32. (d) Since all the verbs in 21–32 are present, it follows that the immoral behaviour described there is ongoing: the defilement in 17–18 therefore cannot have ended. (e) If immorality diminishes Rome's capacity to fight foreign enemies (cf. (a)) and is continuing into the present day (cf. (d)), the implication seems to be that, unless the appropriate measures are taken, the endangerments of 9–16 will recur (cf. *iam*, 9).

17–18 fecunda culpae saecula nuptias | primum inquinauere et genus et domos '<But> generations fertile in fault first defiled marriage, family and home'; the asyndeton of 17 is probably adversative, as H. now reveals that the perils of 9–16 were preceded by an earlier crisis (*primum*: cf. *OLD primum*² 1, 5). He does not make it clear whether the domestic defilement is a further divine punishment, like the military perils, or whether it is simply a pre-existing condition. Moral decline had been identified as starting at various points since at least the early second century BC (A. W. Lintott, *Historia* 21 (1972) 626–38); on the other hand, there is nothing unusual in the notion that descendants of wrongdoers should pay for the latter's misdeeds by a form of punishment which itself is reprehensible (see Watson on *Epo.* 7.17–20).

Since *culpa* often refers to sexual misconduct (*OLD* 3b), *fecunda* is usually said to suggest 'that the generations have been prolific in misconduct rather than children' (N–R); on the other hand, 'generations fertile in fault' might equally suggest a reference to the *delicta maiorum* of line 1 (note *culpa* in a similar connection at *Epo.* 7.14). H. sees the *saecula* (*OLD* 5) as the headwaters of a river (19–20 'hoc fonte deriuata...fluxit'; cf. *OLD fons* 3a). The tense of *inquinauere* does not imply that the defilement has ended, as is shown by 21–32 (17–20n.); the verb has suggestions of a sewer (cf. Fest. 66 'cloacare inquinare'), and the metaphorical contamination here (cf. Front. *Aq.* 91.3 'aquas inquinabat [sc. Anio]'; Rutherford 154) will be contrasted later with the sea stained by enemy blood (34), denoting the heroism of a more distant past. *fecundus*, which is constructed with either genit. or abl., is regular of rivers etc. (e.g. Tac. *A.* 13.57.1 'flumen...fecundum'). For the significance and symbolism of *domos* see R. P. Saller, *Phoenix* 38 (1984) 336–55, esp. 353–4.

19–20 hoc fonte deriuata clades | in patriam populumque fluxit 'it was from this source that there streamed the disaster which inundated fatherland and people'. *clades* refers back to the perils in which Rome recently found herself (9–16) and which, unless something is done (cf. 1–4), seem destined to recur (cf. 21–32). The imagery of 17–18 continues with *hoc fonte deriuata* (cf. Quint. 2.17.40 'ex his fontibus deriuata') and *fluxit* (e.g. Cic. *ND* 3.48 'haec enim omnia ex eodem fonte fluxerunt'). The combination of *fluxit* with *clades* has been questioned, but perhaps cf. Sen. *Thy.* 236 'hinc omne cladis mutuae fluxit malum'. *patriam populumque* is not 'a common formula' (Gow) but relatively rare (Acc. *Praetext.* 6 (p. 326R), Ov. *Met.* 15.572, Sen. *Contr.* 7.1.18, Luc. 9.24–5, Juv. 14.70).

21–2 motus doceri gaudet Ionicos | matura uirgo: *gaudet* is the first of six main verbs applied to the girl in 21–32; since all six verbs are present-tense, yet the girl transitions from unmarried to married (cf. *mox*, 25), it follows that the picture is generalised: her behaviour represents that of a plurality of loose women. Moreover, although there is explicit mention only of her unmarried and married statuses, *doceri* invites speculation about her upbringing and her parents, while *his...parentibus* at 33 condemns the kind of parents that she and her husband will themselves

become. H. brilliantly intimates a dynamic process involving several generations, suggesting the continuing and seemingly inevitable progress of the moral decline which is reflected in the final stanza (45–8).
matura suggests readiness for marriage (e.g. Vitr. 4.1.9 'uirgo...iam matura nuptiis'), which for the average Roman girl would be between the ages of 14 and 15 (A. A. Lelis, W. A. Percy and B. C. Verstraete, *The Age of Marriage in Ancient Rome* (2003) 121). *motus* are dance-moves (e.g. Sen. *Contr.* 1.2.5 'docetur blanditias et in omnem corporis motum fingitur'; *OLD* 2), and *Ionicos* describes a lascivious kind of dance (Plaut. *Pseud.* 1275, *Stich.* 769; cf. Otto 177); see also Adams 194. Dancing of any kind was regarded as unacceptable in respectable women (Sall. *C.* 25.2; Gibson on Ov. *AA* 3.349–80, pp. 240–1), to say nothing of their children (cf. Scipio Africanus, *ORF* 30 'docentur praestigias inhonestas...eunt... in ludum saltatorium inter cinaedos uirgines puerique ingenui!'),[41] and the importation of dancing-girls from Asia in the early second century BC was regarded by Livy (39.6.8) as symbolising the start of moral decline at Rome. Verbs which in the active form take a double accus. (G&L 215–16 §339) may retain an accus. in the passive, as here, although *doceo* is a special case (*NLS* 11–12 §16 (iii)): see further 3.8.5n., 3.9.10n. For the pointed use of *doceri* see also 3.24.56–8n.

22–3 fingitur artibus | iam nunc 'now she is already being shaped by her skills': i.e. she is well on the way to being the finished product described in 25–32 below. For the horror in *iam nunc* cf. *Epi.* 2.1.127 'ab obscenis iam nunc sermonibus'. In a virtuous young woman *artibus* would mean 'good qualities', 'accomplishments', such as those attributed to Cornelia, young wife of Pompey (Plut. *Pomp.* 55.1 'She was well versed in literature, in playing the lyre, and in geometry, and had been accustomed to listen to philosophical discourses with profit' (Loeb trans.)); but here the meaning is more dubious. For *fingitur* see Sen. *Contr.* 1.2.5 (quoted 21–2n.); *OLD* 5a.

23–4 incestos amores | de tenero meditatur ungui: the meaning of the proverbial *de tenero...ungui* (lit. 'from a soft nail') has been much disputed. The ancient commentators agree that it means 'from her earliest childhood' (thus Porphyrio: 'hoc prouerbium de Graeco est, quod dicunt ἐξ ἁπαλῶν ὀνύχων: significant a prima infantia'; Otto 356, Tosi 301 §634), but many modern scholars have preferred 'from the depth of her being'. After surveying all the known exs. in both Latin and Greek, A. Cameron concluded that the ancient commentators were correct (*CQ* 15 (1965)

---

[41] I owe this reference to Dr J. N. Adams.

80–3): in that case the phrase seems to conflict with *matura* (22), which has been much emended. The equivalent Greek phrase occurs in an epigram of Automedon (perhaps a contemporary of H.) on a lascivious Asian *saltatrix* (*Anth. Pal.* 5.129 = 1509–16 G–P) with which H.'s ode seems to have a 'clear relationship' (N–R). Gow and Page ad loc. have argued that the epigram is an exception to Cameron's rule and that the phrase there means 'from her tender finger-tips', although this seems not to be the view of P. Colaclidès & M. McDonald, 'Horace et Automédon', *Latomus* 33 (1974) 382–4. The debate seems set to continue. *meditatur* = 'has been planning/contemplating'.

25–6 mox iuniores quaerit adulteros | inter mariti uina: *mox* introduces a later period, when the immoral girl has been married for a while. The comparative *iuniores* implies the stock figure of an older husband (cf. 3.19.24); to judge from 29–32 below, the girl has no trouble in getting partners: *quaerit* is closer in meaning to 'finds' (*OLD* 7) than 'seeks'. *inter mariti uina* may mean either 'while her husband is drinking' (another conventional scene: cf. McKeown on Ov. *Am.* 1.4.51–4) or 'during her husband's parties' (as Stat. *Silv.* 4.2.17).

It is well known from his legislation of 18–17 BC (the Lex Iulia de maritandis ordinibus and the Lex Iulia de adulteriis coercendis) and later (the Lex Papia Poppaea of AD 9) that Augustus was concerned to promote marriage and curb adultery (Crawford 2.781–6, 801–9): see esp. K. Galinsky, 'Augustus' legislation on morals and marriage', *Philol.* 125 (1981) 126–44 (to the further bibliography at Vell. 93.2n. add Treggiari 572 (index), Edwards chap. 1, *CAH* 10.885–93, T. A. J. McGinn, *Prostitution, Sexuality and the Law in Ancient Rome* (1998) chaps. 3 and 5, W. Eck, 'At Magnus Caesar, and yet! Social resistance against Augustan legislation', in K. Morrell et al. (edd.), *The Alternative Augustan Age* (2019) chap. 6; Wardle on Suet. *Aug.* 34). Whether Augustus tried and failed to pass earlier legislation around the time of our ode, as is often thought (see esp. Cairns, *PRE* 141–55), has been strongly disputed (E. Badian, *Philol.* 129 (1985) 82–98): either way, Livy's famous statement about *uitia* and *remedia* (*praef.* 9), persistently assumed to refer to such legislation (e.g. N–R 99), predates Actium and is thus irrelevant to the debate (Woodman, *RICH* 132–4).

26–8 neque eligit | cui donet impermissa raptim | gaudia luminibus remotis 'and she does not choose someone to whom she can hastily grant unlawful pleasure when the lamps have been removed'. *neque* extends its influence to *luminibus remotis*: darkness was traditional for sexual activity (Prop. 2.15.4 'quantaque sublato lumine rixa fuit!', Tac. *A.* 13.44.3

'pars tenebrarum libidini seposita'); 'only libertines make love' in the light (Gibson on Ov. *AA* 3.807-8), e.g. Mart. 11.104.5-6 'me ludere teste lucerna | et iuuat admissa rumpere luce latus'. *impermissus* occurs nowhere else (Intro. 25). *donet* is most easily described as a generic subjunctive. For the appended abl. abs. see 3.1.30-1n.

29-30 sed iussa coram non sine conscio | surgit marito 'but, having been summoned, she gets up openly with her husband's full knowledge': the lines are a point-by-point negation of 26-8 (*iussa* ~ *eligit, coram* ~ *luminibus remotis, non sine conscio...marito* ~ *impermissa*). *surgit* continues the party scene from 25-6 (*OLD* 1c 'to rise from table'); *coram* (adv.) = 'openly' is extremely common (*TLL* 4.944.82-945.34; *OLD* 2b is misleading). For *non sine* cf. 3.4.20n.
Relevant to this scene is a strange episode described by Tacitus under the year AD 19 (*A.* 2.85.1-3), in which a married woman of a good family had practised prostitution and sought to escape the penalty for adultery by appealing to the old custom of registering her trade with the aediles; her husband, asked why he had not punished his wife for her flagrant misdeeds (thereby laying himself open to a charge of *lenocinium*), escaped punishment by claiming that the time limit for the charge had passed. His wife was banished, and the senate passed decrees against *libido feminarum*. For the legal issues raised see e.g. T. A. J. McGinn, *ZPE* 93 (1992) 273-95, esp. 280-91. For the *leno maritus* see McKeown on Ov. *Am.* 2.19.57-8; and see also below on 3.15.

30 institor: a pedlar or travelling salesman. Such persons 'were known patrons of prostitutes, and in general had a bad reputation for sexual immorality' (Watson on *Epo.* 17.20, with numerous further refs., to which add *Anth. Pal.* 5.159.3).

31 nauis Hispanae magister: Spain was famous for its gold and silver mines (C. Domergue, *Les mines de la péninsule ibérique dans l'antiquité romaine* (1990)); both the *diues amator* (Maltby on Tib. 1.5.47-8) and greedy prostitute (N-H on 2.4.19) are stock figures.

32 dedecorum pretiosus emptor 'the free-spending buyer of disgrace': this meaning of *pretiosus* is very rare and possibly unique (*TLL* 10.2.1204.14-21). *emptor* looks back to *donet* (27): not merely an adulteress but a prostitute.

33-44 non his iuuentus orta parentibus | infecit aequor sanguine Punico...sed rusticorum mascula militum | proles...: the meaning of this three-stanza sentence is clear but its elucidation somewhat complicated. There are two subjects (33 ~ 37–8a), which contrast with each other (*non...sed...*, each having two pairs of nouns + adjs.), and this is one of those cases (like 3.2.21–2, 3.5.37–8, 3.10.1–2) where the main idea is not carried by the main verbs (*infecit, cecidit*): 'It was not young men born from such parents, but the masculine offspring of rustic soldiers, who stained the sea with Punic blood and slaughtered...'

33–4 non his iuuentus orta parentibus | infecit aequor sanguine Punico: these lines clarify the logic of 17–20 (see intro.). The resemblance of children to their parents, a common and usually desirable notion (e.g. Cic. *Phil.* 9.12 'effigiem morum suorum, uirtutis,...filium'; Helzle on Ov. *Ex P.* 2.2.51–2), has disastrous societal consequences if parents are as degenerate as the couple described in 25–32. The contaminated water-source of 17–18 (n.) contrasts with the blood-stained sea here (for the motif cf. N–H on 2.1.35). H.'s reference is to the naval battles of the First Punic War at Mylae in 260 BC, Ecnomus in 256 and Aegates Islands in 241: see *MRR* 1.205, 208, 219–20. There is a pun on *punicus*, one of whose meanings is 'red' (*OLD* 3; cf. N–H on 2.12.3).

35–6 Pyrrhumque et ingentem... | Antiochum: Pyrrhus, king of Epirus, was defeated in 275 BC at Beneventum (or possibly the Arusinian Plains in Lucania); Antiochus III, king of Syria, was defeated in 190 at Magnesia ad Sipylum in western Asia Minor: *ingentem* is an allusion to his name 'the Great'. See *MRR* 1.195 and 356.

36 Hannibalemque dirum: after the Battle of Zama in 202 BC at the end of the Second Punic War Hannibal went into exile, and in the late 180s he committed suicide in Bithynia. *Hannibalemque dirum* (for which see N–H on 2.12.2) is singled out by Quintilian (8.2.9) as an example of 'proper expression', *proprie dictum*. The adj. was derived from *dei ira* (Maltby 190), an appropriate resonance in a poem which opened with neglect of the gods.[42]

37–8 sed rusticorum mascula militum | proles: *mascula...proles* (interlaced) is the second subject of the sentence (33–44n.). The countryside was conventionally a place of virtue (cf. e.g. *Epo.* 2; 3.29.11–12n.), and there was a long-standing association, symbolised by the figure of Cincinnatus (cf. Liv. 3.26.9, Veg. *Mil.* 1.3.5), between the farmer and the soldier (e.g. Cato, *RR praef.* 4, Colum. 1 *praef.* 17–18, Sen. *Ep.* 51.10–11,

---

[42] I owe this point to Ian Du Quesnay.

and esp. Veg. *Mil.* 1.3.1–5 'Vtrum ex agris an ex urbibus utiliores sint tirones'; in Greek cf. Xen. *Oec.* 5.14–16). The expression *rusticorum...militum* would have extra meaning for H.'s contemporaries, who had seen so many veteran soldiers settled on the land (3.4.37–8n.). According to Cicero, *proles* is one of those poetic words which make a speech 'grandior atque antiquior' (*De or.* 3.153).

38–9 Sabellis docta ligonibus | uersare glaebas: the young men's training in domestic tillage ('Sabellis docta') contrasts with the foreign training of the *matura uirgo* at 21 ('doceri...Ionicos'). *ligones* are mattocks (K. D. White, *Agricultural Implements of the Roman World* (1967) Figs. 16–20); the adj. describing them 'means not "Sabine" but "Samnite"' and 'those who continue to write "Sabine" are simply wrong!' (Horsfall on Virg. *Aen.* 7.665): the term typifies 'primitive frugality' (Courtney on Juv. 3.169), as Virg. *G.* 2.167 (cf. Coleman 67). For the Samnite peoples and their territory see S. P. Oakley, *The Hill-forts of the Samnites* (1995) 7–10. For the infin. after *doceo* see *OLD* 4b (very common); *uersare* is the *mot juste* for turning over the ground (*OLD* 2a); some may see a self-referential pointer to the anagrammatic *seuerae*, framing the line.

39–40 seuerae | matris ad arbitrium: the stern mother contrasts with the immoral girl, who will turn out to be a very different kind of mother. The importance of a Roman mother's influence on her child's life is well brought out at Tac. *D.* 28.6 'quae [i.e. of a mother] disciplina ac *seueritas* eo pertinebat ut sincera et integra et nullis prauitatibus detorta unius cuiusque natura toto statim pectore arriperet artes honestas et si...ad rem militarem...inclinasset, id solum ageret, id uniuersum hauriret'; see in general S. Dixon, *The Roman Mother* (1988) 118. *ad arbitrium* = 'in an amount or to a degree to satisfy someone's wishes' (*OLD arbitrium* 7c).

40–1 recisos | portare fustes: two activities are referred to: the young men must lop as well as carry – good military training (Veg. *Mil.* 1.24.4–5).

41–2 sol ubi montium | mutaret umbras 'when [i.e. every time that] the sun altered the shadows from the mountains' (note the chiastic alliteration); the subjunctive is frequentative (as Cat. 63.67 'linquendum ubi esset orto mihi sole cubiculum'; *NLS* 152–3 §196). *mutaret* refers both to the lengthening shadows cast by the evening sun in mountain valleys (cf. Virg. *Ecl.* 1.84 'maioresque cadunt altis de montibus umbrae') and to their change of direction (*Epi.* 1.16.6–7); at Plin. *NH* 2.182 a similar expression refers to the different shadows cast by the sun at different latitudes. See further 3.29.21n. (*umbras*).

42–3 et iuga demeret | bobus fatigatis 'and (the sun) removed the yokes from the exhausted oxen'; the motif goes back to Homer (*Il.* 16.779, *Od.* 9.58 'But when the sun turned to the time for the unyoking of oxen'); note also 'the oxen-loosening time' of Arat. *Phaen.* 825 βουλύσιος ὥρη. For oxen combined with shadows to describe the end of day cf. Virg. *Ecl.* 2.66–7 'aspice, aratra iugo referunt suspensa iuuenci | et sol crescentes decedens duplicat umbras'.

43–4 amicum | tempus agens abeunte curru '(the sun) bringing the kindly time with his departing chariot': *amicum tempus* translates the Greek εὐφρόνη, which means 'the kindly time' and is a euphemism for 'night' (see West on Hes. *WD* 560); the same expr. at Stat. *Silv.* 5.2.38 is different because *amicum* is there followed by a dative (*amicior hora* is at Ov. *Her.* 19.33 and *amica quies* at Claud. *Sext. Cons. Honor. praef.* 2). *abeunte* (the oxymoronic juxtaposition with *agens* is typical of H.: cf. 3.30.4–5n.), *amicum tempus*, *fatigatis* and *umbras* all suggest closure; the sententious final stanza therefore appears παρὰ προσδοκίαν ('contrary to expectation').

45 damnosa quid non imminuit dies?: the question links the idealised past (33–44) with the more immediate generations mentioned below. In the third-person singular the present and perfect forms of *imminuo* are indistinguishable,[43] but the present is significantly more appropriate for the context of the ode: 'What does destructive time not impair?' The question gives every appearance of being rhetorical (G&L 290–1 §451 R.2): i.e. it expects the answer 'Nothing' and is simply another way of expressing the proverbial statement 'tomorrow is always worse than today' (*cotidie est deterior posterior dies*: Tosi 358 §764). Nevertheless the very fact that H. has expressed himself in the form of a question means that he has left open the possibility of a different answer: in this case the answer would be 'time will not impair the future generation' (cf. 48), *provided* the restoration of the temples and statues, mentioned at the beginning of the poem (2–4), is carried out and traditional moral standards are thereby reinstated. See further 47–8n. below. *dies* is equivalent to 'time' here (see Brink on *AP* 293, *OLD* 10), but the choice is pointed after the reference to night in 43–4. *damnosa* and *imminuit* may suggest a financial metaphor, as perhaps Cic. *Att.* 1.16.9.

46–8 The idealised generations of the previous two stanzas are followed in the final stanza by four further generations.[44] The sequence is clearly

---

[43] It is worth noting that the perfect stem of *immineo* is not found.

[44] For the transition from past to present to future at the end of an ode Schrijvers (*OR* 65) compares 1.7.30–2, 1.14.17–20, 1.16.22–8, 1.29.13–16.

related to the Myth of Ages, of which the first example is the five ages described by Hesiod in his *Works and Days* (see West on 106-201). Hesiod was followed by numerous other writers, both Greek and Latin, and there were several variations in the number of ages (see e.g. Lovejoy and Boas 24-53). Of particular interest are the Hellenistic poet Aratus, to whose *Phaenomena* (96-136) H. clearly alludes (see 6n. (?), 42-3n., 47-8n.), and Virgil's Fourth Eclogue, where the Myth of Ages is put into reverse and which shares various motifs with our ode.

46 aetas parentum, peior auis 'the age of our parents, worse than <the age of> our grandparents': such compendious comparisons are common throughout classical literature from Homer onwards.

47 nos nequiores: the blameless addressee of the first stanza (1 *immeritus*) is excluded from this 'us', just as he is, more explicitly, at 1.2.47 'te nostris uitiis iniquum'. *nequam* (declinable only in the comparative and superlative) is largely prosaic and common in political invective.

47-8 mox daturos | progeniem uitiosiorem: *dare* here = 'to bring forth, produce' (*OLD* 23): it thus repeats *tulit* (46); for similar but not identical forms of repetition see Wills 312, 318-19 (cf. 303).

In the course of his account of the Myth of Ages, Aratus introduces the figure of Dike (Justice), who speaks as follows (*Phaen.* 123-4): Οἵην χρύσειοι πατέρες γενεὴν ἐλίποντο | χειροτέρην· ὑμεῖς δὲ κακώτερα τέκνα τεκεῖσθε ('How worse a race the golden fathers have left! But you will bring forth children still more evil' (Loeb trans.)). It is generally recognised that H. is here indebted, whether directly or indirectly, to Aratus' lines. Aratus was translated into Latin by both Cicero and Germanicus, the nephew and adopted son of the emperor Tiberius. Unfortunately Cicero's version of this passage has not survived, but Germanicus renders it thus: 'increpat "o patrum suboles oblita priorum, | degeneres semper semperque habitura minores..."' (126-7).[45] It would be particularly interesting to know whether Cicero anticipated Germanicus in his use of a future participle and thereby influenced H., since without *daturos* H. 'could hardly have packed four generations in three lines' (Shorey).

---

[45] Translated by D. B. Gain (1976) as 'Offspring forgetful of the fathers that have gone before you, destined to have a progeny that is becoming ever more degenerate', but by G. Maurach (1978) as '...who will have children always more degenerate and always more worthless'. The latter defends his version by saying that *minores* is equivalent to *minores pretio*, as if that were a common expression; in fact it is never found.

It is almost universally assumed that with *daturos* H., like Aratus' Dike, is saying that his own generation (47 *nos*) will definitely bring forth a progeny which is even worse; but this conflicts with the first stanza, where *lues* (1), whether it means 'pay for' (on the conventional interpretation) or 'expiate' (on the present interpretation), is conditional upon the restoration of the gods' temples and statues (2–4). 'It is not always seen', says Lyne (*Hor.* 174), 'that there is an invitation to interpret the future participle *daturos* as an implicit apodosis, an apodosis to a protasis which can be inferred from the first stanza.' In other words, a clause such as 'unless the restoration of temples and statues is completed' has to be understood with *daturos*. N–R, who were largely untroubled by the inconsistency between *immeritus* and *nos nequiores* (see intro.), dismiss Lyne's interpretation on the ground that it conflicts with 'the clear allusion to the pessimistic passage of Aratus', but of course alluding authors frequently make adaptations in the course of their allusions. Nevertheless Lyne's interpretation is by no means straightforward; instead I think that 46–8 should be read as a question, thus: [46] 'Has the age of our parents, which is worse than that of our grandparents, brought forth our still more wicked generation in order for us soon to produce an even more degenerate progeny?' (*or* '...brought forth in us a still more wicked generation that will soon produce...'). The answer to the question is naturally negative, because by his programme of restoration Augustus is intervening to stop the seemingly inevitable decline. Questions do not necessarily require an interrogative particle (cf. 1.9.1–4 with N–H, 1.29.1–5, 3.8.1–5; *OLS* 1.321–2), and it is idiomatic of Latin for a question to be inherent in a participle (*daturos*) rather than a main verb (G&L 298 §469, *OLS* 1.337–8; note also Laughton 43–4, 121). The first ode of Book 3, to which the present ode is the companion piece (see Intro. 15), also ends with two questions and a two-word conclusion (cf. also 1.8, 1.29, 2.12).

7

With this ode we move from the public sphere, which has provided the context throughout the Alcaic Hexad, to the intimacy of a married couple whom H. evidently knows well. Asterie has been lamenting the absence of her husband, Gyges, whose return voyage from Asia Minor has been interrupted by seasonal storms, marooning him at Oricum on the west coast of Greece. H. begins the ode by reassuring the young woman that Gyges

---

[46] Evidently this punctuation was proposed also by P. Trenkel, *Zusammenhänge und Beziehungen in Horaz' Römeroden* (1926) 6–7 (*non uidi*).

will be home at the beginning of spring and that in the meanwhile he has remained faithful to her, even though Chloe, his Greek *hospita* in Oricum, is infatuated with him and has communicated her infatuation by means of a *nuntius* or go-between. This scene-setting occupies the first three stanzas of the ode (1–12). The two central stanzas illustrate the kind of mythological stories which the go-between has apparently been using in his attempts at persuading Gyges to succumb to Chloe's charms (13–20). The three final stanzas of the ode begin with the repeated reassurance to Asterie that her Gyges is deaf to the go-between's cunning words (21–2a); but then there is a surprise: H. warns Asterie not to be too attracted herself to her athletic neighbour, Enipeus (22b–32). It therefore transpires at the end of the ode that H.'s insistence on Gyges' *fides* has been aimed at dissuading Asterie from her own potential unfaithfulness.

The ode is thus framed by two triangular relationships, each of them featuring Asterie and Gyges. On the one hand Asterie's husband is advised by a go-between not to resist Chloe; on the other hand Gyges' wife is advised by H. himself that she must resist Enipeus. The reciprocal nature of the relationships is underlined by circular composition: the opening question (1–5), equivalent to a command, corresponds to the imperatives in the final stanza (29–30); Gyges' lonely nights (6–8) correspond to those urged on Asterie (29–32); Chloe's availability (10–12) corresponds to the desirability of Enipeus (25–8); *primo…uere* (2) corresponds to *prima nocte* (29); *tibi* (1) and *tuis* (10) correspond to *tibi* (22) and *te* (31).

The two central stanzas also describe two triangular relationships – from mythology. On the one hand there are Proetus and his wife Anteia (also called Stheneboea), who, when her attempt at seducing Bellerophon, their guest, is rebuffed, plans to have him killed (13–16); on the other hand there is Hippolyte (wife of the unmentioned Acastus), who, when her attempt at seducing Peleus, their guest, is rebuffed, plans to have him killed too (17–18). According to H., these cases are adduced by the go-between in his efforts at persuading Gyges to yield to Chloe, the implied threat being that, if he fails to yield, he may well come to some harm. If the go-between's speech is being correctly reported, however, it is unusually maladroit. (1) Not only does the go-between's threat seem absurd in itself but neither Bellerophon nor Peleus actually came to harm in the end. The threat has no force. (2) It is odd enough to promote a seduction by quoting a precedent which failed, but it is very odd indeed to quote two identical precedents which failed. Hippolyte was no more successful in her seduction than was Anteia/Stheneboea. (3) It is very strange that Anteia/Stheneboea is described contemptuously as a 'faithless wife' (13 'mulier perfida') since she is an analogue for Chloe, who is the go-between's employer.

These oddities require an explanation, which is that the go-between never uttered the words which H. attributes to him: H. has himself chosen the two inept examples from mythology and has pretended that the go-between addressed them to Gyges. His reason for the pretence is that his whole purpose in lines 1–22a is to reassure Asterie of Gyges' faithfulness. Having admitted in 9–12 that Gyges' *constans...fides* (cf. 1–8) is being challenged, he produces a plausibly detailed report which is entirely without foundation but which is designed for comfort: if empty threats and loyal guests are the best that the faithless woman and her *nuntius* can come up with, Asterie need have no fears for Gyges. This interpretation is strongly supported by what is *not* said in lines 13–18. Given that the go-between was trying to promote an affair between his employer and Gyges, an obvious ploy would be to allege to Gyges that Asterie was having an affair in his absence (see also 3.10.15n.). When in the first Mime of Herodas the *lena* tries to persuade the married Metriche to have an affair with Gryllos, a handsome young man who has become infatuated with her, the very first point she makes is that Metriche's husband has now been detained in Egypt for ten months and is bound to have taken a lover (1.21–5, 56–60).[47] Yet no such allegation appears in the speech which H. attributes to Chloe's go-between – and the reason, as will become clear in the last lines of the ode (22b–32), is that the poet knows only too well that Asterie is indeed being tempted. Since the ultimate purpose of 1–22a is to dissuade Asterie from her own affair, an allegation to that effect would be entirely counter-productive.

The situation described in Herodas' mime is so similar to that described in the ode that it prompts the question whether the ode has been influenced by mime. It is known that mime influenced Augustan elegy (J. C. McKeown, *PCPS* 25 (1979) 71–84), with which our ode is thought to have features in common (Cairns, *RL* 352–9), and that one of the most popular mimes was the so-called 'adultery mime' (R. W. Reynolds, *CQ* 40 (1946) 77–84). It is true that the most frequent scenario in this mime involved the fulfilment of an adulterous liaison and its unexpected (and often humorous) discovery by the wronged spouse; but the first Mime of Herodas shows that this plot was by no means invariable. If the ode has indeed been influenced by the adultery mime, that would support the view of many (but not all) scholars that Asterie and Gyges are married (see Cairns, *RL* 366–7); and N–R correctly note that the mythological paradigms of 13–18 scarcely make sense unless Chloe herself is married

---

[47] For the collection of mimes that are attributed to the third-century BC writer Herodas see G. Zanker, *Herodas: Mimiambs* (2009).

(9n.), although her husband, like that of Hippolyte, goes unmentioned. It is perhaps significant that in the two Propertian poems thought to have been influenced by our ode (3.12 and 4.3) the couples in question are married.

Although H. addresses Asterie directly only at the beginning and end of the poem, it is important to remember that he is speaking to her throughout and shows himself to be remarkably well informed: he seems to know not only Gyges' unfortunate circumstances (1–8) but also that Chloe's *nuntius* has been tempting him (9–12). This invites a question: if Gyges is prevented by bad weather from reaching Italy, how is it that news of Gyges has reached H.? Why has the same bad weather not prevented H. from receiving his information? Notions of an 'omniscient narrator', appropriate to epic, seem inappropriate in personal lyric addressed by the poet to Asterie. We may of course assume, if we wish, that H. has simply made up the whole story, as well as the mythological *exempla*, in order to comfort the young girl; but, even so, such comfort would be meaningless unless the basis on which it was offered was plausible. We must remember that Gyges is in charge of a merchant vessel (3), whose size and precious cargo cannot be entrusted to stormy seas: quite simply, he cannot get home until the new sailing season begins. A letter or messenger, however, might risk an unseasonal crossing, or could travel overland via Aquileia, and we must assume that H.'s information will be understood to derive from some such source. Nevertheless we are obliged also to assume that the information cannot have come first-hand from Gyges himself, who, if writing a letter, would presumably prefer to communicate directly with his wife rather than through the mediacy of a third party; H.'s information must derive from a mutual friend, who has either written from Oricum or come back from there with news. None of this dramatic context is explicit in the ode; readers are challenged to work out for themselves that Asterie[1] is being told by H.[2] what he has been told by <a mutual friend[3]>, who has been told by> Gyges[4] that a go-between[5] has been told by Chloe[6] to tell him that she is infatuated with him.

This chain of information is only one aspect of the extreme sophistication of the ode, which, in its wit, eroticism and concern for human relationships shows H. at his most characteristic – and his best.

METRE   Third Asclepiad

1 Quid fles: 'Why are you crying?' is a natural enough question (e.g. Plaut. *Pseud.* 96, and esp. Prop. 2.20.1 'Quid fles?...Quid fles...?'), but here the verb is transitive ('Why are you crying for/over ~ ?': *OLD* 2)

COMMENTARY 7.1–3

and its object is *iuuenem*...*Gygen* (4–5), who is also the antecedent of the *quem*-clause.

Asterie: the name, which is presumably a pseudonym, is a transliteration of the Greek adj. meaning 'star-like' or 'starry'. It was conventional to describe beauty in terms of celestial bodies (3.9.21, 3.19.26): Asteris is the name of an addressee in a fragment ascribed to Anacreon (*Adesp.* 957), as well as the poetic pseudonym of a bride at Stat. *Silv.* 1.2.197–8. Particularly relevant to H.'s addressee, whom H. will advise to avoid any courting by Enipeus (22–32), is the mythical Asterie, who was the sister of Leto (Hes. *Theog.* 409) and took measures to avoid the sexual attentions of Zeus (Callim. *Hymn* 4.37–8): see Cairns, *RL* 370.

1–2 quem tibi candidi | primo restituent uere Fauonii: Favonius is the west wind: although it will be in Gyges' face as he makes his way from Greece (5) back to Italy, it heralds the return of spring and hence the welcome return of the sailing season (1.4.1–2).[48] Elsewhere too (Colum. 10.78) the west wind is described as *candidus*, evidently an equivalent of the Greek ἀργεστής ('cleansing': see Plin. *NH* 2.119; West on Hes. *Theog.* 379) and a reference to its role in clearing away clouds (cf. 1.7.15 and N–H); but here *tibi*, which is to be taken with *candidi* as well as *restituent* (an ex. of *apo koinou*), suggests also the meaning 'lucky' or 'favourable' (*OLD* 7b), as in 'red-letter days' marked with a 'bright mark' on a calendar (e.g. Cat. 68B.148 'quem lapide illa dies candidiore notat', 107.6 'o lucem candidiore nota' (*restituis* occurs twice in the preceding lines), Plin. *Ep.* 6.11.3). *primo uere*, a set phrase = 'at the beginning of spring', indicates that Gyges will return as quickly as he possibly can.[49]

3 Thyna merce beatum: the Thynoi lived on either side of the Bosphorus (*BA* Map 52); the adj. *Thynus* occurs first in Catullus (25.7) and reappears in a slightly different form in a poem of Maecenas (2.4C/185.4H) addressed to H.: on both occasions it seems to be used loosely for 'Bithynian'. When a girl asked Catullus what loot he had brought back to Rome from Bithynia, where he had spent a year on the

---

[48] Favonius is said to be the ultimate origin of the notorious wind known as the Föhn, which is still called Favonio in Ticino; how a benign west wind came to be associated with a famously malign southern wind is unclear (N. Hunt, *Where the Wild Winds Are* (2017) 139).

[49] According to *Orbis* the shortest route from Oricum (5) to Rome – by sea to Brundisium and then overland – would take about three weeks in the spring; it would take less than half that time if one sailed all the way round the foot of Italy and then up the coast.

staff of the governor, the poet, 'ut puellae | unum me facerem *beatiorem*' (10.16–17), concocted a tall story which immediately rebounded on him (10.28–32). Asia Minor in general was fabled for its wealth (cf. Man. 4.758 'Bithynia diues'; W. on Tac. *Agr.* 6.2); Asterie's husband is evidently a merchant who trades between Italy and the Roman province of Bithynia.

4 fide is an archaic genitive, a form supported by Julius Caesar in his work on language (see A. Garcea, *Caesar's De Analogia* (2012) 230–4). For the importance of *fides* in marriage see Treggiari 237–8.

5 Gygēn: the enjambement of the man's name, presumably another pseudonym, is wryly humorous after *beatum* (3): the famous Gyges, king of Lydia (687–652 BC), was legendary for his wealth ('rich in gold', according to Archil. 19). Gyges' ascent to the kingship is told by Herodotus (1.8–12): when the wife of Candaules, the previous king, was seen naked by Gyges, who at the time was her husband's bodyguard, she threatened him with death unless he killed her husband and married her – which he did. The story has some clear similarities to the two later in the poem (13–18), and Cairns (*RL* 362–4) has noted that all three stories appeared in the historical work of Nicolaus of Damascus, biographer of Augustus and contemporary of H. For the accus. *Gygēn*, as in other Greek names of the first declension in *-ēs*, see G&L 32 §65; Housman 2.823–4. The name Gyges is used again for a young man at 2.5.20.

Notis actus ad Oricum: Gyges had been intending to cross from the western coast of Greece to Italy but the southerlies (here contrasting with the *Fauonii* of line 2) had driven him to seek shelter at Oricum (sometimes called Oricus). The port, protected from the open sea by the promontory known as Acroceraunia (cf. Prop. 1.8.19–20 'ut te, felici praeuecta Ceraunia remo, | accipiat placidis Oricos aequoribus!'), was a good place for overwintering ships (cf. Liv. 24.40.17) and in January of 48 BC had been the scene of operations in the civil war (described by Caesar in Book 3 of the *Bellum Ciuile*). The south wind again maroons a young man at 4.5.9–12 (a simile).

6 post insana Caprae sidera: the Goat (today called Capella) is a star in the constellation Auriga: its rising in late September/early October indicated stormy weather and the end of the sailing season (3.1.27–8n.). Yet H. is not merely supplying a date; since anyone called Asterie should know what the stars portend, she should be predisposed to realise that her partner's prolonged absence has an innocent explanation. The fury of the weather conditions (*OLD insanus* 4a) is here transferred to the star (cf. 3.29.19).

6–8 frigidas | noctes…agit: the nights are cold both because it is winter and because Gyges is without Asterie (cf. *CIL* 4.2146 'Vibius Restitutus hic solus dormiuit et Vrbanam suam desiderabat', from the wall of a boarding house in Pompeii). *agit* repeats *actus* (5) in a different form (Wills 325–6) and with a different meaning, but, since there seems to be no special point, the example falls into none of the various and somewhat confusing categories of repetition recognised by ancient theorists (Lausberg 274–98 §§608–64). See Wills 473–7 on 'unfigured repetition'.

7–8 non sine multis | insomnis lacrimis: 'Insomnia is a classic symptom of love' (McKeown on Ov. *Am.* 1.2.1–4, with many exs.); Gyges' tears show that he is as distraught by his separation from Asterie as she is. For *non sine* cf. 3.4.20n.

9 atqui contrasts the following story with Gyges' loyalty to Asterie as proved by his tears (4, 7–8). For *atqui* see 3.5.49–50n.

sollicitae nuntius hospitae 'a/the messenger from his troubled *hospita*'. A *hospita* is a landlady either in her own right or through her marriage to a landlord or *hospes*: that Chloe, like Asterie, is married is suggested by the facts that she discreetly uses a go-between and that the two mythological paradigms are married and rely on messages (see 13–16n. and 17–18n. below). Chloe is certainly of a different social status and function from the lascivious *copa* described in the pseudo-Virgilian poem of that name (cf. V. J. Rosivach, 'The sociology of the *Copa*', *Latomus* 55 (1996) 605–14), although the various terms were considerably fluid (cf. B. W. Frier, *JRS* 67 (1977) 31–3) and some *hospitae* might perform the services of a *copa* (*CIL* 13.10018.95 'futuui hospita(m)'). *sollicitus* is used of the turmoil of passion (e.g. *S.* 2.3.252–3 'meretricis amore | sollicitus') but, since love or infatuation is often seen as a disease (see e.g. Maltby on Tib. 2.5.110), the language of the two conditions often overlaps, as here (cf. Langslow 312).

10–11 suspirare Chloën et miseram tuis | dicens ignibus uri: *tuis* breaks the strict accus. + infin. after *dicens* and is, as it were, spoken by H. to Asterie. *tuis…ignibus* may be taken in one of two ways: *either* 'with the same fires [sc. of passion] as you' (*OLD ignis* 9a, *tuus* 4) *or* 'on account of your flame [i.e. your beloved]', a metonymy (*OLD ignis* 9b); in the latter usage the noun is usually singular but cf. Manil. 4.683 'suos ignes', *Il. Lat.* 72 'solaturque suos alienis ignibus ignes'. The second alternative is perhaps preferable ('Yet a/the messenger from his troubled *hospita*, saying that Chloe is sighing and is wretchedly burning on account of your beloved,...') but it is difficult to be sure (*contra* N–R). See further nn. below.

10 suspirare Chloēn: sighs (again at 3.2.9) are a frequent symptom of love, e.g. Lygd. 6.61 'sollicitus repetam tota suspiria nocte' and NA ad loc. Chloe's name (which reappears at 1.23.1, 3.9.6–19 and 3.26.12) is another transliteration of a Greek adj. (= 'green' and hence 'youthful'); a servant in the imperial household is so called (*CIL* 6.33099). The only other Latin author by whom it is used is Martial (see Henriksén on 9.15). Greek names of the first declension in *-ē* form an accus. in *-ēn* (G&L 32 §65).

10–11 miseram tuis | ...ignibus uri: once again there is a linguistic overlap between love and disease: *miser* is a regular term for the sick (*OLD* 3a), while *uri*, often used of passion (Pichon 301), also suggests feverishness (*OLD* 5a): for the combination of both cf. e.g. *Epo.* 14.13 'ureris ipse miser', Ov. *Her.* 3.138.

12 temptat mille uafer modis: sc. *eum*: 'cunningly attempts to influence him in a thousand ways' (*OLD tempto* 6); for the adverbial use of the adj. (as again in 10) see G&L 206 §325 R. 6. At first glance it is very odd indeed that these thousand ways are illustrated by two examples of the *same* way, but we have seen (intro.) that the stories in 13–18, which duplicate each other, are not the product of the *nuntius*' imagination but have been falsely attributed to him by H. The duplication of the stories is underlined by their chiastic presentation: propositioning woman (13–14) → murder (16a) → *refert* (16b) ≈ *narrat* (17a) → murder (17b) → propositioning woman (18). The present generalisation is then repeated in different words at 19–20, completing a ring.

13–16 ut...refert 'He recalls how a disloyal wife by means of false accusations drove a credulous Proetus to hasten the death of [lit. to] too chaste Bellerophon.' The woman is Anteia (sometimes called Stheneboea), wife of Proetus, king of Argos: she fell in love with Bellerophon while he was a guest at their palace and sent him a message asking for a tryst (Apollod. 2.3.1 προσπέμπει λόγους περὶ συνουσίας); when he rejected her, she accused him to her husband of trying to seduce her, whereupon Proetus attempted, but failed, to arrange for the man's death. See further Ingleheart on Ov. *Tr.* 2.397–8. For *mulier* = 'wife' (again at 3.14.5, (?) 3.24.18) see *OLD* 2.

13 ut Proetum mulier perfida credulum: the chiastically mannered pattern of noun[1] noun[2] ~ adj.[2] adj.[1] facilitates the typically Horatian juxtaposition *perfida credulum*.

14 nimis: just as *mulier perfida* represented the view of H., not the *nuntius* (see intro.), so *nimis* represents the view of the *nuntius*, not H.

15 Bellerophontae: the man's name in Latin is either *Bellerophontēs*, of which the dat. is in *-ae* (as here), or *Bellerophōn*, of which the nom. does not exist except in Hyginus. See *OLD* s.v.; Housman 2.828–9.

16 maturare necem: the verb is quite often found governing words for 'death' (e.g. Cic. *Clu.* 171); for *necem* in particular cf. Liv. 39.50.6, Suet. *Vita Plin.* 'ut necem sibi maturaret'. This seems the earliest ex. of an infin. after *impello* in extant Latin (next in the *Aeneid*, e.g. 1.11).

17–18 narrat paene datum Pelea Tartaro, | Magnessam Hippolyten dum fugit abstinens: Hippolyte, wife of Acastus, fell in love with Peleus, a Thessalian king who was staying with them, and sent him a message asking for a tryst (Apollod. 3.13.3 περὶ συνουσίας προσέπεμψεν αὐτῷ λόγους); when he rejected her, she (a) wrote to his wife, saying that he was about to marry another woman, (b) accused him to her husband of trying to seduce her, whereupon Acastus tried unsuccessfully to have Peleus killed. Hippolyte is described as coming from Magnesia (a town in Thessaly), to distinguish her from the Amazon who shared her name. *dum* seems almost causal here ('in as much as…'). *datum…Tartaro* is constructed on the analogy of such expressions as *dare morti* etc., 'to consign to death' (*OLD do* 20c; cf. 19b), as found in the old legal formula at Varro, *LL* 7.42 'leto datus'. *Pelea* is the accus. of the Greek name *Peleus* see *OLD* s.v.; G&L 32 §65. *abstinens* here = 'chaste' (*TLL* 1.198.9–16, *OLD* 2b).

19–20 peccare docentes | fallax historias mouet 'deceitfully he adduces stories which teach infidelity': since *peccare* has a sexual connotation (*OLD* 3b), its combination with *docentes* is almost a translation of the Greek word ἐρωτοδιδάσκαλοι or 'love-teaching' and alludes self-referentially to the facts that lines 9–20 illustrate erotodidaxis, as scholars have termed it, and that in them H. is attributing to the *nuntius* the role of *praeceptor amoris*.[50] Such *praeceptores* would very often resort to the kinds of mythological *exempla* frequent in erotic poetry, which itself is defined by its deceitfulness (Prop.

---

[50] For this terminology, with bibliography and many practical examples, see Cairns, *GC* 295 (index); Gibson on Ov. *AA* 3, Intro. pp. 13–21.

4.1.135 'fallax opus', Ov. *Tr.* 2.461–2); but here the choice of the word *historias* for these 'stories' (*OLD* 3) simultaneously facilitates parodic allusion to the conventions of genuine historiography, which claimed a didactic function and taught readers moral lessons (Diod. 1.1.1–2, Liv. *praef.* 10, Tac. *A.* 4.33.2 'plures aliorum euentis docentur'). *doceo* is regularly found constructed with the infin. but without an expressed direct object (*TLL* 5.1.1746.29–39). For the adverbial use of the adj. see 12n. above.

fallax is the last of the words picked up by Ovid in an allusion which stretches back to *hospitae* in line 9 (*Tr.* 2.397–8, on Bellerophon): 'Nam quid de tetrico *referam* domitore Chimaerae, | quem leto *fallax hospita paene dedit?*'

Both *mouet* and *monet* are attested by the MSS. An accusative (of a thing) after *moneo* is internal and almost always a neuter pronoun or adj. (e.g. *S.* 1.2.73 'meliora monet'); a noun such as *historias* would be quite exceptional. For *moueo* = 'to bring forward' or 'adduce' see *OLD* 18 and Gibson on Ov. *AA* 3.651–2, where the MSS are similarly divided.

21–2 frustra: nam scopulis surdior Icari | uoces audit: this 'dramatic' use of *frustra*, deferred either to the end of a sentence or the beginning of the next (sometimes depending on editorial preference) and often followed (as here) by *nam(que)*, is regular in verse and prose: e.g. 3.13.6, *S.* 2.7.115, Cat. 21.7, Hirt. *BG* 8.3.4, 8.5.3, *Bell. Alex.* 29.5, Cels. 7.7.6B, Quint. 9.3.60, Mart. 10.35.19, Sil. 6.189. The Icarian Sea (*Icarium*) was in the eastern Aegean (N–H on 1.1.15). For the proverbial deafness of rocks (again at 3.11.1–2) see *Epo.* 17.54–5 and Watson; Otto 313. *uoces* = 'utterances' (*OLD* 7a).

22 adhuc integer 'still morally sound' (*OLD integer* 13a). There is no suggestion that Gyges will succumb to temptation in the future, which would make nonsense of what follows.

22–4 at tibi | ne...caue: at this point H. becomes the *praeceptor fidei* or *castitatis*.

23 uicinus Enipeus: the name (scanned as three syllables: ∪ – –) derives from the Greek ἐνιπή, 'reproof, reproach': if Asterie allowed him to have his way with her, Enipeus would be a source of reproach against her. *uicinus* (again at 3.19.24) does not necessarily mean a next-door neighbour but a dweller in the same *uicus* or neighbourhood (see further 29–30n. below).

24 plus iusto 'more than is proper', a set phrase (*OLD iustum* 2).

25–6 quamuis non alius flectere equum sciens | aeque conspicitur gramine Martio 'although no one else is seen on the Campus Martius equally skilled at handling a horse'; in poetry and post-Augustan prose *quamuis* 'is occasionally used with the indicative, on the analogy of *quamquam*' (*NLS* 204 §249 (*c*) *Note*; cf. G&L 392 §606 N. 1). *sciens* more normally takes a genitive than an infin. (only Quint. 12.3.5 is quoted as parallel in *OLD* 3); *flectere* (*OLD* 7) captures Enipeus' horsemanship more vividly than would the more general *regere*: an epitaph records the deceased as 'flectere doctus equos' (*CLE* 1110.7). Horse-riding was regarded as an important skill (3.2.3–4n.).

The Campus Martius was in the west of the city, near the Tiber. According to H.'s younger contemporary, Strabo, 'the size of the Campus is remarkable, since it affords space at the same time and without interference not only for the chariot races and every other equestrian exercise but also for all that multitude of people who exercise themselves by ball-playing, hoop-trundling and wrestling'. He continues by saying that the Campus 'is covered with grass throughout the year' and 'affords a spectacle that one can hardly draw away from' (5.3.8, Loeb trans.). The expr. *gramine Martio* refers both to the Campus' remarkable verdure (cf. 4.1.39–40) and to Mars' title Gradivus, which was thought to be associated with the word *gramen* (Maltby 262). For other ways of referring to the Campus see Gaertner on Ov. *Ex P.* 1.8.37. See further 1.8.4–7 (and next n.).

28 Tusco denatat alueo: swimming in the Tiber, another manly pursuit, is again juxtaposed with horse-riding in the Campus at 1.8.8; cf. also 3.12.7–9, Tib. 1.4.11–12 and Murgatroyd and Maltby ad loc. The river is described as 'Etruscan' because it rose in Etruria. *denatare* occurs nowhere else in classical Latin: the prefix suggests that Enipeus swims with the current to show off his speed (so Jani).

29 domum claude: *claude* is an allusion to the (would-be) lover who is locked out, for whom the expression *exclusus amator* was used both by Lucr. (4.1177 and Brown's nn.) and by H. himself (*S.* 2.3.259–60 with Muecke); see also next nn. H. might have said *forem claude* (as Ov. *Am.* 2.19.38 'prima claudere nocte forem'), but *domum* has moral resonance (3.6.17–18n.): keeping house symbolised the virtuous female and went hand-in-hand with chastity, as in the epitaph for one Amymone: 'casta, domiseda' (*ILS* 8402).

29–30 neque in uias | sub cantum querulae despice tibiae: 'a negative command is regularly joined to a previous positive command by *nec*' (*NLS* 97 §128 (iii)). *despice* indicates that Asterie's bedroom is upstairs (cf. N–H on 1.25.2); *in uias* contributes to the notion of a neighbourhood 'stud' (cf. Maltby 642-4).

Classical literature has numerous references to young men who, after leaving a drinking party or symposium, parade through the streets of a town, often with torches and musical instruments, and then seek admission through song to the house of their mistress or some other woman, which remains closed to them. (A list of some examples in Cairns, *GC* 284.) The one surviving fragment of Cicero's historical work *De consiliis* describes just such a scene: 'cum uinolenti adulescentes tibiarum etiam cantu (ut fit) instincti mulieris pudicae fores frangerent' (F6C = 4P). The term κῶμος is used for the whole situation of procession and song, although παρακλαυσίθυρον is also found for the latter alone (Plut. *Mor.* 753B). Standard discussions will be found in Copley; Cairns, *GC* 305-6, *PRE* 479, *RL* 519 (indexes in each case), and 'The terms *komos* and *paraclausithyron*', *GRBS* 60 (2020) 262-71. See further 3.10 below, and the passages cited in the previous n.

The serenading of Asterie involves the tibia, originally a Phrygian instrument (Lucr. 2.620) and consisting usually of two pipes (3.19.18-19n.); its shrill sound (1.12.1-2, Cat. 64.264 'barbaraque horribili stridebat tibia cantu') no doubt accounts for its description here as 'plaintive' (also at Lucr. 4.584-5, 5.1384-5), although the adj. also alludes to the term παρακλαυσίθυρον (lit. 'lament at the door', from παρακλαίω, 'to lament beside', + θύρα, 'door'). The tibia is mentioned several times by H. (again in this book at 3.4.1 and 3.19.19); see further Brink on *AP* 202-4; M. L. West (1992) 91-2; *BNP* 9.362-3.

The MSS are divided between *sub cantu* and *sub cantum*. The former is printed by most editors but is unparalleled; *sub cantum*, 'in response to the playing' (*OLD sub* 24b), is paralleled at S. 1.1.10 and seems more likely.

31-2 et te saepe uocanti | duram difficilis mane 'and stay obdurate, though he should often call you hard': *difficilis* (for which see McKeown on Ov. *Am.* 1.6.1-2) starts to be constructed with the dat. in the Augustan age (again at 3.10.11). References to the girl's cruelty are regular in the paraclausithyron (for *dura* see McKeown on Ov. *Am.* 1.9.19-20).

8

The first half of Book 3 comprises fifteen poems: this is the central poem of the fifteen, and in its central stanza (13-16) is an address to Maecenas, to whom the poem is therefore dedicated. On either side of the central stanza is a group of three stanzas, the first (1-12) focussing on H., the second (17-28) on Maecenas. The structure of the ode is thus 3+1+3 (see esp. Marcovich 79–80); as is often the case, there is a dramatic context to be inferred.

H.'s friend and patron is visiting him on the first day of March (1). We are not told whether the visit is in response to an initial invitation, although it is perhaps difficult to imagine the great man just dropping in on the off-chance that the poet would be at home;[51] and in fact Maecenas' astonishment on entering (3 *miraris*) is all the greater if he has been deliberately invited to a celebration which he has not anticipated (see also 1n.). For he finds H.'s place in festal mode, with flowers, incense, an altar, and evidence of a banquet and sacrifice (2–4, 6–7). Maecenas cannot understand it: although 1 March is indeed a festival day, it is a festival for wives – the Matronalia – and H. has no wife (1 *caelebs*).[52] What is going on? H. explains that it is the anniversary of his escape from the falling tree, which he plans to celebrate with a party (7–12).[53] In the central stanza Maecenas is told to start drinking (13 'Sume, Maecenas, cyathos...'), justification for which – the favourable state of foreign affairs – is provided in the last three stanzas. These stanzas are constructed on a ring basis, the imperative of 17 ('mitte...curas') picked up by the three of 26–8 ('parce...et...cape...linque'). Within this frame is a matching list of four foreign successes, presented in parallel fashion and designed to reassure Maecenas that it is not irresponsible to participate in the anniversary party (18–24).

The ode is a perfect blend of the personal and the public, encapsulated in the respective figures of the two friends. In 1–12 the focus is on H., the poet and host, whose encounter with the tree constitutes the background to the celebration. This is not the first time that readers have been told about the infamous tree. In 2.13 the poet delivered an amusing attack on the man who first planted it (1–12), using the episode as a way of paying tribute to Sappho and Alcaeus (21–40). In 2.17, assuring Maecenas that the two of them are destined to die together (1–22), he drew a parallel between his friend's recovery from illness and his own escape from the tree (22–30), and said that each of them must offer sacrifice in thanksgiving for their good fortune (30–2). In 3.4 he aligned the tree episode with the battle of Philippi (commemorated in 2.7) and with an otherwise unrecorded

---

[51] If the ode is set at H.'s Sabine estate (3–4n.), it would take Maecenas the best part of two days to get there (p. 358 n. 142).

[52] Maecenas, however, did have a wife (Terentia), and it may be asked why he is not at home celebrating the Matronalia with her; perhaps we are to imagine that H. has timed his party to coincide with the formal rituals of the festival, from which men may have been absent (cf. Heyworth on Ov. *F.* 3.167–258, p. 115).

[53] Cairns categorises the ode as an example of the *soteria*, an expression of 'rejoicing, congratulations and thanksgiving for the safety of someone who has been rescued from danger' (*GC* 73).

shipwreck and used his survival on all three occasions as evidence of his protection by the Camenae (25–8). The present ode is, as it were, the climax of this highly personal theme, and the decision to commemorate it, perhaps looking back to the commitment of 2.17, illustrates the Romans' 'anniversary mentality' and their 'fascination with anniversary days'. Since the day is also the festival of the Matronalia, it shows not only that 'the new associations of a particular day can overlap or compete with...the old ones' but also that in this case the personal can complement the public.[54]

In 17–28 the focus is on Maecenas, the patron and invitee, with whom H.'s readers will have been very familiar: not only has he featured frequently in H.'s poetry but as an associate of the *princeps* he was a very public, if paradoxical, figure. 'This was the man', said the younger Seneca, 'who always went about in the City with his tunic undone, for, even when he was discharging responsibilities for the absent Caesar, he would be asked for the watchword in a state of undress' (*Ep.* 114.6). Despite twice being placed in charge of the City when Octavian was away (36–33 and 31–29 BC), Maecenas famously insisted on remaining a *priuatus* (17n., 3.16.20n.) and, the moment his official duties were completed, would take himself off for relaxation (Vell. 88.2).[55] Since the ode dates itself to a time when foreign affairs are no longer a worry (see below), Maecenas' notorious hedonism is presented as justified as well as judicious (25–6). Maecenas' unusual lifestyle is used by Seneca to illustrate the dictum 'the style is the man': the examples of stylistic oddities which he quotes (*Ep.* 114.5) are all from Maecenas' prose works, but it is the same with the surviving scraps of his verse, where 'the preciosity and neuroticism of the author come through strongly' (Courtney, *FLP* 276). Since in the ode Maecenas appears to be addressed in literary terms (5 'docte sermones utriusque linguae'), it is possible that in places H. is gently poking fun at the literary extravagances of his cultured friend (7–8n., 10–11n.).

Scholars have recognised that the enemies named in lines 18–24 provide evidence for the date of the ode, though they have not always agreed on what that date is. As we shall see, H. has listed the enemies roughly in the order in which they ceased being a threat. We know that in 25 the Temple of Janus was closed to mark the conquest of the Cantabrians in Spain (21–2n.); we do not know the exact date of the closure, but, since it would presumably have had to follow the end of the campaigning season, Syme's suggestion of the end of 25 seems reasonable (*RP* 3.1180; so

---

[54] The quotations are from Feeney (2007) 148–9. See also J. Griffin, 'Cult and personality in Horace', *JRS* 87 (1997) 54–69, who argues that it is in Book 3 that H. 'exploits the motif of the definite date'.
[55] See also Lyne, *Hor.* 133–5.

too Rich 152-3). Nor do we know anything about the withdrawal of the Scythians (23-4n.), but we may assume that Janus would not have been closed if the Scythians were still considered a menace. Thus the latest date seems to be late 25. Since the dramatic date of the ode is 1 March, it appears likely that H. is referring to the spring of 24 BC, when he was 40 years old.[56] See also Hutchinson 142-3.

METRE Sapphic

1–5 Martiis...linguae: some edd. print the lines as a statement, but they seem far more natural as a question.

1 Martiis caelebs quid agam Kalendis: 'The first day (*Kalends*) of each month was sacred to Juno, and especially the *Kalends* of March when it was customary for husbands to pray for the health of their wives and to give them presents' (Scullard 87). Maecenas is puzzled (3) because H., though engaged in ritual, is unmarried (*caelebs*). H.'s line is imitated by Lygd. 1.1–4, where NA provides further information on the Matronalia. Since the word *Kalendae* was said to derive from Greek καλεῖν 'to summon' (e.g. Varro, *Vita pop. Rom.* fr. 18 'calendae appellatae, quod est tractum a Graecis, qui καλεῖν uocare dixerunt'; Maltby 321), the first day of the month was an appropriate day on which to be summoned to H.'s place for a drink, as Maecenas, whose expertise in Greek is carefully mentioned below (5), may have realised. At the end of the previous book H. had referred to his being summoned by Maecenas (2.20.6–7 'ego quem uocas, | dilecte Maecenas'); perhaps the *bons viveurs* shared a running joke involving reciprocal invitations. For an indir. question after *miror* see *OLD miror* 2c.

2 quid uelint flores 'what the flowers mean' (*OLD uolo* 17). The verb is also to be understood with *acerra* (a casket for holding incense) and *carbo* (charcoal), the three nominatives forming a tricolon crescendo (2–4).

3 miraris: addressees in various genres will often act as a trigger, e.g. Cat. 7.1 'Quaeris quot...', Prop. 4.2.1 'Quid mirare...' (and Hutchinson's n.), Plin. *Ep.* 2.17.1 'Miraris cur...' (and Whitton's n.); N–H on 2.17.1; T. Janson, *Latin Prose Prefaces* (1964) 116–19.

3–4 carbo in | caespite uiuo: as a private citizen H. does not have a permanent altar available in his house, so he has to improvise with one made of fresh turf; such altars (*OLD caespes* 3b) are quite frequently referred to

---

[56] N–R date the ode to 1 March 25 (124–5), but they fudge events in Spain.

COMMENTARY 8.5   191

(N–H on 1.19.13). Was fresh turf easy to come by in Rome? If the charcoal comes from the wood of the fateful tree (8) and has been stored for the purpose of the commemoration,[57] the scene is perhaps on H.'s Sabine estate; but we simply do not know. The link between the third line of a Sapphic stanza and the fourth (the 'adonius') is so close that on three occasions a word is distributed between the lines (1.2.19–20 *u-xorius*, 1.25.11–12 *inter-lunia*, 2.16.7–8 *ue-nale*); this makes it less strange that at the end of 3, 'carb(o) in', the preposition is to be taken with the abl. in 4, as again at 4.6.11–12 'coll(um) in | puluere Teucro'. See also 26 below.

5 docte sermones utriusque linguae: since first-time readers of the ode do not yet know the identity of its addressee,[58] they are as likely to be puzzled by this vocative as is Maecenas by the festal scene in front of him. The phrase *utraque lingua* is extremely common, esp. in Pliny's letters, Quintilian and Gellius, and, unless the context makes clear otherwise (as Varro, *LL* 5.74), refers to Latin and Greek (as Mart. 10.76.6 'lingua doctus utraque'). This seems to rule out a reference to Etruscan as one of the languages here, which is unfortunate: Maecenas claimed Etruscan ancestry (3.29.1n.) and, since the Etruscans were traditionally knowledgeable about religious and calendrical matters, such a reference would be particularly apt in view of lines 1–4.[59] The majority of scholars, however, think that H. is referring to Latin and Greek, but interpretation of H.'s compliment is not straightforward. (1) Educated upper-class Romans aspired to be fluent in Greek and the acquisition of such fluency was regarded as something worthy of being noted (see J. N. Adams, *Bilingualism and the Latin Language* (2003) 10–11). Hence H. may simply be alluding to Maecenas' superior language skills. Yet such an allusion does not quite explain the presence of *sermones*; why did H. not simply say *lingua doctus utraque*, as in Martial (above)? At *S.* 1.10.23 'sermo lingua concinnus utraque' *sermo* is a reference to the satiric genre which is under discussion. (2) Since Maecenas is known to have written prose works in dialogue form (*Symposium* and *Dialogi*), and since *sermo* is the technical term for a literary dialogue (*OLD* 3b), it seems too much of a coincidence if H. were not referring to these works;[60] but in what sense could such dialogues be described as 'in each language'? [i] Apuleius (*Flor.* 18.38–

---

[57] As suggested by Ian Du Quesnay.
[58] I am assuming that the transmitted *titulus* 'Ad Maecenatem' is not authorial (see Tarrant (2016b) 226).
[59] The Etruscan for 'March' is **velcitna* or, in its Latinised form, *uelcitanus*.
[60] Fraenkel's attempt to deny this is refuted by the evidence he quotes (222 n. 2).

43) refers to composing a dialogue between two speakers, one of whom is given Greek to speak and the other Latin. Since only the merest scraps of Maecenas' dialogues have survived, it is impossible to know whether he adopted this format; but it seems unlikely: such bilingualism is a product of Apuleius' own circumstances and, had Maecenas written a work of that type, it would surely have been mentioned in one *testimonium* or another. [ii] Cicero often admitted Greek terms into his Latin dialogues, and, although there is no evidence either in the few surviving fragments or elsewhere that introducing Greek words or phrases was one of Maecenas' stylistic habits, it may be telling that, when Augustus playfully criticised Maecenas' style, he used Greek (Suet. *Aug.* 86.2, Macrob. 2.4.12): perhaps Maecenas' use of Greek was as peculiar as his use of Latin and it is this to which H. is jokingly referring. [iii] Later in Book 3 Messalla Corvinus is said to be 'steeped in Socratic dialogues' (3.21.9–10); perhaps H.'s compliment is that Maecenas' achievement in writing Latin dialogues, one of them with a Socratic title, presupposes a deep familiarity with Greek models. Whatever the precise meaning, however, it is entirely unclear why a reference to Maecenas' dialogues might be relevant to his presence at the poet's celebration. Perhaps one of the dialogues discussed religious festivals.

Whether *doctus* means 'taught' or 'expert/learned in ~ ' depends on the context (3.9.10n.): 'having been taught *sermones* in Latin and Greek' seems less than complimentary, unless it is a joke; the more likely alternative is that *docte* is adjectival = 'learned', as *Epi.* 1.19.1 'Maecenas docte', in which case *sermones* is an accusative of respect or 'Greek' accusative, an idiom to be appreciated by the expert in both languages (3.10.18n.).

6 uoueram: it was customary to pay vows after a lucky escape (N–H on 2.17.30, McKeown on Ov. *Am.* 2.13.23–4). The pluperfect tense seems to imply an unspoken 'but I did not tell you about the vow after I had made it'.

6–7 album | Libero caprum: in Book 2 H. had attributed his survival to Faunus (next n.), earlier in Book 3 to the Camenae (3.4.25–7); Bacchus is chosen here presumably because he is a god of poetic inspiration (cf. 3.25), and, despite the promise of a lamb at 2.17.32, the goat is chosen as victim because goats were notoriously destructive of vineyards, which also came under Bacchus' protection (Virg. *G.* 2.380–1 'non aliam ob culpam Baccho caper omnibus aris | caeditur' and Mynors' n.; Leary on Mart. 13.39). Since *caper* can denote a castrated goat (*OLD* 1a), there may be a link to H.'s self-description (1) as *caelebs*, whose etymology was sometimes associated with castration (Quint. 1.6.36); cf. also 3.22.7n.

The goat is white because 'white was the colour preferred by Romans for animals sacrificed to gods of the upper world' (Oakley on Liv. 7.37.1).

7–8 prope funeratus | arboris ictu 'having been almost laid out by the blow from the tree'. *arboris ictu*, playfully suggesting that the tree deliberately tried to kill H., continues from Book 2 the personification of the tree that was introduced in 2.13; at 2.17.28–9 H. talks of Faunus deflecting the blow of the tree ('nisi Faunus ictum | dextra leuasset'). *funero* usually means 'to carry out the funeral of ~ ' (*OLD* 1); the seemingly unique meaning 'killed', as here,[61] has been explained by A. Bradshaw (*Philol.* 114 (1970) 145–50) as a teasing parody of Maecenas' own famously weird style (see also 10–11n.; N–H 2.290).

9–12 hic dies...Tullo 'As the year comes round again, this festival day will remove the cork, sealed by pitch, of an amphora taught to drink smoke in the consulship of Tullus': *amphorae...institutae* seems better explained as a possessive genitive than as a dat. after a verb of separation. For Tullus see below (12n.).

9–10 hic dies anno redeunte festus | corticem...dimouebit: *dies festus* is a technical expr. for a feast day or holiday (*OLD festus* 1a) and common in H. (3.28.1–2n.); *hic* underlines the 'substitution' of H.'s anniversary for the Matronalia (intro.). While *dies* is often the subject of a transitive verb (e.g. 3.14.13–14), here *corticem...dimouebit* transforms the abstraction into a sommelier (*minister uini*); for the conceit of the day doing what is done on that day see e.g. Tib. 1.7.3–4 and Murgatroyd, Tac. *H.* 2.33.3 and Ash. For *redire* = 'come round again' cf. 3.18.10; *OLD* 9. *anno redeunte* resembles the epic formula περιπλομένου ἐνιαυτοῦ (e.g. Hes. *WD* 386), just as *redeuntibus annis* at Lucr. 1.311 and Virg. *Aen.* 8.47 resembles περιπλομένων ἐνιαυτῶν (e.g. Hom. *Od.* 1.16): cf. *S.* 2.2.83 'siue diem festum rediens aduexerit annus'.

10–11 corticem adstrictum pice...| amphorae fumum bibere institutae: in the production of wine, the juice of the grapes was first poured into vats (*dolia*) for fermenting. After fermentation, the wine was transferred to smaller vessels such as *cadi* (3.14.18, 3.29.2) or *amphorae* (3.28.8), which were then sealed with pitch or resin and stored in an *apotheca* or upstairs storeroom (3.21.7) so that smoke, rising from the fire, could facilitate ageing (Colum. 1.6.20). See 1.20.3 and N–H's n.; Gow on Theocr. 7.147,

---

[61] The translation 'laid out', which exactly captures the ambiguity of the Latin, is owed to Miss D. J. Monk in a Latin class in 1975.

Murgatroyd on Tib. 2.1.27–8, Schmeling on Petr. 34.6–7, Coleman on Stat. *Silv.* 4.8.39; *BNP* 15.668; Thurmond 194, 205–6. The language continues the audaciousness of *funeratus* (8) and perhaps for the same reason (7–8n.): the amphora itself has not only been drinking (*bibere*) instead of being a source of drinks, but has been 'taught' (*institutae*) to do so; and what it has 'drunk' is smoke (cf. Tib. 2.1.27 'fumosos... Falernos', Ov. *F.* 5.518 'fumoso...cado'). See also Leary on Mart. 13.32.

10 dimouebit: the tense does not necessarily imply that there have been no celebrations in previous years: it could be a gnomic future, expressing a general truth (3.1.18–19n.): 'this day is always going to be a holiday!' On the other hand, if there have been previous commemorations, it is surprising that Maecenas is puzzled by H.'s rituals, especially since at 2.17.21–30 the poet goes out of his way to link his survival with that of Maecenas: *miraris* (3) makes better sense if this is the first anniversary (Hutchinson 136). See too next n.

12 consule Tullo: a storage vessel would record – usually by an inscription in red paint on its body or neck – the year it was sealed (3.14.18, 3.21.1, 3.28.8), and perhaps also the year of the vintage, as *ILS* 8580 'Ti. Claudio P. Quinctilio cos. [13 BC] a. d. XIII k. Iun. uinum diffusum quod natum est duobus Lentulis cos. [18 BC], autocr.':[62] see N–H on 1.20.3; Schmeling on Petron. 34.6; Thurmond 210–12. *Tullo* is a reference to L. Volcacius Tullus, presumably the younger (consul in 33) rather than his father (consul in 66). Ideally one wants the date to have point. Some scholars have suggested that 33 was the year in which the tree nearly killed H., but so distant a date conflicts with Maecenas' puzzlement (3 *miraris*). At 1.20.1–8 H. says that he sealed some stocks of Sabine wine to mark the acclamation which Maecenas received in the theatre after recovering from a serious illness; perhaps the acclamation took place in 33 and H., on the first anniversary of his own escape from death, is now offering Maecenas the wine he sealed nine years earlier to celebrate a similar escape of his friend (see intro.). Since Sabine wine evidently required at least seven years' maturation (Cairns, *RL* 237), it would be ready to drink in 24 BC.

13 Maecenas: his name also appears in the central stanza of 4.11 (Moritz 119).

---

[62] *autocratum* means 'self-blended', i.e. 'medium'. The Ti. Claudius of the inscription is the future emperor Tiberius.

13–14 cyathos amici | sospitis centum: a *cyathus* was a ladle for pouring wine (*OLD* 1a), illustrated in one of the paintings on the Tomb of Vestorius Priscus at Pompeii (see Dunbabin 119, Fig. 3), but the term was also used, as here, of the volume of wine a ladle would hold (*OLD* 2a), evidently about a twelfth of a pint or 50 ml. *centum* is not to be taken literally (it would be more than a gallon) but stands for any very large number (*OLD* b), perhaps the length of time for which the survivor wishes from now on (cf. Ov. *F.* 3.531–2 'annosque precantur | quot sumant cyathos'). Shorey calls *amici sospitis* the 'genitive of the toast', but it is presumably possessive, referring to the person being toasted (3.19.9–11n.).

14–15 uigiles lūcernas | perfer in lūcem 'extend the watchful lamps till dawn' (*OLD perfero* 3, *lux* 2b). In his public capacity Maecenas was famous for his watchfulness (Vell. 88.2 'ubi res uigiliam exigeret, sane exsomnis', *Eleg. Maec.* 1.14 'tu uigil urbis eras'); he must now apply himself in the private sphere. H.'s assonance acknowledges the derivation of *lucerna* from *lux* (Varro, *LL* 5.119): whether he and Maecenas also knew that 'its suffix is Etruscan' (De Melo ad loc.) is perhaps doubtful. For other exs. of the play cf. Cic. *Fin.* 3.45, Mart. 11.104.5–6 (quoted 3.6.26–8n.), Apul. *Met.* 2.24.5; for *uigiles* cf. Mart. 14.40 (Meleager, *Anth. Pal.* 5.197.3–4 φιλάγρυπνον | λύχνον).

15–16 procul omnis esto | clamor et ira: perhaps a fleeting allusion to Hom. *Od.* 1.369–70 μηδὲ βοητὺς ἔστω ('let there be no clamour'), but Porphyrio remarks that the future imperative *esto* is here equivalent to *erit*: the expression is one of confidence; there is no chance that the two friends' celebration will degenerate into the kind of drunken scene described at 1.27.1–8.

17 mitte ciuiles super Vrbe curas: *ciuiles* is equivalent to *ciuis* (genit.): 'set aside your citizen's concerns [i.e. the concerns which a citizen has] for Rome' (*OLD mitto* 6, *ciuilis* 6). The expression is variously pointed. (1) In 36–33 BC and again around 31–29 Maecenas was placed by Octavian in charge of the City (~ *super Vrbe*),[63] but he was famous for not wanting formal political advancement (intro.; 3.16.20n.) and on neither occasion did he give up his status as a private citizen (~ *ciuiles...curas*): cf. Vell. 88.2 'erat tunc urbis custodiis praepositus C. Maecenas, equestri... genere natus', Tac. *A.* 3.30.2, 6.11.2 'Augustus bellis ciuilibus Cilnium Maecenatem equestris ordinis cunctis apud Romam atque Italiam praeposuit'. (2) In January 26 BC the official position of *praefectus urbis* was

---

[63] Cf. Dio 49.16.2, 51.3.5 and Reinhold ad loc.

created and given by Augustus to Messalla Corvinus (cos. 31 BC and the honorand of 3.21). Although Messalla resigned after six days, saying '*inciuilem* esse potestatem' (Jer. *Chron.* 18, p. 164H), and seems not to have had a successor until T. Statilius Taurus in 16 BC, contemporaries could have inferred from his appointment that the City would no longer come under the protection of a *priuatus* such as Maecenas.[64] Since the dramatic date of the ode is likely to be 24 BC, *mitte ciuiles super Vrbe curas* is perhaps an allusion to this development, while at the same time reminding readers that during Maecenas' protectorates his power could never have been described as *in-ciuilis*. For *mitte...curas* cf. Virg. *Aen.* 6.85, Liv. 30.3.4, Val. Fl. 4.489.

18 occidit Daci Cotisonis agmen: since Dacians appeared in Octavian's triumph in 29 BC (Dio 51.22.6), it is inferred that they had been defeated by M. Licinius Crassus, the consul of 30, who had been sent out to oppose them (3.6.13–14n.). Although this date is earlier than those implied in 19–24 below, Crassus' own triumph was not celebrated until two years later (4 July 27: cf. EJ p. 35): the triumph is officially described as 'ex...Geteis', but the Getae are regarded as a branch of the Dacians by Dio (51.22.7). Likewise, although the Dacian king is called Cotiso also by Florus (2.27.18 = 4.12.18), he is evidently the same man as is called Coson (his vernacular name) and king of the Getae by Suetonius (*Aug.* 63.2 with Wardle).

19–20 Medus infestus sibi luctuosis | dissidet armis 'the hostile Medes are at variance, their warfare calamitous to themselves'; translation is difficult because of *sibi*, which 'seems equally open to be governed by *infestus*, *luctuosis*, and *dissidet*' (Wickham). The *discordia* of barbarian peoples is a topos of Latin ethnographical writing (Tac. *A.* 3.38.4 and W., 11.8.1 and Malloch), but the internal relations of the Parthians, to whom the collective *Medus* refers (3.3.43–4n., 3.5.9), were particularly volatile in the years 26–25. The sources, esp. Dio (53.33.1–2) and Trogus' epitomator Justin (42.5.6–12), present a confusing picture, and modern scholars do not agree with one another (see the convenient summary in Nabel 308–10); but Parthian coinage (for which see N–R 124, Powell 153 n. 30) indicates that the king, Phraates IV, was ousted by the pro-Roman pretender to his throne, Tiridates II, in May of 26, had regained his kingdom in the summer of that year, was ousted again in March of 25, and then regained his kingdom for the last time in May 25 – a succession of *coups* well reflected in H.'s words. The subsequent movements of Tiridates are disputed, but

---

[64] Agrippa seems to have taken temporary charge of the City around 21/20 BC (cf. Dio 54.6.4-6 and Rich's n.), but he was a three-times consul.

it seems likely that Augustus capitalised on the two leaders' continuing mutual hostility in order to promote his own agenda *vis-à-vis* Parthia (see further Cooley on *RG* 29.2 and 32.1, Rich on Dio 53.33.1–2). *luctuosus* (again at 3.6.8) is a prosaic word and in its commoner meaning of 'calamitous', as here, is a favourite of Cicero. For the metonymy *arma* = 'warfare' see *OLD* 6.

21–2 seruit Hispanae uetus hostis orae | Cantaber sera domitus catena 'the Cantabrian, that old enemy at the edge of Spain, having been belatedly tamed with the chain, is now our slave'; the word order in 21 is chiastic, in 22 interlaced. Prisoners of war would be chained (N–H on 1.29.5) and enslaved (cf. *seruit*), but *domitus* hints also at the conventional view of barbarians as wild animals (W–M on Tac. *A.* 3.47.4). The contrast *uetus hostis ~ sera…catena* is due to the fact that Spain was the first province to be entered (in the third century BC) and the last to be conquered (cf. Liv. 28.12.12 'prima Romanis inita prouinciarum… postrema omnium… perdomita est', Vell. 90.2–4, Tac. *A.* 4.5.1 'recens perdomitae', Just. 44.5.8). Augustus had campaigned in person against the Cantabrians, a people of NW Spain, in 26–25 BC; his success in the latter year was commemorated by H. in 3.14 below (see intro.) and widely celebrated: he was offered a triumph (which he declined) and the Temple of Janus was closed (Dio 53.26.5), though in fact the victory would prove to be merely temporary (Dio 53.29.1–2).

23–4 iam Scythae laxo meditantur arcu | cedere campis: the Scythians occupied a vast region in the north-west hinterland of the Black Sea (*BA* Maps 22: F2 and 23: B2–D1). They were at the peak of their wealth and power in the fifth and fourth centuries BC (see St.J. Simpson & S. Pankova, *Scythians* (2017)), after which they were eclipsed by various neighbouring peoples, with whom they are often confused or identified. In Books 1–2 of the *Odes* they are linked successively with the Parthians (1.19.10–12), Dacians (1.35.9) and (as in our ode) Cantabrians (2.11.1) and seemingly are a warlike threat; in the *Carmen Saeculare* (55) they send a delegation to Augustus (presumably the same delegation as is mentioned at *RG* 31.2), and in Book 4 they and the Parthians seem no longer a threat (4.5.25). Their principal appearance in Book 3 is alongside the Getae, where both peoples are depicted as examples of morality to be imitated (3.24.9–24: see nn.). Their submission in the present ode is to be explained in one of two ways. (1) Actual or threatened Roman force has compelled them into a withdrawal which is otherwise unattested but which, given the closure of Janus in 25 (21–2n.), must have happened before the end of that year. (2) According to Justin (42.5.5–6) it was with Scythian help that

Phraates IV was restored to the throne of Parthia (19–20n.); his successful restoration will have meant that Scythian military activity has ceased. For a full discussion of H.'s numerous references to the Scythians see above all Powell 140–59. For *laxo...arcu* cf. Virg. *Aen.* 11.874, Ov. *RA* 702, Sil. 3.612, Stat. *Theb.* 4.163.

25–6 neglegens ne qua populus laboret, | parce priuatus nimium cauere: this sentence, which clearly looks back to 17 (*populus ~ urbe, priuatus ~ ciuiles, cauere ~ curas*), is extremely awkward. As *ne* + subjunc. is regular with *cauere* but unparalleled with *neglegere*, it seems that *ne...laboret* must depend on *cauere* and that *neglegens*, as Madvig suggested (*Adversaria Critica* (1873) 2.54–5), agrees with *populus*: 'as a private citizen, refrain from taking too much care that the heedless people not be distressed in any way'. H. regularly defers *ne* (e.g. 1.2.5–6 'graue ne rediret | saeculum') and *neglegens* is explained by the two preceding stanzas: the people are paying no heed because all foreign threats have been removed (this is the notion of *metus hostilis*, for which see e.g. D. C. Earl, *The Political Thought of Sallust* (1961) 41–9); for *neglegens* cf. Cato, *ORF* 122 'fortunas secundas neglegentiam prendere solere'. Maecenas, despite its now being a few years since he was placed in official charge of the City (17n.), is tactfully described as still being concerned for its welfare; he must simply reduce the *excessive* concern (*nimium*) which is so characteristic of him; it will be only for a very brief while (27 'praesentis...horae').

27 dona praesentis cape laetus horae: the genitive is either definitive ('the gift consisting of the present moment': plural for singular, as often: N–H on 1.18.5) or, more probably, possessive (cf. 3.29.48 'quod...hora uexit', also to Maecenas): cf. Pind. *Ol.* 1.99–100. Marcovich has argued that the advice applies not just to the imminent party but, like 'carpe diem', is to be taken generally (89–92). For the adverbial adj. (*laetus*, 'happily', as 3.22.6, 3.29.42) see G&L 206 §325 R. 6.

9

Dialogue in the lyric genre goes back to Sappho (114, 137, 140a), and this ode takes the form of a dialogue acted out between a man and a young woman; whether the man represents H. himself is debated, but he seems to be a poet (8n.) and, like H., has a bad temper (23n.). Each of them speaks in turn, as if in a miniature play or mime, such as the *Mimiambi* of Herodas (3.7 intro.). Since each speaker tries to outdo the other, the dialogue takes the form of an *agōn* or 'contest': competitive speaking had featured in literature since the time of Homer (see E.

COMMENTARY 9 199

Barker, *Entering the Agon: Dissent and Authority in Homer, Historiography and Tragedy* (2009); *BNP* 4.1183–4), and was used to comic effect by H. in his satirical account of the journey to Brundisium (*S.* 1.5.51–70). The present contest displays the extra refinement of a series of verbal repetitions, as both speakers take their cue from the other and try to 'cap' his or her performance (1–4 *Donec...nec...uigui...beatior* ~ 5–8 *Donec... neque...uigui clarior*; 9–12 *Me...pro qua...mori, si parcent...fata superstiti* ~ 13–16 *Me...pro quo...mori, si parcent...fata superstiti*). This particular form of competition is known as 'amoebean' (from ἀμοιβαῖος, 'responsive' or 'answering') and was introduced into bucolic by Theocritus, the founder of the genre (e.g. *Id.* 5, 6, 8, 9, 27), from where it was imitated by Virgil in the *Eclogues* (3, 7).

The ode has a simple structure of three sets of exchanges between the two speakers (2 + 2 + 2). Since in the first line the addressee is referred to simply as 'you' (1 *tibi*), it is as if readers are admitted to the conversation only when it is already in progress and the identities of the speakers have already been established. The man is acknowledging that his attractiveness to his beloved belongs to the past (1) and she – the mention of a fair neck indicates that it is a she – is now in the arms of a younger rival (2–3); but his concluding statement that he was never happier than when they were together (4) clearly implies that he wants her back. The girl, whose name is now revealed to be Lydia, responds by saying that, whereas in the past he loved no one more than her, now it is Chloe who principally holds his affections (5–6); and Lydia's concluding statement that she was never more celebrated than when she was with him (8) seems deliberately phrased to avoid repeating the concluding sentiment of her former lover.

What is not made clear in these first exchanges is whether Lydia's disillusion with the man (1) was prompted by his enthusiasm for Chloe or whether the man resorted to Chloe only after a rival proved to have more success with Lydia; this question is not clarified until the final set of exchanges (17–24).

The man, perhaps stung by Lydia's failure to respond to his hint of reconciliation, reacts to her speech with a mixture of defensiveness and bravado: he confirms that his life is now dominated by Chloe (9 *regit*), for whom, he claims, he would be prepared to die (9–12). Although all thoughts of a reconciliation with Lydia seem to be forgotten, this speech can be read as an attempt at making her jealous (he carefully notes that Chloe is musically talented) and hence as another ploy to win her back. But Lydia's reaction is one of defiance: she would be prepared to die *twice* for her Calais (14–16), who, moreover, reciprocates her love (13) – a not-so-subtle suggestion that she doubts whether reciprocal affection is a virtue of the dominating Chloe.

Perhaps the man has been harbouring the same doubts; or perhaps he is simply disappointed that his second attempt at regaining Lydia has backfired. At any rate, when he speaks again, he decides to be more direct in his approach, albeit expressing himself tentatively: what if their former affection is returning, if Chloe is thrown out, and if his house once more welcomes the rejected Lydia (17–20)? Although the reference to rejection seems to imply that the man was after all to blame for their break-up, the possibility of their getting together again is expressed in such a way as to suggest that he thinks it has a chance of success (17–18). And he is right! His last, more direct, tactic has worked: when Lydia replies, she says that, although Calais is strikingly handsome and her previous lover is fickle and irascible, it is nevertheless the latter with whom she would wish to die (21–4).

Her final wish, with its suggestion of a joint death (24n.), recalls and corrects the wishes which each of them had uttered in the course of their conversation: Lydia will no more be dying for Calais than will the man for Chloe (15–16 ~ 11–12). Likewise their shared past life, described in the first two exchanges (1–8), will return in the future, described in the two final exchanges (17–24), the two periods separated from each other by the two central exchanges (9–16), in which their present circumstances are given (9 *nunc*).[65] This movement is very like that in Poem 8 of Catullus, which also moves from past (1–8) through present (9–11 *nunc*) to a future which recalls the past (12–19); but, whereas Catullus' poem constitutes a rejection of love, our ode is (as it were) the converse: it belongs to the category to which the name *oaristys* or 'wooing' has been given and of which other examples are Theocritus 27 and Catullus 45 (Cairns, *RL* 47–76, esp. 60–3 on the ode). The ode is a dazzling example of Horatian humour and wit.

METRE   Fourth Asclepiad. H.'s metrical effects in this ode have been delightfully analysed and discussed by D. West (*HH* 100–7), whose remarks are summarised in his commentary (where there is also an extended comparison of the ode with Catullus 45).

1 Donec 'While', 'As long as' (*OLD* 4), as again in line 5.

gratus 'welcome' or 'acceptable': diplomatically, the speaker is careful not to overstate his previous appeal (cf. Prop. 1.12.7 'olim gratus eram').

---

[65] R. J. Tarrant has noted that this ABA structure is otherwise generally avoided in Book 3 (*HH* 46–9).

2 potior denotes a successful rival (e.g. *Epo.* 15.13 'non feret adsiduas potiori te dare noctes' and Watson's n.), although its only appearance in elegy is Tib. 1.5.69.

2–3 bracchia candidae | ceruici iuuenis dabat: the man is careful to compliment his former beloved, and 'compliments centering on the neck are generally connected with its snow-white colour' (NA on Lygd. 4.27). *dare bracchia* means 'to hold out one's arms' (*OLD do*[1] 18a), as in the famous 'Burst of Joy' photograph of 1973 (there of a daughter to her father); the precise nuance will vary according to context (see e.g. 2.12.18, Prop. 4.3.12, *Aetna* 365). The rueful hint in *iuuenis* that the rival is a younger man is confirmed by *puero* in 16.

4 Persarum uigui rege beatior: evidently the Latin version of the proverbial 'happy as a king' was 'rex sum' (Plaut. *Pseud.* 671; cf. Prop. 1.14.13; Otto 299); but the speaker was even happier than that, he 'thrived more happily than the Persian King', who was known as 'the Great King' and 'King of Kings' (as in the first line of the Behistun Inscription) and was traditionally 'the supreme instance of the *beatus*' (N–H on 2.2.18).[66] For the related idea of 'the lover is a king' see NA on Lygd. 3.23–4. *beatior* is to be taken adverbially (G&L 206 §325 R. 6).

5–6 non aliā magis | arsisti 'you did not burn more for another': *ardere* (*OLD* 7a) + abl. recurs at 2.4.7–8, *Epo.* 14.9 (cf. also Ov. *Am.* 2.8.11). The heat of love is of course a common metaphor (e.g. 3.7.10–11n.; Brown on Lucr. 4.1077).

6–7 neque erat Lydia post Chloen, | multi Lydia nominis 'and Lydia did not take second place to Chloe, Lydia with her great reputation' (*OLD post*[2] 5b). Lydia's 'exotic name suggests luxury and voluptuousness' (N–H on 1.8.1); it reappears also in 1.13 and 1.25 and was the title of a lost work by the neoteric Valerius Cato (Ingleheart on Ov. *Tr.* 2.435–6); for Chloe see 3.7.10n. The device of self-naming, which was a recognised way of generating emotion or *adfectus* (so the scholiast on Virg. *Ecl.* 7.40, *Aen.* 2.479), is used in a wide variety of different genres and for various different effects (out of many discussions see e.g. Horsfall on Virg. *Aen.* 7.401, Tarrant on Virg. *Aen.* 12.11; Rutherford 15); it is esp. frequent in Catullus (Williams, *TORP* 462–3) and Herodas (e.g. 1.76, 87, 2.5, 49, 5.60, 6.23, 45, 7.34, 53), whose mimes have something in common with

---

[66] For the inscription see e.g. D. Asheri et al., *A Commentary on Herodotus Books I–IV* (2007) 529.

the dramatic conversation of our ode (above, intro.). Particularly relevant is *Idyll* 5 of Theocritus, where one of the characters, Lacon, resorts to the device not only in his introductory conversation with Comatas (9, 14) but also in their singing contest (86). In the ode the repetition of the name from one line to the next (epanalepsis) not only suggests indignation and wounded pride ('To think that the famous Lydia is now replaced by Chloe!') but is also a self-referential illustration of *multi... nominis*. The latter (= πολυώνυμος) is a genit. of description (*NLS* 65–8 §§84–5): cf. Gell. 2.3.5 'multi nominis...grammaticum', 13.25.3 (cf. 20.10.2).

8 Romana uigui clarior Ilia: one might have expected a Lydia to come from western Asia Minor and hence perhaps to be more famous than 'the Trojan woman' (*Ilia*), i.e. Helen, esp. since her ex-lover had described himself in terms of a Persian king (4); but Helen had an ambiguous reputation (e.g. *Epo.* 17.42), so, to indicate that she means another Ilia, the mother of Romulus and Remus, Lydia adds *Romana*, thereby also trumping *Persarum*. We may perhaps infer from Lydia's fame that the speaker of 1–4 is a poet, who, by writing about her in his poetry, ensured her celebrity (cf. Prop. 3.2.17–18). If so, the implied tribute to his verse suggests that she may not be as hard-hearted as she appears.

9 Me nunc Thressa Chloe regit: the verb, aptly contrasting with *rege* (4), suggests that the relationship is one of slave (*me*) and mistress (cf. 4.1.4); for the motif of *seruitium amoris* see Lyne, *CP* 85–100, P. Murgatroyd, *Latomus* 40 (1981) 589–606. Chloe's Thracian origin perhaps suggests that she is identical with the Chloe of 3.26.10–12 (see nn.).

10 dulces docta modos et citharae sciens: the man boasts of Chloe's cultural accomplishments in two phrases which are self-evidently complementary: since *sciens* must mean 'knowledgeable on ~ ', *docta* must be adjectival = 'expert in ~ ' rather than participial = 'taught'. It therefore follows that *dulces...modos* is not to be regarded as a so-called 'retained accusative' (as at 3.6.21 'motus doceri gaudet Ionicos': n.) but as an accus. of respect. Of course the two constructions are formally indistinguishable and their separate names are simply a way of indicating what *doctus* + accus. means in any given passage. For ex., at Liv. 6.32.7 ('Latinae maxime legiones longa societate militiam Romanam edoctae') does *edoctae* mean 'taught', 'trained in' or 'expert in'? Each passage must be considered on its merits. Cf. 3.8.5n.; *TLL* 5.1.1759.34–47. Since *citharae* clearly refers to playing, *dulces...modos* presumably refers to singing, as Ov. *F.* 1.444 (*OLD modus* 8b). *sciens* regularly takes a genit., as 1.15.24 (*OLD* 3).

For lyre-playing as a feminine accomplishment, esp. of *meretrices*, see e.g. 2.11.22 and Harrison's n., 3.15.14; Gibson on Ov. *AA* 3.311–28. For the cithara see 3.1.20n.

11–12 pro qua non metuam mori, | si parcent animae Fata superstiti 'for whom I will [*or perhaps* would] not be afraid to die, on condition that the Fates spare my beloved to survive me': for *metuo* + infin. (again at 3.11.10, 3.14.15, as well as in *S*. 2 and *Epi*. 1) see *OLD* 1b; for *anima* = 'beloved' see *OLD* 7b; *superstiti* is proleptic. For the motif see e.g. *CLE* 995 = Courtney, *ML* No. 180.13–16 'Si pensare animas sinerent crudelia fata | et posset redimi morte aliena salus, | quantulacumque meae debentur tempora uitae | pensassem pro te, cara Homonoea, libens' (a dialogue between husband and wife). It is said that Anne of Austria, fourth wife of Philip II of Spain, prayed to die instead of her ailing husband and that her prayer was answered shortly afterwards (see Frazer's n. on Apollod. 1.9.15).

13–14 Me torret face mutua | ...Calais: Lydia resumes the metaphor of heat from her previous statement (5–6) but *face mutua* is difficult: the meaning is *either* 'with a reciprocal flame', i.e. a flame corresponding to mine (*OLD mutuus* 3a), *or* 'the flame being mutual' (*OLD* 5), a loose abl. abs. The only other ex. of the expression ([Sen.] *Oct*. 50 'mutua flagrant face') is easier because the verb is plural, but the text has been variously questioned. For further exs. of *mutuus* in erotic contexts see NA on Lygd. 1.19.

14 Thurini Calais filius Ornyti: in order to out-do the man, Lydia presents her new lover's credentials in chiastic form, mentioning his paternity as well as his origin. So too Daphnis in Theocr. 27 tries to impress the girl by mentioning his parentage (42). The 'real' Calais was a wind-god, son of Boreas/Aquilo and Oreithyia; Lydia's lover is the son of Ornytus, whose name suggests the 'rushing' of wind (from ὄρνυμαι, to rush). Thurii was a Greek colony in the very south of Italy (*BA* Map 46: D2): since it was founded on the site of the notoriously decadent Sybaris and its name suggests a derivation from θούριος ('rushing'), Ornytus' background both maintains the play on rushing wind and underlines the association of Lydia's name with luxury (6n.). The lover of the Lydia addressed in 1.8 is actually called Sybaris.

15 pro quo bis patiar mori: in her enthusiasm to cap the other speaker, Lydia resorts to hyperbole – or perhaps she sees herself as a second Alcestis, whose story is told in Euripides' play: because of her love for her husband, Admetus, she agreed to die in his place and was brought back by Heracles. Lydia will repeat such bravado in the final line of her final speech (24n.). For the expr. commentators compare Eur. *Orest.* 1116 'I am not afraid of dying twice', but the contexts are quite different.

17 quid si prisca redit Venus...: Lydia's *si*-clause (16) is picked up in adversative asyndeton and answered by *quid si...*; the latter (again at e.g. *Epi.* 1.16.10) is a common idiom in which one supplies from the context the verb which has been elided after *quid* (see e.g. Oakley on Liv. 9.18.5; G. W. Williams, *JRS* 47 (1957) 242–3). Here perhaps '<But> what <would be the case> if...?' or, since the four following verbs are in the indicative, '<But> what <happens> if...?'. The indicative mood 'is a hint that the supposition is an actual fact' (Gow).

prisca... Venus is interpreted metonymically by pseudo-Acro as 'our former affection' ('si ad amorem redimus priorem'), which makes good sense, although in line 18 the subject of *cogit* is the goddess herself (n.). (It is theoretically possible that *Venus* refers only to the man's affection; but the plural *diductos* in 18 seems to make it clear that the man detects a change in Lydia's feelings too.) For H.'s numerous refs. to Venus in the *Odes* see A. T. von S. Bradshaw, *CQ* 20 (1970) 144–5.

18 diductosque iugo cogit aëneo: Aphrodite had been described as a charioteer since Sappho (1.9–10), her chariot often drawn by birds of various types (see Hutchinson's n.); here the man, picking up on Lydia's *mutua* (13), imagines Venus as yoking together the former lovers: the contrast between past and present is emphasised by the two prefixes (*di-ductos* ~ *cogit* [= *co-agit*]). For *diducere* of broken friendships etc. see *OLD* 1c; for *cogere* of yoking see Virg. *Aen.* 7.639 'ad iuga cogit equos', *Moret.* 121; for the image see Prop. 3.24.28. Venus is again associated with a bronze yoke at 1.33.10–12 (the bronze chariot at Juv. 7.125 is a statue) and with handling horses/lovers at 4.1.6–7.

19–20 si flaua excutitur Chloe | reiectaeque patet ianua Lydiae 'if fair Chloe is thrown out and my door is open for rejected Lydia': we move from Venus' chariot to the speaker's own house, where Chloe has evidently been living. With *excutitur* we are to understand a word such as *domo* (cf. Ter. *Phorm.* 586 'ut me excutiam atque egrediar domo'); *patere* is the regular word for an open door (*OLD* 1a): for the dat. see e.g. Plaut. *Men.* 362–3 'fores quoi pateant, | magis quam domus tua, domus quom haec tua sit'. Peerlkamp's *reiecto* ('and Lydia's door is open for the one whom she had discarded') is printed by SB (see also *Profile* 94): the sense is unexceptionable in itself and the beloved's doorway is of course a familiar feature of erotic poetry; but the disadvantage of the emendation is that *excutitur* can have no part in the image and is left high and dry.[67]

21 sidere pulchrior: stars were a regular comparandum for beauty (see 3.7.1n.), but, since they were also relied on by sailors for navigation, the maritime motif of 22–3 is anticipated.

22 leuior cortice: 'lighter than cork' suggests an allusion to the 'sea of love' metaphor (for which cf. P. Murgatroyd, *CQ* 45 (1995) 9–25): the man drifts where he is taken by the winds and currents (cf. 9 'nunc... Chloe regit'), the implication being that he was responsible for leaving Lydia in the first place; equally he never sinks underneath the waves, which explains why he is now bobbing up to proposition Lydia once more.

22–3 improbo | iracundior Hadria: the metaphor of the sea (22n.) leads naturally to a comparison with the Adriatic, whose description as *improbus*, not esp. common of the forces of nature (*TLL* 7.1.692.17–23), personifies the sea and so aids the comparison. The storms of the Adriatic were proverbial (3.3.4–5n.). *iracundior* is the third comparative adj. in the final exchange of the dialogue, balancing the three in the first (2 *potior*, 4 *beatior*, 8 *clarior*); such comparatives are a mark of the amoebean style (e.g. Virg. *Ecl.* 7.37–8 ~ 41–2, Sen. *Contr.* 2.2.2).[68] It may be relevant that H. confessed himself to be irascible (*Epi.* 1.20.25 'irasci celerem tamen ut placabilis essem'; cf. *S.* 1.3.29, 2.3.323).

24 tecum uiuere amem, tecum obeam libens: Lydia expresses her final wish with anaphora and in polar terms (*uiuere* ~ *obeam*: see further McKeown on Ov. *Am.* 1.3.17–18), implying that she wants to spend the remainder of her life with her former lover (see e.g. Lygd. 3.7–8 'sed tecum ut longae sociarem gaudia uitae | inque tuo caderet nostra senecta sinu' with NA ad loc.). *tecum obeam libens* in itself may mean simply that she wants to die with her lover at her bedside, a naturally common wish (e.g. Tib. 1.1.59–60 'te spectem suprema mihi cum uenerit hora; | te teneam moriens deficiente manu', and, in the mouth of a woman, *Anth. Pal.* 7.735.5–6 'would that I could die holding your dear hand in mine') and a standard motif of the *consolatio* (see e.g. W. on Tac. *Agr.* 45.5); but the words may also mean, more literally, that she wants to die at the same moment as

---

[67] *iugum excutere* is a set expr. for shaking off the yoke, but, in view of the new *si-*clause, it seems better to regard *excutitur* (nowhere found with abl. *iugo*) as integral with the house-door image of 20 rather than an awkward leftover from 18.

[68] Famously this *controuersia* (see also 24n.) was declaimed by Ovid (cf. 2.2.8).

he (cf. Prop. 2.20.18 'ambos una fides auferet, una dies', 2.28.42 'uiuam, si uiuet; si cadet illa, cadam'; P. Hardie on Virg. *Aen.* 9.444 for other exs.). The latter alternative perhaps seems more likely. H. promised Maecenas in 2.17 that they would die at the same time (and they did). Lydia, as previously when referring to her own death (cf. 15n.), perhaps sees herself in exaggeratedly heroic fashion as a latter-day Evadne, who threw herself on the pyre of her husband to ensure that she died at the same time (Ov. *AA* 3.21-2 and Gibson); and indeed the Romans seem to have been fascinated by the Indian practice of suttee (e.g. Sen. *Contr.* 2.2.1; W. Heckel and J. C. Yardley, *Philol.* 125 (1981) 305-11). For more on the relationship between love and death see e.g. 3.11.33-4n.; Lyne, *CP* 257-66.

10

The seventh ode of the book ended with H.'s advice to Asterie that at nightfall she should shut her door and not give any encouragement to the young suitor who parades to her house in a κῶμος or procession and then calls to her in a serenade or παρακλαυσίθυρον: 'uocanti | ... difficilis mane' (3.7.29-32 and nn.). The present ode resumes (as it were) from where the earlier ode left off. On this occasion the addressee is called Lyce and it is the speaker of the poem who is the suitor. He has arrived at Lyce's door before the poem has begun; the poem is his serenade, his attempt at persuading her to show sympathy to suitors such as himself: 'non... difficilem procis' (11).

The ode does not begin straightforwardly, however, but deceptively with a stanza of fantasy: Lyce is invited, in extravagantly heightened language (1-2n.), to imagine herself a married woman in Scythia, courted by the poet as an *exclusus amator* on her doorstep in a terrible gale (2-4). Since the stanza is constructed as an unreal present condition ('si biberes,... plorares'), readers do not yet know that certain elements of the imaginary scene are in fact part of the dramatic situation; this they learn only gradually, as the ode progresses. In the second stanza they learn that a gale is blowing in Rome, from which they might infer that the poet is indeed an *exclusus amator*; and this inference is confirmed in the following stanza, where we are told that Lyce is playing hard to get (9-12). And from the penultimate stanza (13-16) it emerges that Lyce does in fact have a husband, who at present seems to be abroad in the arms of a mistress, thus providing the speaker with both the opportunity for his serenade and an argument for its success.

Once the purport of the poem becomes clear, the strategy of the first stanza will be recognised for what it is: namely, an example of the so-called 'locus a maiore ad minus', when a writer produces data which 'prove the lesser from the greater' (Quint. 5.10.87 'minora ex maioribus...probant'; Lausberg 187–8 §§395–6). For it will transpire later in the poem that Lyce's husband is a major reason why she refuses to admit the *amator* to her house (15). The function of the first stanza is to counteract this problem in advance: since Lyce would sympathise with the speaker's desperate plight even in a country such as Scythia, where husbands are entitled to kill their adulterous wives, she should surely show sympathy to him in the familiar streets of Rome, where that was not the case.

In the two final stanzas of the ode Lyce is transformed metaphorically into a goddess (13n.) and treated to a parody of a prayer. The prayer is introduced by the interjection *o*, which is separated from the prayer word *parcas* by an extravagant hyperbaton consisting of an entire stanza (13 ~ 17). In between we might have expected to be given a list of the divinity's positive qualities, almost certainly introduced by the words *nam* (cf. 3.11.2–3) or *siue* (cf. 3.21.2–4); instead, however, we are presented with a *quamuis*-clause listing four negatives – and, in case these are not enough, two more are added for good measure after the prayer (17–18).

If we see the first two stanzas as linked by the two gales, and the last two stanzas as linked by the parodic prayer, the central stanza is that in which Lyce seems to be warned in somewhat cryptic terms that she should not pass up opportunities because there will come a time when she is no longer as young and attractive as she is now (9–10). It is therefore interesting that the next time we meet a Lyce in H.'s *Odes* is in Book 4 (13), where her physical ageing is celebrated. 'Although repeated names do not necessarily establish narrative continuities across poems', says R. F. Thomas, the Lyce of Book 4 'looks very much like her namesake' here in Book 3.

The name of the addressee, like the ode itself, raises a number of socio-political questions. Lyce's name ('She-wolf') suggests prostitution or at least easy morals, yet she is married (2, 15) and may live in a grand house (6). Of course her residence and married status are not incompatible with being free with her favours (N–R see her as 'a high-class courtesan'); yet, since she is faithful to her husband despite his own reputed infidelity (15–16), she does not behave like a courtesan. So perhaps she is simply a respectable but desirable married woman. Just as 3.7 expressed approval of husbandly loyalty, so this paraclausithyron is a witty and self-deprecating vehicle for the celebration of wifely fidelity.

METRE   Second Asclepiad

1–2 Extremum Tanain si biberes, Lyce, | saeuo nupta uiro: 'It was an old poetic way of identifying the inhabitants of a country to mention the river that they drank' (N–H on 2.20.20); since the Tanais (mod. Don) was in Scythia (3.4.36n.), this is an elaborate way of saying 'Even if you were living in Scythia…'. H. is not of course interested in the fantasy of Lyce's living in Scythia: at Rome a husband had no right to kill an adulterous wife (Treggiari 269–85), whereas this was not the case in Scythia, or so H. supposes later at 3.24.21–4 ('peccare nefas, aut pretium est mori'). In our ode (as again at e.g. 3.2.21–2, 3.5.37–8, 3.6.33–4) the main idea is conveyed not by the main verb (*biberes*) but by the participle (*nupta*, nom.): even if Lyce were married to a savage Scythian, who would kill her if he caught her in adultery, the speaker's situation is so desperate that she would admit him to her house. The name Lyce suggests a female wolf (cf. Greek λύκος, a (male) wolf); the Latin equivalent is *lupa*, which can mean 'prostitute' (*OLD* 2). *extremum* refers to the ends of the earth (*OLD* 1c), as again at 3.11.47.

2–4 me tamen asperas | porrectum ante fores obicere incolis | plorares Aquilonibus 'you would nevertheless deplore exposing me, stretched out before your cruel door, to the local north-easterlies' (sc. and so you would not expose me): *plorare* is not very common in verse, though liked by H.; for its use + infin. see *OLD* 2b; also Brink on *Epi.* 2.1.9. Prostration before the beloved's door is the conventional pose of the *exclusus amator* (McKeown on Ov. *Am.* 2.19.21–2); here *obicere* (*OLD* 6) humorously suggests that Lyce is personally responsible for the *amator*'s exposure. The *fores* are described as 'asperas' not only because they have taken on the cruelty of their mistress but also because the bad weather has increased their uncongeniality and, being in Scythia, they are inevitably crude. The strong winds are a further conventional element (N–H on 1.25.11): since the Aquilo comes from the north east, it could be regarded as a Scythian wind (cf. Luc. 5.603 'Scythici…rabies Aquilonis'), which would naturally be at its strongest in its native land (hence *incolis*, here adjectival).

5 audis quo strepitu ianua: if this is the closed door which is preventing access to Lyce, as seems required by the context, we have to assume that it is loose on its hinges (a similar situation at Ov. *Am.* 1.6.49–51); a verb such as *sonet* has to be understood from *remugiat* (6) by zeugma: 'Do you hear with what noise the door <is banging>?' Sound was recognised as an important element of *enargeia* (vivid description), conveying realism (e.g. Callim. *Hec.* 260.67–9).

5–7 quo nemus | inter pulchra satum tecta remugiat | uentis: *strepitu* has to be understood from the preceding clause: '(Do you hear) with what <noise> the grove, planted amidst the fine *tecta*, bellows in the wind?' It is possible that *uentis* is dat., influenced by the prefix *re-* ('in response to'),

COMMENTARY 10.7–10

but, despite *strepitu*, abl. of cause seems more natural. Some edd. imagine an elaborate villa complex with incorporated garden(s), although this is perhaps inconsistent with the banging door (5); alternatively H. envisages clumps of trees and bushes growing between houses on an ordinary street, or perhaps in one of the formal gardens dotted around Rome; or he may have in mind a sacred grove, which, 'landscaped with its screen of trees, was a common sight within the urban limits of Rome' (Leach 225). The interspersal of trees and buildings is mirrored in the interlaced word order. Amusingly, despite his desperate circumstances, the komast can still comment on the aesthetic qualities of his surroundings; *pulchra* contrasts with the rough dwellings imagined in Scythia (2). For *remugire* cf. *Epo.* 10.19–20 'Ionius udo...remugiens sinus | Noto'; for its onomatopoeic combination with *nemus* cf. Virg. *Aen.* 12.722 'gemitu nemus omne remugit', Sen. *Thy.* 675–6, Stat. *Theb.* 12.602–3.

7–8 et positas ut glaciet niues | puro numine Iuppiter: a verb of seeing has to be understood from *audis* (5) in a further zeugma (cf. N–H on 1.14.6): 'and <do you see> how Jupiter, his divine power clear, is freezing the lying snow?' *Iuppiter* is here both a god in his own right and a metonymy for the sky (as 1.1.25 'sub Ioue frigido'; cf. *OLD* 2a): as a god, he naturally has his own *numen* (as 4.4.74 'benigno numine Iuppiter'); as the sky, that power can be described as 'clear' (*purus* being a technical term for a clear sky, as 1.34.7; cf. *OLD* 6a). Clear nights often mean hard frosts. *ponor* seems to be technical of snow (Prop. 1.8.7, Ov. *F.* 2.72 'posita sub niue', Sen. *NQ* 5.10.2, *Phoen.* 370), for which Jupiter was the god responsible (Stat. *Theb.* 5.390–1 'talis Hyperborea uiridis niue uerberat agros | Iuppiter'; Watson on *Epo.* 13.1–2).

9 ingratam Veneri pone superbiam: the *exclusus amator* 'typically represents his beloved's refusal of sexual favours as haughtiness' (Myers on Ov. *Met.* 14.715, with numerous exs.); the prologue to Euripides' *Hippolytus*, spoken by Aphrodite, is a disquisition on the theme of such pride being 'unwelcome' to the goddess of love: cf. also *Anth. Pal.* 5.280.7–8. For the repetition *positas* (7) ~ *pone* see 3.7.6–8n.

10 ne currente retro funis eat rota: this probably means 'lest the wheel should run backwards and the rope go <with it>' (*retro* being taken with both *currente* and *eat*). Various attempts have been made to explain H.'s image (e.g. the wheel of fortune: cf. D. M. Robinson, *CP* 41 (1946) 212), but the combination of wheel and rope suggests a simple pulley system such as was used to draw water from a well (see A. T. Hodge, *Roman Aqueducts and Water Supply* (^{2}2002) 54–6 with Fig. 25): if you were to let go of the rope for any reason (perhaps because the water-bucket became too heavy to lift), the wheel would go into reverse and the rope would fly out of your hands and be lost. How does the image apply to Lyce? Perhaps the general message is that she should not let go her opportunities: the lover will not wait for ever (cf. 19–20) and all too soon she will be found no longer desirable (for this topos of the paraclausithyron see N–H on 1.25). For the ageing Lyce of 4.13 see intro.

11–12 non te Penelopen difficilem procis | Tyrrhenus genuit parens: this is a variant on the '*te genuit* topos' (e.g. Cat. 64.154 'quaenam te genuit... leaena'), usually used to express insensibility (Pease on Virg. *Aen.* 4.366); for the same constr. as in H. cf. Ov. *Ex P.* 4.6.27 'lenem te miseris genuit natura'. Tyrrhenus was the eponymous founder of Tyrrhenia, which was the Greek way of referring to Etruria (cf. Tac. *A.* 4.55.3). H.'s sentence, which can be taken in more than one way, probably means: 'Your Etruscan father did not beget you <to be> a Penelope, implacable to suitors.' Since the Etruscans were known for their decadence (N–H on 2.18.8), Lyce ought not to act like a virtuous Penelope – an example of the topos that children should resemble their parents (3.6.33–4n.). Whether the plural *procis* is caused by the comparison with the original Penelope, who in the *Odyssey* has many suitors, or whether this is the first suggestion that Lyce herself has numerous admirers (cf. 14, 16), is unclear.

13 o: the transformation of the beloved into a divinity is a common conceit (McKeown on Ov. *Am.* 1.5.1–8). The interjection *o* introduces the prayer in 16–17 below (*OLD* 3a), and, being often found in prayers (3.13.1n.), is appropriate when a deity is being addressed (13–16n., 16–17n.).

13–16 quamuis...curuat: for *quamuis* + indic. see 3.7.25–6n.; there seems to be no parallel for the use of *curuo* (lit. 'to bend') = 'to sway, influence', but *incuruo* has this meaning at Pers. 1.91. *munera* presumably refers to the flowers and garlands with which the serenader decorates his beloved's door: see Brown on Lucr. 4.1178, who notes that it was conventional to decorate temple doors too with flowers: this, along with *preces*, further underlines Lyce's 'divinity'.

14 tinctus uiola pallor amantium: lovers were conventionally pale (Pichon 224–5) but does H. mean 'the pallor of *your* lovers' or 'the pallor *characteristic* of lovers'? The likelier meaning is the latter, but this is perhaps the second hint in the poem that Lyce has more than one admirer (11, 16). The *pallor* is here 'tinged with violet'; what does this mean? The elder Pliny explains that *uiolae* come in 'plurima genera: purpureae, luteae, albae…' (*NH* 21.27), and, although some scholars have thought of red marks on a generally pale skin, it seems more likely that H. has in mind a paleness tinged with yellow; he may even be echoing Tib. 1.8.51–2 '*parce, precor*,…nimius luto corpora *tingit amor*'. Virgil refers to *pallentes uiolas* at *Ecl.* 2.47.

15 uir Pieria paelice saucius is an example of the *ab urbe condita* idiom (3.4.18–19n.): 'your husband's suffering at the hands of his Macedonian mistress': the speaker claims that Lyce's husband is more interested in his mistress than in his wife, but even this consideration will not influence Lyce. For the ploy of attempting to cause jealousy see 3.7 intro.; since *paelex* stresses the status of the mistress in relation to the wife (J. N. Adams, 'Words for "prostitute" in Latin', *RhM* 126 (1983) 355), it is exactly the right term for the komast to use and confirms Lyce's status as a wife. Metaphors of wounding are common in descriptions of love affairs (Pichon 259; Pease on Virg. *Aen.* 4.1); *saucius* + abl. is regular. Pieria was a region on the western side of the variously named Gulf of Salonica (*BA* Map 50: B3); the implication is that the husband is there with his mistress.

16–17 supplicibus tuis | parcas: the plural probably refers simply to the prostrated *amator* (above, 3), since prostration was the attitude of suppliants (Appel 200–2); but it could be the final hint that Lyce has numerous admirers (cf. 11, 14). The choice of terminology confirms the transformation of the beloved into a divinity (13n.). *parce* 'is a ritual word' (N–H on 2.19.7): cf. 4.1.2 and numerous other exs. in Appel 120.

17 nec rigida mollior aesculo: this and the following *nec…anguibus* agree with the subject of *parcas* (cf. 3.11.5 'nec…neque…'; Nisbet, *OR* 396) and are concessive: 'though <being> no softer than an unyielding oak'.[69] *rigida* contrasts with *curuat* above (16); for the proverbial solidity of oak trees cf. e.g. Virg. *Ecl.* 6.28 'rigidas…quercus', Prop. 1.9.31, Ov. *Am.* 3.7.57–8; M. C. Sutphen, *AJP* 22 (1901) 367–8. The *aesculus*, probably to be identified with the Quercus frainetto or Italian oak, is 'a magnificent tree, native of S. Italy and the Balkans, up to 30 metres in height' (Mynors on Virg. *G.* 2.14–16; see also Sargeaunt 107–9). The ageing Lyce of 4.13 is described in terms of an arid oak (9–10).

---

[69] *nec rigida…anguibus* is translated as a separate sentence by West and Rudd (Loeb), the latter preceding it with an ellipsis ('…'), as if Lyce were being allowed time to respond to the man's appeal and, when she fails to do so, he gives his reaction to her failure. A dramatic pause would indeed be effective here, but neither scholar re-formats the Latin to produce the appropriate syntax.

18 nec Mauris animum mitior anguibus 'and though no kinder in spirit than Moorish snakes': the danger of snakes, esp. African, was proverbial (*S.* 2.8.95 'peior serpentibus Afris'; Tosi 116–17 §252); cf. Plaut. *Merc.* 760–1 'uxor...tua, quam dudum dixeras | te odisse atque anguis'. An accusative after adjectives is a 'purely Greek' construction, and is 'commonest with parts of the body; it is not found until Augustan verse' (E. Courtney, 'The "Greek" accusative', *CJ* 99 (2004) 430): this is said to be the only ex. in H., but that takes no account of the adjectival use of *doctus* (3.8.5n., 3.9.10n.); for *mitis* so used again cf. Stat. *Silv.* 4.6.55.

19–20 non hoc semper erit liminis aut aquae | caelestis patiens latus 'this flank of mine will not always be tolerant of your threshold or of water from the heavens'; the hyperbaton *hoc...latus* throws emphasis on the pronoun ('whatever other people might put up with': see Nisbet, *OR* 384). *latus* often has a sexual connotation (Galán Vioque on Mart. 7.58.3–6; Adams 49, 180), but not here. For *aqua* = 'rain' (again at 3.1.30, 3.17.12) see *OLD* 2; Brink on *Epi.* 2.1.135 says that *aqua caelestis* is poetic (the Greek equivalent is at Pind. *Ol.* 11.2), but its first extant occurrences are in the early books of Livy (4.30.7, 5.15.2) and, apart from a sprinkling of references in H. and Ovid, it is found overwhelmingly in technical texts (Vitruv. Sen. Quint.), esp. those of Columella (15×) and the elder Pliny (25×). Here *caelestis* perhaps hints at Jupiter's role in causing rain, given his masterminding of the weather in 7–8 above. For *aquae...patiens* cf. Ov. *F.* 4.506.

11

H. begins this strange ode with a joint address to Mercury and the lyre (1–3 'Mercuri...tuque, testudo,...'), and each vocative is immediately elaborated according to the conventions of ancient prayers: Mercury is given an explanatory *nam*-clause (1–2), while the lyre is given a series of descriptive phrases (3–6). There then follows a command: both Mercury and the lyre are asked to give a performance which will influence Lyde, a girl who has reached a marriageable age (9–12) but who is deaf to all entreaties: 'dic modos, Lyde quibus obstinatas | applicet aures' (7–8).

A second address now follows, this time to the lyre alone (13 'tu potes...'), and, as before, the address is followed by conventional elaboration, which on this occasion takes up three whole stanzas (13–24) and comprises a list of the lyre's powers as evidenced by its past achievements, ending with its soothing effect on the daughters of Danaus in the Underworld (22–4). As if put in mind of how appropriate the Danaids' story is to Lyde's situation, H. now issues an instruction that Lyde should pay attention to their story (25 'audiat Lyde...'), of which a detailed account, including direct speech, takes up the final seven stanzas of the prayer (25–52). Thus the ode twice follows a similar pattern of address–elaboration–command (1–12 ~ 13–52), except that the instruction for Lyde (25–52) fulfils the command issued in lines 7–8 and, since it involves a mythological narrative which is aimed at a young woman and is longer than the whole of the ode which precedes it, seems almost to take on a life of its own. There is a strong resemblance to 3.27, of which much the same can be said.

The broad outlines of the Danaids' story are that Danaus, the king of Argos, had fifty daughters, who were betrothed to marry their cousins, the fifty sons of king Aegyptus; but Danaus, suspecting that the men intended to usurp his power, extracted from his daughters a pledge that they would murder their husbands on their wedding night. With the one exception of Hypermnestra,[70] who allowed her husband Lynceus to escape, they all proceeded with the murder, for which they were each condemned in the Underworld to fill with water a vat pierced with holes.[71] When H. issues his second command (25–6), it is only the crime and punishment of the forty-nine murderous Danaids to which Lyde must pay attention ('audiat Lyde scelus atque notas | uirginum poenas'); but this turns out to be merely a foil for the story of the one virtuous sister: it is her story which is narrated in the remaining five stanzas of the ode (33–52). The length of her narrative is an indication of its importance, which resides in its illustration of conjugal love. It is clear from the start that it is marriage of which Lyde is afraid (11 'nuptiarum', 12 'marito'); it is equally clear from the story of Hypermnestra that she is described as a standard-bearer for marriage (33–4 'una de multis face nuptiali | digna', 37 'marito'). The point of the last five stanzas of the ode is to show Lyde that marriage is an attractive and desirable condition. If Hypermnestra was prepared to defy her father's orders (37–44), to face the prospect of imprisonment and exile (45–8), and to suffer life-long separation from her husband for his sake (49–52) – then surely

---

[70] N–R on 33–4 state without evidence that 'the correct form' of her name is Hypermestra, which, according to Palmer on Ov. *Her.* 14, is 'always in the best MSS in Latin'. The text of Apollodorus, however, consistently has Ὑπερμνήστρα, and I infer that H. had available to him both forms, from which he could choose as appropriate. Line 51 of the ode suggests that he was thinking of the latter (see 51–2n.).

[71] The Danaid story, summarised here, was the subject of a trilogy by Aeschylus; unfortunately, however, only one play (*Supplices*) survives, and 'the myths surrounding Danaus and his daughters are exceptionally varied and ramified. There are in fact no two sources which give exactly the same versions' (Keuls 47, with a long list of the sources in n. 6).

Lyde should be able to abandon her fears. The extreme circumstances of Hypermnestra are of course far removed from those of Lyde, but Lyde will have known that the heroine's fears proved unfounded and that according to the traditional version of the story she and Lynceus lived happily ever after.[72]

The speech which H. puts into Hypermnestra's mouth (37–52) was described by Fraenkel as 'worthy of tragedy', characterised by 'grandeur' and maintaining 'a dignity of thought and expression' throughout (197). This seems as much a misreading as his ascription of a 'lofty style' to the opening prayer. In the first half of the poem H. wittily capitalises on the misalignment between the address to a humble 'tortoise-shell' and the prayer-formulae which are normally reserved for a powerful divinity. When he says *tu potes* (13), it is as if the shell requires no musician but of its own accord has such powers of enchantment as can tame even Cerberus, whose frightening attributes extend even to his foul breath (13–20). As for Hypermnestra, her speech veers from black humour (37–9) through bravado (45–8) to the elegiac (49–52), each emotion signalled by a young girl's excited anaphora (*Surge...surge...*, *me...me...*, *i...i...*). When discussing the tone of our ode, Cairns draws attention to the term χάρις or 'charm', used by the critic Demetrius (*Comp.* 155) to cover 'a whole range of "para-serious" effects ranging from the funny to the macabre' (*RL* 390); this seems much nearer the mark than Fraenkel.

Five years before the publication of the *Odes*, on 9 October 28 BC (EJ p. 53), Augustus had dedicated the Temple of Palatine Apollo, an event commemorated by H. in an earlier poem (1.31). It was one of the most famous buildings of the principate and incorporated a portico whose columns alternated with statues of the Danaids: see e.g. Prop. 2.31.1–4 (with Miller 197–8 and 218), Ov. *Am.* 2.2.3–4 (with McKeown's n.), *AA* 1.73–4, *Tr.* 3.1.59–62; N–H on 2.14.18. Why Augustus chose the Danaids for his temple adornment remains a mystery: K. Galinsky (*Augustan Culture* (1996) 221–2) unsurprisingly refers to 'multiple meanings' and a 'multiplicity of associations'. In the *Aeneid*, published in 19 BC, the fated belt of Pallas is decorated with the Danaid story (Virg. *Aen.* 10.497–8 with Harrison's n.), and later still Ovid composed for Hypermnestra a letter to her absent husband (*Her.* 14: see nn. below).

---

[72] Cairns, *RL* 391–2, is good on this aspect, but, like many scholars, he believes that H. is trying to coax Lyde into sexual relations with himself. I can see no evidence for this (likewise Quinn ad loc. and S. J. Harrison, 'Horace's Mercury and mercurial Horace', in J. F. Miller and J. S. Clay (edd.), *Tracking Hermes, Pursuing Mercury* (2019) 168 n. 32); 3.11 is different from 1.23 (2.5 is controversial).

COMMENTARY 11.1-4

METRE Sapphic

1-2 Mercuri (nam te docilis magistro | mouit Amphion lapides canendo): the two *Homeric Hymns* to Hermes, as well as H.'s earlier hymn to Mercury (1.10), all begin with the god's name. It is conventional in prayers to have an early explanation, often parenthetic and usually introduced by γάρ in Greek and *nam(que)* or *enim* in Latin (as e.g. Virg. *Aen.* 1.65 'Aeole – namque tibi diuom pater atque hominum rex...', with Austin ad loc. for many parallels). Amphion was famous for having built a wall around Thebes by enchanting the stones to move into place of their own accord (*AP* 394-6 'Amphion, Thebanae conditor urbis, | saxa mouere sono testudinis et prece blanda | ducere quo uellet' and Brink ad loc., Hes. fr. 182 M-W = 125 Most, Paus. 9.5.6-8). The logic of the explanatory parenthesis is this: if Amphion after Mercury's teaching could move stones, perhaps the god will be able to help H. move Lyde, whose stubborn ears are deaf to all appeals (7-8): 'deafer than stones' was a proverbial expression (3.7.21n.). The interposition of *docilis* between *te* and *magistro* is a type of arrangement found frequently in the *Odes* (e.g. 1.8.12 'iaculo nobilis expedito'; Naylor xviii–xix §24). *canendo* refers to lyre-playing as well as singing: since Mercury was famously the most versatile of gods (cf. 1.10) and had many different skills to teach, the gerund is placed last to emphasise the particular skill that is required in the present situation.

3-4 tuque, testudo, resonare septem | callida neruis 'and you, *testudo*, cleverly resounding with seven strings': it is impossible to render in English the ambiguity of *testudo*, which according to context means 'tortoise', 'tortoise-shell' (cf. 5) or (as here) 'lyre';[73] moreover the term 'lyre' is itself ambiguous, sometimes referring to H.'s own imagined lyre (as here), sometimes to an archetypal lyre representative of all lyres (as 6 below). The address to the lyre (as e.g. 1.32.14, Hom. *Hymn Hermes* 30-8, Sappho 118 [next n.], Pind. *Pyth.* 1.1) is a natural accompaniment of the address to Mercury: H. is implicitly following the tradition, found in the *Homeric Hymn* to Hermes (20-67 and Vergados' nn.; also Battezzato 144-5), which attributed the lyre's invention to the god, who is sometimes represented as playing it (see Figs. 5 and 8 in Vergados pp. 653-4). The Hymn also credits Hermes with equipping the lyre with seven strings (51). In hymns or prayers it was customary for a descriptive phrase, often relating to ancestry (5n.), to be attached to the addressee, e.g. 1.10.1 'Mercuri, facunde nepos Atlantis' (and N–H), 1.30.1, 1.35.2-4; for *callidus* + infin.,

---

[73] It follows that a *testudo* was a lyre of the 'bowl' type (M. L. West (1992) 50-1, 56-9; *BNP* 9.355).

first in H., see 1.10.7–8 (where *callidus* is used of Mercury himself) and Mayer's n. Rival traditions attributed the lyre's invention to Orpheus and its stringing to Terpander (see pp. 133–5 of Vergados' commentary).

5 nec loquax olim neque grata 'previously neither eloquent nor welcome': *olim* refers to the time before Mercury transformed the tortoise-shell into a lyre and is a playful allusion to the 'ancestry topos' common in prayers (3–4n.); the tortoise was unwelcome because ugly (Pacuv. 2R 'aspectu truci'). *loquax* alludes to Sappho's address to her lyre (118 χέλυ δῖα... φωνάεσσα, 'divine shell...speaking'); H. has (as it were) omitted Sappho's 'divine' because that is obvious from the co-ordination with Mercury. See also NA on Lygd. 4.38.

5–6 nunc et | diuitum mensis et amica templis: contrasts between 'then' and 'now' are widespread, esp. in Augustan literature (e.g. Virg. *Aen.* 8.348), but they also feature prominently in Greek lyric (Cairns, *RL* 383 and n. 3); here *et...et* correspond to *nec...neque* above. The words *mensis... amica* represent the *Homeric Hymn*'s δαιτὸς ἑταίρη (31), 'friend of the feast', itself an allusion to Hom. *Od.* 17.271; *diuitum* is well illustrated by the *Cena Trimalchionis*, where 'most things happen to musical accompaniment' (N. Horsfall, *The Culture of the Roman Plebs* (2003) 16; also Schmeling on Petron. 28.5). As for *templis*, 'the lyre was played at some Roman sacrifices as an alternative to the pipe' (N–H on 1.36.1).

7–8 dic modos Lyde quibus obstinatas | applicet aures 'express measures to which Lyde can apply her stubborn ears': the subjunctive expresses both characteristic and purpose. The imperative is directed at both Mercury and the lyre (1–2n.) but has a different meaning with each of them (syllepsis):[74] 'Mercury is being asked to supply the words while the lyre will provide the tune' (Cairns, *RL* 387), although it is the lyre alone which is addressed in 13–24. For *dico* of a musical instrument cf. 1.32.3–4 'dic..., | barbite, carmen', *Epi. Sapph.* 200 'nomina dicta lyra' (*TLL* 5.1.989.21–5). The beloved of the Greek poet Antimachus was called Lyde and she famously gave her name to his poem of consolation (Ov. *Tr.* 1.6.1, Plut. *Mor.* 106B–C); the name recurs in 2.11 and 3.28. *applicat aures* recurs at the end of a Sapphic stanza at *CS* 72, where see Thomas' n.

9–10 quae, uelut latis equa trima campis, | ludit exsultim 'who, like a three-year-old mare in the broad fields, plays leapingly' (mimetic syntax),

---

[74] It is tempting to refer *dic* to the lyre alone (so N–R 148–9 and on lines 3–4), but that would leave the voc. *Mercuri* hanging in the air.

an allusion to some famous verses of Anacreon (417.1, 5): πῶλε Θρηικίη,... | νῦν δὲ λειμῶνάς τε βόσκεαι κοῦφά τε σκιρτῶσα παίζεις, 'Thracian filly,...now you graze the meadows and play, leaping lightly'. The scenario described in Anacreon's poem is disputed, but according to one view it is 'a poem about mental states' (Budelmann ad loc.), and the purpose of our ode likewise is to persuade Lyde to change her mind (7–8). On the one hand she has reached the age for sexual relations, as is to be inferred from *equa trima*: Aristotle recommended that mares mate when three years old (*Hist. anim.* 575b24). But it is clear from *metuitque...marito* in 10b–12 that Lyde does not regard herself as yet ready for sexual relations. *ludit*, like παίζεις in Anacreon, is ambiguous: the verb can be used of both women and animals and can refer to innocent or to erotic play. The logic of the ode dictates that Lyde's play be innocent,[75] and *exsultim* suggests that *ludit* participates in the comparison with the mare. But, since the verb is used so often of erotic play (3.12.5n.), we may be invited to infer that her disporting herself is interpreted in sexual terms by third parties. For the horse comparison see 3.26.11–12; Harrison on 2.5.

Adverbs in *-tim* 'abound in early Latin' and were noted by Gellius (12.15) as a particular feature of the historian Sisenna (J. Briscoe, 'The language and style of the fragmentary republican historians', in Reinhardt et al. 55 and 70–1): his extant fragments exhibit the rare *saltuatim*, 'jumpily' (F130C = 127P), but not *exsultim*, which occurs nowhere else in Latin, though *exsultare* was used of horses by Cicero (*Off.* 1.90).

10–12 metuit...tangi | nuptiarum expers et adhuc proteruo | cruda marito 'she is afraid to be touched, being ignorant of marriage and hitherto immature for a rampant husband'. For *metuo* + infin. see 3.9.11–12n.; for the sexual euphemism in *tangi* see Adams 185–7. *cruda* (for which cf. Mart. 8.64.11 'cruda uiro puella') is modified by *adhuc* (*OLD* 1), the point of which is that it allows for H.'s instruction in lines 25–52 to take effect: after paying attention to the Danaid myth and the story of Hypermnestra, Lyde will hopefully change her mind about marriage. It was conventional to describe a future or potential husband in such terms as *proteruo* (e.g. Cat. 61.56 'fero iuueni', 62.23 'iuueni ardenti'). For such expressions as *nuptiarum expers* see Pease on Virg. *Aen.* 4.550.

13–14 tu potes tigres comitesque siluas | ducere 'You have the power to lead tigers and woods as your companions' (*comites* is predicative and to be taken with both nouns: Naylor xxii §33). The reference here, as with

---

[75] That she is a deliberate tease seems ruled out by the context.

the *exempla* listed in lines 15–24 (see nn.), is to the power of the lyre as played by *Orpheus*: the principal intertext is the story of Orpheus at Virgil, *G.* 4.510 '*mulcentem tigres et agentem carmine quercus*' (*carmine mulces* rounds off the list at 24 below), but for Orpheus' tigers cf. also *AP* 393, and for his trees cf. 1.12.7–8 and N–H, 1.24.13–14. Thus, since Orpheus' name has to be understood from the context, lines 13–24 exemplify the 'frequent phenomenon' to which R. O. A. M. Lyne has given the name 'implicit myth' (*Further Voices in Vergil's Aeneid* (1987) 139, quoting our passage). It therefore follows that *tu potes* does not apply to the lyre and Mercury jointly but picks up *tuque* in 3 and refers to the lyre alone (*contra* Cairns, *RL* 384, 387). It is standard in prayers to repeat (ideally three times, as here) the pronoun *tu* (cf. 15), a feature to which German scholars have given the name 'Du-Stil' (cf. 3.13.9–16, 3.18.10, 3.21.13–21), and the presence of the word *potes* is also standard (N–H on 1.28.28): for *tu potes* in particular see e.g. Virg. *Aen.* 7.335 with Horsfall, *Aen.* 10.81 with Harrison, Prop. 3.17.3.

14 riuos celeres morari: for this further power of Orpheus' lyre see 1.12.9–10 and N–H. *morari* is transitive here, as 3.5.52.

15–16 cessit immanis tibi blandienti | ianitor aulae 'the door-keeper of the monstrous hall yielded to your blandishments': Orpheus famously went down into the Underworld to bring back his wife, Eurydice; the story is told at the end of the Fourth Georgic (4.467–527), including the effect of Orpheus' lyre on Cerberus (4.483 'tenuitque inhians tria *Cerberus ora*'), for whom *ianitor* is a regular term (*OLD* b). *immanis*, though used of Cerberus at Virg. *Aen.* 6.417–18, is here better taken with *aulae*, which 'requires some defining epithet' (Gow); cf. also Ov. *F.* 1.139 'caelestis ianitor aulae', Sil. 2.552 'lacrimosae ianitor aulae' (a passage seemingly indebted to our ode). For *aula* of the Underworld see 2.18.31.

17–20 Cerberus, quamuis...ore trilingui: this stanza, though retained by SB and N–R, has been deleted in its entirety by numerous editors, including Goold.[76] Many of the objections to the stanza have been countered by Bradshaw (*RhM* 118 (1975) 311–24), and deletion is impossible if we accept the proportional arrangement of Book 3 (Intro. 31); but it is nevertheless worth adding two further considerations. (a) Cairns has noted (*RL* 384) that the enjambement of a proper name is characteristic of Greek lyric, esp. Pindar (e.g. *Ol.* 10.55, *Pyth.* 9.17, 12.17, *Isth.* 6.35),

---

[76] Tarrant in his forthcoming OCT is evidently inclined to delete the stanza (see Tarrant (2016a) 314–15).

and that the appended concessive clause is paralleled at 2.19.25–7. (b) It seems very likely that, in describing Cerberus, H. had in mind Lucretius' account of the plague at Athens (6.1149 and 1154): '*atque* animi interpres *manabat lingua* cruore...*spiritus ore* foras *taetrum* uoluebat odorem'. That an interpolator had this passage in mind seems very improbable. Questions nevertheless remain over the word *eius* (18): see 18–19n. below.

17–18 quamuis furiale centum | muniant angues caput: the word order is of the 'silver' type (3.1.16n.). H. is 'unusual for his time in suggesting a single, triple-tongued head surrounded by snakes' (*LIMC* 6.1.24); for the three tongues see *ore trilingui* below (20). Cerberus is usually portrayed in literature and art as having three heads (N–H on 2.13.34, 2.19.31); for references to single-headed representations in art see *LIMC* 6.1.25 and 28. *furiale* (*OLD* 2) likens the mane to the hair of the Furies, which was also composed of snakes (2.13.35–6 and, again, Virg. *G.* 4.482–3); *centum* alludes to one of the variant traditions which attribute to Cerberus one hundred heads (2.13.34 with N–H). See further 19–20n. below and, for another ex. of an allusive variant, 3.4.42–4n.

18–19 ...caput atque agatur | spiritus taeter: the transmitted text reads ...*caput eius atque* | *spiritus taeter*, which has been found problematical even by defenders of the stanza as a whole. *eius*, though common in Lucretius, is very rare in Augustan poetry. Taking it for granted that our stanza was spurious, Axelson (72) found one example in the *Odes* (4.8.18) and a mere six in Tibullus, Propertius and Ovid between them; these seven have all been rejected as corrupt by D. Butterfield ('On the avoidance of "eius" in Latin poetry', *RhM* 151 (2008) 151–67), who also dismisses five others, including that in our ode.[77] One might have thought that the two exs. in the transmitted text of the *Odes* would support each other, but unfortunately 4.8 has problems of its own and is best left out of the equation (see Thomas' full discussion ad loc.). In any case, the real objection to *eius* in our ode is not so much its general rarity as its total banality in the present context. Given that *atque* at the end of a Sapphic line is also unusual for H. (but cf. 2.10.21), scholars have suggested emending *eius atque* to (for example) *exeatque* (Bentley) or *aestuatque* (Cunningham). None of the emendations seems very attractive (N–R obelise). I suggest instead that H., who likes *atque* in penultimate position in the Sapphic hendecasyllable (e.g. 25 below), originally wrote *caput atque*, after which

---

[77] The non-Horatian exs. are Cat. 84.5, Tib. 1.6.25, Prop. 4.2.35, 4.6.67, Ov. *Tr.* 3.4.27, *Ex P.* 4.15.6, *Met.* 8.16, Gratt. 224, Sen. *Thy.* 300, Sil. 11.85. For some arguments against Butterfield see D. Kovacs, *JRS* 99 (2009) 34–5.

there was a word which somehow was omitted by a scribe; another scribe, realising that the metre was defective, thought that inserting *eius* was the easiest and least offensive way of rectifying the problem, but, since *atque eius* does not scan, he transposed the words and wrote *eius atque*. Naturally we cannot know what the missing word was, and I have suggested *agatur* merely exempli gratia, although it is the *mot juste* for emitting breath (Tib. 1.8.57–8 'ut lenis agatur | spiritus', Sen. *Ira* 1.3, [Quint.] *Decl.* 2.18, Sil. 11.220–1; *TLL* 1.1372.57–66, *OLD* 9a); it is true that in the *Odes* H. normally prefers not to elide *atque* (cf. D. Butterfield, 'The poetic treatment of *atque* from Catullus to Juvenal', *Mnem.* 61 (2008) 386–413, at 407–8), but cf. 1.33.11, 1.34.4; and for elision at this point in the Sapphic line cf. 1.25.14, 1.32.9. For verbs at the end of successive lines cf. 1.10.17– 18, 2.8.5–7, 3.27.13–14 (all second-person). Thus: 'and (although) foul breath emerges/is emitted from…'.

19–20 saniesque mānet | ore trilingui 'and (although) a discharge drips from his three-tongued mouth': the description perhaps hints (so Cairns, *RL* 384) at the etymology of Cerberus from κρεοβόρος, 'flesh-eating' (Maltby 121). *trilingui* | *ore* at 2.19.31–2 is taken to refer to Cerberus' usual three heads (see N–H) and the identical phrase here is normally given the same meaning (so N–R); but this seems impossible after the singular *caput* at 18 above.[78]

21–2 quin et Ixion Tityusque uultu | risit inuito: the Underworld finale at 2.13.37–40 is likewise introduced by *quin et* ('and furthermore': *OLD quin* 3b); the move from Cerberus to Ixion, Tityus and (below) the Danaids is exactly paralleled in Tib. 1.3.71–80, with the qualification that H. has omitted Tantalus, whom Tib. included. For his murder of a kinsman and for lusting after Hera, Ixion was tied to a revolving wheel, which stopped at the lyre-playing of Orpheus when he descended to the Underworld (Virg. *G.* 4.484). For Tityus see 3.4.77–8n. *risit* illustrates H.'s usual (but not invariable) practice of using a singular verb with a plurality of subjects (3.3.10n.); for *uultu risit* cf. Ov. *Tr.* 1.5.27, Mart. 1.68.7, Sil. 7.467, Stat. *Ach.* 1.194. *uultu…inuito* means that despite their circumstances the two criminals could not help responding (cf. Val. Fl. 7.575).

22–4 stetit urna paulum | sicca, dum grato Danai puellas | carmine mulces: since the tense of *stetit* indicates a once-for-all action, 'came to a halt' (*OLD* 10), it follows that *urna* refers to the pitcher of water carried

---

[78] This objection is denied by N–R, who compare *trina…capita…caput* at Sen. *HF* 784–6, but the text there is probably corrupt (see Fitch's n.).

by each individual Danaid as she runs back and forth between the water-source and the vat (*dolium*, 27); *sicca* indicates that H. is following a version of the myth in which there are holes in the carrying vessels as well as in the vat.[79] The tense of *mulces* indicates that *dum* = 'within the time that' (*NLS* 179 §221): hence 'the urn [sc. of each of them] came to a halt, dry for a short time, while you soothed Danaus' daughters with your welcome music' (*OLD paulum*² 1b, *puella* 1b, *carmen* 5). *stetit urna* is quoted at [Quint.] *Decl.* 12.28; *carmine mulces* is from Virg. *G.* 4.510 (quoted on 13–14 above; later in Ovid and Statius), except that in the ode *carmine* must mean 'music, melody', not 'song'; for *grato...carmine* cf. 1.15.14–15. The Danaids are again referred to as *puellae* at Lucr. 3.1008, where, however, the meaning is 'girls'.

25–6 audiat Lyde scelus atque notas | uirginum poenas: *audiat Lyde* looks back to *Lyde...aures* at 7–8 above ('dic modos, Lyde quibus obstinatas | applicet aures'): the upcoming story of the Danaids (25–52) constitutes the *modi* or 'measures' which H. sought there. *notas*, which applies to *scelus* as well as to *poenas* (Naylor xxii §33), is explained esp. by Augustus' new portico (intro.) and suggests notoriety as well as familiarity (*OLD notus* 7); given that the Danaid story was so well known, *audiat Lyde* must mean 'Lyde should/must pay attention to' (*OLD audio* 10a) rather than e.g. 'hear about'. The subjunctive is probably jussive, although it is not always easy to decide whether an utterance is in fact jussive and not a wish (*OLS* 1.502); and the sentence is programmatic, *scelus* and *poenas* being elaborated in reverse (chiastic) order below (26b–29 ~ *poenas*, 30–2 ~ *scelus*); lines 25–32 as a whole are a foil for the story of Hypermnestra which follows (see intro.).

The description of the Danaids as *uirgines*, which recurs at Prop. 2.1.67 and Stat. *Theb.* 5.118, seems pointed in an instruction for the virgin Lyde (cf. 10–12). In one version of the myth the bridegrooms were so inebriated after the wedding feast that, on retiring, they fell immediately asleep (Ov. *Her.* 14.25–38). This version is used by P. A. Watson (1983: 127 and n. 38) to argue that the sisters are being described as virgins in the technical sense of the term, and it is certainly true that, since they were set on killing their husbands, they had good social reasons for avoiding

---

[79] When the Danaids stopped to listen to the music, the water drained from the *urnae* of those who were on their way from the water-source to the *dolium*, while the *urnae* of those on the return journey were already empty. This seems a more plausible scenario than to imagine (with N–R) that *all forty-nine* girls had already emptied their pitchers into the vat and were temporarily prevented by the music from re-filling them.

intercourse: according to the scholia on Eur. *Hec.* 886, they had agreed to murder their husbands before the latter could have sex with them. Yet at 35 below *uirgo* is also used of Hypermnestra, whose marriage was almost certainly consummated (n.). The rendering 'bride' would suit both occasions, its precise implications being understood from the context in each case; Keuls notes that the Latin poets 'were primarily interested in the story of mass murder' (112).

26–7 et inane lymphae | dolium fundo pereuntis imo 'and the vat empty of water as it runs away at/from the very bottom of the base': *et* (*OLD* 11) is epexegetic (the phrase explains *poenas*). *inanis* is regularly coupled with the genit. (*OLD* 9; cf. 1a); for *pereo* = 'to disappear' through wastage etc. see *OLD* 1a. *fundo...imo*, sometimes accompanied by a preposition (*in*, *ab*), is a common pleonasm of the 'amplificatory' type (J. Diggle, *CQ* 55 (2005) 642–3).

28–9 seraque fata | quae manent culpas etiam sub Orco: since sinners were routinely punished in the Underworld, *etiam* is perhaps more likely to mean 'also' than 'even'. The words constitute a generalisation (note the present tense) but have particular relevance to the Danaids: according to a common version of the story, Lynceus killed his sisters-in-law as punishment for their murdering his brothers (cf. Keuls 48); they were punished *also* in the Underworld by their leaking vessels. *culpas* seems almost = 'guilty persons' here: abstract for concrete is a regular feature of Latin but this particular ex. is impossible to parallel; 'offences' (*OLD* 3a) is a safer rendering. *sub Orco* is interpreted by many as 'under <the rule of> Orcus' (see Brink on *Epi.* 2.1.99 and Appendix 7), but 'down in the Underworld' (so *OLD sub* 2) seems much more plausible (see *OLD Orcus* 2 for the metonymy).

30–2 impiae (nam quid potuere maius?), | impiae sponsos potuere duro | perdere ferro 'the impious women – for what worse thing could they have done? – the impious women brought themselves to destroy their betrothed with hard steel'. The first *potuere* is constructed with the accus. (*OLD* 7a), as 3.4.53–8; the second *potuere* is *OLD* 3 'to be able to bring oneself to do something cruel, unpleasant etc.' (for repetition with a change of meaning see Wills 469–70); for *maius* = 'worse' cf. *S.* 2.8.57 (*TLL* 8.133.73ff.). Danaus had given each daughter a dagger with which to kill her husband; the women are *impiae* because their crime was an offence not only against the gods but against the very individuals to whom they were obligated (*sponsos*, which perhaps also hints at failure to consummate). The gemination of *impiae* frames the parenthesis, a form of 'repetitive resumption' which is rare in poetry before Ov. *Met.* (Wills 66–7). In Ovid's version Hypermnestra stresses her *pietas* towards Lynceus (*Her.* 14.49, 84, 129).

33 una de multis: Hypermnestra. Cf. Pausan. 2.19.6 'she was the only one of the daughters...'; Pindar (*Nem.* 10.6) refers to her μονόψαφον... ξίφος, 'sole-dissenting sword'.

33–4 face nuptiali | digna: torches played a significant role at Roman weddings: see K. K. Hersch, *The Roman Wedding: Ritual and Meaning in Antiquity* (2010) 164–75, who points to the frequency with which authors compared them to funeral torches. For the torches at the Danaids' wedding cf. Ov. *Her.* 14.9–10.

34–5 periurum...in parentem | splendide mendax 'nobly deceitful against her faithless father' (*mendax* constructed with *in* + accus. seems unparalleled). It was not so much that Danaus as father of the brides failed to keep his betrothal promises (for such promises see Treggiari 144), but that he made them with an evil intention. *splendide mendax*, a famous and characteristically Horatian oxymoron, may well be intended to allude to Aeschylus' phrase ἀπάτης δικαίας, 'righteous deceit' (fr. 301N = 601M), which some scholars have assigned to his lost play *Danaides*; it certainly translates Plato's well-known phrase γενναῖόν τι...ψευδομένους, 'lying in some noble way' (*Rep.* 414B), referring to a falsehood which is justified by circumstances. Cf. also Cic. *Lig.* 16 'honesto et misericordi mendacio', *Mil.* 72 'mentiri gloriose', Liv. 2.64.6 'salubri mendacio', Val. Max. 4.7.6 'fideli mendacio', Tac. *H.* 4.50.2 'egregio mendacio'.

35–6 et in omne uirgo | nobilis aeuum: since *nobilis* means 'of noble character' as well as 'famous' (*OLD* 6, 2a), there is a contrast with *notas* above (25n.). Although there was a tradition that Hypermnestra saved Lynceus because he respected her virginity (Apollod. 2.1.5; cf. Ov. *Her.* 14.55 'femina sum et uirgo'), the reference to Venus at 50 below almost certainly refers to the consummation of the marriage (see n.), while 37–9 implies very strongly that Lynceus has dropped off to sleep after intercourse. Here, as probably at 25–6 above (n.), *uirgo* seems to mean 'bride', for which cf. 2.8.23, Lygd. 4.31 '*iuueni* primum uirgo deducta *marito*' and NA ad loc. (the line, in view of its similarity to 37 here, may be indebted to the ode). For further discussion of the term see P. A. Watson (1983) and (1985) 433–4. For the tradition that Hypermnestra saved Lynceus because she fell in love with him see Aesch. *PV* 865–6. *aeuum* (3.5.15–18n.) is commonly combined with *omne* (Woodman, *LH* 63 n. 132), but the phrase's combination with *in* recurs only at *Epi.* 1.2.43 'in omne uolubilis aeuum', Pollio F7C = 5P, Sen. *Cons. Marc.* 5.2.

37–8 'Surge...surge, ne...': the repetition of an imperative is common (e.g. 49–50 below), but those which are expanded in some way (here by a negative purpose clause) are rare in Greek and early Augustan poetry: see Wills 175–6, who suggests that H. has in mind Theocritus' Alcmene, who, sensing danger, rouses her husband with the same repetition (24.35–6 ἄνσταθ', Ἀμφιτρύων... ἄνστα, μηδὲ..., 'Get up, Amphitryon,...get up and do not...'). Ovid's heroine says: 'surge age' (*Her.* 14.73).

38–9 ne longus tibi somnus, unde | non times, detur 'lest you be given a long sleep <by a source> from which you fear no harm' (*OLD timeo* 1c); the source in question is given in 39b–40: if Hypermnestra's father and sisters discover that she has failed to kill Lynceus, they will do the deed for her. *longus*, a euphemism for *perpetuus* (cf. N–H on 2.14.19), indicates that Lynceus has been asleep, presumably resting after the consummation of his marriage. Though death is often described in terms of sleep (1.24.5 and N–H), Hypermnestra's metaphor seems oddly unequal to the circumstances. Cf. Ov. *Her.* 14.74 'nox tibi, ni properas, ista perennis erit'.

41 uelut nactae uitulos leaenae 'like lionesses in possession of/encountering calves' (*OLD nanciscor* 1a, 5). Lions of both sexes were proverbially cruel: see e.g. Lygd. 4.90 'saeua leaena' (and NA ad loc. for the choice noun *leaena*, which H. uses again only at 3.20.2). For calves as their prey see Eur. *IT* 297, Cic. *Fin.* 3.66, Sen. *Thy.* 732–6.

42 singulos...lacerant: i.e. the sisters are killing a man each. *lacerant* is at least as appropriate to lions as to girls (cf. Sen. *Clem.* 1.25.1 'leoni Lysimachum obicias an ipse laceres dentibus tuis'), a linguistic ambiguity which seems to extend to *mollis*, which is regular for gentle animals (*OLD* 14), and *ferio*, which can be used of lions pouncing (Stat. *Theb.* 2.680).

45 me pater saeuis oneret catenis 'My father can load me with cruel chains...' or 'Let my father load me...': the subjunctive, like *releget* in 48, has a concessive force and may be regarded as either jussive or as straightforwardly concessive, the two being 'not always easy to distinguish' (*OLS* 1.509; cf. 502–3). The contrast with *te...neque intra claustra tenebo* (43–4) is underlined by the supposed etymological connection between *catena* and *teneo* (Maltby 114). The reference to chains is dramatic irony: Hypermnestra does not know that after her refusal to carry out her father's command he will imprison her (Apollod. 2.1.5); the letter which Ovid imagines her writing to Lynceus is written from prison in Argos, where she languishes in chains (*Her.* 14.3, 84, 131). For *saeuis...catenis* cf. [Sen.] *Oct.* 939, Sil. 13.609, Stat. *Theb.* 10.562; *catenis onerare* recurs at Ov. *AA* 1.215 and 4× in Tacitus (Heubner on *H.* 1.48.3).

47–8 me uel extremos Numidarum in agros | classe releget: more dramatic irony: her father will indeed put her on trial (Paus. 2.19.6, 20.7, 21.1–2), although she will be acquitted by the Argives. *relegare* is one of the technical terms for exile or banishment in contemporary Rome (F. K. Drogula, 'Controlling travel: deportation, islands and the regulation of senatorial mobility in the Augustan principate', *CQ* 61 (2011) 231–5); *classe*, which is quoted by Serv. *Aen.* 1.39 to illustrate the use of *classis* for a single ship (cf. *TLL* 3.1283.60–8, 1284.4ff.), is strictly redundant but combines with *releget* to suggest the comprehensiveness of legalese; it also perhaps recalls the journey which Danaus and his daughters had made when they first fled from Egypt (Apollod. 2.1.4). Roman exiles were not banished to Numidia, although Africa is one of the destinations of the evicted in Virgil's first Eclogue (1.64). *uel extremos... agros* does not mean 'to even the furthest edge of the Numidians' territory', which would be trivial, but 'to the territory even of the Numidians at the ends of the earth': *extremos* (3.10.1–2n.) is an example of enallage (3.1.42–3n.); for the Numidians at the ends of the earth see Liv. 24.49.5. This is the only ex. of *uel* = 'even' (*OLD* 5c) in the *Odes*.

49 i pedes quo te rapiunt et aurae: Hypermnestra's command embraces travelling by both land and sea (as *Epo.* 16.21–2 'ire pedes quocumque ferent, quocumque per undas | Notus uocabit').

50 dum fauet nox et Venus: darkness would facilitate an escape (cf. Ov. *Her.* 14.77–8 'dum nox sinit'); it is likely that Hypermnestra has added *et Venus* in fond memory of their recent lovemaking. The phrase as a whole may mean 'our night of passion' (hendiadys): cf. Ov. *Her.* 3.116 'noxque Venusque iuuant', where the two nouns 'probably make up one idea' (Palmer). If *Venus* is to be taken separately (she was the protector of lovers: cf. Prop. 3.16.20), we would have to supply another verb by zeugma (e.g. 'and while Venus is able to help'), since there can be no suggestion that Venus' favouring of the married couple is only temporary. When Hypermnestra was acquitted at her later trial, she erected a statue of Aphrodite at Argos in commemoration (Paus. 2.19.6). For *fauet nox* cf. Stat. *Theb.* 11.761; for *f. Venus* cf. Tib. 1.4.71–2, Ov. *Her.* 19.159, Fronto p. 232.19–20 vdH[2].

226   COMMENTARY 12

50–1 i secundo | omine...: repeated imperatives are used frequently to express farewell or to indicate closure (Wills 91–5, 96–9), of which we have both here. Wishes for favourable omens are common in scenes of departure, e.g. *secunda...alite* at *Epo.* 16.23–4 (see above, 49n.).

51–2 et nostri memorem sepulcro | sculpe querelam 'and engrave on my tomb a lament to remember me': since Lynceus is envisaged as being abroad by this time (49), *sepulcro* must refer to a cenotaph; the 'lament' (*OLD querela* 1c) is the epitaph to be inscribed upon it. Hypermnestra does not of course know – as Lyde does – that she will be reunited with Lynceus and after a happy life together will be buried alongside him (cf. Apollod. 2.1.5, Paus. 2.21.2).[80] N–R describe *sculpe* as 'a variant without authority or merit', but its great merit is that it anagrammatises *sepulcro* in a very Horatian manner (Intro. 35). It is true that no earlier ex. of the meaning 'to engrave an inscription' than Val. Max. 3.5.1 is quoted in *OLD* (2a), but Ovid's Hypermnestra uses the verb in a related sense which is likewise previously unattested (*Her.* 14.128–30 'sculptaque sint titulo nostra sepulcra breui: | "exsul Hypermnestra, pretium pietatis iniquum, | quam mortem fratri depulit, ipsa tulit"'); given the relationship between the ode and the elegy, it seems reasonable to infer that Ovid is taking his cue from H. It may or may not be relevant that a traveller to Egypt in the time of Trajan wrote on the Great Pyramid of Giza a lament which clearly alludes to the ode (*CIL* 3.21 = *ILS* 1046a = *CLE* 270): 'Vidi pyramidas sine te, dulcissime frater, | et tibi quod potui lacrimas hic maesta profudi. | Et nostri memorem luctus hanc sculpo querelam' (see Courtney, *ML* No. 74.1–3 and pp. 295–7). *nostri memorem* not only implies that Hypermnestra wants her name incorporated in her epitaph but also suggests its etymology from ὑπέρ ('very') + μνῆστις ('memory, remembrance');[81] for further exs. of the phrase (used differently at 3.27.13–14: see n.) see NA on Lygd. 2.25.

12

The metre of this ode, though unique in the whole of Latin (see below), is found in Greek, one of the examples being a very fragmentary poem

---

[80] In myth (cf. Apollod. 2.2.1) Hypermnestra and Lynceus were grandparents of Acrisius, father of Danae (cf. 3.16.1–7); for convenient family trees see Hornblower and Pelling on Hdt. 6.53.1.
[81] This seems preferable to an etymology from μνηστήρ ('suitor') or μνηστός ('wedded'). For a full discussion of the comparable name Clytemnestra, favouring that spelling, see P. A. Marquardt, 'Clytemnestra: a felicitous spelling in the *Odyssey*', *Arethusa* 25 (1992) 241–54.

of Alcaeus (10B), of which the first line (ἔμε δείλαν, ἔμε παίσαν κακοτάτων πεδέχοισαν, 'Me, poor me, sharing in all miseries') makes it clear that the speaker is a woman. From this evidence many scholars – perhaps the majority – have assumed that H.'s ode is modelled on that of Alcaeus and that it too is therefore spoken by a woman, namely, by Neobule, who appears in an address in line 7.

This scholarly edifice collapses as soon as one compares the ode with the remnants of Alcaeus' poem: apart from the identity of metre, there is not the slightest resemblance between them. Once we rid ourselves of the misconception that the ode is modelled on Alcaeus, there is no evidence whatsoever that H. is impersonating a woman. The ancient commentators rightly assumed that H. was speaking *in propria persona*. The repeated second-person pronouns and the address to Neobule in lines 5–8 are not self-reflexive but illustrate H.'s regular manner of talking to a young girl who is experiencing unrequited love. His purpose is to sympathise with her circumstances (1–8) and to commend the young man who is the object of her affections (9–16). These fundamental points, along with others, are made by Cairns in his analysis of the ode, which is exactly right (*RL* 276–83).

METRE Ionics *a minore*, each metron consisting of ∪ ∪ – –.[82] Ten metra constitute a stanza, but scholars differ on the number and arrangement of lines in each stanza: most seem to prefer three lines per stanza, but, for reasons which are explained elsewhere (Intro. 31), I have followed Goold and Quinn in preferring four-line stanzas.[83] This is one of the rare cases where a metre has not already featured in the 'Parade Odes'.

1–4 Miserarum est neque Amori | dare ludum neque dulci | mala uino lauere aut exanimari metuentes | patruae uerbera linguae 'It is the lot of wretched girls neither to allow Love his sport nor to wash away their troubles with comforting wine, or, if they do, to be scared to death of a tongue-lashing from their paternal uncle.' *miserarum* is a possessive genitive used as a predicate (*NLS* 52 §72 (1) (iii), G&L 233–4 §366 R. 1–2, esp. *OLS* 1.774–5), and the three subjects of *est* are itemised by *neque... neque...aut...* ('not allowing Love his sport...[etc.] is the lot of wretched girls'). Although the first two of these subjects are simple infinitives (*dare*

---

[82] In Ionics *a maiore* the shorts and longs are transposed (– – ∪ ∪).
[83] In printing the text I have preferred Quinn's arrangement (2+2+4+2), which, unlike that of Goold (2+2+3+3), presents in lines 4 and 8 'the typical pattern where adjective and noun frame the line' (N–R 166, who nowhere mention the possibility of four-line stanzas).

and *lauere*), the third is an infinitive (*exanimari*) with an accusative subject (*eas*, which has to be understood and refers back to the wretched girls). For the common construction whereby an accus. + infin. is the subject of a sentence see e.g. Cic. *Deiot.* 1 'est...inusitatum regem reum capitis esse', 'that a king should be on trial for his life is abnormal' (G&L 337 §535, *NLS* 17 §25, *OLS* 1.774 §9.30 (j)). In our sentence *metuentes* agrees with the understood *eas*. Since the girls' wretchedness *consists in* their inability to allow Love his sport etc., *miserarum* is quasi-proleptic; and *aut* (*OLD* 7) is condensed for 'or, if they do [sc. indulge Love or wash away their cares with wine]'.

1-2 neque Amori | dare ludum: *dare ludum* + dat. occurs occasionally elsewhere (*TLL* 7.2.1791.45-55, *OLD ludus* 5c) and seems equivalent to the Eng. 'to give/allow play to ~ ', i.e. 'to indulge'; here it is pointed, since Amor is conventionally a boy who plays with lovers (e.g. Ov. *RA* 23 'puer es, nec te quicquam nisi ludere oportet'; cf. Anacr. 358; Fedeli on Prop. 1.9.23-4), and of course *ludus* is itself often used of love affairs (Adams 162). Another pointed instance at Cic. *Cael.* 42 'detur aliqui ludus aetati... dederit aliquid temporis ad ludum aetatis'.

2-3 neque dulci | mala uino lauere: *lauere*, if the text is correct, is here used in the metaphorical sense of 'to wash away', but the only ex. before H. is Ter. *Phorm.* 973 'uenias nunc precibus lautum peccatum tuom?' and (a more serious objection) the verb recurs in its literal sense at line 10 below, a most awkward repetition; Withof proposed *eluere* (used of washing away cares at 4.12.19-20). For the washing away of (esp. erotic) cares by wine see NA's intro. n. to Lygd. 6 (pp. 460-4); for the ancient prohibition of wine to women see e.g. Cic. *Rep.* 4.6, Val. Max. 2.1.5, 6.3.9; L. Minieri, '*Vini usus feminis ignotus*', *Labeo* 28 (1982) 150-63.

3-4 aut exanimari metuentes | patruae uerbera linguae: paternal uncles were proverbially harsh: see *S.* 2.2.97, 2.3.88; Otto 268, Bettini 21 and nn. 10-11. For metaphorical tongue-lashing see *OLD uerber* 3b, *uerbero* 1b; W. on Tac. *A.* 6.9.4; for metaphorical *exanimari* (*OLD* 4) see 2.17.1 and N-H.

5-8 In this stanza there is a single verb (7 *aufert*), which has two subjects and three objects. In the case of the first two objects (*qualum* and *telas*) the subject is Cupid (5-6); in the case of the third object (*studium*) the subject is *nitor* (7-8). The various divisions are made clear by the patterning of the words. The first two objects are linked by the anaphora of *tibi*; the third object consists of noun + genit. phrase (7) and mirrors the subject, which also consists of noun + genit. phrase (8).

5-6 tibi qualum Cythereae | puer ales, tibi telas: Cytherea is one of the names of Venus (cf. 1.4.5), Cythera being the Aegean island off the SE prong of the Peloponnese where Aphrodite first rose from the sea (Hes. *Theog.* 192-3): see *BA* Map 58: A4-5. *puer* = 'son' (*OLD* 2). *qualus* = a kind of basket; *tela*(*e*) can refer to cloth, the threads of a loom, or the loom itself (see *OLD*): Neobule is envisaged as the kind of virtuous young woman who is defined by her spinning or weaving (for which see e.g. L. Larsson Lovén, '*Lanam fecit*: woolworking and female virtue', in L. Larsson Lovén and A. Strömberg (edd.), *Aspects of Women in Antiquity* (1998) 85-95). Cairns argues strongly that both she and Hebrus (8) are respectable young Romans and that their 'Greek names are only a masquerade' (*RL* 280).

7 operosaeque Mineruae studium aufert, Neobule: Minerva/Athena was the goddess of women's work: H.'s phrase renders in Latin Ἀθηνᾶ Ἐργάνη: although it is to be understood metonymically = 'toilsome weaving/spinning' (*OLD Minerua* 2), the contrast with *Cythereae* should not be lost. *studium* + genit. = 'enthusiasm for ~ ' (*OLD* 2). It was a commonplace that love leads to idleness, e.g. Sappho 102 'I cannot weave my web', Virg. *Aen.* 4.86-8, Ov. *RA* 149 'desidiam puer ille sequi solet, odit agentes' etc. (and Henderson's comm., p. 58), *Ciris* 179, Sen. *Phaedr.* 103. Neobule's name, which appropriately means 'new plan(s)', is famous from Archilochus 118 and 196a.24-5 but is seemingly nowhere else.

8 Liparaei nitor Hebri: the periphrasis (for 'glistening Liparaean Hebrus') adds stylistic elevation: such periphrases (see e.g. 3.3.2, 3.16.2-3, 3.21.10-11, *S.* 2.1.72, *Epi.* 1.12.26 'Claudi uirtute Neronis') are typical of the high style of epic (see e.g. Pease on Virg. *Aen.* 4.132). The young man's glisten is explained by the anointing and swimming referred to in 9-10 below. Hebrus is named after a famous river in Thrace (3.25.10n.), whose water was said by Alcaeus, in a hymn to the river, to be 'like unguent' (45.7): it is therefore interesting that, although young Hebrus is described as coming from Lipara (mod. Lipari), an island off the NE coast of Sicily (*BA* Map 47: F1-2), there was a Cilician river called the Liparis, 'in quo natantes aut lauantes ab ipsa aqua unguuntur' (Vitr. 8.3.8). The Greek adj. λιπαρός means 'shining'.

9-10 simul unctos Tiberinis | umeros lāuit in undis: *simul* = 'as soon as, once' (*OLD* 11a); *lāuit* is the regular perfect indic. used in generalising temporal clauses in the present (*NLS* 175 §217 (2)(c)): 'once he washes...' (lit. 'once he has washed'). The clause explains *nitor*: young Romans would anoint themselves with oil after exercise in the Campus Martius, before going for a swim in the Tiber (*S.* 2.1.7-8; cf. N-H on

1.8.8; also next n.). In Theocr. 2.79–80 Simaetha admires the glistening chests of the men as they leave the wrestling-school. The adj. *Tiberinis* instead of the genit. *Tiberis* continues the elevated style (3.3.26–8n.).

11 eques ipso melior Bellerophontē: the interlaced word order, more pronounced than 9–10, adds a further dimension of elevation. Equestrianism on the Campus Martius is the natural companion of swimming in the Tiber (3.7.25–8nn.). *Bellerophonte* is the abl. of *Bellerophontes* (3.7.15n.); he was famous as rider of the winged horse, Pegasus.

11–12 neque pugno | neque segni pede uictus: the abl. is one of cause, not respect (which would make no sense), and *segni* is to be taken also with *pugno* (Naylor xxii §33): 'and not beaten because of a sluggish fist or foot'. It is not clear whether *pede* refers to a boxer's clever footwork (cf. Virg. *Aen.* 5.430 'pedum melior motu') or to foot-racing (*OLD pes* 5a); either way, Hebrus' excellence as a boxer and (above) rider means that he combines the skills of Castor and Pollux (N–H on 1.12.26).

13–16 celer idem...excipere aprum: *idem* emphasises the potential inconsistency between Hebrus' different qualities of speed (*celer*) and cunning (*catus*): see 3.4.67–8n. The MSS have these adjs. in the opposite order, but *celer* seems more apt for shooting the *fleeing* stags, while *catus* seems more apt for snaring the *lurking* boar. There is a good deal to be said for transposing the transmitted adjs., as was suggested by Bentley. A rather similar case arises at 2.5.13–17, where some scholars wish to transpose *ferox* and *fugax*. The Romans, like the Germans (Caes. *BG* 6.21.3), regarded hunting as training for warfare (Pease on Cic. *ND* 2.161; J. Aymard, *Les chasses romaines* (1951) 469–81). H. is the first to construct *celer* with an infin. (again at 4.6.39–40; then the elder Pliny); for *agito* of hunting or harrying see *OLD* 3b.

15–16 catus arto latitantem | fruticeto excipere aprum 'and cunning at catching the boar lurking in the dense thicket' (*OLD excipio* 13a, *artus*¹ 9a): each word or phrase corresponds to one in the preceding sentence (Intro. 26); the position of *latitantem* between *arto* and *fruticeto* is mimetic. *catus* is 'a quaint archaism' (Brink on *Epi.* 2.2.39): H. is the first to construct it with an infin. (next in Apul.).

13

'Water is best', declared Pindar in 476 BC (*Ol.* 1.1), a sentiment with which few ancient inhabitants of hot Mediterranean countries would have disagreed. When Menander Rhetor in the third century AD wrote his instructions for 'How to describe a city', he stipulated that one of the topics you should discuss is the surrounding countryside, and, when describing that countryside, whether it has a good supply of water, and, if it does, the supply should be treated under the headings of springs, rivers and lakes, which, 'like everything else, are to be judged on grounds of pleasure and utility; a further division may be made in terms of abundance and natural occurrence' (347.7–9, 349.3–4, 25–30). Cool springs feature in early Greek lyric (Sappho 2.5–6), a plentiful supply of water is 'characteristic of earthly paradises' (Watson on *Epo.* 16.47–8, with refs.), and poems on fountains or springs are to be found in the Greek Anthology (9.313, 676, 684, 699) and Martial (7.15, 9.58).[84]

H. in this ode addresses a spring – or, perhaps more accurately (cf. 15–16), a cascade or spout – called Bandusia, just as his model Alcaeus had addressed the River Hebrus (45). Such personifications were facilitated by the fact that rivers and springs were deemed to have their own presiding deity, whether god or nymph, and sometimes it is difficult to know which entity is being referred to. Virgil can describe the Tiber as speaking and then disappearing into himself (*Aen.* 8.66 'dixit, deinde lacu fluuius se condidit alto'), while Ovid 'frequently plays on the dual identity of Achelous as water and god' (P. J. Jones, *Reading Rivers in Roman Literature and Culture* (2005) 67); even more to the point, the Latin word *lympha* can mean 'nymph' as well as 'water' (*OLD* 1) and is indeed so used by H. (*S.* 1.5.97). The whereabouts of Bandusia are today unknown. The slender evidence that it was near Venusia (1n.) tends to be disregarded, because H. elsewhere describes his birthplace as unusually arid (3.30.11, *Epo.* 3.16). Many readers like to imagine that it was the spring near H.'s Sabine farm (cf. 3.16.29), to which reference is made both in the *Satires* (2.6.2 'tecto uicinus iugis aquae fons') and in the *Epistles* (1.16.12–14); some others think that the spring described in the ode is not a particular spring at all but an imagined composite: *fluuii* were a set topic for the *descriptio* (Prisc. *GL* 3.439.8K).

Menander's recommendation that watercourses should be praised on the basis of pleasure and utility, abundance and natural occurrence, coincides with H.'s practice in the ode. The spring is visually and aurally attractive (1, 15–16), but at the same time it provides welcome refreshment for plough oxen and wandering flocks (10–12); it does not fail at even

---

[84] Aelius Aristides wrote a panegyric entitled 'On the Water in Pergamon', thought to refer to an aqueduct (C. P. Jones, *Arch. Anz.* (1991) 111–17). For a wonderful collection of aqueous information see J. E. Lendon, 'Rhetoric and Nymphaea in the Roman empire', *Chiron* 45 (2015) 123–49.

the hottest period of the year (9–10), perhaps owing to the nature of its channel (14–15). Indeed it is the all-round excellence of the spring which supplies the occasion of the ode: on the following day (3) the spring is going to be offered a sacrifice involving wine, flowers and a young kid (2–5). While these offerings align the ode with the dedicatory epigrams collected in Book 6 of the Greek Anthology, many scholars believe that H. is referring specifically to the festival of the Fontinalia, which was celebrated on 13 October; but the promised profusion of flowers (2) does not sit well with an October date, not to mention any problems associated with the breeding seasons of goats (see also 3.18.2–4n.).[85] Perhaps H. is referring to some local and differently timed festival, as in the case of Faunus in 3.18.

Whatever the precise occasion, modern readers have been disconcerted by H.'s picture of the kid's warm red blood mingling with the cool clear stream (6–8). 'Who wants a drink out of the fountain of Bandusia after that?', famously asked A. Y. Campbell (*Horace: A New Interpretation* (1924) 1–2). Yet Campbell seems to have had in mind a rather different poem from the one that H. wrote (perhaps Catullus 68B.57–62): H. never mentions thirsty travellers drinking from the spring; he mentions animals (11–12), which will have been blissfully unaware of the sacrifice that was being performed for their benefit – in thanksgiving for the past year's ceaseless supply of water and in respectful hope that the spring would continue its bounty for the next twelve months. On such reciprocities did life in the ancient world depend.

The poem may be divided into two pairs of stanzas. In 1–8 H. addresses the spring and describes the three forthcoming offerings; in 9–16 he praises the spring for three of its attributes.

METRE   Third Asclepiad

1 O fons Bandusiae: a *fons* was defined by its flowing water (Fest. 84 'fons a fundendo dictus'; Maltby 238), a characteristic to which H. will return (7 *riuos*, 16 *desiliunt*). Many hymns or prayers begin with *O* (e.g. 1.30, 1.35, 3.10.13, 3.26.9, *Epo.* 5), and the form is parodied at 3.21 below. It has sometimes been thought that Bandusia, a name otherwise unattested in classical Latin, is a vernacular rendering of Greek Pandosia, the name of various places in southern Italy, while a papal bull of 1103 contains the words 'in Bandusino fonte apud Venusiam': although this

---

[85] Cairns, who analyses the ode as a dedicatory poem ('anathematikon') cast in the future tense, deals with the goat problem in some detail and concludes by accepting that the day of sacrifice is that of the Fontinalia (*RL* 394–404).

evidence is usually ignored (intro.), it has been defended by Morgan (2009) 132–4. If the name refers to the spring itself, *Bandusiae* will be a genitive of definition, like Virg. *Aen.* 1.244 'fontem... Timaui' (*NLS* 53 §72 (5) *Note* (i)); but, if Bandusia is the name of the local nymph, the genitive will be possessive. The distinction may in any case be unreal, since, as we have seen (intro.), the ancients often did not distinguish between river and deity.

splendidior uitro is the kind of appositional description common in prayers or hymns (3.11.3–5nn.). Since H. is referring to a cold stream or torrent which falls down rocks (9–10, 15–16), his description presumably relates to the sparkling glint of moving water as it catches the rare ray of sunlight which penetrates the shade of the overhanging oak tree (14); the comparison with glass (cf. Publil. Syr. F24 'uitrea...splendet', Callim. *Hecale* 238.16 'the glittering sky more brilliant than glass') is thus different from the transparency of *perlucidior uitro* at 1.18.16 or of the Clitumnus at Plin. *Ep.* 8.8.2, so 'clear and glassy that you can count the coins which have been tossed in and the winking pebbles'. Ovid later uses H.'s words to describe Galatea (*M.* 13.791 'splendidior uitro, tenero lasciuior haedo'). For a relatively recent study of Roman glassware and its properties see e.g. S. Paynter, 'Clarity and brilliance', *Archaeological and Anthropological Sciences* 11 (2019) 1533–55, discussing glass found in Roman Britain.

2 dulci digne mero non sine floribus: it is known from Varro that on the festival of the Fontinalia (see intro.) wreaths[86] were cast into springs and fountains (*LL* 6.22 'et in fontes coronas iaciunt et puteos coronant'); evidently there were occasions on which libations of wine were poured too. Even when the honorand is not itself a water-source, wine unmixed with water (*merum*; again at 3.17.14) had to be used for sacrifices (Festus 474.31ff.); the present wine's acceptability is enhanced by *dulci*, as is the profusion of the flowers by the litotes *non sine* (3.4.20n.). Since *dignus* reappears in the prayer parody at 3.21.6, the word may suggest religious language.

3 cras donaberis haedo: for offerings of flowers (for the Muses) and a goat (for Apollo) see *Anth. Pal.* 6.336, ascribed to Theocritus. For blood sacrifices to springs see e.g. Ov. *F.* 3.300, Mart. 6.47.

---

[86] Perhaps of decorative leaves rather than flowers, since the festival took place in mid-October.

4 cui: the use of the 'sympathetic dative' (3.1.17–18n.) rather than a possessive genitive prepares for the poignancy of *frustra* below (6n.).

4–5 frons turgida cornibus | primis: *turgida* aptly describes the swelling effect when a kid's nascent horns or 'buds' start to appear; for this sense of *primus* see Sen. *Tro.* 538 'primis...cornibus'; *OLD* 8. Others think *primis* refers to the tips of the little horns. Cf. 4.2.57–60 (a calf).

5 et uenerem et proelia destinat: the repetition of *et* may be intended to suggest the range of the kid's potential activities: the pursuits of Venus and Mars. On the other hand, since billy goats' head-butting battles over females were evidently proverbial (Tosi 647 §1429), the nouns may be a form of hendiadys ('promises battles for love').

6 frustra: the 'dramatic' use of *frustra* (3.7.21–2n.) here conveys pathos: the life to which the kid could have looked forward (5) is about to be cut short. H. makes a similar point about a young boar at 3.22.7–8.

6–7 nam gelidos inficiet tibi | rubro sanguine riuos: the words which so disconcerted A. Y. Campbell (intro.) are a classic illustration of the so-called *schema Horatianum* (3.4.46–7n.), in which H. presents two parallel phrases, an adj. in each implying its opposite in the other. Thus on *pinus ingens albaque populus* (2.3.9) Wickham comments: 'The double contrast between the *slight* poplar white in the wind and the *gloom* of the heavier pine is indicated, after Horace's manner, by one epithet with each of the pair of substantives' (emphasis added). In our example we have to infer from *gelidos ~ rubro* that the water is clear (≠ *rubro*) and the blood is warm (≠ *gelidos*): the standard discussion is E. A. Schmidt, *WS* 103 (1990) 57–98 (66–8 for the present case); also R. Gaskin, 'Bentley's classicism, "Paradise Lost", and the "Schema Horatianum"', *Int. Journ. Class. Trad.* 17 (2010) 360–1. The device was called antallage by Bell (340–50); see also Mayer on *Odes* 1, p. 245 (index). According to one account *riuus* was derived ἀπὸ τοῦ ῥεῖν ('from its flow': see Maltby 528); here *riuos* no doubt refers to the stream as it flows from the bottom of the cascade (15–16), although conceivably H. is also thinking of the blood finding its way into the tributaries or irrigation channels which the *fons* supplies (cf. N–H on 1.7.13 'mobilibus...riuis'). For *nam* following *frustra* see 3.7.21–2n.; *tibi*, another 'sympathetic dative' (3.1.17–18n.), helps to maintain the deification of the stream.

8 lasciui suboles gregis: the primary meaning of *suboles* is 'shoot'; in the sense of 'offspring, scion' (*OLD* 2a) it was considered elevated and archaic by Cicero (*De or.* 3.153), and its distribution 'shows that the usage was largely the property of the poets' (Oakley on Liv. 6.7.1); it recurs in H. at 4.3.14 and *CS* 17. Goats were proverbially lascivious (Servius on *Ecl.* 3.8 'hircos libidinosa constat esse animalia'); here the grandiose circumlocution for 'kid' not only enhances its value as a victim but is a further reminder that the kid is destined not to take part in the kinds of ritual which resulted in his birth (5 *uenerem*).

9–16 In the two final stanzas H. lists three attributes of the spring: each is itemised by the triple repetition of the second-person pronoun *te...tu... tu...* ('Du-Stil': cf. 3.11.13–14n.) and they are arranged as a tricolon crescendo (9–10a, 10b–12, 13–16). The first two attributes are those which the spring provides for others (its ceaseless flow and refreshing water); the third is the fame with which it will be provided by H. (14 'me dicente'), although, in a final reciprocity, it transpires that the spring plays a part in the poet's eloquence too (15–16n.).

The wording of the stanzas is typically Horatian: each noun except *uomere* is qualified by an adj., only *lymphae* having two adjs. The arrangement is: <a¹ a² n² n¹> | <n³ a³ | a⁴ n⁴> | <n⁵ a⁵ ‖ a⁶ n⁶> | <a⁷ a⁸ n⁸ | n⁷> a⁹ | n⁹ a⁹. In 9–12 each group is contained within a single line, an arrangement which is varied in 13–16; the first four pairs are mirrored chiastically by the second four (see the angle brackets), with the words *loquaces* | *lymphae...tuae*, summarising (as it were) the theme of the poem outside the frame at the very end.

9–10 te flagrantis atrox hora Caniculae | nescit tangere 'The terrible season of the burning Dog-star cannot reach you' (*OLD nescio* 3a, *tango* 7); this meaning of *hora* (*OLD* ¹6) is first in H. The rising of Sirius, or the Dog-star, took place on 18 July (Plin. *NH* 2.123) and heralded the hottest time of the year (3.1.31–2), the so-called 'dog days' (3.29.18; N–H on 1.17.17). H.'s spring is in the shade of the oak tree (14): compare the *fons* at Ov. *Met.* 3.412 'siluaque sole locum passura tepescere nullo'. For *atrox* of weather etc. see *OLD* 1b.

10 frigus amabile: the words contrast with *flagrantis* and *atrox* respectively. Coldness is always a desirable feature of springs: see N–H on 2.3.12, adding Plin. *Ep.* 8.8.4 'rigor aquae certauerit niuibus' (of the Clitumnus).

11 fessis uomere tauris: there was a distinction between *boues* and *tauri* (Virg. *Ecl.* 1.45 'pascite ut ante boues, pueri, submittite tauros') and normally the former term was used for plough oxen (Mynors on Virg. *G.* 1.45); but cf. Cat. 64.40, Virg. *G.* 3.515, Ov. *F.* 2.295, which all have *uomere* *taurus* at the end of the line. *uomer*, lit. 'ploughshare', here = 'plough' by synecdoche. For *fessus* see 3.4.37–8n.

12 pecori uago: cf. Cat. 63.13 'uaga pecora', Liv. 2.50.6 (Calp. *Ecl.* 1.37–8 'uagetur...pecus').

13 fies nobilium tu quoque fontium: the partitive genitive follows directly after the verb (as *Epi.* 1.9.13 'scribe tui gregis hunc', 'enrol him as <one> of your herd'): see *OLS* 1.777. Hence 'you too will become <one> of the famous springs' (*OLD nobilis* 2b). Scholars in the Hellenistic age were extremely interested in making lists and catalogues (see e.g. Pfeiffer): Callimachus, for example, produced a work entitled 'On the rivers of the world' (frr. 457–9 Pf), while a list of 'the most beautiful springs' (κρῆναι κάλλι[σται]) has been preserved on a Ptolemaic papyrus (H. Diels, 'Laterculi Alexandrini aus einem Papyrus ptolemäischer Zeit', *Abhandl. Preuss. Akad. Wiss.*, Phil.–Hist. Klasse, 2 (1904) 13–14): it includes Arethusa, Castalia and Peirene, amongst others. Just as H. wants to be inserted into the canon of lyric poets (1.1.35), so he promises here that, as a result of his producing this poem (14 'me dicente'), Bandusia too will be inserted into the canon of springs which have left anonymity behind and become famous (*tu quoque*, mimetic syntax); no doubt he is thinking principally of those associated with poetic inspiration, like Hippocrene and Castalia (3.4.61n.). Some scholars think that *palma...nobilis* at 1.1.5 has the extra meaning of *nobilitans*, 'making famous'; perhaps the same is true of *nobilium* here: the spring has provided him with a topic and inspiration. For the opposite cf. Callim. *Hymns* 4.131 μόνος ἐν ποταμοῖσιν ἀτιμότατος καλέεσθαι ('alone to be called the least honoured amongst rivers', of the Peneus).

14–15 me dicente cauis impositam ilicem | saxis: for the appended abl. abs. cf. 3.1.30–1n.; *dicente* = 'telling of' (*OLD* 7b): 'because of my telling of the holm-oak perched over the hollow rocks' (the reference is to the present ode). The ilex is 'an impressive evergreen tree which grows to a considerable height' (Watson on *Epo.* 15.5); for *impositam* see *OLD* 2a. The rocks themselves are not, of course, hollow: H. has in mind either a cave (cf. Virg. *Ecl.* 9.41–2 'populus antro | imminet') or, perhaps more likely, a channel formed by rocks. The combination of rocks, tree and water suggests the conventional *locus amoenus* and has been compared with the painted panel in the Casa di Livia on the Palatine (Leach 229).

15–16 unde loquaces | lymphae desiliunt tuae: Catullus had mentioned the laughing of Lake Garda (31.14 'ridete quidquid est domi cachinnorum'), presumably referring to the sound of the water gently lapping the shore; here H. describes the waters of the spring as speaking, as they leap down from their rocky source (see Intro. 35). There seems to be a suggestion that H.'s descriptive eloquence (14 'me dicente') derives, at least in part, from that of the spring itself: for this see the oracular well at *Anacreontea* 12.5–8 οἱ δὲ Κλάρου παρ' ὄχθαις | δαφνηφόροιο Φοίβου | λάλον πιόντες ὕδωρ | μεμηνότες βοῶσιν ('Some drink the babbling water of bay-bearing Phoebus by the slopes of Claros and go mad and shout' (Loeb trans.)); Antipater of Sidon referred to the 'eloquent water' of Mt Helicon (*Anth. Pal.* 11.24.1–2 ὕδωρ | εὐεπές). The reputations of poet and spring are inter-dependent (*dicente ~ loquaces*); for the motif, common in Latin literature, of water as a source of inspiration see N–H on 1.26.6; Crowther; Morgan (2009) 134–6. *desiliunt* (of water again at *Epo*. 16.48) here alludes to the derivation of *lympha* 'ab aquae lapsu lubrico' (Varro, *LL* 5.71); this final reference to the water's flow attests to the permanence and vitality of the source.

14

On 16 January 27 BC, in recognition of his services to the Roman state, Octavian was given the name Augustus, as he proudly recorded in the *Res Gestae* (34.2); later that year he departed for Gaul and thence, in due course, to Spain, where he would spend the years 26–25 on campaign against the Cantabrians and Astures in the north west of the country (Syme, *RP* 2.825–7, 843–8). It was the second and last of the two occasions on which he would campaign in person (Suet. *Aug.* 20). Although he fell ill in 25 and was obliged to withdraw to Tarraco for the purposes of convalescence (Dio 53.25.7), the campaign was concluded in his absence and celebrated as a great victory. The senate voted him a triumph, which he took pride in refusing (Flor. 2.33.53 = 4.12.53, Dio 53.26.5; cf. *RG* 4.1). Symbolising the establishment of peace, the Temple of Janus was closed in 25 (Dio 53.26.5), which was also the year with which the *princeps* decided to bring his autobiography to a close (Suet. *Aug.* 85: see Rich 157–61). The Augustan conquest of Spain constituted the finale of the history by the contemporary historian, Trogus (cf. Just. 44.5.8), while more than half a century later another historian, Velleius Paterculus, would choose the conquest of Spain to illustrate the *pax Augusta* (90.2–4: see 3.8.21–2n.).

Augustus' victorious return to Rome was delayed because of his continuing convalescence at Tarraco, but in 24 it was reported that he was at last approaching the City (Dio 53.28.1); it is in response to this news that H.'s ode is imagined as being written (3 'Caesar...repetit penates'). In the first three stanzas the poet assumes the role of a public orator addressing the Roman people (1n.): he announces the news of the approaching *princeps* (3-4), exhorts the great man's wife and sister, along with the Roman *matronae*, to turn out to greet him (5–10), and concludes his address by focussing on the youngest members of his imagined audience (10 'o pueri et puellae') and commanding them to look out for the arrival of their leader (11n.).

In the central stanza, speaking as if it were now already the day of Augustus' arrival (13 'hic dies'), H. reverts to the statement mode of 1–4; but the emphasis upon himself (13 'uere *mihi* festus', 14 '*ego* nec...metuam') implies a transition from public address to private reaction, which is then elaborated in the three final stazas. Here he begins by commanding a slave boy (17 'puer') to arrange a celebratory party (17–20) and to summon the melodious Neaera (21–4); he concludes with a wistful acknowledgement that, should Neaera fail to come, he would not regret it as much as he would have done when he was younger.

It is therefore clear that the ode consists of two sets of three stanzas arranged chiastically around a central stanza (see also Marcovich 72–4):

Public address (1–2)

Statement (1–4) → exhortation + command (5–12)

Transitional (13–16)

Private reaction (17–28)

Command + exhortation (17–24) → statement (25–8).

Although scholars have very often expressed unease about the move from public address to private reaction,[87] we as readers must simply accept that such changes of voice, context and mood are an intrinsic element of ancient poetry (e.g. Prop. 4.6); it has been argued above that the first ode of the Alcaic Hexad is an analogous example. In the present case the private reaction is particularly poignant. Although lines 17–24 look to the future, as if to illustrate the promises made in 13–16 ('eximet', 'nec... metuam'), the description of the ancient vintage (18–20) brilliantly recalls the violent past which, thanks to Augustus, H. and his fellow citizens have escaped (~ 14–16). This is a change which H. embodies in his own person, as if to guarantee the genuineness of the earlier expressions

---

[87] See the survey of opinions in Evans 215 n. 166; Fraenkel refers to it as a 'clash' (291).

of public joy. Two decades earlier his enthusiasm for the *militia amoris* had coexisted with the conflicts of the civil war, in which he had taken part at Philippi (cf. 25–8); now he is older and more relaxed about lovemaking, but at the same time he and his contemporaries are enjoying the benefits of the Augustan peace. His enthusiasm for the latter, on which the whole ode depends, is in wonderful tension with his regret at the former.

METRE Sapphic

1–4 The opening stanza is deceptively difficult. *modo* suggests a specific time, while the perfect *petiisse* requires to be seen in light of the fact that Augustus was already in Spain when he fell ill in 25 (Dio 53.25.7). The inference must be that news of his illness got back to Rome, whereupon, exactly as had happened when he fell ill in 42 BC after the battle of Philippi (Dio 48.3.1, 3), people assumed the worst and that he was dying or already dead: they are imagined as having said to one another 'he sought a triumph but it is going to [*or* has] cost him his death'. In fact, however, Aug. recovered and was now, in 24, returning to Italy victorious, a reversal of fortune which is represented by the repetition *petiisse* ~ *repetit* (for some analogous cases see Macleod 227-8; also Wills 443-51).

How does the comparison with Hercules fit into this scenario? As scholars have noted, *Herculis ritu* ('Like Hercules...') could be taken either with *petiisse* (2) or with *repetit* (3). Although Hercules risked his life when he performed his series of labours, it is perhaps unflattering to Aug. if his enforced absence from the field is compared to the hero's personal dangers. The key point of contact between Hercules and Aug. was that each travelled victorious from Spain to Italy, Hercules after killing the monster Geryon, Aug. after defeating the natives. In other words, as indicated by my punctuation of the text, *Herculis ritu* is to be taken closely with *Hispana...ab ora*, and *modo dictus...laurum* is almost concessive: 'Caesar, recently said to have sought a triumph procurable only at the cost of his death, is returning home victorious from Spain, like Hercules.' H.'s words are doubtless intended to recall an earlier association with Hercules, when, on Aug.'s return from Actium in 29 BC, his triple triumph on 13–15 August (EJ p. 50) followed the very day after the celebration of Herculus Inuictus at the Ara Maxima (Scullard 171-3): see Du Quesnay, *HH* 177-8 = *OR* 326–7. For Aug. and Hercules see further 3.3.9–10n. and, for the hero's relevance to the present ode, the interesting discussion of Ll. Morgan, *CQ* 55 (2005) 190–203 (who believes that the ambiguity of the opening stanza is deliberate and should not be removed by punctuation). For *ritu* + genit. = 'like' (again at 3.29.33-4) see *OLD ritus* 2a.

1 o plebs: the noun *plebs* strictly referred *either* to Roman citizens who were not patricians *or* (in the later republic) to those citizens below the senatorial and equestrian ranks; this seems to be the first occasion on which it is used for the whole Roman people (*TLL* 10.1.2387.17–28). The form of address is unique (Fraenkel 289 and n. 1), although H. had previously adopted the role of public speaker in 3.1 and earlier in *Epo.* 7 and 16 (see Watson, esp. on the former). The position of the vocative between *modo dictus* and *morte...laurum* seems significant: H. is addressing the very people amongst whom had spread the rumour, implied by *dictus*, that Aug. had died (see 1–4n. and 2n.).

2 morte uenalem petiisse laurum: since a laurel crown was worn by the *triumphator* (2.1.15–16; Beard 50, 246–7), *laurum* here stands for the triumph itself (metonymy); *morte* is abl. of price, as 2.16.7, although *uenalem* is of course metaphorical.

The emphasis of the line falls on *morte uenalem*, since it is the false rumour of Aug.'s dying that is corrected in the main sentence by the statement of his return; but the words *petiisse laurum* are deliberately chosen to correct a second false rumour as well. The words evoke the set phrase *triumphum petere*, used of the long-standing convention whereby a victorious general was obliged to ask the senate for permission to celebrate a triumph. The immediately preceding decade, 36–26 BC, had seen six different generals make successful requests for triumphs for their achievements in Spain (Rich 147 and n. 7), and, when Aug. travelled to Spain in 26, people no doubt assumed that he intended to add his name to this distinguished list; but they were mistaken. Although he accepted an imperial salutation for his Spanish victory (Syme, *RP* 3.1200), he took pride in refusing the triumph that was offered to him on his return (intro.), thus confounding, by his restraint, the suggestion in *petiisse laurum* that he had been seeking personal glory.[88]

3–4 Hispana...|...ab ora: the same phrase at 3.8.21 seems to indicate the northern (Atlantic) shore of Spain, but on the present campaign Aug.'s illness required convalescence at Tarraco on the Mediterranean coast (Dio 53.25.7). It was presumably from there that he returned to Italy.

4 uictor underlines the comparison to Hercules: there were two temples to Hercules Victor in Rome (Oakley on Liv. 10.23.3), in addition to the Ara Maxima Herculis Inuicti (*OCD* Hercules).

---

[88] He seems also to confound Virg. *G.* 1.504 'hominum...curare triumphos'. Cf. W. on Vell. 122.1.

5 unico gaudens mulier marito: scholars disagree both on whether *unico* means 'one and only' (*OLD* 1a) or 'singular' (*OLD* 2b) and, in either case, on whether the word would remind readers that Livia had been previously married (to Ti. Claudius Nero, father of the future emperor Tiberius). Aug. and his wife were in fact famously devoted to each other. Cunningham's *unice* has much to recommend it, although the paradosis is supported by the chiastic word grouping, which is extremely common (Naylor xv §10). For her see *BNP* 7.738–40 [2]; Barrett. For *mulier* = 'wife' see *OLD* 2.

6 prodeat: sc. to greet him. 'The entry of a great man into the city, with the welcome he receives, is a traditional topic' (T. E. V. Pearce, *CQ* 20 (1970) 314; also W. on Vell. 103–104.1: each has a wealth of illustrative material), and his actual meeting of the reception committee (ἀπάντησις) was, along with the appropriate sacrifices, an important feature (Du Quesnay, *HH* 135–7 = *OR* 279–81).[89] Some modern historians believe that Livia was by her husband's side as he convalesced at Tarraco (*CAH* 10.82; Barrett 35), but H.'s ode suggests that she remained in Rome and, as Aug.'s wife, could be expected to play a prominent part in the welcoming ceremony.

iustis operata sacris: *operatus*, though perfect in form, is present in sense and, when not used absolutely, is followed by a dative: it resembles *deditus* and means 'devoted (to)', often with reference to religious observances (*OLD* 1–2). The MSS are divided between *sacris* and *diuis*, each of which is well attested with *operatus* (for *sacris* cf. Liv. 1.31.8, Val. Max. 6.6.1, Mela 3.37, *Ciris* 142; for *deo vel sim.* cf. Tib. 2.1.9 and Maltby's n.): the former seems a significantly better accompaniment of *iustis*, which means either 'rightful, due' or 'appropriate' (*OLD* 2a, 6a). Hence the meaning is: 'devoting herself to the due/appropriate rituals'. Having been described in terms of her wifely affection (5), Livia is now described in terms of First Lady, 'Livia wife of Imp. Caesar Augustus', as she is styled on a Greek inscription of 17–12 BC (EJ 76). The point is analogous to that made in Tacitus' obituary of her: 'sanctitate domus priscum ad morem' (*A.* 5.1.3).

7 soror clari ducis: sc. *prodeat* from above. Aug.'s sister was Octavia (b. 69 BC): by her first husband she was mother of the young Marcellus, who was with Aug. in Spain (Dio 53.26.1) but would die in the second half of

---

[89] See also J. Rich, 'Consensus rituals and the origins of the principate', in *Il princeps romano* (ed. J. L. Ferrary & J. Scheid, 2015) 121–38 ('From triumph to aduentus').

23 (3.2.1–3n.); her second and last marriage was to Mark Antony (*BNP* 10.19–20 [2]; Syme, *AA* Table III). *clarus* is regularly used as an epithet with *dux*; its connotations of 'brightness' will become relevant at 13–14 below (n.).

8 supplice uitta: Roman women wore a linen head-band (*OLD uitta* 1), but *supplice* indicates rather an item worn or carried in a *supplicatio* or ritual thanksgiving (*OLD uitta* 2c, *supplicatio* b), of which there were many during the Augustan principate (*RG* 4.2 with Cooley).

9–10 uirginum matres iuuenumque nuper | sospitum: sc. *prodeant* from above (cf. 3.3.10n.). Doubts have been cast over *nuper*, on the grounds that the young men are returning home safely 'now' rather than 'recently'; but, since the *iuuenes* will have been safe since the fighting stopped in 25, why not assume that *sospitum* refers to this moment rather than, as usually supposed, to the moment of home-coming? On this assumption, the young men returning home in 24 will have been 'recently safe' since 25. It follows that *sospitum* refers only to the young men and not also, as some have thought, to the *uirgines*, who were unaffected by the war in Spain. Now that the young men are almost home, the mothers of both parties can start thinking of marriage. It has seemed odd to some scholars that no exhortation is addressed to adult males resident in Rome, such as the husbands of the *matres*; but perhaps matchmaking is seen here as principally a female responsibility: 'Roman mothers and aunts took a vigorous interest in the activity' (Horsfall on Virg. *Aen.* 11.581, q.v.). For marriage as a panegyrical topos see W. on Vell. 103.5.

10–11 uos, o pueri et puellae, | iam uirum expectate: the vocative alludes to the convention whereby 'all ages' were present at an *aduentus* (e.g. Vell. 89.1 'omnium...aetatium', on Octavian's return to Rome in 29).

Line 11 is 'probably the most vexed line in the *Odes*' (Quinn). The MSS read *iam uirum expertae*, but it is highly unlikely that, after the mention of *uirgines*, a seemingly younger group would be identified by their *non*-virginal status. Some scholars read *non* for *iam* or *expertes* for *expertae*: these are not only open to the opposite objection (they repeat a reference to virginity) but they strike a crudely blunt note (yet cf. *Epi.* 2.1.132 'castis cum pueris ignara puella mariti'). Gow proposed an entirely different approach, emending *expertae* to *expectate* and understanding *uirum* to mean 'the hero' (i.e. Aug.). The change is minimal and the use of *uir* idiomatic, as Quinn noted when accepting Gow's proposal (cf. e.g. Virg. *Aen.* 6.791–2 'hic uir, hic est, tibi quem promitti saepius audis, | Augustus

Caesar'); its only possible drawback is that it introduces a break after the sixth (rather than the fifth) syllable of the line, which does not occur elsewhere in Book 3; such a break does occur, however, in Books 1 (e.g. 25.11) and 2 (e.g. 6.11) and is common in Book 4 (e.g. 6.27 'Dauniae defende decus Camenae') and the *Carmen Saeculare* (see N–H 1.xliv). *iam* + imper. is extremely common (*TLL* 7.1.104.6ff.). See also next n.

11–12 male ominatis | parcite uerbis: if *expertae* or some other trisyllabic word is read in 11, the line will not scan unless *male ominatis* is tolerated as a hiatus. Most scholars therefore accept either the alternative reading *male nominatis*, which is said to represent the Greek δυσώνυμος, or an emendation such as Bentley's *male inominatis*, where *male* is intensive (as 1.9.24) and *inominatis* paralleled only at *Epo.* 16.38. By providing an extra syllable, however, Gow's *expectate* eliminates the troublesome hiatus, which is another argument in its favour (commended by J. Trappes-Lomax, 'Hiatus in Vergil and in Horace's *Odes*', *PCPS* 50 (2004) 156). *parcere uerbis* is a common phrase = 'refrain from speaking' (*OLD parco* 2b); *ominatus* = 'omened' does not occur elsewhere in Latin and is not recognised in *TLL*, but, if H. can produce the singular *inominatus* in the *Epodes*, he can presumably produce the equally singular *ominatus* in the *Odes*.

13 hic dies uere mihi festus: the anticipated day of Aug.'s arrival, whose exact date is not known. An inscription tells us that he was ill on 13 June 24 BC (*Inscr. Ital.* 13.1, p. 150), from which it is inferred that he was in Rome, or at least back in Italy, on that day. At any rate, this appears to be 'the latest date in Books 1–3' (Hutchinson 143). In panegyrical contexts such as this it was conventional to stress the significance of 'the day itself' (e.g. Vell. 103.4 'laetitiam illius diei...quam ille omnibus fauerit' with W.); *uere mihi* personalises the happiness and helps the transition to the upcoming party (17–24). For *festus* and festival days see also 3.8.9n., 3.28.1–2n.

13–14 atras | eximet curas: as at 4.15.18, the MSS are divided between *eximet* and *exiget*. The latter is never found with *dies* as its subject, whereas this is not the case with *eximere* (cf. Virg. *Aen.* 6.745–6, 9.447, Ov. *AA* 2.653); *curas* is the object of *exigere* = 'to banish' only at Gratt. *Cyn.* 475–6 'Liber...curas | exigit', whereas its combination with *eximere* is a little more common (*TLL* 5.2.1501.78–81). This evidence suggests that *eximet* is likelier to be the correct reading. The expr. 'black care(s)', perhaps derived from Homer's 'black pains' (*Il.* 4.117 μελαινέων...ὀδυνάων), recurs at 4.11.35–6 and is memorably personified at 3.1.38–40 (n.).

14–15 nec tumultum | nec mori per uim metuam: *metuo* + infin., a frequent construction in H., here means 'I shall not fear a violent death' (*OLD* 2f) and is thus different from 3.9.11 'pro qua non metuam mori', 'for whom I shall not be afraid to die' (*OLD* 1b). *tumultus* is a term especially associated with uprisings in Cisalpine Gaul (Cic. *Phil.* 8.3 [cf. 5.31], Tac. *A.* 3.42.3; Oakley on Liv. 7.9.6); the war in Spain also coincided with a revolt by the Salassi (Dio 53.25.2–5), who lived uncomfortably close in the Aosta valley and controlled the Alpine passes (*BA* Map 39: A2). Thus *mori per uim* evidently refers to invading hordes and being slaughtered in one's bed. The picture is deliberately exaggerated (compare 2.11.1 'Quid bellicosus Cantaber et Scythes |…cogitet Hadria | diuisus obiecto remittas | quaerere') in order to emphasise the *pax Augusta*, symbolised by the closing of the Temple of Janus in 25 (Dio 53.26.5). In fact the Cantabrians and Astures rebelled again almost as soon as Aug. left Spain (Dio 53.29.1–2), and the Alps were not finally pacified until a decade later.

15–16 tenente | Caesare terras 'holding sway over', as Virg. *Aen.* 1.139 'qui terras omnes dicione tenerent'; *OLD* 9b. For the appended abl. abs. see 3.3.17–18n.; H. likes to end a Sapphic stanza with the name 'Caesar' (1.2.52, 1.12.52, 4.2.48).

17–18 i, pete unguentum, puer, et coronas | et cadum: 'Wine, perfume, and flowers are often associated by Horace as symbols of the symposium' (N–H on 2.3.13). The address to a slave boy (cf. Dickey 253) is traditional in sympotic contexts (3.19.9–11; Watson on *Epo.* 9.33), and the instruction to him resembles the so-called 'shopping-list motif', e.g. Philodem. *Anth. Pal.* 11.35.5–6 = 28.5–6 Sider '*Boy, get us* wine *and wreaths and* sandals *and* myrrh' (Giangrande 142, N–H on 1.38, intro.).

18 cadum Marsi memorem duelli: other authors refer to the *bellum Marsicum*: both forms refer to the Social War of 91–89 BC, in which the Marsi in central Italy (3.5.9n.) took a leading role in demanding Roman citizenship. The war would have had a special resonance for H. if, as has been suggested, his father was taken prisoner at the siege of Venusia and enslaved (Intro. 2). A *cadus* (κάδος) was a storage jar for wine, and, although the term had a wide range of meanings, it was often used as a synonym for an amphora (see K. D. White, *Farm Equipment of the Roman World* (1975) 127–30), and, like an amphora, it would bear some indication of the consular year in which the wine was bottled (3.8.12n.): *memorem* thus means primarily 'commemorative of the Marsian War' (*OLD memor* 6), *duelli* being substituted for the more normal *belli* to sound an appropriately old-fashioned note (3.5.38n.); but a secondary meaning 'mindful of'

COMMENTARY 14.19–22

(*OLD memor* 1b; cf. 4), personifying the jar, is impossible to exclude (see also next n.). H. does not specify the type of wine, although there was a *uinum Marsicum* local to the region (Scrib. Larg. 57).

19–20 Spartacum si quā potuit uagantem | fallere testis: in 73–71 BC Spartacus led a famous slave revolt which started in Capua and eventually spread all over Italy: see B. D. Shaw, *Spartacus and the Slave Wars* (2001), T. Urbainczyk, *Spartacus* (2004). The MSS read *testa*, which, since it means an earthenware jar (1.20.2, 3.21.4; *OLD* 1a), 'seems repetitious after *cadum*' (N–R). *cista* ('hamper') was proposed by Nisbet to replace it; more plausible, I suggest, is *testis*, which picks up and sustains the metaphor of *memorem* (there being a natural association between witnessing and memory): 'if there is any way the witness could have escaped the notice of marauding Spartacus'. There is agreeable humour in the notion that Spartacus would have been unlikely to leave evidence of his drunken looting; and, while wars are more normally witnessed by *campi* or *flumina* (e.g. 4.4.37–8 with Thomas), a *cadus* is as good at witnessing events as is a finger-ring (cf. Ter. *Ad.* 347) or a hazel bush (Virg. *Ecl.* 5.21). H. likes to personify a whole range of objects, such as the 'devoted jar' at 3.21.4 or the 'reluctant amphora' at 3.28.8 or the autoptic statue at *S.* 1.8.44. The corruption may have arisen because *qua*, which has to scan as a long syllable and hence is abl. (*OLD quā* 9), was mistakenly interpreted as nominative, as by Williams, and a feminine noun was sought with which it might easily be seen to agree. Brink offered no reason for being attracted to the reading *Spartacum... uagacem* (Intro. to *AP*, pp. 34–5), but, despite the typically Horatian assonance of -*ac*-, it seems very bold to prefer an otherwise unattested adj. on the strength of a single quotation by the grammarian Charisius (*GL* 1.66.2K).

21 dic et argutae properet Neaerae: the name Neaera suggests youth (νέα) and 'connotes loose morals' (Lightfoot on Parthen. *Erot. Path.* 18.1); it reappears at *Epo.* 15.11 and is also that of Lygdamus' beloved (1.6 *al.*); like Chloe (3.9.10n.) and Phyllis (4.11.34–5), she evidently includes singing amongst her specialisms. *dico* + subjunc. to express an indirect command is regular (*OLD* 2c).

22 murreum nodo cohibere crinem: N–R print Muretus' *cohibente* on the grounds that H.'s 'chief point is that Neaera should come quickly, not that she should make haste to put her hair in a band'; yet not only is the abl. abs. limp in the extreme but the editors have mistaken the point. A *nodus* was a particular form of hair-styling whereby 'a segment of hair is combed forward from the middle of the crown and then back up from the hairline to form a knot above the forehead; the remainder of the hair is drawn back into a chignon' (Gibson on Ov. *AA* 3.139–40). The *nodus* style, which is famously illustrated on busts and statues of the empress Livia (see Barrett, plates 12–18), 'appears to have become something of a Roman cultural symbol, and more than half of surviving female portraits of the period display it'. H. takes it for granted that Neaera will not emerge into the street unless she is at her most fashionable; he is merely asking that she hurries up in achieving the desired look so that she can get to him as quickly as possible (for *propero* + infin. = 'to hurry to ~ ', a constr. favoured by H., cf. *OLD* 3b). He issues a very similar instruction for Lyde at 2.11.22–4, but there are textual problems. *murreus* almost certainly refers to fragrance (e.g. Prop. 1.2.3 'crines perfundere myrrha'), although *OLD*, like some commentators, prefers 'Having the colour of myrrh, i.e. reddish-brown'.

23–4 si per inuisum mora ianitorem | fiet: *mora* is a euphemistic reference to the possibility that, when the *puer* arrives at Neaera's abode with the poet's summons, she may be entertaining another man and needs the doorkeeper to be obstructive until she has finished (*per* = 'through the agency of': *OLD* 15a): hence *inuisum*, which otherwise is simply a trite allusion to the conventional uncooperativeness of doorkeepers (see e.g. McKeown on Ov. *Am.* 1.6).

24 abito looks back to the imperative with which the address to the *puer* began (17). When future imperative forms are used, it is often in conjunction with a conditional clause, as here (see *OLS* 1.517–18).

25–8 Although H. is hoping to round off his party (17–20) with some vigorous lovemaking (26), his advancing years mean that, if his message to Neaera fails to reach her (23–4), he will not take it too badly (25), as he would have done twenty years ago in his youth (27–8). The middle-aged self-reference is characteristically Horatian, and the closural diminuendo is akin to the techniques mentioned at 3.20.13–14n. (see also Schrijvers, *OR* 64–5).

25 albescens...capillus: H. was born on 8 December 65 BC; if we assume that Aug. returned from Spain in early or mid-24, the poet was in his forty-first year at the dramatic date of the ode. *canities* is a frequent metonymy for old age (*OLD* 2c), but at *Epi.* 1.20.24 H. actually describes himself as 'praecanus'. Here the reference to hair perhaps has extra point in the context of the erotic *proelia* mentioned in line 26: in the *militia amoris* (3.26.2n.) 'attacks on the hair are a standard feature' (McKeown on Ov.

Am. 1.7.11–12); for cases where a girl attacks the man's hair cf. Prop. 3.8.5, 3.15.13, 4.8.61. For H. such 'battles' are now largely a thing of the past. *capillus,* generally the most prosaic of the words for 'hair', is used more frequently by H. (18×) than *coma* (11×) or *crinis* (12×), although he uses all three more or less indifferently in Book 3 (3:3:2); here *capillus* (collective sing.) varies *crinis,* used of the girl in 22. For statistics in various authors see *TLL* 3.314.25–49. H. uses the almost exclusively poetic *caesaries* only at 1.15.14. *animos* = 'feelings' (*OLD* 10b).

26 litium et rixae cupidos proteruae 'desirous of reckless/shameless disputes and quarrelling'. *rixae* is the *mot juste* for bedroom battles (1.13.9–11 with N–H, 3.21.3; Pichon 254) and *proteruus* very often has erotic connotations (as 3.11.11–12); the adj. here applies also to *litium,* which is again used of lovers' fights at Prop. 4.5.40 (where some edd. prefer Heinsius' *dentibus*).

27–8 non ego hoc ferrem calidus iuuenta | consule Planco: these words probably mean '<but> I would not have tolerated this as a hot-headed young man in the consulship of Plancus' (for this use of the imperf. potential subjunc. to refer to the past see *NLS* 91–2 §121); but some scholars prefer an elliptical conditional sentence, '<but> I would not be tolerating this if I were a hot-headed young man and Plancus were consul [*or perhaps* as I was in the consulship of Plancus]'. *hoc* refers to the obstructiveness mentioned at 23–4 above.

28 consule Planco: 42 BC: 'few of Horace's contemporaries were likely to have forgotten the year of the battle of Philippi' (Fraenkel 290); they will perhaps also have remembered that that was another occasion on which one of Aug.'s illnesses was thought falsely to have denoted his death (ring composition with 1–4, where see n.). L. Munatius Plancus, the addressee of 1.7 (see J. L. Moles, *JRS* 92 (2002) 86–109), is an archetypal example of the many who, like H. himself, became reconciled to Aug.

15

This short ode tells the story of a family: the husband is Ibycus (1), his wife is Chloris (8), and their daughter is Pholoe (7), who is in love with young Nothus (11). Chloris should put an end to her notorious promiscuity (2–3), since she is now too old for such behaviour (4–6), which would be more appropriate in Pholoe (7–10), who has the excuse of her love for Nothus (11–12). Chloris should take up working with wool, now that her time as a party girl has passed (13–16).

Women had been denigrated by poets since the early days of Greek poetry: a now famous example is the 'First Cologne Epode' of Archilochus (196a.24–38).[90] The denigration features in a variety of genres and has been much studied by modern scholars (see e.g. Henriksén on Mart. 9.37, Watson and Watson, Intro. to Juv. 6, pp. 26–35, each with numerous further refs.). H. included two notorious examples in his *Epodes* (8 and 12: see Watson's comm.), where the detailed description of the women's decrepitude assigns these poems to the category to which German scholars have given the name of '*Vetula*-Skoptik' or 'Mockery of an old woman' (σκώπτειν means 'to mock'). Although such detail is absent from the enigmatic ode 1.25 (on which see N–H and Mayer), it recurs in a modified form in 4.13, which features a woman of the same name as that in 3.10. While acknowledging that our ode 'may seem rather a savage poem', Lyne sees in the contrast between Chloris and her daughter an illustration of Horace's belief – 'a belief which he shares with a wide range of thinkers, including conventional Roman thinkers' – that 'There is a time in life when love is appropriate and there is a time in life when it is not. Love is the province of youth. It ends (or should end) with age' (*LLP* 204–5; see further C. C. Esler, 'Horace's old girls: evolution of a topos', in T. M. Falkner and J. de Luce (edd.), *Old Age in Greek and Latin Literature* (1989) 172–82).

The ode is constructed on a 'ring' basis, the four central lines (7–10) framed by the first and last six: address (1 *Uxor* ~ 13 *te*), reference to old age (4 *maturo propior...funeri* ~ 16 *uetulam*), four activities (2 *nequitiae*, 3 *laboribus*, 5 *ludere*, 6 *spargere* ~ 13 *lanae*, 14 *citharae*, 15 *flos*, 16 *cadi*). The central panel serves to introduce the daughter with whom Chloris will be contrasted in 11–16 (*illam...te...*).

METRE   Fourth Asclepiad

1 Vxor pauperis Ibyci: the address ('Wife of impoverished Ibycus') is humorously formulated, the point being that Chloris' husband shares a name with the well-known sixth-century Greek lyric poet who allegedly lived in luxury (Ar. *Thesm.* 161–3). Though *uxor* is the regular word for 'wife' (P. A. Watson (1985) 431–2), its use with the genit. to address someone else's wife seems unusual (Dickey 362), but it underlines the adulterous nature of Chloris' liaisons, adding to her culpability (cf. 3.6.25–32).

2–3 tandem nequitiae fige modum tuae | famosisque laboribus: *nequitia* is sexual promiscuity and the like (cf. 3.4.78–9); it would be nice

---

[90] See L. Swift, *Archilochus: The Poems* (2019) 364–84.

COMMENTARY 15.4-8 249

to think that *labor* was a euphemism like the modern 'working girl', but there seems to be no exact parallel (cf. Adams 157). *fige modum* ('put an end to ~ ') is exceptionally rare in classical Latin, paralleled only at Cic. *Parad. Stoic.* 3.25 as emended by Lambinus (the MSS have *fingere*). Since the verb is frequently used of posting up a notice on a wall for public information (*OLD* 3), is H. inviting a comparison between Chloris and a prostitute, who would post a *titulus*, advertising her rates and specialities, at the door to her *cella* (Sen. *Contr.* 1.2.5, 7, Petron. 7.3, Mart. 11.45.1, Juv. 6.123, *Hist. Ap. Reg. Tyr.* 33)? This would give point both to *famosis* and to the description of her husband as poor (cf. T. A. J. McGinn, *The Economy of Prostitution in the Roman World* (2004) 57). For imputations of prostitution in misogynistic poetry see e.g. Juv. 6.114-32 and the Watsons' nn. (and also p. 318 Index). H. would be implying that Chloris should now advertise her retirement instead. For *modus* as equivalent to *finis* see N-H on 1.16.2. *tandem* ('after all this time...') + imper., an Horatian idiom (1.23.11, 2.9.17-18, *Epo.* 17.6), contributes to the notion of Chloris' being too old.

4 maturo propior...funeri: *maturus*, a word of many meanings, here = 'occurring at the proper time' (*OLD* 7): cf. Stat. *Silv.* 3.3.136-7 'qui funera patris | haud matura putas' (Ar. *Wasps* 1365 ὡραίας σοροῦ). It was a convention in this type of poetry to mention the woman's proximity to death (Mankin and Watson on *Epo.* 8.12, adding e.g. *Anth. Pal.* 11.71); the compar. perhaps implies 'now closer to death than you once were'.

5 inter ludere uirgines: *uirgines* 'here means simply "young (as opposed to old) women"' (P. A. Watson (1983) 127). Some think that *ludere* refers to choral dancing, which seems quite out of place. The verb can be used of a wide range of provocative or sexual activity (*OLD* 4; Adams 162-3): here 'to be promiscuous', as Ov. *Am.* 1.8.43-4 (see McKeown), would make good sense: Chloe's general behaviour, inappropriate in a woman of her age, diverts attention from the attractive young women (6). The verb's position between *inter* and *uirgines* is mimetic. Cf. 4.13.2-4 'fis anus et tamen...ludis'.

6 candidis: the adj. is regular of young women (*OLD* 5a), e.g. Cat. 13.4.

7-8 non, si quid Pholoen satis, | et te, Chlori, decet 'Whatever <befits> Pholoe well enough does not befit you too, Chloris': *si quid* lit. = 'if something'; for *satis* cf. *OLD* 9a. For the notion of appropriateness being dictated by one's age see esp. *Epi.* 1.14.36 'nec lusisse pudet, sed non incidere ludum', Plaut. *Merc.* 984, Cic. *Off.* 1.123, Philodem. 5.5-6 (Sider); also

above (intro.). The two names are likewise juxtaposed at 2.5.17–18.
Pholoe is the name of a mountain in the Peloponnese (*BA* Map 58: B2);
Chloris derives from the Greek χλωρός ('green'): if intended to suggest
freshness, it is presumably ironical, although 'greenness attends various
medical conditions in the Hippocratic corpus' (Budelmann on Sappho
31.14–15).

8–9 filia rectius | expugnat iuuenum domos: the inference from 7–8
seems to be that Pholoe is Chloris' daughter: 'your daughter more prop-
erly storms the homes of young men'. The traditional storming of the
beloved's house (cf. 3.26.6–8nn.) is performed by each of the women
(cf. Plaut. *Mil.* 1249–50, Sen. *NQ* 4A *praef.* 6; Gibson on Ov. *AA* 3.69–70),
thereby illustrating ironically the convention that children should resemble their parents (3.6.33–4n.), but, whereas in Chloris' case *iuuenum* is a
genuine plural (indicating her desperation), in Pholoe's case it is a rhetorical plural and refers only to Nothus, as will be explained in 11–12.
expugnare is regularly used metaphorically (*S.* 1.9.55; *OLD* 1c): this seems
to be the only ex. with *domos* (-*um*), but cf. Ter. *Eun.* 773 'aedes expug-
nabo...uirginem eripiam'.

10 pulso Thyias uti concita tympano 'like a Bacchante roused by the
beating of a drum' (another ex. of the *ab urbe condita* idiom: see 3.4.18–
19n.). *Thyias* (*Thyi-* is scanned as one long syllable) is variously etymolo-
gised (Maltby 610), including a derivation from θυίειν, 'to rush' (N–H on
2.19.9). For the music accompanying a serenade see 3.7.29–30n.

11 amor Nothi 'her love for Nothus.' The name, which means 'bastard'
or 'spurious', is attested on inscriptions. 'Though "bastard" was not a regular term of abuse in antiquity, it may hint at a background which is not
quite respectable' (N–R).

12 lasciuae...capreae: it is goats (*caprae*), not roe-deer (*capreae*), which
are proverbially lustful (3.13.8n.); H. seems to have used the latter term
for the former. A similar usage occurs at Virg. *Aen.* 10.725 'capream aut...
ceruum', where the allusion to Hom. *Il.* 3.24 makes it almost certain that
Virgil means 'goat or...stag'. Isidore implies that both animals could be
called by the same name (*Orig.* 12.1.15–16 'idem autem et capreae'; cf.
Varro, *LL* 5.101 'caprea a similitudine quadam caprae'). See also W. on
Tac. *A.* 4.67.1.

ludere here refers to behaviour which will attract and retain Nothus'
interest.

COMMENTARY 16   251

13–14 te lanae prope nobilem | tonsae Luceriam: the verb is *decent*, to be supplied from the end of 14, and with *te* we have to supply *uetulam* from the last line of the ode, a remarkable and emphatic hyperbaton. *lanae... tonsae* is not a further ex. of the *ab urbe condita* idiom, as in line 10, but means 'wool shorn near famous Luceria': the wool has to be shorn from the sheep before it can be worked by *lanificae*. For a woman's transition from love to working with wool in old age see Tib. 1.6.77–80, *Anth. Pal.* 6.283; since wool-working was taxing (Juv. 6.289 'labor' with Courtney), the implication is that Chloris should replace her *famosi labores* (3) by virtuous *labor* (for which see 3.12.5–6n.). Luceria (mod. Lucera) was a town in Apulia (*BA* Map 45: B1), a region famous (*nobilem*) for its wool (Strabo 6.3.9, Plin. *NH* 8.190, Mart. 14.155.1–2 and Leary's n.).

14 non citharae decent: lyre-playing was an expected accomplishment of young women, esp. *meretrices* (3.9.10n.).

15 nec flos purpureus rosae: sc. *te decet*. The rose was sacred to Venus (Galán Vioque on Mart. 7.89.3–4) and symbolises partying (cf. e.g. 1.36.15 with N–H, 3.19.22); the circumlocution with *flos* or *flores* is a Horatian favourite (again at 2.3.14, 3.29.3, 4.10.4): cf. the very similar expr. at Archil. 30 ῥοδῆς τε καλὸν ἄνθος, where ῥοδῆς is alleged to mean 'rose-bush'. *purpureus* can be applied specifically to roses (e.g. *Culex* 399, *Copa* 14) but is also a common adj. with *flos*, esp. in Virgil.

16 nec poti...faece tenus cadi: 'nor do jars drunk down to the dregs <befit you>'; the application of *potus* to the vessel rather than to the liquid seems unique in classical Latin (*TLL* 10.2.365.4–5): even if *cadi* is not to be taken literally, the term suggests a large receptacle and undiluted wine (3.14.18n.); *faece tenus* adds to the picture of excess (cf. Sen. *Ep.* 58.32 'ille ultra modum deditus uino est qui amphoram exsiccet et faecem quoque exsorbet'). Since drinking was traditionally discouraged in women on the grounds that it led to lecherous behaviour (3.12.2–3n.), hypersexed older women were conventionally accused of excessive drinking (e.g. 4.13.2–6). H. in the *Odes* is generally sparing with diminutives (Bo 3.216–19): here *uetulam* is dismissive.

16

At the start of the second half of the book H. addresses an ode to Maecenas and refers to his patron's distinguished equestrian status (20), exactly as he had done in the corresponding ode in Book 1 (20.5 'clare Maecenas eques'). Given the central position of each, both odes serve to reinforce the dedication of all three books of *carmina* to Maecenas, but, whereas 1.20 is an invitation poem, the present ode expresses gratitude for Maecenas' generosity (Du Quesnay (1981) 98–101), although this does not become clear for some time. The ode is structured in three parts, two outer sections of identical length (1–16 ~ 29–44) framing a pivotal section (17–28) which contains not only the address to Maecenas but also, in the exact centre of the ode (21–2), a moralising *sententia* (Moritz 118–19).

In 1–16 H. demonstrates the corrupting power of gold by means of four examples of bribery, two of them mythological (1–13a Danae, Eriphyle), two historical (13b–15 Philip II, Caesar's pirates), and in all cases except the third the result was the death of the bribees and/or of someone close to them. These four stanzas thus illustrate, in an extreme fashion, the dangers associated with a desire for gold, an illustration which allows H. to begin the central section of the ode with the statement that trouble always follows the desire for gain (17–18); by contrast, the more one denies to oneself, the greater the rewards that one will receive from the gods (21–2): H. himself is more content with his modest circumstances than if he possessed great wealth (25–8). This contentment is elaborated in the final section of the ode (29–44). H.'s estate is lovingly described – first in positive terms (29–32), then by negation (33–6), and lastly by counter-factuals (39–42). The praise of his benefactor with which the description is punctuated (37–8) and concluded (42–4) is respectively explicit and implicit, repeating H.'s satisfaction at what Maecenas has given him (38–9 *plura...deneges...cupidine* ~ 21–2 *plura negauerit...plura...cupientium*). The final section as a whole constitutes a deft and diplomatic statement of personal gratitude in the public context of Book 3, *quod satis est* in the last line (44) echoing *quod satis est* in the ode which began the first half of the book (3.1.25).

It is suggestive that the last section of the ode is so very different from the first, where the illustrations of the power of gold evidently act as an extended foil for the poem as a whole. The arresting opening (1) introduces an excursion into myth (1–13), and all four stanzas are characterised by allusive naming (11–12, 14, 15–16), grandiose phraseology (2–3), humour (5–8), and vivid metaphor (9–10, 15–16). The pivotal central section, where Maecenas is addressed for the first time (20), alternates *sententiae* (17–18, 21–2) and personal statements (18–19, 22–4), as the poet addresses the question of the proper attitude to wealth. Finally, in the last section, we are given details of the relationship between H. and his patron, who is obliquely accorded divine status in the gnomic conclusion to the poem (42–4). Almost every one of these features can be paralleled in the odes of Pindar, and, although there seem to be few (if any) verbal

COMMENTARY 16.1-8   253

parallels between our poem and the Pindaric corpus, it is worth asking
whether H. was working to a Pindaric template.

METRE Second Asclepiad

1-8 The two opening stanzas are almost a parody of a situation commonly found in love elegy. All the key elements are present: a desired
woman (1) is kept from would-be lovers (4) by a *custos* (6); but Venus is
on the side of love (6) and the *custos* may be bribable (8). See McKeown
on Ov. *Am.* 2.2, Gibson on Ov. *AA* 3.611-58, 651-2. The key differences
are that Danae is a virgin (5), the would-be lover is Jupiter (6), and it is
the woman, not the *custos*, who is bribed (8).

1 Inclusam Danaen turris aënea: Danae was the daughter of Acrisius
(5), king of Argos and grandson of Hypermnestra and Lynceus (3.11.51-
2n.). Terrified (6 *pauidum*) by an oracular prophecy that he would be
killed by a grandson, he confined his daughter to prevent her from coming into contact with potential suitors (*inclusam* = 'imprisoned': *OLD
includo* 2). In some accounts she is confined in an underground chamber,
but H. prefers a tower and is perhaps the first author to do so. Doubtless
his preference would catch the attention of the poem's addressee, whose
house was famously equipped with a *turris* (3.29.10n.). See further Ov.
Am. 2.19.27 'si numquam Danaen habuisset aenea turris' and McKeown's
nn., 3.8.29-34 (quoted below, 8n.), *AA* 3.415-16, 631-2 and Gibson's
nn.; also above, *C.* 3.3.65n.

2 robustae: 'oaken' seems a commoner meaning than 'strong' (*OLD* 1,
5a) and is a better match for *aenea*; but both make sense here. In lines 2-4
each adj. is followed by its noun, whereas in 1 the arrangement is chiastic.

2-3 uigilum canum | tristes excubiae 'the grim vigils of watchful dogs', an
elevated periphrasis of the type familiar in epic (3.12.8n.); for *uigilum...
excubiae* cf. Virg. *Aen.* 9.159 'uigilum excubiis'. Dogs are a conventional
feature of love poetry, since their bark signals the approach of an illicit
lover (McKeown on Ov. *Am.* 2.19.39-40, Ingleheart on Ov. *Tr.* 2.459-60);
but here *tristes*, suggesting the fierceness of wild animals (*OLD* 5e), indicates that Acrisius' dogs are intended as practical deterrents too.

3-4 munierant satis | nocturnis ab adulteris: since the verb in the pro-
tasis is pluperfect subjunc. (7), this is a so-called 'mixed' condition (N-H
on 2.17.28; *NLS* 157 §200 (iii)): '...had satisfactorily defended <and
would have continued to do so>..., had not...'. *satis* indicates that Danae's

protection consisted exclusively of the fortified tower and the dogs (1–3a) and that this combination would have been a perfectly adequate defence against the human suitors whom Acrisius anticipated; but he reckoned without the intervention of Jupiter and Venus, thereby misjudging the situation, as his name suggests (5–7n.). The construction of *munio* with *ab* is relatively uncommon (cf. *OLD* 2a). *adulter* can be used of any illicit lover (*OLD adulter*¹), but Jupiter (6–8) was of course a married divinity; for *nocturnis* cf. Juv. 8.144.

5–7 si non Acrisium...Iuppiter et Venus | risissent   'had not Jupiter and Venus made a mockery of...Acrisius' (*OLD rideo* 6a); for their conventional laughter see 3.27.67n. and 3.29.31–2n. In Danae's case it is her father who is her *custos*, and his guardianship is aimed at protecting not her but himself (1n.); yet his very name symbolises his tragedy (ἀκρισία = 'misjudgement') and in due course he would be killed, albeit accidentally, by Perseus, the offspring of Danae's intercourse with Zeus/Jupiter (Apollod. 2.4.4). For *uirginis...custodem* cf. Virg. *Aen.* 7.791; *custodem... uirgini* is at Acc. 386R.

7 fore enim tutum iter et patens: *sciebant* or *inter se dicebant* or similar has to be understood from the context. *tutum* looks back to the menacing dogs (2–3), *patens* to the tower and doors (1–2): *patens* is used of gates etc. standing open and of clear, unimpeded routes (*OLD patens* 1, 2a).

8 conuerso in pretium deo: if H. had written *in aurum*, he would have been following the usual version of the story, according to which 'Zeus, having changed into gold and streamed through the roof into Danae's lap, had intercourse with her' (Apollod. 2.4.1); but *in pretium*, a noun regularly used of paying for sex (*TLL* 10.2.1209.8–25; NA on Lygd. 1.7), suggests a rationalised version: Jupiter metamorphosed into a bribe, presumably of gold coins, with which Danae was persuaded to admit him to her presence. Amusingly left to the reader's imagination are the details of how this might have been accomplished: the king of gods and men will have had to establish contact with Danae, presumably by shouting up to her through a window, showing her his gold, and promising her that it would all be hers if only she would open the door and keep the dogs off.[91] Cf. Ov. *Am.* 3.8.29–34 'Iuppiter, admonitus nihil esse potentius auro, | corruptae *pretium* uirginis ipse fuit. | dum merces aberat, durus

---

[91] *pretium*, like *aurum* in 9, is a kind of metonymy = 'a man with payment' (cf. *Anth. Pal.* 5.31.5–6 'I think that Zeus came to Danae not as gold but carrying a hundred gold pieces').

pater, ipsa seuera, | aerati postes, ferrea turris erat; | sed postquam sapiens
in munere uenit adulter, | praebuit ipsa sinus et dare iussa dedit'. *deo* may
be dat., but the appended position of the phrase suggests rather an abl.
abs. (3.1.30–1n.).

9–16 In these stanzas two statements of the persuasiveness of gold –
one generalised (9–11a) and one specific (13b–15a) – alternate with two
examples of its fatal effect on those who profit from bribery (11b–13a,
15b–16).

9–11 aurum per medios ire satellites | et perrumpere amat saxa potentius | ictu fulmineo 'Gold loves to make a way through the middle of
bodyguards and to burst through stone more effectively/powerfully than
a lightning-bolt' (*OLD amo* 12). The paradoxical ability of gold to break
through physical obstacles is proverbial (Otto 50), while the corruptibility of doorkeepers and other bodyguards is likewise conventional
(*S.* 1.9.57, Juv. 3.184 and Courtney). The sentence is a generalisation,
but *ictu fulmineo* looks forward to the case of Amphiaraus (11–13n.). A
verb of motion + *per medios* is a regular form of expression for passing
through the middle of a group of people (often enemies, e.g. Val. Fl.
1.438 'medios...ire per hostes'); *fulmineo*, as at Ov. *Met.* 14.618, is more
elevated than the genit. *fulminis* (3.3.26–8n.). For *perrumpere...saxa* cf.
Vitr. 8.6.9.

11–13 concidit auguris | Argiui domus ob lucrum | demersa exitio: this
story, which has similar elements to the story of Danae, follows 9–11a
in adversative asyndeton: '<but> the house of the Argive seer collapsed,
plunging to destruction on account of gain'. Eriphyle, the wife of the
Argive seer Amphiaraus, was bribed by a golden necklace to persuade
her husband to take part in the expedition of the Seven against Thebes;
her persuasion was successful, even though, with his gift of foresight,
Amphiaraus knew that he would die. When his attack on Thebes was
driven off and he fled, he was swallowed up in a chasm made by Zeus's
lightning bolt (Apollod. 3.6.8). Eriphyle was slain by their son to avenge
his father's death. *concido* is regular to describe the collapse of physical
buildings (*OLD* 2), but here *domus* is metaphorical = 'family' (so too e.g.
Cic. *Div.* 1.121 'domum funditus concidisse'). *demersa* (*OLD* 1d) alludes
to the manner of Amphiaraus' death (cf. Eur. *Suppl.* 926 'into the recesses
of the earth', Diod. 4.65.8 'falling into the chasm'), *exitio* being dat. of
direction (3.23.1n.), as Sen. *Ag.* 523 'mitti...exitio'; Housman prefers abl.
(3.916), but it is difficult to explain. *ob lucrum* is felt with *concidit* as well
as with *demersa*.

13–15 diffidit urbium | portas uir Macedo…muneribus 'The man from Macedon split open the gates of cities…with bribes': *uir Macedo* translates Μακεδὼν ἀνήρ, Demosthenes' well known phrase (*Phil.* 1.10; cf. [Long.] *Subl.* 18.1) for Philip II (father of Alexander the Great), who in 348 BC captured Olynthus by bribing Lasthenes and Euthycrates, two of its leading citizens (Juv. 12.47 with Mayor's n.); he was famous for his view that any fortress could be stormed by gold (Cic. *Att.* 1.16.12, Plut. *Mor.* 178B), while the two bribees became proverbial for treachery (cf. Demosth. *Fals. leg.* 342). Being a member of the Argead dynasty, Philip has an Argive link to both Amphiaraus and Acrisius. For the proverbial power of *munera* see Otto 233, Tosi 609 §1353.

14–15 aemulos | reges: since the same expr., used of two rivals of Alexander the Great, appears in Justin (12.1.5), it may have been used by the historian Pompeius Trogus, H.'s contemporary, whom Justin epitomised.

15–16 munera nauium | saeuos illaqueant duces '<but> bribes ensnare the savage captains of ships' (adversative asyndeton again); for another ex. of polyptoton used to link sentences see 3.1.21 (n.). The episode is unidentified, but I suggest that H. is referring to the well-known story of the young Julius Caesar, who, when captured by pirates, bribed them to release him and, once released, returned with a strong force and killed them (Plut. *Caes.* 1.8–2.7 with Pelling's nn.): they were thus hoist with their own petard. *illaqueo* is exceptionally rare in classical Latin: used metaphorically it is found earlier in Pacuv. 210R and Cic. *Har. Resp.* 7; in its literal sense it is not found until Amm. 20.11.15 (*TLL*).

17 crescentem sequitur cura pecuniam: the relationship between wealth and anxiety was a commonplace of popular philosophy (Tosi 805 §1801, Oltramare 267) and treated memorably at 3.1.38–40 (n.). *sequitur* may suggest pursuit (cf. *S.* 2.7.114–15 'comes atra [i.e. *cura*] premit sequiturque fugacem'; also Lucr. 2.48 'curaeque sequaces' with Fowler's n.), but the coordination of *cura* with *fames* indicates that H. is perhaps thinking rather in medical metaphors (18n.): *sequi* is exceptionally frequent to describe the onset of symptoms etc. in Celsus (e.g. 4.11.3 'saepe quidem euenit ut sanguinem pus sequatur'), for whom *crescere* too is a regular verb (e.g. 3.18.7 'continuata quoque febris…non tamen crescit'). *pecunia* (again at 3.24.61) is largely prosaic (Axelson 108).

18 maiorumque fames 'and the hunger for more': *maiorum* is neut. (cf. *Epi.* 1.10.32 'fuge magna'), a unique ex. of the gender of *maiora* not being

COMMENTARY 16.18-22

clarified by the context or in some other way (*TLL* 8.147.27). Line 17 implies that *maiora* refers to riches and to the paradox *crescit amor nummi quantum ipsa pecunia creuit* (Juv. 14.139; cf. Theocr. 16.64, Ov. *F.* 1.211; Tosi 808 §1809); but, since the noun does not exclude more general advancement, it also prepares the way for the next sentence (18–19n.). Hunger is a common analogy for avarice, most memorably in Virgil's 'accursed hunger for gold' (*Aen.* 3.57 'auri sacra fames'; cf. Tosi 809 §1810); H. perhaps has in mind a correspondence such as that found in Plutarch, who compares the avaricious man to one who eats but is never filled and consults a physician on how to rid himself of his affliction (*Cup. Div.* 524A–D).

18–19 iure perhorrui | late conspicuum tollere uerticem: the disadvantages of wealth, just outlined in 17–18a, lead us to expect 'it is with good reason that I have recoiled from accumulating wealth'; instead, however, H. says 'it is with good reason that I have recoiled from lifting my head so that it be visible far and wide' (*late conspicuum* is proleptic). H. has substituted a statement about social status for one about financial resources, it being proverbial that 'money is the man' (*S.* 1.1.62; Tosi 797–8 §1784); his substitution allows him to draw a parallel between his own position and that of his patron, since Maecenas, though extremely wealthy, was famous for recoiling from *political* recognition (below, 20n.). H.'s reference to height (for *tollere uerticem* in this sense cf. 1.18.15) suggests the proverbial difficulty of living one's life in an elevated position (Sall. *C.* 51.12 'qui...in excelso aetatem agunt, eorum facta cuncti mortales nouere', with Vretska's parallels). His rejection of elevation suggests allegiance to the Epicurean doctrine of keeping a low profile (λάθε βιώσας), one of his constant themes (e.g. *Epi.* 1.18.103). *perhorresco* + inf. seems paralleled only at Val. Max. 6.3.2 (cf. *TLL* 10.1.1444.67–70); *late conspicuum* renders a Greek compound adj. such as τηλεφανής or τηλέσκοπος.

20 Maecenas, equitum decus: the reference to Maecenas as an *eques* is pointed, since he was famous for not seeking political advancement but remaining within the *equester ordo* (ps.-Acro ad loc. 'nec uoluit transire in ordinem senatorium'): cf. 3.8.17n., *S.* 1.6.97–8, Prop. 3.9.2 'intra fortunam qui cupis esse tuam', Vell. 88.2 'angusto clauo...contentus', Tac. *A.* 3.30.2 'Maecenatem aemulatus sine dignitate senatoria', Dio 55.7.4. *decus* is used again of Maecenas at 1.1.2, 2.17.4, *Eleg. Maec.* 1.18.

21–2 quanto quisque sibi plura negauerit, | ab dis plura feret: in the main clause *tanto* is to be supplied with *plura*, which refers to spiritual benefits, in contrast to the material benefits of 21; *feret* = 'get, acquire' (*OLD* 36). The wording is recalled and varied at 38 below.

22–4 nil cupientium | nudus castra peto et transfuga diuitum | partes linquere gestio: it is important to recognise that this statement is the result of that expressed in 21–2: the logic is 'Since one's rewards from the gods are in direct proportion to one's degree of self-denial, I'd better leave the party of the rich and make for the camp of those who desire nothing'. This paraphrase ought to make it clear that lines 22–4 are an illustration of H.'s famous irony: he was never one of the rich,[92] and, as the remainder of the ode amply attests, he is already supremely contented with Maecenas' generosity and desires nothing more.

Military metaphors of various types are extremely common to express the sentiments of popular philosophy (e.g. Sen. *Ep.* 51.6; Oltramare 56 n. 4, 280–1, Rutherford 240–1); for metaphorical *transfuga* cf. e.g. Sen. *Ep.* 2.5 (and for *castra* see further *TLL* 3.563.31ff.). *nudus* here is taken to mean 'destitute' in *OLD* (10a), but H. explicitly says that he is not destitute (37 'importuna...pauperies abest'); the metaphorical context suggests rather 'unarmed' (*OLD* 4a). For *partes*, used of Maecenas himself at Prop. 3.9.60 'ferar in partes ipse fuisse tuas', see *OLD* 16a. Since one cannot join the opposition camp until one has left one's own, the lines exemplify *hysteron proteron*.

25–7 contemptae dominus splendidior rei | quam si quidquid arat impiger Apulus | occultare meis dicerer horreis '...being more illustrious as a master of scorned means than if I were reputed to store in my own granaries everything that an energetic Apulian ploughs'. Normally an unreal comparative clause ('quam si') follows the sequence of tenses, as at 40–2 below ('porrig<u>am</u>...quam si...continu<u>em</u>') and 3.28.6 (n.), but here we have the imperfect subjunctive, which is used only when 'it is particularly desired to stress the unreality' (*NLS* 210 §255). *rei* refers to property or wealth (*OLD* 1a): scholars debate whether it is scorned (*contemptae*) by others, contemptuous of its modesty (cf. Cic. *Parad. Stoic.* 6.47 'meam... pecuniam contemnis'), or by H. himself: being a master of property which one has rejected perhaps qualifies as a typically Horatian surrealism, but we know that people criticised H. for being a friend of Maecenas (*S.* 1.6.46–7) and criticism would balance *dicerer* in the comparative clause (27). Either way, the enjambed phrase is the converse of that at 28 below (n.). Since *splendidus* is almost technical of distinguished

---

[92] Obviously we are talking in relative terms: in comparison with most people H. was well off, but not when compared with the *really* rich, like Maecenas. Some scholars (e.g. Lyne, *Hor.* 124–6) think that *diuitum* is a reference to Maecenas (cf. 3.29.13), but it is inconceivable that, in an ode which is an expression of gratitude to his patron, H. should express a longing to abandon him.

equestrians such as Maecenas (W. on Vell. 88.2), the adj. provides a further link between poet and patron.

Elsewhere *occultare* means 'to conceal' and not 'to store', which is nevertheless the meaning required here; evidently H. is using the word on the analogy of *condere*, which has both meanings (cf. 1.1.9–10 'si proprio condidit horreo | quidquid de Libycis uerritur areis', where see N–H for the symbolism of granaries). *arat* is almost equally odd, since *quidquid*, its object, refers not to the land which is ploughed but to the crops which grow as a result of the ploughing (cf. Sen. *Clem.* 1.6.1 'consumitur quidquid terris omnibus aratur'). For the artificial lengthening *arāt* at this point in an asclepiad line cf. 1.13.6 (N–H 1.xxxix, Brink (1982) 31, 33). In a long letter on the simple life, Seneca appears to allude to our passage (*Ep.* 87.7). For the fertility of Apulia cf. Varro, *RR* 1.2.6, 1.57.3, Strabo 6.3.9; H. again refers to his fellow Apulians as typically vigorous at *Epo.* 2.42.

28 magnas inter opes inops: the point of this enjambed phrase is that, if H. were surrounded by wealth, he would be spiritually poor: this is the converse of 25, where he is wealthy (*dominus*) despite means which are scorned (*contemptae*). Philosophical reflections on riches and poverty lent themselves to paradox (e.g. Sen. *Ep.* 74.4 'in diuitiis inopes'; Otto 51); plays on *inops ~ opes* and the like are very common (e.g. Sall. *J.* 14.7 'inops alienas opes expecto', Tac. *Agr.* 30.4 'opes atque inopiam'), and for the type of oxymoron which arises 'from the combination of a noun and a contrary adjective', e.g. *Epi.* 1.12.19 'concordia discors', see Wills 455.

29–32 This is an extremely awkward sentence. The subjects of the verb, *fallit*, are the three nouns *riuus*, *silua* and *fides*; with *beatior*, which agrees with each of those subjects, we have to understand the participle 'being' (which of course does not exist in Latin). The question is how the understood participle is to be construed. Commentators explain the use of *fallo* as analogous to λανθάνω + participle in Greek (*OLD* 6a); it recurs at *Epo.* 3.7, 5.67–8, *Epi.* 1.17.10 and is a favourite of Livy, who uses it as early as 2.19.7 (see Oakley on 8.20.5). Thus: 'A river of pure water and a wood of a few acres...escape the notice of X *in being* a more enriching destiny/lot'. However, it may be simpler to understand the entire sequence as an example of the *ab urbe condita* idiom (3.4.18–19n.) but featuring a nominative present participle and to translate as 'the fact that...' (3.21.23–4n.). Thus: '*The fact that* a river of pure water and a wood of a few acres...*are* a more enriching destiny/lot escapes the notice of X'. See also next nn.

29 purae riuus aquae: presumably the Digentia (*Epi.* 1.18.104), mod. Licenza. In the unfolding description of his estate, which recalls that at

S. 2.6.2-3 'iugis aquae fons | et paulum siluae', H. varies the positioning of nominatives and genitives and of adjs. and nouns.

29-30 iugerum | paucorum: it is striking that a few sure acres, along with a wood and a stream, are used by an anonymous poet to sum up Maecenas' own choice of life-style (*Eleg. Maec.* 1.33-4 'maluit umbrosam quercum lymphasque cadentes | *pauca*que pomosi *iugera certa* soli'): the poet is once again following the example of his patron (see 18-20 above).

30 segetis certa fides meae: since farming was an unreliable activity (cf. 3.1.30 'fundus...mendax'), Nisbet was worried by *certa*, which he seems to have regarded as a transferred epithet; but the emphasis is perhaps on possession (like Virg. *Ecl.* 1.46 'ergo tua rura manebunt') rather than the harvests themselves, *fides* + genit. meaning 'belief in' (*OLD* 12a) rather than 'promise of' (*OLD* 2a). We should remember that H., like Alcaeus (130B.5-9), had once been dispossessed (*Epi.* 2.2.50-1). Cf. Stat. *Silv.* 2.6.66 'fidem messesque' (hendiadys).

31 fulgentem imperio fertilis Africae 'one who is resplendent in his dominion over fertile Africa.' Africa was proverbial for the richness of its land (1.1.10 and N–H, *S.* 2.3.87; Schmeling on Petron. 48.3; Otto 8) and supplied significantly more grain for Rome even than Egypt (G. Rickman, *The Corn Supply of Ancient Rome* (1980) 67-71). Whether H. is the first to use *fulgens* of persons is unclear (cf. Liv. 26.22.13); *imperium* is here being used in a non-technical sense.

32 sorte beatior: the adj. refers both to riches (here metaphorical) and to happiness, as often, and here has an active sense ('making richer/happier': *OLD* 1b); it is very frequently constructed with an abl. ('in respect of my lot/destiny', like *Epi.* 1.10.44 'laetus sorte tua'). H.'s first satire opens with the theme of contentment with one's lot (*S.* 1.1.1-3).

33-4 The argument is as follows: Although I am not rich, nevertheless I am not poor and, if I wanted more, you would not deny me (33-8); <but I don't want more:> by limiting my desires, I make my income go further than if I were extremely rich (39-42). Those who ask for a lot lack a lot; the man who has enough is the happy one (42-4).

33 nec Calabrae...apes: for the excellence of Calabrian honey see N–H on 2.6.14. For 'description by negation', of which this stanza is a good ex., see 3.1.25-6n.

34–5 nec Laestrygonia Bacchus in amphora | languescit mihi: the Laestrygonians, man-eating giants in the *Odyssey* (10.80–132), were associated both with Leontini in Sicily and, more recently, with Formiae on the southern coast of Latium (see intro. to 3.17). Wine came from both Sicily and Formiae, but Sicilian was seemingly a lesser vintage (Plin. *NH* 14.66); scholars assume that, as in the 'twin' poem to this (1.20.11–12 with Cairns, *RL* 232–9), H. is saying that it is Formian wine of which he has no stocks. (His own estate apparently produced no wine of its own: cf. *Epi.* 1.14.23.) *languescit* seems to mean 'mellows' (cf. 3.21.8); *Bacchus*, mimetically placed, is of course a common metonymy for wine.

35–6 nec pinguia Gallicis | crescunt uellera pascuis: sc. *mihi*: 'nor do I have thick fleeces growing in Gallic pastures': Cisalpine Gaul was famous for its wool (Plin. *NH* 8.190), although elsewhere (e.g. Mart. 6.11.7) *pinguis* is used to describe the greasiness of its fabrics. *uellera* is a form of synecdoche; for *cresco* of animals growing up cf. 3.23.11 (*OLD* 2a). The word order forms a 'golden' sequence (3.18.5n.).

39–42 contracto melius parua cupidine | uectigalia porrigam | quam si Mygdoniis regnum Alyattēī | campis continuem 'by contracting my desire I shall extend my small income more advantageously than if I were to join the kingdom of Alyattes to the Mygdonian plains' (for the present subjunc. see 25–7n. above). *contracto...cupidine* (the noun is always masc. in H.) looks back to *nil cupientium* (22). *parua...uectigalia* (again at Sall. *H.* 2.47.7M/2.43.7R) seems to be a reference to income from tenant farmers (cf. *Epi.* 1.14.2–3), but, while it is self-evidently true that one's money will go further if one's desires are few, the extravagance of the paradoxical comparison ('quam si') suggests that *uectigalia* also has a metaphorical dimension (cf. e.g. Cic. *Parad. Stoic.* 6.49 'quam magnum uectigal sit parsimonia', 51 'non esse emacem uectigal est'). H. expresses the paradox here more pointedly (*contracto ~ porrigam*) than in the similar 2.2.9–12 'latius regnes auidum domando | spiritum quam si Libyam remotis | Gadibus iungas' (and N–H). The motif of joining one region to another to symbolise great wealth, memorably expressed by Seneca (*Ep.* 89.20, 90.39), is, as it were, parodied in Petron. 48.3 (see Schmeling's n.). See also next nn.

41–2 Mygdoniis...campis: dat. (*OLD continuo*² 1b). Mygdon was a legendary Homeric chief (*Il.* 3.186), and Mygdonia was the name given to various areas in western Asia Minor and northern Greece which the ancients no doubt had difficulty distinguishing from one another (*BNP* 9.404–5); Sallust says that it is an earlier name for Bithynia (*H.* 3.70M/3.90R;

cf. Amm. 22.8.14), a rich area (3.7.3). The adj. 'Mygdonian', seemingly popularised in the Hellenistic age (Lightfoot on Parthen. fr. 3, Schol. 23–5; also pp. 554–5), is frequently used by the Augustan poets and others to mean 'Phrygian' (N–H on 2.12.22); since H. is the only Latin author to refer to 'Mygdonian plains', it is worth noting that the alternative name for Mygdonia was 'Plain of Mygdonia' (Strabo 13.1.13; cf. 12.3.22).

41 regnum Alyattĕī: Alyattes was the father of Croesus, king of Lydia (Hdt. 1.6 etc.), both of them conventionally associated with riches; Lydia was not only proverbial for its wealth, like most of Asia (3.7.3n.), but allegedly responsible for settling Etruria, from where Maecenas originated (*S.* 1.6.1–2 and Gowers ad loc.). The genit. is like *Ulixĕī* at 1.6.7 or *Achillĕī* at 1.15.34 (G&L 33 §65; Housman 2.834).

42–3 multa petentibus | desunt multa is the converse of Democr. fr. 284 'If you do not desire a lot (πολλῶν), a little will seem a lot (πολλά)' (cf. also Otto 232). The technical term for framing repetition is *redditio* (Lausberg 280–1 §625, Wills 426–7). *multa petentibus* contrasts with *si plura uelim* (38: see n.) and *nil…peto* (22–3), while *desunt multa* looks back to *maiorum… fames* (18).

43–4 bene est cui deus obtulit | parca quod satis est manu: sc. *ei*: 'Happy is he to whom a god, with sparing hand, has offered <only> what is enough' (reminiscent of the *makarismos* formula 'beatus…qui…', for which see Watson on *Epo.* 2.1–8): for *bene est* + dat. see *OLD bene* 9b; here the dat. antecedent is omitted before the following relative, an idiom for which see 3.1.17–18n. At *S.* 2.6.3–4 H. thanked the gods for the blessing of his estate ('auctius atque | di melius fecere. bene est. nil amplius oro'); here *deus* is a final complimentary allusion to Maecenas, since it was regular to refer to benefactors in divine terms (e.g. 3.25 intro., Virg. *Ecl.* 1.6 'deus nobis haec otia fecit'). Words for 'only' are often omitted in Latin (W. on Vell. 68.5). For *parca…manu* cf. Val. Max. 6.4 *praef.*, Mart. 12.62.11 (*parcentis…dexteras* at 3.19.21 below). *quod satis est* recalls 3.1.25 (n.) and also the address to Maecenas at the end of the first epode (1.31–2 'satis superque me benignitas tua | ditauit'); references to 'enough' are a common closural signal (e.g. *S.* 1.1.120, *Epi.* 2.2.214, Virg. *Ecl.* 10.70, 77).

17

It is generally accepted that the addressee of this ode is L. Aelius Lamia, homonymous son of Cicero's friend and supporter, L. Aelius Lamia, who had been praetor in 42 BC (*MRR* 2.359; Kaster on Cic. *Sest.* 29) and is the first Aelius Lamia of whom anything is known. After Augustus left Hispania Tarraconensis in 24 BC (3.14 and nn.), the younger Lamia was *legatus Augusti pro praetore* there from 24 to 22 (Dio 53.29.1 with Rich's n.); he was also *quindecimuir sacris faciundis* – from which scholars infer that he had been elevated to the patriciate in 29 (see *RG* 8.1 with Scheid and Cooley ad loc.) – and father of the consul of AD 3. Little else is known about him; he is assumed to have died before his political career could progress any further. (See Syme, *AA* 394–5; Cairns, *RL* 415; Rüpke 510 no. 470.)

Lamia seems to have been a good friend of H., since he is almost certainly the same man as is named at 1.26.8, 1.36.7 (where he and H. welcome back a mutual friend from Spain) and *Epi.* 1.14.6. The cognomen is strange and distinctive. The Latin noun *lamia* means either a shark or a child-eating witch (see *OLD*). According to the ode's opening lines, however, Lamia's family was popularly supposed to derive its name from a legendary figure called Lamus, of whom three are known. A Rutulian called Lamus is mentioned by Virgil (*Aen.* 9.334); another Lamus, a son of Hercules, was founder of the Thessalian city of Lamia (Diod. 4.31.8), which had been sacked by the Romans in the early second century; the third, a son of Neptune/Poseidon, was founder of the city of Telepylos, home of Homer's man-eating giants, the Laestrygonians (*Od.* 10.81–2). An additional complication was the fact that Lamia was the name of a daughter of Neptune/Poseidon who was queen of the Laestrygonians (schol. Theocr. 15.40). Such complexity of background was by no means uncommon, and, if a family was interested in its line of descent, it is not surprising that 'the identity of the person from whom it was derived was the subject of speculation' (C. J. Smith, *The Roman Clan* (2006) 41).

There was a long-standing and well-established tradition, attested as early as Hesiod (fr. 150.56 M–W = 98.26 Most), that the Laestrygonians' home, Telepylos, was to be located in Sicily and identified with the town of Leontini (Thuc. 6.2.1, Theopomp. fr. 225, Plb. 8.9.13 with Walbank, Strabo 1.2.9; cf. 1.2.11, 32). But Cicero, writing to Atticus in 59 BC, identified the place with Formiae on the coast of southern Latium (*Att.* 2.13.2 'Τηλέπυλον... Λαιστρυγονίην, Formias dico'). It is striking both that Cicero is the earliest author in whom this identification is found and that 'the learned Atticus needs to have the allusion explained' (Parker 170). The inference seems to be that this alternative identification of Telepylos with Formiae was very recent; to Diodorus, a contemporary, Formiae was associated with the Argonauts (4.56.6), while Strabo says that it was founded by the Laconians (5.3.6). We do not know how or why the different identification in Cicero originated, but, since Telepylos had been founded by a Lamus, the association will have mattered to the Lamiae if, as seems likely (6n.), they owned property at Formiae.⁹³ They may have had before them the precedent of the Gellii, who, at roughly the same period, were advertising their descent from Neptune via his daughter Lamia, whose other name was Gello.⁹⁴ Such a scenario, almost every element of which is entirely speculative, would explain why H. not only devotes half his ode to endorsing his friend's ancestry but carefully distinguishes the recent version (5–9) from its much vaguer predecessors (2–4). (See further 2–9n. and 6n. below.)

After the elaborate tracing of Lamia's ancestry, H. presents his addressee with a weather forecast: there is going to be a storm tomorrow (9–13), so Lamia is advised to gather dry wood while he can (13–14). The implication is that a fire will be needed, and so it proves: in the final sentence of the poem H. reminds Lamia that on the following day the consumption of wine will be accompanied by the sacrifice of a young pig (14–16). Tomorrow is evidently a very special day – almost certainly, as some scholars have suggested, Lamia's birthday. The case is argued in great detail by Cairns as part of his masterly discussion of the ode as a *genethliakon* or birthday poem (*RL* 412–40, at 424–36): 'if the occasion is not Lamia's birthday', he says, 'then the ode is well-nigh incomprehensible' (434).

METRE   Alcaic

1 Aeli uetusto nobilis ab Lamo 'Noble Aelius <descended> from an ancient Lamus' (the word order is grammatically interlaced and formally chiastic): the preposition incorporates the notion of descent (*OLD* 17b), and perhaps also that of name-derivation (cf. *OLD* 15b). Whether Aelius Lamia was technically a *nobilis* will depend upon one's understanding of the term: many scholars believe it was restricted to individuals with a consular ancestor (cf. *OLD* 1018, *BNP* 9.784–5; Berry on Cic. *Sull.* 37), something which would not apply to Lamia. Genealogical writing, such as

---

⁹³ Parker speculates that the identification may have originated with the Lamiae themselves – either Cicero's friend, the praetor of 42, or his father. It is tempting to see a role for Varro's *De familiis Troianis*, but we do not know its date (Drummond in *FRH* 1.421 suggests 'the mid-to-late 40s'). The identification of Telepylos with Formiae was repeated later (Plin. *NH* 3.59, Sil. 7.276, 410) but did not oust that with Leontini (see Strabo 1.2.9, noted above).
⁹⁴ For the Gellii see Wiseman, *RS* 214–18, 381 (217 n. 2 for Gello). Noting that in the early empire a Gellius was a local magistrate at Minturnae (*CIL* 10.6017), Wiseman wondered whether the family had connections there in the republic. If so, this would have further encouraged the Lamiae's ancestral interests, since Minturnae lies at the mouth of the River Liris (lines 7–8 of the ode), less than 10 miles south-east of Formiae.

the lost *De familiis Troianis* by Varro (n. 93), was popular in the late republic; the whole subject of 'legendary genealogies' is discussed in a famous paper by T. P. Wiseman (*RS* 207–18; cf. 381).

2–9 quando...late tyrannus 'since they say that it was from hence [i.e. from a Lamus] that the early Lamiae and the entire line of descendants down through the memorialising *fasti* took their name, you derive your origin from that particular patriarch who...': i.e. we have to supply (i) *esse* with *denominatos* in 3, and (ii) *denominatum esse* with *nepotum...genus omne* in 3–4; the latter ellipse is facilitated by *et...et...*, which signposts the two subjects of the accus. + infin. after *ferunt*. Lines 2–9 give rise to more questions than it is possible to deal with here. With reference to the interpretation proposed above, N–R object that it 'produces the banal truism "since the Lamiae are all descended from Lamus, you are descended from Lamus"'; like most modern edd., they prefer to adopt the emendation *ducit* (so too Tarrant (2016a) 302–4). But the objection takes no account of the fact that there was more than one Lamus. *quando* = 'as, since' occurs only here in the *Odes*; otherwise exclusively in *S*. 2 (4×).

2 priores 'early' (*OLD prior* 3), and accus. rather than (as in some editions) nominative.

hinc 'from hence': the adverb (*OLD* 7) reflects the fact that *ab Lamo* (1) means 'from *a* Lamus': H. cannot be more specific because there was more than one of them (intro.). There is a strong contrast with *auctore ab illo* below (5).

4 per memores...fastos: strictly the *fasti* were the lists of the *consules ordinarii* who gave their names to the year (*OLD* 3); it is generally assumed that the word is here being used non-technically (as at 4.13.15) and refers to family records, although there was a 'fashion in Italian cities of the early empire for setting up *Fasti* and other commemorative monuments' (Cairns, *RL* 417). We are invited to imagine a domestic list of ancestors with the name 'Lamus' at the top, like that which Brutus evidently had in his house (Cic. *Att.* 13.40.1, Nep. *Att.* 18.3; see further Sen. *Ben.* 3.28.2 and Courtney on Juv. 8.1–9). As again at 4.14.4 (see Thomas), the MSS are divided between *fastos* and *fastūs*, as were those seen by the sixth-century grammarian Priscian (*GL* 2.256.16–20K): it is very difficult to know what to print (see also Brink on *Epi.* 2.1.48), but *memores...fastos* recurs at Stat. *De bello Germanico* line 3 (*FLP* p. 360). *memor* = 'commemorative, memorialising' (3.14.18n.).

5 auctore ab illo ducis originem: *auctore ab illo* contrasts emphatically with the vague *hinc* (2n.), while *ducis* likewise contrasts with *ferunt* (2–9n.): *this particular* Lamus is the one from whom Lamia himself claims derivation (*OLD duco* 27b). If *auctor* is not to be a redundant anticipation of *princeps* below (7), it here denotes founder of a family (*OLD* 15) rather than of a town. *ducere originem* is probably first here, although the same expr. at Just. 43.5.11 may derive from Trogus (see also 3.16.14–15n.); otherwise it seems not to become common until the late first century AD and beyond (*TLL* 9.2.989.25–7).

6 Formiarum: Formiae lies on the Via Appia, about two-thirds of the way between Rome and Naples, at the northern end of the bay known in ancient times as the Sinus Amy(n)clanus (*BA* 44: E3); it was the 'city of the Mamurrae' (*S.* 1.5.37 with Gowers), the family whose notorious bankrupt was pilloried by Catullus (41.4, 43.5). According to Strabo (5.3.6) its original name was *Hormiae* because it had a good ὅρμος ('anchorage'; cf. Maltby 240). Despite the impression given by modern scholarship (e.g. N–R 212–13, S. Treggiari, 'Cicero, Horace, and mutual friends: Lamiae and Varrones Murenae', *Phoenix* 27 (1973) 246–53), H.'s ode is the only evidence for a connection between the Lamiae and Formiae, and the evidence, though cogent, has to be inferred from the relationship between lines 5–9a and 9b–13a (9–12n.).

dicitur: the 'Alexandrian footnote' (3.5.41–3n.) endows the story with all the authority of tradition.

7–8 princeps...tenuisse 'first to have held sway over' (*OLD princeps*[1] 1, *teneo* 9b).

innantem...Lirim: the River Liris (N–H on 1.31.7) debouches into the sea at Minturnae, just down the coast from Formiae. The area was well known for its marshes (Mayor on Juv. 10.276), in which Marius hid himself when trying to escape from Sulla's forces; Marica is the local goddess (cf. Vell. 2.19.2 on Marius: 'extractus harundineto circa paludem Maricae, in quam se fugiens consectantes Sullae equites abdiderat'): sometimes identified with various other divinities or supernatural beings, she is associated also with a famous grove (Liv. 27.37.2 'lucum Maricae', Luc. 2.424, Mart. 13.83.1 with Leary's n.).

9 late tyrannus: nouns which imply some action, as here ('ruling' *vel sim.*), may be modified by an adverb, as Virg. *Aen.* 1.21 'populum late regem', Sen. *Suas.* 6.5 'foris uictores'; edd. compare Greek compound

COMMENTARY 17.9–13   267

adjs. formed from εὐρυ-, such as εὐρυάναξ ('wide-ruling'). The words refer
to the ten miles of coast between Formiae and Minturnae over which
Lamus held sway.

9–12 cras...tempestas... | sternet 'tomorrow a storm will strew...' (for
sterno + abl. = 'to strew X with Y' see *OLD* 4b); the word order seems
to be mimetic (the grove is enveloped by leaves, the shore by seaweed),
while *sternet* perhaps points self-referentially to the scattering of the storm
('mu̱lti̱s et alga li̱tu̱s inu̱tili̱'). Since it would seem perverse to understand
litus as referring to anything other than 'Marica's shores', just mentioned
(7–8), it follows that *nemus* must refer to the goddess's famous grove
(7–8n.) and that the storm is being predicted to hit Formiae. Thus the
ode is set at Formiae, where, it is implied, Lamia had an establishment;
and we are invited to imagine that H. has come down from Rome for
his friend's birthday party, otherwise he could not have heard the crow
and issued his weather warning for 'tomorrow'.[95] Some regard the storm
as merely symbolic, but this seems unlikely because the repeated *cras* at
14 below clearly denotes a particular day. Cairns not only argues that we
can identify the day but suggests why H. knows that it will be stormy (*RL*
426–7). The pig to be sacrificed will be two months old (15): since pigs
were conceived in February and born five months later (Colum. 7.9.3),
it follows that the sacrifice must fall in September. The likeliest time for
storms in that month will be the autumn equinox (cf. Plin. *NH* 2.108),
which for Columella falls between 24 and 26 September (11.2.66). Cairns
notes further that 23 September was Augustus' birthday (Suet. *Aug.* 5.1;
cf. Hor. *Epi.* 1.5.9) and wonders whether Lamia shared a birthday with
the *princeps*.

10 alga...inutili: seaweed was proverbially worthless (*S.* 2.5.8; Otto 13).

12–13 aquae nisi fallit augur | annosa cornix 'unless the aged crow,
prophet of rain, deceives me'. Crows were famously long-lived (4.13.25,
Hes. fr. 304 M–W = 254 Most, Arat. *Phaen.* 1022, Phaedr. *App.* 24(26).6)
and their powers of predicting rain were proverbial (3.27.10, Lucr.
5.1083–6 with Campbell, Virg. *G.* 1.381–9 with Mynors, Ov. *Am.* 2.6.34
with McKeown). *aquae...augur* translates a Greek term such as ὑετόμαντις
(cf. Euphor. fr. 114L ὑετόμαντις ὅτε κρώξειε κορώνη, 'when the crow, the
rain-prophet, should croak'); *augur* is pointed in an ode addressed to a
member of a priestly college (intro.), while the choice of *aqua* = 'rain' is

---

[95] According to *Orbis*, a journey down the Via Appia from Rome to Formiae
would take at least four and a half days.

significant because a crow's cawing resembles *aqua* repeated (*aqua* is put to a similar use for ducks in the joke at Plaut. *Rud.* 533–4: see W. Beare, *CR* 44 (1930) 166–7 and n. 1).

13 dum potes is a set phrase (e.g. Plaut. *Merc.* 553, Ov. *Met.* 2.147, Mart. 4.30.14); *dum + potis* (indecl. adj.), the alternative reading, is unparalleled.

14 compone lignum: we might have expected *ligna*, as Cato, *RR* 37.5 'ligna...compone' (where, however, the verb means 'heap' and not, as here, 'gather'); *lignum* is a collective singular (*TLL* 7.2.1386.32–46).

14–15 cras Genium mero | curabis et porco bimenstri 'tomorrow you will care for your Genius with neat-wine and a two-month-old pig' (for *merum* in sacrifices see 3.13.2n.). The Genius was a person's guardian spirit, who protected him throughout his life (cf. *Epi.* 2.2.187–9 with Brink ad loc. and his Appendix 19). Since offerings to one's Genius were above all due on one's birthday (see e.g. Tib. 1.7.49–54, 2.2.3–9 with Murgatroyd and Maltby; Cairns, *RL* 432), H.'s statement virtually guarantees that 'tomorrow' is Lamia's birthday. There is nevertheless one problem with this conclusion: the third-century AD writer Censorinus in his 'birthday book' appeals to a (now lost) work of Varro for the view that 'our ancestors' (*maiores nostri*) did not make blood-sacrifices to the Genius on their birthday (*De die natali* 2.2). One solution to this difficulty is to assume that *genium curare* does not refer to Lamia's Genius at all but means simply 'to enjoy oneself', like *genio indulgere* or ψυχῇ χαρίζεσθαι, and this indeed is the view of some commentators and standard works of reference (*TLL* 6.2.1838.56–7, *OLD genius* 1b); but this not only deprives the ode of all point but fails to explain the participation of holidaying slaves (16), which one would expect only on some special day (cf. Cic. *Leg.* 2.29 'feriarum festorumque dierum ratio...requietem habet...in seruis operum et laborum'). There are in fact two partial parallels for a blood-sacrifice on one's birthday. At 4.11.6–8 Maecenas' birthday is to be celebrated by the sacrifice of a lamb, although Maecenas is not conducting the sacrifice himself and it is not stated explicitly that the sacrifice is in honour of his Genius; likewise at Stat. *Silv.* 2.7.17–18 Lucan's birthday is to be celebrated by blood-sacrifices, but Lucan himself is dead and again there is no explicit reference to his Genius. Although neither is precisely parallel to the situation in our ode, these two passages, along with other evidence, have been used to support the view that *Genium...curabis* cannot be other than a reference to a birthday sacrifice (see, in addition to Cairns, Du Quesnay (1981) 108-9, 164–5).

16 cum famulis operum solutis: the abl. is more usual after *solutus* (*OLD* 10a) but adjs. expressing separation can sometimes take the genitive: 'H. liked experimenting with this type of construction in place of the Ciceronian abl. or *ab*' (Brink on *AP* 212). For *famulus* see 3.1.34–6n.

18

The Faunalia were celebrated officially on 13 February (Ov. *F.* 2.193); apart from this ode, there is no evidence that Faunus had another festival, which according to the transmitted text of the ode (line 10) was celebrated on 5 December in at least one area of the Italian countryside (Scullard 201):

> Here we have the essence of true Roman country religion: the appeal to the vague and possibly dangerous spirit that guards the flocks to be present, but not to linger too long; the smoking altar of earth; the simple offering of wine and kid; the gambolling sheep; the quiet relaxation after the year's toil, and the dance on the hated land which had demanded so much labour.

Yet H.'s description of the god's festival (9, 11–16) scarcely accords with a date in early December; the details seem far more suggestive of spring, which is the season depicted in the opening of the poem (1–4). For this reason I have suggested elsewhere that a copyist, thinking wrongly that the phrase *pleno...anno* in line 5 referred to the end of the calendar year, substituted *Decembres* for H.'s original *Apriles*, the two words happily having the same prosody (see 'Now that April's there: Horace, *Odes* 3.18', *G&R* 67 (2020) 247–53). If this suggestion, admittedly radical, is accepted, the entire ode is set in springtime.[96]

The structure of the ode is simple enough. In the first half (1–8) H. makes a bargain with Faunus: he prays that the god's visitation will be benign (3 *lenis*, 4 *aequus*) if there is an annual sacrifice to him (5–8). In the second half (9–16) H. gives a vivid account of the festival during which the sacrifice will take place. The ode was rightly described by Fraenkel as 'a little masterpiece' (205 n. 2); with its local setting, it is part of the sequence consisting of the ode to the Bandusian spring (3.13), the prayer to Diana (3.22), and the address to the countrywoman Phidyle (3.23).

---

[96] For another case where a transmitted date seems to conflict with other evidence see Pliny's famous letter (6.16.4) on the eruption of Vesuvius (cf. R. K. Gibson, *Man of High Empire* (2020) 77–8 n. 25), as Dr Salvador Bartera reminds me.

COMMENTARY 18.1-4

METRE Sapphic

1 Faune, Nympharum fugientum amator: Faunus is a recurrent deity in the *Odes*. His frequent visits to H.'s farm provide the background for an invitation (1.17); sacrifice to him marks the beginning of spring (1.4.11–12); and he is credited with saving H. from the falling tree (2.17.28–30). A rustic and especially woodland god (below, 14n.), he was often identified with Pan (hence his dwelling on Mt Lycaeus at 1.17.2; cf. Ov. *F.* 2.424) and associated with (usually fleeing) Nymphs (cf. e.g. Stat. *Silv.* 2.3.8). Being an 'insatiable erotomaniac' (*BNP* 5.368–70), he is sometimes also called Inuus or the god of intercourse: see further *LIMC* 8.1.582–3. For the formula of address + descriptive phrase in apposition, a feature of prayers and hymns, see e.g. 3.11.3–4n., 3.13.1n.

The regular genit. plur. of participles is formed in -*ium*, but for metrical reasons poets from the earliest times had adopted 'the common, indispensable alternative form' in -*um* (Horsfall on Virg. *Aen.* 6.728: see e.g. Enn. *Ann.* 76 'altiuolantum', Cat. 34.12 'sonantum', Virg. *G.* 3.111 'sequentum'), and *fugientum* is found occasionally in Silius and Statius. See also 3.27.9–12n.

2–4 per meos fines et aprica rura | lenis incedas abeasque paruis | aequus alumnis 'may your progress across my land and the sunlit countryside be gentle, and may your departure be favourable to my young little animals'. The humorous implication of this chiastically arranged prayer seems to be that Faunus' visit to H.'s estate should be a preferable alternative to his amorous pursuit of Nymphs (1). Although Faunus had a protecting role, the epiphany of any divinity could be terrifying, especially if he was associated with the unpredictable Pan (cf. G. Petridou, *Divine Epiphany in Greek Literature and Culture* (2016) 201–5). It was therefore conventional to pray that a god's visitation be benign, for which *lenis* is almost technical (1.19.16 and N–H). It is unusual for a god to be told to depart (see Thomas on 4.1.7) but the emphasis is on the *manner* of his departure, as of his arrival (cf. translation): *aequus* + dat. means 'favourable to ~ ' (*OLD* 7a) and perhaps alludes to the derivation of Faunus' name from *faueo* (Maltby 226): cf. *CS* 65. *alumni* are young animals (*OLD* 1b), a meaning first found in H. (again at 3.23.7). The reference is almost certainly to young kids and lambs (cf. 5, 13). The former are born in spring when the woods are sprouting with new foliage (Varro, *RR* 2.3.8, Colum. 7.6.6 'iam propinquante uere...cum primum siluae noua germinant fronde', Plin. *NH* 8.200);[97] lambs too were born

---

[97] For more on the life cycle of goats see Cairns, *RL* 399–400.

in the spring (Colum. 7.3.11; cf. 11.2.14), although they might also be born at the very end of autumn (Varro, *RR* 2.2.14). For *aprica rura* cf. Colum. 7.5.2.

5 si tener pleno cadit haedus anno: a 'golden' line (adj.[1] adj.[2] verb noun[1] noun[2]): see Wilkinson, *GLA* 215–16, 219. At 1.4.11–12 Faunus is offered the choice of a kid or (as at Ov. *F.* 4.653 'prima cadit Fauno') a lamb; for *cado* = 'to be sacrificed' see *OLD* 9b. *pleno...anno*, a regular combination (cf. *TLL* 10.1.2416.9–17), here means 'when the annual cycle is completed', i.e. twelve months since the previous festival (cf. 3.8.9 'anno redeunte'): cf. Cic. *Mil.* 24 'plenum annum'.

Prayers conventionally deploy conditional clauses, of which the various types are sometimes confused. (1) Divine addressees are reminded *either* of their proper function(s), as in Cat. 76.17 'O di, si uestrum est misereri', *or* of their past services, as in Cat. 76.17–18 'si quibus umquam | extremam...tulistis opem'. (2) Suppliants remind the divine addressee of their own good standing, as in Cat. 76.19 'si uitam puriter egi'. (3) Suppliants make a bargain with the divine addressee, as here and 3.23.1–4 (see intro.). None of these conditional clauses implies doubt; they merely constitute a diplomatic way of expressing oneself to a powerful supernatural being.

6–7 larga nec desunt Veneris sodali | uina creterrae probably means 'and the bowl, that companion of Venus, does not lack generous helpings of wine' (for *creterrae* rather than the variant *craterae*, a form avoided by poets, see W. Clausen, *CQ* 13 (1963) 85–7). The close connection between wine and lovemaking, or between Liber and Venus (cf. 3.21.21), was proverbial (Otto 366), but the reference to Venus gains added point if, as suggested (see intro.), the sacrifice takes place in April, Venus' own month (4.11.15–16; Maltby 44). For the metaphorical use of *sodalis* cf. 1.25.19–20 'hiemis sodali | ...Euro'. *uina* is often plur. for sing. in H. but here the qualification *larga* suggests a distributive use, in the same way as *ligna* can mean 'pieces of wood'; the same expr. at Ov. *F.* 2.636 is metonymical and means 'generous cups of wine'.

7–8 uetus ara multo | fumat odore: *ara fumat* is a regular expr. (*OLD fumo* 1b), perhaps (in view of the coincidence of *fumantibus aris* at Cic. fr. 22.8 Morel and Cat. 64.393) orig. Ennian; but the addition of *multo odore* is unparalleled (it is unclear whether *odor* refers to incense or to the smell from the sacrifice itself or both). *uetus* implies an often repeated ritual and hence looks forward to 10 below; see also D. Feeney, *Literature and Religion at Rome* (1998) 133–4.

9 ludit herboso pecus omne campo: grassy fields usually symbolise spring (cf. 4.7.1 'redeunt iam gramina campis'); the verb is regular of playful animals (*OLD* 1b), e.g. 3.11.9–10, Ov. *F.* 1.156 'ludit et in pratis luxuriatque pecus' (springtime).

10 cum tibi Nonae redeunt Apriles: *tibi*, emphatically placed and repeated at 14 below, belongs to the so-called 'Du-Stil' of prayers (3.11.13–14n., 3.13.9–16); for *redire* = 'to come round again' see 3.8.9n. For *Apriles* rather than the transmitted *Decembres* see intro.; unlike Propertius and Ovid, H. scans the word with a short first syllable (4.11.16 'findit Aprilem').

11–12 otioso | cum boue: oxen would rest on a sacred day, because the ploughman did no ploughing (Tib. 2.1.7–8).

12 pagus 'countryfolk' (cf. *TLL* 10.1.93.80ff., esp. 94.7–17), the place standing for its inhabitants (as in our 'the whole village came out to celebrate').

13 inter audaces lupus errat agnos: for the effect of Faunus' visit cf. 1.17.8–9 'nec...metuunt... haediliae lupos' (the hostility of wolves to lambs was proverbial: cf. *Epo.* 15.7). There is perhaps a hint at the name Lupercal, although the god associated with the place thus named was Pan himself (Serv. *Aen.* 8.343 'lupos non sinat in oues saeuire'; Maltby 351–2). *lupus errat* is mimetic syntax.

14 spargit agrestis tibi silua frondes: the word order suggests (and most scholars agree) that *agrestis* qualifies *frondes*, but the qualification seems otiose (contrast Virg. *Ecl.* 10.24 'uenit et agresti capitis Siluanus honore'); perhaps, as Williams has it, *agrestis* qualifies *silua* (cf. Ov. *Met.* 7.242, Curt. 8.10.14), underlining the fact that the wild wood is paying honour to the god. Faunus himself is called *siluicola* by Virgil (*Aen.* 10.551; cf. Hor. *AP* 244), and *agrestis* is one of his own epithets (Ov. *F.* 2.193). Influenced by the transmitted *Decembres* in 10, scholars assume that H. is referring to trees shedding their leaves (cf. *Epo.* 11.5–6 'December...siluis honorem decutit') in honour of Faunus; but dry and dead leaves, elsewhere used to symbolise an ageing courtesan (1.25.19), seem quite inappropriate for this purpose: if Horace is referring to springtime, on the other hand, it is a flattering conceit to pretend that the trees are spreading their new leaves (cf. 2–4n.) in his honour (for this sense of *spargo* cf. Plin. *NH* 25.84 'spargens folia'; *OLD* 3).

15–16 inuisam pepulisse fossor | ter pede terram: the *fossor* hates the earth because it costs him so much labour. *ter pede* implies the *tripudium* or 'three-step' (*OLD* 1). For the perf. infin. see 3.4.51–2n.

19

The poem opens with H. chiding a friend – unnamed, but identified at the end as Telephus (26)[98] – for being more interested in antiquarian lore (1–4) than in their present plight: they need to buy wine and get a hot bath (or, less probably, a hot toddy), and they are freezing cold and do not know who will offer them hospitality (5–8). H. then addresses a serving boy and orders toasts to the new moon, to the middle of the night, and to Murena the augur (9–11). The order is followed by instructions for the appropriate amounts of wine (11–18), by references to loud music and roses (18–24), and by allusions to the respective love-lives of H. and Telephus (25–8).

This 'extraordinary composition' (Gow) is one of H.'s most difficult odes. The principal problem, as will be clear from the preceding summary, concerns the relationship between lines 5–8 and what follows: in 5–8 H. is evidently outdoors in the cold and looking to buy wine, whereas in 9–28 a drinking party or symposium appears to be in full swing and he is calling for toasts. What has happened? What kind of transition is envisaged from 5–8 to 9–28?

Scholars have responded variously to this problem. (i) H. in 9–28 *imagines* himself at the party which he had craved in 5–8. Nothing in the text supports this view, which seems quite implausible. (ii) The whole poem is set at a party, which H. interrupts at 5–8 to ask what the arrangements are for the *next* party, to be held at some future date. There is no evidence for this theory, either. (iii) N–R suggest that 1–8 are set at a dinner party and 9–28 at a symposium in another house: H. is worried that he will be cold (8) as he walks from the first venue to the second. This seems desperately artificial. (iv) West thinks that the whole poem is set at a symposium but that the verbs *narras* and *taces* in 1–8 are *generalising* : 'Telephus, you're always going on about antiquarian matters but you never give a thought to the really important questions. Come on! Let's drink a toast or two!' This ingenious interpretation is attractive, but there is no indication in the text that the two verbs are to be so taken ('always' and 'never' have to be inserted into the translation).

---

[98] SB says that 'an opening address to a person not named later in the poem seems to be unique' (*Profile* 97), but of course a person *is* named later in the poem – Telephus. SB evidently adopts the same position as N–R (238), who say that Telephus 'cannot be' the person to whom the verbs *narras* and *taces* (3, 8) apply. Why not? It is an article of faith in Horatian scholarship that each ode has a named addressee: there are almost no exceptions (Heinze, *OR* 11–12). It seems inconceivable that for 24 lines we would be led to think that this ode is one of the exceptions and that H. is not naming his addressee but that then in the final 4 lines we are somehow obliged suddenly to divine that the addressee named there is not the ode's addressee but someone different altogether. Porphyrio was surely right to identify Telephus as the subject of *narras* and *taces*.

We have to remember that, like 1.27 or *Epode* 9, the ode is a mimetic poem: that is, it dramatises a developing situation in which the poet participates.[99] In the present case the drama is a nocturnal *comissatio*, as the two friends drink their way along the streets of Rome, rather in the manner for which Augustus' daughter Julia was notorious (cf. Sen *Ben.* 6.32.1 'pererratam nocturnis comissationibus ciuitatem'), and, like the *cenae captatores* whom we meet in Petronius (cf. 3.3 'ficti adulatores...cenas diuitum captant') or comedy (also Cat. 44.9, 47.6–7), they are hoping to find a generous host who will take them in. Telephus' antiquarian ramblings (1–4), and H.'s apparent impatience with him, suggest that the two have been drinking since before the start of the poem (3n.): when H. complains that Telephus has given no thought to how they can buy a jar of Chian (5), it is because their supplies are running dangerously low and he does not want their drinking to stop. There is no reason why the serving boy (10) should not be part of the outdoor scene, since guests on their way to a dinner party would bring along their own slaves (n.). Indeed, as members of the elite, the pair are also accompanied by musicians (18–20). Toasting the new moon and midnight seems more appropriate if the two friends are out in the open (9–10), while the toast for Murena is perhaps offered more in hope than in gratitude (10–11): it is not that Telephus and H. have been admitted to Murena's house, where it would surely be unthinkable for the music to have stopped playing (18–20), but, finding themselves in the vicinity, pray that the great man will let them in out of the cold. Once the music has resumed in response to H.'s grumble, his wish for the 'mad din' (*dementem strepitum*) to be heard by the locals (22–4) is more appropriate for an outdoor revel than for a performance inside Murena's grand establishment. Since *dementem* (23), like *insanire* (18), suggests that the two friends become increasingly inebriated as the ode progresses, it is no surprise that H. ends with a maudlin contrast between Telephus' love life and his own (25–8); and, while it was conventional to praise someone by likening them to a star, the specific comparison of Telephus to the evening star (26n.) implies that the action is still taking place outdoors under the night sky. Finally, if the scene is (as is usually assumed) an indoor *conuiuium*, one would expect an allusion to other guests apart from Telephus: in this respect our ode is very different from 1.27, with which it otherwise has so much in common.

Given the uncertainty surrounding almost every aspect of the ode, none of this can be proved. Perhaps the one certain feature of the poem is that

---

[99] N–R 229 refer to N–H on 1.27, where the mimetic nature of the ode is unfortunately misunderstood (contrast Fraenkel 181); for *Epo.* 9 see my discussion in A. J. Woodman and J. Wisse (edd.), *Word and Context in Latin Poetry* (2017) 43–60.

it is based on the 'magic' number 3. It divides into three parts (1–11a, 11b–18a, 18b–28), the first and last being of identical length. There are three objects of *narras* in 1–4, three subjunctives in 5–8, three toasts in 9–10a. The central part deals in 3 or multiples thereof (11b *tribus aut nouem*, 13 the nine Muses, 14 *ternos ter*, 15 *tres*, 16–17 the three Graces). There are three musical instruments in 18b–20 and three pairs of actual or would-be lovers in 22–8.

METRE Fourth Asclepiad

1–2 Quantum distet ab Inacho | Codrus: legend had it that Inachus was the first king of Argos, Codrus the last king of Athens: *distet*, referring to the lengthy period of time which separated them (*OLD* 2a), points with self-referential wit to the juxtaposition of their names in H.'s text. There had been a recent flourishing of chronometrical writing with Nepos, Atticus and Varro (*PH* 123–4, *LH* 61–4); for more on the 'interval-spacing mentality' see Feeney (2007) 13–14 and n. 27. The nerdy Telephus is made to sound rather like the future emperor Tiberius, who specialised in obscure mythological questions (Suet. *Tib.* 70.3).

2 pro patria non timidus mori: the story was that, in a war with the Dorians, Codrus invited his own death because it had been prophesied that the enemy would win if they spared the life of the king (Cic. *TD* 1.116, where he is cited as an example of 'clarae mortes pro patria oppetitae'). For the motif of dying for one's country (again at 4.9.51–2 'non… timidus perire') see 3.2.13n.; for *timidus* + infin. see *OLD* 1c (this the earliest ex. quoted).

3 narras is followed both by the indir. question of 1–2 and by the accusatives *genus* and *bella* (3–4), a common form of *uariatio*. For the commonplace that drinking leads to garrulity (again at 3.21.13–14) see Plut. *Mor.* 503E–504B, 614E; Watson on *Epo.* 11.14. For *narras* ('go on about') cf. perhaps Cat. 9.6–8, Petron. 44.1 (similar to our passage); the verb contrasts with *taces* below (8): we have to imagine a strong 'but' between lines 4 and 5 (adversative asyndeton).

genus Aeaci: Aeacus, a son of Zeus, was father of Telamon (father of Ajax and Teucer) and Peleus (father of Achilles, whose son was Neoptolemus).

4 pugnata sacro bella sub Ilio: the word order is interlaced, as often; *pugno* is an intransitive verb but can take a cognate accus. (*OLD* 1d): the expr. recurs at *Epi.* 1.16.25, Cat. 37.13, Virg. *Aen.* 8.629, Val. Fl. 1.770.

sacro indicates that *Ilio* is neuter here, although in the Homeric formula to which H. is alluding the noun is feminine (*Il.* 4.46 Ἴλιος ἱρή, etc.), as at 3.3.18 (n.): hence *sacra* was suggested by Haupt. *sub* is a reference to the walls of Troy, beneath which the action of the Trojan War takes place (e.g. *Il.* 12.264, 22.144; J. S. Clay, *Homer's Trojan Theater* (2011) 38).

5–6 quo Chium pretio cadum | mercemur: this and the two following subjunctives represent deliberative questions in direct speech: 'For what price are we to buy a jar of Chian?' (for the abl. of price see *NLS* 68–70 §§86–7). For indir. questions with *taceo* (8) see *OLD* 4a. For the excellence of Chian wine see Watson on *Epo.* 9.34, Murgatroyd on Tib. 2.1.27–8.

6 quis aquam temperet ignibus 'who is to regulate the water with fire' (*OLD tempero* 5b). Some think that the reference is to the Roman practice (11–12n., below) of diluting wine with water, which might sometimes be warmed up; but, if so, it seems very odd not to mention the wine at all, while *ignibus* seems a quite bizarre way of referring to the rather elegant charcoal-burning water-heaters which were used for warming the water (see Dunbabin 120–5). Others think that the two shivering friends (cf. 8) are looking forward to a hot bath (cf. *Epi.* 1.11.12–13), such as one might take before a meal (Mart. 6.53.1, 10.48.3ff., 11.52.3, Plin. *Ep.* 3.1.8–9). If so, the reference must be to a pool in a private house, since no one would be interested in who heated the water in a public baths.

7–8 quo praebente domum et quotā | Paelignis caream frigoribus: *horā* has to be understood with *quotā*, but the abl. abs. *quo praebente* makes the clause awkward to render in English: '(you are silent about) under whose roof and at what hour I am to escape the Paelignian cold' (thus Bennett). *praebente domum* denotes a potential host (cf. *S.* 1.5.38 'Murena praebente domum': see further 10–11n. below): the pair's ignorance of the hoped-for host's identity resembles that of Petronius' anti-heroes before the start of the *Cena Trimalchionis*: 'cum maesti deliberaremus quonam genere praesentem euitaremus procellam, unus seruus Agamemnonis interpellauit trepidantes et "quid uos?", inquit, "nescitis hodie apud quem fiat?"' (26.8–9). The Paeligni were a people of the central Apennines, where the mountains can rise to almost 10,000 ft; one of their towns was Sulmo (*BA* Map 44: E1), birthplace of Ovid. 'Paelignian' is explained by the area's proverbial coldness (Ov. *F.* 4.81, Plin. *NH* 17.250); one cannot safely infer from it that H. and his friend are not in Rome. *careo* here = 'to be free from' (*OLD* 3a), as 3.29.23–4.

9–11 da lunae propere nouae, | da noctis mediae, da, puer, auguris | Murenae: sc. *cyathum/-os* or similar with each imperative, an elliptical use of the verb for which there seems to be no parallel (cf. *TLL* 5.1.1666.70–2). Where we might toast someone with the words 'Raise your glass(es) to X', the Romans could say 'Present X's ladleful(s)' (cf. 3.8.13–14n.): in other words, the genitives of 9–11 are possessive. It is not to be imagined that the *puer* (next n.) will actually perform the toast; his role is simply to serve the wine to H. and Telephus so that they can do the toasting.

On these lines Quinn comments as follows: 'A toast to the new month, to the new day which begins at midnight, to Murena as *augur*: i.e., a toast in three stages (timed to begin at midnight) to celebrate Murena's assumption of office on the first of the month (probably January 1st in view of 8).' Other commentators adopt a similar view, of which an essential component is that *lunae...nouae* 'refers not to the new moon...but the new month when Murena assumed his augurate' (N–R); but this cannot be right. It is true that *luna* is sometimes used as an equivalent of 'month', but the present passage is not listed under this equivalence in *TLL*, where the examples are either significantly different or non-classical or both (7.2.1833.25–51).[100] If the toast to midnight is intended to indicate the start of the first day of a new month, it is incompatible with a toast to the new moon, since new moons are visible in the sky for only a very short time just after sunset: at midnight the new month, if indicated by the new moon, is either already several hours old or has not yet started (depending on whether one is calculating from the first or second day of the new moon's appearance). If H. had wanted to indicate a new month, he could easily have substituted *mensis...noui* for *lunae...nouae*, but why should he wish to refer to a new month at all? There is no evidence that augurs took up office at the start of a new year or a new month or at midnight (a strange time for priests whose function was auspicy). The whole hypothesis is flimsy in the extreme.

H. toasts the new moon because it is visible in the sky as he and his friend walk through Rome; but this first toast has to be made quickly (*propere* is placed between *lunae* and *nouae*) because the moon, as already explained, will soon disappear. The toast *noctis mediae* need not indicate the dot of midnight: H. is anticipating that his *comissatio* will continue well into (i.e. the middle of) the night.

10 puer: commands to a slave or *puer* are conventional in sympotic literature (3.14.17–18n.), and most editors think that this vocative points to the scene being in Murena's house. If so, it seems that, amusingly, H.

---

[100] The same qualifications apply to the examples meaning 'day of the lunar month' (ibid. 52–82), the difference being esp. clear in the two cases where the expression *luna noua* occurs (Cic. *Att.* 10.5.1, Caes. *BG* 1.50.5).

has taken upon himself the duties of symposiarch (for which see Lyne, *CP* 317–18), like the drunken Alcibiades when he arrives at the house of Agathon in Plato's *Symposium* (213E). But there is no reason why the *puer* should not be H.'s own, since it was the custom to take one's own slave along to a party (cf. *BNP* 2.496 §5).

10–11 auguris | Murenae: the number of contemporary (and often polyonymous) Murenae is bewildering and controversial. This Murena is likely to be the same Murena as is mentioned at *S.* 1.5.38, where the same phraseology is used of him as appears in line 7 above (7–8n.); but who is he? Some have thought that the likeliest candidate is A. Terentius Varro Murena, conqueror of the Salassi in 25 (Strabo 4.6.7, Dio 53.25.3–4): see Arkenberg 349–50 no. 35 (but note also pp. 345–6 no. 27). The difficulty is that this man was consul elect for 23 but failed to take up office, presumably because he died in the interval after his designation (cf. M. Swan, 'The consular *fasti* of 23 BC and the conspiracy of Varro Murena', *HSCP* 71 (1966) 235–47): it seems highly unlikely that H. would permit the publication in 23 of an ode which referred playfully to a consul designate whose very recent death had prevented his being *consul ordinarius* in that same year. An alternative candidate is L. Licinius Varro Murena, brother-in-law of Maecenas (who was married to Terentia, the man's sister) and usually thought to be brother of the consul designate (Arkenberg 350–1 no. 36); this was the man who conspired against Augustus (almost certainly in 22) and whom some have thought identical with the Licinius addressed in 2.10 (so N–H ad loc. and N–R 227; *contra* Syme, *AA* 387–92). A third possibility is that H. is referring to an otherwise unknown Murena. See also Rüpke 135, 917 (no. 3235); W. on Vell. 91.2 and Tac. *A.* 4.40.6.

Augurs constituted the second most important priestly college after the *pontifices* (the next in line were the *quindecimuiri sacris faciundis* and the *epulones*), and appointment to the augurate (by co-optation) was a great honour (Rüpke 7–9, *BNP* 2.339–41, *OCD* 205). Even if Murena's identity were secure, we would not know the date at which he was co-opted. While the toast to Murena as augur is certainly complimentary, it seems entirely misguided to regard his co-optation (which, after all, is nowhere mentioned) as the *raison d'être* of the whole poem. Another augur, Messalla Corvinus, will be complimented in 3.21.

11–12 tribus aut nouem | miscentur cyathis pocula commodis? 'Are the drinks being mixed with three or nine ladlefuls [sc. of wine], as appropriate?' (*OLD cyathus* 2b, *poculum* 2a). The Romans, like the Greeks, normally diluted their wine with water (Galán Vioque on Mart. 7.20.19, Leary on Mart. 14.105.1), a process for which a *crater(a)* would be used

(Dunbabin 116–20). Printed as a statement, as by most edd., H.'s words are banal; they are a question, equivalent to a command,[101] and they continue the address to the *puer* which began in line 9. H. wants to ensure that the *puer* is mixing two correct sets of drinks, one of them three times stronger than the other.[102] The amusing reason is given in 13–17: since H. is a poet inspired by the nine Muses, he feels entitled to drinks based on nine ladlefuls of wine (13–15a);[103] since Telephus is not a poet, he is expected to make do with drinks which are only a third of that strength (15b–17). *commodis* (*OLD* 2) is to be taken predicatively (cf. *OLS* 1.30), its end position 'carefully marking' the distribution outlined in 13–17 (Page). *poculum* (= the contents of a cup) is often combined with *misceo*, e.g. Ov. *AA* 2.336, *Met.* 10.160, Mart. 14.112.1.

13 qui Musas amat impares: after Telephus' antiquarian lecture (1–4), it is now H.'s turn to harangue his friend. The fronting of the relative clause suggests sententiousness (as Plin. *Ep.* 8.22.3 'qui uitia odit, homines odit' and several of Publilius Syrus' *sententiae*) or legalese (as in some of the clauses in the Twelve Tables, e.g. X.7 'qui coronam parit ipse…'); only in 14–15 do we discover that there is a specific antecedent: 'attonitus…uates'. Conventionally the Muses' assistance to poets is seen in metaphorical terms as draughts of pure water and the like (e.g. Lucil. 1008M/1061W 'quantum haurire animus Musarum e fontibus gestit'; 3.13.15–16n.), the relevance of which will become clear immediately below (14–15n.).

14–15 attonitus petet | uates: H. begins *Epi.* 1.19 with the long-standing antithesis between poets as 'water-drinkers' and as 'wine-drinkers', coming down in support of the latter: 'poetry is a matter of inspiration, so that the poet must be mad or, in more homely terms, drunk' (Macleod 266–7): see esp. Archil. 120 'my wits thunderstruck with wine'. Yet the *attonitus uates* has already been described as 'a lover of the Muses' (13 and n.), thus reflecting not only the combination of water and wine in the friends' actual drinks but also the fact that in Latin 'it is not uncommon

---

[101] SB and Goold print Rutgers' *miscentor*, a third-person plural passive imperative ('let them be mixed'), but the word is unattested elsewhere in literature. N–R obelise *miscentur*.
[102] *aut* is used because the sentence does not comprise two alternative questions (it is not a matter of whether there are nine or three ladlefuls) but two subdivisions of the same question (*NLS* 128 §170 *Note*). *aut* here is almost equivalent to *et*, as S. 1.1.101–2.
[103] H.'s occupation of poet is the ninth to be listed in 1.1 (29–32), alongside mention of the Muses (33) and (nine) canonical lyricists (35).

for poets to seek inspiration both from holy streams and wine' (Crowther 10–11; cf. 3.13.15–16n.). *petet* is a gnomic future (3.1.18–19n.), but of course H. is referring to himself. For the term *uates* see H. D. Jocelyn, '*Poeta* and *Vates*: concerning the nomenclature of the composer of verses in republican and early imperial Rome', in *Studia Classica I. Tarditi oblata* (1995) 1.19–50, esp. 47–9.

15–17 tres prohibet supra | rixarum metuens tangere Gratia | nudis iuncta sororibus 'linked with her naked sisters, the Grace, fearful of quarrels, forbids tasting more than three <ladlefuls>' (*OLD prohibeo* 7, *tango* 5c, *supra*² 5a); for the dislocation of *supra* cf. e.g. Sisenn. 66C/107P, Virg. *G.* 4.236. Just as Varro discussed the appropriate number of dinner-guests by contrasting the nine Muses with the three Graces (cf. Gell. 13.11.1–2), so here H. uses the same groups to contrast ladlefuls of wine. For drunken quarrels see esp. 1.27.1–4, also 3.8.15–16; the genit. with *metuens* is regular (see *OLD*).

18 insanire iuuat: proverbial (N–H on 2.7.28).

18–19 cur Berecyntiae | cessant flamina tibiae? 'Why have the blasts from the Berecyntian *tibia* stopped?' (this is the only ex. of *flamen* of a wind instrument in classical Latin: see *TLL* 6.1.861.4–5). Just as the wine seemed to be running low earlier (5–6), so now the escorting musicians are taking a well-earned 'breather'.

The Berecyntes were a mythical Phrygian tribe who worshipped Cybele, the Great Mother: hence the adj. comes to be used of the goddess or her attributes (*OLD* 2). The 'Berecyntian *tibia*', comprising one curved pipe and one straight (3.7.29–30, Virg. *Aen.* 9.618 with Hardie), was used on 4 April to introduce the Ludi Megale(n)ses (Ov. *F.* 4.181–2), which were held in Cybele's honour and lasted for several days (Scullard 100–1). In an unpublished paper J. G. F. Powell has acutely noted that it was at this festival that leading citizens entertained one another in their houses according to an ancient practice called *mutitatio* (cf. Ov. *F.* 4.353–6, Gell. 2.24.2 'id est mutua inter sese dominia agitarent', 18.2.11). Suggesting further that Augustus revived the augural meeting which had possibly taken place on 5 April but which had fallen into disuse by Cicero's day (cf. *Div.* 1.96), Powell hypothesises that H.'s poem depicts the night of 4 April, as H. and Telephus take advantage of *mutitatio* on the eve of Murena's installation as augur the following day.[104] It is a most attractive hypothesis, but it should

---

[104] I am most grateful to Professor Powell for allowing me to refer to his paper, 'Horace and the calendar', here and on 3.30.8–9.

be noted (i) that the evidence suggests that *mutitatio* was a much more elaborate and organised ritual than is implied by lines 5–8 of the ode – Ovid refers to *indictas...dapes*, 'formally invited dinners' (Fantham) – and (ii) that elsewhere H. can conjoin the Berecyntian *tibia* with the lyre and pipes in a context which has nothing to do with the Megale(n)sia (4.1.22–4). Since music was a standard element of the komos (3.7.29–30n.), there is no reason why it should not feature prominently in a nocturnal *comissatio*: indeed, when the inebriated Alcibiades knocks at Agathon's door demanding to join the ongoing symposium, he is accompanied by a flute-girl (Plato, *Symp.* 212c), an episode which provides a parallel to that suggested for our ode (intro.).

20 cur pendet tacitā fistula cum lyra? 'Why is the pan-pipe idle, with the lyre silent?' For the *fistula* see M. L. West (1992) 109–12; *pendet* refers to hanging from one's belt or similar and hence embraces the wider sense of 'being silent, inactive' (NA on Lygd. 4.38). Strictly a *lyra* (again at 3.28.11; cf. 3.3.69) was a bowl lyre of the type legendarily invented by Mercury (3.11.3–4n.); for *cum* indicating attendant circumstances see *OLD cum*[1] 9a. *tacita...lyra* is perhaps an allusion to the 'silent lyre' at Callim. *Hymn* 2.12 σιωπηλὴν κίθαριν.

22 odi 'I reject' (N–H on 1.38.1); see also 3.1.1n.

sparge rosas!: roses were a standard accompaniment of all types of banquet and the like (3.15.15n.), regardless of season (N–H on 1.38.4): if they could feature in the water-parties at Baiae (Sen. *Ep.* 51.12 'fluitantem toto lacu rosam'), there seems no reason why they should not be carried in baskets by the slave(s) accompanying the *comissatores*. At Ov. *AA* 3.72 '*sparsa nec inuenies limina mane rosa*' it seems more natural to think of scattered petals than the komast's withered garland (see also McKeown on *Am.* 1.2.39–40). Roses would have a special significance for Telephus since his girlfriend was called Rose (27).

22–3 audiat inuidus | dementem strepitum: Propertius refers to an indoor party which can be heard outside in the street (3.10.26 'publica uicinae perstrepat aura uiae'; cf. also Cic. *Rosc. Am.* 134); in our ode H. and Telephus are actually partying in the street (see intro.).

23–4 Lycus | et uicina seni non habilis Lyco 'Lycus and the neighbour unsuitable for old Lycus' (the dat. is to be taken *apo koinou* with *uicina* and *non habilis*); the anonymous girl's unsuitability presumably resides in her youth. Line-final repetition, sometimes with polyptoton, is relatively common in H., as in other poets (Wills 421–3); there is a Lycus ('wolf') at Theocr. 14.24 and 47, where too the name is repeated and in the former line he is implied to be a neighbour. For *uicina* see 3.7.23n.

25–6 spissa te nitidum coma, | puro te similem, Telephe, Vespero: the repeated word order mimics, as it were, what Rhode says to herself about Telephus' attractions – his thick, shiny hair, his star-like appearance. A Telephus reappears at 1.13.1, where it is his actual name which is repeated (see N–H), and 4.11.21. The name suggests 'far-shining' (τῆλε = 'far off' + φῶς = 'light'), like the evening star to which he is compared. Comparisons with stars are as old as Homer (*Il.* 6.401; cf. 3.9.21, 3.15.6; N–H on 1.12.47), but that with Vesper seems rare and possibly unique. *purus* is often used of heavenly bodies (*OLD* 6a; also 3.10.7–8n.); *spissus* is an unusual word for hair, though used of *comae* = 'leaves' at 4.3.11; for *coma* = 'hair' see 3.14.25n.

27 tempestiua petit Rhode: the girl's name means Rose and, unlike the neighbour pursued by Lycus (24), it is she who pursues Telephus and is at just the right season of life (*OLD tempestiuus* 2a). A Telephus is pursued by Phyllis at 4.11.21.

28 me lentus Glycerae torret amor meae: 'No name perhaps had a more definite connotation to a Greek or Roman than the name Glycera. It was one of the most common names of *hetaerae*, and Horace might just as well have used the common noun *meretrix*, except that it would be less refined and romantic' (B. L. Ullman, *AJP* 33 (1912) 152). A Glycera (the name means 'sweet') had appeared thrice in Book 1 (19.5, 30.3, 33.2). *Glycerae...meae* is of course objective genit., and the word order is mannered (adj.[1] noun[2] verb noun[1] adj.[2], with line-framing by *me...meae*). *torret* indicates that *amor* is being seen as a slow-burning fire, as at Tib. 1.4.81 'quam Marathus lento me torret amore!' (*OLD lentus* 4b); see also 1.13.7–8, Ov. *AA* 3.573.

20

This complex ode, one of the most challenging of all H.'s odes, features both a love triangle and the battle of the sexes. The three protagonists are Pyrrhus (the addressee), an unnamed woman, and Nearchus, a beautiful youth who is an object of desire for the other two. Each of these three is described metaphorically: Pyrrhus is a hunter (4), the woman a lioness, and Nearchus her cubs (2). Since metaphor of its nature is a comparative device, we expect a relationship between the literal and the metaphorical (or, to use more technical terminology, between 'tenor' and 'vehicle');[105] the complexity of the ode arises partly from the fact that the comparative element is elided and the metaphor takes on a life of its own. That is: although the metaphor conveys essential truths about the interactions of the three protagonists, it is not possible to explain every element of the metaphor in terms of how each of the three is imagined as reacting in real life. Nevertheless the deployment of leonine imagery, which is largely at home in epic, is a source of wit and humour in an erotic context (see e.g. Lyne, *LLP* 230–3).

Further complexity arises when we try to understand how the interactions of the three protagonists unfold, a matter which is by no means straightforward. H. begins by remarking that Pyrrhus seems not to know the danger involved in stealing Nearchus from the unnamed woman (1–2). The lines neither disclose what the danger is nor make it clear whether Pyrrhus has already stolen Nearchus or is only planning to do so.[106] Of course Pyrrhus himself knows what he has done, and he almost certainly knows what risk he is running, but readers do not yet know either of these things: they learn in the immediately following lines the nature of the danger (3–10), but it is not until lines 11–16 that they discover from the tense of the main verb (13 *fertur...recreare*) what the present situation is: these lines strongly suggest (but admittedly do not prove) that Nearchus no longer belongs to the woman; his behaviour suggests freedom from her possessiveness, from which it appears that Pyrrhus has already stolen him away from her.

Since Pyrrhus has stolen Nearchus, a showdown between Pyrrhus and the woman is in prospect (3–4 *dura...proelia*, a poetic plural), for which the two of them are presently making their respective preparations (9–10 *tu...haec...*); but after a short while the woman will become involved in a great tussle with Pyrrhus' friends to determine whether Nearchus (whom she thinks they are protecting) will be won by her or by Pyrrhus (5–8), at which point Pyrrhus himself will lose his nerve and will decline to participate in the impending showdown altogether (3 'post paulo fugies inaudax'). In the meantime (9 *interim*), as yet unaware that he will be returning to the woman by default, Nearchus himself is shown to be less interested in the outcome of the expected showdown than in the state of his beautiful hair (11–16). The concluding focus upon Nearchus and the

---

[105] I. A. Richards' terms are those used by M. S. Silk, *Interaction in Poetic Imagery* (1974).
[106] On the latter question editors are divided; N–R (240) seemingly embrace each alternative in the same paragraph (they also have Lyne saying the exact opposite of what he does say).

brilliance of his description indicate that the purpose of the ode is not to warn Pyrrhus that he will be the loser but to console him for his loss by signalling Nearchus' indifference to him.

When H. describes the woman as a lioness (2 *leaenae*), Nearchus as her cubs (2 *catulos*) and Pyrrhus as a hunter (4 *raptor*), he seems to have attributed to the 'lioness' similar behaviour to that which Pomponius Mela (3.43) and the elder Pliny (*NH* 8.66) later ascribe to a tigress: when a hunter, for whom both authors use the term *raptor*, has seized a tigress's *catuli*, he withdraws in flight (a *profugus raptor*, as Mela describes him), but he is pursued by the tigress until she has retrieved as many of her young as possible. The linguistic similarities are suggestive, but the description of Nearchus as an onlooker in charge of a victory palm (11–12 *arbiter...palmam*) implies that by the end of the third stanza the imagery has changed: facilitated by the ambiguity of the term *praeda* (7), the metaphor of a hunt in the wild develops into that of a *uenatio* in the arena:[107] fights between men and lions had taken place at Rome since 186 BC (Liv. 39.22.2). The trick which H. has to pull off is to sustain the images while not losing sight of the fact that the mother lioness is a possessive lover.

In the *Satires* an interlocutor accuses H. of rampant bisexuality (2.3.325), and in the *Epodes* H. describes himself as susceptible to boys and girls alike (11.4, 23–8 and Watson's nn.). In Latin literature, as in Greek (e.g. Callim. *Epigr.* 25, Meleager, *Anth. Pal.* 12.109), love triangles are sometimes bisexual (see e.g. Tib. 1.8, 1.9.39–46; Courtney, *Companion* 49–50, 222–3); and, whereas such themes used to be said to be literary constructs without much reference to everyday life, there is now a much greater readiness to accept that a reality lay behind them (cf. Griffin 25–6, S. Harrison, 'Hidden voices: homoerotic colour in Horace's Odes', in S. Matzner and S. Harrison (edd.), *Complex Inferiorities: The Poetics of the Weaker Voice in Latin Literature* (2018) 169–84). There may never have been a Pyrrhus or a Nearchus, but in Augustan Rome there will have been many like them.[108]

METRE Sapphic

1 Non uides quanto moueas periclo...? 'Don't you see how dangerous it is for you to move...?' With a name like Pyrrhus (2n.), H.'s addressee ought to know from his Homer (*Il.* 18.318–22), if not from elsewhere, how dangerous it is to steal the cubs of a lion(ess) (see also Soph. *Aj.*

---

[107] There is exactly the same development at Tac. *Agr.* 34.3 (see W.).
[108] It is impossible to know the putative ages of the various protagonists in the ode; Cicero portrays Clodia, then in her late 30s, as pursuing *adulescentuli* (*Cael.* 36).

986–7; later at e.g. Ov. *Met.* 13.547–8, Stat. *Silv.* 2.1.8–9 with van Dam). *moueo* in the sense of 'remove' (as Virg. *Aen.* 8.213) seems required by the context, although many edd. prefer 'disturb'; *quanto...periclo* is abl. of attendant circumstances (*NLS* 31 §43 (5) (ii)), as e.g. Cic. *Sull.* 28 'non sum nescius quanto periculo uiuam'. Pyrrhus' means of stealing Nearchus (e.g. slandering the woman or bribing the youth) are left unsaid.

2 Pyrrhe: in Greek myth Pyrrhus ('red-haired') is an alternative name for Neoptolemus, Achilles' son and a warrior at Troy. It was also the name of the third-century king of Epirus (3.6.35–6n.), from whom we get the proverbial 'Pyrrhic victory'; a reference to the latter (so Quinn and West) would certainly be neat, but whether the king's words (Plut. *Pyrrh.* 21.9) already constituted a proverb in H.'s time is unknown.

Gaetulae catulos leaenae: lions 'are conventionally Gaetulian' (N–H on 1.22.15), the adj. being loosely used for 'African' (1.23.10; *OLD*). The *leaena*, a choice noun which recurs in H. only at 3.11.41 (n.), represents the woman from whom Pyrrhus has just stolen Nearchus. For the repeated *-ae-* sounds cf. 1.2.42–3 'almae...Maiae', Virg. *Aen.* 3.386 'Aeaeae'.

3–5 dura post paulo fugies inaudax | proelia raptor | cum... 'After a short while, as a *faint-hearted* hunter/ravisher/thief, you will avoid the harsh battle [sc. with the lioness] when she...' (*OLD fugio* 11–12). With one exception (4.14.14), *proelium* is always plur. in H.: the present instance is a 'poetic' plural, as often in Virgil (Williams on *Aen.* 5.98), and refers to the showdown (11 *pugnae*) which the lioness and Pyrrhus seem destined to have but in which, as is predicted here, Pyrrhus will decline to participate (for *proelium* of fights with animals see *TLL* 10.2.1651.53–5). No reason is offered for H.'s confidence that Pyrrhus, despite his success in stealing Nearchus from the woman, will prove faint-hearted in the long run; we must just assume that H. knows what he is talking about, based on his familiarity with the addressee. For some other erotic competitions see Bowie on Longus, *D&C* 1.15.4. The combination *dura... proelia* recurs once each in Liv. Prop. Sil. (Virg. *Aen.* 7.806–7 is disputed). *raptor* is multiply suggestive (*OLD* 1–2); its combination with *inaudax*, a rendering of ἄτολμος which occurs only here in extant Latin, is characteristically Horatian (Intro. 25, 26). *post paulo* (again at *S.* 1.2.120, *Epi.* 1.6.43, 1.18.33) recurs in Caesar, Sallust, Livy and Quintilian; *paulo post* is the normal order in Cicero.

5–6 cum per obstantes iuuenum cateruas | ibit insignem repetens Nearchum 'when she is going [lit. will be going] through the bands of young men obstructing her, to reclaim her beautiful Nearchus' (*OLD repeto* 5a; cf. 8a): *ibit* indicates that the woman's actions are contemporaneous with that of Pyrrhus in 3–4: while she is grappling with the young men, he will withdraw in fear from the impending duel. In metaphorical terms Pyrrhus seems to acquire a retinue of fellow hunters, who, perhaps by forming a cordon, will try to obstruct the lioness's attempts at reaching her young. A non-metaphorical reading of the lines is more difficult. The *iuuenes* are Pyrrhus' comrades, who, empathising with his love for the 'young leader' (Nearchus = νέος + ἄρχων),[109] will try to prevent the woman from getting him back. *obstantes* is of course not to be taken too literally (contrast 4.9.43 'per obstantes cateruas', Sen. *Contr.* 5.5): perhaps we are to imagine the youths offering themselves to the woman in an attempt to distract her from Nearchus; the scene is the converse of that in Cat. 55, where it is girls who use their charms in the hope of distracting the poet in his search for his beloved Camerius. The use of the present participle to express purpose, esp. with a verb of seeking (as here, *repetens*), is a feature of Cicero's late writings, e.g. *ND* 2.125 (Laughton 30–1); see also *OLS* 1.544 for exs. from Livy.

7–8 grande certamen, tibi praeda cedat | an magis illi 'a great contest, <to see whether> the prize will fall to you or rather to her'. *grande certamen*, usually taken to be accus., is in apposition to the *cum*-clause (5–6): i.e. it summarises the young men's interaction with the lioness/woman. For an accus. in apposition to a clause or sentence see *NLS* 10 §15, G&L 204 §324; *certamen* in various of its meanings is regularly followed by an indir. question (see *OLD*); here *utrum* has been omitted, as often in alternative questions. *grandis* 'probably had a freshness which *magnus* may have lacked' (Brink on *Epi.* 2.2.178–9). As *praeda* can mean 'prey' (*OLD* 2), it sustains the metaphor of Pyrrhus as hunter; but *praeda* is also the 'prize' (*OLD* 3) for which Pyrrhus and the woman are competing jointly: the term is appropriate not only for an erotic competition (Pichon 238) but also for a contest in the arena (11–13). For *praeda cedat* cf. Liv. 23.33.11, 26.26.3, Tac. *A.* 13.39.4.

The transmitted text reads *praeda... | maior an illi*. The phrase *praeda maior* (again at *Epi.* 1.15.38) is regular, esp. in Livy (e.g. 10.17.6), but the comparative here is problematic, since there is only one prize – Nearchus. No satisfactory defence of the paradosis has been suggested; the translation 'the rather large prize', proposed by some edd., is inadequate to the

---

[109] Cf. Theog. 1319–20 'Boy, since the Cyprian goddess gave you a beauty that arouses desire and all the young men are obsessed with your looks...' (Loeb trans.).

COMMENTARY 20.9–14 287

context. Rudd and seemingly also Nisbet favour the view that H. is referring to the question 'whether the man or the woman will get greater pleasure from the sexually ambiguous Nearchus', but this seems very difficult to extract from the Latin. Peerlkamp offered *maior an illă*, 'or whether she is the winner/stronger', but the omission of *sit* would be unique in the *Odes* and the required meaning of *maior* is not easy to parallel. I suggest *an magis*, a common combination found again at *S*. 2.3.67 'tune insanus eris si acceperis an magis excors...?' A scribe mistakenly wrote the almost synonymous *magis an* (another regular combination, e.g. Curt. 5.9.10 'quorum nos pudeat magis an paeniteat, incertum est') instead of *an magis*; subsequently it was realised that this will not scan, but, instead of transposing the words, *magis* was 'corrected' to *maior*. For the shape of the line cf. 12 below, 3.18.12, 16, 3.27.16.

9–14 interim...fertur...capillis: these lines describe what is happening in the interval (*interim*) between the woman's loss of Nearchus (1–2) and the expected showdown (3–8) in the near future (*post paulo*, to which *interim* looks back).

9–10 dum tu...acuit timendos: the two-part *dum*-clause (*tu...haec...*) performs the function of arming scenes in epic, such as those of Turnus and Aeneas in the *Aeneid* (12.81–112 with Tarrant: note 108 'Aeneas acuit Martem'). *promis* and *acuit* are the regular present tenses to be expected in a *dum*-clause (3.21.23–4n.).

9 celeres sagittas: *celeris* is regular to describe *sagitta* in verse, perhaps because of an alleged etymological connection (Isid. *Orig.* 18.8.1 'sagitta a sagaci ictu, id est ueloci ictu'; Maltby 538). Arrows would naturally be used by a hunter; the evidence for their use against wild beasts in the arena (11–13) is unfortunately scarce (Dio 63.3.2).

10 haec dentes acuit timendos '<and> she is sharpening her fearsome teeth' (asyndeton, pointed by *tu* ~ *haec*). Teeth-sharpening is usually illustrated by a boar (Hom. *Il*. 11.416, 13.474, Virg. *G*. 3.255, [Tib.] 3.9.3, Plin. *NH* 18.2, Sen. *Ira* 1.1.6, 3.4.1, *Phaedr*. 346–7) but cf. *Rhet. Herenn.* 4.51 'sicut e cauea leo emissus aut aliqua taeterrima belua soluta ex catenis...acuens dentes'.

11–13 arbiter pugnae posuisse nudo | sub pede palmam | fertur: *pugnae* refers to the showdown for which Pyrrhus and the woman are currently preparing (9–10) but which Pyrrhus will soon decline when he loses his nerve (3–4). Although many edd. think that *arbiter* means 'judge' here

(*OLD arbiter*[1] 2) and that Nearchus himself will decide which of the rivals he favours, this is inconsistent with his implied description in 1–10 as the possession of one or other of them. *arbiter* must have its primary meaning of 'onlooker' (as Sen. *Tro.* 1070 'arbiter belli' (*OLD* 1); compare Deianira at Soph. *Trach.* 523–5), which complements nicely the indifference on display in 13b–14: as the prize in the expected showdown, Nearchus is unconcerned whether he is won by Pyrrhus or the woman. *fertur* is not easy to explain: perhaps we are to imagine that word of Nearchus' indifference has emerged from wherever Pyrrhus has secured him (cf. 5–6): '*the talk is that* Nearchus has put the palm [sc. of victory] under his naked foot'. The palm is symbolic of the winner's prize (Murgatroyd on Tib. 1.9.81–2), which is Nearchus himself; because his hands are too busy rearranging his hair (13–14n.), he is said to have trapped the palm under his foot, emphasising his unconcern about the eventual winner. His foot is unshod perhaps to show that he is 'beautifully ankled' (καλλίσφυρος), although this is more normally an attribute of girls.

13–14 et leni recreare uento | sparsum odoratis umerum capillis is said to mean 'and in the soft breeze to be fanning [*or* cooling] his shoulder, covered with his perfumed hair'. This is impossible to believe; why would anyone fan their shoulder? I think the meaning is: 'and that in the soft breeze he is rearranging the spread of his perfumed hair on his shoulder' (lit. 'his spread-with-his-perfumed-hair shoulder', as if the hair and shoulder were a single, artfully composed feature which has been slightly disturbed in the gentle breeze). *recreare* means 'to restore to a previous condition', as again at 3.24.16. Gorgeous long hair was the defining characteristic of *pueri delicati* such as Nearchus (cf. 4.10.3 with Thomas; Watson on *Epo.* 11.28; Schmeling on Petr. 27.1). This final stanza with its concluding simile (15–16) resembles those at 1.8.13–16, 2.5.21–4 and 4.1.37–40: such 'lingering vignettes' are 'an established form of Horatian closure in the *Odes*' (Harrison on 2.5.21–4; see also Schrijvers, *OR* 68 and n. 44) and for hair in particular as a closural motif see Oliensis (100–3 for our ode). Compare the description of Ganymede at Eur. *Tro.* 835–7 'while by the throne of Zeus you keep that face, young in its charms, in its beautiful serenity' (Loeb trans.). For the prosaic *capillus* see 3.14.25n.

15 qualis...Nireus fuit '<one> such as Nireus was', i.e. 'the image of Nireus'. Nireus was the most handsome of the Greeks at Troy apart from Achilles (Hom. *Il.* 2.673–4); used again as an example of beauty at *Epo.* 15.22, where see Mankin. *fuit* seems flat, but Peerlkamp's *puer* is unpersuasive.

15–16 aquosa | raptus ab Ida '<the one> snatched from well-watered Mt Ida' (*raptus* looks back to 4 *raptor*). The reference is to Ganymede, a frequent *exemplum* of a sexually attractive youth (Henriksén on Mart. 9.11.7) and famous for his lovely hair (Mart. 9.16.6 'Ganymedeas... comas'). He was seized from Mt Ida by the eagle of Zeus/Jupiter to be the divine cup-bearer (4.4.1–4 and Thomas ad loc., Virg. *Aen.* 5.254–5; Pease on Cic. *ND* 1.112); H.'s omission of his name attests to the familiarity of the story. *aquosa* (again at Ov. *F.* 6.15 'aquosae...Idae') represents the Homeric Ἴδην...πολυπίδακα, 'Ida with many springs' (*Il.* 8.47, *al.*; cf. 11.183).

21

This ode consists of two sets of three stanzas. It begins as a cletic or 'summoning' prayer to a wine-jar (4–7 'pia testa...descende') and exhibits wittily many of the formulaic features that are to be found in a real prayer to a divinity (e.g. 2n., 5–6n.). One such feature is the repeated use of the second-person pronoun (2 *tu*, 10 *te*); but, when this use becomes dominant in the second half of the ode, being repeated five times in lines 13–24, the pronoun also illustrates what is called 'container/content' metonymy (cf. *Rhet. Herenn.* 4.43 'ab eo quod continet, id quod continetur'; Lausberg 258 §568.1d), since H. is no longer addressing the jar but the wine contained within it (see also 1n.). The prayer thus develops into, or includes, an encomium of wine, the latter belonging to a noble tradition to which H. alludes elsewhere (1.18.3–6, *Epi.* 1.5.16–20) and which can be traced back as far as Homer (*Od.* 14.463–6; cf. Pind. fr. 124ab, Bacchyl. fr. 20B, Ov. *AA* 1.237–42, 589–602, *Anth. Pal.* 9.524; NA on Lygd. 6).

The transition between the first half of the ode and the second is managed by the reference to M. Valerius Messalla Corvinus (7–12), the extremely distinguished statesman and orator whom H. has invited to a *conuiuium* and in whose honour the ode is therefore written (7–8n.). The man's political affiliations had followed a similar trajectory to those of H. himself. Like H., Corvinus studied in Athens as a young man and subsequently fought on the side of Brutus and Cassius at Philippi in 42 BC but was eventually reconciled to Octavian; unlike H., he had a public career and was rewarded for his support by being made consul along with Octavian in 31 BC, the year of Actium, where he was one of the commanders. He celebrated a triumph in 27 and in the following year was *praefectus urbis*, though he resigned after six days (3.8.17n.; Tac. *A.* 6.11.3 with W.). Like Maecenas, Messalla was both patron and poet; he was the dedicatee of the *Panegyricus Messallae* and *Catalepton* 9;[110] and he featured in H.'s *Sermones* (1.10.29, 85). His literary circle, which included Lygdamus, Ovid and Sulpicia, also embraced poets addressed by H., such as Tibullus (1.33, *Epi.* 1.4) and Valgius Rufus (2.9).[111] These literary interactions are well illustrated by the work of Maecenas, who is known to have written a Platonic dialogue entitled *Symposium* which featured, among others, Virgil and Messalla Corvinus along with H. himself (3.8.5n.). And it is surely relevant to H.'s encomium of wine that Corvinus is known to have spoken in praise of wine in the dialogue (Serv. *Aen.* 8.310): 'ex persona Messallae de ui uini loqueretur, ita: "idem umor ministrat faciles oculos, pulchriora reddit omnia, et dulcis iuuentae reducit bona"'. This is one of those odes where external evidence indicates something of the social relationships which lie behind them.[112] H.'s reference to an 'auspicious day' (6 'bono die') suggests that there was a special occasion which led to the composition of the ode; but what that occasion was – whether Corvinus' birthday or some other celebration (cf. Tib. 1.7) – is unknown.

METRE Alcaic

1 O nata mecum consule Manlio: H. was born on 8 December 65 BC (*Epi.* 1.20.2-8,[113] Suet. *Vita Hor.*; Bradshaw, *TC* 2-10) in the consulship of L. Manlius Torquatus (*MRR* 2.157), whose magistracy is again used affectionately to date wine at *Epo.* 13.6 'uina Torquato moue consule pressa meo' (see Watson). *nascor*, a verb with a very wide set of applications (including wine, as *S.* 2.8.47, *ILS* 8580 (quoted at 3.8.12n.); *OLD* 7), here denotes the year when the wine-jar was filled (3.8.12n.) rather than (as Mart. 14.101.1 'calices de puluere natos') the year it was manufactured. This prepares for the fact that H. is mostly talking about the contents of the jar rather than the jar itself (see intro.). If Corvinus was born in 65 BC rather than (as is usually thought) 64, he will have been the same age as the *testa* and as H. himself (so Nisbet, *TC* 83; cf. Bradshaw, *TC* 6-7). Birth and ancestry were conventional topics in hymns and prayers (N-H on 1.10.1): *nata mecum* suggests a twin sister, rather like Diana for Apollo;

---

[110] He is also thought to have been the dedicatee of the *Ciris*, though this is denied by Lyne (pp. 54-5 of his edition).
[111] The Codrus who features in Valgius fr. 2C/166H is thought by some to be Corvinus (see Hollis ad loc.).
[112] Not everyone agrees that the speaker in the dialogue is our Messalla (Syme, *AA* 385 and n. 15), but the identification seems overwhelmingly likely.
[113] In this passage H. mentions his age at the time of writing (cf. 2.4.23-4, 4.1.6, *Anth. Pal.* 12.46.1 (Asclepiades), Enn. ap. Gell. 17.21.43, Aug. *RG* 35.2, Ov. *Tr.* 4.10.5-6).

H. does not reveal immediately that he is referring to a wine-jar or that *mecum* merely indicates contemporaneity (*OLD cum*[1] 6a). For the initial *O*, a feature of prayers, see 3.13.1n.

2–4 seu tu...somnum: prayers or hymns conventionally exhibit one or more *si*-clauses to name the function(s) of the divine addressee (3.18.5n.). Here H. lists the activities which are facilitated by the contents of the wine-jar: lovers' *rixae* (3.14.25–6), *ioci* and affairs (*Epi.* 2.2.56), easy sleep (2.11.5–8), all of which he elsewhere associates with youth. When the ode was published, Corvinus was in his early 40s, and in Maecenas' *Symposium* he is represented as praising wine precisely for bringing back the 'dulcis iuuentae bona' (intro.): see Evans 198–200.

2 seu tu querellas siue geris iocos: *querellae* suggests maudlin complaints about one's love life (Pichon 248), to which drinkers are esp. liable (3.19.28, *Epo.* 11 with Mankin and Watson); wine and wit are natural partners (Cat. 12.2, 50.6, Ov. *AA* 1.594, Lygd. 6.20 'uina iocosa'; also 15–16 below). *geris* = 'contain, hold' (*OLD* 2a), as Mart. 4.88.6 'testa... quae cottana parua gerit'; the conceit is that the jar contains the effects of its contents. For *tu* see 13–14n.

3 rixam et insanos amores: *rixam* indicates *either* lovers' quarrels (cf. 1.13.9–11 'seu tibi candidos | turparunt umeros immodicae mero | rixae', 3.14.26) *or* brawls in general (cf. 1.18.8–9 'rixa super mero | debellata', 1.27.1–4); the former is made more likely by the co-ordination (*et*) with *insanos amores* (contrast *siue* in 2). For the association of wine with sex see 3.18.6–7n.; for the insanity of love see Pichon 172.

4 seu facilem, pia testa, somnum: the address to the wine-jar (as *Anth. Pal.* 9.229.3) is an extension of such personifications as that of the amphora at 3.28.8. For the soporific effects of wine see e.g. Enn. *Ann.* 292, Virg. *Aen.* 2.265, Ov. *Am.* 1.4.53–4 and McKeown, Sil. 7.205. For *facilis* used of *somnus* cf. 2.11.8, Ov. *Her.* 11.29, Stat. *Theb.* 8.217. *pius* is an appropriate word for H.'s 'twin' (1n.), since its application to relatives ('devoted': *OLD* 3c) is regular (cf. Syndikus 2.181 n. 7); N–R prefer to think of its application to divinities ('kindly'), but admit that this is a 'rare usage'.

5–6 quocumque lectum nomine Massicum | seruas: this is a joke. In hymns/prayers it was conventional to add a so-called 'blanket clause', in which, to prevent offending the divinity being addressed, one said 'by whatever (other) name you wish to be called' *uel sim.*, e.g. Cat. 34.21–2 'sis quocumque tibi placet | sancta nomine' (N–H on 1.32.15, pp. 366–7). Our clause uses the same formula but, since it actually names the wine ('Massicum'), must have a different meaning: '*for whatever purpose* you are preserving the choice Massic' (*OLD nomen* 26a: 'perh. always abl., w. pron. adjs. or w. gen.', quoting this ex.), thus adding the catch-all formula to the possible purposes already specified by *seu...siue...seu...seu...* (for *seruo* = 'preserve' see *OLD* 7; for *lectus* = 'choice, excellent' cf. Lucr. 5.965 'pira lecta'; *OLD lectus*¹ 2). Monte Massico is just inland from the coastal town of Sinuessa (*BA* Map 44: E3); the local wine (again at 1.1.19, 2.7.21, *S.* 2.4.51) was famous (Virg. *G.* 2.143, *al.*, Plin. *NH* 3.60, Colum. 3.8.5 etc.). In Book 2 H. urges Massic wine upon a fellow veteran of Philippi in order to forget (2.7.21 'obliuioso...Massico'); here he chooses the same wine to help another veteran of Philippi to remember (Bradshaw, *TC* 6–7).

6 moueri digna bono die 'worthy of being removed [sc. from your store] on an auspicious day' (*OLD bonus* 17b): see intro. *dignus* perhaps illustrates prayer language (3.13.2n.); it may also be relevant that *dignus* + infin. occurs twice in *Catalepton* 9 (8, 16), addressed to Corvinus: was it a mannerism of his? For *moueri* cf. *Epo.* 13.6 (quoted above, 1n.); the reference is to the *apotheca* (next n.).

7 descende: another joke. In a cletic or 'summoning' hymn/prayer one might ask a divinity to 'descend' from heaven (3.4.1n.); here the wine-jar is being summoned from the upstairs *apotheca*, where it has been maturing since 65 BC (3.8.10–11n.). The imperative strongly suggests that H. is the host and Corvinus the guest and not, as some have thought, the other way round.

7–8 Coruino iubente | promere languidiora uina: sc. *me* (the accus. is regularly omitted with *iubeo*, e.g. 2.3.14). Unless H.'s guest has pre-empted the role of *magister bibendi* (3.19.10n.), which seems unlikely (next n.), *iubente* probably has its weakened sense of 'ask' (*OLD* 7a): when H. issued his invitation, he perhaps urged Corvinus, whose special day it was (intro.), to suggest what kind of wine he would like (cf. *S.* 2.8.16–17); Corvinus' acceptance of the invitation will then have been accompanied by an indication, expressed in humorous terms which prompted reciprocation in the ode, of his preference for *languidiora uina*. The adj. *languidus* (evidently = 'mellow') seems not to be technical of wine (cf. 3.16.34–5); *uina* is plur. for sing., as often. For M. Valerius Messalla Corvinus see Syme, *AA* 200–43 and Table IX; *BNP* 15.187–8 [II 16]; and esp. Nisbet (*TC* 80–92, a masterly discussion of the ode) and A. Drummond (*FRH* 1.463–6). For the appended abl. abs. see 3.1.30–1n.

9–10 non ille, quamquam Socraticis madet | sermonibus, te neglegit horridus 'Although he is steeped in Socratic dialogues, he is not the man to neglect you sternly': the sentence is a generalisation (for the metaphor cf. Plin. *Ep.* 3.12.1 'Socraticis... sermonibus abundet', an allusion to our ode). The third-person *ille* strongly suggests that, when the jar of Massic is summoned (1–7), Corvinus is not yet present at the poet's house: he has provided in advance an indication of the kind of wine he would like (7–8n.). Since *madeo* can mean 'to be drunk' (*OLD* 3), there is the ironical suggestion that Corvinus will arrive at H.'s house already inebriated; and, since wine was a traditional obstacle to wisdom (3.28.4n.), there are the further ironies that Corvinus is not only able to combine philosophising with drinking but that this ability will be in evidence on his visit. *horridus* is an apt adj. for grim philosophers (e.g. Cic. *Fin.* 4.78; *OLD* 5).

11–12 narratur et prisci Catonis | saepe mero caluisse uirtus: *narratur* introduces an *exemplum* in defence of Corvinus' drinking as described in 9–10: 'it is said that even virtuous old Cato often warmed with neat-wine' (for *merum* used in contexts of heavy drinking cf. 1.13.10, 1.36.13, 2.12.5). *prisci* identifies Cato as the Elder (cos. 195 BC, censor 184 BC; *MRR* 1.339, 374–5), who was well known for his extended *conuiuia* (23–4n. below) and at *Epi.* 2.2.117 is again described as *priscus*, which was said to have been his original cognomen (Plut. *Cato Mai.* 1.2). Yet the elevated periphrasis *Catonis...uirtus* (= 'virtuous Cato': cf. 3.12.8n.), combined with *Socraticis... sermonibus* in the couplet of which lines 11–12 are adduced as support, suggests also a reference to Cato the Younger, who was the personification of *uirtus* (e.g. Vell. 35.2 'homo Virtuti simillimus', Luc. 9.371 'uirtus... Catonis'), whose suicide in 46 BC was famously Socratic, and who was also a notorious drinker (Plut. *Cato Min.* 6.2 'at night over the wine he would converse with philosophers'). Nisbet's suggestion that there are 'hints' of the younger Cato is most attractive (*TC* 86): Roman poets elsewhere 'conflate' the characters of history (see Cairns, *PRE* 197–211).

caleo is often used of persons warmed by wine (e.g. *Epo.* 11.13–14 'calentis...feruidiore mero', Mart. 8.45.6, Stat. *Theb.* 5.263), but the Platonic reference in 9–10 may mean that the words *mero caluisse uirtus* have an additional resonance. In Books 1–2 of his *Laws* (e.g. 671B–C) Plato formulates the theory that wine restores in older persons some of the fire which they had in their youth, making them more educable in the pursuit of virtue (see E. Belfiore, 'Wine and catharsis of the emotions in Plato's *Laws*', *CQ* 36 (1986) 421–37). This notion accords well with a wine chosen for its nostalgic resonances (1n., 5–6n.), and the positive attitude to wine in these lines prepares neatly for the encomium which follows in the second half of the ode. For such terms as *narratur* to enhance the authority of an *exemplum* and the like see 3.5.41–3n.; for the elder Cato as an *exemplum* see N–H or Harrison on 2.15.11. Messalla Corvinus' own *uirtus* is singled out at the start of the *Panegyricus Messallae* ([Tib.] 3.7.1 'cognita uirtus').

13–14 tu lene tormentum ingenio admoues | plerumque duro 'You apply mild torture to a generally dour character': *admoues* looks back to *moueri* (6) and represents a follow-up activity (cf. 3.14.1–4n.). *tormentum admouere* is a set phrase (Curt. 6.11.31, 9.7.8), and torture was often used to get people to speak (cf. Liv. 27.43.3 'metus tormentorum admotus fateri uera coegit'): see esp. *AP* 434–5 'reges dicuntur multis urgere culillis | et torquere mero', *Epi.* 1.18.38 'commissumque teges et uino tortus et ira'; for the general notion that drinking leads to garrulity cf. 3.19.3n. For the oxymoron *lene tormentum* (here underlined by the polar tension with *ingenio... duro*) cf. Bacchyl. fr. 20B.6 γλυκεῖ' ἀνάγκα, 'sweet compulsion' (also of wine: see below, 19–20n.), Mart. 7.29.1 'tormentum dulce' (with Galán Vioque); *lenis*, a natural antithesis to *durus* (e.g. Ov. *Am.* 2.1.22), is often used of wine (3.29.2; *OLD* 3). Use of the second-person pronoun, often repeated (as in this ode), is a regular feature of prayers/hymns (see 3.11.13–14n.). *plerumque* (again at 3.29.13) is a prosaic word (N–H on 1.34.7).

14–16 tu sapientium | curas et arcanum iocoso | consilium retegis Lyaeo: these lines, which are almost a free translation of Hom. *Od.* 14.463–6, evidently illustrate the proverbial *in uino ueritas* (Otto 372, Tosi 343 §732). *sapientium curas* relates to the question, which is to be answered in the affirmative, 'whether philosophy is a fitting topic over a drink' (Plut. *Mor.* 612E: see esp. 613C 'Dionysus is...the Loosener [Λυαῖος]...and especially unbridles the tongue', 614A 'to philosophise without seeming to philosophise and to accomplish in jest the issues of the earnest'). *arcanum... consilium* may have a similar reference but more probably relates to private issues (cf. *Epo.* 11.13–14 'calentis...feruidiore mero arcana promorat loco'), although Corvinus can be confident that H. knows how to keep a secret (3.2.25–9). *sapientium* = 'philosophers' (*OLD sapiens*[2] b); *retego* = 'to uncover, disclose' (*OLD* 3). It is hard to know whether *iocoso...Lyaeo* (for which cf. 4.15.26 'iocosi...Liberi', Lygd. 6.20 'uina iocosa') is dat. or abl., and, if the latter, what kind of abl. ('Lyaeus being fond of a joke'?); Lyaeus, 'the Loosener' (from λύω), is another name for Bacchus (cf. *Epo.* 9.38): the motif is continued in *Liber* and *soluere* below (21–2).

17 tu spem reducis mentibus anxiis: as in the invitation to Torquatus at *Epi.* 1.5.16–18 ('ebrietas...operta recludit, | spes iubet esse ratas,...| sollicitis animis onus eximit'), H. transitions to the notion that wine soothes cares (Otto 372, Tosi 345 §736), another favourite proverb (1.18.4 and N–H, 2.11.17–18). H. likes to repeat *re-*compounds (e.g. 1.16.27–8, 1.29.11–12, 3.5.25–8 *repensus…redibit…refert*); here the prefix has two different nuances (as 1.24.15–17 *redeat…recludere*, 2.1.37–8 *relictis…retractes*, 2.3.6–7 *remoto…reclinatum*).

18–20 uiresque et addis cornua pauperi: it is disputed whether *-que* co-ordinates *spem* and *uires* ('hope and strength') or *reducis* and *addis* ('and you impart strength and horns to the pauper', as if *uiresque addis et cornua*): the latter supposes a dislocation of conjunction which would be typical of H. (3.1.12–13n.), while the co-ordination of abstract and concrete is a pleasing bonus. Horns symbolise strength (Otto 94), as Ov. *AA* 1.239 'pauper cornua sumit' (a passage which echoes our ode).

19–20 post te neque iratos trementi | regum apices neque militum arma '(the pauper) who, after you, quakes neither at the crowns of angry kings nor at the weapons of soldiers' (*apices* are the peaks of oriental crowns, and *iratos* is a transferred epithet). After sampling the contents of a wine-jar (for the brachylogical use of *post* see N–H on 1.18.5 'post uina') the poor man thinks he can do anything: the fantasy is a modified version of Bacchyl. fr. 20B (mentioned at 13–14n. above): 'wine sends a man's thoughts soaring on high: immediately he is destroying the battlements of cities, and he expects to be monarch over all the world' (lines 10–12, Loeb trans.); cf. also Pind. fr. 124AB.7–8. For the transitive use of *tremo* see *OLD* 2.

21–3 Liber et (si laeta aderit) Venus 'Liber and (if she is happy to attend) Venus…': these two are the first of the four subjects of *producent* (23). As the final honour for the *testa*, H. envisages a *conuiuium* attended by various appropriate divinities which will last all night until Phoebus as the sun god returns (24); H.'s exclamation at *S.* 2.6.65 ('O noctes cenaeque deum!') suggests that divine parties were proverbial (cf. also Suet. *Aug.* 70). The gods are both themselves and, in the present case, metonymical for wine and lovemaking (for the connection between the two see 3.18.6–7n.): for such fusions see 3.13 intro. *laeta* 'suggests the gracious pleasure of a visiting deity' (N–H on 1.2.46); *aderit* alludes to the ritual imperative *ades*, conventional in cletic prayers (NA on Lygd. 6.1), although it is also the appropriate verb for attending a *conuiuium* (Suet. *Tib.* 61.6): see also 3.27.66n.

22 segnesque nodum soluere Gratiae 'and the Graces loath to loosen the link [sc. between them].' The Graces, one of whom is again co-ordinated with Bacchus in *Catalepton* 9 (60), addressed to Corvinus, symbolise dancing: since in Roman times 'the Graces were normally portrayed naked' (N–H on 1.30.5–6 'solutis...zonis'; also 3.19.17, 4.7.6), *nodus* seems more likely to refer to their linked hands (3.19.17) than to their girdles, although the latter meaning is easier to parallel than the former (cf. *OLD nodus* 2c, 6a). For *segnis* + inf. cf. Ov. *Tr.* 5.7.19.

23–4 uiuaeque producent lucernae, | dum rediens fugat astra Phoebus 'and the lighted lamps will keep you going, until the return of Phoebus puts the stars to flight': *uiuus* is technical of fire or lamps (*OLD* 5); for the sense of *produco* see Winterbottom on [Quint.] *Decl.* 260.16, though none of his exs. is quite the same as this, which seems an extension of such expressions as *cenam producere* (S. 1.5.70) or *noctem producere* (Mart. 2.89.1). It may be relevant that both Catos (cf. 11–12n.) were well known for their extended symposia (respectively Cic. *Senec.* 46 'conuiuiumque...ad multam noctem quam maxime possumus vario sermone producimus' and Plut. *Cato Min.* 6.1 'he would often pass the time till dawn in drinking'). The rule for *dum* = 'until' is as follows: 'When the main verb is future, imperative, or an expression that refers to the future, *and is not negatived*, the present indicative (*not* the future simple) is used in the temporal clause' (*NLS* 182 §223 (*a*)). The use of a nom. present participle in the *ab urbe condita* idiom (for which see 3.4.18–19n.) is first in Cicero (see *NLS* 76 §95, Laughton 96–9); see also 3.16.29–32n. above. *fugare astra* returns with Statius (*Silv.* 3.2.12, *Theb.* 8.274; cf. also Ferri on *Octav.* 1–2).

22

Artemis was the subject of two short *Homeric Hymns* (9 and 27) and of Callimachus' long third *Hymn*; she was also addressed by Anacreon (348) and seemingly by other Greek lyric poets (cf. Menand. rhet. 334.28–30 with Russell–Wilson). Diana, her Roman equivalent, was the subject of a well-known hymnic poem of Catullus (34) and, along with her brother Apollo, had been hymned by H. in Book 1 of the *Odes* (21). As is clear from line 5, our poem is formally a dedication (see esp. Cairns, *RL* 441–61), a category amply exemplified in Book 6 of the Greek Anthology. Although one could dismiss the ode as merely a literary exercise, the fact that dedications to Diana have survived on inscriptions (see Courtney, *ML* Nos. 139–42, pp. 136–9) suggests that matters are not so straightforward. In particular, in 17 BC, Augustus celebrated the Ludi Saeculares, for which H. wrote his *Carmen Saeculare*, and Diana featured prominently both in the ritual and in the poem (see Thomas's commentary on the latter). Our ode may reflect an episode in H.'s life; we simply do not know.

METRE Sapphic

1 Montium custos nemorumque uirgo: the *Homeric Hymns* to Artemis, Callimachus' Hymn to Artemis, and Catullus' hymn to Diana all begin, as does *Odes* 1.21, with the goddess's name; here we have to infer her name from her cult-titles or roles, an inference assisted translinguistically by *uirgo*: the name Artemis was supposedly derived from ἀρτεμής, 'whole, intact'. Artemis asked Zeus to be assigned all mountains, and it was on mountains that she proposed to dwell (Callim. *H.* 3.18, 20); for Catullus she is 'montium domina' (34.9). *custos* is a regular term for tutelary deities (*OLD* 1a): *montium custos* is unparalleled, but, since ὀρει- compounds are common in Greek, is perhaps intended to hint at a learned compound, 'mountain-guard'. *nemorumque* is an allusion to Diana's cult-title of Nemorensis, by which she was worshipped at Lake Nemi, just south of Rome (*BA* 43: Map c3): cf. Virg. *Aen.* 9.405 'nemorum Latonia custos'. Most editors place commas round *uirgo*, indicating a vocative noun (cf. Callim. *H.* 3.72); but it seems better to take it adjectivally ('Virgin guardian of mountains and groves'), as Cic. *Rep.* 2.63, Ov. *Met.* 12.28–9.

2–3 quae laborantes utero puellas | ter uocata audis: it is standard procedure in ancient prayers or hymns for the address to the divinity to be followed by one or more relative clauses (e.g. 1.2.34 with Mayer, 1.10.2–4, 3.26.9–11, Cat. 34.7–8). *audis* = 'heed, give ear to' (*OLD* 10b); *puellas* here refers to young married women and is an appropriate term for those who are pregnant (P. A. Watson (1983) 135), emphasising their vulnerability (McKeown on Ov. *Am.* 2.13.19–20 'laborantes utero...puellas'). *laboro* is technical of childbirth (*OLD* 6a). As a magic or ritual number, 'three' is often found in prayers or hymns; *ter uocata* translates the Greek τρίλλιστος. As goddess of childbirth, Diana was identified or associated with Juno Lucina (e.g. *CS* 13–15, Cat. 34.13–14), but once again H. omits any name.

3 adimisque Leto 'and you remove (them) from Death' (dat. after a verb of taking away: *NLS* 43–4 §61, *G&L* §345 R. 1); the choice of verb is pointed, since it is often used absolutely of being taken off by Death (e.g. 2.4.10 'ademptus Hector', 2.9.10). Death in childbirth was a real danger in the ancient world and the mere 18 Latin inscriptions recording such deaths are out of all proportion to their presumed frequency:[114]

---

[114] For this figure see A. G. Hug, '*Fecunditas, sterilitas*, and the politics of reproduction at Rome', diss. York University (2014) 273–80, a reference I owe to Dr Anna Bonnell Freidin.

well-known cases are Cicero's daughter, Tullia, and the two daughters of the younger Helvidius Priscus (Plut. *Cic.* 41.7, Plin. *Ep.* 4.21.1). Although *letum* (again at 3.27.61) is regarded as more 'poetic' than *mors*, the latter is used twice as often in the *Aeneid* and by H. (P. A. Watson (1985) 442). It is a remarkable oddity that *Leto* transliterates Λητώ, the mother of Artemis.

4 diua triformis has been taken in two different ways. (a) The goddess conventionally had three aspects and corresponding names: Diana, Luna and Hecate. This is almost certainly the explanation of her address as 'Delia uirgo triformis' at *CIL* 2.2660 (Courtney, *ML* No. 141.2). (b) Diana was worshipped at cross-roads as Hecate or Trivia (of which *diua triformis* incorporates an anagram) and was depicted as having three faces: cf. Ov. *F.* 1.141–2 'ora uides Hecates in tres uertentia partes, | seruet ut in ternas compita secta uias'. Of these, (b) seems the more likely. It would be odd to refer to three aspects when only two have been mentioned in 1–3. See Pease on Virg. *Aen.* 4.511 and 609.

5 imminens uillae tua pinus esto 'let the pine-tree overlooking the villa be yours'. In the past, according to the elder Pliny, trees 'were temples of the divinities, and in accordance with ancient ritual simple country places even now dedicate an outstandingly tall tree to a god' (*NH* 12.3), although it has been noted (Hunt 228) that there is only a 'minimal amount of evidence for the idea of arboreal dedication' in the Roman world and that only in our ode is the relationship between tree and deity conceptualised as one of belonging ('tua'). The Italian stone pine is also known as the umbrella pine, because its branches and foliage spread out like an umbrella at the top of the trunk (Sargeaunt 101). It is the tree to which Pliny likened the ash cloud erupting from Vesuvius (*Ep.* 6.16.5–6).

6–8 quam...donem: it is almost universally assumed that the antecedent of *quam* is *pinus* and that the relative clause is one of purpose ('so that I can present it with...'); but it is very odd, in a poem addressed to Diana, either to talk about sacrificing to a pine tree or to maintain that 'a sacrifice to the goddess's tree is a sacrifice to the goddess herself' (N–R). No parallels are produced for such a sacrifice-at-one-remove, and, though N–R follow Cairns (*RL* 454) in referring to W. H. D. Rouse, *Greek Votive Offerings* (1902) 50–1, the ritual illustrated there is the very different one of hanging antlers and the like on trees (for which see Courtney, *ML* No. 141, pp. 346–7). Macleane proposed that the antecedent of *quam* is 'you' (i.e. Diana), inferred from *tua*, a so-called *constructio ad sensum* (synesis) of a very common type (e.g. Ter. *Andr.* 97–8 'laudare fortunas meas, | qui gnatum haberem... praeditum', Cic. *Vat.* 29 'nostra acta, quos tyrannos uocas'). If Macleane is right, the subjunctive will be adhortative ('and let me happily present you with...'): this use of the first person singular pres. subjunc. is 'not uncommon in poetry' (*OLS* 1.497).

6 per exactos...annos: *per* is distributive (N–H on 2.3.6): the meaning is 'at the completion of each successive year'. For an annual sacrifice combined with a one-off dedication see Virg. *Ecl.* 7.33–5 'Sinum lactis et haec te liba, Priape, quot annis | exspectare sat est: custos es pauperis horti. | Nunc te marmoreum pro tempore fecimus.'

laetus: *libens* is a regular self-description in prayers; sometimes it is accompanied by *laetus*, as Plaut. *Trin.* 821 'Neptuno laetus libens laudes ago', *CIL* 3.11128 'uotum soluit laetus libens': here H. has used *laetus* alone, as *CIL* 6.643 (Cairns, *RL* 458 and n. 84). Cf. 3.30.16n.

7 uerris obliquum meditantis ictum: *meditantis* cannot mean 'intending' (so *OLD* 2a), since it does not make sense for H. to wish that every year he will sacrifice a boar just as it is planning to attack him. *meditantis* means 'practising' (*OLD* 5a) and is a vivid way of indicating that his annual victim will be young, like the kid at 3.13.3–5.[115] Unlike the wild boar sacrificed to Artemis at *Anth. Pal.* 6.240.6, the victim here, as in the next ode (3.23.4), is a domestic animal: *uerres* = 'an uncastrated male pig' (*OLD*), appropriate for the untouched virgin goddess (1n.); cf. also 3.8.6–7n. Its practice blow is 'sideways' because the tusks of a boar do not point forwards and the animal has to swing its head when it attacks (cf. Hom. *Od.* 19.451, Ov. *Her.* 4.104 'obliquo dente timendus aper').

23

In this ode H. assures a countrywoman named Phidyle that, if she sacrifices to the Lares, her various crops and livestock will not suffer from bad weather or blight (1–8). There is no need for costly sacrificial victims; a simple ritual is enough (9–16). At this point the ode has come to a logical conclusion, yet there remains a final stanza which contains three surprise elements: (1) the Penates, not the Lares, are now the recipients of sacrifice; (2) the Penates are hostile rather than friendly; (3) there is no sacrificial victim at all. The stanza is evidently intended as a 'locus a maiore ad minus' (Quint. 5.10.87: see 3.10 intro.): if *even* a victimless sacrifice will

[115] For the sacrifice of pigs in connection with sacred groves see Cato, *RR* 139; Hunt 137–51.

mollify the hostile Penates, Phidyle should think how much more efficaciously her humble sacrifices to the Lares will be.

Commentators have noted that in his *De agri cultura* the elder Cato specifies that the wife of a farm's *uilicus* (bailiff) must make an appropriate offering to the Lares on the Kalends, Ides and Nones of every month (143.1–2 'uilicae…officia…: Kalendis, Idibus, Nonis…Lari familiari pro copia supplicet'). H.'s assurances to Phidyle clearly relate to these rites, but there is also a further point. Farmers would make bargains with the gods (cf. Virg. *Ecl.* 5.79–80 'uota quot annis | agricolae facient'), and Cato in the immediately preceding sections of his work (139–41) illustrates the prayers with which a farmer was expected to accompany his various regular sacrifices: each of these prayers, esp. the famous one to Mars (141.2–4),[116] is of the *uotum* type: 'since I am making this sacrifice, protect my crops and livestock'. As this is the burden of H.'s ode too, it would seem that he has transposed to the second person (1–4 'si tuleris…, si… placaris…') the kind of ritual utterance that country persons would make in their own name.[117]

The combination of frugality and piety makes this a thoroughly 'Augustan' poem, complementing 3.22 and leading in to 3.24. In his *Res gestae* the *princeps* recorded that he had built temples to the Lares and Penates respectively (19.2 with Cooley's nn.; Flower 259–62).

METRE Alcaic

1 Caelo: in verse the dat. may be used instead of *ad* + accus. for direction towards, e.g. 3.16.13, Virg. *Aen.* 5.451 'it clamor caelo' (*NLS* 39–40 §57, G&L 228 §358).

supinas 'up-turned', regularly used of the hands and 'esp. in supplication' (*OLD* 1c; also Horsfall on Virg. *Aen.* 3.176–7).

si tuleris 'if you stretch out' (*OLD fero* 15a); the verb is often used of hands. The fut. perf. indic. is of course regular in the protasis of a future vivid condition (see also 3n. below). For this 'bargaining' type of conditional clause see 3.18.5n.

2 nascente luna: i.e. a new moon (as *S.* 2.4.30, Cic. *Acad. post.* 2 fr. 6, Man. 2.103, Plin. *NH* 18.349), which in the old lunar calendar marked

---

[116] See E. Courtney's commentary (*Archaic Latin Prose* (1999) 62–7).
[117] See further Cairns, *RL* 405–6, who categorises the ode as an *anathematikon* or dedication poem.

the Kalends (A. K. Michels, *The Calendar of the Roman Republic* (1967) 21): see further intro.

Phidyle: like the dialogists in Varro's work on farming, who have such names as Fundanius and Agrius etc., the name Phidyle, a transliteration of the infrequently attested Greek name Φειδύλη, relates to the theme of the ode: it means 'thrifty, frugal'. Cato (see intro.) had specified that the *uilica*'s offerings to the Lar should be *pro copia*, a set expr. meaning 'as one's circumstances allow' (*OLD copia* 5c).

3 ture: for incense as a regular offering to the Lares see Plaut. *Aul.* 24, 385–6, Tib. 1.3.34, Ov. *F.* 2.631, Juv. 9.138.

placarīs: apart from the first person sing., the fut. perf. indic. is indistinguishable in form from the perf. subjunc. Originally, the perf. subjunc. was characterised by a long *ī* and the fut. perf. indic. by a short *i*, but the forms have become interchangeable in classical Latin poetry. H. again has a long final syllable of the fut. perf. indic. at 4.7.20–1 (twice; short at 4.10.6): for further statistics and discussion see R. Wallace, 'Perfect subjunctive and future perfect paradigms', *CJ* 84 (1988/89) 162–6.

3–4 horna | fruge: since *hornus* refers to produce of the current year, the reference is presumably to *primitiae* (ἀπαρχαί) or 'first fruits' (as *S.* 2.5.12–14, Calp. *Ecl.* 2.64–5), consisting of a representative range of a farm's yield.

4 Lares: the Lares were guardians of a person's whole estate (see intro. on Cato), and images of them feature in H.'s description of country life at *Epo.* 2.66 (cf. also 4.5.34); their help is sought by the Arval Brethren at the very beginning of the *Carmen Aruale* (3.1.1n.). See further Maltby on Tib. 1.1.20, *BNP* 7.247–9, *OCD* 794, and esp. Flower 40–5.

auidaque porca: pigs were 'the preferred sacrificial gift' for the Lares (Flower 55): see *S.* 2.3.164–5, Plaut. *Rud.* 1206–8, Tib. 1.10.26. The proverbial greediness of pigs meant that they were fat and hence esp. acceptable as sacrificial victims (Ov. *F.* 1.349 'prima Ceres auidae gauisa est sanguine porcae').

5–6 nec pestilentem sentiet Africum | fecunda uitis: a destructive wind from Africa (again at 3.29.57–8) suggests the scirocco, which peaks in March and November but is also associated with summer and autumn (8n. below); since it would be strange to refer to the vine as *fecunda* in November, H. must be imagining the March onslaught: the stanza proceeds from spring to autumn (see below). *sentiet* illustrates H.'s usual (but not invariable) practice of using a singular verb with a plurality of subjects (3.3.10n.); here, the last of those subjects is itself plural (7): cf. 3.4.49–51, 3.14.5–10. For *sentire* used of an inanimate subject see *AP* 66 and Brink; for the meaning 'to be affected by' see 3.27.22, Sen. *Ep.* 76.13 'non sentiens uentum'; *OLD* 5a.

6–7 sterilem...robiginem: *robigo* is blight or mildew (Virg. *G.* 1.151): there was a divinity, Robigo or Robigus, who was worshipped at the Robigalia on 25 April 'ne robigo frumentis noceat' (the Fasti Praenestini, *Inscr. Ital.* 13.2.17: see Scullard 108, 261). *sterilis* here seems to have an active meaning, 'sterilising'.

7 alumni: young animals (3.18.2–4n.).

8 pomifero graue tempus anno: *grauis* is often constructed with the dat. ('harmful to ~ '), but *pomifero...anno* cannot be dat. because it would imply that, though the *alumni* escape the malign effects of autumn, the fruit crops do not – and this would contradict the logic of the sentence. The expr. must be abl. ('the harmful climate/conditions of [lit. at] fruit-bearing season'): for the proverbial unhealthiness of autumn see 2.14.15 (and N–H) and *S.* 2.6.18 (and Muecke), where the Auster or south wind, often identified with the scirocco, is mentioned. For *annus* = 'season' cf. *Epo.* 2.29 'annus hibernus' (*OLD* 7); for *tempus* = 'climate, conditions' see *OLD* 11b. *pomifer* is not found before H. (again at 4.7.11). The phrase is chiastic grammatically but not formally (adjs. ~ nouns).

9 nam: the explanation is not given until 13b–16 below; the intervening lines are a kind of 'foil'.

9–13 quae...uictima...tinguet: *uictima* – a collective singular, as *multa caede bidentium* (14) shows – is the antecedent of the relative clause: depending on whether editors think that the antecedent is included within the rel. clause or whether the rel. clause precedes its antecedent, they place a comma either before or after *uictima* (or not at all). It is simplest to assume that the rel. clause precedes its antecedent, as at 3.7.1–5.

9 niuali pascitur Algido: Algidus is the name both of a pass and of a mountain in Latium (see *BA* Map 43: C–D2–3): though the former played an important part in early Roman history (Ogilvie on Liv. 3.2.6), H. is usually assumed to be referring to the latter (cf. *niuali*), normally identified with the modern Monte Artemisio, SE of Rome; it is roughly 3,000 feet high and part of the same range as the Alban Hills (11 below). The name ('cold') lent itself to etymologies (N–H on 1.21.6), here pointed by *niuali*. For *pascor* + abl. = 'feed/graze on' see *OLD* 6a.

10 deuota: the context indicates that the word means 'destined' or 'marked out' (as Cic. *Har. resp.* 6 'deuota...hostia'); but at this halfway point of the ode there is perhaps also a reference to the bargain (*uotum*) which a sacrificer strikes with the gods and which H. has incorporated into his poem (see intro.). For such self-referentiality see 3.7.19–20n.; W. on Tac. *Agr.* 15.5.

quercus inter et ilices: *quercus* is the common oak; *ilex*, evidently a feature of the Algidus (cf. 4.4.57–8), is the holm oak (3.13.14–15n.), whose 'leaves are much darker than those of the common oak and usually untoothed' (Sargeaunt 62). The two are often mentioned together (e.g. Enn. *Ann.* 176) and H. had both on his farm (*Epi.* 1.16.9–10). For the interposed *inter* cf. *Epi.* 1.4.12 (Bo 3.276): the order is 'characteristic of poetry' (Mayer ad loc., referring to *TLL* 7.1.2147.28–34).

11 crescit Albanis in herbis: scholars have inferred from Dion. Hal. *AR* 3.29.6 (a speech) that certain areas of the Alban Hills were reserved for rearing sacrificial animals. For *crescit* cf. 3.16.35–6.

12–13 uictima pontificum secures | ceruice tinguet: this is a so-called 'concessive future', as 1.6.1 'Scriberis', 1.7.1 'Laudabunt': the priests will perform an extravagant sacrifice, *but* there is no need for such an offering from you. Normally an axe would be used only to stun the victim, which would then be despatched with a knife (Horsfall on Virg. *Aen.* 2.224); here axes are envisaged as the lethal instruments: the verb is used esp. of staining with blood (*ceruice* is elliptical for *ceruicis sanguine*, as Prop. 4.1.111–12 'ferrum ceruice puellae | tinxit'; cf. *OLD tingo* 4). A similar scene at 3.13.6–8.

13–16 te nihil attinet | temptare multa caede bidentium | paruos coronantem...deos '<but> *you* have no need to try to influence the little gods by slaughtering many sheep, provided you crown them with...': *te* is a strong adversative asyndeton, and *paruos...deos*, which is to be taken *apo koinou* with *temptare* and *coronantem*, is sylleptic: with *temptare* (*OLD* 6) it refers to the actual Lares, with *coronantem*, which is to be understood in a conditional sense (*NLS* 73 §92),[118] it refers to their statues, which

---

[118] Rudd's relative clause ('the little gods whom you decorate with rosemary and brittle myrtle') is an alternative; West's quite different interpretation ('There is no call for you to crown your little gods with rosemary and brittle myrtle...') runs counter to the argument of the poem.

were conventionally small (e.g. 3.29.14 (?), Ov. *F.* 5.130 'signaque parua deum', Juv. 9.137 'o parui nostrique Lares', 12.87–8 'parua...simulacra', a heavily Horatian passage). The crowning of statues was routine (*OLD corona* 1c, *corono* 1a). *attinet* is one of H.'s prosaic terms (N–H on 1.19.12).

14 multa caede bidentium: the contrast between an extravagant sacrifice and a humble offering is conventional (e.g. Ov. *Tr.* 2.75–6 'sed tamen, ut fuso taurorum sanguine centum, | sic capitur minimo turis honore deus', with Ingleheart ad loc., [Tib.] 3.7.14–15, Stat. *Silv.* 1.4.127–31; N–R 262). *multa caedes* is a very common expr., esp. in abl. and in Livy, in whom it is first found (8×); in our passage the adj. has perhaps been transferred from *bidentium* (enallage: cf. 3.1.42–3n.), as translated above (13–16n.). *bidens* (lit. 'having two teeth') is used esp. of sheep in their role of sacrificial victims (Pease on Virg. *Aen.* 4.57).

15–16 marino | rore 'rosemary' (*OLD ros* 3), which 'gets its name from its liking for sea coasts and spray' (Sargeaunt 110).

16 fragili seems an odd adj. to describe a wood which was used above all for crowns and wreaths (*TLL* 8.1751.36ff., esp. 48–52 for its use with *coronare*); *gracili* or similar would seem more appropriate (e.g. Philoxen. 836.3 στέφανον | λεπτᾶς ἀπὸ μυρτίδος, 'a crown...of slender myrtle'). Naylor suggests 'sprigs', as if equivalent to *fracta*, 'broken off' (*OLD frango* 3d). Myrtle, associated with the Lares also at Tib. 1.10.27–8, is again coupled with rosemary at Ov. *AA* 3.690 and Colum. 12.25.4; it too has a 'liking for the shore' (Sargeaunt 82).

17–20 Though the final stanza comes as something of a surprise (intro.), it is formally linked to the first through ring composition (17 *si...manus* ~ 1 *si...manus,* 19 *molliuit...Penates* ~ 3–4 *placaris... Lares*).

17 immunis aram si tetigit manus: although Porphyrio took *immunis* to mean 'pure, innocent', this meaning is not found without a dependent genit. or abl. etc. (as Ov. *Her.* 14.8 'immunes caedis... manus'), which is why Unger emended *manus* to *malis*. Bentley preferred 'without a gift, empty-handed', which is the meaning of the word elsewhere in H. (4.12.23, *Epi.* 1.14.33) and at Gell. 7.13.2 (*TLL* 7.1.505.47–52). Gow reasonably asks 'how can a hand, which brings meal and salt, be described as "bringing no gift" at all?' But the answer is that the mixture of meal and salt (20) was not usually regarded as an offering in its own right (see below). *tetigit* is the regular perfect tense found in the protasis of present general conditions (*NLS* 148 §193): 'Whenever a giftless hand touches the altar...'; for the ritual touching of an altar see Pease on Virg. *Aen.* 4.219.

18 non sumptuosa blandior hostia: there are almost as many different interpretations of this controversial line as there are interpreters. In my view there are four key elements: (i) *blandior* agrees with *manus* (for the expr. cf. Ov. *Am.* 1.11.14, *Met.* 2.691, Sen. *HF* 1002, Mart. 6.23.3); (ii) *sumptuosa...hostia* is an abl. of cause (for a similar abl. enclosing a comparative adj. cf. 3.5.39–40; note also 3.28.1); (iii) *non* negatives the three-word phrase; (iv) the line is concessive and to be taken with 19–20. Thus: 'though not more persuasive by reason of an expensive victim' (i.e. though there is no expensive victim to make the offering more persuasive: the persuasiveness of the offering is not dependent on the expensiveness of the victim). *hostia* seems here to be used simply as a synonym for *uictima* (12), though the terms could be seen as different (e.g. [Fronto] *Diff.* 7.532.13K 'uictima maior est, hostia minor'): see Bömer on Ov. *F.* 1.335–6.

19 molliuit auersos Penates: *molliuit* is regarded as a 'gnomic perfect', stating a general rule (3.5.1–2n.). The Penates were gods specifically of the household: since they are quite often mentioned alongside the Lares, they are appropriate to use as a clinching argument (see intro.): see further *BNP* 10.717–19, *OCD* 1102. *auersus* is regular of ill-disposed divinities, e.g. Ov. *Tr.* 1.3.45 'auersos... Penates'; NA on Lygd. 3.28.

20 farre pio et saliente mica 'with sacred meal and leaping grains <of salt>.' The words refer to *mola salsa* (again at *S.* 2.3.200), a mixture of meal and salt: in earlier times the mixture was regarded by the gods as an offering in its own right (Plin. *NH* 12.83 'nec minus propitii erant mola salsa supplicantibus') but its more usual function was as a sacrificial accessory, being sprinkled both on the animal to be killed and on the altar and fire on which it was to be killed and then burned (for the details see NA on Lygd. 4.10 'farre pio placant et saliente sale', a line imitating that of H.). This ambiguity explains why the hand of the sacrificer can be described as 'without a gift' (17n.). For *pius* see e.g. Virg. *Aen.* 5.745 'farre pio'; *OLD* 2b. *saliente* puns on the noun *sal*, which H. has avoided using (cf. Isid. 16.2.3 'sal quidam dictum putant quod in igne exsiliat'; Maltby 539); the same pun recurs at Ov. *F.* 4.409 'micae...salientis'. The grains do not themselves leap in the fire but make the flames appear to leap up: *mĭca* is another collective singular and perhaps also another pun, since *mĭcare* is used of flames flickering and flashing.

24

This poem constitutes the longest passage of sustained moralising anywhere in the *Odes*. Many modern readers find it not to their taste, but the importance which H. attached to its message is suggested not only by its length – the same as the great address to Maecenas at the end of the book (3.29) – but also by the significance of its setting: between a celebration of rustic ritual (3.23) and the promise of an inspired treatment of Augustus (3.25). The ode divides into two equal halves (1–32, 33–64). It opens with a figure familiar from elsewhere in H.'s work: the rich and impious builder who ignores the boundaries of nature and, despite his mortality, has an insatiable compulsion to keep on building (1–8). Better lives, with features even of the Golden Age, are lived by the Scythians and Getae, who have neither fixed abodes nor long-term routines (9–16): their women in particular epitomise social morality (17–24). At Rome the reining in of unbridled *licentia* is a precondition of the eradication of civil war, and the statesman who tackles this menace will be honoured as the father of his people (27 *pater*), although his true distinction will be recognised only after his death (25–32).

The second half of the ode is a varied reprise of the first. The rich builder of 1–8 is replaced by a second familiar type, the overseas merchant, who finds himself compelled to undertake extreme journeys to the farthest-flung regions of the earth in pursuit of gain (33–44). We should jettison the luxury imports which such journeys produce (45–50), and we should educate boys in morality rather than allow a villainous father (59 *patris*) to encourage them in idle and enervating pastimes (51–64). Thus each half of the ode concludes with contrasting father figures, and throughout both halves the argument is driven forward by a series of doubled expressions (e.g. 3–7 *licet*... ~ *si*..., 9–13 *Scythae, quorum*... ~ *Getae*,... *quibus*..., 33–44 *Quid...si non*... ~ *quid...si neque*..., 45–50 *uel nos*... ~ *uel nos*...).

Although the ending of civil war is cast in the future (25 *uolet*), no one disputes that the dramatic date of the ode is later than Actium; but the very reference to 'rabiem...ciuicam' (26) indicates that the conflict is recent and still a live issue, as it was for Livy in his early books (7.40.2, 9.19.15, 17: see Woodman, *RICH* 134–5). The danger is that it will break out again, unless *licentia* (28–9) is curbed. Numerous scholars think that, coming as it does after a description of chaste barbarian women (21–4), *licentia* is a reference to sexual licence and that the subsequent mention of *leges* (35) is an allusion to the first round of marriage legislation which Octavian is supposed to have introduced and then withdrawn in the early 20s. But it is implausible to see adultery as likely to cause a renewal of civil war,[119] and it is quite possible that early legislation against adultery never existed in the first place (3.6.25–6n.). *licentia* means for H. what it meant for Sallust, whose analysis of Rome's socio-political decline he is following closely (see on 3–4, 9–10, 42, 49): *licentia* is the condition which allows individuals to become hybristic (*BC* 6.7 'per licentiam insolescere animum humanum') and manifests itself above all in the pursuit of power and wealth (*BC* 10.3–13.5). In the aftermath of Octavian's victory at Actium it would be unrealistic to refer to the pursuit of power, but H. could certainly criticise the corrupting pursuit of riches, which is where the emphasis of the poem lies (1–8, 36–50, 58–64).

H. says that the statesman – unnamed, but of course the *princeps* is meant – must tackle the problem of *licentia* if he wishes to be called 'father' (27–9), although the poet adds with regret that we reject the man of *uirtus* when he is alive and seek him only after he has been removed from our sight (31–2), a form of words which suggests the apotheosis of Romulus (cf. Liv. 1.16.1 'ut conspectum eius...abstulerit'). This is not the first time that the reader of the *Odes* has encountered this combination of ideas: H. concluded the second ode of Book 1 by referring to the *princeps* as 'father' and by describing his death in terms of that of Romulus (1.2.47–50 'neue te nostris uitiis iniquum | ocior aura | tollat; ... | hic ames dici pater atque princeps'). The likelihood is that the two odes reflect the same period, namely, the interval between Actium and Octavian's acquisition of the name Augustus in 27 BC (see Woodman (2022)). But, whereas 1.2 presented an emergency which required immediate attention (cf. 1.2.25–6 'ruentis | imperi rebus'), H. here offers a programme of moral reform for the long-term future.

METRE   Fourth Asclepiad

1–8   The logic is: 'Your fabulous wealth allows you to build on the sea as well as on the land, but, given that you are subject to Destiny, you will not escape Death.' The theme is that of 2.18, esp. 17–21 'tu secanda marmora | locas sub ipsum funus et sepulcri | immemor struis domos | marisque Bais obstrepentis urges | summouere litora'.

1–3 Intactis opulentior | thesauris Arabum et diuitis Indiae: *opulentior* (perhaps vocative: cf. e.g. 1.16.1, 3.10.17–18) provides the reason why the addressee is able to build so extravagantly: '(You who are) wealthier than the untouched treasures of the Arabs and of rich India, although you...'

---

[119] 'None, even of the Roman historians, was so naïve as to attribute the civil wars to a decline in sexual morality' (Williams (1962) 32).

(i.e. 'wealthier than the rich Arabs and Indians with their untouched treasures', a form of transferred comparison): *diuitis* perhaps goes also with *Arabum* (Naylor); cf. [Tib.] 3.8.18 'diues Arabs'. Since Rome already enjoyed luxury products associated with both Arabia and India (48n.), *Intactis* does not mean literally 'untouched' but refers to those treasures that still remained to be exploited. In the event it was the *princeps* who through the agency of Aelius Gallus, prefect of Egypt, invaded Arabia in 26/25 BC (1.29.1–5; *RG* 26.5 'meo iussu et auspicio', with Cooley); but Augustus famously used wealth for state purposes (46n.). India was never invaded by Rome but sent its first embassy to Augustus in 25 BC (*RG* 31.1 with Cooley); it is regularly coupled with Arabia in Latin texts (note esp. Prop. 2.10.15–16 'India quin, Auguste, tuo dat colla triumpho, | et domus intactae te tremit Arabiae'): their counterparts will be the Scythians and Getae below (9–24). In general see G. W. Bowersock, *Roman Arabia* (1983), and G. R. Parker, *The Making of Roman India* (2008). The expr. *intacti thesauri* recurs 3× in Book 29 of Livy (8.9, 18.4, 18.7) and nowhere else.

3–4 caementis licet occupes | terrenum omne tuis et mare publicum: the ode, very unusually, has no named addressee; the second-person singular forms with which it opens and closes (3, 4, 8, 57, 58) are the anonymous 'you' whom we meet in satire and similar genres (N–H on 2.18.17). Cicero, with reference to the Four Element theory, had used the expr. *terrenum omne* to refer to 'everything earthen' (*ND* 3.31): it thus makes an excellent counterpart to *mare*: wealthy Romans, having taken over all of the land, are now building on the sea (cf. esp. Sall. *BC* 13.1 'a priuatis compluribus subuorsos montes, maria constrata esse', 20.11 'in exstruendo mari et montibus coaequandis'; also above, 3.1.33–5nn., and note too W. on Tac. *Agr.* 30.4).[120] *publicum* = 'available to, shared or enjoyed by, all members of the community' (*OLD publicus*¹ 4); though the combination with *mare* is unparalleled, the adj. is commonly applied to waterways and the like and has almost a legal nuance (cf. *ager publicus*; *TLL* 10.2.2462.17–33). H.'s point is ironical: the builders have taken advantage of the sea's proverbial commonality (see also e.g. Plaut. *Rud.* 975 'mare quidem commune certost omnibus', Cic. *Rosc. Am.* 72), of which they are now depriving everyone else. *occupo* has many shades of meaning:

---

[120] Many scholars prefer the better attested reading *Tyrrhenum* to *terrenum*, but not only does this deprive us of the conventional motif of land and sea but we should then expect *mare* to be qualified by a proper adj., for which neither of the transmitted alternatives is at all plausible: the Apulian Sea 'was not a place for luxury building' and 'the Black Sea was far too remote' (N–R).

perhaps foremost here are 'to fill up an area with ~ ' (*OLD* 8), reinforcing *omne*, and 'to appropriate to oneself, seize to the exclusion of others' (*OLD* 2a), contrasting with *publicum* and constituting an ironical juxtaposition with *licet* (lit. 'it is permitted'). The actual meaning of *licet* + subjunc. here is of course 'although' (for which see *NLS* 202–5 §§248, 249 (*d*), G&L 392 §607); *caementa* (again at 3.1.35) is a kind of metonymy, the rubble standing for building projects (for another critique of which see 2.15 and N–H).

5–7 si figīt adamantinos | summis uerticibus dira Necessitas | clauos: although it is awkward to have a concessive clause (3–4) followed immediately by a conditional clause, the transmitted text does not require change: *si* has a causal nuance ('since, given that'), as again at e.g. 36 below, Plaut. *Amph.* 817 (also 3.18.5n.); for the logic see 1–8n. above. What does *summis uerticibus* mean? The words have been taken to refer to (i) the heads of the nails ('up to the heads'), (ii) the heads of the builders, (iii) the roofs of the houses being built. (iii) seems the least implausible: although *uertex* of a house roof seems paralleled only at Mart. 8.36.11–12, the houses of the wealthy were often crowned with a tower (3.29.9–10n.), for which *uertex* seems highly suitable (cf. Oros. 2.6.25). Necessity, equivalent to Fate or Fortune (3.1.14–15n.), was conventionally seen as being equipped with nails to fix a person's destiny (N–H on 1.35.17–18; Tosi 424–5 §906); here she is imaginatively described as a roofer, planting her nails in the rich man's mansion, the structure dearest to his heart. Hence: 'given that it is dire Necessity who fixes her adamantine nails in the tops of your pinnacles'. *summis*, an adj. which often qualifies *uertex* (sing. and plur.), here perhaps has the additional nuance of 'finishing touch' (*OLD summus* 5); the phrase is presumably abl. (so *TLL* 6.1.714.10). There is no parallel for the artificial lengthening of present-tense *figīt*, but experts regard the anomaly as 'not certainly wrong' (N–R; see Brink (1982) 31).

7 metu: some understand *mortis* from 8.

8 non Mortis laqueis expedies caput: Death is an executioner who has each person's neck in a noose, ready to draw it tight. *expedire* means 'release, disengage' (*OLD* 1a), as Cic. *II Verr.* 2.102 'ex nullo [sc. laqueo] se umquam expediet'. For similar imagery cf. Sen. *NQ* 2.59.6–8 (*laqueis mortis* at Apul. *Met.* 10.24.2 is perhaps different).

9–16 The syntax of these lines is debatable. The Scythians and Getae, to both of whom *melius...uiuunt* applies, are each given an adj. (*campestres* ~

rigidi) and a relative clause (*quorum ~ quibus*); although there is a case for continuing the *quibus*-clause as far as *uicarius* (16), it is easier to punctuate after *ferunt* (13) and to regard *nec cultura...uicarius* (14–16) as a separate sentence.

9–11 campestres melius Scythae, | quorum plaustra uagas rite trahunt domos, | uiuunt: *melius* goes with *uiuunt*: H. is not suggesting that the Romans should adopt the nomadic existence of Scythians, but, by praising the latter's lifestyle, he is inviting the rich to question their own: 'living well' (*bene uiuere*) is not what the wealthy builder imagines it to be (a familiar trope, e.g. N–H on 2.16.13). *campestres* contrasts with *mare* (4): the Scythians are regularly associated with *campi* or steppes (3.8.23–4n.) and are here seen as the archetypal 'noble savages' (see esp. Lovejoy and Boas 287–90, 315–44); for their nomadic way of life see Pind. fr. 105AB.4–6 and esp. Sall. *H.* 3.76M/3.96R 'Scythae nomades tenent, quibus plaustra sedes sunt' (quoted by Porphyrio here), Just. 2.2.3; *trahunt domos* translates their description by Herodotus as φερέοικοι, 'home-carriers' (4.46.2–3, where see Corcella). *rite* (*OLD* 3) underlines the propriety of their habitation, in contrast to that of the Romans, which is both improper (3 *occupes*) and unnatural (4 *mare*). For the Roman view of nomadic peoples see Dauge 620–6; there is a very full study by R. Batty, *Rome and the Nomads: The Pontic-Danubian Realm in Antiquity* (2007).

11 et rigidi Getae: sc. *melius uiuunt*. The Getae, in Latin texts often associated (or confused) with the Scythians, straddled the Lower Danube in the direction of the Black Sea, including Tomis, the place of Ovid's exile (*BA* Maps 22: C4 and 23: B3). Ovid uses a large number of uncomplimentary adjs. to describe them (see Gaertner on *Ex P.* 1.2.76), including *rigidus* (*Tr.* 5.1.46), which for H. seems rather to indicate moral uprightness or severity (*OLD* 5a), with perhaps a hint of climatic frigidity (cf. 2.9.20); there is also a contrast with the Arabs (2), whose very name was thought to be associated with softness (Maltby on Tib. 2.2.4). See further Corcella on Hdt. 4.93.1; *BNP* 5.842–4.

12 immetata...iugera: a *iugerum* was strictly a measure of land (approx. 240 × 140 Roman feet: see *OLD*): the oxymoronic phrase generates an implicit contrast with Rome, where surveying was a necessary element of building activity (2.15.14–15 'decempedis | metata'). *immetatus* occurs only here (Intro. 25); unpartitioned land is a feature of the Golden Age (Virg. *G.* 1.126–7 'ne signare quidem aut partiri limite campum | fas erat'; the passage is continued in the following n.) but also attributed to the Scythians at Just. 2.2.3.

12–13 liberas | fruges et Cererem ferunt: since *Cererem* is 'grain' by metonymy (*Cererem ferre* renders the Greek adj. πυροφόρος, used of Asia by Strabo 7.3.9), *fruges* must refer to other produce. *liberas*, which applies to both nouns, evidently = 'not privately owned' (so *OLD* 7b; absent from *TLL*), but Getic farming again has hints of Golden Age abundance: cf. Licin. Calv. 20C/42H 'terra omnia liberius ferente', Virg. *G.* 1.127–8 'ipsaque tellus | omnia liberius...ferebat' (see previous n.), Stat. *Silv.* 1.6.41 'non sic libera uina tunc [i.e. in the Golden Age] fluebant'.

14 nec culturā placet longior annuā: with *annuā* we must understand *culturā*, and *placet* (sc. *eis*) conveys a variety of nuances such as acceptability, formal approval etc. (see *OLD*): hence something like 'and they do not approve of a cultivation which is lengthier than a year-long <cultivation>'. For the same practice cf. Caes. *BG* 4.1.7 'neque longius anno remanere uno in loco incolendi causa licet', 6.22.2, Tac. *G.* 26.2 (and Rives); C. B. Krebs, 'Borealism: Caesar, Seneca, Tacitus, and the Roman discourse about the Germanic North', in E. S. Gruen (ed.), *Cultural Identity and the Peoples of the Ancient Mediterranean* (2010) 206–7.

15–16 defunctumque laboribus | aequali recreat sorte uicarius 'and a substitute revives, on a comparable basis, the man who has completed his toils' (*-que* is epexegetic): this is a rather elliptical way of saying that the agricultural labourer will be revived after a period's toil by being replaced by someone else (*uicarius*), who himself will be replaced after a further period ('aequali...sorte'), and so on. For another alternating system see Caes. *BG* 4.1.4. For *aequali...sorte* cf. Manil. 2.458; for *recreat* cf. 3.20.13–14.

17 illic: similarly of the Germans at Tac. *G.* 18.1 'seuera illic matrimonia', 19.3 'nemo enim illic uitia ridet'.

17–18 matre carentibus | priuignis mulier temperat innocens 'a blameless wife is moderate in her conduct towards her motherless stepchildren' (for this sense of *temperare* + dat. see *OLD* 2b). Stepmothers at Rome, commonplace because divorce was frequent, were proverbial for their cruelty (P. A. Watson, *Ancient Stepmothers* (1995) 11–12, 92–134, esp. 104; Tosi 653–4 §1448), but amongst the virtuous Scythians and Getae the presence of a stepmother is to be explained rather by death in childbirth (hence *matre carentibus*, for which expr. cf. Virg. *Aen.* 12.209, of a branch removed from a tree); and her fostering is such that she can be described by a benign periphrasis rather than by the censorious *nouerca* (*OLD* b). *mulier* perhaps = 'wife' here (3.14.5n.).

19 nec dotata regit uirum 'nor does a well-dowered woman rule the roost over her husband': again the antithesis of Rome, where 'dowry is a powerful lever. Whatever her legal position, the wife with a big dowry was never really in her husband's control' (Treggiari 329). On the steppes such dowries are unknown. The substantival use of *dotata* is uncommon (Plaut. *Aul.* 535, Ter. *Phorm.* 940) but cf. next n.

20 coniunx nec nitido fidit adultero 'and no wife places her trust in a sleek adulterer'. If *coniunx* is taken with *dotata*, as is usual, it could be implied that at Rome rich wives were gulled by their lovers; this is not only implausible but strikes the wrong note, since it elicits the reader's sympathy for the rich wives. Emendations of *fidit* are unpersuasive, but the problem is largely eliminated by re-punctuating the sentence so that *nec* is postponed (as e.g. 1.8.6, 3.4.77, *Epo.* 10.11) and the unqualified *coniunx* becomes the subject of *fidit*: H. is praising marital fidelity and the absence of adultery amongst the Scythians and Getae, praise which implies criticism of the opposite at Rome (see esp. 3.6.25–32).

21–3 dos est magna parentium | uirtus et metuens alterius uiri | …castitas 'the great dowry from her parents is her virtue and the chastity which…is fearful of another man'. These lines repeat positively what was said negatively in 19–20: *dos* looks back to *dotata*, and *alterius uiri* etymologises *adultero* (Fest. 22 'ad alterum'; Maltby 9–10); for the conceit see e.g. Hippon. 182.1–2, Plaut. *Amph.* 839–40 'non ego illam mi dotem duco esse quae dos dicitur, | sed pudicitiam et pudorem et sedatum cupidinem'. Normally the Scythians and associated peoples are described as anything but monogamous; it may be that 'views of the genuine nomadic Scythians have been conditioned by what was believed about their supposed kinsmen in Parthia' (Powell 181; cf. 149): see below, 24n. (*aut*). Elsewhere in H. the genit. plur. of *parens* = 'parent' is *–um* (e.g. 3.6.46); *metuens* + genit. is regular (3.19.15–17n.).

23 certo foedere is either an abl. of description loosely attached to *castitas* ('chastity with its firm bond') or an abl. abs. ('the bond [sc. of marriage] being firm'); for *foedus* used of the marriage bond cf. e.g. Cat. 64.335, 373, Ov. *Tr.* 2.536. The derivation of the noun from *fides* (Maltby 237) provides another link back to 19–20 (~ *fidit*).

24 peccare nefas: sc. *est*. For *peccare* of sexual offences see *OLD* 3b. There is a contrast with Rome below (30 'heu nefas!').

aut pretium est mori 'otherwise the price is death' (for *aut*, again at 3.12.3, see *OLD* 7). The same point is made about the Scythians, contrasting with

Rome, at 3.10.1–2 (n.), and implied about the Parthians by Trogus (Just. 41.3.1). Death brings to a close the ethnographical section of the ode, as it did the domestic (8).

25–9 o quisquis uolet impias | caedes et rabiem tollere ciuicam, | si quaeret..., indomitam audeat | refrenare licentiam: the order is convoluted: the clause *quisquis...ciuicam* is the subject both of the *si*-clause and of the main clause; *o* at the start is to be taken with *audeat* and indicates a wish (3.10.13n.): 'If whoever aims to dispel impious slaughter and the madness of civil war seeks to..., may he dare to curb untamed licence!' *quisquis* is here used of a person not yet identified (*OLD* 4) but of course refers obliquely to Augustus. *uolet* is a 'gnomic' future (3.1.18–19n.): for the sense 'aim' see *OLD* 16. For the connection between civil war and *licentia* see intro.: only when *licentia* is curbed will Aug. be entitled to be described in paternal terms as a benefactor (cf. 4.15.10–11 [below, 28–9n.]). For *impia caedes* cf. Liv. 5.4.14, Curt. 8.8.4, Sen. *Ag.* 219, Oct. 598; for *rabies ciuica* cf. Flor. 2.9.5 = 3.21.5 (*r. ciuilis* at Luc. 6.63, Tac. *H.* 3.80.2): 'madness' words are commonly applied to civil war (Jal 421–5). *tollere* can be used of dispelling illness (Scrib. Larg. 11 'capitis dolorem... tollit') and is perhaps so used here (cf. 27–8n., 34n., 35–6n.).

27–8 si quaeret 'PATER' urbium | subscribi statuis: for *quaero* + infin. see 3.4.39n.; *subscribere* is here followed by a predicate, as *describere* (*OLD* 4a) or *inscribere* (*OLD* 4a) or indeed the simple *scribere* (e.g. 1.6.1 'Scriberis... fortis', 'You will be written of *as* brave'): the prefix *sub-* refers to the fact that inscriptions were often placed on the base of statues. The meaning is 'if he seeks to be captioned as...'.

Scholars are divided on (a) whether *urbium* is to be taken with *pater* or with *statuis* or with both, (b) whether *subscribi* is followed by an example of the actual caption ('as "Father"') or merely by a description ('as a father'). Now it so happens that the Greek expression πατὴρ τῆς πόλεως ('Father of the City') is commonly found on inscriptions from eastern cities in the late empire to praise a benefactor, although sometimes πατήρ alone is used, either with or without an accompanying adjective (e.g. λαμπρότατος, 'most distinguished'): see C. Roueché, 'A new inscription from Aphrodisias and the title πατὴρ τῆς πόλεως', *GRBS* 20 (1979) 173–85. Unfortunately no example of πατὴρ τῆς πόλεως survives from the classical period,[121] but it is nevertheless noteworthy that no extant inscription illustrates a plural genitive: the plural form is found only in legislative

---

[121] I gratefully acknowledge the help of Dr J. Nelis-Clément here. The examples quoted by L. Robert ('Épigrammes d'Aphrodisias', *Hellenica* 4 (1948) 130–1, and

documents, when reference is being made to the class of 'benefactors of cities', as in *Cod. Iust.* 10.27.2.12 οἱ πατέρες τῶν πόλεων. Despite the interval of time separating the ode from the inscriptions, it therefore seems highly unlikely that H. could have written *pater urbium* as a title; he must have written *pater* alone: the word order is interlaced, a favourite of his. It may nevertheless be objected that one cannot be certain of the reference of the genitive *urbium*, but this is not quite the case (for discussion of some other such genitives see e.g. N–H on 1.35.6; Fraenkel 342). *pater urbium* is an almost meaningless phrase. Moreover, if *urbium* is to be taken with *pater*, the likeliest inference is that the statues are in Rome; but it seems inconceivable that anyone would trouble to set up statues in the capital which commemorated Augustus' paternalism in various nameless cities of the empire. In fact *pater urbium* is unparalleled elsewhere in Latin literature; when *pater* is combined with *urbs*, the genitive is always in the singular (thus e.g. *pater...urbis* at Stat. *Silv.* 1.4.95, 4.8.20, of the emperor). Although the title *pater patriae* was not given to Augustus officially until 2 BC (*RG* 35.1 with Cooley), H. had referred to him as *pater* at 1.2.50 (see intro.) and in our ode he envisages a time when *pater* is the caption on the statues of the *princeps* which adorned cities all across the Roman empire (for which see e.g. J. Edmondson, 'Cities and urban life in the western provinces of the Roman Empire, 30 BCE–250 CE', in D. S. Potter (ed.), *A Companion to the Roman Empire* (2006) 263–4).

Some scholars infer from the practice attributed to the Elder Cato (Plin. *NH* 29.14–15, Plut. *Cato Mai.* 23.3–4) that it was traditionally the *paterfamilias* who took charge of the health of his household: if true, this would provide a link between the title here and such medical language as *tollere* (25–9n.). For medical metaphors and the ruler as doctor see *PH* 162–80, B. Walters, *The Deaths of the Republic: Imagery of the Body Politic in Ciceronian Rome* (2020). On *pater* see also Weinstock 203–4, Wardle on Suet. *Aug.* 58.1.

28–9 indomitam audeat | refrenare licentiam: the image is that of reining in an untamed horse (Lucil. 1042 'Tessalam ut indomitam frenis subigamque domemque', Liv. 34.2.13 'date frenos...indomito animali', Ov. *Tr.* 5.4.16 'more nec indomiti frena recusat equi'); although the image is not quite the same, H. perhaps had in mind the end of *Georgics* 1, where civil war is described as a chariot out of control (514 'neque audit currus habenas'): cf. *Trag. incert.* 126R 'repriment ualidae legum habenae atque

'Inscriptions grecques de Sidè en Pamphylie', *Rev. Phil.* 32 (1958) 50) all date from the late empire.

COMMENTARY 24.30-3

imperi insistent iugo'. By 13 BC the task was said to be complete (4.15.10–11 'euaganti frena licentiae | iniecit', where Thomas defines *licentia* as 'a debasement of political freedom').

30 clarus postgenitis, quatenus… 'famous <only> to those yet to be born, since…' (*OLD quatenus* 8); *postgenitus* is unique in classical Latin. The word 'only' is often omitted in Latin.

heu nefas: *nefas* is a common exclamation (*OLD* 3c) but its combination with *heu* is found again only at 4.6.17.

31–2 uirtutem incolumem odimus, | sublatam ex oculis quaerimus inuidi: *inuidi* is not to be taken with *quaerimus*, with which it makes no sense; rather, it explains the relationship between both parts of the sentence: 'it is through jealousy that we hate excellence while it is still alive and search for it only when it is removed from our sight'. The contrast is a topos (e.g. Mimn. 25; N–H on 2.20.4 (note their ref. to Vell. 92.5); Tosi 186 §401), but H. may have in mind Thuc. 2.64.5, the last speech of Pericles, a much earlier first citizen (Thuc. 2.65.9). Although H. expresses the contrast in abstract terms, *uirtus* is almost equivalent to 'an excellent man', meaning Augustus; for similar conceits cf. Vell. 35.2 'homo Virtuti simillimus' (of the younger Cato), Tac. *A.* 16.21.1 'uirtutem ipsam exscindere concupiuit' (of Thrasea Paetus and Barea Soranus). *incolumem*, an adj. found in *uota* 'pro incolumitate principis' and the like (e.g. W. Henzen, *Acta Fratrum Arvalium* (1874) 122–3), strikes an official note, while *sublatam ex oculis* seems intended to recall the apotheosis of *pater* Romulus (see intro.), a name which the *princeps* and/or his supporters briefly considered for himself, until in 27 BC 'Augustus' was chosen instead (cf. Suet. *Aug.* 7.2 with Wardle). For *uirtutem incolumem* cf. Sen. *Ep.* 71.18 'uirtus…si manet etiam comminuto corpore incolumis', although in H. the adj. = 'still alive' (*OLD* 1c), as Sen. *Clem.* 1.21.2 'plusque eius nomini confert incolumis quam si ex oculis ablatus esset'. For the play *ex oculis* ~ *in-uidi* cf. Nep. *Chabr.* 3.4 'tantum se ab inuidia putabant futuros quantum a conspectu suorum recesserint'; for *inuidia uirtutis* cf. R. A. Kaster, *Emotion, Restraint, and Community in Ancient Rome* (2005) 182–3 n. 15.

33 quid tristes querimoniae: sc. *proficiunt* from 36; *quid* is an internal accus., as often with *proficio* (*OLD* 1a). The complaints are presumably those of contemporaries, but H. says that there is no point in their complaining about *licentia* unless they are prepared to see something done about it. *tristes* = 'bitter' (*OLD* 2).

34 si non supplicio culpa reciditur 'if wrongdoing is not cut away by punishment': the metaphor is surgical (e.g. Ov. *M.* 1.190–1, Curt. 6.3.11, Luc. 2.141–2 'putria membra recidit | ...medicina') and continues the medical language of *tollere* (26); for *culpa* see *OLD* 3. Punishment presupposes laws (*OLD supplicium* 3a), but laws themselves presuppose *mores* (35–6n.).

35–6 quid leges sine moribus | uanae proficiunt, si neque...: although this question is formally similar to that at 33–4 ('quid...si non...'), the conditional element is in fact inherent in *sine moribus uanae*, which is equivalent to *si uanae sine moribus sunt*; the *si*-clause in 36–41 is effectively causal (see below). The question is the corollary to 33–4: what good is legislation, when it is futile without morality? That is, the *princeps* can only do so much; it is the mindset of the people – illustrated in 36–44 – which needs to change, and it is the purpose of H.'s ode to help change it. The combination of *leges* and *mores* is as old as Ennius (*Euhem.* 6 G–M 'Iouem leges hominibus moresque condentem') and exceptionally common. According to Suetonius, Augustus later 'recepit et morum legumque regimen' (*Aug.* 27.5), but neither from this (controversial) statement[122] nor from later passages elsewhere in H. (4.5.22 'mos et lex maculosum edomuit nefas', *Epi.* 2.1.2–3 'res Italas armis tuteris, moribus ornes, | legibus emendes', both addressed to Aug.) can it be inferred that in our passage the reference is to any putative social legislation: (a) Aug.'s social legislation was intended to correct morality, whereas here H. has *leges* and *mores* the other way round; (b) the illustration of *sine moribus* in 36–41 below has nothing to do with adultery or marriage. *proficiunt* sustains the medical imagery of 26 and 34: cf. e.g. Sen. *Ep.* 69.2 'plurimum remedia continuata proficiunt'; *OLD* 2.

36–41 si neque...nauitae: there is no doubt about the journeys of the *nauitae*. *si* has a causal sense ('given that'), as elsewhere (5–7n.), and the clause illustrates the absence of *mores* mentioned in 35.

According to ancient geographical theory the world was divided vertically into (usually) five zones, of which those at the top and bottom are extremely cold; the central zone is extremely hot and separated from the cold zones by a temperate zone on either side, of which the northern is the one we inhabit (see e.g. Cic. *Rep.* 6.21, Varro Atac. 112H/17C with Hollis' nn., Diog. Laer. 7.156; D. Dueck, *Geography in Classical Antiquity* (2012) 84-6). The unnaturalness of the *mercator*'s journeys to two of the extreme zones (*neque...nec...*) mirrors the unnatural behaviour of the addressee in lines 3–4.

---

[122] The corresponding passage at *RG* 6.1–2 is only available in the Greek version.

36–8 feruidis | pars inculta caloribus | mundi: *pars* ('region, clime, zone', as at 3.3.38–9) and *caloribus* are 'geographical' terms (e.g. Cic. *ND* 2.25 'partes mundi...calore fultae', Sall. *J.* 17.2–3 'loca...ob calorem... minus frequentata sunt;...in parte tertia'; N–H on 1.35.32). In the paradosis *pars* is qualified by *inclusa*. Although this verb is also regular in geographical contexts, where it means 'to surround with a border, fence in' (*TLL* 7.1.953.58–67, *OLD* 4), this meaning is impossible here, both because none of the five zones is fenced in by hot zones (36–41n.) and because H. clearly means that the *pars...mundi* is itself hot. Nisbet proposed to read *exclusa* ('shut off by its boiling heat'), but perhaps better is *inculta* ('uninhabited because of its boiling heat'): for this meaning cf. *TLL* 7.1.1069.46–59, quoting *inter al.* Cic. *TD* 1.69 'ceteras partis incultas, quod aut frigore rigeant aut urantur calore'. For *feruidi calores* cf. Vitr. 8.2.3. The word order is again interlaced (27–8n.).

38 Boreae finitimum latus 'the region nearest to the North Wind', i.e. the topmost zone of extreme cold. *latus*, varying *pars*, is again technical (*OLD* 7a); *mundi* is to be taken with *latus* as well as *pars* (cf. 1.22.19 'mundi latus').

39 durataeque solo niues 'snows hardened on the ground' (abl. of place); in the topmost zone the snow is imagined as never melting.

40 abigunt 'deter, repel' (*OLD* 4a).

40–1 horrida callidi | uincunt aequora nauitae: a 'golden' sequence (3.18.5n.); *horrida...aequora* (earlier at Cat. 64.205–6, later at Stat. *Silv.* 3.3.160–1) is oxymoronic, since *horrida* = 'rough' and *aequora* = lit. 'level surface' (cf. Lucr. 2.1). For the metaphor see Tac. *Agr.* 25.1 'uictus Oceanus' (and W.); for *nauita* see 3.4.29–31n.

42 magnum pauperies opprobrium: another ex. of mannered word order, this time the 'schema Cornelianum', so called because allegedly introduced into Latin poetry by Cornelius Gallus (in whose few surviving lines, however, there is no example); it consists of a bracketing phrase which explains, or is explained by, the centralised word or phrase in apposition: the standard ex. is Virg. *Ecl.* 1.57 'raucae tua cura palumbes' (see J. B. Solodow, *HSCP* 90 (1986) 129–53). H. is not saying that poverty is shameful (cf. 3.2.1) but that, as at Sall. *BC* 12.1 'paupertas probro haberi', it is an accusation which is laid by others ('the great reproach of "poverty"') and which, once laid, compels men to do anything to escape the reproach. For *pauperies/paupertas* see 3.2.1–3n.

iubet: the verb often lacks an expressed object (cf. 3.21.7–8n.): in this case we need to understand e.g. *quemlibet* or *hominem*. See also next n.

44 uirtutisque uiam deserit arduae: the subject is 'he', inferred from the unexpressed object of *iubet* (last n.); *-que* is almost epexegetic (*OLD* 6). The 'path to virtue' is a common image (e.g. Hes. *WD* 287–92, Xen. *Mem.* 2.1.21, Sall. *J.* 1.3; E. Fantham, *Comparative Studies in Republican Latin Imagery* (1972) 70–1, Rutherford 176 and n. 138). Sometimes *ardua* is applied to the path ('steep, difficult'), e.g. Sil. 2.578 'ardua uirtutem profert uia', sometimes to virtue itself (perhaps 'lofty'), e.g. Stat. *Silv.* 5.2.98. Since poverty is virtuous (3.29.54–6) and conventionally associated with lowness (e.g. *Octav.* 896–7; cf. 3.16.18–19n.), there is irony in *uirtutis...arduae*. If *arduam* were to be read here, as Lambinus proposed, there would be an ironic contrast with the difficult journeys which, in his pursuit of riches, the merchant *has* chosen to undertake (36–41).

45–50 uel nos...uel nos...mittamus: the repeated pronouns are subject of *mittamus*, which is slightly sylleptic: with *in Capitolium* it means 'send' or 'arrange to be conveyed' (*OLD* 14, 17a–b) but with *in mare* it means 'drop' (*OLD* 8). Of the two alternatives introduced by *uel*, only the first is realistic (next nn.).

in Capitolium: i.e. to the Temple of Jupiter Optimus Maximus on the Capitol (3.3.42–3n.), for its adornment; Suet. chooses the same ex. of Augustus' *liberalitas* (next nn.).

46 quo clamor uocat et turba fauentium 'to where the noisy crowd of supporters demands' (hendiadys): H. is thinking of Augustus, who donated a fortune to the temple following his victory at Actium (*RG* 21.2, Suet. *Aug.* 30.2 [next n.], Dio 51.22.3). Cf. Livy on the Oppian Law (34.1.4): 'Capitolium turba hominum fauentium aduersantiumque legi complebatur'.

48 gemmas et lapides aurum et inutile: Suet. lists Augustus' donations as 'sedecim milia pondo auri gemmasque ac margaritas quingenties sestertium' (*Aug.* 30.2), whence it is deduced that H.'s *lapides* refers to pearls (cf. also Tib. 1.8.39 'lapis...gemmaeque'). Since pearls were associated esp. with India (e.g. Plin. *NH* 9.106) and Arabia was a notable source of various gems (e.g. Plin. *NH* 37.84–91), there is a link back to 1–2.

49 summi materiem mali: H. is reversing the philosophical term *summum bonum* (cf. Cic. *Fin.* 1.29) and alluding to the proverbial notion that *auaritia* is the cause of all evil (Tosi 809–10 §1811). *materies/-ia mali* (as

Ov. *Ex P.* 4.16.50, Sen. *Ben.* 3.30.2, 7.1.7) and *m. malorum* (as *Rhet. Herenn.* 2.34, Sen. *Ep.* 98.2) draw from translators a wide variety of renderings (e.g. 'substance', 'source', 'raw material'); in the passage which H. seems to be imitating (Sall. *BC* 10.3 'primo pecuniae, deinde imperi cupido creuit: ea quasi materies omnium malorum fuit') the image is probably one of disease. *materies* 'appears to have an archaic and poetic flavour' compared with *materia* (Brink on *AP* 131).

50 scelerum si bene paenitet 'if we *really* regret our crimes': *scelus* seems to refer to civil war, as often (Watson on *Epo.* 7.18; Jal 450–60), and to look back to 25–6 above. If the ode belongs to the period 31–28 (intro.), plots such as that of the young M. Lepidus (3.6.13–14n.) meant that the renewal of civil war always seemed a possibility. *bene* = 'thoroughly' (*OLD* 13a): cf. Ov. *Ex P.* 1.1.58 'bene peccati paenituisse' with Gaertner.

51–2 eradenda cupidinis | praui sunt elementa 'the rudiments of perverted desire must be erased'. Moral advice was esp. directed at the young (3.1.4n.) and H. envisages (as it were) a classroom demonstration, in which the basic elements of greed, written on a board or wax tablet as things to be avoided, are then symbolically rubbed out, and the pupils' minds directed elsewhere. For the metaphor of the alphabet see *S.* 1.1.25–6 and Gowers; for *cupidinis praui* cf. Sall. *BJ* 1.4 (*p. cupiditas* at Liv. 7.9.4, Val. Max. 5.1.3).

52–4 tenerae nimis | mentes asperioribus | formandae studiis: if *tener* = 'young' (*OLD* 2), *nimis* will mean 'very', as it sometimes does (*OLD* 3a), and *asperioribus* will mean 'strict' (*OLD* 12b); but *asperioribus* also suggests, as at Virg. *Ecl.* 10.49, a rough ~ soft contrast with *tenerae* = 'soft' (*OLD* 7), in which case *nimis* will have its more regular meaning of 'too'. *formare* is a technical term of education (*OLD* 4a), e.g. Quint. 10.1.59 'formanda mens'; here it suggests also the rigid shaping of a mould (cf. *OLD forma* 16a), in contrast to the training in crooked desire.

54–5 nescit equo rudis | haerere ingenuus puer 'untrained on horseback, the free-born boy does not know how to cling on [sc. to his horse]' (the 'fronted' *equo* is *apo koinou*): horse-riding was a valued skill (3.7.25–6n.): the boy's inability to ride constitutes a reflection of the unbridled *licentia* in society at large (28–9n.); he will never be the brave and hardy *puer eques* of 3.2.2–4. *puer* continues the theme of youth from 51–4a, while *rudis*, regularly accompanied by an abl. (e.g. Vell. 73.1 'studiis rudem' and W.), continues the theme of education, which will be sustained by *doctior* (56) below. For *haerere* cf. *OLD* 2a (numerous exs. with abl.).

56 uenarique timet: 'The first pursuit that a young man just out of boyhood should take up is hunting' (Xen. *Cyneg.* 2.1), which was regarded as training for warfare (cf. 3.12.13–16n.).

56–8 ludere doctior | seu Graeco iubeas trocho | seu malis uetita legibus alea: once again *seu* (*siue*) = *uel si* (3.4.3–4n.); in full the clauses would read: 'ludere doctior uel Graeco trocho, si iubeas, uel, si mālis,... alea' ('more learned in playing either with the Greek hoop, should one so order, or, should one prefer it, with the dice forbidden by law'). For the indefinite second-person singular subjunctive in a generalising condition see *NLS* 151–2 §195. *doctior* contrasts with *rudis* (as e.g. Cic. *Off.* 1.1); the cynical implication is that vice is something to be learned (cf. e.g. 3.6.21, Licin. Calv. 1C/34H 'talis...pereruditus', Tac. *Agr.* 16.3, *A.* 3.54.3), and there were in fact handbooks on gambling (Ov. *Tr.* 2.471, Suet. *Claud.* 33.2). *trochus* is a Greek loan word for a metal hoop (see Leary on Mart. 14.168–9); the noun 'could itself convey contempt' (N–R), but H. underlines its Greekness by *Graeco*.

58 uetita legibus alea: gambling was disapproved of because it led to debt (next n.), and *aleator* is a regular term of abuse in Cicero (e.g. *Phil.* 2.66–8); legislation against the practice went back to the third century BC (Plaut. *Mil.* 163–4) but was routinely flouted: Augustus himself was a regular player (Suet. *Aug.* 71.1–3). See further J. P. V. D. Balsdon, *Life and Leisure in Ancient Rome* (1969) 154–6; Griffin 13–14; Edwards 190–1; N. Purcell, 'Literate games: Roman urban society and the game of alea', *P&P* 147 (1995) 3–37; Ingleheart on Ov. *Tr.* 2.471–2.

59–62 cum periura patris fides | consortem <et> socium fallat et hospites, | indignoque pecuniam | heredi properet: the indulged son is able to gamble at will (58) 'since his father's perjurious loyalty/credit deceives his coheritor and his business partner and his guests, and hastens the money to his undeserving heir' (*periura...fides* is an oxymoron). Since the transmitted *consortem socium* seems to say the same thing twice, Bentley introduced a distinction between the terms by inserting *et* and interpreting *consortem* in its technical primary sense (*OLD* 1): the father shares an inheritance (e.g. with a sibling) but defrauds his coheritor to fund his son's gambling debts. *socium* is a business partner (*OLD* 3a): defrauding a partner is a commonplace idea (*Epi.* 2.1.122–3 and Brink), and *socium fallere* is a regular phrase (e.g. Cic. *Rosc. Com.* 16 'aeque enim perfidiosum et nefarium est fidem frangere...et socium fallere qui se in negotio coniunxit'). Although the conventions of hospitality were of great importance in the ancient world, and infringing them was worthy of note (*TLL*

6.3.3021.8-19), it is not clear how the father's favouring of his unworthy son could inflict financial loss on persons to whom he was bound 'by personal or inherited ties of hospitality' (*OLD hospes*¹ 3); perhaps the father has borrowed from the *hospites* on a promise of investment and repayment which he knows he is not going to keep. For transitive *propero* see *OLD* 5a; for *pecunia* see 3.16.17.

62-4 *scilicet* both affirms an obvious fact and prepares for a following contrast (*OLD* 2c). *sententiae* and the like are a regular form of closure, here assisted by ring composition (*diuitiae* ~ *diuitis* (2), *improbae* ~ *occupes*...*mare publicum* (3-4), *curtae*...*rei* ~ *intactis* (1)) and the universalising *semper* (Schrijvers, *OR* 62-3, 66-7).

63-4 tamen | curtae nescioquid semper abest rei 'but something is always missing from one's incomplete resources': i.e. no matter how much a man acquires, he thinks his pile is insufficient and so he always wants more. Such expressions as *semper auarus eget* (*Epi.* 1.2.56) are proverbial (for a series of them see Tosi 808-11); for *absum* = 'to be missing' see *OLD* 13. H.'s lines are alluded to by Pers. 6.33-4 'cenam funeris heres | negleget iratus quod rem curtaueris', where, unlike 61-2 here, the heir sees his father as having deprived him and hence seeks to deprive the father in his turn.

25

In AD 14 some voyagers from Alexandria were putting in at Puteoli and, as the *princeps* sailed past in his own craft, they cried out that 'per illum se uiuere, per illum nauigare, libertate atque fortunis per illum frui' (Suet. *Aug.* 98.2). The triple *per illum* becomes, in direct speech, *per te*, a ritual formula of prayers (McKeown on Ov. *Am.* 2.9.47-8): the gratitude which ordinary people felt towards their great benefactor was such that they regarded him as a living god. The world was very different in 23 BC, almost forty years earlier, when H. published his *Odes*, yet citizens already had reason to be grateful to Augustus for ending twenty years of civil war. As early as the second ode H. describes the *princeps* as a god on earth and prays that his return to heaven be delayed as long as possible (1.2.45 'serus in caelum redeas'), a motif which soon became popular (see N-H). Beneficiaries felt it incumbent upon themselves to express their gratitude, which, in the case of a great man such as Augustus, took the form of deification on earth (Du Quesnay (1981) 99-106), which in turn led to apotheosis in the afterlife (see 3.3.11-12).

The present ode is addressed to Bacchus as the inspirer of poetry and it explains the subject of the poem which H. will be inspired by Bacchus to write: the apotheosis of Augustus (3–6). The promise of the poem is both unqualified and insistent (7 *dicam*, 18 *loquar*), but it does not follow that the poet ever intended to write such a poem: the ode itself constitutes its own praise, but it gives the *impression* of an intention, and that is what is important.[123] That the *princeps*' death should be delayed as long as possible goes without saying.

The poem displays a series of triads: three questions in tricolon crescendo in 1–6 (*Quo, quae..., quibus*), three objectives in 2–4 (*nemora, specus, antris*), three qualities in 7–8 (*insigne, recens, indictum*), three place names in 10–12 (Hebrus, Thrace, Rhodope), and three further qualities in 17–18 (*nil paruum aut humili modo, nil mortale*). The arrangement of the poem can also be seen as triadic, in so far as it exhibits three separate elements, two of which are repeated chiastically to produce a ring structure:

A¹   1–3a With the god: address (*Bacche*), travel (*me...rapis, agor*), ecstasy (*uelox mente noua*)
B¹   3b–8a Proposed project: brilliant, fresh, original (*insigne, recens, adhuc indictum*)
C   8b–14a Destination
B²   14b–18a Proposed project: important, elevated, immortal (*nil paruum aut humili modo, nil mortale*)
A²   18b–20 With the god: address (*o Lenaee*), travel (*sequi*), ecstasy (*dulce periculum*)

The structure reveals that the ode has a dramatic form. In 1–8a the poet, possessed by Bacchus, imagines himself in the process of being conveyed by the god to another place where he can write his poem on Augustus. In 8b–14a he has arrived at his destination. In 14b–20 his acknowledgement of what he has experienced indicates that he is in a position to begin the promised poem. The drama is somewhat similar to that in another ode of inspiration, 3.4, where we have to envisage a dramatic interval between lines 1–4 and 5–8 (see nn.).

Augustus' apotheosis is to take two forms: a new star will be visible in the sky and he will join Jupiter's Council of the Gods as a member (6). Stars were regularly associated with celestial immortality (cf. 3.3.10) and

---

[123] N–R take a similar view (298), but the work of E. L. Bundy, to which they refer, has now been superseded by I. L. Pfeijffer, *First Person Futures in Pindar* (1999). The strange notion that the promised poem is the so-called 'Roman Odes' (Fraenkel 259) is a non-starter.

became especially prominent in the aftermath of the murder of Julius Caesar, the *princeps*' adoptive father, whose temple was dedicated in 29 BC (Weinstock 370–84, esp. 379, 383–4 for Augustus, 399–400 for the temple). Indeed the elder Pliny says that Augustus inferred his own apotheosis from the manifestation of that of Caesar (*NH* 2.94). Membership of the *concilium deorum* seems a less usual expression of divinity but occurs alongside catasterism in the prologue to Virgil's first Georgic, where he addresses Octavian (as he still was) in bold prophetic terms (1.24–8, 32):[124]

> tuque adeo, quem mox quae sint habitura deorum
> concilia incertum est, urbesne inuisere, Caesar,   25
> terrarumque uelis curam, et te maximus orbis
> auctorem frugum tempestatumque *potentem*
> accipiat *cingens* materna *tempora* myrto;...   28
> anne nouum tardis sidus te mensibus addas...   32

and as for you, Caesar, it is uncertain which councils of the gods will have you <as a member> in due course, whether you will choose to visit cities and have care of the earth, and the great globe, encircling your temples with your mother's myrtle, will accept you as the originator of crops and in charge of the weather/seasons; ...or whether you will add yourself as a new star when the months have slowed down...

Virgil refers to a plurality of councils because he fancifully imagines that there is one council for each of the four areas of the universe, of which the first mentioned is the earth and the third is the heavens. It cannot be known whether H. took from his friend the ideas of a divine council and a new star and combined them, but the overlapping vocabulary is obviously interesting. The likelihood of a relationship is increased when we consider that the prologue to the second Georgic begins with an address to Bacchus (2.2–6):

> nunc te, *Bacche*, canam, nec non siluestria tecum
> uirgulta et prolem tarde crescentis oliuae.

---

[124] The Latin is difficult and translation uncertain. Membership of the *concilium deorum* is to be distinguished from the motif in which a mortal is summoned to appear before the *concilium* to receive advice or orders (Quint. 11.1.24; Pease on Cic. *Div.* 1.49).

> Huc, pater *o Lenaee*, tuis hic omnia *plena*
> muneribus, tibi *pampineo* grauidus autumno   5
> floret ager, spumat plenis uindemia labris;
> huc, pater *o Lenaee*, ueni...
>
> now I shall sing of you, Bacchus, as well as the woodland shrubs with you, and the product of the slow-growing olive. Hither, o father Lenaeus! Here everything is full of your gifts, for you the laden field flourishes with autumn vines, and the vintage foams in full vats; come hither, o father Lenaeus...

Like H.'s first line, the passage begins with a monosyllable and a pronoun followed by the vocative *Bacche* and a two-syllable verb. *o Lenaee*, which Virgil has twice, recurs in this precise form only once more in Latin literature, in H.'s ode (19); *tuis...plena muneribus* becomes *tui plenum* (1–2); and *pampineo* features as *pampino* in H.'s final line (20). It seems that H. is paying tribute to Virgil as well as to Bacchus and Augustus.

The cult of Bacchus at Rome had famously been the subject of repressive legislation in 186 BC (Liv. 39.8–19 with Briscoe), but references to the god are abundant in Augustan literature (see e.g. Ov. *Met.* 4.1–30). It is significant that throughout the 30s Mark Antony had demanded to be called Nouus Liber Pater (Vell. 82.4 and W.); after Actium 'this divine identity was appropriated by the future Augustus' (Harrison on 2.19, p. 225, with further refs.). West appears to see the ode as a form of dithyramb, which is an ecstatic choral poem in praise of Bacchus/Dionysus (*BNP* 4.560–2, *OCD* s.v.), but a choral aspect seems incompatible with the poet's journey and his promise of a new poem.[125] More striking, perhaps, are the evocations of Orpheus, the allegedly eponymous founder of Orphism. Not only had Bacchus himself achieved divine status from being mortal (cf. 3.3.13–15), but the transition to apotheosis is one which appears also in the Orphic Fragments (487.4, 488.9 'you will be a god instead of mortal'): see F. Graf and S. I. Johnston, *Ritual Texts for the Afterlife: Orpheus and the Bacchic Gold Tablets* (2007) 8–9, 12–13. The address to Bacchus in 14–15 has a very close parallel in one of the Orphic Hymns (54.6), and Orpheus himself is closely associated with the places mentioned in 10–12 (see nn. ad locc.). These elements are not to be seen

---

[125] For bibliography on the dithyramb in contemporary Rome see A. Hardie's discussion of 4.2 (*CQ* 65 (2015) 253–85).

as evidence of some special knowledge of a closely related cult,[126] but they contribute to the general air of mystical enthusiasm and hence support the notion that H. is to be taken seriously when he promises a poem on the apotheosis of the emperor.

METRE Fourth Asclepiad

1 Quo me...rapis: the first in a series of anaphoric questions with polyptoton: 'Where are you sweeping me off to?', as *Epi.* 1.1.15 'quo me cumque rapit tempestas'. Scholars compare the three questions which introduce the Bacchic lyric by the fifth-century BC Pratinas (708), although there is nothing necessarily Bacchic about such an introduction (cf. 1.12.1–6).

1–2 tui | plenum: phrases such as *deo/dei plenus*, equivalent to the Greek ἔνθεος (3.4.20n.), are common to describe the inspired prophet or poet (see 2.19.6 'plenoque Bacchi pectore' and N–H; Horsfall on Virg. *Aen.* 6, App. 1, pp. 627–9):[127] H. is about to foretell the apotheosis of the *princeps*.

2 quae nemora: sc. *in* from later in the line. For the association of groves and poetic inspiration see 3.4.6–8n.

specus: for caves as a Bacchic location see Dodds on Eur. *Bacch.* 120.

3 uelox mente noua: *uelox* is adverbial with *agor* (3.3.70–2n.); *mente noua* is usually translated as an abl. of attendant circumstances or abl. abs., '(with) my mind altered'; the juxtaposition with *uelox* may even suggest a causal abl. (*NLS* 32 §45), 'quickly because of my altered mind', the paradox of *agor* ~ *mente* underlining the visionary nature of the experience. Although *nouus* refers primarily to ecstasy (*OLD* 9b), it also anticipates the poetic originality of line 8 (n.).

3–4 quibus | antris...audiar: since *nemus* means 'grove' and *specus* means 'cave, grotto', *antris* is perhaps intended to embrace both meanings (for this ambiguity see further 3.4.40n.); the noun is probably abl. (of place 'where'): since H. will be practising (6 *meditans*) and alone (13 'uacuum

---

[126] Everything relating to Orphism is complex and much discussed: for the relationship with Bacchus see e.g. Bremmer 70–80.
[127] In theory *tui plenum* could be equivalent to *uini plenum*, a common phrase (cf. Quint. 9.3.1); one has to assume that this meaning is precluded by the words *Quo...rapis*.

nemus'), we are presumably to interpret *audiar* in terms of an echo.[128] That *audiar* is fut. indic. rather than pres. subjunc. is perhaps suggested by *dicam* below (7).

4–6 egregii Caesaris... | aeternum meditans decus | stellis inserere et concilio Iouis 'practising to install amongst the stars and in Jupiter's council the everlasting adornment of [i.e. which consists of] exceptional Caesar'. *egregii Caesaris* is a genitive of definition, like *Epo.* 5.7 'purpurae decus', Manil. 4.194 'decus linguae' (*NLS* 53 §72 (5), *OLS* 1.1023–5). Although N–R prefer the variant *consilio* because it suggests 'the informal group of advisers that played such an important part in Roman public and private life', they acknowledge that *concilium* is the term used for the divine council. The more normal expr. is *concilium deorum* (see 3.3.intro.), but it was under the 'chairmanship' of Jupiter (Virg. *Aen.* 10.2), as again in Seneca's *Apocolocyntosis*. Since *grex* can be used of a group of stars (*OLD* 1d), there is likely to be play with *e-gregii* (cf. Maltby 201). Apart from 1.6.11 (the *recusatio* where H. declines to write in praise of Augustus), *egregius* is used elsewhere with the name *Caesar* only at Cic. *Fam.* 10.28.3 in a complimentary description of the young Octavian (early 43 BC); the adj. is not commonly found with *princeps* but does occur in later texts (Suet. *Galba* 14.1, Tac. *A.* 14.48.3 (a speech), Fronto p. 87.12–13 vdH²). *aeternum decus* is an exclusively poetical expr. (*TLL* 5.1.244.57–8). For *insero* (again at 1.1.35, where the object is H. himself) see *OLD insero*² 3; for the notion that the writer does what he describes (*inserere*) see N–H on 2.1.18, W. on Tac. *A.* 6.38.1 (n. 112). For *meditor* + infin. see *OLD* 5a.

7–8 dicam insigne, recens, adhuc | indictum ore alio 'I shall utter something brilliant, fresh, and still unuttered by another voice'; *insignis*, itself often used of stars (*TLL* 7.1.1904.22–34), also suggests the noun *signum*, which can mean 'star' (2.8.11): the term thus looks back to *stellis inserere*. H.'s promises echo, both explicitly and implicitly, those expected of a speaker who is trying to gain his audience's attention: 'attentos habebimus si pollicebimur nos de rebus *magnis, nouis*, inusitatis uerba facturos, aut de iis quae ad rem publicam pertineant aut...ad deorum immortalium religionem' (*Rhet. Herenn.* 1.7; cf. Cic. *Inv.* 1.23; Lausberg 126

---

[128] In AD 21 a poet called Clutorius Priscus, having been rewarded by Tiberius for a poem in which he had mourned the dead Germanicus, had tried to capitalise on his success by writing a poem in which he anticipated the death of Drusus, Tiberius' son, who was ill. Unfortunately he made the mistake of trying out his poem in front of an invited audience before Drusus actually died; he was executed (Tac. *A.* 3.49–51 and W–M ad loc.).

§270). The promise of novelty, here emphasised by the assonantal play of positive *dicam* ~ negative *indictum* (for which see Wills 455–8), is self-evidently closely connected with the so-called '*primus*-motif' (for which cf. 3.30.13–14n.): H.'s promised poem will be as original as his popularisation of Alcaeus in the *Odes* (*Epi.* 1.19.32–3 'hunc ego, non alio dictum prius ore, Latinus | uulgaui fidicen').

8–14a This is a very awkward sentence. The accepted interpretation is that *non secus* (8) is correlative with *ut* (12). This is problematic, because initial *non* (or *haud*) *secus* ('not otherwise', 'no differently') is invariably followed by *quam* or *ac* ('than'). On the rare occasions when *ut* or an equivalent is correlative with *non secus*, the *ut*-clause invariably precedes (*Il. Lat.* 488–92 'ut lupus...auidus ruit, haud secus Hector | inuadit Danaos' ('just as the wolf...rushes greedily, no differently does Hector attack the Greeks'), Stat. *Theb.* 6.854–9 'ueluti...non secus...', Gell. 12.1.14 'sicut... non secus...'), which is what one would expect (see Thomas on 4.14.25–9). Our example falls foul of each of these conventions, and indeed it makes no sense to say 'no differently is the Bacchante astonished..., just as I am delighted to wonder...'. Those who retain *ut* appeal to the one case where *non secus* allegedly precedes *ut* (Ov. *Met.* 15.179–80 'ipsa quoque adsiduo labuntur tempora motu, | non secus ut flumen'): this text is approved by Housman and printed by Tarrant, presumably on the grounds that *non secus* is equivalent in meaning to 'in the same way'; but *ut* is in fact a variant, the majority of MSS having *ac*. Some editors, such as N-R, adopt the variant *ac* for *ut* in line 12, but this involves the consequent change of *ac* to *et* in 11, and in any case H. never uses *ac* = *quam* in the *Odes* (3.27.42–4n.). The only alternative for line 12 seems to be to adopt Porphyrio's lemma, which reads *quam*: it is true that this results in a momentary ambiguity after the feminine sing. *lustratam Rhodopen*, but there is a somewhat similar sequence at 1.7.11–12.

8–10 in iugis | exsomnis stupet Euhias | ...prospiciens: the ridges are presumably those of Rhodope, which the Bacchante has climbed (11–12n.) and from which she is now enjoying a panorama. Euhias, which occurs only here in Latin, transliterates the Greek term for a female follower of Bacchus/Dionysus and derives from the Bacchic cry εὐοῖ (*euhoe*: 2.19.5, 7); the noun is a collective singular, standing for a plurality of Bacchantes, but it facilitates the comparison with the poet himself ('non secus...quam mihi...'). All-night rituals were a feature of Bacchic worship (Soph. *Ant.* 1150); for *exsomnis* in particular see *Orph. Hymn* 54.5, where the Bacchic Silenus (14–15n. below) is addressed as φιλάγρυπνε, 'wakeful'. Since H. does not elsewhere construct *stupeo* with an accus., it is likely that *prospiciens* (10) governs the following three proper names (10–12). *stupet* is pres. tense because H. is visualising a timeless scene, perhaps as represented by a work of art: cf. the coverlet on which Ariadne 'saxea ut effigies bacchantis *prospicit*' (Cat. 64.61), a familiar passage (cf. 3.2.9n.) which H. may well have in mind again here (~ 'Euhias... *prospiciens*').

10 Hebrum: a principal river of Thrace (mod. Maritsa) which debouches into the northern Aegean (*BA* Map 51: G1–3) and plays a major part in the story of Orpheus (Virg. *G.* 4.524).

10–11 niue candidam | Thracen: Thrace, the homeland of Bacchus (McKeown on Ov. *Am.* 1.14.21–2), was regarded by the ancients as 'un pays exceptionnellement froid et fortement enneigé', and its 'snowy mountains' appear as early as Hom. *Il.* 14.227 (P.-J. Dehon, *Hiems Latina: études sur l'hiver dans la poésie latine des origines à l'époque de Néron* (1993) 48, with many refs. in n. 89).

11–12 pede barbaro | lustratam Rhodopen: Rhodope is the mountain range – over 7,000 feet at its highest point – by which Thrace is defined (*BA* Map 51: B–E1–2) and, like the Hebrus, it features in the myth of Orpheus (Virg. *Ecl.* 6.30, *G.* 4.461); the traversing of mountains (ὀρειβασία) is characteristic of Bacchantes (e.g. Alcm. 56.1), as of their leader (e.g. Anacr. 357.4–5). *pede* refers to the Bacchante herself, although the meaning of *barbaro* is unclear. The woman's astonishment (9 *stupet*) suggests that she is a stranger in the Thracian massif, but *barbarus* in the sense of *externus* or *alienus* seems impossible to parallel. N–R see a reference to the 'outlandish' Bacchic custom of bared feet, which is conceivably how H.'s phrase was interpreted by Seneca (cf. *Med.* 753 'secreta nudo nemora lustraui pede').

12 deuio suggests both 'off-course' and 'remote'. H.'s transplantation to the Bacchic landscape matches that of the Bacchante (~ *barbaro*), but there is also an allusion to the 'untrodden paths' by which Callimachean poetry was symbolised (e.g. *Aet.* 1.27 and Harder's n., *Epig.* 28.1–2 (quoted on 3.1.1), Lucr. 1.926–7 'auia Pieridum peragro loca nullius ante | trita solo', Prop. 3.1.18 'intacta...uia').

13 rupes et uacuum nemus: the MSS read *ripas* but there was no mention of banks (or rivers) as H.'s destination (2–4); *rupes*, a typically Bacchic landscape (2.19.1), refers back to the caves of line 2, as *nemus* picks up the groves (cf. Prop. 1.18.2–4 'uacuum...nemus...saxa'). *uacuum* suggests, in addition to solitude, a reference to the poetic originality claimed in lines 7–8 (cf. *Epi.* 1.19.21 'libera per uacuum posui uestigia princeps').

COMMENTARY 25.14-19

14 mirari ~ stupet...prospiciens (9–10).

14–15 o Naïadum potens | Baccharumque: the address resembles that to Silenus at *Orph. Hymn* 54.6 'leader of Naiads and Bacchantes'. Nymphs of one sort or another are frequent attendants of Bacchus/Dionysus (e.g. Pratinas 708.4, *Orph. Hymn* 51.1–3). *potens* is a regular term for a divinity, and the accompanying genitive ('powerful over': *OLD* 2a) 'is often used in religious contexts' (N–H on 1.3.2).

15–16 ualentium | proceras manibus uertere fraxinos 'able to uproot tall ash trees with their hands' (the Bacchantes uproot fir trees at Eur. *Bacch.* 1109–10); the adj. is not idle, since the common ash 'out-towers the manna ash [3.27.58n.], and is sometimes nearly a hundred feet high' (Sargeaunt 48). *uertere* seems to be used for *euertere* (*OLD* 3c). Is H. recalling Enn. *Ann.* 177–8 *'fraxinus* frangitur atque abies consternitur alta, | pinus *proceras* per*uortunt*' (describing the felling of timber)? *ualere* commonly takes an infin. (*OLD* 6a).

17 nil paruum aut humili modo: *paruum* denotes something small-scale, non-epic; *humili* not only means 'humble' but activates the metaphor of 'low-level' genres (*Epi.* 2.1.250 'repentes per humum'): see Brink on *AP* 28 *humi*, Harder on Callim. *Aetia* 112.9. H. gives the impression that he is promising a poem of epic proportions (3.3.70–2n.), although in reality the present ode performs the fulfilment of the promise.

18 nil mortale alludes to H.'s topic (Augustus' apotheosis), to his inspired state (cf. Virg. *Aen.* 6.50 'nil mortale sonans') and to the immortality of his poetry (for which see on 3.30 below).

dulce periculum: while it was good to be chosen by a god for some select task (1–8), it was nevertheless dangerous to be in a god's presence (3.18.2–4n.), especially a god as capable of violence as Bacchus: cf. 2.19.5–7 'recenti mens trepidat metu | plenoque Bacchi pectore turbidum | laetatur'. Similar oxymoron at 3.4.5–6 'amabilis | insania'; the same phrase at Stat. *Silv.* 4.5.25 (a very Horatian poem).

19 o Lenaee: there was a close connection between wine and inspiration (3.19.14–15n.), and, when H. discussed the matter in *Epi.* 1.19, he chose the epic poets Homer and Ennius as his examples of wine-drinkers (1.19.6–8). Thus it was naturally relevant here to address Bacchus, the god of both, as 'god of the wine-press'. For more details on the name, which was thought to be derived from the Greek ληνός (Diod. 3.63.4), see NA on Lygd. 6.38.

sequi deum: the verb, which is not to be taken as meaning that H. had any choice in the matter (cf. 1–2 'rapis...agor'), is an acknowledgement that the journey which was beginning in lines 1–6 has been completed. Note that *sequi* has other connotations apart from movement: see esp. *OLD* 11a 'to attend as a client or servant', 12b 'to be an adherent of (a teacher)'.

20 cingentem uiridi tempora pampino 'encircling his temples with the green vine-shoot.' Despite the juxtaposition of *cingentem* with *deum*, scholars have debated whether *cingentem* and *tempora* may not refer rather to H. himself, who is associated with ivy at 1.1.29–30; but the primary reference here is surely to Bacchus, 'the ivy-knowing god' (Pind. *Dithyramb* 4, fr. 75.9). Yet perhaps the ambiguity of the Latin, if it is present,[129] hints at the fact that the god has taken possession of the poet (1–2 'tui plenum'). For the expr. cf. Virg. *Aen.* 5.539 'cingit uiridanti tempora lauro' (also *G.* 1.28: see intro.).

26

It is night-time and a komast is walking through the streets of some anonymous town, perhaps at the seaside (5), carrying his lyre (4) and accompanied by slaves holding torches (6–7). He is on his way to Chloe's door, but Chloe likes to give herself airs (12), and he knows that he is unlikely to be granted admission; but he has had the foresight to bring along crowbars in order to threaten or effect a forced entry (7–8).[130] Then he stops in his tracks and thinks to himself: he's not the man he was; he is now too old for this kind of game (1–2). As he comes to this grim realisation, he happens to be passing a wayside shrine, or perhaps a little local temple, to Maritime Venus: here is the ideal place to hang his torches and crowbars on the goddess's wall by way of dedication, signalling the end of his erotic career (3–8): 'hic...hic, hic...'. But then he has second thoughts. This is not just any deity: it's *Venus!* Perhaps a considered prayer to her will soften Chloe's heart for one final encounter (9–12). So he resumes his journey to her door with rekindled hope.

On this reading, 3.26 is another of those mimetic poems where the dramatic background has to be filled in from hints provided by the poem

---

[129] The alternative interpretation requires (i) that *periculum* be followed by an accus. + infin., for which the only parallel before H. is Acc. *Trag.* 206–8R (*TLL* 10.1.1471.1–3), and (ii) that *me* be supplied as its accus. subject. This all seems very difficult and unnatural; if the reference were to H., we should surely expect *cingenti*.

[130] Crowbars seem highly unlikely in the hands of H. himself and their mention suggests very strongly that the 'I' of the ode, even if of a similar age to the poet, is not to be identified with him (Intro. 20–1).

COMMENTARY 26.1 331

itself; and its charm resides in the *volte face* which takes place in the final stanza, where, after appearing to give up on love, the speaker changes his mind back again. Other readings are of course possible. Most scholars see the poem as a straightforward *renuntiatio amoris*: the former lover is on his way to Venus' shrine to dedicate his accoutrements, but in the last stanza, when he prays to Venus, his rejection of love turns out to be 'a sham' (N–R).[131] This interpretation seems to me not only feeble[132] but also implicitly contradicted by details in the poem itself.[133] Night is the traditional time for an actual komos and explains the reference to burning torches; no one would set out at night-time to dedicate torches, which would be needed to light the return journey home. Why would anyone choose to hang up their komastic equipment in a shrine specified as that of *Maritime* Venus, goddess of the sea and seafaring? That he came across the shrine by happy accident is indicated by the threefold repetition of *hic*, which suggests a serendipitous encounter rather than an intended destination. Moreover the description of the lover's accoutrements as 'a threat to enemy doors' (8) appears entirely redundant unless he had been intending to use them.

The poem deploys a wide variety of familiar elements: the ageing philanderer, the *militia amoris*, the komos, the epitaph, the dedication, the prayer for help. There is a particular reverberation with the famous Pyrrha ode, the fifth in Book 1, just as this is the fifth-last in Book 3. It is natural to see the poem as divided into three parts: in 1–6a he is thinking or speaking reflectively to himself; in 6b–8 he gives orders to his attendant slaves; and in 9–12 he prays to Venus.

METRE Alcaic

1 Vixi puellis nuper idoneus: these apparently simple words are not as straightforward as they are often taken. Although the phraseology is similar to that in some epitaphs (e.g. *CLE* 381.1 'uixi uiro cara'), the

---

[131] Comparable is the allegation that the poem illustrates 'the motif of pretended impotence' (Giangrande 112 n. 2). A change of mind is said to be a regular feature of the *renuntiatio amoris* (Cairns, *GC* 139), but it is striking that the ode features in only two of the nine topoi by which Cairns defines the *renuntiatio amoris* (*GC* 80–1), and one of them ('contentment' in the 'state of mind' topos) is contradicted immediately afterwards (82 'conflict of mind').

[132] This objection would be removed if in lines 11–12 the speaker were praying that Chloe should experience an unrequited love affair with a third party; but see ad loc.

[133] Some think that 'love-poetry, rather than love-life, is the primary target of renunciation' (Davis 64; cf. N–R 311), but the problem here is that the next ode but one is a love poem (3.28).

similarity is only formal, since epitaphic *uixi* is difficult to reconcile with *nuper*.[134] In the ode *uixi* is being used in the sense of *fui* (*OLD uiuo* 2; cf. 3.27.13–14), a colloquial usage and thus appropriately combined with the prosaic *idoneus* (N–H on 2.19.26). *idoneus*, a word often used of military fitness, is only rarely constructed with a personal dat. such as *puellis* (*TLL* 7.1.231.23–7), and the meaning is not immediately clear (Franke suggested *duellis*). There seem to be two possibilities. (i) *puellis* is elliptical and the words mean 'Recently I was fit for <dealing with> girls' (so, implicitly, Commager 147); (ii) *puellis* is a dat. 'of the person judging' (*NLS* 47 §65, G&L 225 §350.1) and the words are equivalent to 'Recently girls thought me suitable' (so Copley 56n.). Either way, the contrast between previous sexual prowess and present diminished powers is a conventional motif (see e.g. Sider's commentary on Philod. 19 = *Anth. Pal.* 11.30).

2 militaui non sine gloria: the *militia amoris* is one of the commonest tropes in Latin love poetry (P. Murgatroyd, *Latomus* 34 (1975) 59–79), the classic example being Ov. *Am.* 1.9 'Militat omnis amans' (see McKeown). *militauit* is frequently found in soldiers' epitaphs (*TLL* 8.965.78ff.), a formula to which H. alludes here (see further 1n.): N–R compare *ILS* 2030 'C. Iulius...Gemellus...uixit ann. XVIII militauit ann. II in coh. VII pr.'. For erotic *gloria* see McKeown on Ov. *Am.* 2.12.11; for *non sine* see 3.4.20n.

3–4 nunc arma...hic paries habebit: the retired 'soldier' dedicates his weapons as does the former gladiator at *Epi.* 1.1.4–5 'armis | Herculis ad postem fixis' (see further 6n. below; also *Anth. Pal.* 6.127–32). The future tense perhaps has a jussive sense (as e.g. Cic. *Off.* 1.18; G&L 162 §243): 'but now [adversative asyndeton] let this wall...'. *nunc* contrasts (and alliterates) with *nuper* (1); *hic* is deictic, like *harum* at 2.14.22, and is further specified by the following relative clause (5–6).

defunctumque bello | barbiton: music was an essential element of the komos (3.7.29–30n.); the *barbitos*, a Greek word for a Greek instrument (again at 1.1.34, 1.32.4), was a bowl lyre (*BNP* 9.355–7; M. L. West (1992) 50–1, 57–9, Battezzato 144, all with illustrations): the lyre was supposedly 'unwarlike' (1.6.10 'imbellisque lyrae'), but of course H. is talking about metaphorical warfare. *defunctum...bello* (again at Liv. 25.35.5, 32.21.18) = 'finished with/discharged from war' (*OLD defungor* 2a) and applies to *arma* as well as *barbiton*.

---

[134] Different again is *uixi* at 3.29.43 (*contra OLD uiuo* 7b).

COMMENTARY 26.5-7   333

5-6 laeuum Marinae qui Veneris latus | custodit: '(this wall,) which guards the left-hand side of Maritime Venus'. The goddess stands for her temple or shrine, a common form of metonymy (3.5.12n.) which here suggests that the wall is actually guardian of Venus herself (cf. Mart. 6.76.1 'sacri lateris custos'). *Marinae* is usually explained in terms of Venus' birth from the sea (cf. Thomas on 4.11.15, the only other ex. of the phrase), but there is ample evidence that she was a goddess of the sea and seafaring, which seems a far more probable explanation: see N–H on 1.3.1 and 1.5.16, where they quote the dedication at *ILS* 3179 'Veneri Pelagiae', to which *Marinae...Veneris* is equivalent. Perhaps we are to infer that the imagined location is near the sea.

6 hic, hic ponite: the address is to the accompanying slaves. The repeated adverb picks up *hic paries* (4) and suggests delight at having just come across the place ('This is the very place for...!'); the verb is being used in its technical sense of hanging up one's decommissioned weapons (3-4n.) or other votive objects at a temple or suchlike (Ov. *Tr.* 4.8.21-2 'miles ubi emeritis non est satis utilis annis, | ponit ad antiquos, quae tulit, arma Lares'; *TLL* 10.1.2644.63-2645.35).

6-7 lucida | funalia et uectes acutos 'bright torches and sharp crowbars'. *funalia*, lengths of rope smeared with a flammable substance, seem to be used almost exclusively in torchlight processions and the like (*TLL* 6.1.1545.79-1546.16), and it is obviously true that on his way through the streets at night the komast would be accompanied by slaves carrying torches (Prop. 1.3.10); but line 8 indicates that, once the door of the beloved was reached, the torches would be available for a different use: the locked-out lover conventionally threatens to break down and/or, albeit less commonly, burn down the beloved's door (cf. Theocr. 2.128 'axes and torches'; McKeown on Ov. *Am.* 1.6.57-8). Such behaviour was, however, unsuitable for the older lover (Ov. *AA* 3.565-7 'ille uetus miles...| nec franget postes nec saeuis ignibus uret'), as the komast has just come to acknowledge. *lucida* has been questioned on the ground that one cannot hang up burning torches; obviously they would be extinguished before being dedicated.

In the MSS the torches and crowbars are accompanied by bows ('et arcus'), which would not be much use against a stout door. The notion that the bows here symbolise a lover, as if he were some kind of Cupid figure (see Kenney on Apul. *Met.* 4.30.4), seems quite out of place; some edd. have suggested that H. is referring to an otherwise unattested kind of siege-engine (Amm. 24.2.13, quoted in *TLL*, is not a parallel for this usage), but such a machine would be impossible to fix to a wall. A large number of conjectures have been proposed: Bentley's clever *securesque* has proved the most popular, although the resulting elision is very rare (only 2.3.27–8, 3.29.35–6).[135] I suggest *acutos*, referring to the flattened point at the business end of the implement (examples of which have been found at Vindolanda, the famous Roman site just south of the Hadrian's Wall in Northumberland).

8 oppositis foribus minaces: the description refers pointedly to the intended use of the torches and crowbars, which has been temporarily abandoned (next n.). *oppositis* looks back to *ponite* (6); *minaces* is to be taken with *funalia* as well as *uectes*.

9 o, quae beatam, diua, tenes Cyprum: we have to imagine a brief interval between lines 8 and 9 (cf. 3.4.5 and n.), to allow time for the speaker to realise that the presence of Venus could be put to a different purpose than simply the dedication of his 'weapons' (see intro.). For initial *o* in prayers see 3.13.1n.; here the accompanying vocatives both interrupt (*diua*) and follow (11 *regina*) the relative clause, a feature of heightened style (cf. 3.4.1–2n.). For relative clauses as a formal element of hymns and prayers see 3.22.2–3n. *teneo* here means either 'inhabit' or 'rule over' (*OLD* 8, 9b): Venus had a famous cult centre on Cyprus at Paphos (3.28.13–15n.); *beatam* is not only explained by Cyprus' association with Venus (*OLD beatus* 2b) but translates the Greek adj. Makaria, an earlier name for the island (Plin. *NH* 5.129).

10 Memphin carentem Sithonia niue: Memphis was an Egyptian town on the Nile (*BA* Map 75: E1) and the location of a temple of 'foreign Aphrodite' (Hdt. 2.112.2 with Lloyd's n., Strabo 17.1.31); Bacchylides had referred to ἀχείμαντόν...Μέμφιν, 'winter-/storm-free Memphis' (fr. 30), of which H.'s words are a close rendering. Sithonia is the central promontory of Chalcidice and often used loosely for Thrace (N–H on 1.18.9): like Thrace (3.25.10–11n.), it was famous for its snow (Virg. *Ecl.* 10.66, Ov. *Am.* 3.7.8). H.'s specification of Sithonian snow suggests a connection with Chloe (12), since 3.9 features a 'Thracian Chloe' (9 'me nunc Thressa Chloe regit'), with whom the present Chloe is perhaps to be identified. See also next n.

11–12 sublimi flagello | tange Chloen semel arrogantem 'touch arrogant Chloe just once with your raised whip': *semel* (*OLD* 1b) is to be taken with *tange*. Since Chloe seems to have a connection with Thrace (10n.) and

---

[135] Interlinear elision is technically called synaloepha.

'Thracian horses were famous from Homer's time onwards' (Campbell on Anacr. 417; cf. West on Hes. *WD* 507–8), *flagello* suggests that Chloe is being portrayed as a young horse, a common image (3.11.9–10n.); for horse-whips see *OLD flagellum* 1b. For this use of *tango* see e.g. Stat. *Theb.* 7.579 'tactas...flagello' (the Fury maddens two tigers with her whip); *OLD* 1b. *sublimi* seems = 'raised high' (*OLD* 1c): Venus, often seen as a charioteer (3.9.18n.), is envisaged with whip poised (as was conventional for charioteers in Roman art); she is also equipped with a whip at Mart. 6.21.9, but without the equine image.

After the elaborate build-up in 9–10, the prayer to Venus could have been of any type (e.g. thanksgiving for a successful love life); the speaker has delayed as long as possible the revelation that he wants one final attempt at Chloe. N–R are sympathetic to the view of C. P. Jones (*HSCP* 75 (1971) 81–3) that the speaker is praying, not that Chloe admit him, but that, in revenge for her rejection of him, she should fall in love with someone else who will fail to reciprocate her affections. But *semel* is problematic for this view: if the idea was that Chloe should have a taste of her own medicine, the suppliant would hardly want to restrict it to one solitary occasion.

27

This ode is addressed to a girlfriend called Galatea, who is set upon leaving H. for a new lover overseas. The poem takes the form of a propemptikon or 'send-off', of which there were various types: in the basic type the speaker simply offers the addressee good wishes for his or her journey; in the so-called 'inverse' propemptikon the speaker does the opposite, issuing bad wishes for, and a disastrous outcome to, the addressee's journey (a standard example is *Epo.* 10); in the 'schetliastic' propemptikon the speaker makes every attempt to dissuade the addressee from departing, although there will often be a reaction in which the speaker, recognising that the attempts have failed, becomes reconciled to the addressee's departure and offers good wishes for the journey.[136]

The ode divides itself into two parts, since it concludes with a mythological *exemplum* (25–76) which is more than twice as long as the six stanzas which precede (1–24). The first six stanzas exhibit a circular structure. H. begins (1–7a) by listing five evil omens, each with its own epithet or equivalent, which should befall travellers guilty of *impietas*. These

---

[136] On all this see Cairns, *GC* index 310–12 'propemptikon' and 320 'schetliastic'; for this ode in particular see *GC* 189–92.

lines resemble an inverse *propemptikon*. In the central panel (7b–16) H. reveals himself to be speaking as an *auspex* and promises to supply a good omen for Galatea's journey and, after offering her good wishes for the future, prays to prevent evil omens from delaying her departure. These lines resemble a basic *propemptikon*. H. ends (17–24) by listing six aspects of the November weather, each with its own epithet or equivalent, in order to deter Galatea from leaving. These lines resemble a schetliastic *propemptikon*. Thus the argument of the first six stanzas is: 'Let the *impii* be accompanied by evil omens when they travel (1–7a); I shall seek good omens for you, Galatea (7b–16); but don't you realise how bad the travel conditions are (17–24)?' The argument appears straightforward, but all is not as it seems. Galatea, through her disloyalty to H., is one of the *impii* (1). H.'s promise of a good omen is one which self-evidently cannot be fulfilled, and, even if it could, he gets his augural details exactly the wrong way round (9–12n.). Likewise the two evil omens which he seeks to avert are evidence of the same augural mispractice as before (15–16nn.). The central panel is the opposite of what it says it is; H.'s claim to augural status is jocular and his accounts of augural procedure are mere hocus-pocus. That this is how we – and Galatea – are expected to interpret the panel is suggested by the poem's opening list of evil omens, which seems disproportionately long and indicative of over-kill (cf. 2.13.1–10).

In the mythological *exemplum* (25–76) H. tells the story of Europa and her abduction by Jupiter in the form of a bull. As is attested by the legends of Pasiphae, Io, the Proetides, and others, the ancient world was greatly taken with narratives featuring bulls or cows, and the story of Europa was alluded to or told by Hesiod (fr. 141 M–W = 90 Most), Stesichorus (195), Simonides (562/253P), Bacchylides (*Ode* 17; fr. 10), Moschus in his *Europa* and later by Ovid (*Met.* 2.833–75, *F.* 5.603–20). According to Moschus' epyllion, which H. seems certainly to have read, Aphrodite sent Europa a dream in which the royal maiden saw the two continents of the world competing for her affections. When she woke up, she joined her companions in picking flowers by the seashore, where she was spotted by Zeus. Overcome by her beauty, but not wanting to frighten her, Zeus adopted the form of a quasi-magical bull. Intrigued and attracted, Europa climbed onto the bull's back, whereupon the animal suddenly whisked her off, skimming over the sea, to Crete; as they travelled, he revealed his real identity to the terrified girl and promised that he would make her the wife of Zeus. Readers are left to assume that, as a wedding gift, Zeus named the continent of Europe after her.

H.'s version inevitably differs: the initial dream, for example, is replaced by a later one (39–42a), nor does the bull reveal his identity on the journey: once Europa is deposited on Crete, she is abandoned by the bull and utters a terrified soliloquy which comprises the greater part of the narrative (34b–66a). The soliloquy takes the form of an address to her absent father (34b–56), whose imagined reply constitutes the final lines of her speech (57–66a). Although there seem to be few, if any, verbal reminiscences, the situation has rightly reminded scholars of Ariadne in Poem 64 of Catullus: 'abandonment on an island, the lament uttered on the shore, guilt over issues of filial piety, the possibility of being eaten by beasts, the final happy ending of a divine marriage' (Lowrie 310, with refs. to earlier scholarship; also below, 73n.). Yet, whereas Ariadne is a tragic figure, Europa's speech is melodramatic in the extreme. Europa's threats against the bull (45–8) are absurdly unrealistic and her proposed method of suicide (51–6) combines bizarreness with gothic horror. Her father's imagined response to her proposed suicide ('What are you waiting for?', 58) and his concern for her maidenly girdle (59) are the essence of black humour. It is hardly surprising that Venus, who in the best traditions of comedy has been eavesdropping on the soliloquy, finds Europa's words highly amusing (66b–9) and takes her time in explaining to the poor girl the truth of the situation (69–76): she is to be Jupiter's wife.

Europa's story, which H. presents as an explicit parallel to Galatea (25 'sic et Europe...'), constitutes another instance of a 'locus a maiore ad minus' (see 3.10 intro.). Each young girl is associated with a journey to a lover, but, whereas Galatea is proposing to undertake her journey despite advance warning of its dangers (17–24), Europa has no advance warning of danger or even of a journey (25–6 'doloso | ...tauro'), but she experiences both nevertheless (26–66a). If this is what can happen when there are no warning signs, Galatea must think how much worse it might be for her, who has warning signs aplenty. Yet, since Europa's story has a happy ending (66b–76), how can it act as a deterrent for Galatea? The explanation seems to be that Europa's eventual happiness actualises the happiness which H. wishes for Galatea (13–14): despite all his attempts at dissuasion, he has to reconcile himself to the seeming inevitability of her departure and so, in a reaction characteristic of the propemptic speaker, he hopes that she will be as happy as Europa proved to be.

And yet H. must have hoped against hope that Galatea's mind would be changed at the last minute when she read the exceptional ode which he had written for her. It is the second longest ode (after 3.4) in Books 1–3, and only the third ode of the Alcaic Hexad has a longer narrative (by two lines) than the story of Europa and the bull (Lowrie 301). Moreover the ode 'is part of the final climax of this boldly innovative collection, coming between two exquisite love poems and before the greatest of all Horace's lyrics, 3.29, and the proud claim of 3.30' (West, *DP* 223). Throughout its length H. sustains the most outrageous wit and humour, the pseudo-augury of 1–24 complemented by the tragicomedy of 25–76. The ode is clearly designed as a dazzling and spectacular *tour de force*: if a girl could be won over by the *uenustas* of Caecilius' poem on Cybele (Cat. 35.11–18; cf. Prop. 2.34.57–8), surely Galatea could be won over by the *uenustas* on such ample display here.

This is one of the most controversial of H.'s odes and has attracted a wide range of views.[137] Fraenkel, who deemed it a failure, called it a 'heavy ode' and saw Europa's monologue as characterised by 'unmitigated seriousness' (196, 194). Yet the tragic motifs to which he alluded, and which were illustrated by Harrison (1988), are all set in a parodic context. West, who helpfully summarises a number of different views, interprets the ode in terms of 'burlesque' (*DP* 233–5). It is nevertheless possible that there is a further dimension at the close. Readers of Moschus have been concerned that, although Zeus has sex with Europa at the end of his epyllion, there is no reference to the expected naming of Europe. In H. it is almost the converse: here it is the absence of intercourse which has troubled readers (see Lowrie 311 n. 109, N–R 319), but the poem ends with the naming of Europe. The aetiology may well have had contemporary relevance. When the *Odes* were published, the battle of Actium was less than a decade in the past. The Augustan poets, as is well known, portrayed the battle as a conflict between West and East, but it was also possible to portray the opposing sides in terms of the continents of Europe and Asia (Philo, *Leg. Gai.* 144). At the end of his poem H. reminds his readers of the origin of the continent which the victorious Augustus championed.

METRE Sapphic

1–4 H. does not need to spell things out for Galatea, since they both know that she is set to leave Italy; but for readers the first stanza is elliptical: a journey has to be inferred from *ducat* (2) and its route – the Via Appia – from the reference to Lanuvium (3); only at *iter institutum* (5) is the topic made clear. From *Hadriae* (19) we infer that Galatea's destination is Brundisium, the port of embarcation for the Adriatic, on the far side of which, it seems, her new lover resides.

---

[137] For a recent study see F. Hadjittofi, 'Sleeping Europa from Plato Comicus to Moschus and Horace', *CQ* 69 (2019) 264–77, with many refs. to earlier discussions.

1-2 Impios parrae recinentis omen | ducat 'Let the omen of a *parra*'s repetitive call lead out the *impii*', an ex. of the *ab urbe condita* idiom (3.4.18–19n.) with the present participle (cf. 3.21.23–4n.); the genit. is one of definition (*NLS* 53 §72 (5), *OLS* 1.1023–5), as often with *omen* (*TLL* 9.2.577.66–78). The subjunctive, like *rumpat* in 5, has a concessive force and may be regarded either as jussive or as straightforwardly concessive (3.11.45n.). Lines 1–7a function as a foil for 7b–12 and the tone is dismissive: 'Let the *impii* experience as many ill omens as possible; *I* will provide only good omens for my beloved.' The complication is that *impius* can be used of disloyal lovers (2.18.19; Pichon 171), a category that includes Galatea, who is therefore at risk of the very omens which H. specifies here; indeed their relevance is suggested by the fact that at least four of them, and perhaps all five, are female. A *parra* is an ill-omened bird of uncertain identity, perhaps an owl (see *OLD*); *recino* here = 'sing repeatedly' (*OLD* 1c): contrast 3.28.11 (n.). *ducat* poses difficulties. While 'lead out' suits an omen at the start of a journey, neither that meaning nor any of the many other meanings of *ducere* is appropriate for the other animals of ill-omen to be encountered *en route* (2–4):[138] with them we must supply a different verb (e.g. 'influence') by zeugma and understand that it applies to successive stages of the journey. For the various types of omen and the like in lines 1–16 see P. Struck, 'Animals and divination', in G. L. Campbell (ed.), *The Oxford Handbook of Animals in Classical Thought and Life* (2014) 310–22, esp. 313–14 on birds.

2-3 ab agro | …Lanuuino: Lanuvium was a town about 20 miles SE of Rome, on the western side of the Via Appia (*BA Map* 44: C2) and hence on the unlucky side for a traveller journeying south.

3 raua is 'a dark colour between grey and yellow' (*OLD*): since the coat of the so-called grey wolf goes from grey on its back to yellowish on its flanks, the adj. seems well chosen.

4 feta means either 'having recently given birth' or 'pregnant' (*OLD* 1, 2a); the former is perhaps more likely, since the dog of line 2 is pregnant.

5 rumpat et serpens iter institutum 'and let a snake interrupt the journey on which they have embarked/the course of their journey', perhaps

---

[138] Contrast ἡγεμονέοι at Posid. 22.4 A–B ('But let a crane from Thrace lead…'), where the crane is evidently envisaged as flying ahead of the sailors for the duration of their voyage (see D. Sider, 'Posidippus on weather signs and the tradition of didactic poetry', in K. Gutzwiller (ed.), *The New Posidippus* (2005) 164–82). Cf. also Callim. *Aet.* fr. 43.66 (with Harder on 43.61–7).

another ex. of the *ab urbe condita* idiom (above, 1n.); for *rumpat* see *OLD* 9. *iter institutum* recurs at Cic. *Fam.* 15.5.3, Plin. *Ep.* 9.14 (to Tacitus).

6–7 si per obliquum similis sagittae | terruit mannos 'whenever like an arrow it terrifies their ponies from the side'. *si* + perf. indic. represents a general condition (*NLS* 150–1 §194): whenever a snake darts across the road in front of them (*OLD obliquus* 8b), it should be regarded as an omen and hence should interrupt their journey. *manni* were ponies of foreign origin and usually regarded as a sign of luxury (see e.g. Hutchinson on Prop. 4.8.15–16).

7–8 ego, cui timebo | prouidus auspex: sc. *ei* (see 3.1.17–18n.): '<But> I, being a provident diviner <for the one> on whose behalf I shall be afraid,…': the adversative asyndeton marks the transition from the imprecations directed at the *impii* (1–7a) to H.'s invocation of good omens for his (as yet unnamed) addressee, to whom he refers with the anonymity of intimacy. He is afraid for her because of the dangers of her imminent journey. *timeo* + dat. is regular (*OLD* 1b); *pro-uidus* 'etymologises' *auspex*, which is derived 'ab inspiciendis auibus' (Maltby 69). *auspicia* were divided into the two classes of *publica* and *priuata* (cf. Val. Max. 2.1.1) and were discussed in books by various experts: one of the most recent was that by the long-term augur M. Valerius Messalla Rufus (cos. 53), who died c. 26 BC (Rüpke 941 no. 3417): see Gell. 13.14.1, 15.3, 16.1. Obviously it is *auspicia priuata* which provide the context in the ode.

9–12 antequam stantes repetat paludes | imbrium diuina auis imminentum, | oscinem coruum prece suscitabo | solis ab ortu 'with a prayer I shall summon from the east an oracular raven, before the bird, the foreteller of imminent rain, can return to its standing marshes'. Auspices fell into the two categories of those which were sought (*impetratiua*), as in the present case (cf. *prece*), and those which were not sought (*oblatiua*): see e.g. Serv. *Aen.* 6.190. In some cases omens were derived from a bird's call, in others from its flight (cf. e.g. Prob. *In Virg. Ecl.* 9.13): *oscinem* (11) suggests that it is the raven's call which matters, but *suscitabo solis ab ortu* (11–12) clearly implies flight; H. as *auspex* seems unclear which is important. To a person facing south, as would an *auspex*, the east was on the left, which in Roman culture is usually favourable (cf. Plin. *NH* 2.142 'laeua prospera existimantur'); but we happen to know that, in the case of ravens, the *right* was the favourable side (Plaut. *Asin.* 260–1, Cic. *Div.* 1.85 'a dextra coruus', Prob. loc. cit.). Not only does H. get his orientation wrong but avian behaviour is not something which it is within his gift to promise. For the raven predicting rain see Plin. *NH* 18.362;

only H. constructs *diuinus* + genit. = 'foretelling of' (again at *AP* 218). The ancients derived *oscen* from *os* + *cano* (Maltby 436; Pease on Cic. *Div.* 1.120). The subjunctive with *antequam* is regular when the idea of design or anticipation or prevention is involved, as here (*NLS* 183–5 §§225, 227); for *stare* in the sense of 'stagnant' see *OLD* 7c. In 10 the MSS, like the editors, are divided between *imminentum* and *imminentium*. The latter requires an interlinear elision which otherwise occurs in Sapphics only at 2.2.18, 2.16.34 and 4.2.22; it seems more probable that H. wrote *imminentum* (see further 3.18.1n.).

13–14 si licet, felix, ubicumque mauis, | et memor nostri, Galatea, uiuas: two problems are raised by *sis licet felix*, the transmitted text. (1) The sense 'you can be happy wherever you prefer to be' is inappropriate since the words could be taken to imply an indifference which is at odds with H.'s present concern for Galatea. (2) The co-ordination with *et memor...uiuas* makes it appear that these words too depend on *licet*, whereas *memor nostri* is clearly an instance of the 'remember me' topos, a feature of the propemptikon (cf. Tib. 1.3.2 and Maltby, Ov. *Am.* 2.11.37–8 and McKeown), and therefore 'must be an independent wish' (N–R). To avoid these problems SB follows Page in making *licet* a one-word parenthesis (*Profile* 97), which seems too jerky. Although the *scilicet* of Courtney (2016: 44–5) is preferable to Nisbet's *ilicet*, a word not found elsewhere in H. and completely implausible, I suggest *si licet*, 'if it is allowed' (i.e. by the gods),[139] an amusing anticipation of the upcoming story of Europa, whose happiness became entirely dependent on a god. *uiuas*, which now has to be taken with both adjs., has the sense of *sis*, as at 3.26.1 (n.): 'may you be happy (if it is allowed) wherever you prefer to be, and mindful of me, Galatea'; cf. Lygd. 5.31 'uiuite felices, memores et uiuite nostri', where NA discusses the leave-taking formulae (add Augustus' last words at Suet. *Aug.* 99.1). *memor nostri* is a belated indication to readers that Galatea and H. have been lovers. The name Galatea, commonly found of slaves and freedwomen on Roman inscriptions, does not feature elsewhere in H. but is used several times in the *Eclogues* by Virgil, who takes it from Theocritus. The most well-known Galatea is a sea nymph, described as 'white' by both Theocr. (*Id.* 11.19) and Virg. (*Ecl.* 7.38), suggesting the derivation of her name from γάλα, 'milk'; if we are intended to think of H.'s Galatea as 'white', that provides another connection with Europa (25–6). It is perhaps not simply coincidental that the nymph features in Propertius' first propemptikon (1.8.18).

---

[139] For the use of a present tense instead of a future see G&L 156–7 §228.

15 laeuus...picus: a woodpecker on the left was supposed to be favourable (cf. Plaut. *Asin.* 260–1), whereas H.'s argument requires mention of an *un*favourable omen.

16 uaga cornix: by contrast with the raven (11 above), from which it is to be distinguished (see Pease on Cic. *Div.* 1.12), the crow, like the woodpecker (15n.), has to fly on the *left* if it is to be favourable (Cic. *Div.* 1.85 'a sinistra cornix'). H. should thus be mentioning right-sided rather than random flight (*uaga*); perhaps he is referring to the possibility of an *auspicium oblatiuum* (above, 9–12n.), viz. a crow flying on what H. considers to be the unfavourable side. Crows were generally regarded as unfavourable birds (Plin. *NH* 10.30; cf. *C.* 3.17.13).

17–18 sed uides quanto trepidet tumultu | pronus Orion? 'But do you see with what turbulence Orion rushes downwards?' (*OLD trepido* 2a): if the travel conditions are terrible, perhaps Galatea will change her mind about leaving. *quanto...tumultu* is an abl. of attendant circumstances (*NLS* 31 §43 (5) (ii)) and refers to the stormy conditions which accompanied the setting of the constellation Orion in early November, marking the end of the furthest limit of the sailing season (3.1.27–8n.; Watson on *Epo.* 10.10). *pronus* is a technical term of constellations etc. (*TLL* 10.2.1931.35–48); for its adverbial use, as here, cf. Germ. *Phaen.* 481 'pronus deuoluitur inde' (of the sun).

18–19 ego quid sit ater | Hadriae nōui sinus 'I know what the black gulf of the Adriatic is like': *ater* is regular of threatening waters (*OLD* 2c), and the notorious storms of the Adriatic (3.3.4–5n.) are here given extra authenticity by H.'s claim of personal experience (αὐτοπάθεια). The insertion of a main verb within the subordinate clause which depends on it, as here (*noui*), is 'hard to explain, but well attested' (Harder on Callim. *Aet.* 6, with Greek exs.; note also e.g. Williams, *TORP* 715–16). For this particular nuance of *quid* see *OLD quis*[1] 3a.

19–20 et quid albus | peccet Iapyx 'and in what way the clearing Iapyx misbehaves': Iapyx was the name of the WNW wind which facilitated crossing from Italy to Greece (N–H on 1.3.4); *albus* evidently refers to the clearing away of clouds and is equivalent to *candidus* (3.7.1–2n.): H.'s point is that the wind can change its nature or direction unexpectedly, an anticipation of the theme of 'deceit' which features prominently in the upcoming myth (25 *doloso*, 27 *fraudes*, 40 *ludit*, 67 *perfidum*, 73 *nescis*). *peccare*, personifying the wind, is regularly constructed with an internal accus. such as *quid* (see *OLD*).

21 hostium uxores puerique: travel conditions are so bad that one would wish them upon one's enemies (for the proverbial *hostibus eueniat* see esp. Virg. *G.* 3.513 'di meliora piis, erroremque hostibus illum!' and e.g. McKeown on Ov. *Am.* 2.10.16). Women and children are specified because they are the unfortunate survivors of a hypothetical conflict in which the men have been killed.

21–2 caecos | ...motus orientis Austri 'the unforeseen disturbances of a south wind getting up': for *motus* of wind see *TLL* 8.1534.78–81; for *caecus* see *OLD* 7c; for *sentiant* see 3.23.5–6n.

23–4 trementes | uerbere ripas: the shores are being lashed by the winds of 21–2 (as Sen. *NQ* 4a.2.23 'Etesiae litus Aegyptium uerberant') and the waves of 23 (as Ov. *F.* 3.568 'insula quam Libyci uerberat unda freti'). *ripa* much more commonly refers to a river-bank but cf. *OLD* b (also N–H on 2.18.22). *uerber* is a defective noun which in the singular is found almost exclusively in verse and only in the genit. (very rare) and abl. (very common).

25 sic et Europe: like οὕτως in Greek (Fraenkel on Aesch. *Ag.* 718), *sic* introduces the *exemplum* (again at *Epi.* 1.81.41). Later (57) Europa puts the Greek form of her name (for which cf. G&L 32 §65) into the mouth of her father. Interestingly, Europa was a name in regular use, being that of a *symphoniaca* in the imperial household (*CIL* 6.33372).

25–6 niueum doloso | credidit tauro latus: *latus* must mean 'body' here (synecdoche), as Plin. *Pan.* 23.2 'latus tuum crederes omnibus', though *doloso* reminds us that later she will be compelled to entrust to Jupiter her *latus* in a sexual sense (3.10.19–20n.); the five words are an illustration of 'silver' ordering (3.1.16n.), the juxtaposition *doloso credidit* being particularly Horatian (Intro. 26). Bacchylides had referred to Europa as 'white-armed' (*Ode* 17.54): if Galatea's name is intended to suggest her 'whiteness' (above, 13–14n.), *niueum...latus* establishes, at the start of the *exemplum*, a parallel between the two women. The phrase is borrowed from Virg. *Ecl.* 6.53 and reused by Ov. *Met.* 2.865, although both authors apply it to the bull rather than to Pasiphae and Europa respectively; Ovid then defers to the start of Book 3 an apparent allusion to H.'s *doloso... tauro* (3.1 'fallacis...tauri').

26–7 scatentem | beluis pontum 'the deep teeming with beasts': perhaps *scatentem beluis* represents a Greek compound adj. such as θηριώδης (e.g. Hdt. 6.44.3 θηριωδεστάτης ἐούσης τῆς θαλάσσης, 'the sea being infested by beasts'): cf. 1.3.18 'monstra natantia' and N–H, 4.14.47–8 'beluosus… Oceanus', Sen. *Suas.* 1.4 'immanes… beluas', Tac. *A.* 2.24.4. The sea is the eastern Mediterranean between her home in Sidon (Phoenicia is regarded as Europa's native land) and Crete; for the grecising *pontus* see 3.3.37–8n.

27 medias…fraudes is often taken to mean 'the snares by which she was surrounded', which is excellent sense but doubtful Latin; Bell 329 suggests an equivalence to *medii ponti fraudes*, 'mid-sea snares'; N–R prefer 'intervening' (on the journey).

28 palluit 'grew pale at': this is the perfect form of both *pallesco* and *palleo*, each of which is almost always intransitive (see *OLD*). Blanching was to be expected of those endangered at sea (*Epo.* 10.16), but Europa's body was already snow-white (25–6): are we being invited to think that her face had caught the sun while she was in the meadows (cf. S. Lilja, 'Sunbathing in antiquity', *Arctos* 21 (1987) 53–60)? The juxtaposition with *audax* is typically Horatian; Lambinus compared the Greek compound adj. θρασύδειλος (Arist. *Eth. Nic.* 1115b32), meaning initially bold but subsequently cowardly.

29 studiosa florum 'intent on flowers', evidently choosing which ones to pick (cf. 43–4): flower-picking is 'often a precursor to seduction' (Swift on Archil. 30–1). *studiosus* regularly takes a genit.

31–2 nocte sublustri nihil astra praeter | uidit et undas 'in the dimness of the night she saw nothing but stars and waves', an allusion to Moschus' *Europa*, where the heroine sees nothing 'but air above and the boundless sea [πόντος] below' (133), but cf. also Lucr. 4.434 'nil aliud nisi aquam caelumque tuentur', Virg. *Aen.* 3.193 and Horsfall. The nearest parallels for *nocte sublustri* (Naev. *Pall.* 4 (p. 6R) 'sublustri noctu', Liv. 5.47.2 'nocte sublustri', Virg. *Aen.* 9.373 'sublustri noctis in umbra') suggest an elevated expr., as here, though one which can be put to comic use. The anastrophe of *praeter* is also elevated (*TLL* 10.2.1000.1–7).

33–4 quae simul centum tetigit potentem | oppidis Creten 'And as soon as she reached Crete, powerful with its hundred towns…': *simul* = *simul ac*; for *tetigit* see *OLD* 7a. As at *Epo.* 9.29 'centum nobilem Cretam urbibus', H. is alluding to the Homeric Κρήτην ἑκατόμπολιν (*Il.* 2.649), the Greek form of the island's name complementing that of the heroine (25n.). The allusion is teasingly anachronistic: Zeus/Jupiter chose Crete as their destination because he had been born there (e.g. Mosch. *Eur.* 158–9):

after his subsequent intercourse with Europa, she gave birth to Minos, the first king of Crete, and it was only in his time that there was established (in legend) the power symbolised by the island's 'hundred cities'. Minos' wife Pasiphae mated with a bull belonging to Minos and gave birth to the Minotaur, which inhabited the Labyrinth on Crete; it was also at Cnossos on Crete that the famous bull-leaping fresco was discovered. 'In Cretan culture, the bull is ubiquitous' (J. McInerney, *The Cattle of the Sun: Cows and Culture in the World of the Ancient Greeks* (2010) 54).

34 Pater: the bull has left her (cf. 45–6),[140] and she now begins a soliloquy which lasts until 66. The soliloquy takes the form of an address to her father, who at 57 she imagines as replying to her ('pater urget absens'). The sentence which begins with the vocative *Pater* is completed in 37 by the words *unde, quo ueni?* (the intervening words are parenthetical). Some think that *pater* is co-ordinated with *pietas* (35) by *-que* and that only *o relictum filiae nomen* is parenthetical, but the two three-word participial phrases seem a parallel pair. Europa's father is Phoenix in Homer (*Il.* 14.321) and Moschus (*Eur.* 7) but Agenor in Herodotus (4.147.4) and Ovid (*Met.* 2.858): see Apollod. 3.1.1 and Frazer's nn.

34–6 o relictum | filiae nomen pietasque... | uicta furore: *o* is used in exclamations expressing horror (3.5.38n.), and *pietasque* shows that *nomen* too must be nominative (cf. Enn. *Ann.* 4 'o pietas animi', though Skutsch says this is a vocative). *o...nomen* may mean: (a) 'Oh, only the name [sc. of father] left to your daughter', i.e. she will never see her father himself again; (b) 'Oh, the name abandoned by your daughter' (dat. of agent), where *nomen* virtually = 'you'; (c) 'Oh, only the name of your daughter left [sc. to you]', i.e. he will never see her again. That (c) is the likeliest of these is suggested both by its co-ordination with *pietas*, which refers to Europa, and by the recurrence of her name at the end of the poem (75–6). *furor* is the madness of love (Pichon 158): the implication is that she should have stayed with her family, and in particular with her father, rather than succumb to her mad infatuation with the bull. (Since the bull is in fact Jupiter, *pietas...uicta* takes on a paradoxical nuance.) For *uicta furore* cf. *Culex* 110 (of Agave); for *pietas...uicta* cf. Prop. 3.13.48, Ov. *Met.* 1.149, 13.663, 15.173.

---

[140] Jupiter will return in his divine manifestation after the end of the ode, at which point he has sex with Europa for the first (and only) time. That he does not have sex with her before this seems to me obvious, though the matter is hotly disputed (see intro.). Her speech is melodramatic because 'she regards her indiscretion at Sidon as serious enough to deserve death' (N–R on 50, whose own view differs).

346 COMMENTARY 27.37-42

37 unde, quo ueni?: such questions are formulaic (e.g. *S.* 2.4.1 'Vnde et quo Catius?', Plato, *Lysis* 203A 'where are you going and from where?'), but they are not normally first-person, as here: although Europa may not know where she has arrived at, she obviously knows where she has come from: the question is rhetorical, expressing bewilderment at the journey she has made (how can she have got to here from there?) – if indeed she has made a journey at all and is not simply dreaming (39–42). Commentators compare Virg. *Aen.* 10.670 'quo feror? unde abii?'

37–8 leuis una mors est | uirginum culpae 'A single death is mild for the misconduct of maidens' (compare Prop. 4.4.17 'nec satis una malae potuit mors esse puellae', though the line is controversial). *culpa* is technical of sexual immorality (3.6.17–18n.): Europa considers herself 'shameless' (*impudens*, 49, 50), and hence guilty, on account of her attraction to the bull. *leuis* is regular of punishments (*TLL* 7.2.1214.21–33). For further variations on the theme of *una mors* cf. Eur. *Heracl.* 959–60, Virg. *Aen.* 9.140, Sen. *HO* 866 'leuis una mors est', Petron. 108.14 (line 7).

38–9 uigilansne ploro | turpe commissum 'Am I awake and bewailing a shameful crime...?' In 38–42 Europa, whose whole tale, according to Moschus, began with a dream sent by Venus/Aphrodite 'as if it were real' (*Eur.* 17), poses chiastically the question 'Do I wake or sleep?'; intention was an important element in Roman law and she is to be blamed only if she is awake (cf. Liv. 1.58.9 'mentem peccare, non corpus, et unde consilium afuerit, culpam abesse', Sen. *Phaedra* 735 'mens impudicam facere non casus solet'); Pasiphae makes a similar point (Eur. fr. 472e.10 Kannicht 'my sin was not freely willed'). *turpe commissum* is reminiscent of legal language, e.g. Cic. *II Verr.* 2.180 'commissa...turpia', Sen. *Ag.* 278 'nil esse crede turpe commissum tibi'; for *ploro* see 3.10.2–4n.

39–42 an uitiis carentem | ludit imago | uana, quam...somnium ducit? 'or am I without fault and deceived by an empty image, which is being brought on by a dream as it flees from the Ivory Gate?' Europa desperately tries to make the less credible alternative more plausible by alluding to the authority of Homer, in whom false dreams are said to emerge from an ivory gate (*Od.* 19.562–5, famously alluded to by Virg. *Aen.* 6.893–9: see Horsfall). The MSS here read *quae*: while the ancients could talk of real-life images entering the mind and producing dreams during sleep (e.g. Plut. *Mor.* 735A), that rationale makes no sense here, since the context requires that the *imago* not be real (cf. *uana*). Sanadon, the eighteenth-century Jesuit, was surely right to change to *quam* ('fort. recte', according to SB). *imago uana* (again at 1.24.15) and *uitiis carere* are both common expressions, the latter again reminiscent of legal language (cf. Cic. *Leg.* 3.28–9). For *ludo* = 'deceive' see 3.4.5–6n.; for *duco* = 'bring on' cf. *Epo.* 14.3; *OLD* 15b. *fugiens* ~ *ducit* is another Horatian oxymoron.

42–4 meliusne fluctus | ire per longos fuit an recentes | carpere flores?: *melius fuit* has to be repeated with *an...flores*: 'Was it better to travel across the endless waves or <would it have been better> to pick fresh flowers?' The change of mood is required in English because Europa travelled across the sea *instead of picking* fresh flowers, but in Latin certain expressions, of which *melius fuit* is one, retain the indicative even when the notion is one of potentiality (G&L 167–9 §254): *melius fuit* ('was better') can also mean 'would have been better' (e.g. Cic. *ND* 3.78, 81 (*bis*); H. J. Roby, *A Grammar of the Latin Language* (1896) Part II, p. 227). E. Baehrens (*Lectiones Horatianae* (1880) 20) argued that *an* was a scribal error under the influence of -*ne...an* in 38–9 and that H. originally wrote *ac* (= *quam*): 'Was it better to travel across the endless waves *than* to pick fresh flowers?' The sense is excellent, yet, although this use of *ac/atque* after comparatives (*OLD atque* 15) is frequent in H., there is no ex. in the *Odes* at all; and indeed there is no ex. of *melius esse ac/atque* anywhere in Latin. *longi... fluctus* at Virg. *G.* 3.200 means 'big waves', and this may be the meaning here; but, despite Mosch. *Eur.* 154 πόντιον οἶδμα ('sea swell'), 'endless waves' seems more likely (cf. Stat. *Ach.* 2.92 'longas...per undas'; see also 3.3.37–8n.). Europa, whose tone combines bitterness and regret, is perhaps reflecting that the journey was so long that the flowers she was considering (29) will be no longer fresh.

45–6 siquis infamem mihi nunc iuuencum | dedat iratae... 'I'm angry, and if someone were now to present me with the discredited bullock...' (*nunc* is equivalent to 'after everything I've been through'). *infamem* is slightly odd: the bullock is not actually notorious but 'deserving of ill repute as far as I'm concerned' (*OLD infamis* 3); *mihi* is not only indir. object with *dedat* but perhaps also dat. of the person judging with *infamem* (cf. Liv. 27.20.11). The dramatic irony is hilarious: she will indeed be presented with the bullock again, except that Jupiter will have resumed his divine form and will make her his wife.

46–8 lacerare ferro et | frangere enitar modo multum amati | cornua monstri 'I would strive to rend with a knife and break the horns of the monster that recently I loved so much' (note her furious alliteration and assonance); that the object of *lacerare* is *cornua* and not *iuuencum* (understood from 45) is suggested by *laceranda...cornua* at 71–2. The bull's horns seem a bizarre body-part on which to vent her fury, especially since her language suggests an impractical desire to saw them off (and besides she has no knife); but a bull's horns were its glory (Tac. *G.* 5.1 'gloria frontis'), and those of Europa's bull were a defining feature (Mosch. *Eur.* 87–8, 153 'the well-horned bull'): had it not been for the horns, which she was obliged to grasp during her journey (Mosch. *Eur.* 126, Ov. *Met.* 2.874), she would have fallen off the bull's back. *cornu* can be used as a metaphor for the penis (Adams 22), but this does not become relevant until 71–2 below (n.). For *lacerare ferro* cf. Val. Max. 6.2.8, 9.2.1, *Octav.* 956; *enitor* + infin. occurs before H. at Ter. *Andr.* 596, Sall. *J.* 14.1. For *multum amati* cf. *Epo.* 17.20.

49 liqui patrios Penates: cf. Mosch. *Eur.* 146–7 'Alas! How very unlucky I am! Leaving my father's house and going with this bull' (Loeb trans.).

50 Orcum moror 'I am keeping Orcus waiting' (*OLD moror* 1b): unaware that she is to be married to Jupiter (73), she speaks as if, having left her *patrios Penates*, she is a reluctant bride – of Death (for the common associations of marriage and death see e.g. 3.11.33–4n.; R. Seaford, *JHS* 107 (1987) 106–7).

50–1 o deorum | si quis haec audis: it will turn out later that Venus has been listening (66–7). For the partitive genit. address cf. *Epo.* 5.1 'o deorum quidquid...regit'; *si quis* + second-person verb is a mannerism of Ovid, e.g. *Am.* 1.7.2.

51–2 utinam inter errem | nuda leones: Europa does not know where she is (37), but she assumes that the place is inhabited by helpfully wild animals. The hyperbaton of *inter...leones* allows her vulnerable wandering to be placed in between (mimetic); whether *nuda* means 'unarmed' (as 3.16.23) or actually 'naked' is unclear: somewhere in the background to this picture 'lie the sadistic pleasures of watching in the amphitheatre' (Griffin 107).

53–6 antequam turpis macies decentes | occupet mālas teneraeque sucus | defluat praedae, speciosa quaero | pascere tigres 'Before disgusting emaciation can take control of my comely cheeks and the sap flow out of their tender prey, I intend, while still attractive, to be food for tigers.' Evidently she despairs of finding any sustenance in her new location and prays that she will encounter a troop of hungry tigers before starvation renders her too unappetising for them; ironically *tener* would normally be used of an animal, not a human, as food (*OLD* 3a). For *quaero* + infin. = 'to intend' see *OLD* 6b; *turpis macies* recurs at Sen. *HO* 119, for *m. occupet* cf. [Tib.] 3.10.5.

COMMENTARY 27.57–62

57–8 'Vilis Europe', pater urget absens, | 'quid mori cessas?': her father's imagined reply takes up the remainder of Europa's soliloquy (to 66); for such *sermocinatio* or *prosopopoeia* see Lausberg 366–9 §§820–5. *urget* combines the notions of urging to a course of action and urging to hurry up (*OLD* 10–11). *uilis*, 'contemptible' or 'considered of no account' (*OLD* 3–4), is not only doubly dramatic irony – the identity of her abductor is unknown to Europa and hence, by definition, to the father whom she is impersonating – but also a 'corrective' allusion to Mosch. *Eur.* 15, where Europa is described as a 'prize' (γέρας). *quid mori cessas?* recalls Cat. 52 'quid moraris emori?' (cf. Ov. *Her.* 9.146 'quid dubitas... mori?'), but the motif derives from tragedy (Tarrant on Sen. *Ag.* 198).

hac ab orno: the manna ash is common across southern Europe and is 'regarded by the Latin poets as the typical hillside tree of central and southern Italy' (Sargeaunt 93); since there are references to its barrenness (Virg. *G.* 2.111, Claud. *Rapt. Pros.* 3.73, Pallad. *Insit.* 63), the girl's impersonated father may have regarded it as an *infelix arbor* and hence suitable for her death.

58–60 potes...laedere collum: suicide is a motif of tragedy, the novel and some other genres, and very often the three options envisaged by a desperate character are those of hanging, stabbing and jumping off rocks (cf. *Epo.* 17.70–3 with Watson's nn.; Courtney, *Companion* 146–7). Europa's father mentions hanging and (below) rocks (61–3); Europa herself has already substituted wild animals for the sword (51–6). *laedere* is a euphemism for 'crush'; *pendulum* seems equivalent to *pendendo* (cf. 3.6.16 *missilibus*).

59 zona bene te secuta 'with your girdle, which fortunately came with you': hilariously she envisages her father as concerned about her virginity, symbolised by her *zona* (*OLD* 2b), even as he urges her to kill herself. *bene* both commends his daughter for her presence of mind and expresses relief that she has the means to hang herself (cf. Aesch. *Suppl.* 457–65, where the chorus have breast-bands and girdles to hang themselves, Tac. *A.* 15.57.2, where the heroic Epicharis hangs herself with her breast-band). Europa's girdle features prominently in Moschus (*Eur.* 73, 164).

61–2 siue te...delectant: as if choosing a violent method of suicide were a delightful prospect! *siue* = *uel*, *si*..., as often (3.4.3–4n.). *acuta leto* = 'sharp for death' (*acuo* + dat. is at *Epi.* 1.3.23, Colum. 10.1.105). For the poetic *letum* see 3.22.3n.; *delecto* is absent from Lucr. Virg. Tib. *al.* and was described by Axelson (106) as prosaic.

62 procellae: the atmospheric condition that will aid her plunge: the noun suggests a derivation from *procellere*, 'to throw violently forward' (*TLL* 10.2.1509.39–43).

63–6 nisi erile mauis | carpere pensum | regius sanguis dominaeque tradi | barbarae paelex 'unless, of course, you – royal blood – prefer to pluck her ladyship's wool and be handed over to a foreign mistress as a concubine'. *pensum* (from *pendo*) is the amount of wool which has been weighed out, evidently by the *era*, for spinning by slave girls; *carpere* 'does not seem to mean anything more definite than the rapid passing of the wool through the fingers' (Conington on Virg. *G.* 4.335): cf. *G.* 1.390 'carpentes pensa puellae', Prop. 3.6.13–14 'tristis erat domus, et tristes sua pensa ministrae | carpebant'. *paelex* is a term which tends to stress the status of a man's concubine in relation to his wife (3.10.15n.), which is exactly the case here. The point of the clause, which is ironic ('of course'), is that, having been a princess, Europa will become the slave of a barbarian couple – another tragic motif (Harrison (1988) 431–2). Her previous status is emphasised by the 'grandiloquent' use of *sanguis* = 'progeny' (N–H on 2.20.5), while the reversal is underlined by *carpere*, previously used to describe the ladylike pastime of picking flowers (44).

66 aderat: the verb is technical of divinities (*OLD* 13) but is also used of being present as a listener (*OLD* 5) and as a supporter (*OLD* 11a, with dat.). Cf. also 3.21.21–3n.

67 perfidum ridens Venus: laughter (again at 1.2.33, 2.8.13, 3.16.5–7) is 'a frequent attribute of the goddess of love' (Pease on Virg. *Aen.* 4.128); *perfidum* is explained by the fact that Europa's plight is Venus' responsibility, both by stirring the girl's emotions in the initial dream (Mosch. *Eur.* 1–15; above, 38–9n.) and by making Zeus/Jupiter fall for her (Mosch. *Eur.* 75–6). Venus and Cupid (cf. 68) have presumably been invisible up to this moment: scenes of overhearing are a staple ingredient of comedy and the comic novel (e.g. G. F. Franko, *AJP* 125 (2004) 27–59). For the adverbial accusative cf. 1.22.23, Tac. *A.* 4.60.2 'falsum renidens'; *NLS* 10 (top).

67–8 remisso…arcu 'with his bow slack' (*OLD remitto* 8a). Cupid has no need of his arrows, since Jupiter has already been smitten and is about to return to Europa in his divine form.

69 ubi lusit satis 'when she had had enough fun'. *ludere* + *satis* (again at *Epi.* 2.2.214) is 3× in Catullus (61.125–6, 61.225, 68A.17).

69–70 Abstineto | ...irarum calidaeque rixae: Venus' divine speech is characterised by an archaising future imperative and a grecising use of the genit. instead of the more usual (*ab* +) abl. (again at 4.9.37–8; see *OLD abstineo* 8a). *irarum* looks back to *iratae* (46). Quarrels are often 'heated' in English, but *calida rixa* is unparalleled in Latin.

71–2 cum tibi inuisus laceranda reddet | cornua taurus: Venus' words are an ironic and suggestive echo of Europa's own (46–8), to which she was listening: the girl understands the goddess to mean 'the hated bull' (*OLD inuisus*[1]), but Venus knows that, at the next encounter, the bull will remain 'unseen' (*OLD inuisus*[2]) since it will be Jupiter that returns to her; and it will not be his horns but another 'horn' that he will present to her (46–8n.): for *reddet* cf. Petron. 134.11 'nisi illud [sc. 'penis'] tam rigidum reddidero quam cornu', though the meaning is different. *tibi* is to be taken *apo koinou* with *inuisus*, *laceranda* and *reddet*.

73 uxor inuicti Iouis esse nescis? 'Don't you know that you are the wife of invincible Jupiter?' Venus continues her grecising with a nom. + infin. construction (*OLD nescio* 1b; Coleman 84; J. Clackson and G. Horrocks, *The Blackwell History of the Latin Language* (2007) 196); since on the present reading of the ode the marriage has yet to be consummated, one could regard the present infin. as substituting for the future, as often (*OLS* 1.525). Some think that the meaning is 'You don't know how to be the wife...', which is admittedly the regular use of *nescio* + infin. (*OLD nescio* 3a), but the act of revelation, so typical of dramatic genres (anagnorisis), is much more effective if made explicitly. Scholars have noted the similarity to the Ariadne story told by the scholiast on Hom. *Od.* 11.322 'As Ariadne was lamenting, Aphrodite appeared and advised her to cheer up: she would be the wife of Dionysus and would become famous.' Conversely the emperor Claudius did not know that his wife had left him (Tac. *A.* 11.30.2 '"An discidium...tuum nosti?"'). Iuppiter Inuictus had a temple in Rome (Cic. *Leg.* 2.28, Ov. *F.* 6.650).

75–6 tua sectus orbis | nomina ducet 'half the world will take your name': Venus' speech ends as Europa's began (34–5), with her name, although now its significance is transformed. *nomina* is plur. for sing., as 4.2.4 (see Thomas); *sectus orbis*, lit. 'the halved world' (*OLD seco* 1d), is a nom. example of the *ab urbe condita* idiom (3.4.18–19n.). The ancients divided the world into either two continents of Europe and Asia (as Varro, *LL* 5.31) or three (adding Africa: cf. Sall. *J.* 17.3; Pease on Cic. *ND* 2.165). The former division, as in H., naturally had the attraction of appealing to the age-old conflict between Europe and Asia (cf. Gh. Ceauşescu, 'Un topos de la littérature antique: l'éternelle guerre entre l'Europe et l'Asie', *Latomus* 50 (1991) 327–41). The elder Pliny, while acknowledging formally the tripartite division (*NH* 3.3), nevertheless offers geopolitical and aesthetic grounds for believing Europe to be really half the world (*NH* 3.5): 'de Europa altrice uictoris omnium gentium populi longeque terrarum pulcherrima, quam plerique merito non tertiam portionem fecere uerum aequam' (see intro.). *nomen ducere* is regular Latin for 'to derive a name' (as *S.* 2.1.66 'duxit ab oppressa Carthagine nomen'; *OLD duco* 27a), but *tua* indicates that here *ducet* means 'borrow' or 'acquire' (*OLD* 27d).

28

This is one of those dramatic or mimetic odes which, like 3.9 (see intro.), begins with a conversation already in progress; the difference from 3.9 is that on this occasion we hear only the voice of H. and have to imagine what Lyde has been saying to him. It seems that the poet has been preparing to celebrate a divinity's feast day (cf. 3.8.2–4), preparations which Lyde has evidently questioned. As the ode begins, H. responds by asking her what could be more important (1–2a). It is already late morning, verging towards afternoon, and, since he wishes to start drinking in order to get his celebration under way, he instructs Lyde to fetch a jar of wine from its storage place in his house (2b–8). There is to be singing as they drink, and in the second half of the ode H. lists the divinities who will be sung, ending with Venus (9–15). The reference to Venus invites the conjecture that their singing will be interrupted by an interval during which H. and Lyde make love; their lovemaking will last into the evening, whereupon they will sing their gratitude to Night (16).

METRE Fourth Asclepiad

1–2 Festo...die | Neptuni: H. is extremely fond of focussing on a particular day (cf. 3.8 intro.): sometimes *dies* is qualified by its common epithet *festus* (e.g. 3.8.9, 3.14.13, *S.* 2.2.83, *Epi.* 1.5.9–10), sometimes the day is an identifiable feast day (e.g. 2.12.19–20 'sacro | Dianae celebris die'), and sometimes the day is mentioned at the very beginning of an ode (e.g. 2.13.1 'nefasto...die'); all these variants are combined here. The feast day of Neptune is usually identified with the Neptunalia on 23 July, although sacrifices to Neptune were also made on the anniversary of the Battle of Actium (2 September) and the birthday of Augustus (23 September); but H. is perhaps thinking transculturally, as his later reference to the Nereids may suggest (10n.), and Bradshaw (*TC* 8–10) has acutely noted that, in the Athenian calendar, December was called the month of Poseidon and the eighth day of that month was Poseidon's actual feast day (J. D. Mikalson, *The Sacred and Civil Calendar of the Athenian Year* (1975) 89). Now 8 December was also H.'s birthday; what better day on which to celebrate with wine, woman and song?

quid potius…|…faciam? is perhaps a colloquial expression; the position of *potius* suggests that it is the neuter of *potior* (*OLD potior*²) rather than the adverb, but it is difficult to be sure (see Gaertner on Ov. *Ex P.* 1.5.43). *faciam* is deliberative subjunctive (*NLS* 129–30 §172): 'what better am I to do?'

2 prome: the regular verb for fetching wine from where it is kept (*OLD* 1c); see further 7n. *reconditum* suggests a wine deep in the cellar (cf. 2.3.6–8 'per dies | festos…| interiore nota Falerni'); also next n.

3 Lyde: if she is the out-of-the-way girl of the same name who needs to be enticed from her house at 2.11.21–2 ('deuium scortum', where see Harrison), she is ideally suited to fetch an inaccessible jar of wine ('reconditum'). A Lyde also features in 3.11.

strenua is to be taken adverbially (3.3.70–2n.), as at *Epi.* 1.7.71; it anticipates the military image in 4.

Caecubum: Caecuban wine, mentioned only here in Book 3, was one of the finest Italian wines, suitable for putting aside for special occasions (*Epo.* 9.1, where see Watson; also N–H on 1.20.9, Cairns, *RL* 232–9). It came from the Caecubus Ager, on the Sinus Amy(n)clanus (3.17.6n.), between Terracina and Fundi (Vitr. 8.3.12, Plin. *NH* 14.61): see *BA* Map 44: D3.

4 munitaeque adhibe uim sapientiae 'and bring its strength to bear on well-fortified philosophy' (*OLD munitus* 1a). It was conventional to see philosophy metaphorically as a stronghold (e.g. Cic. *Fam.* 16.23.3; N–H on 2.6.21), and *uis* is the technical term for the 'strength' of a wine or other liquid (*OLD* 9d): just as Hannibal famously ordered the Alpine rocks to be split apart by the agency of vinegar (Liv. 21.37.2, Plin. *NH* 23.57 'domitrix *uis haec* non ciborum modo est uerum et rerum plurimarum. saxa rumpit infusum', Juv. 10.153), so H. is ordering his 'subordinate' Lyde to use wine against the sturdy defences of philosophy. There was a proverbial antithesis between wine and wisdom (see 21.9– 10n., Plin. *NH* 23.41 'sic quoque in prouerbium cessit sapientiam uino obumbrari'; Tosi 345–6 §737), although we are presumably not to take seriously the notion that H. or Lyde have actually been deep in Plato or Aristotle. *adhibere uim* is a very common expr. (e.g. Liv. 5.43.1, 36.10.7). The juxtaposition *uim sapientiae*, like *prome reconditum* above, is typically Horatian (Intro. 26).

5 inclinare meridiem: *meridiem* must be pregnant for 'the midday sun' (the closest parallel seems to be Apul. *Met.* 6.12.4 'meridies solis'); for intrans. *inclinare* cf. Juv. 3.316 'sol inclinat'; *OLD* 4b. The day is evidently passing quickly (cf. 1n. (*quid*), 6n.), and H. is keen to start the party. The middle of the day was regarded as a good time for sex by Catullus (32.3) and Ovid (*Am.* 1.5.1).

6 et, ueluti stet uolucris dies 'and yet, as if the flying day were standing still' (*OLD et* 14a). *uolucris dies* recurs at 4.13.16 and Sen. *HF* 178. The pres. subjunc. in an unreal comparative clause in the present is regular (see 3.16.41–2; G&L 389 §602).

7 parcis deripere 'you refrain from grabbing' (*OLD parco* 2c).

horreo: to be taken *apo koinou* with the surrounding words (Grimm 11, 22): it is separative ('from') with *deripere* but locative ('in') with *cessantem*. The noun is here assumed to mean 'wine store' (*OLD* 2), perhaps identical with the *apotheca* (3.8.10–11n.).

8 cessantem Bibuli consulis amphoram: M. Calpurnius Bibulus was Julius Caesar's colleague as consul in 59 BC. *amphoram* activates the obvious pun on his name (cf. Tac. *A.* 3.52.2 and W–M); not only is *cessantem* appropriate for a wine which has been lurking at the back of the storeroom (2 *reconditum*) for well over thirty years but it exactly describes Bibulus' famous non-cooperation when he withdrew to his house for most of 59 in order to frustrate Caesar's legislation (cf. e.g. Cic. *Vat.* 22 'Bibulum... inclusum domi', *Fam.* 1.9.7, Vell. 44.5 'Bibulus...domi se tenuit'). The amphora has taken on his defining behaviour. For the dating of a wine-jar by the consular year when it was filled see 3.8.12n.

9–10 nos cantabimus inuicem...: some think that *nos* = 'I' (~ *tu*, 11): not only is this extremely confusing in the context but it seems impossible alongside *inuicem*. The clearest (and most amusing) way of interpreting these and the following lines is if we assume that H. sings of Neptune, the god whose feast day it is, and Lyde sings of the Nereids in her turn ('inuicem'); but then Lyde is expected to continue singing alone (11 'tu') about the three goddesses listed in 11–15 (11n.): she thus ends up doing most of the singing.

10 uirides Nereideum comas: the Nereids were sea nymphs, offspring of Nereus and Doris; like other sea deities, they take on the colour of their surroundings (Knox on Ov. *Her.* 5.57 'uirides Nereidas oro'; Gibson on Ov. *AA* 3.130). The Nereids are more usually associated with the Greek Poseidon than with Neptune, his Roman equivalent (J. M. Barringer, *Divine Escorts: Nereids in Archaic and Classical Greek Art* (1995)); but cf. Sil. 3.412–13. For *coma* see 3.14.25n.

11 curua recines lyra: the Lyde of 2.11 also has a lyre (22); the description as 'curved' is conventional (N–H on 1.10.6; *BNP* 9.355–7). *recines* perhaps = 'sing again, continue singing' (contrast 3.27.1 and n.).

12 Latonam et celeris spicula Cynthiae: Latona (Leto in Greek) gave birth to Diana on Mt Cynthus on the island of Delos; as a fabled huntress Diana is expected to be swift (again at Ov. *Met.* 4.304, *Ciris* 297).

13 summo carmine, quae...: *either* 'in the last song...', thereby constituting 'a touching *mise en abîme* of...the last love poem' in *Odes* 1–3 (Barber 151), *or* 'at the end of the song...'. Scholars differ on whether the verb continues to be *recines* (11), in which case the understood antecedent of *quae* will be *eam* and the sentence will end at *oloribus* (15), or whether a new sentence starts with *summo carmine*, in which case the main verb will be *dicetur* (16) and the understood antecedent of *quae* will be *ea*. N–R assume the latter, but it is significantly inferior in terms of both structure and drama (see nn. below).

13–15 quae Cnidon | fulgentesque tenet Cycladas et Paphon | iunctis uisit oloribus: the understood antecedent of *quae* is *eam* (13n.). As at Cat. 36.11–15 the goddess's name is omitted, but, from the cult centres which H. mentions, Lyde will infer that he wishes her to end her singing with Venus (cf. 1.30.1 'O Venus, regina Cnidi Paphique'). As Quinn rightly remarks, the symbolic strategy of H.'s musical programme now becomes clear: Venus is involved at the conclusion of the programme in order that she may favour the lovemaking which is to follow. Cnidos was in Caria in SW Turkey (*BA* Map 61: E4) and famous for its devotion to Aphrodite (N–H on 1.30.1); Paphos (*BA* Map 72: B3) was on the western shore of Cyprus and the place where Aphrodite made landfall after Cythera (Hes. *Theog.* 193; cf. 3.12.5–6n.); the Cyclades are a group of islands in the Aegean Sea (*BA* Map 57): they are conventionally described as 'shining'

(N–H on 1.14.19), though *fulgentes* does not recur. *tenet* = 'inhabit, frequent' or 'rule over', as at 3.26.9 (n.); *uiso* is technical of divine visitations (N–H on 1.4.8).

15 iunctis...oloribus: Venus' chariot here has a team of swans, as at 4.1.10, Prop. 3.3.39, Ov. *Met.* 10.708 'iunctis...cycnis'; in Sappho 1.10 she famously has sparrows (where see Hutchinson for her various other avian transporters).

16 dicetur merita Nox quoque nenia: *merita* suggests that the song to Night will be sung after an anticipated session of lovemaking (see intro.); if so, *nenia* cannot have its commonest meaning of 'dirge' but must simply be a synonym for *carmen* or similar: the noun occasionally has non-funereal applications (see *OLD*; Dyck on Cic. *Leg.* 2.62). *dico* is often used of the subject of song (3.13.14; *OLD* 7b); the passive form 'allows us to suppose that both parties are now participating' (N–R). Night is a common and natural means of closure (Smith 176), here concluding the sequence *die* (1), *meridiem* (5), *dies* (6); for the personification see Maltby on Tib. 2.1.87–90.

29

In the first ode of Book 1 H. had praised Maecenas for his royal ancestry and had declared that, if his patron passed a favourable verdict on his lyric poetry, it would bring him the greatest happiness. These elements are resumed in, and distributed between, the last two odes of Book 3. In the present poem H. praises Maecenas for his royal ancestry, and in the last poem of all he himself gives his own verdict on his lyric achievement. Book 1 of the *Epistles* has a somewhat similar arrangement.

As Fraenkel recognised (223–9), the greatness of our ode resides in its combination and treatment of widely divergent themes: N–R refer to the 'breadth and majesty of its scope' (347). There are eight central stanzas (17–48), framed by two sets of four. In lines 1–16 the focus is on Maecenas rather than H. (in 49–64 it will be the other way round):[141] the poet urges his patron to stop tarrying in Rome, gazing out east and south from his Esquiline tower at resorts nestling in the foothills within a fifteen-mile radius of the city; instead he should travel twice as far afield to H.'s villa, where he would find that a *cadus* of wine has long since been put aside for him. Rich men enjoy a change of scene and they find relaxation in modest fare and modest surroundings.

---

[141] Compare 3.8, where in 1–12 the focus is on H. and in 17–28 on Maecenas.

The central section (17–48) begins by offering a further reason why Maecenas should accept H.'s invitation to the country (17–24): time has been hurrying by and it is already midsummer (*iam...iam...iam...*), *par excellence* the season for drinking (18n.), but Maecenas is anxious about the city and is worried what preparations are being made by potentially hostile states for the future (25–8). Although these three stanzas continue the invitation to H.'s patron, they also serve to concentrate attention on the theme of time, which takes up the remainder of the ode's central section (29–48) and in which the future (cued by *quid...parent*, 27–8) is contrasted with the present. The contrasts are set down twice, each time on a 'ring' basis:

[1A¹] 29–32a: But only god is permitted to know the future (the implication being that Maecenas is worrying pointlessly and should accept H.'s invitation). [1B] 32b–33a: The important thing, expressed in a *sententia* in the exact centre of the ode, is to adopt an appropriate attitude to the present; [1A²] 33b–41a: everything else (i.e. the future) will take its own course, described in a magnificent simile as the River Tiber, which sometimes flows calmly between its banks and at other times is a raging and destructive torrent.

[2A¹] 41b–43a: That man will spend a happy life in control of himself who can look back on each present day and say 'I have lived'. [2B] 43b–45a: Jupiter – making a ring with *deus* in 29–32a – can bring clouds or sunshine tomorrow; [2A²] 45b–48: but he cannot undo the present blessings which the fleeting hour – making a closural ring with the speed of time at 17–24 (see above) – has already brought.

It will be seen that in **1** the ring is formed by the future and in **2** by the present and that future and present alternate throughout. To the final section [2A²] on the present, however, H. has added that Jupiter also cannot undo the past (45b–6), a surprising addition to the argument which will become relevant in the final section of the poem.

The limitations of Jupiter's power act as a foil for the all-powerful capriciousness of Fortuna, with which the final four stanzas of the ode begin (49–64). The last we heard of H. was in line 5 ('apud me'), and the successive reflections on time (29–48) mean that Maecenas too – last mentioned in 25–8 – has faded from view. But now H. returns to himself (52 *mihi*) and, by referring to his privileged lifestyle (51 *honores*), returns also, by implication, to his patron. The poet has assured us that nothing, not even Jupiter, can deprive him of the benefits which Maecenas has bestowed upon him and which he continues to enjoy; but Fortuna is a different matter and she can change things in an instant (51–2): if she takes to wing and deserts him, he will adapt unprotestingly to a reduction in his circumstances (53–6). Should there be a storm, he has no rich merchant's vessel to worry about (57–61); his little rowing boat will carry him safely to the end of his voyage (62–4).

It is difficult to do justice to the subtlety and tact of this tribute to Maecenas. H. begins by issuing an invitation born of friendship and camaraderie: in its explicit form it effectively takes up almost half of the ode (1–28), and the temporal contrasts of 29–48, despite their generalising nature, are also predicated on it, in as much as they emphasise the present at the expense of the future; but, when we eventually return to H. himself (49ff.), the generosity from which he benefits (52 *benigna*), and which results from the friendship symbolised by the invitation, is not attributed to Maecenas by name at all: the poet's gratitude and contentment have to be read between the lines of the references to Fortuna, and the metaphor of his negotiating the stormy seas safely in his little boat is less a statement of improbable independence than an assurance that there will be no further call on his patron's generosity. In these respects the ode is very different from, and considerably more powerful than, the earlier and more open acknowledgements of *Epode* 1 (25–34).

Maecenas cannot have failed to be enchanted by 'the greatest of all Horace's lyrics' (West, *DP* 223). Its majestic sweep both claims attention in its own right and allows the combination of widely different opposites: poet and patron, town and country, present and future, human and divine, foreign and domestic, the personal and the philosophical. The philosophy is not that of any given school but the kind of popular wisdom that Maecenas will have come to expect from H.; and the prosaic language in which some of the concepts are expressed (32 'quod adest', 46 'quodcumque retro est', 48 'quod...hora uexit') casts into brilliant relief the vivid particularity of his description of the Tiber (34–41). We may surmise that, if this invitation was issued in real life, Maecenas will have summoned his carriage immediately and travelled the thirty or so miles to H.'s villa.[142]

---

[142] The journey would have taken him along the Via Tiburtina to Tibur, after which he would follow the Via Valeria up the Anio valley for another 7 miles or so, before branching north up the valley of the Digentia. It is worth reflecting that the whole journey will have taken the best part of two days: *Orbis* calculates almost a full day's travel to Tibur, which is only just over halfway (although Pliny says that it takes him only half a day to get from Rome to his Laurentine villa, which is roughly the same distance as Tibur but in the opposite direction: *Ep.* 2.17.2). Perhaps a visitor to H. would break the journey overnight at Tibur, where a house belonging to the poet was still being pointed out in Suetonius' day (see N–H on 1.7.13, Harrison on 2.6.5–8).

METRE Alcaic

1 Tyrrhena regum progenies illustrates enallage (3.1.42–3n.): the meaning is 'Offspring of Etruscan kings'. The 'Grecising' note of *Tyrrhena* (cf. 3.10.11–12n.) is maintained by *balanus* (4) and *Telegoni* (8), both transliterations of Greek, and 'well characterises the Hellenophile Etruscan' (Coleman 65–6): see further 3.8.5n. Maecenas, whose full name seems to have been C. Maecenas Cilnius (W. on Tac. *A.* 6.11.2), was descended from the Cilnii of Arretium in northern Etruria (Lyne, *Hor.* 132–3). Augustus addressed him as 'Cilniorum smaragde' (Macrob. 2.4.12), and his Etruscan lineage is mentioned again at *S.* 1.6.1–2, Prop. 3.9.1, *Eleg. Maec.* 1.13.

1–5 tibi...iamdudum apud me est 'for a long time there has been...for you in my keeping/at my house'. An English translation cannot bring out the emphatic nature of *tibi* or the long deferment of *apud me*; in the context it is difficult to distinguish between the two senses of *apud* (*OLD* 4a, 9a).

2 non ante uerso lene merum cado 'mellow neat-wine in a jar not previously upended', i.e. it has been kept specially for Maecenas, in whose dialogue *Symposium* the qualities of wine were featured (3.21 intro.); since the wine is still in its original container, it is as yet unmixed with water (*merum*, as 1.9.8). *lenis* is used 'esp. of wine' (*OLD* 3): for the suggestion that H. is referring obliquely to Alban wine (Plin. *NH* 23.33, 36), perhaps a favourite of Maecenas (cf. *S.* 2.8.16–17), see West, *DP* 256–9. *uerto* is technical of pouring from a container (*OLD* 6a); the line is mimetic, the wine contained within the undisturbed jar.

3 cum flore, Maecenas, rosarum: the roses, an essential accompaniment of any party (3.15.15n., 3.19.22n.), encircle Maecenas' name, as a garland would encircle his head (again mimetic). For the availability of roses in summer (cf. 17–20) see N–H on 1.38.3–4 'rosa...sera'.

4 pressa tuis balanus capillis 'pounded be(he)n-nut for your hair': another essential party element was perfumed ointment (3.14.17–18n.), in this case the product of a nut from Egypt (Plin. *NH* 12.100), where Maecenas seems to have had estates (Lyne, *Hor.* 133). Maecenas was notoriously foppish, and Augustus' dismissal of his literary style as 'perfume-dripping locks' (Suet. *Aug.* 86.2) may well have been chosen because of his friend's attention to his hair;[143] on the other hand we are

---

[143] Note C. S. Kraus, 'Hair, hegemony, and historiography: Caesar's style and its earliest critics', in Reinhardt et al. 97–115, esp. 104 n. 24.

told that, when Maecenas appeared in public, he covered his head with a kind of turban, with only his ears peeping out (Sen. *Ep.* 114.6). For *capillus* see 3.14.25n.

5 eripe te morae: H. has been waiting quite some time (*iamdudum*). Since *morae* is an anagram of *Romae* (12: also line-end), there is perhaps the suggestion that the capital is inherently delaying and exerts its pull on Maecenas (cf. Prop. 1.12.2, Ov. *Tr.* 1.3.62). For the reflexive construction see *OLD* 5b. *morae* is presumably dat. (cf. 3.22.3n.), although Coleman (80–1) suggests a genit. on the analogy of Greek (e.g. ἐρύομαι).

6–8 ne semper udum Tibur et Aefulae | decliue contempleris aruum et | Telegoni iuga parricidae: the three locations form an arc bordering (roughly) the south-east quadrant of the Roman hinterland. Tibur (3.4.22–4n.) was situated on the River Anio about 15 miles ENE of Rome along the Via Tiburtina and had an elaborate irrigation system (N–H on 1.7.13); it is *udum* again at Ov. *F.* 4.71. Aefula was in the hills due south of Tibur and a short distance from it (*BA* Map 43: D2). The 'ridges of Telegonus' is a reference to Tusculum, a city in the Alban Hills c. 15 miles SE of Rome just off the Via Latina (*BA* Map 43: C2): according to legend it was founded by Telegonus, son of Odysseus and Circe (cf. *Epo.* 1.29–30 'superni… Tusculi | Circaea…moenia'), who ended up unwittingly killing his father. *ne…contempleris* indicates that Maecenas is imagined as gazing out from his famous tower (9–10n.), wondering to which fashionable resort – each 'is within sight of persons in Rome' (Strabo 5.3.11) – he should escape in the midsummer heat (17–20nn.). Elsewhere in H. a present subjunc. expressing a prohibition is introduced by both *ne* (1.33.1) and *nec* (2.11.4): since the MSS here are divided, it is difficult to know which to choose; I have opted for *ne* (a constr. regarded as early and colloquial: cf. *NLS* 96 §126 *Note* (ii), *OLS* 1.499), since two asyndetic commands mirror those in 9–12 and also help to render *eripe te morae* more emphatic.

9–10 fastidiosam desere copiam et | molem propinquam nubibus arduis: the villas of wealthy Romans would often boast a *turris* (e.g. Sen. *Ep.* 86.4, Mart. 3.58.46, Plin. *Ep.* 2.17.12–13 with Whitton's nn.), but whether the references are literally to a tower or to an extra storey is not always clear (see P. Grimal, *Les jardins romains* (1943) 276–7; D'Arms, Plate 15A; T. P. Wiseman, *PBSR* 84 (2016) 141–4): in his estate on the Esquiline Hill, in the eastern quarter of Rome, Maecenas had such an edifice (cf. *Epo.* 9.3 'sub alta…domo'), the so-called *turris Maecenatiana*, from which Nero is said to have watched the Great Fire (Suet. *Nero* 38.2). The *turris* is wittily described as being 'neighbour of the lofty clouds'; similarly Tacitus notes that, when the city's tenement blocks were demolished in the path of the Great Fire, their inhabitants left 'the sky unoccupied' (*A.* 15.40.1 'uelut uacuum caelum'). For the conceit *propinquam nubibus* see e.g. Sen. *Ag.* 92–3 'nubibus ipsis inserta caput | turris' and Tarrant, *Anth. Pal.* 9.58.6; Pease on Virg. *Aen.* 4.89, and Fraenkel 225 n. 3. *fastidiosam* is active (*OLD* 4), as again at *Epo.* 17.73: Williams translates 'a plenty that creates boredom', but, given the context, there is perhaps play also with *fastigium* (theme and variation), as at 3.1.22–3 (n.).

11–12 ŏmitte mirari beatae | fumum et opes strepitumque Romae: for Rome as a 'city of marvels' see C. Edwards, *Writing Rome* (1996) 96–102; H.'s ironical description of Maecenas admiring Rome's drawbacks (*fumum, strepitum*) as much as its attractions (*beatae, opes*) defines him as a city-dweller. *beatus*, like εὐδαίμων (e.g. Xen. *Anab.* 1.2.6, 1.2.20, 1.4.1, 1.4.19; Dunbar on Ar. *Birds* 36–8), is commonly applied to cities (*TLL* 2.1918.34–57), as at Liv. 5.7.10 'beatam urbem Romanam', but seems not to qualify *Roma* in any other literary text (it is on Constantinian coins: see *RIC* 8.286–7 nos. 372, 376–7). *strepitus* is almost conventional for the noise and bustle of the capital (*Epi.* 2.2.79–80, Cic. *Arch.* 12, Plin. *Ep.* 1.9.7): see R. Jenkyns, *God, Space, and City in the Roman Imagination* (2013) 38–9, who notes also that references to the smokiness of Rome (again at 3.6.4, Sen. *Ep.* 104.6 'grauitatem urbis...et illum odorem culinarum fumantium') are rare. The counterpart to these lines will come in the description of the countryside at 21–4 below, both passages relating to the commonplace 'rusticane uita an urbana potior' (Quint. 2.4.24), a regular Horatian theme (e.g. *Epi.* 1.10, 1.14; S. J. Harrison, *CCH* 235–47). Compare Sejanus' attempts at persuading Tiberius to leave the capital and retire to the country (Tac. *A.* 4.41.3 and W.). For *omitto* + inf. = 'stop' see *OLD* 5b; for *ŏmitte* see Intro. 30.

13 plerumque gratae diuitibus uices: sc. *sunt* ('The rich generally welcome change'). H. presents Maecenas' fabled wealth as a reason why he should accept the poet's modest invitation. The prosaic *plerumque* (3.21.13–14n.) combines with *mundae...cenae* (next n.) to suggest that the language of the invitation reflects the plainness of the promised meal.

14–15 mundaeque...cenae: the adj., which seems colloquial, is 'used often by H. to suggest a mean between luxurious superfluity and sordid lack' (Mayer on *Epi.* 1.4.11 'mundus uictus'). *cena*, common in H.'s hexameters, is absent from epic and is another of his prosaic terms (N–H on 2.14.28; P. A. Watson (1985) 436).

14 paruo sub Lare: since *paruus* is the regular word for statues of the Lares (3.23.15–16n.), this probably means 'under the authority of a little Lar' (*OLD sub* 15a), but 'under the shelter of a little house/home' (*OLD sub* 4, *Lar* 2) cannot be excluded. *sub Lare* recurs only at Ov. *Ex P.* 1.1.10, 1.7.58. *pauperum* seems to go with both *Lare* and *cenae* (Naylor).

15 sine aulaeis et ostro: perhaps 'purple tapestries', a hendiadys like Virg. *G.* 2.192 'pateris...et auro'. Maecenas seems to have liked the colour (Juv. 12.38–9); for tapestries as a sign of luxury see *S.* 2.8.54 (the *cena Nasidieni*) with Muecke.

16 sollicitam explicuere frontem: the verb ('unfold') indicates that *sollicitam* refers to furrowing or creasing: cf. *S.* 2.2.125 'explicuit uino contractae seria frontis'; the reasons for Maecenas' anxiety are given at 25–8 below (~ *sollicitus*). For *frons* as a mirror of one's feelings see *OLD* 2; the tense is a 'gnomic perfect' (3.5.1–2n.): unpretentious dinners *are* a source of relaxation.

17–21 iam...iam...iam...: H. ticks off the reasons why it is high time for Maecenas to visit him – but the great man hasn't arrived (25 *tu*, adversative asyndeton).

17–18 clarus occultum Andromedae pater | ostendit ignem: Andromeda was famously chained to a rock as a sacrifice to a sea monster; her father was Cepheus, king of the Ethiopians and husband of Cassiopeia, who gave his name to a constellation which according to Columella rose on 9 July (11.2.51), although edd. point out that from Rome the constellation never sets: Columella's statements are true of an observer in Alexandria; he seems likely to have been relying on an Alexandrian text, and perhaps the same was true of H. as well. *clarus* is regular of stars and the like (*OLD* 2); its juxtaposition with *occultum* is typical of H. *ostendere ignem*, first in Cat. 62.7, is used by other authors too of visible celestial phenomena (e.g. Germ. *Phaen.* 258). It is generally inferred from 2.17 that Maecenas had a special interest in astronomy and astrology (see Harrison's intro., p. 198).

18 Procyon furit: the name (Προκύων) means Pre-Dog (cf. Cic. *ND* 2.114 'Ante Canem, Procyon Graio qui nomine fertur' and Pease) and refers to the star which according to Columella rose on 15 July (11.2.52). The Dog-star itself (Sirius) rose on 18 July (3.13.9–10n.) and was conventionally associated with exhortations to drink (Hes. *WD* 582ff. (and West on 585), Alc. 347, 352, Theog. 1039–40; also below, 21n.).

19 stella uesani Leonis: on 29 July 'Leonis in pectore clara stella exoritur' (Colum. 11.2.53); since this is now the hottest season of the year, the constellation to which the star belongs is conventionally described as violent or mad (see Henriksén on Mart. 9.90.12).

20 dies...siccos: an expr. used also by Columella (2.11.8, 7.3.12, 12.19.3, 12.41) and the elder Pliny (*NH* 11.38). For the appended abl. abs. see 3.1.30–1n.

21–2 pastor umbras...fessus quaerit: the shepherd is an appropriate figure to evoke summer heat (Virg. *Ecl.* 2.1–13), while *fessus* (again at Ov. *Tr.* 4.1.11–12) recalls the description of men in summertime as 'at their weakest' (Hes. *WD* 586) or 'feeble' (Alc. 347.5). Virgil's description of summer (*G.* 3.327–34, based on Varro, *RR* 2.2.11) likewise features shade, 'a natural connection in the Italian landscape, and an important bucolic component' (Thomas ad loc.); in the *Eclogues*, *umbra* (17×) is a 'key word' (P. L. Smith, 'Lentus in umbra', *Phoenix* 19 (1965) 298). Yet, since shepherds had long been regarded as analogues for political leaders (3.1.5–6n.) and *umbra* can also denote retirement from the stresses of public life (*OLD* 5), the wording has particular relevance to Maecenas (cf. Prop. 3.9.29 'in tenues humilem te colligis umbras', addressed to Maecenas),[144] whose love of retirement was well known (3.8 intro.), and is esp. relevant in a poem of invitation (25–32 below). For *fessus* see 3.4.37–8n.

21 cum grege languido: Varro describes as *languidae* those sheep which are starved for three days before being plucked (*RR* 2.11.9); but, since plucking was presumably an alternative to shearing, and the latter was supposed not to extend beyond the summer solstice in June (ibid. 2.11.6), H. must be referring to general lethargy brought on by the heat in July/August.

22–3 et horridi | dumeta Siluani: *dumeta* is a third object of *quaerit*; some think that the word is nom. and that *carent* has to be supplied from *caret* below, but (i) this dislocation seems far more difficult than that illustrated by 3.1.12–13 (n.), (ii) the interlaced word order of 24 seems to restrict *uagis...uentis* to the river-bank. Silvanus was a god of flocks (Virg. *Aen.* 8.601 'pecoris...deo') and, as suggested by his name and epithet (again at Mart. 10.92.6), woodland; see P. F. Dorcey, *The Cult of Silvanus* (1993).

---

[144] Note the subtitle of P. Le Doze, *Mécène: ombres et flamboyances* (2014).

23–4 caretque | ripa uagis taciturna uentis: *caret* = 'is free from' (3.19.7–8n.); *taciturnus*, a favourite adj. of H., is more expressive than *tacitus* (N–H on 1.31.8); for *uagis…uentis* cf. Cat. 65.17.

25–6 tu ciuitatem quis deceat status | curas: for an indir. qu. after *curo* see *OLD* 8d. The sing. nom. masc. forms of the interrogative adj. (*qui*) and interrog. pronoun (*quis*) 'are in practice not well distinguished' (*OLS* 1.974; cf. 336) and one can find the latter when strictly one might expect the former. The usage (*OLD quis*[1] 5) is fairly common in H. (e.g. 1.5.1), although this is the only ex. in Book 3. *ciuitatis status* is an extremely common phrase, esp. in Cicero and Livy, and will regularly mean something like 'the condition of the community' or 'the state of affairs in the community' (*OLD status* 6–7). Here, however, the verb *deceat* suggests that the meaning is 'civic constitution' (*OLD status* 8a), and discussions of the best or most appropriate constitution are found from Herodotus (3.80–2) through Plato, Cicero and others to pseudo-Plutarch (*Mor.* 826–7); one of the most striking occurs in Dio, who under the year 29 BC puts opposing speeches into the mouths of Agrippa and Maecenas about whether Augustus should restore the republic or consolidate his monarchy (52.1.1–40.2). No one believes that these speeches are authentic, but it is obviously possible that the three leaders did hold such discussions, and it is certainly credible that Maecenas was indeed concerned about the constitutional direction of the state.[145] What is remarkable is that H. should refer to his patron's concerns in the public medium of a poem. We know from the *Satires* (2.6) that contemporaries saw H. as having the ear of Maecenas, while he himself protests that he knows no state secrets but only the merest trivialities; yet here in the ode he chooses to touch on a matter which must have been of the greatest political sensitivity. In the event, of course, Augustus sided with Dio's 'Maecenas' in favour of monarchy, often choosing the term *status* to describe it (Suet. *Aug.* 28.2, Gell. 15.7.3). See further next n.

26–7 et Vrbi sollicitus times | quid…: since *sollicitus* appears not to be constructed with a dat. in classical Latin, these words probably mean: 'and you fear for the City, anxious as to what…' (for the indir. qu. see *OLD sollicitus* 2c). Edd. infer from these words that the ode relates to a time when Augustus was absent from Rome, such as 27–24 BC (3.14 intro.), i.e. the period immediately preceding the so-called second constitutional settlement of 23 (Intro. 10). For Maecenas' anxieties see further 3.8.17–26nn.

---

[145] See also Lyne, *Hor.* 134–6, on Augustus' advisers.

COMMENTARY 29.27-33	365

27-8 quid Serēs et regnata Cyro | Bactra parent Tanaisque discors: for the short *-ēs* ending of a Greek plural noun see G&L 33 §66 *Note* 4; Housman 2.821, 836. It is conventional to translate *Seres*, mentioned again at 1.12.56 and 4.15.23, as 'Chinese', but H.'s contemporaries knew them simply 'as a people beyond the eastern border of Parthia who controlled the supply of valuable commodities' (Powell 163). Bactria, of which Bactra (neut. plur.) was the chief city (*BA* Map 99: A3), lay on Parthia's northern border, while the Tanais flowed through Scythia (3.4.36n.). 'The combination of the three geographical references', says Powell (165), 'points clearly to one single area: the north-eastern frontier of the Parthian empire'. For Cyrus' rule over Bactria see e.g. Xen. *Cyr.* 1.1.4; the passive of *regno* and the dat. of agent, again at 2.6.11, 'are alike Grecizing and grandiloquent' (N–H ad loc.; also Horsfall on Virg. *Aen.* 3.14). *discors* alludes to the internal dissensions conventionally attributed to barbarian peoples (3.8.19–20n.): since their *discordia* suggests that they are no threat to Rome, Maecenas' worries are implied to be misplaced.

29-30 prudens futuri temporis exitum | caliginosa nocte premit deus: *futuri temporis* is to be taken *apo koinou* both with *prudens* and with *exitum*, so *prudens* is to be translated two different ways: '*Having foreknowledge* of future time, the god *prudently* hides the outcome [sc. of future time] in dark night.' The god's prudence is explained by the commonplace that it was undesirable for men to know the future (Pease on Cic. *Div.* 2.22). For *premit* see *OLD* 17; the coupling with *nocte* is common. For the darkness of the future cf. Pind. *Ol.* 12.8–9, Bacchyl. *Ode* 16.32–3, Theog. 1077–8, Juv. 6.556.

31-2 ridetque, si mortalis ultra | fas trepidat: laughter is quite often ascribed to the gods, esp. Jupiter (3.16.6–7, Enn. *Ann.* 446–7, Virg. *Aen.* 1.254–5); here the god laughs if a mortal tries to encroach upon divine competence by looking into the future. *ultra fas* is paralleled only at Sen. *Ep.* 95.23.

32-3 quod adest memento | componere aequus 'Be sure to arrange calmly what is at hand', the same constr. as 1.7.17–18 'sapiens finire memento | tristitiam' and, though without the adverbial adj., 2.3.1–2 'Aequam memento...seruare mentem', *Epi.* 1.8.16 (cf. *OLD memini* 4a, *compono* 16, *aequus* 8b). Since the ode is 64 lines long, the *sententia* is placed at the exact centre (Fraenkel 227). For *componere* cf. Sen. *Ep.* 12.8

'sic ordinandus est dies'.[146] *quod adest*, a common expr., here suggests a contrast such as that found at Pind. *Pyth.* 3.22 on the man 'who scorns what is at hand and peers at things far away' (also *Paean* 4.34–5): see further D. C. Young, *Three Odes of Pindar* (1968) Appendix 1 (pp. 116–20). Equanimity, a commonplace of popular philosophy, is one of H.'s most characteristic themes (N–H on 2.3.1).

33–4 cetera fluminis | ritu ferentur 'everything else will take its course like a river' (*OLD fero* 5b); for *ritu* cf. 3.14.1–4n. *cetera*, a favoured usage (1.9.9,[147] *Epo.* 13.7) and here contrasting with *quod adest*, refers to future events; *ferentur*, the reading of the oldest MS (R), seems much more natural than *feruntur*: given the imperative *memento* in 32–3, one might also consider *ferantur*, 'let everything else…' (cf. *occupato* at 44 below). Plato has Heraclitus 'likening everything to the flow of a river' (*Crat.* 402A), but this relates to the proverbial 'you cannot step into the same river twice'; for other comparisons of life to a river see 2.14.2 and N–H; Rutherford 147–8. H.'s comparison, as is often the way with similes, is extended and takes on a life of its own.

34–8 nunc…nunc… 'sometimes…at other times…': any great river which rises in the Alps or the Apennines can change its character very quickly depending on the conditions, and indeed the Tiber is prone to flooding: cf. Plin. *Ep.* 8.17.2; G. S. Aldrete, *Floods of the Tiber in Ancient Rome* (2007).

34 medio alueo: i.e. as opposed to bursting over its banks into the adjacent countryside (Plin. cit.).

35–6 cum pace delabentis Etruscum | in mare: *delabentis*, like *uoluentis* below (38), agrees with *fluminis* (33); *cum pace* ('peacefully') is a fairly common expr. The final syllable of *Etruscum* is elided before *in* in the following line (synaloepha), as at 2.3.27–8. *Etruscum mare* (again at Liv. 4.52.5, 40.41.3) is the Tyrrhenian Sea, into which the Tiber debouches

---

[146] On the correspondence between our ode and Sen. *Ep.* 12 see nn. below, G. Vogt-Spira, 'Time in Horace and Seneca', in Stöckinger et al. 187–93, and Edwards' commentary on the letter.

[147] To N–H's parallels here add Sappho's 'Brothers Poem' (see T. Phillips, 'A new Sapphic intertext in Horace', *Archiv für Papyrusforschung* 60 (2014) 283–9). A more general indebtedness of 3.29 to Sappho is argued by Ll. Morgan, 'The reception of Sappho's Brothers Poem in Rome', in A. Bierl and A. Lardinois (edd.), *The Newest Sappho* (2016) 296–9.

– an appropriately named destination in an ode addressed to the Etruscan Maecenas (1n.).

36 lapides adesos: the river's debris ranges from inanimate matter through animate and animals to dwellings (*domos* perhaps implying also their occupants). For somewhat similar descriptions cf. Lucr. 1.281–9, Virg. *Aen.* 2.496–9, 12.523–5, Ov. *Met.* 1.285–90, Stat. *Theb.* 1.364–9. The stones are surely those which the river has already eroded (cf. Theocr. 22.49–50, Ov. *Her.* 10.26) rather than those which are now being dislodged from the river's banks.

37 stirpesque raptas 'the saplings it has seized.'

38 una: either 'all together' or 'along with it'. For *non sine* cf. 3.4.20n.

39 clamore 'echo.'

40–1 cum fera diluuies quietos | irritat amnes 'when a wild flood arouses its quiet waters': since *amnes* presumably refers to the river itself rather than to tributaries, and since *diluuies* and *amnes* refer to the same entity, the words illustrate the type of pleonasm known as 'disjunctiveness', e.g. Virg. *Aen.* 10.103 'premit placida aequora pontus' (see Harrison; also W. on Tac. *Agr.* 1.1). *quietos* looks back to *cum pace* at the beginning of the simile (35). *diluuies* (again at 4.14.28, Lucr. 5.255, 6.292, Sen. *NQ* 3.29.8 [conjecture], Plin. *NH* 9.8) is a rare equivalent of *diluuium*. Personification, often used of rivers in general (3.13 intro.) and of the Tiber in particular (e.g. Tac. *A.* 1.79.3), is here implied by the unparalleled application of *irrito* to waters ('quasi animantes': *TLL* 7.2.429.83–4): Fraenkel (224 n. 1) believed the usage was suggested by ὀρόθυνον at Hom. *Il.* 21.312, where the river Scamander tells the river Simois to 'arouse all your torrents'.

41–3 ille potens sui | laetusque deget cui licet in diem | dixisse 'Vixi' 'That man will exist in control of himself and happily who is permitted to say/ have said each day "I have lived"': for intrans. *dego* + predicative adj. see *OLD* 2a. *potens sui* (*OLD potens* 2a), which renders the Greek terms αὐτάρκης or ἐγκρατὴς ἑαυτοῦ, implicitly contrasts with what one is *not* in control of – the future. According to Plut. *Cic.* 22.4, the perfect tense of *uiuere* is a Roman euphemism for death (thus *uixerunt* = 'they have lived', i.e. are no longer alive), but H.'s *uixi* has a different meaning: I have lived to the full today, so it does not matter what tomorrow may bring (43–5 'cras…'): see *OLD uiuo* 7. *dixisse* is perhaps used for *dicere* (cf. 3.4.52 *imposuisse*), but may be intended to suggest the end of each day as seen from the viewpoint of tomorrow (cf. Sen. *Ep.* 12.9 'quisquis *dixit* "uixi" cotidie ad lucrum surgit' and contrast Ov. *Met.* 3.136–7 '*dici*que beatus | *ante* obitum nemo...debet').[148] For other exs. of the '*uixi* motif' see Pease on *Aen.* 4.653; for pregnant uses of *uiuere* in other tenses see e.g. Mart. 1.15.11–12 with Howell, 2.90.3 with C. A. Williams. *in diem* is a regular phrase = 'daily' (*OLD dies* 3b).

44 polum Pater occupato 'let the Father fill the sky with...' (*OLD polus* 2a, *occupo*¹ 8). The Father is Jupiter, the sky- and weather-god (e.g. 3.10.7–8n., 19–20n.); *occupato* is third-person fut. imperative.

45 sole puro 'bright sunshine' (*OLD purus* 6a).

45–6 non tamen irritum | quodcumque retro est efficiet 'but he will not make void whatever is behind' (the subject is Father Jupiter, continued from 44). For the association of the past with what is 'behind', as in *CIL* 8.10570 'per tot retro annos', see Bettini 121–33 ('Localizing Future and Past'), esp. 122–3. That the past cannot be undone is proverbial (Theogn. 583–4, Simon. 603/311P, Pind. *Ol.* 2.15–17, Plato, *Prot.* 324B, Arist. *Eth. Nic.* 6.2.6, Plin. *NH* 2.27; Otto 129–30). *irritum efficere*, again at e.g. Sen. *Ben.* 1.5.2, is a variant on the legal *irritum facere* (*OLD irritus* 1a).

46–8 neque | diffinget infectumque reddet | quod fugiens semel hora uexit 'nor will he re-shape or render undone that which the fleeting hour has once brought' (*-que* is here equivalent to *-ue*: cf. 3.2.28–9n.). H. had referred to 'the gifts of the present hour' (3.8.27 'dona praesentis... horae') in a previous ode to Maecenas, and this seems to be the meaning of *quod...uexit* here, with *hora* hinting perhaps at the Greek *Horai* or Seasons, who in their cycle 'always bring with them some gift' (Theocr. 15.105). But, just as the cycle of seasons is fixed (and hence the arrival of their gifts is assured), so the individual seasons slip by quickly (and the time of their gift-giving has passed); this latter thought, implied by *fugiens*, prepares for the transition to the changeableness of Fortune which follows (49–56). *diffingo* is found only in H. (again at 1.35.39 and perhaps *S.* 1.10.37).

49 Fortuna saeuo laeta negotio: adversative asyndeton: '<But> Fortune, delighting in her savage task...': the interlaced word order generates the

---

[148] The passage of Seneca is one reason for rejecting Vollmer's notion that the direct speech of line 43 is not restricted to *uixi* but continues to the end of the poem.

typically Horatian juxtaposition of *saeuo laeta* (see also 50n.). The savagery of Fortuna is commonplace (*TLL* 6.1.1183.3–5, 1187.61–2); for her *negotium* see e.g. Sen. *Tranq. an.* 8.7 'age tuum negotium, Fortuna', *Ep.* 98.14, Petron. 55.2 'Fortuna negotia curat'.

50 ludum insolentem ludere pertinax 'persistent at playing her arrogant game': *pertinax* is nowhere else constructed with an inf. (Intro. p. 25). For the 'game of Fortune' cf. 2.1.3 and N–H; *ludum* is a 'cognate' accus., as Ter. *Eun.* 586–7 'luserat...ludum' (*NLS* 8 §13 (i), G&L 210–11 §333.2), and generates a *figura etymologica* (Wills 243–8). Since *insolens* can also mean 'unaccustomed', there is a surreal contrast with *pertinax*.

51 transmutat incertos honores: the noun seems almost to mean 'favours' here (Quinn): '(she) switches her undependable honours/privileges', i.e. from one person to another (cf. N–H on 1.34.12–13). *transmutat*, an exceedingly rare verb evidently inherited from Lucretius (2.488), is explained by the next line.

52 nunc mihi, nunc alii benigna: cf. Pind. *Ol.* 7.11 'Charis [Kindness] looks favourably now on one man, now on another'. Fortuna is *benigna* again at Sen. *Cons. Marc.* 26.2.

53 laudo manentem: sc. *eam* (i.e. Fortune): 'I praise her when she stays [sc. with me].' The expr. *fortuna manet* recurs at Ov. *Tr.* 3.4.77, Petron. 80.9, and on the coinage of Commodus (*RIC* 3.427 no. 534); but perhaps H. was alluding to Lucr. 5.1121, a passage (1105–35) with which he was evidently familiar (see 3.3.49–52n.).

53–4 si celeris quatit | pennas: the verbs in this conditional sentence are present for future, a vivid usage normally considered colloquial (*NLS* 150 §194 (*a*)). For Fortune represented as winged cf. Curt. 7.8.25, Petron. 120.78, Fronto p. 155.1–3 vdH², Amm. 27.11.2. It is assumed that *celeris* qualifies *pennas*, but the point is not the speed at which Fortune flies but the suddenness with which she can take off. Adjs. expressing speed or slowness are often used adverbially: is it possible that *celeris* is nom. and that the meaning is 'if she is quick to flap her wings'? *quatio* is a regular word for flapping wings (*OLD* 1b); the deliberately light-hearted picture conceals the devastating effect that a change of fortune can have – a characteristically Horatian technique.

54 resigno quae dedit: *resigno*, again at *Ep.* 1.7.34, is apparently a financial term and means 'to enter as a debt' (*OLD* 2a). Some think that the meaning is 'hand over, give up' (*OLD* 2b), but that is already implied by Fortune's departure.

54–5 mea | uirtute me inuoluo 'I shall wrap myself in my own *uirtus*' (*mea* is emphatic), a metaphor said to be indebted to Plato, *Rep.* 457A '(the Guardians' women) will be clothed with *arete* instead of garments'; note too Varro, *Men.* 571 'non quaerenda est homini qui habet uirtutem paenula in imbri', Athen. 281d. As suitor to Poverty (55–6n.), H. will be attired as best he can. For the contrast with Fortuna see esp. Acc. *Trag.* 619–20R 'si a me regnum Fortuna atque opes | eripere quiuit, at uirtutem non quiit'.

55–6 probamque | Pauperiem sine dote quaero: *sine dote*, a regular expr. in comedy, indicates that H. is speaking in metaphorical terms of marriage: virtuous Poverty (the adj. is often used of women: *OLD probus* 4b) is a potential bride (for the verb cf. *Epi.* 1.2.44–5 'quaeritur...uxor'). Poverty, described as a sister at Alc. 364 and Petr. 84.4, is often personified (e.g. Theog. 267–70, 351–4, 649–52; Otto 268–9). For *pauperies/paupertas* see 3.2.1–3n.

57–64 In the last two stanzas H. deploys the metaphor of the 'voyage of life' (for which see e.g. C. W. Mendell, *CP* 33 (1938) 145–56, C. Bonner, *Harv. Theol. Rev.* 34 (1941) 49–67) in order to elaborate and emphasise the points made in the previous two stanzas (49–56). He contrasts two vessels caught in a storm (57–8, 62). The first, which is *not* applicable to him (57 'Non est meum'), is a rich merchantman carrying precious cargo which its owner-captain is desperate to save (58–61); this ship acts merely as a foil for the little skiff which represents H.'s life and which will carry him safely to his destination if a storm should strike (62–4). It is often thought that the two ships constitute a single image and that in the storm H. escapes the larger ship by means of a lifeboat (cf. Plaut. *Rud.* 75 'de naui timidae desiluerunt in scapham', 366); but it seems inconceivable that H. would wish to be associated with a rich merchantman, an image which is usually deployed to indicate greed and vice (cf. Davis 180–1). For other contrasts between types of vessel see *Epi.* 1.1.92–4 (and Cucchiarelli), 2.2.200–4 (and Brink).

57 non est meum... 'It is not in my character (to...)' (*OLD meus* 6).

57–8 si mugiat Africis | mālus procellis 'if the mast were to bellow in African gales': present subjunc. in a remote future condition, *non est meum...decurrere* being equivalent in meaning to 'I would not ~ ' in the apodosis. Gales from Africa were notorious (3.23.5–6n.); the verb suggests that *malus* is synecdochic and refers also to the sail attached to the mast (see also N–H on 1.14.6).

59 decurrere 'to have recourse to, descend to' (*OLD* 9). For *miseras preces* cf. Cic. *Att.* 3.19.2.

59–61 uotis pacisci | ne Cypriae Tyriaeque merces | addant auaro diuitias mari 'by means of vows to make a bargain [sc. with the gods] that goods from Cyprus and Tyre should not add their riches to the greedy sea': the *ne*-clause follows *pacisci* (*OLD paciscor* 3), whose application to a trader is pointed; for such prayers during a storm at sea see e.g. Watson on *Epo.* 10.18, Pease on Cic. *ND* 3.89. Cyprus was famous for its timber and copper (*OCD* 404), Tyre for its purple dye and garments (Mayor on Juv. 1.27). The sea is not elsewhere described as *auarus*, but for *auidus* cf. 1.28.18, Lucr. 1.1031.

62 tum 'in that event' (*OLD* 5a), i.e. if there were to be a storm. The MSS are divided between *tum* and *tunc*. Most edd., if not all, print *tunc*, presumably because it 'avoids the assonance with *tutum* and *tumultus*' (N–R); but the assonance is exactly in H.'s manner (Intro. p. 35). Cf. E. Courtney, '*Tum* and *Tunc*', *Prometheus* 29 (2003) 235–40.

62–4 me biremis praesidio scaphae | tutum per Aegaeos tumultus | aura feret geminusque Pollux 'a breeze from the twin Polluxes will carry me safely through the turbulent Aegean with the aid of my two-oared skiff' (almost a hendiadys): for the gods' ability to provide a magically soft breeze during a storm cf. Cat. 68B.63–5 'in nigro iactatis turbine nautis | lenius aspirans aura secunda uenit | iam prece Pollucis, iam Castoris implorata'. A *biremis scapha* is a one-person rowing boat (*OLD biremis*[1]) and thus manageable by H. alone; as *aura feret* implies, such boats would usually have a mast and sail as well as oars (Casson 329). *praesidium* is a prosaic word (see N–H on 1.1.2, where it is applied to Maecenas himself); *praesidio* + genit. can mean 'in the protection of' or 'with the aid of' (*OLD* 1c, 2a). The idiom whereby *gemino...muro* means 'twin walls' (Virg. *Aen.* 3.535) or *solem geminum* means 'twin suns' (ibid. 4.470) suggests that *geminus...Pollux* means 'the twin Polluxes', i.e. Castor and Pollux: it was apparently conventional for one name to stand for both (Serv. *G.* 3.89 'ambo libenter et Polluces et Castores uocantur'). Ovid repeats the idiom but applies it to Castor (*AA* 1.746): see also Bell 3ff., 64. For Aegean storms see 2.16.1 and N–H.

30

It stands to reason that authors will give careful thought to how a work or collection should end. Book 1 concluded with a two-stanza ode (38) which embodies H.'s characteristic technique of diminuendo. In the final ode of Book 2 (20) the poet will avoid death by being transformed into a swan, preparing to fly to far-distant lands where his lyric poetry will be read (see Harrison ad loc.). Since the last ode in Book 3 serves as the conclusion not only to the book but also to the collection as a whole, there is an expectation of climax in terms of both content and presentation – more expansive claims, more arresting expression.

Ancient poets often took advantage of the closural device known as the 'seal' or σφραγίς. This would be a few lines, or perhaps a complete poem, in which they identified themselves by means of some personal details (often including their name) and said something about the nature of their poetry (see e.g. N–H on 2.20 intro. (p. 335), Harder on Callim. *Aetia* 112 (p. 856); *BNP* 13.735). The standard Latin example is the final paragraph of Virgil's *Georgics* (4.559–66). The present ode, despite the pointed omission of the poet's name, includes many of the conventional elements of a *sphragis*, as is generally recognised, but H. has combined them strikingly with the metaphor of the *monumentum* which he announces in the very first line: the three books of odes are his memorial or grave-monument, and the present ode is the epitaph inscribed thereon (see esp. Korzeniewski; *PH* 86–9).

The ode falls into three main parts: description of the *monumentum* (1–5), H.'s future fame (6–14a), concluding prayer to the Muse (14b–16). The first two of these are themselves triadic: 1–5 three descriptions (*perennius, altius, quod*); 6–14a three statements of increasing length (6–7a, 7b–9, 10–14a). Lines 1–14a are also loosely chiastic: the description of the *monumentum* turns into a prediction of its future (1–5), while H.'s future (6–12a) is based on his poetic achievement (12b–14a), which is his *monumentum*. Lines 1–5 juxtapose Roman and Egyptian monuments (1–2) and allude memorably to the Greek lyrics of Pindar (2n., 3–4n.). Lines 6–14a begin at one of the most famous places in Rome, the symbolic Capitol, where the silent Vestal climbs upward in haunting perpetuity; they end at the roaring River Aufidus, the poet's birthplace, the genesis of his fame as 'numerosus Horatius' (Ov. *Tr.* 4.10.49), Italy's metrical master. He is not unnaturally proud of his achievement, but his pride is complemented by gratitude to the Muse, Melpomene (14b–16).

The brilliance of this final ode is such that it was immediately imitated by Propertius (3.2.17–26) and Ovid (*Met.* 15.871–9), and it enjoys a fame which has lasted into modern times (*PH* 102–3, N–R 367).

COMMENTARY 30.1-2

METRE First Asclepiad. The only other ode in Books 1-3 in this metre is 1.1, so the collection has a metrical 'frame'. See also Intro. 7.

1 Exegi monumentum aere perennius: the noun *monumentum*, associated etymologically with both *memoria* and *monere* (Maltby 392), accommodated itself easily to H.'s sepulchral metaphor (see intro.) since it could be used of monuments, memorials and tombs (see *OLD*) and written records, books, and literature (see *TLL* 8.1464.28-1465.23). Compare the 4th-cent. AD Themistius (*Or.* 4.59D): 'books and writings are the tombs of these spirits'. *aere* does not mean that H. envisages a bronze memorial; the point of the comparison is that bronze was famous for its durability and hence was the Romans' preferred medium for the display of official texts (cf. Plin. *NH* 34.99 'usus aeris ad perpetuitatem monumentorum iam pridem tralatus est tabulis aereis, in quibus publicae constitutiones inciduntur'; C. Williamson, 'Monuments of bronze: Roman legal documents on bronze tablets', *CA* 6 (1987) 160-83). Some grave-monuments could carry a bronze inscription, as in the case of Augustus' Mausoleum.

Although *exigo* had been used before H. of 'finishing off' (e.g. a marble slab), seemingly it had not had a whole building as its object before our passage, where the 'building' is metaphorical. After our passage the meaning 'to perfect' becomes common (e.g. Ov. *RA* 811, *Met.* 15.871-2) and is used of the refinement expected of the Callimachean poet (Prop. 3.1.8 'exactus tenui pumice uersus eat'): see Brink on *Epi.* 2, App. 5, pp. 421-4. The combination of first-person past-tense verb with *monumentum* evokes sepulchral inscriptions such as *hoc monumentum feci* (*CLE* 127.2) or *monumentum apsolui* (*CLE* 89.3); sometimes epitaphs declare that the tomb will last for ever (e.g. *CLE* 467.1 'Aeternam tibi sedem...dicaui'; Korzeniewski 385): H. goes one better by changing *perennis*, which is used of literary longevity by Cat. 1.10, Lucr. 1.118 and Stat. *Silv.* 5.1.12 and has an 'implication of immortality' (*OLD* 3b), into an oxymoronic comparative. When Ovid picks up H.'s phrase and applies it to constellations, he reverts to the positive (*F.* 2.265 'antiqui monumenta perennia facti').

2 regalique situ pyramidum aptius: I have discussed the numerous problems in this line, which as transmitted reads not *aptius* but *altius*, in Woodman (2021), the main points of which are summarised here. (a) Some think that *situ* means 'decay' (*OLD situs*³), support for which is sought in Simonides' famous poem on the dead at Thermopylae (531.4-5/261P), in which a burial (ἐντάφιον), because metaphorical, will not be destroyed by physical decay (εὐρώς): see e.g. Harrison (2001) 263-4. But not only is it no compliment to compare a monument to a decayed ruin, but the pyramids were known to be 'undecayed' in H.'s day (Diod. 1.63.5). We need a parallel with line 1, where the whole point of *monumentum aere perennius* is that bronze resists decay. (b) Others (e.g. Syndikus 2.260, N–R) think that *situ* means 'site' (*OLD situs*² 1). A reference to 'the royal site of the pyramids' makes excellent sense in itself: the Giza pyramids were sited with remarkable precision according to astronomical principles (see P. A. Clayton, 'The Great Pyramid of Giza', in *The Seven Wonders of the Ancient World* (ed. P. A. Clayton and M. Price, 1990) 21), and the Giza burial site, almost a square mile in area, was the most impressive site of memory in the ancient world. Yet a comparison with 'the royal site of the pyramids' makes little sense of the transmitted *altius*, since the point about the pyramids is not that they occupy a conspicuously high site but that they themselves are famously high (Prop. 3.2.19, Plin. *NH* 36.75–82, Tac. *A.* 2.61.1): the Great Pyramid at Giza is in fact two-and-a-half times the height of the plateau on which it stands.[149] (c) A further problem with *altius* is that, however suitable it may be to describe a grave-monument, it is far from suitable to describe the poetry for which the *monumentum* is a metaphor. Such meanings as 'elevated, noble, lofty' (*OLD* 13b) are hardly an appropriate description for a collection which includes repeated invitations to sex and drink and which the poet himself elsewhere characterises as 'playthings', the product of a 'light-hearted lyre' (3.3.69 'iocosae...lyrae'; cf. *Epi.* 1.1.10 'ludicra').

altus and *aptus* are variant readings at Prop. 3.22.42 and Ov. *Am.* 3.1.14, *F.* 2.216, *Ibis* 212. Although the manuscripts at Lucr. 6.357 are unanimous in transmitting *alta*, the poet's evident allusion to an Ennian phrase (*Ann.* 27, 145, 348) means that Turnebus was almost certainly right to emend *alta* to *apta*. At *Aen.* 1.429 the manuscripts again transmit *alta*, but, since the same word appears in the same *sedes* two lines earlier, one of them is likely to be an error; Bentley emended the second *alta* to *apta*, which is printed by Mynors and Austin. Is it possible that H. wrote *aptius* rather than *altius*? It is generally accepted that in lines 3–4 (see below) H. is alluding to Pind. *Pyth.* 6.7–14:

ἑτοῖμος ὕμνων
θησαυρὸς ἐν πολυχρύσῳ
Ἀπολλωνίᾳ τετείχισται νάπᾳ·

<u>τὸν οὔτε</u> χειμέριος <u>ὄμβρος</u>, ἐπακτὸς ἐλθών
ἐριβρόμου νεφέλας
στρατὸς ἀμείλιχος, <u>οὔτ' ἄνεμος</u> ἐς μυχούς
ἁλὸς ἄξοισι παμφόρῳ χεράδει τυπτόμενον.

---

[149] According to *OLD* (*situs*² 2) Horace's meaning is 'structure', but there is no parallel.

a ready treasure house of hymns has been built in Apollo's valley rich in gold, one which neither winter rain, coming from abroad as a relentless army from a loudly rumbling cloud, nor wind shall buffet and with their deluge of silt carry into the depths of the sea. (Loeb trans., slightly adapted)

Since Pindar describes his 'treasure house of hymns' as ἑτοῖμος ('ready'), there must be a strong likelihood that H. described his *monumentum* of odes as *aptius*, which regularly means 'ready' (*OLD* 5). Here, however, the adj. will mean 'better adapted to its purpose' (i.e. as a memorial), for which see Pease on Cic. *ND* 2.47. H.'s paradoxical point is that, despite the fame of the pyramids, there was no agreement about which kings they commemorated (Plin. *NH* 36.79 'inter omnes non constat a quibus factae sint, iustissimo casu obliteratis tantae uanitatis auctoribus'). *uanitas* means 'futility, pointlessness' as well as 'foolish pride' (*OLD* 1c, 2b). H.'s *monumentum* will succeed where the world's most famous necropolis had failed. Moreover *aptus*, unlike *altus*, is frequently used in literary criticism and has a wide variety of applications: in particular it is one of the terms used to express the key virtue of τὸ πρέπον, 'appropriateness' (Lausberg 117–18 §258, 460–4 §§1055–62).

It is striking that an Egyptian papyrus of c. 1200 BC says of ancient scribes that 'their teachings are their pyramids' (quoted in N–R 366): it is possible that H.'s comparison came to him through some now lost Alexandrian intermediary. Quite apart from its economic value to the Romans, Egypt had always been a source of cultural and intellectual interest (cf. V. A. Foertmeyer, 'Tourism in Graeco-Roman Egypt' (diss. Princeton, 1989) 104–256). Augustus' Mausoleum – which began to be built in the late 30s – is thought to have been inspired in part by the pyramids (*PH* 181–2), and the *princeps* had two Egyptian obelisks placed on either side of its entrance (Amm. 17.4.16). In 26 BC attention may have been directed specifically at the pyramids because the poet Cornelius Gallus as first prefect of the new province of Egypt is said to have inscribed his achievements on them (Dio 53.23.5) and been compelled to commit suicide (cf. B. J. Gibson, *CQ* 47 (1997) 312–14). Whatever H.'s motivation, he was no doubt aware of the well-known fact that the Giza necropolis consists of three vast pyramids (cf. e.g. Strabo 17.1.33, Plin. *NH* 36.76, Mela 1.55), the 'magic' number suggesting the three books of *Odes*.[150] A decade after the publication of the *Odes* a substantial pyramidal tomb

---

[150] The necropolis also includes two sets of three much smaller pyramids, making three triads in all.

monument, faced in marble, was constructed at the Porta Ostiensis in Rome for the former praetor C. Cestius (see Toynbee, plate 33), while at Ostia there is a miniature pyramidal tomb for one C. Annaeus Atticus from Gaul (Toynbee 102–3).

3–4 quod non imber edax, non Aquilo impotens | possit diruere: scholars are reminded of Pindar, *Pyth.* 6.7–14 (see above, 2n.), where also there are a relative clause, double negative, and pairing of the same two elements. *diruere* is not commonly found with *monumentum* (only Liv. 31.30.5, Suet. *Dom.* 8.5); *possit* is a subjunctive of characteristic in a rel. clause ('the like of which...cannot destroy') and explains the reason why H.'s *monumentum* is superior to bronze and the pyramid complex. *impotens*, seemingly rare of natural forces (*OLD* 3c), helps to personify the wind (cf. 3.27.2on.): here the primary meaning is 'out of control', but *impotens* is an autantonym and also has the opposite meaning of 'powerless' (*OLD* 1), which, since the wind is ineffective, comes to be activated proleptically.

4–5 innumerabilis | annorum series et fuga temporum: perhaps enallage: 'the succession of countless years and the flight of time'. For *annorum series* cf. Ov. *Ex P.* 4.12.21, Colum. 3.10.6, 4.19.1; for *innumerabilis* of time cf. e.g. Muc. Scaev. 1C/91H 'canescet saeclis innumerabilibus' (on the immortality of Cicero's poem *Marius*): on the expr. see Feeney in Rudd (1993) 57–9 (= *OR* 227–9). For *fuga temporum* (*-is*) cf. Colum. 11.1.29, Sen. *Brev. vit.* 9.3; it is a paradox that time 'can destroy by running away' (N–R).

6–7 non omnis moriar multaque pars mei | uitabit Libitinam 'Not all of me will die: a significant part of me will avoid Libitina' (the goddess of funerals: cf. Varro, *LL* 6.47, Plut. *Numa* 12.1–2): *-que* is epexegetic (*OLD* 6a). The immortality of the *Odes* is the reason why not all of H. will die; his poetry is part of him, a conceit which modulates to *ego* in 7–8 (n.): cf. 2.20.6–8 'non ego...obibo | nec Stygia cohibebor unda'. A grave-monument carries, in its epitaph, only the name of the deceased (cf. Laber. 91.27P/124R (p. 360) 'sepulcri similis nil nisi nomen retineo'); H.'s epitaph does not record his name, because his decease will not be absolute: he will survive in his *Odes*, by which he will be identified. Claims of poetic immortality go back at least as far as Sappho (147, 193; cf. 55); likewise various expressions of immortal memory feature in epitaphs (R. Lattimore, *Themes in Greek and Latin Epitaphs* (1942) 243–6). H. is echoed by Ovid (*Am.* 1.15.41–2 'ergo etiam cum me supremus adederit ignis, | uiuam, parsque mei multa superstes erit', *Met.* 15.875–6 'parte tamen meliore mei super alta perennis | astra ferar').

COMMENTARY 30.7-10 377

7-8 usque...dum...: *usque* (*OLD* 4b) is correlative with *dum* (*NLS* 177-8 §219): 'for exactly as long as...'.

ego postera | crescam laude recens: the expr. is often compared with Virg. *Ecl.* 7.25 'hedera crescentem [*v.l.* nascentem] ornate poetam', but the meaning there is 'developing, advancing' (as Quint. 1.2.30 'laude crescit et impetu augetur', of the *animus*). Our passage seems to be equivalent to *recenti posterorum laude crescam*, 'I shall grow with the praise of posterity ever fresh': *recens*, regular of fresh memories (*OLD* 5), has been transferred to the subject of the verb; and the growth is not that of the poet but of the praise (as Nep. *Cato* 2.4 'quoad uixit, uirtutum laude creuit'; cf. Hor. *Epi.* 2.2.101 'cognomine crescit'). H. means that, as each future generation encounters his poetry, they will praise it/him afresh, and the praise will therefore accumulate over time. Cf. *CLE* 1552.41-3 'sciat hic tantam faciem superesse sepulchri | perpetua nouitate sui, sic stare nitentes | consensus lapidum...' (= Courtney, *ML* No. 199A). *ego* seems to continue the conceit of 6-7 (n.) but also prepares for the first-person *dicar* of 10, which can only refer to the poet himself. The association of *postera* with *recens* is a typically Horatian oxymoron.

8-9 dum Capitolium | scandet cum tacita Virgine pontifex: the *pontifices* constituted the most important priestly college, and the Pontifex Maximus, who in H.'s day was the former triumvir M. Aemilius Lepidus (cos. 46, 42 BC), had supervision of the six Vestal Virgins (see Rüpke 7). H.'s evocative image has caused puzzlement, but, since it is known that the *pontifices* made a calendrical announcement on the Capitol on the first day of each month (Varro, *LL* 6.27), J. G. F. Powell in an unpublished paper has suggested that this is the ritual to which H. refers. The 'regular, predictable and frequent ritual...could easily be seen as a symbol of the eternity of Rome', and, since Augustus was himself a *pontifex* and no doubt took part in the ritual from time to time, H.'s reference 'is surely also a compliment to Augustus'. For the eternity of Rome (3.5.11n.) as symbolised by the Capitol (3.3.42-3n.) note esp. Virg. *Aen.* 9.446-9 'Fortunati ambo! si quid mea carmina possunt, | nulla dies umquam memori uos eximet aeuo, | dum domus Aeneae Capitoli immobile saxum | accolet imperiumque pater Romanus habebit'; also Amm. 22.16.12. It was a commonplace that empires and cities fall as well as rise (e.g. Vell. 2.11.3), but such thoughts are inappropriate here.

10 dicar is to be taken with *deduxisse* below (14). Perhaps another epitaphic feature (Prop. 4.11.36 'in lapide hoc uni nupta fuisse legar', *CLE* 1038.6 'diceris coniunxs una fuisse uiri'; compare the *sphragis* at Theogn.

22 'everyone will say this'); but, although post-Callimachean poets sought to appeal especially to a learned and elite readership (3.1.1n.), more general approval was required if one wanted, as did H. (1.1.35), to join a literary canon (R. Mayer, *PLLS* 8 (1995) 291–2). Aristotle maintained that 'the general public is a better judge of the works...of the poets' (*Pol.* 3.6.4; cf. 3.10.5), and H. himself admitted that 'interdum uulgus rectum uidet' (*Epi.* 2.1.63 and Brink).

10–12 qua uiolens obstrepit Aufidus | et qua pauper aquae Daunus agrestium | regnauit populorum: the river Aufidus (mod. Ofanto), which rises in the Apennines, flows through Apulia before debouching into the Adriatic just east of Cannae (*BA* Map 45: C2–D2); Daunus was a legendary king of Apulia and father-in-law of Diomedes. If readers couple this information with the explicit reference to Apulia at 3.4.9–16, they will infer correctly that the *qua*-clauses allude to H.'s birthplace (cf. 4.9.2 'longe sonantem natus ad Aufidum'). Cf. also 4.14.25–6. It was conventional to designate inhabitants by reference to their local river: see 3.10.1–2n.

Scholars have disputed keenly whether the *qua*-clauses are to be taken with *dicar* (10) or with *deduxisse* (14). The fatal objection to the latter is that H.'s poetic career was not spent in his birthplace but in Rome. Fraenkel rightly supports the former by noting (305) that numerous Latin authors refer to local pride in their achievements (Cic. *Planc.* 20, Prop. 4.1.63–4, Ov. *Am.* 3.15.7–8, Mart. 1.61.1–2), a pride which therefore presupposes widespread fame. See also 11–12n. below. West, noting that *obstrepere* can mean 'to protest against' (*OLD* 3), suggests that H. humorously sees the Aufidus as disagreeing with the local verdict.

11 pauper aquae: Apulia's notorious lack of water (*Epo.* 3.16 'siticulosae Apuliae', with Watson) seems oddly juxtaposed with the Aufidus, yet Canusium was situated on the Aufidus (Mela 2.66 'adtingens Aufidum') and evidently suffered from a poor supply of water (*S.* 1.5.91). The paradox of Apulia was typified by (and perhaps had its origin in?) its coastal wetlands, where the water was plentiful but unhealthy and presumably undrinkable (Vitr. 1.4.12 'umores graues et pestilentes'). *pauper* + genit. is first in H. (*S.* 1.1.79, 2.3.142) and almost exclusive to him (*TLL* 10.1.848.4–9).

11–12 agrestium | regnauit populorum: since there was an antithesis between rusticity and modern, post-Callimachean, poetry (cf. L. Watson, *PLLS* 6 (1990) 13–33), there is an implied contrast between H.'s local contemporaries, who can appreciate his achievement (10–12n.), and their unqualified ancestors. Cf. also *Epi.* 2.1.157 'agresti Latio'. The unique *regnare* + genit., modelled on the Greek ἄρχω or βασιλεύω, is 'a syntactic reflection of the fusion of Italian and Greek in the final quatrain of the ode' (Coleman 81).

12 ex humili potens 'powerful from <having been> lowly' (*OLD ex* 13). Social or professional advancement is a common theme in epitaphs (Korzeniewski 386 and n. 25), e.g. *ex paruo creuit*, proposed by Trimalchio for his own epitaph (Petron. 71.12). H. was proud of his humble origins, which at 2.20.5-6 ('ego pauperum | sanguis parentum') he contrasts with his friendship with the powerful Maecenas; one might have expected a similar contrast here (for *humilis/potens* elsewhere cf. Phaedr. 1.30.1, Vell. 126.3), but, if so, it is only hinted at in *humili* by contrast. *potens*, which 'seems to have been fertile ground for punning – "powerful" in its different connotations' (Brink on *AP* 289–90 'potentius...linguā'), here refers to a capability in poetry (as 4.8.26–7 'lingua potentium | uatum', Hygin. *Fab.* 194.1 'arte citharae potens', Mart. 9.86.2; *TLL* 10.1.278.62–3, 284.8–22).

13-14 princeps Aeolios carmen ad Italum | deduxisse modos: in pre-archaic times the island of Lesbos had been settled by colonists from Aeolia on the west coast of Asia Minor: 'Aeolian' is thus synonymous with 'Lesbian' and refers to Sappho and Alcaeus, who both came from the island of Lesbos. *Aeolium carmen* in the transmitted text will thus mean, as it does again at 4.3.12,[151] the poetry of Sappho and Alcaeus, and H. will be claiming that he composed Aeolian/Lesbian poetry to Italian metres ('ad Italos...modos'). The problem with this claim, as everyone has recognised, is that it is the opposite of the truth: the metres that H. uses 'are not "Italian" but Greek' (Page). The only way of retaining the transmitted text is to assume that *carmen*, which means 'poetry', refers to metres and that *modos*, which means 'metres', refers to poetry.[152] This explanation, though adopted by N–R and others (e.g. *PH* 98 n. 44), seems completely counter-intuitive. In 1840 J. D. Fuss proposed transposing the cases (*Aeolios... Italum*), thereby resolving the problem at a stroke, but his proposal sank without trace until D. Kovacs came up with the same transposition independently (*CQ* 65 (2015) 682–8, including a full and convincing defence of the resulting word order). The hypothesis is that a scribe mistakenly assimilated the cases of the adjs. to the nearest nouns. On the emended text, as printed here, the process is exactly the same as that described at

---

[151] Cf. also Pind. *Ol.* 1.102 Αἰοληΐδι μολπᾷ ('Aeolic song').
[152] Collinge was reduced to suggesting 'double hypallage' (32 n. 1), i.e. taking *Aeolium* and *Italos* as if they referred to *modos* and *carmen* respectively.

1.32.3-4, where H. addresses the lyre of Alcaeus: 'dic *Latinum*, | barbite, *carmen*'.

In defence of the paradosis it should be acknowledged that *carmen deducere* is a regular expression, although its meaning varies depending on context (e.g. *AP* 129 'rectius Iliacum carmen deducis in actus', Virg. *Ecl.* 6.5, Prop. 1.16.41, Ov. *Met.* 1.4, *Tr.* 1.1.39). The meaning of the transmitted text here has been much debated. (1) Some think *deduxisse* = 'to have adapted' (cf. *TLL* 5.1.282.3-27, but not quoting our passage). (2) Many scholars have seen a reference to a triumph (cf. 1.37.31-2 'deduci... triumpho', Virg. *G.* 3.10-11 'primus ego in patriam me cum, modo uita supersit, | Aonio rediens *deducam* uertice Musas'; *OLD* 10a). (3) Perhaps the commonest preference has been 'to spin': not only is spinning a regular metaphor for composing poetry (e.g. *S.* 2.1.3-4) but *deducere* in this sense is used esp. of the Callimachean artistry expected of late-republican and Augustan poets (Virg. *Ecl.* 6.5 'deductum dicere carmen'; Brink on *AP* 224-5): in this case *ad* will perhaps have the sense of 'so as to produce' (*OLD* 46).[153] None of these possible meanings is clearly incompatible with the emended text, and a combination of (1) and (2) is tempting: 'to have adapted Aeolian metres triumphantly to Italian song'; certainly the upcoming references to *superbia* (cf. 1.35.3-4 'superbos...triumphos', 1.37.1-2 'superbo...triumpho') and laurel (cf. 3.14.2n.) suggest that (2) cannot be excluded.

princeps here is adjectival, 'first' (*OLD princeps*¹ 1), as again at 3.17.7, *Epi.* 1.19.21 'libera per uacuum posui uestigia princeps'. Claims of originality, a feature of epitaphs (e.g. *CLE* 427.11 'primus qui talia gessi'), were regularly made by ancient poets (the so-called '*primus*-motif': for many exs. see N–H on 1.26.6 and 10), which in the case of Latin poets often meant priority in introducing a Greek genre to Rome, as in our passage and *Epi.* 1.19.23-4 'Parios ego primus iambos | ostendi Latio'. See further Intro. 31-4.

14-15 sume superbiam | quaesitam meritis: for a *sphragis* incorporating a prayer see esp. the so-called 'seal' of Posidippus (118 A–B): see H. Lloyd-Jones, *JHS* 73 (1963) 92-3, 96. *superbiam* is explained by the achievement mentioned in the previous lines (esp. 13-14, if there is a reference there to a triumph: see n.); but are the *merita* those of Melpomene or of H.? Taken by themselves, the words *sume...meritis* suggest the former: 'the pride should really be yours, since it was thanks to you that I achieved

---

[153] Numerous scholars have sought an analogy in the expressions *deducere coloniam* or *colonos*, but none of the examples seems constructed with *ad* (*TLL* 5.1.273.27-80).

poetic eminence'. But the words are co-ordinated with a request for a victor's crown (15–16), which, despite the acknowledgement of Melpomene at 4.3.21–4, comes oddly after an admission that H.'s achievements were all the Muse's doing. Besides, the expression (*pro*) *meritis* is regularly used of the deceased in epitaphs (e.g. *CLE* 423.5, 467.7; Korzeniewski 387 and n. 32). But the decision is a difficult one. For *quaero* = 'to obtain as a result of one's efforts', as Prop. 3.2.25 'ingenio quaesitum nomen', see *OLD* 7a, quoting our passage.

15–16 et mihi Delphica | lauro cinge uolens, Melpomene, comam: 'Delphic laurel' was evidently a recognised species of laurel (Cato, *RR* 133.2), but here the name cannot fail to evoke the oracle of Delphi, the athletic and artistic contests that were held there (the Pythian Games), and the presiding god, Apollo (cf. Lucr. 6.154 'Phoebi Delphica laurus'). Scholars have noticed that Pindar's collection of Olympian Odes ends with the word 'hair' in the accusative case, governed by the verb 'crowned' (*Ol.* 14.24 ἐστεφάνωσε ...χαίταν), corresponding to *cinge*... *comam* here: in Pindar the hair is that of the Olympic victor, but in H.'s ode the victor and the poet are one and the same. An allusion to Pindar, 'laurea donandus Apollinari' (4.2.9) and already imitated at the start of the ode (2n.), is doubly appropriate, since victory in the Olympian Games opened Book 1 of the *Odes* (1.1.3). Since laurel was also used to crown *triumphatores* at Rome (3.14.2n.), some scholars, pointing out that *deduxisse* above can have triumphal associations (13–14n.), have argued that H. also sees himself as a Roman general celebrating a triumph (A. Hardie, *Stud. Class.* 21 (1983) 49–57): this perhaps requires *Delphica* to be understood more loosely, 'Apolline' (see Miller 310–12 and n. 32).

16 uolens 'if you are willing': the word, analogous to the Greek θέλων (Fraenkel on Aesch. *Ag.* 664), is usually found alongside *propitius*; the present passage seems unique (Appel 122–3). Cf. 3.22.6n.

Melpomene, comam: ring composition with the very first ode, where he had mentioned Euterpe and Polyhymnia and the crown of his head (1.1.33, 36). In later antiquity Melpomene came to be regarded as the muse of tragedy; H. is using the name generically, as again in his thanks to her at 4.3.1 (see Thomas). For *coma* see 3.14.25n.; in Lygdamus' poetic collection (6.64) *comas* likewise comes at the end.

SELECT BIBLIOGRAPHY

THE *ODES*: EDITIONS, COMMENTARIES, TRANSLATIONS

The following have been consulted:

Bennett, C. E. (1914). London/New York
Bo, D. (1958–60). Turin etc. [Vols. 1 and 3]
Campbell, A. Y. (1945). Liverpool/London *and* (1953). Liverpool
Fedeli, P. and Ciccarelli, I. (2008). Florence [Book 4 only]
Goold, G. P. (1977). Groton
Gow, J. (1906 [1st edn 1896]). Cambridge
Harrison, S. J. (2018). Cambridge [Book 2 only]
Jani, C. D. (1778–82). Leipzig
Keller, O. and Holder, A. (2nd edn 1899). Leipzig
Kiessing, A. and Heinze, R. (11th edn 1964). Zurich/Berlin
Klingner, F. (1959). Leipzig
Macleane, A. J. (1881). London
Mayer, R. G. (2012). Cambridge [Book 1 only]
Moore, C. H. (1902). New York/Cincinnati/Chicago
Nisbet, R. G. M. and Hubbard, M. (1970, 1978). Oxford [Books 1–2 only]
Nisbet, R. G. M. and Rudd, N. (2004). Oxford [Book 3 only]
Orelli, J. C. (3rd edn 1850). Zurich
Page, T. E. (1895 [1st edn 1893]). Repr. London/Basingstoke
Peerlkamp, P. H. (1834). Haarlem
Quinn, K. (1980). Walton on Thames
Rudd, N. (2004). Cambridge, MA/London
Shackleton Bailey, D. R. (1985, ⁴2001). Stuttgart
Shorey, P. (1909 [1st edn 1898]). Boston
Thomas, R. F. (2011). Cambridge [Book 4 and *CS* only]
Vollmer, F. (1907). Leipzig
West, D. (1998–2002). Oxford
Wickham, E. C. (3rd edn 1896). Oxford
Williams, G. (1969). Oxford [Book 3 only]

I have referred freely to standard commentaries on other texts but without providing bibliographical details here.

OTHER WORKS

As a general rule, works are referred to by author's name and page-number only. Where an author is responsible for several works, these are distinguished either by an abbreviated title or by date. Where reference is given to a reprinted work, full details of the original publication will be found in the following list.

Adams, J. N. (1982). *The Latin Sexual Vocabulary*. London
Appel, G. (1909). *De Romanorum precationibus*. Giessen
Arkenberg, J. S. (1993). 'Licinii Murenae, Terentii Varrones, and Varrones Murenae: 1. A prosopographical study of three Roman families', *Historia* 42.326–51
Axelson, B. (1945). *Unpoetische Wörter*. Lund
Barber, D. T. (2010). 'Speaker and Addressee in Horace's *Odes*', Diss. University of Virginia
Barchiesi, A. (2009). 'Lyric in Rome', *CCGL* 319–35
(2009). 'Rituals in ink: Horace on the Greek lyric tradition', *OR* 418–40 (= M. Depew and D. Obbink (edd.), *Matrices of Genres: Authors, Canons, and Society* (Cambridge, MA 2000) 167–82)
Barrett, A. A. (2002). *Livia: First Lady of Imperial Rome*. New Haven
Battezzato, L. (2009). 'Metre and music', *CCGL* 130–46
Beard, M. (2007). *The Roman Triumph*. Cambridge, MA/London
Bell, A. J. (1923). *The Latin Dual and Poetic Diction*. London/Toronto
Bettini, M. (1991). *Anthropology and Roman Culture. Kinship, Time, Images of the Soul*. Baltimore
Bo, D. (1960). *Q. Horati Flacci Opera*. Vol. 3 *Indices*. Turin etc.
Bradshaw, A. (2002). 'Horace's birthday and deathday', *TC* 1–16
Bremmer, J. N. (2014). *Initiation into the Mysteries of the Ancient World*. Berlin/Boston
Brink, C. O. (1982). 'Horatian notes III', *PCPS* 28.30–56
Cairns, F. (1972). *Generic Composition in Greek and Roman Poetry*. Edinburgh [*GC*]
(2006). *Sextus Propertius. The Augustan Elegist*. Cambridge [*SP*]
(2007). *Papers on Roman Elegy 1969–2003*. Bologna [*PRE*]
(2012). *Roman Lyric. Collected Papers on Catullus and Horace*. Berlin/Boston [*RL*]
Casson, L. (1971). *Ships and Seamanship in the Ancient World*. Rev. edn. Princeton

Citroni, M. (2007). 'Occasion and levels of address in Horatian lyric', *OR* 72–105 (= 'Occasione e piani di destinazione nella lirica di Orazio', *MD* 10–11 (1983) 133–214)
Coleman, R. G. G. (1999). 'Poetic diction, poetic discourse and the poetic register', in J. N. Adams and R. G. Mayer (edd.), *Aspects of the Language of Latin Poetry* (*PBA* 93) 21–93. Oxford
Collinge, N. E. (1961). *The Structure of Horace's Odes*. London
Commager, S. (1962). *The Odes of Horace. A Critical Study*. Bloomington
Cooley, A. E. (2009). *Res Gestae Divi Augusti: Text, Translation, and Commentary*. Cambridge
Copley, F. O. (1956). *Exclusus amator: A Study in Latin Love Poetry*. Ann Arbor
Courtney, E. (1995). *Musa Lapidaria: A Selection of Latin Verse Inscriptions*. Atlanta [*ML*]
—— (2001). *A Companion to Petronius*. Oxford [*Companion*]
—— (2003). *The Fragmentary Latin Poets*. Rev. edn. Oxford [*FLP*]
—— (2016). 'Three passages in Horace's *Odes*', *MH* 73.42–6
Crawford, M. H. (1996). *Roman Statutes*. Vols. 1–2. London
Crowther, N. B. (1979). 'Water and wine as symbols of inspiration', *Mnem.* 32.1–11
D'Arms, J. H. (1970). *Romans on the Bay of Naples*. Cambridge, MA
Dauge, Y. A. (1981). *Le barbare*. Brussels
Davis, G. (1991). *Polyhymnia: The Rhetoric of Horatian Lyric Discourse*. Berkeley/Los Angeles/Oxford
Dickey, E. (2002). *Latin Forms of Address*. Oxford
Dunbabin, K. M. D. (1993). 'Wine and water at the Roman *convivium*', *JRA* 6.116–41
Du Quesnay, I. M. Le M. (1981). 'Vergil's First *Eclogue*', *PLLS* 3.29–182
—— (1984). 'Horace and Maecenas', in A. J. Woodman and D. West (edd.), *Poetry and Politics in the Age of Augustus* 19–58 and 200–11. Cambridge
—— (1995). 'Horace, *Odes* 4.5', *HH* 128–87 (= *OR* 271–336)
—— (2002). '*Amicus certus in re incerta cernitur*: Epode 1', *TC* 17–37 and 195–210
Edwards, C. (1993). *The Politics of Immorality in Ancient Rome*. Cambridge
Erskine, A. (2001). *Troy between Greece and Rome: Local Tradition and Imperial Power*. Oxford/New York
Evans, C. (2016). 'Time in the *Odes* of Horace.' Diss. University of Virginia
Feeney, D. C. (1984). 'The reconciliations of Juno', *CQ* 34.179–94
—— (2007). *Caesar's Calendar*. Berkeley/Los Angeles/London
—— (2009). 'Horace and the Greek lyric poets', *OR* 202–31 (= Rudd (1993) 41–63)
—— (2011). '*Hic finis fandi*: On the absence of punctuation for the endings (and beginnings) of speeches in Latin poetic texts', *MD* 66.45–91

Flower, H. I. (2017). *The Dancing Lares and the Serpent in the Garden*. Princeton/Oxford
Fraenkel, E. (1957). *Horace*. Oxford
Giangrande, G. (1969). 'Sympotic literature and epigram', in *L'épigramme grecque* 93–177. Vandoeuvres/Geneva
Griffin, J. (1985). *Latin Poets and Roman Life*. London
Grimm, J. C. M. (1928). *The Construction ΑΠΟ ΚΟΙΝΟΥ in the Works of Horace*. Philadelphia
Hardie, A. (2008, 2009). 'An Augustan hymn to the Muses', *PLLS* 13.55–118, 14.191–317
— (2016). 'The Camenae in cult, history and song', *CA* 35.45–85
Hardie, P. (1986). *Virgil's Aeneid: Cosmos and Imperium*. Oxford
Harrison, S. J. (1988). 'A tragic Europa? Horace, Odes 3.27', *Hermes* 116.427–34
— (2001). 'Simonides and Horace', in D. Boedeker and D. Sider (edd.), *The New Simonides* 261–71. Oxford
— (2007). *Generic Enrichment in Vergil and Horace*. Oxford
— (2007). 'Town and country', *CCH* 235–47
Heinze, R. (2009). 'The Horatian ode', *OR* 11–32 (= 'Die horazische Ode', *NJ* 51 (1923) 153–68)
Heyworth, S. J. (1995). 'Dividing poems', in O. Pecere and M. D. Reeve (edd.), *Formative Stages of Classical Traditions: Latin Texts from Antiquity to the Renaissance* 117–48. Spoleto
Housman, A. E. (1972). *Classical Papers*. Vols. 1–3. Cambridge
Hunt, A. (2016). *Reviving Roman Religion: Sacred Trees in the Roman World*. Cambridge
Hutchinson, G. O. (2007). 'Horace and archaic Greek poetry', *CCH* 36–49
— (2008). *Talking Books*. Oxford
Jal, P. (1963). *La guerre civile à Rome*. Paris
Keppie, L. (1983). *Colonisation and Veteran Settlement in Italy 47–14 BC*. London
Keuls, E. (1974). *The Water Carriers in Hades*. Amsterdam
Korzeniewski, D. (1972). 'Exegi monumentum. Hor. carm. 3, 30 und die Topik der Grabgedichte', *Gymn.* 79.380–8
Langslow, D. R. (2000). *Medical Latin in the Roman Empire*. Oxford
Laughton, E. (1964). *The Participle in Cicero*. Oxford
Lausberg, H. (1998). *Handbook of Literary Rhetoric*. Leiden/Boston/Cologne
Leach, E. W. (1988). *The Rhetoric of Space*. Princeton
Lovejoy, A. O. and Boas, G. (1935). *Primitivism and Related Ideas in Antiquity*. Baltimore/London

Lowrie, M. (1997). *Horace's Narrative* Odes. Oxford
Lyne, R. O. A. M. (1980). *The Latin Love Poets from Catullus to Horace.* Oxford [*LLP*]
 (1995). *Horace: Behind the Public Poetry.* New Haven/London [*Hor.*]
 (2007). *Collected Papers on Latin Poetry.* Oxford [*CP*]
McDonnell, M. (2006). *Roman Manliness.* Virtus *and the Roman Republic.* Cambridge
Macleod, C. (1983). *Collected Essays.* Oxford
Maltby, R. (1991). *A Lexicon of Ancient Latin Etymologies.* Leeds
Marcovich, M. (1980). 'Eight Horatian "bridges"', *ICS* 5.72–93
Miller, J. F. (2009). *Apollo, Augustus, and the Poets.* Cambridge
Moles, J. (2007). 'Philosophy and ethics', *CCH* 165–80
Morgan, Ll. (2009). 'The one and only *Fons Bandusiae*', *CQ* 59.132–41
 (2010). *Musa Pedestris. Metre and Meaning in Roman Verse.* Oxford
Moritz, L. A. (1968). 'Some "central" thoughts on Horace's *Odes*', *CQ* 18.116–31
Myers, K. S. (2009). *Ovid: Metamorphoses Book XIV.* Cambridge
Nabel, J. (2015). 'Horace and the Tiridates episode', *RhM* 158.304–25
Naylor, H. D. (1922). *Horace: Odes and Epodes. A Study in Poetic Word-Order.* Cambridge
Nisbet, R. G. M. (2007). 'Horace: life and chronology', *CCH* 7–21
 (2009). 'The word order of Horace's *Odes*', *OR* 378–400 (=J. N. Adams and R. Mayer (edd.), *Aspects of the Language of Latin Poetry* (*PBA* 93, 1999) 135–54)
Oakley, S. P. (1997, 1998, 2005). *A Commentary on Livy Books VI–X.* Vols. 1–4. Oxford
Oliensis, E. (2002). 'Feminine endings, lyric seductions', *TC* 93–106
Oltramare, A. (1926). *Les Origines de la diatribe romaine.* Lausanne
Orbis. The Stanford geospatial network model of the Roman world (orbis.stanford.edu)
Otto, A. (1890). *Die Sprichwörter und sprichwörtlichen Redensarten der Römer.* Leipzig
Parker, L. P. E. (2016). 'Micae Horatianae', *MH* 73.167–78
Pfeiffer, R. (1968). *History of Classical Scholarship.* Vol. 1. Oxford
Pichon, R. (1902). *Index verborum amatoriorum.* Paris
Powell, J. G. F. (2010). 'Horace, Scythia, and the East', *PLLS* 14.137–90
Quinn, K. (1963). *Latin Explorations.* London [*LE*]
Reinhardt, T., Lapidge, M. and Adams, J. N. (edd.) (2005). *Aspects of the Language of Latin Prose.* (*PBA* 129.) Oxford
Rich, J. W. (2009). 'Cantabrian closure: Augustus' Spanish War and the ending of his memoirs', in C. Smith and A. Powell (edd.), *The Lost*

Memoirs of Augustus and the Development of Roman Autobiography 145–72. Swansea
Ross, D. O. (1975). *Backgrounds to Augustan Poetry. Gallus, Elegy and Rome.* Cambridge
Rossi, L. (2009). 'Horace, a Greek lyrist without music', *OR* 356–77 (= 'Orazio, uno lirico greco senza musica', *Seminari Romani di cultura greca* 1 (1998) 163–81)
Rudd, N. (ed.) (1993). *Horace 2000: A Celebration.* Ann Arbor
Rüpke, J. (2008). *Fasti Sacerdotum.* Oxford
Rutherford, R. B. (1989). *The Meditations of Marcus Aurelius: A Study.* Oxford
Santirocco, M. S. (1986). *Unity and Design in Horace's Odes.* Chapel Hill/London
Sargeaunt, J. (1920). *The Trees, Shrubs and Plants of Virgil.* Oxford
Schrijvers, P. H. (2009). 'How to end an ode? Closure in Horace's short poems', *OR* 56–71 (= 'Comment terminer une ode?', *Mnem.* 26 (1973) 140–59)
Scullard, H. H. (1981). *Festivals and Ceremonies of the Romam Republic.* London
Shackleton Bailey, D. R. (1982). *Profile of Horace.* London [*Profile*]
Silk, E. T. (1973). 'Towards a fresh interpretation of Horace *Carm.* III.1', *YCS* 23.131–45
Smith, B. H. (1968). *Poetic Closure.* Chicago/London
Stöckinger, M., Winter, K. and Zanker, A. T. (edd.) (2017). *Horace and Seneca: Interactions, Intertexts, Interpretations.* Berlin/Boston
Syme, R. (1979–91). *Roman Papers.* Vols. 1–7. Oxford [*RP*]
(1986). *The Augustan Aristocracy.* Oxford [*AA*]
Syndikus, H. P. (2001). *Die Lyrik des Horaz.* 3rd edn. Vols. 1–2. Darmstadt
Tarrant, R. J. (2016a). 'A new critical edition of Horace', in R. Hunter and S. P. Oakley (edd.), *Latin Literature and its Transmission* 291–321. Cambridge
(2016b). 'The protohistory of the text of Horace', in J. Velaza (ed.), *From the Protohistory to the History of the Text* 223–44. Frankfurt am Main
Thurmond, D. L. (2017). *From Vines to Wines in Classical Rome.* Leiden/Boston
Tosi, R. (2007). *Dizionario delle sentenze latine e greche.* 16th edn. Milan
Toynbee, J. M. C. (1971). *Death and Burial in the Roman World.* London
Treggiari, S. (1991). *Roman Marriage.* Oxford
Tsitsiou-Chelidoni, C. (2018). 'Horace's "persona<l> problems": on continuities and discontinuities in poetry and in classical scholarship', in S. Harrison, S. Frangoulidis & Th. Papanghelis (edd.), *Intratextuality and Latin Literature* 173–97. Berlin

Vergados, A. (2013). *The Homeric Hymn to Hermes*. Berlin
Watson, P. A. (1983). 'Puella and virgo', *Glotta* 61.119–43
(1985). 'Axelson revisited: the selection of vocabulary in Latin poetry', *CQ* 35.430–48
Weinstock, S. (1971). *Divus Julius*. Oxford
West, D. (1973). 'Horace's poetic technique in the *Odes*', in C. D. N. Costa (ed.), *Horace* 29–58. London
(2002). *Horace Odes III: Dulce Periculum*. Oxford [*DP*]
West, M. L. (1992). *Ancient Greek Music*. Oxford
Wilkinson, L. P. (1945). *Horace and his Lyric Poetry*. Cambridge [*HLP*]
(1963). *Golden Latin Artistry*. Cambridge [*GLA*]
(n.d.). *Facets of a Life*. Privately printed [*FL*]
Williams, G. (1962). 'Poetry in the moral climate of Augustan Rome', *JRS* 52.28–46
(1968). *Tradition and Originality in Roman Poetry*. Oxford [*TORP*]
Wills, J. (1996). *Repetition in Latin Poetry*. Oxford
Wiseman, T. P. (1987). *Roman Studies Literary and Historical*. Liverpool [*RS*]
Woodman, A. J. (1988). *Rhetoric in Classical Historiography*. London [*RICH*]
(2012). *From Poetry to History*. Oxford [*PH*]
(2015). *Lost Histories. Selected Fragments of Roman Historical Writers*. Histos Suppl. 2. Newcastle upon Tyne [*LH*]
(2020). 'Horace's "Roman Odes"', *CJ* 115.276–82
(2021). 'Horace's monument', *CCJ* 67 (forthcoming)
(2022). 'Horace's second ode', *MH* 79 (forthcoming)

INDEXES

GENERAL INDEX

All dates are BC

ablative absolute, appended 88, 110, 117, 148, 151, 236, 244, 255, 292
abstract for concrete 143, 222, 315
ab urbe condita idiom 130, 131, 150, 165, 211, 250, 259, 296, 339, 340, 351
accusative, 'Greek' 192, 212
Acrisius, king of Argos and father of Danae 253–4
acrostic 79
Actium, battle 1, 5, 134, 136, 141–2, 143, 167, 239, 289, 306–7, 338, 352
addressees, addresses 16, 18–19, 42, 126, 161–3, 190, 240, 244, 248, 273 (n. 98), 277, 308, 333; addresses to the young 80, 81, 94, 238, 319
adjectives: adverbial use of 89, 121, 183, 185, 198, 201, 325, 342, 353, 365, 369; continuative 117; in *-ax* 106, in *-osus* 24; + infinitive 25, 118, 215–16, 230, 275; instead of genitive 113, 230, 255; instead of gerund(ive) 167, 349; negative 25, 101, 153, 162; placement 108
Adriatic Sea 107, 205, 342
aduentus 241, 242, 243
adultery 23, 170, 171, 178, 207, 208, 248–51, 254, 306, 312
adverb, modifying noun 266
Aedes Herculis Musarum 80
Aelius Gallus, L., prefect of Egypt 308
Aelius Lamia, L., praetorian legate in Spain 262–9
Aemilius Lepidus, M., conspirator 167, 319
Aeschylus 213 (n. 71), 223
aetiology 338; *see also* etymologies
Aetna 144–5
Africa 260, 301; proverbially fertile 260
agon 198–9; amoebean 199, 205
Alcaeus 28–30, 32–4, 227, 229, 231, 260, 327, 379; Alcaic metre 29–30, 121, 153
Alcaic Hexad 12–16, 31, 80
Alexander the Great 118, 256

'Alexandrian footnote' 113, 158, 266, 293
alliteration 34–5, 94, 98, 143, 145, 173, 332, 347
Amor 228
Amphiaraus, Argive seer 255
Anacreon, Anacreontea 127 (n. 22), 217, 237
anagrams 34–5, 90, 132, 138, 145, 173, 226, 298, 360
anaphora 81, 100, 106, 108, 109, 134, 138, 142, 143, 165, 205, 214, 228, 325
anastrophe 108, 344
ancestral records 100, 265
Anne of Austria 203
antallage 234
Antonius, M. (cos. 44), Mark Antony 1, 4–5, 95, 96, 105, 109, 165, 166, 167, 242, 324
apo koinou (ἀπὸ κοινοῦ) 95, 99, 115, 149, 154, 180, 196, 209, 255, 281, 303, 317, 319, 347, 351, 354, 362, 365
Apollo 124, 126, 141, 381; Palatine Temple 123, 135, 214
apotheosis 103–20, 148, 307, 315, 321–29
April 269–72
Apulia 2, 122, 123, 128, 150, 251, 259, 378
Arabia 308, 318
Aratus 165, 174, 175–6
archaisms *see* words
Archilochus 229, 248, 251
Ariadne 337, 351
Aristides Quintilianus 33
Asclepiad metre(s) 7, 29–31, 259, 373
Asia 169, 181, 262
assonance 34–5, 79, 98, 138, 145, 159, 195, 245, 327, 347, 371; *see also* paronomasia, wordplay
asyndeton 25, 77, 86, 157, 167, 204, 255, 256, 275, 287, 303, 332, 340, 360, 362, 368

389

Atilius Regulus, M. (cos. 267, 256) 146–7, 151–60
Aufidus, river 372, 378
augurs 278
augury 336, 340
Augustus (Octavian) 1, 3–8, 22, 78, 82, 90, 94, 100, 102, 116, 132–6, 143, 145, 147–9, 161–5, 176, 196, 197, 214, 237–44, 267, 280, 296, 300, 306–29, 338, 352, 364, 377; apotheosis of 103–110, 322, 323, 325, 326; consulship 135; and Jupiter 81, 148, 164; literary interests 122–5, 135–6; concern for morals 170, 316; nomenclature 109, 110, 148, 164, 244, 315, 326; *onus imperii* 135, 163; as *pater* 313–14; *Res Gestae* 81, 163, 164, 237, 300, 316 (n. 122); shield 100, 106
Ausonius 114
auspicia 340
autantonym 376
Automedon, Greek epigrammatist 160, 170

Bacchante 250, 327–8
Bacchus 109, 192, 294, 322–30
Bacchylides 129, 295, 334
Baiae 131, 281
Bandusia, spring 231–7
benefactors 108, 110, 252, 262, 313–14, 321; deification of 108, 321
birds 340–2; birdsong 85; bird calls mimicked 268; *see also* crows
Britain, Britons 119, 132–3, 149
bronze 373
Brutus *see* Junius Brutus, M.
builders 88–9, 306, 307–9
bull 336–7, 345, 347–8, 351

callida iunctura see words: word combinations
Callimachus 79, 80, 81, 102, 121, 122, 127, 158, 236, 281, 296–7, 328, 373, 378, 380
Calliope 121–30
Calpurnius Bibulus, M. (cos. 59) 354
Camenae 122–42
Campus Martius 83, 186, 229
canons: heroic benefactors 108, 110; lyric poets 32, 236, 378; springs 236
Cantabrians 6, 95, 189, 197, 237, 244; *see also* Spain

Capitol, Capitoline Hill 107, 115, 148, 151, 164, 318, 372, 377
Carmen Aruale 78, 82, 301
Carrhae, battle 3, 95, 145–51
Carthage 146, 151–9
Castalia 141, 236
Castor and Pollux 108, 230, 371
Catalepton 9 290, 292, 295–6
Cato the Elder 293, 296, 300, 314
Cato the Younger 293, 296
Catullus 28, 30 (n. 101), 32, 33, 97, 111, 133, 149, 180–1, 200, 201, 271, 286, 296–7, 328, 337, 349, 364
cenae captatores 274, 276
centaurs 140
Cerberus 218–20
'charm' (*gratia*, χάρις), literary quality 33, 214
chiasmus, chiastic arrangement 25, 81, 84, 107, 142, 143, 149, 154, 173, 183, 184, 197, 203, 221, 235, 238, 241, 253, 264, 270, 302, 322, 346, 372
Churchill, Winston 90
Cicero 24, 81, 84, 152, 175, 187, 192, 263, 298
Cinara (Cinura, Cinyra) 3–4
civil war 3, 115, 135, 142, 239, 306–7, 313, 314, 319, 321
Claudius Caecus, Ap. (cos. 307, 296) 143
Claudius Marcellus, C., nephew of Augustus 95, 131, 241
Claudius Marcellus, M. (cos. 222, 215, 214, 210, 208) 96, 100
Claudius Nero, Ti. (pr. 42), father of Tiberius 241
clientela, clientes 83, 160
closure 18, 84, 121, 122, 145, 147, 159, 160, 174, 226, 246, 262, 288, 321, 356, 357, 372; 'break-off' 120
comic scene 350
comissatio 274
commonplaces (topoi): activity ~ leisure 135–6; anxiety and wealth 256; children resemble parents 172, 210, 250; decline of cities 377; defying nature 88, 316; defrauding a partner 320; corruptible doorkeepers 255; drink and garrulity 275, 294; dying for one's country 98, 147, 275; from east to west 117; the end lies with the gods 165; envied less

INDEXES

after death 315; savage Fortune 369; ignorance of the future 365; love and idleness 229; accompanying a perjurer 103; humble sacrifices 304; *quod satis est* 80; self-destruction 142; sleep of the poor 86; *te genuit* 210; town or country 361; *uis ~ consilium* 142; *see also* proverbs
concilium deorum 104–20, 322, 323, 326
conditional sentences, mixed 107, 253, 370; *see also* prayers
coniunctio see hyperbaton
consolatio 205
constructio ad sensum (synesis) 298–9
contentment 77–92, 252, 258–62, 358
conuiuium, symposium, party 187, 244, 251, 273, 278, 281, 289–96; commands to slave 244, 277; roses 251, 281, 359; 'shopping list motif' 244
Cornelius Gallus, C., elegist and prefect of Egypt 96, 126, 127, 317, 375
countryside 22, 77, 86, 92, 161, 172, 231, 269, 299–305, 358, 361
Crassus *see* Licinius Crassus, M.
Crinagoras, Greek epigrammatist 95
crows 267, 342
Cybele 280

Dacians 166, 196, 197
Damocles 84–5
Danae 253–55
Danaids 212–14, 220–6
dancing 168–70
dative: of direction 255, 300; 'sympathetic' 85, 234
dedication 232, 296–9, 300 (n. 117)
Dellius, Q., historian 96
Delphi 381
Demosthenes 256
description by negation 87, 260
Diana 296–9
Dio Cassius 364
Dionysius I, tyrant of Syracuse 84–5
dithyramb 324
'divided allusion' 106
doors 92, 187, 204, 206, 208, 210, 249, 254, 330, 333; doorkeeper 218, 246, 255
Douglas, Keith 90
dreams 126–7, 346

Egypt 96, 118, 226, 260, 308, 334, 359, 375

Elegiae in Maecenatem 260
elegy 253
Eleusinian Mysteries 102
enallage 91, 154, 225, 304, 359, 376
enjambement 89, 181, 218, 258, 259
Ennius 98, 104, 113, 116, 120, 271, 329, 374
epanalepsis 119, 202
epic 92, 104, 107, 121, 193, 229, 253, 283, 287, 329
Epicureanism 148, 257
epitaphs 226, 331–2, 372–81
erotodidaxis 184
Ethiopians 118, 166
ethnographical motifs 133, 196, 197, 310–12, 365
Etruria, Etruscans 186, 191, 195, 210, 262, 359, 366
etymologies 78, 79, 101, 172, 187, 192, 195, 224, 232, 234, 237, 287, 312, 340, 341, 373; of names 119, 125, 132, 140, 143, 145, 185, 186, 190, 203, 207, 208, 220, 226, 229, 245, 250, 254, 266, 270, 272, 282, 294, 297, 301, 302–3, 310
Euripides 103, 141, 203, 209
Europa 336–8, 343–52
Evadne 206
exclusus amator 186, 206, 208, 209, 333; *see also* komos, paraclausithyron
exempla 77, 177–8, 184, 252, 255, 289, 293, 335, 336, 343; *see also* myth
exploration 118

'Father of the City' (πατὴρ τῆς πόλεως) 313–14
Faunus 269–72; Faunalia 269
figura etymologica 138, 369
Föhn, wind 180 (n. 48)
Fontinalia 232
Formiae 263–9
Fortuna 357, 358, 368–70
Fraenkel, E. 38

gambling 320
Ganymede 288–9
Gellii 264
Gellius, Aulus 79
Geloni 134
gender, dualism of 33
generic interaction 104, 121
genethliakon (birthday poem) 264

genitive: archaic 181; in drinking rituals 195, 277; grecising 351, 360; irregular 151; possessive with *est/sunt* 81
Genius 268
geography 118, 316–17, 351; cliché of 138–9, 361; *see also* language
Germanicus, nephew and adopted son of Tiberius 81, 175
Getae 196–7, 310–12
Giants, Gigantomachy 82, 122, 124, 139–41, 164
glassware 233
Glycera 282
gold *see* wealth
Golden Age 86, 306, 310, 311
Gow, J. 37
grecising 102, 125, 130, 133, 137, 144, 174, 184, 202, 229, 257, 266, 267, 285, 297, 310, 311, 334, 343, 344, 351, 359, 365, 367, 379
Greek, knowledge of 191
Greek lyric 28, 29 (n. 94), 32, 124, 125, 216, 231, 296; *see also* Alcaeus, Anacreon, Bacchylides, Pindar, Sappho, Simonides
Greek names, forms of 181, 183, 184, 230, 262, 365
groves 127, 135, 209, 266–7, 297, 299 (n. 115), 325, 328

hair 245–6, 288, 381; *nodus* style 245–6
Hannibal 116, 156, 172, 353
Hebrus, Thracian river 229, 231, 328
Helvidius Priscus, the younger 298
hendiadys 83, 125, 225, 234, 260, 318, 362, 371
Hercules 108, 239–40
Herodas 178, 198, 201
heroes 108
Hesiod 124–45, 175
hiatus 243
historiography 185
Homer, Homeric motifs 91, 95, 99, 107, 112, 113, 118, 128, 139, 143, 195, 216, 243, 276, 289, 294, 344, 346, 367
Horace: name 7; birthplace 2, 128, 378; date of birth 2, 290, 353; childhood 122, 127–30; life and career 1–8, 132; Sabine farm 5, 77, 92, 130, 231, 356; date of *Odes* 1–3 6, 243; date of death 8; self-description 246; position as poet 7, 123; *see also* Philippi
horsemanship 95–6, 186, 230, 319
hospita 182
houses, villas 89, 92; *see also* builders
Housman, A.E. 36 (n. 128), 108
hunting 230, 320
hyperbaton 114, 127, 150, 207, 212, 251, 348; 'conjunct hyperbaton' (*coniunctio*) 78
Hypermnestra 213, 223–6, 253
hysteron proteron 84, 156, 258

Ibycus 248
Ilium, Ilion 105; *see also* Troy
imagery *see* metaphor
imperialism 149
India 132, 308, 318
inspiration 130–1, 325
interlacing 25, 100, 107, 110, 124, 143, 144, 155, 164, 172, 197, 209, 230, 264, 275, 314, 317, 363, 368
invitation poems 19, 187, 289–96, 356–71
irony 91, 121, 130, 144, 155, 156, 250, 258, 293, 308, 318, 348, 350, 351, 361; dramatic irony 224, 225, 347, 349

Janus, Temple of 189, 197, 237, 244
Julius Caesar, C. (cos. 59) 1–3, 81, 105, 181, 256, 323, 354
Junius Brutus, M. (pr. 44) 3–4, 99, 166, 289
Juno 104–20, 141, 190
Jupiter 16, 77–8, 81–2, 103–11, 122, 137–41, 148, 149, 164, 209, 212, 254, 322, 326, 336–51, 357, 365, 368; Temple of Iuppiter Inuictus 351; of Iuppiter Optimus Maximus 115, 151, 318; of Iuppiter Tonans 107, 148, 151
Juvenal 131, 254, 304

Kalends 190, 300–1
Keats, John 126
komos ('serenade'), komast 20, 187, 206–12, 330–5; *see also exclusus amator*, paraclausithyron

Laestrygonians 261, 263
Lamus 263–5

language: elevated 24, 89, 106, 113,
  114, 135, 151, 229, 230, 253, 255,
  293, 344 (*see also* periphrasis);
  euphemistic 115; geographical 115,
  119, 317; official, legal or technical
  82, 106, 137, 148, 158, 184, 193,
  225, 308, 315, 346, 347, 368;
  religious 233, 292 (*see also* prayers);
  see also words
Lar, Lares 299–304, 362
laughter, divine 254, 350, 365
laurel 381
leno 160, 171
Leontini 263, 264 (n. 93)
licentia 306–7, 313–15
Licinius Crassus, M. (cos. 70, 55) 2,
  95, 149, 165
Licinius Crassus, M. (cos. 30) 166, 196
lions 97–8, 224, 284
Liris, Italian river 266
lives of poets 127–30
Livia, wife of Augustus 241, 246
Livy 111, 136, 152, 159, 164, 170, 306
locus a maiore ad minus 207, 299, 337
locus amoenus 85, 86, 127, 236
love 248; and death 206; **commonplaces
  of**: divinised beloved 210; warning
  dogs 253; doorway 204 (*see also*
  komos, *exclusus amator*); ageing lover
  332; *militia amoris* 239, 246, 247, 332;
  seruitium amoris 202; **symptoms of**:
  heat 183, 201, 282; insomnia 182;
  pallor 210; sighs 97, 183; emotional
  turmoil 182; wounds 211
Lucilius 2, 100, 104
Lucretius 83, 91, 97, 117, 219, 369
Ludi Megale(n)ses 280–1
Ludi Saeculares, Secular Games 6–7,
  296
Lygdamus 190, 223, 290, 305, 341
Lynceus 222–6, 253
lyre 86, 212, 215–20, 281, 332

Macaulay, Lord 160
Maecenas 1, 5–8, 17–18, 19, 22, 83,
  102, 167, 180, 187–98, 251–62,
  278, 356–71, 379; equestrian status
  195, 257; as *littérateur* 189, 191–2,
  290
Manlius Torquatus, L. (cos. 65) 290
Manlius Torquatus, T. (cos. 235, 224)
  152, 159
Marcellus *see* Claudius Marcellus, C.

Marius, C. (cos. 107, 104–100, 86)
  157, 266
marriage 23, 150, 160, 169, 170, 176,
  178, 212, 213, 217–26, 242, 306,
  312, 348; *see also* wedding, wife
Mars 109–14, 147, 150, 186, 300
Marsi 150, 244
Matronalia 188, 190
Menander Rhetor 231
merchants 87, 179, 181, 306, 370
Mercury 212, 215–18
Messalla Corvinus *see* Valerius Messalla
  Corvinus, M.
metaphor, imagery: alphabet 319; boat
  358, 370; clothing 370; disease 182,
  183, 319; executioner 309; financial
  174, 369; horse 217, 335; wild horse
  314; horse-rider 90; hunger 257;
  hunter 282–8; broken limbs 155;
  lion cubs 282–8; lioness 282–8;
  madere 293; marriage 370; masonry
  107; medical 91, 256, 313, 314,
  316; military 258, 332; *monumentum* 372–6; pulley 209; river 168,
  366; *scandere* 89; sea of love 205;
  sewer 168; shepherd 81, 363; sleep
  224; sortition 84; stronghold 353;
  spinning 380; surgery 316; tongue-
  lashing 228; triumph 380; *uenatio*
  370; *uincere* 317; voyage 370; water
  237, 279; yoke 204; *see also* love
metonymy 83, 86, 100, 108, 116, 120,
  151, 182, 197, 204, 209, 222, 229,
  240, 246, 254 (n. 91), 261, 272,
  289, 295, 309, 311, 333, 362
metre, metrical features, prosody
  13–14, 29–34, 91, 121, 136, 153,
  165, 191, 200, 243, 259, 309, 366,
  379–80; Ionics *a minore* 31, 226–7;
  see also Alcaeus, Sappho
metus hostilis 198
middles, central positioning 17–18,
  77, 78, 80, 86, 111, 121, 122, 147,
  162, 187, 194, 238, 248, 251, 252,
  303, 356, 357, 365
military life 92–102
mime 36, 178, 198, 201
Minerva 141, 229
mola salsa 305
monumentum 372–6
moon, new 277, 300
morality, decline of 145, 149–51,
  160–76, 306–21

Moschus 336, 344, 348, 349
'motto', epigraph 28
Munatius Plancus, L. (cos. 42) 247
Murenae, identity of 278
Muses 77, 80, 90, 92, 121, 122, 130, 135-7, 142, 279, 280, 372, 381; *see also* Camenae
mutitatio 280-1
myth 213, 252, 336; allusive reference to 114, 138, 219; conflation of 137; implicit myth 218; Myth of Ages 175; *see also exempla*, rationalisation

names 207, 241
Necessitas 83-4, 309
Neptune 352
Nicolaus of Damascus 181
Nile, river 116, 117
Nisbet, R. G. M. 37, 40
nobiles, nobilitas 83, 264
nomads 310
noui homines 83
numerology 14-15
Numidia 225

oaristys (wooing) 200
Octavia, sister of Augustus 241
odes, mimetic or dramatic 19-20, 36, 77-92, 187-98, 198-206, 206-12, 237-47, 274-82, 322-30, 330-5, 352-6; performed (?) 35-6
omens 335-6, 339-42
'only' often omitted in Latin 86, 262, 315
Oricum 181
originality, poetic 32, 80, 325, 327, 328, 380
Orpheus 126, 216, 218, 220, 324, 328; Orphic Fragments 78
Ovid 126, 136, 164, 185, 205 (n. 68), 214, 221-6, 224, 233, 254, 276, 290, 295, 310, 343, 348, 372, 373, 376
Owen, Wilfred 98
oxymoron 119, 259; *see also* paradox, words: word combinations

Page, T. E. 13, 38
Pan 270, 272
Panegyricus Messallae 290, 294
Paphos 334, 355
paraclausithyron 187, 206-12; *see also exclusus amator*, komos

paradox 143, 257, 261, 325, 345, 375, 376; *see also* oxymoron, words: word combinations
para prosdokian (παρὰ προσδοκίαν) *see* surprise element
Paris 111-15
paronomasia 81; *see also* assonance
Parthia, Parthians 3, 15, 94-9, 106, 116, 145-53, 160, 165-7, 196, 197, 312, 313, 365; *see also* Persians, Persae
participles: future 175-6; present to express purpose 286; present genitive plural in *-um* 270, 341
party *see conuiuium*
patrons 83, 357, 358
Paulinus of Nola 95
peace 151, 154, 237, 239, 244
Pegasus 102
Penates 299, 305
periphrasis 106, 229, 253, 293, 311
Persians, Persae 149, 201
Persius 321
persona, roles 2, 20-1, 42, 77, 80, 163, 227, 238, 240; speaking role 77-90 (priest), 163-5 (prophet?), 238-43 (public orator), 336 (pseudo-*auspex*); *see also* komos, komast
personification 41, 86, 89, 90, 99, 100, 101, 103, 144, 151, 155, 193, 205, 231, 243, 245, 291, 342, 356, 367, 370, 376
Philip II, king of Macedon 256
Philippi, battle 4, 22, 131, 155, 188, 239, 247, 289, 292
philosophy 259, 293, 294; popular 80, 86, 256, 258, 358, 366
Phraates IV, Parthian ruler 94, 147, 196, 198
Pindar 93, 124, 127-8, 128, 142, 252-3, 372, 374-5, 381
Plato 130, 223, 278, 281, 293, 370
pleonasm: 'amplificatory' 222; disjunctiveness 367
Pliny the Younger 293
'polar tension' 26, 294; *see also* words: word correspondences or contrasts
polyptoton 81, 82, 86, 256, 281, 325
Pompeius Trogus, historian 237, 256, 266
Pomponius Mela 284
pontifices 278, 303, 377
Porphyrio 13, 39, 169, 195, 273 (n. 98), 304, 327

praefectus urbis 195–6, 289
Praeneste 131
prayers, hymns 212, 214, 232, 233, 289, 296, 380; parodied 207, 289–96; **formulae of**: *ades* 295; ancestry 216, 290; appositional description 215, 233, 270; 'blanket' clause 291–2; conditional clauses 125, 271, 291, 300; *nam(que)* 215; *o* 210, 232, 334; *parce* 211; *potens* 329; relative clause 297, 334; *tu* ('Du-Stil') 218, 235, 272, 289, 294 (*per te* 321, *tu potes* 218)
Priam 112–15
propemptikon (send-off poem) 335–52
Propertius 80, 94, 104, 341, 372
prosopopoeia 349
prostitution, prostitutes 160, 171, 207, 208, 211, 249
proverbs, proverbial expressions or ideas: *ab Ioue principium* 164; autumn unhealthy 302; *semper auarus eget* 321; avarice the root of all evil 318; Sicilian banquets 85; *caelum ruit* 108; *cenae deum* 295; crows predict rain 267; *de tenero ungui* 169–70; deafer than rocks 185, 215; death and the runaway 99; goats battling 234, lascivious 235, 250; rivalling the gods 164; power of gold 255, 256; happy as a king 201; *hostibus eueniat* 343; Lasthenes and Euthycrates 256; cruel lions 224; Persian luxury 91; *noli leonem tangere* 98; money is the man 257; nothing to excess 87; solid as an oak 211; the past irreversible 368; popular favour 101; *Punica fides* 156; retribution slow but sure 103; seaweed worthless 267; silence is best 102; dangerous snakes 212; cruel stepmothers 311; tomorrow always worse 174; *in uino ueritas* 294; harsh uncles 228; wine and sex 271, 291, 295; wine soothes cares 294–5; wine and wisdom 293, 294, 353; wolves and lambs 272; *see also* commonplaces
punctuation 41–2, 125, 166, 239
puns 116, 172, 305, 326, 354, 379; *see also* word play
Punic Wars: First 146, 151–9, 172; Second 156, 172; Third 157

pyramids 226, 373–6
Pyrrhus, king of Epirus 172, 285

Quintilian 33

rationalisation (of myth etc.) 103, 133, 254
reading 36, 136; recitation 36
Regulus *see* Atilius Regulus, M.
relative clause, antecedent omitted 85, 137, 262, 340
renuntiatio amoris 331
Rhodope, mountain range in Thrace 327–8
ring composition 15, 17, 18, 90, 122, 147, 163 (n. 39), 177, 183, 188, 247, 248, 304, 321, 322, 357, 381, 335–6
rivers, springs 207, 230–7, 259, 366–7; *see also* Aufidus, Bandusia, Hebrus, Liris, Nile, Tanais, Tiber
'Roman Odes' *see* Alcaic Hexad
Rome 356, 360–1; eternal 115, 151, 377; future of 105, 115, 119; name 116
Romulus 104, 106, 109–20, 307, 315
Rudd, N. 37

Sabine region 92
sacrifices 133, 188–94, 232–5, 241, 264, 267, 268, 269, 270, 271, 298–305
Salassi, Alpine tribe 132, 134, 244, 278
Sallust 307, 319
Samnium 173
Sappho 28–30, 32–4, 216, 366 (n. 147), 379; Sapphic metre 29–30, 191
schema Cornelianum 317
schema Horatianum 128, 234
Scythia, Scythians 149, 197–8, 206–8, 310–12
seafaring, season of 87, 179, 180, 181, 342
self-naming 201
self-referential cues 119, 173, 184, 202, 267, 275, 303
Seneca the Younger 83, 138, 148, 259, 328, 365–8
sententiae, aphorisms 26, 93, 98, 142, 143, 252, 321, 357, 365
sermocinatio 349
Shorey, P. 37

silence 93, 102–3
Silius Italicus 97, 108, 133, 153, 218, 355
Simonides 93, 99, 101, 102, 373
Social War (91-89) 2, 244
soteria (poem of congratulation and thanksgiving) 188 (n. 53)
Spain 6, 95, 107, 117, 132, 133, 171, 189, 197, 237–46, 263; *see also* Cantabrians
Spartacus 245
speech 16–17, 41–2, 90, 104, 136–7, 153, 154, 337; *genus deliberatiuum* 110, 154, 158
sphragis (σφραγίς), 'seal' 17, 372–80
springtime 180, 269–72
stars 87, 88, 91, 108, 180, 181, 205, 235, 282, 322, 323, 326, 362, 363
Statius 329
stepmothers 311
Stoicism 103
structure, arrangement (within poems) 78, 93, 110–11, 123, 162, 177, 187–98, 199, 200, 232, 238, 252, 269, 322, 331, 356; *see also* ring composition
subjunctive: concessive 224, 339; imperfect = futurity from past point of view 129; jussive 221, 224, 339; optative 221; *see also* verbs, subjunctive
Suetonius 2, 4, 5, 6, 8
suicide 349
surprise element (παρὰ προσδοκίαν) 174, 177, 299, 331, 357
surrealism 82, 149, 158, 166, 258; *see also* words: word combinations
swimming 186, 229
syllepsis 85, 113, 127, 128, 216, 303, 318
symposium *see conuiuium*
synecdoche 100, 109, 128, 236, 261, 343, 371

Tacitus 171
Tanais, river 134, 208, 365
Tarentum 160
Tauri 133
teichoskopia 96, 98
Telepylos 263–4
Tempe 86
theme and variation 99, 100, 125, 361
Theocritus 199, 202, 203, 224, 282, 341

Thrace 202, 328, 334–5
three, significant or 'magic' number 275, 297, 322, 372, 375
Thucydides 315
Thurii 203
Tiber, river 186, 229, 357, 366
Tiberius, emperor 79, 81, 175, 194 (n. 62), 241, 275, 326 (n. 128), 361
tibia 125, 187, 280–1
Tibullus 211, 220
Tibur 131, 358 (n. 142), 360
tigers 109, 284, 348
time 7 (n. 26), 21–2, 105–6, 189, 238–9, 246–7, 248, 249, 357, 365–8
Tiridates II, Parthian ruler 196
Titans, Titanomachy 124, 137
Tityus 145
toga 151
towers 89, 253, 356, 360–1
tragedy 214, 338, 349, 350, 351
trees 298; vocal 88; 'Horace's tree' 132, 188, 191, 193, 194
tricolon crescendo 142, 190, 235, 322
triumph, *triumphator* 82, 109, 196, 237, 239, 240, 380, 381
Trogus *see* Pompeius Trogus
Troy 111–20; *see also* Ilium
tyrant 77, 84–5, 107

uirtus 83, 93, 99–102, 147, 155, 315
uncles 228

Valerius Messalla Corvinus, M. (cos. 31) 192, 196, 289–94
Valgius Rufus, C. (cos. suff. 12) 145, 290
Venafrum 160
Venus 129, 204, 225, 229, 254, 271, 330–5, 350–1, 355–6
Venusia 2, 3, 129, 231, 232, 244
verbs: causative 89; extended meaning 25, 86, 259; singular verb with multiple subjects 108, 112, 220, 302; main idea not conveyed by main verb 101, 156–7, 172, 208; **tenses: indicative**: future 121; concessive future 303; gnomic future 85, 194, 280, 313; jussive future 332; perfect in generalising clauses 131, 134, 229, 304, 340; gnomic perfect 148, 305, 362; future perfect/perfect subjunctive 301; present for future 369; **infinitive**: perfect for present

140, 272, 367; **subjunctive**: in unreal comparative clauses 159, 258, 261, 354; imperfect potential referring to the past 247
Vesta 151; Vestal Virgins 377
veteran soldiers 134–5
'*Vetula*-Skoptik', mockery of old women 248
vines *see* wine(s)
Virgil 28, 87, 88, 94, 97, 101, 104–5, 106, 111, 116, 119, 121, 125, 126, 127, 136, 139, 175, 218, 219, 221, 290, 323–4, 343, 372
Volcacius Tullus, L. (cos. 33) 194
vows, prayer-bargaining, *uota* 192, 271, 300, 303, 315, 371

water 86, 230–7; as source of inspiration 236, 237, 279
wealth, riches, gold 252–62, 307–21; and territorial acquisition 261
wedding 223, 348; wedding torches 223
wife, wives 16, 23, 150, 158, 169, 171, 177, 183, 188, 190, 206–12, 311–12
Wilkinson, L. P. 36, 38 (n. 135)
wine(s) and vines: vigneron 77, 82, 87; plantations 82; grape harvest 88; vintage 194, 290, 354; production and storage 193, 194, 244, 292; wine-jar 289–96; unmixed wine 233, 293, 359; diluted wine 276, 278; toasts 277; wine and inspiration 279, 329, and lovers' complaints 274, 291, and wit 291; wine forbidden to women 228, 251; soporific effects 291; encomium of wine 289, 290; **types of wine**: Alban 359, Caecuban 353, Chian 276, Falernian 91, Formian 261, Marsian 245, Massic 292, Sabine 194, Sicilian 261
wool-working 229, 251
women 18, 23, 228, 229, 242, 248, 251
word order 25–7, 215, 235, 260, 282; 'golden' 25, 261, 271, 317; mimetic 26, 88, 114, 156, 216, 230, 236, 249, 261, 267, 272, 348, 359; 'silver' 25, 84, 219, 343; *see also* chiasmus, interlacing
wordplay 34–5, 84, 113, 139, 143, 195, 259, 315, 326, 361; *see also* assonance, paronomasia, puns
words: archaisms 24, 96–7 (*hosticus*), 103 (*Diespiter*), 129 (*forem*), 132 (*nauita*), 153 (*pubes*), 157 (*duellum*), 181 (*fide*, gen.), 230 (*catus*), 234–5 (*suboles*), 319 (*materies*), 351 (fut. imper.); new words, meanings or usages 24–5, 86 (*fastidire* 'look down on'), 91 (*costum*), 117 (*irrepertus*), 184 (*impello* + inf.), 215–16 (*callidus* + inf.), 226 (*sculpere* 'engrave an inscription'), 230 (*celer* + inf.), 230 (*catus* + inf.), 235 (*hora* 'season'), 240 (*plebs*), 259 (*occultare* 'store'), 270 (*alumnus* 'young animal'), 302 (*pomifer*), 378 (*pauper* + gen.); 'prosaic' words 24, 82 (*ordinare*), 102 (*merces*), 153 (*condicio*), 155 (*flagitium*), 159 (*atqui*), 160 (*negotium*), 175 (*nequam*), 197 (*luctuosus*), 247 (*capillus*), 256 (*pecunia*), 294 (*plerumque*), 304 (*attinet*), 332 (*idoneus*), 349 (*delectare*), 361 (*cena*), 371 (*praesidium*); unique or rare words, meanings or usages 24–5, 101 (*intaminatus*), 144 (*temptator*), 171 (*impermissus*), 171 (*pretiosus* 'free-spending'), 186 (*denatare*), 193 (*funerare* 'kill'), 210 (*curuare* 'influence'), 217 (*exsultim*), 223 (*mendax in* + acc.), 243 (*ominatus*), 280 (*flamen* of instruments), 285 (*inaudax*), 310 (*immetatus*), 327 (*Euhias*), 340–1 (*diuinus* + gen.), 368 (*diffingere*), 369 (*pertinax* + inf.), 379 (*regnare* + gen.); word combinations for effect (suggestive, surreal, oxymoronic etc.) 26, 109, 114, 126, 137, 155, 156, 159, 174, 184, 223, 285, 294, 310, 317, 320, 329, 343, 344, 347, 354, 362, 369, 377; word correspondences or contrasts 26, 90, 92, 100, 101, 107, 112, 117, 128, 129, 148, 159, 173, 177, 181, 197, 199, 202, 211, 224, 229, 230, 234, 235, 248, 262, 266, 275, 306, 310, 319, 320, 357, 369 (*see also* ring composition); word repetition 86, 111, 130, 154, 175, 182, 222, 224, 228, 239, 262, 281; *see also* language

zeugma 97, 119, 128, 164, 208, 209, 225, 339

LATIN WORDS

See also General Index s.vv. 'language' and 'words'.

Assyrius 'Indian' 132
atque 220

cadus 244
capillus/coma/crinis/caesaries 247
capra/caprea 250
cena 361
consenescere 150
cunctus 82

damnare 112
dare, elliptical use 277
deducere 380
de tenero ungui 169–70
diluuies/diluuium 367
doceri, doctus 169, 192, 202
duellum 157, 244

eius 219–20
ensis/gladius 85
exigere 373

fallere 259
famulus/seruus 89
fastidire 'look down on' (?) 86
fessus/lassus 135
fides, genitive of 181
forem/essem 129
frustra, 'dramatic' use of 185, 234

Ilios, Ilion 111, 276
immunis 304
insultare 115

lamia 263
letum/mors 298

materies/materia 319
melius fuit 347
Mygdonius 261–2

nidus 'eyrie' 129
nobilis = *nobilitans* (?) 236
non (haud) secus 327
non sine 130, 233

o 157, 313, 345
occultare 'store' (?) 259
odisse 78

paelex 211, 350
pauperies/paupertas 95
plebs 240
pro, interjection 150
proles 173

quamuis + indic. 186, 210
-que: dislocated 83, 128, 130, 295; = *-ue* 86, 102, 368
quid si 204
quis and *qui* (interrogative) 364

recreare 288
redonare 113
Romane (vocative) 161–3

Sabellus 173
seu (siue) = *uel, si* 125, 320, 349
situs 373–4
suboles 234–5

–tim, adverbs in 217
tumultus 244

uir: 'hero' 242; used instead of *alius, alter* 82
uirgo 97, 221–2, 223, 249
uiuere, perfect tense of 367
uxor/coniunx 120